AFRICAN-AMERICAN Classics Collection:

Frederick Douglass's Narrative of the Life,
Booker T. Washington's Up From Slavery,
W.E.B. Du Bois's The Souls of Black Folk &
Solomon Northup's Twelve Years a Slave

SANAGE
PUBLISHING HOUSE

Paperback: 978-939089660-8

Sanage Publishing House LLP
Mumbai, India

sanagepublishing@gmail.com

CONTENTS

UP FROM SLAVERY

THE SOULS OF BLACK FOLK

NARRATIVE OF THE LIFE OF FREDERICK DOUGLASS

TWELVE YEARS A SLAVE

UP FROM SLAVERY

BOOKER T. WASHINGTON

SANAGE
PUBLISHING HOUSE

Booker Taliaferro Washington (April 5, 1856 – November 14, 1915) was an American educator, author, orator, and adviser to multiple presidents of the United States. Between 1890 and 1915, Washington was the dominant leader in the African American community and of the contemporary black elite.Washington was from the last generation of black American leaders born into slavery and became the leading voice of the former slaves and their descendants. They were newly oppressed in the South by disenfranchisement and the Jim Crow discriminatory laws enacted in the post-Reconstruction Southern states in the late 19th and early 20th centuries.

Preface

This volume is the outgrowth of a series of articles, dealing with incidents in my life, which were published consecutively in the Outlook. While they were appearing in that magazine I was constantly surprised at the number of requests which came to me from all parts of the country, asking that the articles be permanently preserved in book form. I am most grateful to the Outlook for permission to gratify these requests.

I have tried to tell a simple, straightforward story, with no attempt at embellishment. My regret is that what I have attempted to do has been done so imperfectly. The greater part of my time and strength is required for the executive work connected with the Tuskegee Normal and Industrial Institute, and in securing the money necessary for the support of the institution. Much of what I have said has been written on board trains, or at hotels or railroad stations while I have been waiting for trains, or during the moments that I could spare from my work while at Tuskegee. Without the painstaking and generous assistance of Mr. Max Bennett Thrasher I could not have succeeded in any satisfactory degree.

INTRODUCTION

The details of Mr. Washington's early life, as frankly set down in "Up from Slavery," do not give quite a whole view of his education. He had the training that a coloured youth receives at Hampton, which, indeed, the autobiography does explain. But the reader does not get his intellectual pedigree, for Mr. Washington himself, perhaps, does not as clearly understand it as another man might. The truth is he had a training during the most impressionable period of his life that was very extraordinary, such a training as few men of his generation have had. To see its full meaning one must start in the Hawaiian Islands half a century or more ago.[1] There Samuel Armstrong, a youth of missionary parents, earned enough money to pay his expenses at an American college. Equipped with this small sum and the earnestness that the undertaking implied, he came to Williams College when Dr. Mark Hopkins was president. Williams College had many good things for youth in that day, as it has in this, but the greatest was the strong personality of its famous president. Every student does not profit by a great teacher; but perhaps no young man ever came under the influence of Dr. Hopkins, whose whole nature was so ripe for profit by such an experience as young Armstrong. He lived in the family of President Hopkins, and thus had a training that was wholly out of the common; and this training had much to do with the development of his own strong character, whose originality and force we are only beginning to appreciate.

In turn, Samuel Armstrong, the founder of Hampton Institute, took up his work as a trainer of youth. He had very raw material, and doubtless most of his pupils failed to get the greatest lessons from him; but, as he had

[1] For this interesting view of Mr. Washington's education, I am indebted to Robert C. Ogden, Esq., Chairman of the Board of Trustees of Hampton Institute and the intimate friend of General Armstrong during the whole period of his educational work.

been a peculiarly receptive pupil of Dr. Hopkins, so Booker Washington became a peculiarly receptive pupil of his. To the formation of Mr. Washington's character, then, went the missionary zeal of New England, influenced by one of the strongest personalities in modern education, and the wide-reaching moral earnestness of General Armstrong himself. These influences are easily recognizable in Mr. Washington to-day by men who knew Dr. Hopkins and General Armstrong.

I got the cue to Mr. Washington's character from a very simple incident many years ago. I had never seen him, and I knew little about him, except that he was the head of a school at Tuskegee, Alabama. I had occasion to write to him, and I addressed him as "The Rev. Booker T. Washington." In his reply there was no mention of my addressing him as a clergyman. But when I had occasion to write to him again, and persisted in making him a preacher, his second letter brought a postscript: "I have no claim to 'Rev.'" I knew most of the coloured men who at that time had become prominent as leaders of their race, but I had not then known one who was neither a politician nor a preacher; and I had not heard of the head of an important coloured school who was not a preacher. "A new kind of man in the coloured world," I said to myself—"a new kind of man surely if he looks upon his task as an economic one instead of a theological one." I wrote him an apology for mistaking him for a preacher.

The first time that I went to Tuskegee I was asked to make an address to the school on Sunday evening. I sat upon the platform of the large chapel and looked forth on a thousand coloured faces, and the choir of a hundred or more behind me sang a familiar religious melody, and the whole company joined in the chorus with unction. I was the only white man under the roof, and the scene and the songs made an impression on me that I shall never forget. Mr. Washington arose and asked them to sing one after another of the old melodies that I had heard all my life; but I had never before heard them sung by a thousand voices nor by the voices of educated Negroes. I had associated them with the Negro of the past, not with the Negro who was struggling upward. They brought to my mind the plantation, the cabin, the slave, not the freedman in quest of education. But on the plantation and in the cabin they had never been sung as these thousand students sang them. I saw again all the old plantations that I had ever seen; the whole history of the Negro ran through my mind; and the inexpressible pathos of his life found expression in these songs as I had never before felt it.

And the future? These were the ambitious youths of the race, at work with an earnestness that put to shame the conventional student life of most educational institutions. Another song rolled up along the rafters. And as soon as silence came, I found myself in front of this extraordinary mass of faces, thinking not of them, but of that long and unhappy chapter in our country's history which followed the one great structural mistake of the Fathers of the Republic; thinking of the one continuous great problem that generations of statesmen had wrangled over, and a million men fought about, and that had so dwarfed the mass of English men in the Southern States as to hold them back a hundred years behind their fellows in every other part of the world—in England, in Australia, and in the Northern and Western States; I was thinking of this dark shadow that had oppressed every large-minded statesman from Jefferson to Lincoln. These thousand young men and women about me were victims of it. I, too, was an innocent victim of it. The whole Republic was a victim of that fundamental error of importing Africa into America. I held firmly to the first article of my faith that the Republic must stand fast by the principle of a fair ballot; but I recalled the wretched mess that Reconstruction had made of it; I recalled the low level of public life in all the "black" States. Every effort of philanthropy seemed to have miscarried, every effort at correcting abuses seemed of doubtful value, and the race friction seemed to become severer. Here was the century-old problem in all its pathos seated singing before me. Who were the more to be pitied—these innocent victims of an ancient wrong, or I and men like me, who had inherited the problem? I had long ago thrown aside illusions and theories, and was willing to meet the facts face to face, and to do whatever in God's name a man might do towards saving the next generation from such a burden. But I felt the weight of twenty well-nigh hopeless years of thought and reading and observation; for the old difficulties remained and new ones had sprung up. Then I saw clearly that the way out of a century of blunders had been made by this man who stood beside me and was introducing me to this audience. Before me was the material he had used. All about me was the indisputable evidence that he had found the natural line of development. He had shown the way. Time and patience and encouragement and work would do the rest.

It was then more clearly than ever before that I understood the patriotic significance of Mr. Washington's work. It is this conception of it and of him that I have ever since carried with me. It is on this that his claim to our gratitude rests.

To teach the Negro to read, whether English, or Greek, or Hebrew, butters no parsnips. To make the Negro work, that is what his master did in one way and hunger has done in another; yet both these left Southern life where they found it. But to teach the Negro to do skilful work, as men of all the races that have risen have worked,—responsible work, which IS education and character; and most of all when Negroes so teach Negroes to do this that they will teach others with a missionary zeal that puts all ordinary philanthropic efforts to shame,—this is to change the whole economic basis of life and the whole character of a people.

The plan itself is not a new one. It was worked out at Hampton Institute, but it was done at Hampton by white men. The plan had, in fact, been many times theoretically laid down by thoughtful students of Southern life. Handicrafts were taught in the days of slavery on most well-managed plantations. But Tuskegee is, nevertheless, a brand-new chapter in the history of the Negro, and in the history of the knottiest problem we have ever faced. It not only makes "a carpenter of a man; it makes a man of a carpenter." In one sense, therefore, it is of greater value than any other institution for the training of men and women that we have, from Cambridge to Palo Alto. It is almost the only one of which it may be said that it points the way to a new epoch in a large area of our national life.

To work out the plan on paper, or at a distance—that is one thing. For a white man to work it out—that too, is an easy thing. For a coloured man to work it out in the South, where, in its constructive period, he was necessarily misunderstood by his own people as well as by the whites, and where he had to adjust it at every step to the strained race relations—that is so very different and more difficult a thing that the man who did it put the country under lasting obligations to him.

It was not and is not a mere educational task. Anybody could teach boys trades and give them an elementary education. Such tasks have been done since the beginning of civilization. But this task had to be done with the rawest of raw material, done within the civilization of the dominant race, and so done as not to run across race lines and social lines that are the strongest forces in the community. It had to be done for the benefit of the whole community. It had to be done, moreover, without local help, in the face of the direst poverty, done by begging, and done in spite of the ignorance of one race and the prejudice of the other.

No man living had a harder task, and a task that called for more wisdom to do it right. The true measure of Mr. Washington's success is, then, not his teaching the pupils of Tuskegee, nor even gaining the support of philanthropic persons at a distance, but this—that every Southern white man of character and of wisdom has been won to a cordial recognition of the value of the work, even men who held and still hold to the conviction that a mere book education for the Southern blacks under present conditions is a positive evil. This is a demonstration of the efficiency of the Hampton-Tuskegee idea that stands like the demonstration of the value of democratic institutions themselves—a demonstration made so clear in spite of the greatest odds that it is no longer open to argument.

Consider the change that has come in twenty years in the discussion of the Negro problem. Two or three decades ago social philosophers and statisticians and well-meaning philanthropists were still talking and writing about the deportation of the Negroes, or about their settlement within some restricted area, or about their settling in all parts of the Union, or about their decline through their neglect of their children, or about their rapid multiplication till they should expel the whites from the South—of every sort of nonsense under heaven. All this has given place to the simple plan of an indefinite extension among the neglected classes of both races of the Hampton-Tuskegee system of training. The "problem" in one sense has disappeared. The future will have for the South swift or slow development of its masses and of its soil in proportion to the swift or slow development of this kind of training. This change of view is a true measure of Mr. Washington's work.

The literature of the Negro in America is colossal, from political oratory through abolitionism to "Uncle Tom's Cabin" and "Cotton is King"—a vast mass of books which many men have read to the waste of good years (and I among them); but the only books that I have read a second time or ever care again to read in the whole list (most of them by tiresome and unbalanced "reformers") are "Uncle Remus" and "Up from Slavery"; for these are the great literature of the subject. One has all the best of the past, the other foreshadows a better future; and the men who wrote them are the only men who have written of the subject with that perfect frankness and perfect knowledge and perfect poise whose other name is genius.

Mr. Washington has won a world-wide fame at an early age. His story of his own life already has the distinction of translation into more languages, I think, than any other American book; and I suppose that he has as large a personal acquaintance among men of influence as any private citizen now living.

His own teaching at Tuskegee is unique. He lectures to his advanced students on the art of right living, not out of text-books, but straight out of life. Then he sends them into the country to visit Negro families. Such a student will come back with a minute report of the way in which the family that he has seen lives, what their earnings are, what they do well and what they do ill; and he will explain how they might live better. He constructs a definite plan for the betterment of that particular family out of the resources that they have. Such a student, if he be bright, will profit more by an experience like this than he could profit by all the books on sociology and economics that ever were written. I talked with a boy at Tuskegee who had made such a study as this, and I could not keep from contrasting his knowledge and enthusiasm with what I heard in a class room at a Negro university in one of the Southern cities, which is conducted on the idea that a college course will save the soul. Here the class was reciting a lesson from an abstruse text-book on economics, reciting it by rote, with so obvious a failure to assimilate it that the waste of labour was pitiful.

I asked Mr. Washington years ago what he regarded as the most important result of his work, and he replied:

"I do not know which to put first, the effect of Tuskegee's work on the Negro, or the effect on the attitude of the white man to the Negro."

The race divergence under the system of miseducation was fast getting wider. Under the influence of the Hampton-Tuskegee idea the races are coming into a closer sympathy and into an honourable and helpful relation. As the Negro becomes economically independent, he becomes a responsible part of the Southern life; and the whites so recognize him. And this must be so from the nature of things. There is nothing artificial about it. It is development in a perfectly natural way. And the Southern whites not only so recognize it, but they are imitating it in the teaching of the neglected masses of their own race. It has thus come about that the school is taking a more direct and helpful hold on life in the South than anywhere else in the country. Education is not a thing apart from life—not a "system," nor a philosophy; it is direct teaching how to live and how to work.

To say that Mr. Washington has won the gratitude of all thoughtful Southern white men, is to say that he has worked with the highest practical wisdom at a large constructive task; for no plan for the up-building of the freedman could succeed that ran counter to Southern opinion. To win the support of Southern opinion and to shape it was a necessary part of the task; and in this he has so well succeeded that the South has a sincere and high regard for him. He once said to me that he recalled the day, and remembered it thankfully, when he grew large enough to regard a Southern white man as he regarded a Northern one. It is well for our common country that the day is come when he and his work are regarded as highly in the South as in any other part of the Union. I think that no man of our generation has a more noteworthy achievement to his credit than this; and it is an achievement of moral earnestness of the strong character of a man who has done a great national service.

Walter H. Page.

Chapter 1. A Slave Among Slaves

I was born a slave on a plantation in Franklin County, Virginia. I am not quite sure of the exact place or exact date of my birth, but at any rate I suspect I must have been born somewhere and at some time. As nearly as I have been able to learn, I was born near a cross-roads post-office called Hale's Ford, and the year was 1858 or 1859. I do not know the month or the day. The earliest impressions I can now recall are of the plantation and the slave quarters—the latter being the part of the plantation where the slaves had their cabins.

My life had its beginning in the midst of the most miserable, desolate, and discouraging surroundings. This was so, however, not because my owners were especially cruel, for they were not, as compared with many others. I was born in a typical log cabin, about fourteen by sixteen feet square. In this cabin I lived with my mother and a brother and sister till after the Civil War, when we were all declared free.

Of my ancestry I know almost nothing. In the slave quarters, and even later, I heard whispered conversations among the coloured people of the tortures which the slaves, including, no doubt, my ancestors on my mother's side, suffered in the middle passage of the slave ship while being conveyed from Africa to America. I have been unsuccessful in securing any information that would throw any accurate light upon the history of my family beyond my mother. She, I remember, had a half-brother and a half-sister. In the days of slavery not very much attention was given to family history and family records—that is, black family records. My mother, I suppose, attracted the attention of a purchaser who was afterward my owner and hers. Her addition to the slave family attracted about as much attention as the purchase of a new horse or cow. Of my father I know even less than of my mother. I do not even know his name. I have heard reports to the effect that he was a white man who lived on one of the near-by plantations. Whoever he was, I never heard of his taking the least interest in me or providing in any way for my rearing. But I do not find especial fault with him. He was simply another unfortunate victim of the institution which the Nation unhappily had engrafted upon it at that time.

The cabin was not only our living-place, but was also used as the kitchen for the plantation. My mother was the plantation cook. The cabin was without glass windows; it had only openings in the side which let in the light, and also the cold, chilly air of winter. There was a door to the cabin—that is, something that was called a door—but the uncertain hinges by which it was hung, and the large cracks in it, to say nothing of the fact that it was too small, made the room a very uncomfortable one. In addition to these openings there was, in the lower right-hand corner of the room, the "cat-hole,"—a contrivance which almost every mansion or cabin in Virginia possessed during the ante-bellum period. The "cat-hole" was a square opening, about seven by eight inches, provided for the purpose of letting the cat pass in and out of the house at will during the night. In the case of our particular cabin I could never understand the necessity for this convenience, since there were at least a half-dozen other places in the cabin that would have accommodated the cats. There was no wooden floor in our cabin, the naked earth being used as a floor. In the centre of the earthen floor there was a large, deep opening covered with boards, which was used as a place in which to store sweet potatoes during the winter. An impression of this potato-hole is very distinctly engraved upon my memory, because I recall that during the process of putting the potatoes in or taking them out I would often come into possession of one or two, which I roasted and thoroughly enjoyed. There was no cooking-stove on our plantation, and all the cooking for the whites and slaves my mother had to do over an open fireplace, mostly in pots and "skillets." While the poorly built cabin caused us to suffer with cold in the winter, the heat from the open fireplace in summer was equally trying.

The early years of my life, which were spent in the little cabin, were not very different from those of thousands of other slaves. My mother, of course, had little time in which to give attention to the training of her children during the day. She snatched a few moments for our care in the early morning before her work began, and at night after the day's work was done. One of my earliest recollections is that of my mother cooking a chicken late at night, and awakening her children for the purpose of feeding them. How or where she got it I do not know. I presume, however, it was procured from our owner's farm. Some people may call this theft. If such a thing were to happen now, I should condemn it as theft myself. But taking place at the time it did, and for the reason that it did, no one could ever make me believe that my mother was guilty of thieving. She was simply a victim of the system of slavery. I cannot remember having slept in a bed until after our family was declared free by the Emancipation Proclamation. Three children—John, my older brother, Amanda, my sister, and myself—had a pallet on the dirt floor, or, to be more correct, we slept in and on a bundle of filthy rags laid upon the dirt floor.

I was asked not long ago to tell something about the sports and pastimes that I engaged in during my youth. Until that question was asked it had never occurred to me that there was no period of my life that was devoted to play. From the time that I can remember anything, almost every day of my life had been occupied in some kind of labour; though I think I would now be a more useful man if I had had time for sports. During the period that I spent in slavery I was not large enough to be of much service, still I was occupied most of the time in cleaning the yards, carrying water to the men in the fields, or going to the mill to which I used to take the corn, once a week, to be ground. The mill was about three miles from the plantation. This work I always dreaded. The heavy bag of corn would be thrown across the back of the horse, and the corn divided about evenly on each side; but in some way, almost without exception, on these trips, the corn would so shift as to become unbalanced and would fall off the horse, and often I would fall with it. As I was not strong enough to reload the corn upon the horse, I would have to wait, sometimes for many hours, till a chance passer-by came along who would help me out of my trouble. The hours while waiting for some one were usually spent in crying. The time consumed in this way made me late in reaching the mill, and by the time I got my corn ground and reached home it would be far into the night. The road was a lonely one, and often led through dense forests. I was always frightened. The woods were said to be full of soldiers who had deserted from the army, and I had been told that the first thing a deserter did to a Negro boy when he found him alone was to cut off his ears. Besides, when I was late in getting home I knew I would always get a severe scolding or a flogging.

I had no schooling whatever while I was a slave, though I remember on several occasions I went as far as the schoolhouse door with one of my young mistresses to carry her books. The picture of several dozen boys and girls in a schoolroom engaged in study made a deep impression upon me, and I had the feeling that to get into a schoolhouse and study in this way would be about the same as getting into paradise.

So far as I can now recall, the first knowledge that I got of the fact that we were slaves, and that freedom of the slaves was being discussed, was early one morning before day, when I was awakened by my mother kneeling over her children and fervently praying that Lincoln and his armies might be successful, and that one day she and her children might be free. In this connection I have never been able to understand how the slaves throughout the South, completely ignorant as were the masses so far as books or newspapers were concerned, were able to keep themselves so accurately and completely informed about the great National questions that were agitating the country. From the time that Garrison, Lovejoy, and others began to agitate for freedom, the slaves throughout the South kept in close touch with the progress of the movement. Though I was a mere child during the preparation for the Civil War and during the war itself, I now recall the many late-at-night whispered discussions that I heard my mother and the other slaves on the plantation indulge in. These discussions showed that they understood the situation, and that they kept themselves informed of events by what was termed the "grape-vine" telegraph.

During the campaign when Lincoln was first a candidate for the Presidency, the slaves on our far-off plantation, miles from any railroad or large city or daily newspaper, knew what the issues involved were. When war was begun between the North and the South, every slave on our plantation felt and knew that, though other issues were discussed, the primal one was that of slavery. Even the most ignorant members of my race on the remote plantations felt in their hearts, with a certainty that admitted of no doubt, that the freedom of the slaves would be the one great result of the war, if the northern armies conquered. Every success of the Federal armies and every defeat of the Confederate forces was watched with the keenest and most intense interest. Often the slaves got knowledge of the results of great battles before the white people received it. This news was usually gotten from the coloured man who was sent to the post-office for the mail. In our case the post-office was about three miles from the plantation, and the mail came once or twice a week. The man who was sent to the office would linger about the place long enough to get the drift of the conversation from the group of white people who naturally congregated there, after receiving their mail, to discuss the latest news. The mail-carrier on his way back to our master's house would as naturally retail the news that he had secured among the slaves, and in this way they often heard of important events before the white people at the "big house," as the master's house was called.

I cannot remember a single instance during my childhood or early boyhood when our entire family sat down to the table together, and God's blessing was asked, and the family ate a meal in a civilized manner. On the plantation in Virginia, and even later, meals were gotten by the children very much as dumb animals get theirs. It was a piece of bread here and a scrap of meat there. It was a cup of milk at one time and some potatoes at another. Sometimes a portion of our family would eat out of the skillet or pot, while some one else would eat from a tin plate held on the knees, and often using nothing but the hands with which to hold the food. When I had grown to sufficient size, I was required to go to the "big house" at meal-times to fan the flies from the table by means of a large set of paper fans operated by a pulley. Naturally much of the conversation of the white people turned upon the subject of freedom and the war, and I absorbed a good deal of it. I remember that at one time I saw two of my young mistresses and some lady visitors eating ginger-cakes, in the yard. At that time those cakes seemed to me to be absolutely the most tempting and desirable things that I had ever seen; and I then and there resolved that, if I ever got free, the height of my ambition would be reached if I could get to the point where I could secure and eat ginger-cakes in the way that I saw those ladies doing.

Of course as the war was prolonged the white people, in many cases, often found it difficult to secure food for themselves. I think the slaves felt the deprivation less than the whites, because the usual diet for slaves was corn bread and pork, and these could be raised on the plantation; but coffee, tea, sugar, and other articles which the whites had been accustomed to use could not be raised on the plantation, and the conditions brought about by the war frequently made it impossible to secure these things. The whites were often in great straits. Parched corn was used for coffee, and a kind of black molasses was used instead of sugar. Many times nothing was used to sweeten the so-called tea and coffee.

The first pair of shoes that I recall wearing were wooden ones. They had rough leather on the top, but the bottoms, which were about an inch thick, were of wood. When I walked they made a fearful noise, and besides this they were very inconvenient, since there was no yielding to the natural pressure of the foot. In wearing them one presented and exceedingly awkward appearance. The most trying ordeal that I was forced to endure as a slave boy, however, was the wearing of a flax shirt. In the portion of Virginia where I lived it was common to use flax as part of the clothing for the slaves. That part of the flax from which our clothing was made was largely the refuse, which of course was the cheapest and roughest part. I can scarcely imagine any torture, except, perhaps, the pulling of a tooth, that is equal to that caused by putting on a new flax shirt for the first time. It is almost equal to the feeling that one would experience if he had a dozen or more chestnut burrs, or a hundred small pin-points, in contact with his flesh. Even to this day I can recall accurately the tortures that I underwent when putting on one of these garments. The fact that my flesh was soft and tender added to the pain. But I had no choice. I had to wear the flax shirt or none; and had it been left to me to choose, I should have chosen to wear no covering. In connection with the flax shirt, my brother John, who is several years older than I am, performed one of the most generous acts that I ever heard of one slave relative doing for another. On several occasions when I was being forced to wear a new flax shirt, he generously agreed to put it on in my stead and wear it for several days, till it was "broken in." Until I had grown to be quite a youth this single garment was all that I wore.

One may get the idea, from what I have said, that there was bitter feeling toward the white people on the part of my race, because of the fact that most of the white population was away fighting in a war which would result in keeping the Negro in slavery if the South was successful. In the case of the slaves on our place this was not true, and it was not true of any large portion of the slave population in the South where the Negro was treated with anything like decency. During the Civil War one of my young masters was killed, and two were severely wounded. I recall the feeling of sorrow which existed among the slaves when they heard of the death of "Mars' Billy." It was no sham sorrow, but real. Some of the slaves had nursed "Mars' Billy"; others had played with him when he was a child. "Mars' Billy" had begged for mercy in the case of others when the overseer or master was thrashing them. The sorrow in the slave quarter was only second to that in the "big house." When the two young masters were brought home wounded, the sympathy of the slaves was shown in many ways. They were just as anxious to assist in the nursing as the family relatives of the wounded. Some of the slaves would even beg for the privilege of sitting up at night to nurse their wounded masters. This tenderness and sympathy on the part of those held in bondage was a result of their kindly and generous nature. In order to defend and protect the women and children who were left on the plantations when the white males went to war, the slaves would have laid down their lives. The slave who was selected to sleep in the "big house" during the absence of the males was considered to have the place of honour. Any one attempting to harm "young Mistress" or "old Mistress" during the night would have had to cross the dead body of the slave to do so. I do not know how many have noticed it, but I think that it will be found to be true that there are few instances, either in slavery or freedom, in which a member of my race has been known to betray a specific trust.

As a rule, not only did the members of my race entertain no feelings of bitterness against the whites before and during the war, but there are many instances of Negroes tenderly caring for their former masters and mistresses who for some reason have become poor and dependent since the war. I know of instances where the former masters of slaves have for years been supplied with money by their former slaves to keep them from suffering. I have known of still other cases in which the former slaves have assisted in the education of the descendants of their former owners. I know of a case on a large plantation in the South in which a young white man, the son of the former owner of the estate, has become so reduced in purse and self-control by reason of drink that he is a pitiable creature; and yet, notwithstanding the poverty of the coloured people themselves on this plantation, they have for years supplied this young white man with the necessities of life. One sends him a little coffee or sugar, another a little meat, and so on. Nothing that the coloured people possess is too good for the son of "old Mars' Tom," who will perhaps never be permitted to suffer while any remain on the place who knew directly or indirectly of "old Mars' Tom."

I have said that there are few instances of a member of my race betraying a specific trust. One of the best illustrations of this which I know of is in the case of an ex-slave from Virginia whom I met not long ago in a little town in the state of Ohio. I found that this man had made a contract with his master, two or three years previous to the Emancipation Proclamation, to the effect that the slave was to be permitted to buy himself, by paying so much per year for his body; and while he was paying for himself, he was to be permitted to labour where and for whom he pleased. Finding that he could secure better wages in Ohio, he went there. When freedom came, he was still in debt to his master some three hundred dollars. Notwithstanding that the Emancipation Proclamation freed him from any obligation to his master, this black man walked the greater portion of the distance back to where his old master lived in Virginia, and placed the last dollar, with interest, in his hands. In talking to me about this, the man told me that he knew that he did not have to pay the debt, but that he had given his word to the master, and his word he had never broken. He felt that he could not enjoy his freedom till he had fulfilled his promise.

From some things that I have said one may get the idea that some of the slaves did not want freedom. This is not true. I have never seen one who did not want to be free, or one who would return to slavery.

I pity from the bottom of my heart any nation or body of people that is so unfortunate as to get entangled in the net of slavery. I have long since ceased to cherish any spirit of bitterness against the Southern white people on account of the enslavement of my race. No one section of our country was wholly responsible for its introduction, and, besides, it was recognized and protected for years by the General Government. Having once got its tentacles fastened on to the economic and social life of the Republic, it was no easy matter for the country to relieve itself of the institution. Then, when we rid ourselves of prejudice, or racial feeling, and look facts in the face, we must acknowledge that, notwithstanding the cruelty and moral wrong of slavery, the ten million Negroes inhabiting this country, who themselves or whose ancestors went through the school of American slavery, are in a stronger and more hopeful condition, materially, intellectually, morally, and religiously, than is true of an equal number of black people in any other portion of the globe. This is so to such an extent that Negroes in this country, who themselves or whose forefathers went through the school of slavery, are constantly returning to

Africa as missionaries to enlighten those who remained in the fatherland. This I say, not to justify slavery—on the other hand, I condemn it as an institution, as we all know that in America it was established for selfish and financial reasons, and not from a missionary motive—but to call attention to a fact, and to show how Providence so often uses men and institutions to accomplish a purpose. When persons ask me in these days how, in the midst of what sometimes seem hopelessly discouraging conditions, I can have such faith in the future of my race in this country, I remind them of the wilderness through which and out of which, a good Providence has already led us.

Ever since I have been old enough to think for myself, I have entertained the idea that, notwithstanding the cruel wrongs inflicted upon us, the black man got nearly as much out of slavery as the white man did. The hurtful influences of the institution were not by any means confined to the Negro. This was fully illustrated by the life upon our own plantation. The whole machinery of slavery was so constructed as to cause labour, as a rule, to be looked upon as a badge of degradation, of inferiority. Hence labour was something that both races on the slave plantation sought to escape. The slave system on our place, in a large measure, took the spirit of self-reliance and self-help out of the white people. My old master had many boys and girls, but not one, so far as I know, ever mastered a single trade or special line of productive industry. The girls were not taught to cook, sew, or to take care of the house. All of this was left to the slaves. The slaves, of course, had little personal interest in the life of the plantation, and their ignorance prevented them from learning how to do things in the most improved and thorough manner. As a result of the system, fences were out of repair, gates were hanging half off the hinges, doors creaked, window-panes were out, plastering had fallen but was not replaced, weeds grew in the yard. As a rule, there was food for whites and blacks, but inside the house, and on the dining-room table, there was wanting that delicacy and refinement of touch and finish which can make a home the most convenient, comfortable, and attractive place in the world. Withal there was a waste of food and other materials which was sad. When freedom came, the slaves were almost as well fitted to begin life anew as the master, except in the matter of book-learning and ownership of property. The slave owner and his sons had mastered no special industry. They unconsciously had imbibed the feeling that manual labour was not the proper thing for them. On the other hand, the slaves, in many cases, had mastered some handicraft, and none were ashamed, and few unwilling, to labour.

Finally the war closed, and the day of freedom came. It was a momentous and eventful day to all upon our plantation. We had been expecting it. Freedom was in the air, and had been for months. Deserting soldiers returning to their homes were to be seen every day. Others who had been discharged, or whose regiments had been paroled, were constantly passing near our place. The "grape-vine telegraph" was kept busy night and day. The news and mutterings of great events were swiftly carried from one plantation to another. In the fear of "Yankee" invasions, the silverware and other valuables were taken from the "big house," buried in the woods, and guarded by trusted slaves. Woe be to any one who would have attempted to disturb the buried treasure. The slaves would give the Yankee soldiers food, drink, clothing—anything but that which had been specifically intrusted to their care and honour. As the great day drew nearer, there was more singing in the slave quarters than usual. It was bolder, had more ring, and lasted later into the night. Most of the verses of the plantation songs had some reference to freedom. True, they had sung those same verses before, but they had been careful to explain that the "freedom" in these songs referred to the next world, and had no connection with life in this world. Now they gradually threw off the mask, and were not afraid to let it be known that the "freedom" in their songs meant freedom of the body in this world. The night before the eventful day, word was sent to the slave quarters to the effect that something unusual was going to take place at the "big house" the next morning. There was little, if any, sleep that night. All as excitement and expectancy. Early the next morning word was sent to all the slaves, old and young, to gather at the house. In company with my mother, brother, and sister, and a large number of other slaves, I went to the master's house. All of our master's family were either standing or seated on the veranda of the house, where they could see what was to take place and hear what was said. There was a feeling of deep interest, or perhaps sadness, on their faces, but not bitterness. As I now recall the impression they made upon me, they did not at the moment seem to be sad because of the loss of property, but rather because of parting with those whom they had reared and who were in many ways very close to them. The most distinct thing that I now recall in connection with the scene was that some man who seemed to be a stranger (a United States officer, I presume) made a little speech and then read a rather long paper—the Emancipation Proclamation, I think. After the reading we were told that we were all free, and could go when and where we pleased. My mother, who was standing by my side, leaned over and kissed her children, while tears of joy ran down her cheeks. She explained to us what it all meant, that this was the day for which she had been so long praying, but fearing that she would never live to see.

For some minutes there was great rejoicing, and thanksgiving, and wild scenes of ecstasy. But there was no feeling of bitterness. In fact, there was pity among the slaves for our former owners. The wild rejoicing on the part of the emancipated coloured people lasted but for a brief period, for I noticed that by the time they returned to their cabins there was a change in their feelings. The great responsibility of being free, of having charge of themselves, of having to think and plan for themselves and their children, seemed to take possession of them. It was very much like suddenly turning a youth of ten or twelve years out into the world to provide for himself.

In a few hours the great questions with which the Anglo-Saxon race had been grappling for centuries had been thrown upon these people to be solved. These were the questions of a home, a living, the rearing of children, education, citizenship, and the establishment and support of churches. Was it any wonder that within a few hours the wild rejoicing ceased and a feeling of deep gloom seemed to pervade the slave quarters?

To some it seemed that, now that they were in actual possession of it, freedom was a more serious thing than they had expected to find it. Some of the slaves were seventy or eighty years old; their best days were gone. They had no strength with which to earn a living in a strange place and among strange people, even if they had been sure where to find a new place of abode. To this class the problem seemed especially hard. Besides, deep down in their hearts there was a strange and peculiar attachment to "old Marster" and "old Missus," and to their children, which they found it hard to think of breaking off. With these they had spent in some cases nearly a half-century, and it was no light thing to think of parting. Gradually, one by one, stealthily at first, the older slaves began to wander from the slave quarters back to the "big house" to have a whispered conversation with their former owners as to the future.

Chapter 2. Boyhood Days

After the coming of freedom there were two points upon which practically all the people on our place were agreed, and I found that this was generally true throughout the South: that they must change their names, and that they must leave the old plantation for at least a few days or weeks in order that they might really feel sure that they were free.

In some way a feeling got among the coloured people that it was far from proper for them to bear the surname of their former owners, and a great many of them took other surnames. This was one of the first signs of freedom. When they were slaves, a coloured person was simply called "John" or "Susan." There was seldom occasion for more than the use of the one name. If "John" or "Susan" belonged to a white man by the name of "Hatcher," sometimes he was called "John Hatcher," or as often "Hatcher's John." But there was a feeling that "John Hatcher" or "Hatcher's John" was not the proper title by which to denote a freeman; and so in many cases "John Hatcher" was changed to "John S. Lincoln" or "John S. Sherman," the initial "S" standing for no name, it being simply a part of what the coloured man proudly called his "entitles."

As I have stated, most of the coloured people left the old plantation for a short while at least, so as to be sure, it seemed, that they could leave and try their freedom on to see how it felt. After they had remained away for a while, many of the older slaves, especially, returned to their old homes and made some kind of contract with their former owners by which they remained on the estate.

My mother's husband, who was the stepfather of my brother John and myself, did not belong to the same owners as did my mother. In fact, he seldom came to our plantation. I remember seeing him there perhaps once a year, that being about Christmas time. In some way, during the war, by running away and following the Federal soldiers, it seems, he found his way into the new state of West Virginia. As soon as freedom was declared, he sent for my mother to come to the Kanawha Valley, in West Virginia. At that time a journey from Virginia over the mountains to West Virginia was rather a tedious and in some cases a painful undertaking. What little clothing and few household goods we had were placed in a cart, but the children walked the greater portion of the distance, which was several hundred miles.

I do not think any of us ever had been very far from the plantation, and the taking of a long journey into another state was quite an event. The parting from our former owners and the members of our own race on the plantation was a serious occasion. From the time of our parting till their death we kept up a correspondence with the older members of the family, and in later years we have kept in touch with those who were the younger members. We were several weeks making the trip, and most of the time we slept in the open air and did our cooking over a log fire out-of-doors. One night I recall that we camped near an abandoned log cabin, and my mother decided to build a fire in that for cooking, and afterward to make a "pallet" on the floor for our sleeping. Just as the fire had gotten well started a large black snake fully a yard and a half long dropped down the chimney and ran out on the floor. Of course we at once abandoned that cabin. Finally we reached our destination—a little town called Malden, which is about five miles from Charleston, the present capital of the state.

At that time salt-mining was the great industry in that part of West Virginia, and the little town of Malden was right in the midst of the salt-furnaces. My stepfather had already secured a job at a salt-furnace, and he had also secured a little cabin for us to live in. Our new house was no better than the one we had left on the old plantation in Virginia. In fact, in one respect it was worse. Notwithstanding the poor condition of our plantation cabin, we were at all times sure of pure air. Our new home was in the midst of a cluster of cabins crowded closely together, and as there were no sanitary regulations, the filth about the cabins was often intolerable. Some of our neighbours were coloured people, and some were the poorest and most ignorant and degraded white people. It was a motley mixture. Drinking, gambling, quarrels, fights, and shockingly immoral practices were frequent. All who lived in the little town were in one way or another connected with the salt business. Though I was a mere child, my stepfather put me and my brother at work in one of the furnaces. Often I began work as early as four o'clock in the morning.

The first thing I ever learned in the way of book knowledge was while working in this salt-furnace. Each salt-packer had his barrels marked with a certain number. The number allotted to my stepfather was "18." At the close of the day's work the boss of the packers would come around and put "18" on each of our barrels, and I soon learned to recognize that figure wherever I saw it, and after a while got to the point where I could make that figure, though I knew nothing about any other figures or letters.

From the time that I can remember having any thoughts about anything, I recall that I had an intense longing to learn to read. I determined, when quite a small child, that, if I accomplished nothing else in life, I would in some way get enough education to enable me to read common books and newspapers. Soon after we got settled in some manner in our new cabin in West Virginia, I induced my mother to get hold of a book for me. How or where she got it I do not know, but in some way she procured an old copy of Webster's "blue-back" spelling-book, which contained the alphabet, followed by such meaningless words as "ab," "ba," "ca," "da." I began at once to devour this book, and I think that it was the first one I ever had in my hands. I had learned from somebody that the way to begin to read was to learn the alphabet, so I tried in all the ways I could think of to learn it,—all of course without a teacher, for I could find no one to teach me. At that time there was not a single member of my race anywhere near us who could read, and I was too timid to approach any of the white people. In some way, within a few weeks, I mastered the greater portion of the alphabet. In all my efforts to learn to read my mother shared fully my ambition, and sympathized with me and aided me in every way that she could. Though she was totally ignorant, she had high ambitions for her children, and a large fund of good, hard, common sense, which seemed to enable her to meet and master every situation. If I have done anything in life worth attention, I feel sure that I inherited the disposition from my mother.

In the midst of my struggles and longing for an education, a young coloured boy who had learned to read in the state of Ohio came to Malden. As soon as the coloured people found out that he could read, a newspaper was secured, and at the close of nearly every day's work this young man would be surrounded by a group of men and women who were anxious to hear him read the news contained in the papers. How I used to envy this man! He seemed to me to be the one young man in all the world who ought to be satisfied with his attainments.

About this time the question of having some kind of a school opened for the coloured children in the village began to be discussed by members of the race. As it would be the first school for Negro children that had ever been opened in that part of Virginia, it was, of course, to be a great event, and the discussion excited the wildest interest. The most perplexing question was where to find a teacher. The young man from Ohio who had learned to read the papers was considered, but his age was against him. In the midst of the discussion about a teacher, another young coloured man from Ohio, who had been a soldier, in some way found his way into town. It was soon learned that he possessed considerable education, and he was engaged by the coloured people to teach their first school. As yet no free schools had been started for coloured people in that section, hence each family agreed to pay a certain amount per month, with the understanding that the teacher was to "board 'round"—that is, spend a day with each family. This was not bad for the teacher, for each family tried to provide the very best on the day the teacher was to be its guest. I recall that I looked forward with an anxious appetite to the "teacher's day" at our little cabin.

This experience of a whole race beginning to go to school for the first time, presents one of the most interesting studies that has ever occurred in connection with the development of any race. Few people who were not right in the midst of the scenes can form any exact idea of the intense desire which the people of my race showed for an education. As I have stated, it was a whole race trying to go to school. Few were too young, and none too old, to make the attempt to learn. As fast as any kind of teachers could be secured, not only were day-schools filled, but night-schools as well. The great ambition of the older people was to try to learn to read the Bible before they died. With this end in view men and women who were fifty or seventy-five years old would often be found in the night-school. Some day-schools were formed soon after freedom, but the principal book studied in the Sunday-school was the spelling-book. Day-school, night-school, Sunday-school, were always crowded, and often many had to be turned away for want of room.

The opening of the school in the Kanawha Valley, however, brought to me one of the keenest disappointments that I ever experienced. I had been working in a salt-furnace for several months, and my stepfather had discovered that I had a financial value, and so, when the school opened, he decided that he could not spare me from my work. This decision seemed to cloud my every ambition. The disappointment was made all the more severe by reason of the fact that my place of work was where I could see the happy children passing to and from school mornings and afternoons. Despite this disappointment, however, I determined that I would learn something, anyway. I applied myself with greater earnestness than ever to the mastering of what was in the "blue-back" speller.

My mother sympathized with me in my disappointment, and sought to comfort me in all the ways she could, and to help me find a way to learn. After a while I succeeded in making arrangements with the teacher to give me some lessons at night, after the day's work was done. These night lessons were so welcome that I think I learned more at night than the other children did during the day. My own experiences in the night-school gave me faith in the night-school idea, with which, in after years, I had to do both at Hampton and Tuskegee. But my boyish heart was still set upon going to the day-school, and I let no opportunity slip to push my case. Finally I won, and was permitted to go to the school in the day for a few months, with the understanding that I was to rise early in the morning and work in the furnace till nine o'clock, and return immediately after school closed in the afternoon for at least two more hours of work.

The schoolhouse was some distance from the furnace, and as I had to work till nine o'clock, and the school opened at nine, I found myself in a difficulty. School would always be begun before I reached it, and sometimes my class had recited. To get around this difficulty I yielded to a temptation for which most people, I suppose, will condemn me; but since it is a fact, I might as well state it. I have great faith in the power and influence of facts. It is seldom that anything is permanently gained by holding back a fact. There was a large clock in a little office in the furnace. This clock, of course, all the hundred or more workmen depended upon to regulate their hours of beginning and ending the day's work. I got the idea that the way for me to reach school on time was to move the clock hands from half-past eight up to the nine o'clock mark. This I found myself doing morning after morning, till the furnace "boss" discovered that something was wrong, and locked the clock in a case. I did not mean to inconvenience anybody. I simply meant to reach that schoolhouse in time.

When, however, I found myself at the school for the first time, I also found myself confronted with two other difficulties. In the first place, I found that all the other children wore hats or caps on their heads, and I had neither hat nor cap. In fact, I do not remember that up to the time of going to school I had ever worn any kind of covering upon my head, nor do I recall that either I or anybody else had even thought anything about the need of covering for my head. But, of course, when I saw how all the other boys were dressed, I began to feel quite uncomfortable. As usual, I put the case before my mother, and she explained to me that she had no money with which to buy a "store hat," which was a rather new institution at that time among the members of my race and was considered quite the thing for young and old to own, but that she would find a way to help me out of the difficulty. She accordingly got two pieces of "homespun" (jeans) and sewed them together, and I was soon the proud possessor of my first cap.

The lesson that my mother taught me in this has always remained with me, and I have tried as best as I could to teach it to others. I have always felt proud, whenever I think of the incident, that my mother had strength of character enough not to be led into the temptation of seeming to be that which she was not—of trying to impress my schoolmates and others with the fact that she was able to buy me a "store hat" when she was not. I have always felt proud that she refused to go into debt for that which she did not have the money to pay for. Since that time I have owned many kinds of caps and hats, but never one of which I have felt so proud as of the cap made of the two pieces of cloth sewed together by my mother. I have noted the fact, but without satisfaction, I need not add, that several of the boys who began their careers with "store hats" and who were my schoolmates and used to join in the sport that was made of me because I had only a "homespun" cap, have ended their careers in the penitentiary, while others are not able now to buy any kind of hat.

My second difficulty was with regard to my name, or rather A name. From the time when I could remember anything, I had been called simply "Booker." Before going to school it had never occurred to me that it was needful or appropriate to have an additional name. When I heard the school-roll called, I noticed that all of the children had at least two names, and some of them indulged in what seemed to me the extravagance of having three. I was in deep perplexity, because I knew that the teacher would demand of me at least two names, and I had only one. By the time the occasion came for the enrolling of my name, an idea occurred to me which I thought would make me equal to the situation; and so, when the teacher asked me what my full name was, I calmly told him "Booker Washington," as if I had been called by that name all my life; and by that name I have since been known. Later in my life I found that my mother had given me the name of "Booker Taliaferro" soon after I was born, but in some way that part of my name seemed to disappear and for a long while was forgotten, but as soon as I found out about it I revived it, and made my full name "Booker Taliaferro Washington." I think there are not many men in our country who have had the privilege of naming themselves in the way that I have.

More than once I have tried to picture myself in the position of a boy or man with an honoured and distinguished ancestry which I could trace back through a period of hundreds of years, and who had not only inherited a name, but fortune and a proud family homestead; and yet I have sometimes had the feeling that if I had inherited these, and had been a member of a more popular race, I should have been inclined to yield to the temptation of depending upon my ancestry and my colour to do that for me which I should do for myself. Years ago I resolved that because I had no ancestry myself I would leave a record of which my children would be proud, and which might encourage them to still higher effort.

The world should not pass judgment upon the Negro, and especially the Negro youth, too quickly or too harshly. The Negro boy has obstacles, discouragements, and temptations to battle with that are little known to those not situated as he is. When a white boy undertakes a task, it is taken for granted that he will succeed. On the other hand, people are usually surprised if the Negro boy does not fail. In a word, the Negro youth starts out with the presumption against him.

The influence of ancestry, however, is important in helping forward any individual or race, if too much reliance is not placed upon it. Those who constantly direct attention to the Negro youth's moral weaknesses, and compare his advancement with that of white youths, do not consider the influence of the memories which cling about the old family homesteads. I have no idea, as I have stated elsewhere, who my grandmother was. I have, or have had, uncles and aunts and cousins, but I have no knowledge as to where most of them are. My case will illustrate that of hundreds of thousands of black people in every part of our country. The very fact that the white boy is conscious that, if he fails in life, he will disgrace the whole family record, extending back through many generations, is of tremendous value in helping him to resist temptations. The fact that the individual has behind and surrounding him proud family history and connection serves as a stimulus to help him to overcome obstacles when striving for success.

The time that I was permitted to attend school during the day was short, and my attendance was irregular. It was not long before I had to stop attending day-school altogether, and devote all of my time again to work. I resorted to the night-school again. In fact, the greater part of the education I secured in my boyhood was gathered through the night-school after my day's work was done. I had difficulty often in securing a satisfactory teacher. Sometimes, after I had secured some one to teach me at night, I would find, much to my disappointment, that the teacher knew but little more than I did. Often I would have to walk several miles at night in order to recite my night-school lessons. There was never a time in my youth, no matter how dark and discouraging the days might be, when one resolve did not continually remain with me, and that was a determination to secure an education at any cost.

Soon after we moved to West Virginia, my mother adopted into our family, notwithstanding our poverty, an orphan boy, to whom afterward we gave the name of James B. Washington. He has ever since remained a member of the family.

After I had worked in the salt-furnace for some time, work was secured for me in a coal-mine which was operated mainly for the purpose of securing fuel for the salt-furnace. Work in the coal-mine I always dreaded. One reason for this was that any one who worked in a coal-mine was always unclean, at least while at work, and it was a very hard job to get one's skin clean after the day's work was over. Then it was fully a mile from the opening of the coal-mine to the face of the coal, and all, of course, was in the blackest darkness. I do not believe that one ever experiences anywhere else such darkness as he does in a coal-mine. The mine was divided into a large number of different "rooms" or departments, and, as

I never was able to learn the location of all these "rooms," I many times found myself lost in the mine. To add to the horror of being lost, sometimes my light would go out, and then, if I did not happen to have a match, I would wander about in the darkness until by chance I found some one to give me a light. The work was not only hard, but it was dangerous. There was always the danger of being blown to pieces by a premature explosion of powder, or of being crushed by falling slate. Accidents from one or the other of these causes were frequently occurring, and this kept me in constant fear. Many children of the tenderest years were compelled then, as is now true I fear, in most coal-mining districts, to spend a large part of their lives in these coal-mines, with little opportunity to get an education; and, what is worse, I have often noted that, as a rule, young boys who begin life in a coal-mine are often physically and mentally dwarfed. They soon lose ambition to do anything else than to continue as a coal-miner.

In those days, and later as a young man, I used to try to picture in my imagination the feelings and ambitions of a white boy with absolutely no limit placed upon his aspirations and activities. I used to envy the white boy who had no obstacles placed in the way of his becoming a Congressman, Governor, Bishop, or President by reason of the accident of his birth or race. I used to picture the way that I would act under such circumstances; how I would begin at the bottom and keep rising until I reached the highest round of success.

In later years, I confess that I do not envy the white boy as I once did. I have learned that success is to be measured not so much by the position that one has reached in life as by the obstacles which he has overcome while trying to succeed. Looked at from this standpoint, I almost reached the conclusion that often the Negro boy's birth and connection with an unpopular race is an advantage, so far as real life is concerned. With few exceptions, the Negro youth must work harder and must perform his tasks even better than a white youth in order to secure recognition. But out of the hard and unusual struggle through which he is compelled to pass, he gets a strength, a confidence, that one misses whose pathway is comparatively smooth by reason of birth and race.

From any point of view, I had rather be what I am, a member of the Negro race, than be able to claim membership with the most favoured of any other race. I have always been made sad when I have heard members of any race claiming rights or privileges, or certain badges of distinction, on the ground simply that they were members of this or that race, regardless of their own individual worth or attainments. I have been made to feel sad for such persons because I am conscious of the fact that mere connection with what is known as a superior race will not permanently carry an individual forward unless he has individual worth, and mere connection with what is regarded as an inferior race will not finally hold an individual back if he possesses intrinsic, individual merit. Every persecuted individual and race should get much consolation out of the great human law, which is universal and eternal, that merit, no matter under what skin found, is, in the long run, recognized and rewarded. This I have said here, not to call attention to myself as an individual, but to the race to which I am proud to belong.

Chapter 3. The Struggle For An Education

One day, while at work in the coal-mine, I happened to overhear two miners talking about a great school for coloured people somewhere in Virginia. This was the first time that I had ever heard anything about any kind of school or college that was more pretentious than the little coloured school in our town.

In the darkness of the mine I noiselessly crept as close as I could to the two men who were talking. I heard one tell the other that not only was the school established for the members of any race, but the opportunities that it provided by which poor but worthy students could work out all or a part of the cost of a board, and at the same time be taught some trade or industry.

As they went on describing the school, it seemed to me that it must be the greatest place on earth, and not even Heaven presented more attractions for me at that time than did the Hampton Normal and Agricultural Institute in Virginia, about which these men were talking. I resolved at once to go to that school, although I had no idea where it was, or how many miles away, or how I was going to reach it; I remembered only that I was on fire constantly with one ambition, and that was to go to Hampton. This thought was with me day and night.

After hearing of the Hampton Institute, I continued to work for a few months longer in the coal-mine. While at work there, I heard of a vacant position in the household of General Lewis Ruffner, the owner of the salt-furnace and coal-mine. Mrs. Viola Ruffner, the wife of General Ruffner, was a "Yankee" woman from Vermont. Mrs. Ruffner had a reputation all through the vicinity for being very strict with her servants, and especially with the boys who tried to serve her. Few of them remained with her more than two or three weeks. They all left with the same excuse: she was too strict. I decided, however, that I would rather try Mrs. Ruffner's house than remain in the coal-mine, and so my mother applied to her for the vacant position. I was hired at a salary of $5 per month.

I had heard so much about Mrs. Ruffner's severity that I was almost afraid to see her, and trembled when I went into her presence. I had not lived with her many weeks, however, before I began to understand her. I soon began to learn that, first of all, she wanted everything kept clean about her, that she wanted things done promptly and systematically, and that at the bottom of everything she wanted absolute honesty and frankness. Nothing must be sloven or slipshod; every door, every fence, must be kept in repair.

I cannot now recall how long I lived with Mrs. Ruffner before going to Hampton, but I think it must have been a year and a half. At any rate, I here repeat what I have said more than once before, that the lessons that I learned in the home of Mrs. Ruffner were as valuable to me as any education I have ever gotten anywhere else. Even to this day I never see bits of paper scattered around a house or in the street that I do not want to pick them up at once. I never see a filthy yard that I do not want to clean it, a paling off of a fence that I do not want to put it on, an unpainted or unwhitewashed house that I do not want to paint or whitewash it, or a button off one's clothes, or a grease-spot on them or on a floor, that I do not want to call attention to it.

From fearing Mrs. Ruffner I soon learned to look upon her as one of my best friends. When she found that she could trust me she did so implicitly. During the one or two winters that I was with her she gave me an opportunity to go to school for an hour in the day during a portion of the winter months, but most of my studying was done at night, sometimes alone, sometimes under some one whom I could hire to teach me. Mrs. Ruffner always encouraged and sympathized with me in all my efforts to get an education. It was while living with her that I began to get together my first library. I secured a dry-goods box, knocked out one side of it, put some shelves in it, and began putting into it every kind of book that I could get my hands upon, and called it my "library."

Notwithstanding my success at Mrs. Ruffner's I did not give up the idea of going to the Hampton Institute. In the fall of 1872 I determined to make an effort to get there, although, as I have stated, I had no definite idea of the direction in which Hampton was, or of what it would cost to go there. I do not think that any one thoroughly sympathized with me in my ambition to go to Hampton unless it was my mother, and she was troubled with a grave fear that I was starting out on a "wild-goose chase." At any rate, I got only a half-hearted consent from her that I might start. The small amount of money that I had earned had been consumed by my stepfather and the remainder of the family, with the exception of a very few dollars, and so I had very little with which to buy clothes and pay my travelling expenses. My brother John helped me all that he could, but of course that was not a great deal, for his work was in the coal-mine, where he did not earn much, and most of what he did earn went in the direction of paying the household expenses.

Perhaps the thing that touched and pleased me most in connection with my starting for Hampton was the interest that many of the older coloured people took in the matter. They had spent the best days of their lives in slavery, and hardly expected to live to see the time when they would see a member of their race leave home to attend a boarding-school. Some of these older people would give me a nickel, others a quarter, or a handkerchief.

Finally the great day came, and I started for Hampton. I had only a small, cheap satchel that contained a few articles of clothing I could get. My mother at the time was rather weak and broken in health. I hardly expected to see her again, and thus our parting was all the more sad. She, however, was very brave through it all. At that time there were no through trains connecting that part of West Virginia with eastern Virginia. Trains ran only a portion of the way, and the remainder of the distance was travelled by stage-coaches.

The distance from Malden to Hampton is about five hundred miles. I had not been away from home many hours before it began to grow painfully evident that I did not have enough money to pay my fare to Hampton. One experience I shall long remember. I had been travelling over the mountains most of the afternoon in an old-fashion stage-coach, when, late in the evening, the coach stopped for the night at a common, unpainted house called a hotel. All the other passengers except myself were whites.

In my ignorance I supposed that the little hotel existed for the purpose of accommodating the passengers who travelled on the stage-coach. The difference that the colour of one's skin would make I had not thought anything about. After all the other passengers had been shown rooms and were getting ready for supper, I shyly presented myself before the man at the desk. It is true I had practically no money in my pocket with which to pay for bed or food, but I had hoped in some way to beg my way into the good graces of the landlord, for at that season in the mountains of Virginia the weather was cold, and I wanted to get indoors for the night. Without asking as to whether I had any money, the man at the desk firmly refused to even consider the matter of providing me with food or lodging. This was my first experience in finding out what the colour of my skin meant. In some way I managed to keep warm by walking about, and so got through the night. My whole soul was so bent upon reaching Hampton that I did not have time to cherish any bitterness toward the hotel-keeper.

By walking, begging rides both in wagons and in the cars, in some way, after a number of days, I reached the city of Richmond, Virginia, about eighty-two miles from Hampton. When I reached there, tired, hungry, and dirty, it was late in the night. I had never been in a large city, and this rather added to my misery. When I reached Richmond, I was completely out of money. I had not a single acquaintance in the place, and, being unused to city ways, I did not know where to go. I applied at several places for lodging, but they all wanted money, and that was what I did not have. Knowing nothing else better to do, I walked the streets. In doing this I passed by many food-stands where fried chicken and half-moon apple pies were piled high and made to present a most tempting appearance. At that time it seemed to me that I would have promised all that I expected to possess in the future to have gotten hold of one of those chicken legs or one of those pies. But I could not get either of these, nor anything else to eat.

I must have walked the streets till after midnight. At last I became so exhausted that I could walk no longer. I was tired, I was hungry, I was everything but discouraged. Just about the time when I reached extreme physical exhaustion, I came upon a portion of a street where the board sidewalk was considerably elevated. I waited for a few minutes, till I was sure that no passers-by could see me, and then crept under the sidewalk and lay for the night upon the ground, with my satchel of clothing for a pillow. Nearly all night I could hear the tramp of feet over my head. The next morning I found myself somewhat refreshed, but I was extremely hungry, because it had been a long time since I had had sufficient food. As soon as it became light enough for me to see my surroundings I noticed that I was near a large ship, and that this ship seemed to be unloading a cargo of pig iron. I went at once to the vessel and asked the captain to permit me to help unload the vessel in order to get money for food. The captain, a white man, who seemed to be kind-hearted, consented. I worked long enough to earn money for my breakfast, and it seems to me, as I remember it now, to have been about the best breakfast that I have ever eaten.

My work pleased the captain so well that he told me if I desired I could continue working for a small amount per day. This I was very glad to do. I continued working on this vessel for a number of days. After buying food with the small wages I received there was not much left to add on the amount I must get to pay my way to Hampton. In order to economize in every way possible, so as to be sure to reach Hampton in a reasonable time, I continued to sleep under the same sidewalk that gave me shelter the first night I was in Richmond. Many years after that the coloured citizens of Richmond very kindly tendered me a reception at which there must have been two thousand people present. This reception was held not far from the spot where I slept the first night I spent in the city, and I must confess that my mind was more upon the sidewalk that first gave me shelter than upon the recognition, agreeable and cordial as it was.

When I had saved what I considered enough money with which to reach Hampton, I thanked the captain of the vessel for his kindness, and started again. Without any unusual occurrence I reached Hampton, with a surplus of exactly fifty cents with which to begin my education. To me it had been a long, eventful journey; but the first sight of the large, three-story, brick school building seemed to have rewarded me for all that I had undergone in order to reach the place. If the people who gave the money to provide that building could appreciate the influence the sight of it had upon me, as well as upon thousands of other youths, they would feel all the more encouraged to make such gifts. It seemed to me to be the largest and most beautiful building I had ever seen. The sight of it seemed to give me new life. I felt that a new kind of existence had now begun—that life would now have a new meaning. I felt that I had reached the promised land, and

I resolved to let no obstacle prevent me from putting forth the highest effort to fit myself to accomplish the most good in the world.

As soon as possible after reaching the grounds of the Hampton Institute, I presented myself before the head teacher for an assignment to a class. Having been so long without proper food, a bath, and a change of clothing, I did not, of course, make a very favourable impression upon her, and I could see at once that there were doubts in her mind about the wisdom of admitting me as a student. I felt that I could hardly blame her if she got the idea that I was a worthless loafer or tramp. For some time she did not refuse to admit me, neither did she decide in my favour, and I continued to linger about her, and to impress her in all the ways I could with my worthiness. In the meantime I saw her admitting other students, and that added greatly to my discomfort, for I felt, deep down in my heart, that I could do as well as they, if I could only get a chance to show what was in me.

After some hours had passed, the head teacher said to me: "The adjoining recitation-room needs sweeping. Take the broom and sweep it."

It occurred to me at once that here was my chance. Never did I receive an order with more delight. I knew that I could sweep, for Mrs. Ruffner had thoroughly taught me how to do that when I lived with her.

I swept the recitation-room three times. Then I got a dusting-cloth and dusted it four times. All the woodwork around the walls, every bench, table, and desk, I went over four times with my dusting-cloth. Besides, every piece of furniture had been moved and every closet and corner in the room had been thoroughly cleaned. I had the feeling that in a large measure my future depended upon the impression I made upon the teacher in the cleaning of that room. When I was through, I reported to the head teacher. She was a "Yankee" woman who knew just where to look for dirt. She went into the room and inspected the floor and closets; then she took her handkerchief and rubbed it on the woodwork about the walls, and over the table and benches. When she was unable to find one bit of dirt on the floor, or a particle of dust on any of the furniture, she quietly remarked, "I guess you will do to enter this institution."

I was one of the happiest souls on Earth. The sweeping of that room was my college examination, and never did any youth pass an examination for entrance into Harvard or Yale that gave him more genuine satisfaction. I have passed several examinations since then, but I have always felt that this was the best one I ever passed.

I have spoken of my own experience in entering the Hampton Institute. Perhaps few, if any, had anything like the same experience that I had, but about the same period there were hundreds who found their way to Hampton and other institutions after experiencing something of the same difficulties that I went through. The young men and women were determined to secure an education at any cost.

The sweeping of the recitation-room in the manner that I did it seems to have paved the way for me to get through Hampton. Miss Mary F. Mackie, the head teacher, offered me a position as janitor. This, of course, I gladly accepted, because it was a place where I could work out nearly all the cost of my board. The work was hard and taxing but I stuck to it. I had a large number of rooms to care for, and had to work late into the night, while at the same time I had to rise by four o'clock in the morning, in order to build the fires and have a little time in which to prepare my lessons. In all my career at Hampton, and ever since I have been out in the world, Miss Mary F. Mackie, the head teacher to whom I have referred, proved one of my strongest and most helpful friends. Her advice and encouragement were always helpful in strengthening to me in the darkest hour.

I have spoken of the impression that was made upon me by the buildings and general appearance of the Hampton Institute, but I have not spoken of that which made the greatest and most lasting impression on me, and that was a great man—the noblest, rarest human being that it has ever been my privilege to meet. I refer to the late General Samuel C. Armstrong.

It has been my fortune to meet personally many of what are called great characters, both in Europe and America, but I do not hesitate to say that I never met any man who, in my estimation, was the equal of General Armstrong. Fresh from the degrading influences of the slave plantation and the coal-mines, it was a rare privilege for me to be permitted to come into direct contact with such a character as General Armstrong. I shall always remember that the first time I went into his presence he made the impression upon me of being a perfect man: I was made to feel that there was something about him that was superhuman. It was my privilege to know the General personally from the time I entered Hampton till he died, and the more I saw of him the greater he grew in my estimation. One might have removed from Hampton all the buildings, class-rooms, teachers, and industries, and given the men and women there the opportunity of coming into daily contact with General Armstrong, and that alone would have been a liberal education. The older I grow, the more I am convinced that there is no education which one can get from books and costly apparatus that is equal to that which can be gotten from contact with great men and women. Instead of studying books so constantly, how I wish that our schools and colleges might learn to study men and things!

General Armstrong spent two of the last six months of his life in my home at Tuskegee. At that time he was paralyzed to the extent that he had lost control of his body and voice in a very large degree. Notwithstanding his affliction, he worked almost constantly night and day for the cause to which he had given his life. I never saw a man who so completely lost sight of himself. I do not believe he ever had a selfish thought. He was just as happy in trying to assist some other institution in the South as he was when working for Hampton. Although he fought the Southern white man in the Civil War, I never heard him utter a bitter word against him afterward. On the other hand, he was constantly seeking to find ways by which he could be of service to the Southern whites.

It would be difficult to describe the hold that he had upon the students at Hampton, or the faith they had in him. In fact, he was worshipped by his students. It never occurred to me that General Armstrong could fail in anything that he undertook. There is almost no request that he could have made that would not have been complied with. When he was a guest at my home in Alabama, and was so badly paralyzed that he had to be wheeled about in an invalid's chair, I recall that one of the General's former students had occasion to push his chair up a long, steep hill that taxed his strength to the utmost. When the top of the hill was reached, the former pupil, with a glow of happiness on his face, exclaimed, "I am so glad that I have been permitted to do something that was real hard for the General before he dies!" While I was a student at Hampton, the dormitories became so crowded that it was impossible to find room for all who wanted to be admitted. In order to help remedy the difficulty, the General conceived the plan of putting up tents to be used as rooms. As soon as it became known that General Armstrong would be pleased if some of the older students would live in the tents during the winter, nearly every student in school volunteered to go.

I was one of the volunteers. The winter that we spent in those tents was an intensely cold one, and we suffered severely—how much I am sure General Armstrong never knew, because we made no complaints. It was enough for us to know that we were pleasing General Armstrong, and that we were making it possible for an additional number of students to secure an education. More than once, during a cold night, when a stiff gale would be blowing, our tent was lifted bodily, and we would find ourselves in the open air. The General would usually pay a visit to the tents early in the morning, and his earnest, cheerful, encouraging voice would dispel any feeling of despondency.

I have spoken of my admiration for General Armstrong, and yet he was but a type of that Christlike body of men and women who went into the Negro schools at the close of the war by the hundreds to assist in lifting up my race. The history of the world fails to show a higher, purer, and more unselfish class of men and women than those who found their way into those Negro schools.

Life at Hampton was a constant revelation to me; was constantly taking me into a new world. The matter of having meals at regular hours, of eating on a tablecloth, using a napkin, the use of the bath-tub and of the tooth-brush, as well as the use of sheets upon the bed, were all new to me.

I sometimes feel that almost the most valuable lesson I got at the Hampton Institute was in the use and value of the bath. I learned there for the first time some of its value, not only in keeping the body healthy, but in inspiring self-respect and promoting virtue. In all my travels in the South and elsewhere since leaving Hampton I have always in some way sought my daily bath. To get it sometimes when I have been the guest of my own people in a single-roomed cabin has not always been easy to do, except by slipping away to some stream in the woods. I have always tried to teach my people that some provision for bathing should be a part of every house.

For some time, while a student at Hampton, I possessed but a single pair of socks, but when I had worn these till they became soiled, I would wash them at night and hang them by the fire to dry, so that I might wear them again the next morning.

The charge for my board at Hampton was ten dollars per month. I was expected to pay a part of this in cash and to work out the remainder. To meet this cash payment, as I have stated, I had just fifty cents when I reached the institution. Aside from a very few dollars that my brother John was able to send me once in a while, I had no money with which to pay my board. I was determined from the first to make my work as janitor so valuable that my services would be indispensable. This I succeeded in doing to such an extent that I was soon informed that I would be allowed the full cost of my board in return for my work. The cost of tuition was seventy dollars a year. This, of course, was wholly beyond my ability to provide. If I had been compelled to pay the seventy dollars for tuition, in addition to providing for my board, I would have been compelled to leave the Hampton school. General Armstrong, however, very kindly got Mr. S. Griffitts Morgan, of New Bedford, Mass., to defray the cost of my tuition during the whole time that I was at Hampton. After I finished the course at Hampton and had entered upon my lifework at Tuskegee, I had the pleasure of visiting Mr. Morgan several times.

After having been for a while at Hampton, I found myself in difficulty because I did not have books and clothing. Usually, however, I got around the trouble about books by borrowing from those who were more fortunate than myself. As to clothes, when I reached Hampton I had practically nothing. Everything that I possessed was in a small hand satchel. My anxiety about clothing was increased because of the fact that General Armstrong made a personal inspection of the young men in ranks, to see that their clothes were clean. Shoes had to be polished, there must be no buttons off the clothing, and no grease-spots. To wear one suit of clothes continually, while at work and in the schoolroom, and at the same time keep it clean, was rather a hard problem for me to solve. In some way I managed to get on till the teachers learned that I was in earnest and meant to succeed, and then some of them were kind enough to see that I was partly supplied with second-hand clothing that had been sent in barrels from the North. These barrels proved a blessing to hundreds of poor but deserving students. Without them I question whether I should ever have gotten through Hampton.

When I first went to Hampton I do not recall that I had ever slept in a bed that had two sheets on it. In those days there were not many buildings there, and room was very precious. There were seven other boys in the same room with me; most of them, however, students who had been there for some time. The sheets were quite a puzzle to me. The first night I slept under both of them, and the second night I slept on top of them; but by watching the other boys I learned my lesson in this, and have been trying to follow it ever since and to teach it to others.

I was among the youngest of the students who were in Hampton at the time. Most of the students were men and women—some as old as forty years of age. As I now recall the scene of my first year, I do not believe that one often has the opportunity of coming into contact with three or four hundred men and women who were so tremendously in earnest as these men and women were. Every hour was occupied in study or work. Nearly all had had enough actual contact with the world to teach them the need of education. Many of the older ones were, of course, too old to master the text-books very thoroughly, and it was often sad to watch their struggles; but they made up in earnest much of what they lacked in books. Many of them were as poor as I was, and, besides having to wrestle with their books, they had to struggle with a poverty which prevented their having the necessities of life. Many of them had aged parents who were dependent upon them, and some of them were men who had wives whose support in some way they had to provide for.

The great and prevailing idea that seemed to take possession of every one was to prepare himself to lift up the people at his home. No one seemed to think of himself. And the officers and teachers, what a rare set of human beings they were!

They worked for the students night and day, in seasons and out of season. They seemed happy only when they were helping the students in some manner.

Whenever it is written—and I hope it will be—the part that the Yankee teachers played in the education of the Negroes immediately after the war will make one of the most thrilling parts of the history of this country. The time is not far distant when the whole South will appreciate this service in a way that it has not yet been able to do.

Chapter 4. Helping Others

At the end of my first year at Hampton I was confronted with another difficulty. Most of the students went home to spend their vacation. I had no money with which to go home, but I had to go somewhere. In those days very few students were permitted to remain at the school during vacation. It made me feel very sad and homesick to see the other students preparing to leave and starting for home. I not only had no money with which to go home, but I had none with which to go anywhere.

In some way, however, I had gotten hold of an extra, second-hand coat which I thought was a pretty valuable coat. This I decided to sell, in order to get a little money for travelling expenses. I had a good deal of boyish pride, and I tried to hide, as far as I could, from the other students the fact that I had no money and nowhere to go. I made it known to a few people in the town of Hampton that I had this coat to sell, and, after a good deal of persuading, one coloured man promised to come to my room to look the coat over and consider the matter of buying it. This cheered my drooping spirits considerably. Early the next morning my prospective customer appeared. After looking the garment over carefully, he asked me how much I wanted for it. I told him I thought it was worth three dollars. He seemed to agree with me as to price, but remarked in the most matter-of-fact way: "I tell you what I will do; I will take the coat, and will pay you five cents, cash down, and pay you the rest of the money just as soon as I can get it." It is not hard to imagine what my feelings were at the time.

With this disappointment I gave up all hope of getting out of the town of Hampton for my vacation work. I wanted very much to go where I might secure work that would at least pay me enough to purchase some much-needed clothing and other necessities. In a few days practically all the students and teachers had left for their homes, and this served to depress my spirits even more.

After trying for several days in and near the town of Hampton, I finally secured work in a restaurant at Fortress Monroe. The wages, however, were very little more than my board. At night, and between meals, I found considerable time for study and reading; and in this direction I improved myself very much during the summer.

When I left school at the end of my first year, I owed the institution sixteen dollars that I had not been able to work out. It was my greatest ambition during the summer to save money enough with which to pay this debt. I felt that this was a debt of honour, and that I could hardly bring myself to the point of even trying to enter school again till it was paid. I economized in every way that I could think of—did my own washing, and went without necessary garments—but still I found my summer vacation ending and I did not have the sixteen dollars.

One day, during the last week of my stay in the restaurant, I found under one of the tables a crisp, new ten-dollar bill. I could hardly contain myself, I was so happy. As it was not my place of business I felt it to be the proper thing to show the money to the proprietor. This I did. He seemed as glad as I was, but he coolly explained to me that, as it was his place of business, he had a right to keep the money, and he proceeded to do so. This, I confess, was another pretty hard blow to me. I will not say that I became discouraged, for as I now look back over my life I do not recall that I ever became discouraged over anything that I set out to accomplish. I have begun everything with the idea that I could succeed, and I never had much patience with the multitudes of people who are always ready to explain why one cannot succeed. I determined to face the situation just as it was. At the end of the week I went to the treasurer of the Hampton Institute, General J.F.B. Marshall, and told him frankly my condition. To my gratification he told me that I could reenter the institution, and that he would trust me to pay the debt when I could. During the second year I continued to work as a janitor.

The education that I received at Hampton out of the text-books was but a small part of what I learned there. One of the things that impressed itself upon me deeply, the second year, was the unselfishness of the teachers. It was hard for me to understand how any individuals could bring themselves to the point where they could be so happy in working for others. Before the end of the year, I think I began learning that those who are happiest are those who do the most for others. This lesson I have tried to carry with me ever since.

I also learned a valuable lesson at Hampton by coming into contact with the best breeds of live stock and fowls. No student, I think, who has had the opportunity of doing this could go out into the world and content himself with the poorest grades.

Perhaps the most valuable thing that I got out of my second year was an understanding of the use and value of the Bible. Miss Nathalie Lord, one of the teachers, from Portland, Me., taught me how to use and love the Bible. Before this I had never cared a great deal about it, but now I learned to love to read the Bible, not only for the spiritual help which it gives, but on account of it as literature. The lessons taught me in this respect took such a hold upon me that at the present time, when I am at home, no matter how busy I am, I always make it a rule to read a chapter or a portion of a chapter in the morning, before beginning the work of the day.

Whatever ability I may have as a public speaker I owe in a measure to Miss Lord. When she found out that I had some inclination in this direction, she gave me private lessons in the matter of breathing, emphasis, and articulation. Simply to be able to talk in public for the sake of talking has never had the least attraction to me. In fact, I consider that there is nothing so empty and unsatisfactory as mere abstract public speaking; but from my early childhood I have had a desire to do something to make the world better, and then to be able to speak to the world about that thing.

The debating societies at Hampton were a constant source of delight to me. These were held on Saturday evening; and during my whole life at Hampton I do not recall that I missed a single meeting. I not only attended the weekly debating society, but was instrumental in organizing an additional society. I noticed that between the time when supper was over and the time to begin evening study there were about twenty minutes which the young men usually spent in idle gossip. About twenty of us formed a society for the purpose of utilizing this time in debate or in practice in public speaking. Few persons ever derived more happiness or benefit from the use of twenty minutes of time than we did in this way.

At the end of my second year at Hampton, by the help of some money sent me by my mother and brother John, supplemented by a small gift from one of the teachers at Hampton, I was enabled to return to my home in Malden, West Virginia, to spend my vacation. When I reached home I found that the salt-furnaces were not running, and that the coal-mine was not being operated on account of the miners being out on "strike." This was something which, it seemed, usually occurred whenever the men got two or three months ahead in their savings. During the strike, of course, they spent all that they had saved, and would often return to work in debt at the same wages, or would move to another mine at considerable expense. In either case, my observations convinced me that the miners were worse off at the end of the strike. Before the days of strikes in that section of the country, I knew miners who had considerable money in the bank, but as soon as the professional labour agitators got control, the savings of even the more thrifty ones began disappearing.

My mother and the other members of my family were, of course, much rejoiced to see me and to note the improvement that I had made during my two years' absence. The rejoicing on the part of all classes of the coloured people, and especially the older ones, over my return, was almost pathetic. I had to pay a visit to each family and take a meal with each, and at each place tell the story of my experiences at Hampton. In addition to this I had to speak before the church and Sunday-school, and at various other places. The thing that I was most in search of, though, work, I could not find. There was no work on account of the strike. I spent nearly the whole of the first month of my vacation in an effort to find something to do by which I could earn money to pay my way back to Hampton and save a little money to use after reaching there.

Toward the end of the first month, I went to a place a considerable distance from my home, to try to find employment. I did not succeed, and it was night before I got started on my return. When I had gotten within a mile or so of my home I was so completely tired out that I could not walk any farther, and I went into an old, abandoned house to spend the remainder of the night. About three o'clock in the morning my brother John found me asleep in this house, and broke to me, as gently as he could, the sad news that our dear mother had died during the night.

This seemed to me the saddest and blankest moment in my life. For several years my mother had not been in good health, but I had no idea, when I parted from her the previous day, that I should never see her alive again. Besides that, I had always had an intense desire to be with her when she did pass away. One of the chief ambitions which spurred me on at Hampton was that I might be able to get to be in a position in which I could better make my mother comfortable and happy. She had so often expressed the wish that she might be permitted to live to see her children educated and started out in the world.

In a very short time after the death of my mother our little home was in confusion. My sister Amanda, although she tried to do the best she could, was too young to know anything about keeping house, and my stepfather was not able to hire a housekeeper. Sometimes we had food cooked for us, and sometimes we did not. I remember that more than once a can of tomatoes and some crackers constituted a meal. Our clothing went uncared for, and everything about our home was soon in a tumble-down condition. It seems to me that this was the most dismal period of my life.

My good friend, Mrs. Ruffner, to whom I have already referred, always made me welcome at her home, and assisted me in many ways during this trying period. Before the end of the vacation she gave me some work, and this, together with work in a coal-mine at some distance from my home, enabled me to earn a little money.

At one time it looked as if I would have to give up the idea of returning to Hampton, but my heart was so set on returning that I determined not to give up going back without a struggle. I was very anxious to secure some clothes for the winter, but in this I was disappointed, except for a few garments which my brother John secured for me. Notwithstanding my need of money and clothing, I was very happy in the fact that I had secured enough money to pay my travelling expenses back to Hampton. Once there, I knew that I could make myself so useful as a janitor that I could in some way get through the school year.

Three weeks before the time for the opening of the term at Hampton, I was pleasantly surprised to receive a letter from my good friend Miss Mary F. Mackie, the lady principal, asking me to return to Hampton two weeks before the opening of the school, in order that I might assist her in cleaning the buildings and getting things in order for the new school year. This was just the opportunity I wanted. It gave me a chance to secure a credit in the treasurer's office. I started for Hampton at once.

During these two weeks I was taught a lesson which I shall never forget. Miss Mackie was a member of one of the oldest and most cultured families of the North, and yet for two weeks she worked by my side cleaning windows, dusting rooms, putting beds in order, and what not. She felt that things would not be in condition for the opening of school unless every window-pane was perfectly clean, and she took the greatest satisfaction in helping to clean them herself. The work which I have described she did every year that I was at Hampton.

It was hard for me at this time to understand how a woman of her education and social standing could take such delight in performing such service, in order to assist in the elevation of an unfortunate race. Ever since then I have had no patience with any school for my race in the South which did not teach its students the dignity of labour.

During my last year at Hampton every minute of my time that was not occupied with my duties as janitor was devoted to hard study. I was determined, if possible, to make such a record in my class as would cause me to be placed on the "honour roll" of Commencement speakers. This I was successful in doing. It was June of 1875 when I finished the regular course of study at Hampton. The greatest benefits that I got out of my life at the Hampton Institute, perhaps, may be classified under two heads:—

First was contact with a great man, General S.C. Armstrong, who, I repeat, was, in my opinion, the rarest, strongest, and most beautiful character that it has ever been my privilege to meet.

Second, at Hampton, for the first time, I learned what education was expected to do for an individual. Before going there I had a good deal of the then rather prevalent idea among our people that to secure an education meant to have a good, easy time, free from all necessity for manual labour. At Hampton I not only learned that it was not a disgrace to labour, but learned to love labour, not alone for its financial value, but for labour's own sake and for the independence and self-reliance which the ability to do something which the world wants done brings. At that institution I got my first taste of what it meant to live a life of unselfishness, my first knowledge of the fact that the happiest individuals are those who do the most to make others useful and happy.

I was completely out of money when I graduated. In company with other Hampton students, I secured a place as a table waiter in a summer hotel in Connecticut, and managed to borrow enough money with which to get there. I had not been in this hotel long before I found out that I knew practically nothing about waiting on a hotel table. The head waiter, however, supposed that I was an accomplished waiter. He soon gave me charge of the table at which there sat four or five wealthy and rather aristocratic people. My ignorance of how to wait upon them was so apparent that they scolded me in such a severe manner that I became frightened and left their table, leaving them sitting there without food. As a result of this I was reduced from the position of waiter to that of a dish-carrier.

But I determined to learn the business of waiting, and did so within a few weeks and was restored to my former position. I have had the satisfaction of being a guest in this hotel several times since I was a waiter there.

At the close of the hotel season I returned to my former home in Malden, and was elected to teach the coloured school at that place. This was the beginning of one of the happiest periods of my life. I now felt that I had the opportunity to help the people of my home town to a higher life. I felt from the first that mere book education was not all that the young people of that town needed. I began my work at eight o'clock in the morning, and, as a rule, it did not end until ten o'clock at night. In addition to the usual routine of teaching, I taught the pupils to comb their hair, and to keep their hands and faces clean, as well as their clothing. I gave special attention to teaching them the proper use of the tooth-brush and the bath. In all my teaching I have watched carefully the influence of the tooth-brush, and I am convinced that there are few single agencies of civilization that are more far-reaching.

There were so many of the older boys and girls in the town, as well as men and women, who had to work in the daytime and still were craving an opportunity for an education, that I soon opened a night-school. From the first, this was crowded every night, being about as large as the school that I taught in the day. The efforts of some of the men and women, who in many cases were over fifty years of age, to learn, were in some cases very pathetic.

My day and night school work was not all that I undertook. I established a small reading-room and a debating society. On Sundays I taught two Sunday-schools, one in the town of Malden in the afternoon, and the other in the morning at a place three miles distant from Malden. In addition to this, I gave private lessons to several young men whom I was fitting to send to the Hampton Institute. Without regard to pay and with little thought of it, I taught any one who wanted to learn anything that I could teach him. I was supremely happy in the opportunity of being able to assist somebody else. I did receive, however, a small salary from the public fund, for my work as a public-school teacher.

During the time that I was a student at Hampton my older brother, John, not only assisted me all that he could, but worked all of the time in the coal-mines in order to support the family. He willingly neglected his own education that he might help me. It was my earnest wish to help him to prepare to enter Hampton, and to save money to assist him in his expenses there. Both of these objects I was successful in accomplishing. In three years my brother finished the course at Hampton, and he is now holding the important position of Superintendent of Industries at Tuskegee. When he returned from Hampton, we both combined our efforts and savings to send our adopted brother, James, through the Hampton Institute. This we succeeded in doing, and he is now the postmaster at the Tuskegee Institute. The year 1877, which was my second year of teaching in Malden, I spent very much as I did the first.

It was while my home was at Malden that what was known as the "Ku Klux Klan" was in the height of its activity. The "Ku Klux" were bands of men who had joined themselves together for the purpose of regulating the conduct of the coloured people, especially with the object of preventing the members of the race from exercising any influence in politics. They corresponded somewhat to the "patrollers" of whom I used to hear a great deal during the days of slavery, when I was a small boy. The "patrollers" were bands of white men—usually young men—who were organized largely for the purpose of regulating the conduct of the slaves at night in such matters as preventing the slaves from going from one plantation to another without passes, and for preventing them from holding any kind of meetings without permission and without the presence at these meetings of at least one white man.

Like the "patrollers" the "Ku Klux" operated almost wholly at night.

They were, however, more cruel than the "patrollers." Their objects, in the main, were to crush out the political aspirations of the Negroes, but they did not confine themselves to this, because schoolhouses as well as churches were burned by them, and many innocent persons were made to suffer. During this period not a few coloured people lost their lives.

As a young man, the acts of these lawless bands made a great impression upon me. I saw one open battle take place at Malden between some of the coloured and white people. There must have been not far from a hundred persons engaged on each side; many on both sides were seriously injured, among them General Lewis Ruffner, the husband of my friend Mrs. Viola Ruffner. General Ruffner tried to defend the coloured people, and for this he was knocked down and so seriously wounded that he never completely recovered. It seemed to me as I watched this struggle between members of the two races, that there was no hope for our people in this country. The "Ku Klux" period was, I think, the darkest part of the Reconstruction days.

I have referred to this unpleasant part of the history of the South simply for the purpose of calling attention to the great change that has taken place since the days of the "Ku Klux." To-day there are no such organizations in the South, and the fact that such ever existed is almost forgotten by both races. There are few places in the South now where public sentiment would permit such organizations to exist.

Chapter 5. The Reconstruction Period

The years from 1867 to 1878 I think may be called the period of Reconstruction. This included the time that I spent as a student at Hampton and as a teacher in West Virginia. During the whole of the Reconstruction period two ideas were constantly agitating in the minds of the coloured people, or, at least, in the minds of a large part of the race. One of these was the craze for Greek and Latin learning, and the other was a desire to hold office.

It could not have been expected that a people who had spent generations in slavery, and before that generations in the darkest heathenism, could at first form any proper conception of what an education meant. In every part of the South, during the Reconstruction period, schools, both day and night, were filled to overflowing with people of all ages and conditions, some being as far along in age as sixty and seventy years. The ambition to secure an education was most praiseworthy and encouraging. The idea, however, was too prevalent that, as soon as one secured a little education, in some unexplainable way he would be free from most of the hardships of the world, and, at any rate, could live without manual labour. There was a further feeling that a knowledge, however little, of the Greek and Latin languages would make one a very superior human being, something bordering almost on the supernatural. I remember that the first coloured man whom I saw who knew something about foreign languages impressed me at the time as being a man of all others to be envied.

Naturally, most of our people who received some little education became teachers or preachers. While among those two classes there were many capable, earnest, godly men and women, still a large proportion took up teaching or preaching as an easy way to make a living. Many became teachers who could do little more than write their names. I remember there came into our neighbourhood one of this class, who was in search of a school to teach, and the question arose while he was there as to the shape of the earth and how he could teach the children concerning the subject. He explained his position in the matter by saying that he was prepared to teach that the earth was either flat or round, according to the preference of a majority of his patrons.

The ministry was the profession that suffered most—and still suffers, though there has been great improvement—on account of not only ignorant but in many cases immoral men who claimed that they were "called to preach." In the earlier days of freedom almost every coloured man who learned to read would receive "a call to preach" within a few days after he began reading. At my home in West Virginia the process of being called to the ministry was a very interesting one. Usually the "call" came when the individual was sitting in church. Without warning the one called would fall upon the floor as if struck by a bullet, and would lie there for hours, speechless and motionless. Then the news would spread all through the neighborhood that this individual had received a "call." If he were inclined to resist the summons, he would fall or be made to fall a second or third time. In the end he always yielded to the call. While I wanted an education badly, I confess that in my youth I had a fear that when I had learned to read and write very well I would receive one of these "calls"; but, for some reason, my call never came.

When we add the number of wholly ignorant men who preached or "exhorted" to that of those who possessed something of an education, it can be seen at a glance that the supply of ministers was large. In fact, some time ago I knew a certain church that had a total membership of about two hundred, and eighteen of that number were ministers. But, I repeat, in many communities in the South the character of the ministry is being improved, and I believe that within the next two or three decades a very large proportion of the unworthy ones will have disappeared. The "calls" to preach, I am glad to say, are not nearly so numerous now as they were formerly, and the calls to some industrial occupation are growing more numerous. The improvement that has taken place in the character of the teachers is even more marked than in the case of the ministers.

During the whole of the Reconstruction period our people throughout the South looked to the Federal Government for everything, very much as a child looks to its mother. This was not unnatural. The central government gave them freedom, and the whole Nation had been enriched for more than two centuries by the labour of the Negro. Even as a youth, and later in manhood, I had the feeling that it was cruelly wrong in the central government, at the beginning of our freedom, to fail to make some provision for the general education of our people in addition to what the states might do, so that the people would be the better prepared for the duties of citizenship.

It is easy to find fault, to remark what might have been done, and perhaps, after all, and under all the circumstances, those in charge of the conduct of affairs did the only thing that could be done at the time. Still, as I look back now over the entire period of our freedom, I cannot help feeling that it would have been wiser if some plan could have been put in operation which would have made the possession of a certain amount of education or property, or both, a test for the exercise of the franchise, and a way provided by which this test should be made to apply honestly and squarely to both the white and black races.

Though I was but little more than a youth during the period of Reconstruction, I had the feeling that mistakes were being made, and that things could not remain in the condition that they were in then very long. I felt that the Reconstruction policy, so far as it related to my race, was in a large measure on a false foundation, was artificial and forced. In many cases it seemed to me that the ignorance of my race was being used as a tool with which to help white men into office, and that there was an element in the North which wanted to punish the Southern white men by forcing the Negro into positions over the heads of the Southern whites. I felt that the Negro would be the one to suffer for this in the end. Besides, the general political agitation drew the attention of our people away from the more fundamental matters of perfecting themselves in the industries at their doors and in securing property.

The temptations to enter political life were so alluring that I came very near yielding to them at one time, but I was kept from doing so by the feeling that I would be helping in a more substantial way by assisting in the laying of the foundation of the race through a generous education of the hand, head, and heart. I saw coloured men who were members of the state legislatures, and county officers, who, in some cases, could not read or write, and whose morals were as weak as their education.

Not long ago, when passing through the streets of a certain city in the South, I heard some brick-masons calling out, from the top of a two-story brick building on which they were working, for the "Governor" to "hurry up and bring up some more bricks." Several times I heard the command, "Hurry up, Governor!" "Hurry up, Governor!" My curiosity was aroused to such an extent that I made inquiry as to who the "Governor" was, and soon found that he was a coloured man who at one time had held the position of Lieutenant-Governor of his state.

But not all the coloured people who were in office during Reconstruction were unworthy of their positions, by any means. Some of them, like the late Senator B.K. Bruce, Governor Pinchback, and many others, were strong, upright, useful men. Neither were all the class designated as carpetbaggers dishonourable men. Some of them, like ex-Governor Bullock, of Georgia, were men of high character and usefulness.

Of course the coloured people, so largely without education, and wholly without experience in government, made tremendous mistakes, just as many people similarly situated would have done. Many of the Southern whites have a feeling that, if the Negro is permitted to exercise his political rights now to any degree, the mistakes of the Reconstruction period will repeat themselves. I do not think this would be true, because the Negro is a much stronger and wiser man than he was thirty-five years ago, and he is fast learning the lesson that he cannot afford to act in a manner that will alienate his Southern white neighbours from him. More and more I am convinced that the final solution of the political end of our race problem will be for each state that finds it necessary to change the law bearing upon the franchise to make the law apply with absolute honesty, and without opportunity for double dealing or evasion, to both races alike. Any other course my daily observation in the South convinces me, will be unjust to the Negro, unjust to the white man, and unfair to the rest of the state in the Union, and will be, like slavery, a sin that at some time we shall have to pay for.

In the fall of 1878, after having taught school in Malden for two years, and after I had succeeded in preparing several of the young men and women, besides my two brothers, to enter the Hampton Institute, I decided to spend some months in study at Washington, D.C. I remained there for eight months. I derived a great deal of benefit from the studies which I pursued, and I came into contact with some strong men and women.

At the institution I attended there was no industrial training given to the students, and I had an opportunity of comparing the influence of an institution with no industrial training with that of one like the Hampton Institute, that emphasizes the industries. At this school I found the students, in most cases, had more money, were better dressed, wore the latest style of all manner of clothing, and in some cases were more brilliant mentally. At Hampton it was a standing rule that, while the institution would be responsible for securing some one to pay the tuition for the students, the men and women themselves must provide for their own board, books, clothing, and room wholly by work, or partly by work and partly in cash. At the institution at which I now was, I found that a large portion of the students by some means had their personal expenses paid for them. At Hampton the student was constantly making the effort through the industries to help himself, and that very effort was of immense value in character-building. The students at the other school seemed to be less self-dependent. They seemed to give more attention to mere outward appearances. In a word, they did not appear to me to be beginning at the bottom, on a real, solid foundation, to the extent that they were at Hampton. They knew more about Latin and Greek when they left school, but they seemed to know less about life and its conditions as they would meet it at their homes. Having lived for a number of years in the midst of comfortable surroundings, they were not as much inclined as the Hampton students to go into the country districts of the South, where there was little of comfort, to take up work for our people, and they were more inclined to yield to the temptation to become hotel waiters and Pullman-car porters as their life-work.

During the time I was a student at Washington the city was crowded with coloured people, many of whom had recently come from the South. A large proportion of these people had been drawn to Washington because they felt that they could lead a life of ease there. Others had secured minor government positions, and still another large class was there in the hope of securing Federal positions. A number of coloured men—some of them very strong and brilliant—were in the House of Representatives at that time, and one, the Hon. B.K. Bruce, was in the Senate. All this tended to make Washington an attractive place for members of the coloured race. Then, too, they knew that at all times they could have the protection of the law in the District of Columbia. The public schools in Washington for coloured people were better then than they were elsewhere. I took great interest in studying the life of our people there closely at that time. I found that while among them there was a large element of substantial, worthy citizens, there was also a superficiality about the life of a large class that greatly alarmed me. I saw young coloured men who were not earning more than four dollars a week spend two dollars or more for a buggy on Sunday to ride up and down Pennsylvania Avenue in, in order that they might try to convince the world that they were worth thousands. I saw other young men who received seventy-five or one hundred dollars per month from the Government, who were in debt at the end of every month. I saw men who but a few months previous were members of Congress, then without employment and in poverty. Among a large class there seemed to be a dependence upon the Government for every conceivable thing. The members of this class had little ambition to create a position for themselves, but wanted the Federal officials to create one for them. How many times I wished then, and have often wished since, that by some power of magic I might remove the great bulk of these people into the county districts and plant them upon the soil, upon the solid and never deceptive foundation of Mother Nature, where all nations and races that have ever succeeded have gotten their start,—a start that at first may be slow and toilsome, but one that nevertheless is real.

In Washington I saw girls whose mothers were earning their living by laundrying. These girls were taught by their mothers, in rather a crude way it is true, the industry of laundrying. Later, these girls entered the public schools and remained there perhaps six or eight years. When the public school course was finally finished, they wanted more costly dresses, more costly hats and shoes. In a word, while their wants have been increased, their ability to supply their wants had not been increased in the same degree. On the other hand, their six or eight years of book education had weaned them away from the occupation of their mothers. The result of this was in too many cases that the girls went to the bad. I often thought how much wiser it would have been to give these girls the same amount of maternal training—and I favour any kind of training, whether in the languages or mathematics, that gives strength and culture to the mind—but at the same time to give them the most thorough training in the latest and best methods of laundrying and other kindred occupations.

Chapter 6. Black Race And Red Race

During the year that I spent in Washington, and for some little time before this, there had been considerable agitation in the state of West Virginia over the question of moving the capital of the state from Wheeling to some other central point. As a result of this, the Legislature designated three cities to be voted upon by the citizens of the state as the permanent seat of government. Among these cities was Charleston, only five miles from Malden, my home. At the close of my school year in Washington I was very pleasantly surprised to receive, from a committee of three white people in Charleston, an invitation to canvass the state in the interests of that city. This invitation I accepted, and spent nearly three months in speaking in various parts of the state. Charleston was successful in winning the prize, and is now the permanent seat of government.

The reputation that I made as a speaker during this campaign induced a number of persons to make an earnest effort to get me to enter political life, but I refused, still believing that I could find other service which would prove of more permanent value to my race. Even then I had a strong feeling that what our people most needed was to get a foundation in education, industry, and property, and for this I felt that they could better afford to strive than for political preferment. As for my individual self, it appeared to me to be reasonably certain that I could succeed in political life, but I had a feeling that it would be a rather selfish kind of success—individual success at the cost of failing to do my duty in assisting in laying a foundation for the masses.

At this period in the progress of our race a very large proportion of the young men who went to school or to college did so with the expressed determination to prepare themselves to be great lawyers, or Congressmen, and many of the women planned to become music teachers; but I had a reasonably fixed idea, even at that early period in my life, that there was a need for something to be done to prepare the way for successful lawyers, Congressmen, and music teachers.

I felt that the conditions were a good deal like those of an old coloured man, during the days of slavery, who wanted to learn how to play on the guitar. In his desire to take guitar lessons he applied to one of his young masters to teach him, but the young man, not having much faith in the ability of the slave to master the guitar at his age, sought to discourage him by telling him: "Uncle Jake, I will give you guitar lessons; but, Jake, I will have to charge you three dollars for the first lesson, two dollars for the second lesson, and one dollar for the third lesson. But I will charge you only twenty-five cents for the last lesson."

Uncle Jake answered: "All right, boss, I hires you on dem terms. But, boss! I wants yer to be sure an' give me dat las' lesson first."

Soon after my work in connection with the removal of the capital was finished, I received an invitation which gave me great joy and which at the same time was a very pleasant surprise. This was a letter from General Armstrong, inviting me to return to Hampton at the next Commencement to deliver what was called the "post-graduate address." This was an honour which I had not dreamed of receiving. With much care I prepared the best address that I was capable of. I chose for my subject "The Force That Wins."

As I returned to Hampton for the purpose of delivering this address, I went over much of the same ground—now, however, covered entirely by railroad—that I had traversed nearly six years before, when I first sought entrance into Hampton Institute as a student. Now I was able to ride the whole distance in the train. I was constantly contrasting this with my first journey to Hampton. I think I may say, without seeming egotism, that it is seldom that five years have wrought such a change in the life and aspirations of an individual.

At Hampton I received a warm welcome from teachers and students. I found that during my absence from Hampton the institute each year had been getting closer to the real needs and conditions of our people; that the industrial teaching, as well as that of the academic department, had greatly improved. The plan of the school was not modelled after that of any other institution then in existence, but every improvement was made under the magnificent leadership of General Armstrong solely with the view of meeting and helping the needs of our people as they presented themselves at the time. Too often, it seems to me, in missionary and educational work among underdeveloped races, people yield to the temptation of doing that which was done a hundred years before, or is being done in other communities a thousand miles away. The temptation often is to run each individual through a certain educational mould, regardless of the condition of the subject or the end to be accomplished. This was not so at Hampton Institute.

The address which I delivered on Commencement Day seems to have pleased every one, and many kind and encouraging words were spoken to me regarding it. Soon after my return to my home in West Virginia, where I had planned to continue teaching, I was again surprised to receive a letter from General Armstrong, asking me to return to Hampton partly as a teacher and partly to pursue some supplementary studies. This was in the summer of 1879. Soon after I began my first teaching in West Virginia I had picked out four of the brightest and most promising of my pupils, in addition to my two brothers, to whom I have already referred, and had given them special attention, with the view of having them go to Hampton. They had gone there, and in each case the teachers had found them so well prepared that they entered advanced classes. This fact, it seems, led to my being called back to Hampton as a teacher. One of the young men that I sent to Hampton in this way is now Dr. Samuel E. Courtney, a successful physician in Boston, and a member of the School Board of that city.

About this time the experiment was being tried for the first time, by General Armstrong, of educating Indians at Hampton. Few people then had any confidence in the ability of the Indians to receive education and to profit by it. General Armstrong was anxious to try the experiment systematically on a large scale. He secured from the reservations in the Western states over one hundred wild and for the most part perfectly ignorant Indians, the greater proportion of whom were young men. The special work which the General desired me to do was to be a sort of "house father" to the Indian young men—that is, I was to live in the building with them and have the charge of their discipline, clothing, rooms, and so on. This was a very tempting offer, but I had become so much absorbed in my work in West Virginia that I dreaded to give it up. However, I tore myself away from it. I did not know how to refuse to perform any service that General Armstrong desired of me.

On going to Hampton, I took up my residence in a building with about seventy-five Indian youths. I was the only person in the building who was not a member of their race. At first I had a good deal of doubt about my ability to succeed. I knew that the average Indian felt himself above the white man, and, of course, he felt himself far above the Negro, largely on account of the fact of the Negro having submitted to slavery—a thing which the Indian would never do. The Indians, in the Indian Territory, owned a large number of slaves during the days of slavery. Aside from this, there was a general feeling that the attempt to educate and civilize the red men at Hampton would be a failure. All this made me proceed very cautiously, for I felt keenly the great responsibility. But I was determined to succeed. It was not long before I had the complete confidence of the Indians, and not only this, but I think I am safe in saying that I had their love and respect. I found that they were about like any other human beings; that they responded to kind treatment and resented ill-treatment. They were continually planning to do something that would add to my happiness and comfort. The things that they disliked most, I think, were to have their long hair cut, to give up wearing their blankets, and to cease smoking; but no white American ever thinks that any other race is wholly civilized until he wears the white man's clothes, eats the white man's food, speaks the white man's language, and professes the white man's religion.

When the difficulty of learning the English language was subtracted, I found that in the matter of learning trades and in mastering academic studies there was little difference between the coloured and Indian students. It was a constant delight to me to note the interest which the coloured students took in trying to help the Indians in every way possible. There were a few of the coloured students who felt that the Indians ought not to be admitted to Hampton, but these were in the minority. Whenever they were asked to do so, the Negro students gladly took the Indians as room-mates, in order that they might teach them to speak English and to acquire civilized habits.

I have often wondered if there was a white institution in this country whose students would have welcomed the incoming of more than a hundred companions of another race in the cordial way that these black students at Hampton welcomed the red ones. How often I have wanted to say to white students that they lift themselves up in proportion as they help to lift others, and the more unfortunate the race, and the lower in the scale of civilization, the more does one raise one's self by giving the assistance.

This reminds me of a conversation which I once had with the Hon. Frederick Douglass. At one time Mr. Douglass was travelling in the state of Pennsylvania, and was forced, on account of his colour, to ride in the baggage-car, in spite of the fact that he had paid the same price for his passage that the other passengers had paid. When some of the white passengers went into the baggage-car to console Mr. Douglass, and one of them said to him: "I am sorry, Mr. Douglass, that you have been degraded in this manner," Mr. Douglass straightened himself up on the box upon which he was sitting, and replied: "They cannot degrade Frederick Douglass. The soul that is within me no man can degrade. I am not the one that is being degraded on account of this treatment, but those who are inflicting it upon me."

In one part of the country, where the law demands the separation of the races on the railroad trains, I saw at one time a rather amusing instance which showed how difficult it sometimes is to know where the black begins and the white ends.

There was a man who was well known in his community as a Negro, but who was so white that even an expert would have hard work to classify him as a black man. This man was riding in the part of the train set aside for the coloured passengers. When the train conductor reached him, he showed at once that he was perplexed. If the man was a Negro, the conductor did not want to send him to the white people's coach; at the same time, if he was a white man, the conductor did not want to insult him by asking him if he was a Negro. The official looked him over carefully, examining his hair, eyes, nose, and hands, but still seemed puzzled. Finally, to solve the difficulty, he stooped over and peeped at the man's feet. When I saw the conductor examining the feet of the man in question, I said to myself, "That will settle it;" and so it did, for the trainman promptly decided that the passenger was a Negro, and let him remain where he was. I congratulated myself that my race was fortunate in not losing one of its members.

My experience has been that the time to test a true gentleman is to observe him when he is in contact with individuals of a race that is less fortunate than his own. This is illustrated in no better way than by observing the conduct of the old-school type of Southern gentleman when he is in contact with his former slaves or their descendants.

An example of what I mean is shown in a story told of George Washington, who, meeting a coloured man in the road once, who politely lifted his hat, lifted his own in return. Some of his white friends who saw the incident criticised Washington for his action. In reply to their criticism George Washington said: "Do you suppose that I am going to permit a poor, ignorant, coloured man to be more polite than I am?"

While I was in charge of the Indian boys at Hampton, I had one or two experiences which illustrate the curious workings of caste in America. One of the Indian boys was taken ill, and it became my duty to take him to Washington, deliver him over to the Secretary of the Interior, and get a receipt for him, in order that he might be returned to his Western reservation. At that time I was rather ignorant of the ways of the world. During my journey to Washington, on a steamboat, when the bell rang for dinner, I was careful to wait and not enter the dining room until after the greater part of the passengers had finished their meal. Then, with my charge, I went to the dining saloon. The man in charge politely informed me that the Indian could be served, but that I could not. I never could understand how he knew just where to draw the colour line, since the Indian and I were of about the same complexion. The steward, however, seemed to be an expert in this manner. I had been directed by the authorities at Hampton to stop at a certain hotel in Washington with my charge, but when I went to this hotel the clerk stated that he would be glad to receive the Indian into the house, but said that he could not accommodate me.

An illustration of something of this same feeling came under my observation afterward. I happened to find myself in a town in which so much excitement and indignation were being expressed that it seemed likely for a time that there would be a lynching. The occasion of the trouble was that a dark-skinned man had stopped at the local hotel. Investigation, however, developed the fact that this individual was a citizen of Morocco, and that while travelling in this country he spoke the English language.

As soon as it was learned that he was not an American Negro, all the signs of indignation disappeared. The man who was the innocent cause of the excitement, though, found it prudent after that not to speak English.

At the end of my first year with the Indians there came another opening for me at Hampton, which, as I look back over my life now, seems to have come providentially, to help to prepare me for my work at Tuskegee later. General Armstrong had found out that there was quite a number of young coloured men and women who were intensely in earnest in wishing to get an education, but who were prevented from entering Hampton Institute because they were too poor to be able to pay any portion of the cost of their board, or even to supply themselves with books. He conceived the idea of starting a night-school in connection with the Institute, into which a limited number of the most promising of these young men and women would be received, on condition that they were to work for ten hours during the day, and attend school for two hours at night. They were to be paid something above the cost of their board for their work. The greater part of their earnings was to be reserved in the school's treasury as a fund to be drawn on to pay their board when they had become students in the day-school, after they had spent one or two years in the night-school. In this way they would obtain a start in their books and a knowledge of some trade or industry, in addition to the other far-reaching benefits of the institution.

General Armstrong asked me to take charge of the night-school, and I did so. At the beginning of this school there were about twelve strong, earnest men and women who entered the class. During the day the greater part of the young men worked in the school's sawmill, and the young women worked in the laundry. The work was not easy in either place, but in all my teaching I never taught pupils who gave me much genuine satisfaction as these did. They were good students, and mastered their work thoroughly. They were so much in earnest that only the ringing of the retiring-bell would make them stop studying, and often they would urge me to continue the lessons after the usual hour for going to bed had come.

These students showed so much earnestness, both in their hard work during the day, as well as in their application to their studies at night, that I gave them the name of "The Plucky Class"—a name which soon grew popular and spread throughout the institution. After a student had been in the night-school long enough to prove what was in him, I gave him a printed certificate which read something like this:—

"This is to certify that James Smith is a member of The Plucky Class of the Hampton Institute, and is in good and regular standing."

The students prized these certificates highly, and they added greatly to the popularity of the night-school.

Within a few weeks this department had grown to such an extent that there were about twenty-five students in attendance. I have followed the course of many of these twenty-five men and women ever since then, and they are now holding important and useful positions in nearly every part of the South. The night-school at Hampton, which started with only twelve students, now numbers between three and four hundred, and is one of the permanent and most important features of the institution.

Chapter 7. Early Days At Tuskegee

During the time that I had charge of the Indians and the night-school at Hampton, I pursued some studies myself, under the direction of the instructors there. One of these instructors was the Rev. Dr. H.B. Frissell, the present Principal of the Hampton Institute, General Armstrong's successor.

In May, 1881, near the close of my first year in teaching the night-school, in a way that I had not dared expect, the opportunity opened for me to begin my life-work. One night in the chapel, after the usual chapel exercises were over, General Armstrong referred to the fact that he had received a letter from some gentlemen in Alabama asking him to recommend some one to take charge of what was to be a normal school for the coloured people in the little town of Tuskegee in that state. These gentlemen seemed to take it for granted that no coloured man suitable for the position could be secured, and they were expecting the General to recommend a white man for the place. The next day General Armstrong sent for me to come to his office, and, much to my surprise, asked me if I thought I could fill the position in Alabama. I told him that I would be willing to try. Accordingly, he wrote to the people who had applied to him for the information, that he did not know of any white man to suggest, but if they would be willing to take a coloured man, he had one whom he could recommend. In this letter he gave them my name.

Several days passed before anything more was heard about the matter. Some time afterward, one Sunday evening during the chapel exercises, a messenger came in and handed the general a telegram. At the end of the exercises he read the telegram to the school. In substance, these were its words: "Booker T. Washington will suit us. Send him at once."

There was a great deal of joy expressed among the students and teachers, and I received very hearty congratulations. I began to get ready at once to go to Tuskegee. I went by way of my old home in West Virginia, where I remained for several days, after which I proceeded to Tuskegee. I found Tuskegee to be a town of about two thousand inhabitants, nearly one-half of whom were coloured. It was in what was known as the Black Belt of the South. In the county in which Tuskegee is situated the coloured people outnumbered the whites by about three to one. In some of the adjoining and near-by counties the proportion was not far from six coloured persons to one white.

I have often been asked to define the term "Black Belt." So far as I can learn, the term was first used to designate a part of the country which was distinguished by the colour of the soil. The part of the country possessing this thick, dark, and naturally rich soil was, of course, the part of the South where the slaves were most profitable, and consequently they were taken there in the largest numbers. Later, and especially since the war, the term seems to be used wholly in a political sense—that is, to designate the counties where the black people outnumber the white.

Before going to Tuskegee I had expected to find there a building and all the necessary apparatus ready for me to begin teaching. To my disappointment, I found nothing of the kind. I did find, though, that which no costly building and apparatus can supply,—hundreds of hungry, earnest souls who wanted to secure knowledge.

Tuskegee seemed an ideal place for the school. It was in the midst of the great bulk of the Negro population, and was rather secluded, being five miles from the main line of railroad, with which it was connected by a short line. During the days of slavery, and since, the town had been a centre for the education of the white people. This was an added advantage, for the reason that I found the white people possessing a degree of culture and education that is not surpassed by many localities. While the coloured people were ignorant, they had not, as a rule, degraded and weakened their bodies by vices such as are common to the lower class of people in the large cities. In general, I found the relations between the two races pleasant. For example, the largest, and I think at that time the only hardware store in the town was owned and operated jointly by a coloured man and a white man. This copartnership continued until the death of the white partner.

I found that about a year previous to my going to Tuskegee some of the coloured people who had heard something of the work of education being done at Hampton had applied to the state Legislature, through their representatives, for a small appropriation to be used in starting a normal school in Tuskegee. This request the Legislature had complied with to the extent of granting an annual appropriation of two thousand dollars. I soon learned, however, that this money could be used only for the payment of the salaries of the instructors, and that there was no provision for securing land, buildings, or apparatus. The task before me did not seem a very encouraging one. It seemed much like making bricks without straw. The coloured people were overjoyed, and were constantly offering their services in any way in which they could be of assistance in getting the school started.

My first task was to find a place in which to open the school. After looking the town over with some care, the most suitable place that could be secured seemed to be a rather dilapidated shanty near the coloured Methodist church, together with the church itself as a sort of assembly-room. Both the church and the shanty were in about as bad condition as was possible. I recall that during the first months of school that I taught in this building it was in such poor repair that, whenever it rained, one of the older students would very kindly leave his lessons and hold an umbrella over me while I heard the recitations of the others. I remember, also, that on more than one occasion my landlady held an umbrella over me while I ate breakfast.

At the time I went to Alabama the coloured people were taking considerable interest in politics, and they were very anxious that I should become one of them politically, in every respect. They seemed to have a little distrust of strangers in this regard. I recall that one man, who seemed to have been designated by the others to look after my political destiny, came to me on several occasions and said, with a good deal of earnestness: "We wants you to be sure to vote jes' like we votes. We can't read de newspapers very much, but we knows how to vote, an' we wants you to vote jes' like we votes." He added: "We watches de white man, and we keeps watching de white man till we finds out which way de white man's gwine to vote; an' when we finds out which way de white man's gwine to vote, den we votes 'xactly de other way. Den we knows we's right."

I am glad to add, however, that at the present time the disposition to vote against the white man merely because he is white is largely disappearing, and the race is learning to vote from principle, for what the voter considers to be for the best interests of both races.

I reached Tuskegee, as I have said, early in June, 1881. The first month I spent in finding accommodations for the school, and in travelling through Alabama, examining into the actual life of the people, especially in the court districts, and in getting the school advertised among the class of people that I wanted to have attend it. The most of my travelling was done over the country roads, with a mule and a cart or a mule and a buggy wagon for conveyance. I ate and slept with the people, in their little cabins. I saw their farms, their schools, their churches. Since, in the case of the most of these visits, there had been no notice given in advance that a stranger was expected, I had the advantage of seeing the real, everyday life of the people.

In the plantation districts I found that, as a rule, the whole family slept in one room, and that in addition to the immediate family there sometimes were relatives, or others not related to the family, who slept in the same room. On more than one occasion I went outside the house to get ready for bed, or to wait until the family had gone to bed. They usually contrived some kind of a place for me to sleep, either on the floor or in a special part of another's bed. Rarely was there any place provided in the cabin where one could bathe even the face and hands, but usually some provision was made for this outside the house, in the yard.

The common diet of the people was fat pork and corn bread. At times I have eaten in cabins where they had only corn bread and "black-eye peas" cooked in plain water. The people seemed to have no other idea than to live on this fat meat and corn bread,—the meat, and the meal of which the bread was made, having been bought at a high price at a store in town, notwithstanding the fact that the land all about the cabin homes could easily have been made to produce nearly every kind of garden vegetable that is raised anywhere in the country. Their one object seemed to be to plant nothing but cotton; and in many cases cotton was planted up to the very door of the cabin.

In these cabin homes I often found sewing-machines which had been bought, or were being bought, on instalments, frequently at a cost of as much as sixty dollars, or showy clocks for which the occupants of the cabins had paid twelve or fourteen dollars. I remember that on one occasion when I went into one of these cabins for dinner, when I sat down to the table for a meal with the four members of the family, I noticed that, while there were five of us at the table, there was but one fork for the five of us to use. Naturally there was an awkward pause on my part. In the opposite corner of that same cabin was an organ for which the people told me they were paying sixty dollars in monthly instalments. One fork, and a sixty-dollar organ!

In most cases the sewing-machine was not used, the clocks were so worthless that they did not keep correct time—and if they had, in nine cases out of ten there would have been no one in the family who could have told the time of day—while the organ, of course, was rarely used for want of a person who could play upon it.

In the case to which I have referred, where the family sat down to the table for the meal at which I was their guest, I could see plainly that this was an awkward and unusual proceeding, and was done in my honour. In most cases, when the family got up in the morning, for example, the wife would put a piece of meat in a frying-pan and put a lump of dough in a "skillet," as they called it. These utensils would be placed on the fire, and in ten or fifteen minutes breakfast would be ready. Frequently the husband would take his bread and meat in his hand and start for the field, eating as he walked. The mother would sit down in a corner and eat her breakfast, perhaps from a plate and perhaps directly from the "skillet" or frying-pan, while the children would eat their portion of the bread and meat while running about the yard. At certain seasons of the year, when meat was scarce, it was rarely that the children who were not old enough or strong enough to work in the fields would have the luxury of meat.

The breakfast over, and with practically no attention given to the house, the whole family would, as a general thing, proceed to the cotton-field. Every child that was large enough to carry a hoe was put to work, and the baby— for usually there was at least one baby—would be laid down at the end of the cotton row, so that its mother could give it a certain amount of attention when she had finished chopping her row. The noon meal and the supper were taken in much the same way as the breakfast.

All the days of the family would be spent after much this same routine, except Saturday and Sunday. On Saturday the whole family would spent at least half a day, and often a whole day, in town. The idea in going to town was, I suppose, to do shopping, but all the shopping that the whole family had money for could have been attended to in ten minutes by one person. Still, the whole family remained in town for most of the day, spending the greater part of the time in standing on the streets, the women, too often, sitting about somewhere smoking or dipping snuff. Sunday was usually spent in going to some big meeting. With few exceptions, I found that the crops were mortgaged in the counties where I went, and that the most of the coloured farmers were in debt. The state had not been able to build schoolhouses in the country districts, and, as a rule, the schools were taught in churches or in log cabins.

More than once, while on my journeys, I found that there was no provision made in the house used for school purposes for heating the building during the winter, and consequently a fire had to be built in the yard, and teacher and pupils passed in and out of the house as they got cold or warm.

With few exceptions, I found the teachers in these country schools to be miserably poor in preparation for their work, and poor in moral character. The schools were in session from three to five months. There was practically no apparatus in the schoolhouses, except that occasionally there was a rough blackboard. I recall that one day I went into a schoolhouse—or rather into an abandoned log cabin that was being used as a schoolhouse—and found five pupils who were studying a lesson from one book. Two of these, on the front seat, were using the book between them; behind these were two others peeping over the shoulders of the first two, and behind the four was a fifth little fellow who was peeping over the shoulders of all four.

What I have said concerning the character of the schoolhouses and teachers will also apply quite accurately as a description of the church buildings and the ministers.

I met some very interesting characters during my travels. As illustrating the peculiar mental processes of the country people, I remember that I asked one coloured man, who was about sixty years old, to tell me something of his history.

He said that he had been born in Virginia, and sold into Alabama in 1845. I asked him how many were sold at the same time. He said, "There were five of us; myself and brother and three mules."

In giving all these descriptions of what I saw during my month of travel in the country around Tuskegee, I wish my readers to keep in mind the fact that there were many encouraging exceptions to the conditions which I have described.

I have stated in such plain words what I saw, mainly for the reason that later I want to emphasize the encouraging changes that have taken place in the community, not wholly by the work of the Tuskegee school, but by that of other institutions as well.

Chapter 8. Teaching School In A Stable And A Hen-House

I confess that what I saw during my month of travel and investigation left me with a very heavy heart. The work to be done in order to lift these people up seemed almost beyond accomplishing. I was only one person, and it seemed to me that the little effort which I could put forth could go such a short distance toward bringing about results. I wondered if I could accomplish anything, and if it were worth while for me to try.

Of one thing I felt more strongly convinced than ever, after spending this month in seeing the actual life of the coloured people, and that was that, in order to lift them up, something must be done more than merely to imitate New England education as it then existed. I saw more clearly than ever the wisdom of the system which General Armstrong had inaugurated at Hampton. To take the children of such people as I had been among for a month, and each day give them a few hours of mere book education, I felt would be almost a waste of time.

After consultation with the citizens of Tuskegee, I set July 4, 1881, as the day for the opening of the school in the little shanty and church which had been secured for its accommodation. The white people, as well as the coloured, were greatly interested in the starting of the new school, and the opening day was looked forward to with much earnest discussion. There were not a few white people in the vicinity of Tuskegee who looked with some disfavour upon the project. They questioned its value to the coloured people, and had a fear that it might result in bringing about trouble between the races. Some had the feeling that in proportion as the Negro received education, in the same proportion would his value decrease as an economic factor in the state. These people feared the result of education would be that the Negroes would leave the farms, and that it would be difficult to secure them for domestic service.

The white people who questioned the wisdom of starting this new school had in their minds pictures of what was called an educated Negro, with a high hat, imitation gold eye-glasses, a showy walking-stick, kid gloves, fancy boots, and what not—in a word, a man who was determined to live by his wits. It was difficult for these people to see how education would produce any other kind of a coloured man.

In the midst of all the difficulties which I encountered in getting the little school started, and since then through a period of nineteen years, there are two men among all the many friends of the school in Tuskegee upon whom I have depended constantly for advice and guidance; and the success of the undertaking is largely due to these men, from whom I have never sought anything in vain. I mention them simply as types. One is a white man and an ex-slaveholder, Mr. George W. Campbell; the other is a black man and an ex-slave, Mr. Lewis Adams. These were the men who wrote to General Armstrong for a teacher.

Mr. Campbell is a merchant and banker, and had had little experience in dealing with matters pertaining to education. Mr. Adams was a mechanic, and had learned the trades of shoemaking, harness-making, and tinsmithing during the days of slavery. He had never been to school a day in his life, but in some way he had learned to read and write while a slave. From the first, these two men saw clearly what my plan of education was, sympathized with me, and supported me in every effort. In the days which were darkest financially for the school, Mr. Campbell was never appealed to when he was not willing to extend all the aid in his power. I do not know two men, one an ex-slaveholder, one an ex-slave, whose advice and judgment I would feel more like following in everything which concerns the life and development of the school at Tuskegee than those of these two men.

I have always felt that Mr. Adams, in a large degree, derived his unusual power of mind from the training given his hands in the process of mastering well three trades during the days of slavery. If one goes to-day into any Southern town, and asks for the leading and most reliable coloured man in the community, I believe that in five cases out of ten he will be directed to a Negro who learned a trade during the days of slavery.

On the morning that the school opened, thirty students reported for admission. I was the only teacher. The students were about equally divided between the sexes. Most of them lived in Macon County, the county in which Tuskegee is situated, and of which it is the county-seat. A great many more students wanted to enter the school, but it had been decided to receive only those who were above fifteen years of age, and who had previously received some education. The greater part of the thirty were public-school teachers, and some of them were nearly forty years of age. With the teachers came some of their former pupils, and when they were examined it was amusing to note that in several cases the pupil entered a higher class than did his former teacher. It was also interesting to note how many big books some of them had studied, and how many high-sounding subjects some of them claimed to have mastered. The bigger the book and the longer the name of the subject, the prouder they felt of their accomplishment. Some had studied Latin, and one or two Greek. This they thought entitled them to special distinction.

In fact, one of the saddest things I saw during the month of travel which I have described was a young man, who had attended some high school, sitting down in a one-room cabin, with grease on his clothing, filth all around him, and weeds in the yard and garden, engaged in studying a French grammar.

The students who came first seemed to be fond of memorizing long and complicated "rules" in grammar and mathematics, but had little thought or knowledge of applying these rules to their everyday affairs of their life. One subject which they liked to talk about, and tell me that they had mastered, in arithmetic, was "banking and discount," but I soon found out that neither they nor almost any one in the neighbourhood in which they had lived had ever had a bank account. In registering the names of the students, I found that almost every one of them had one or more middle initials. When I asked what the "J" stood for, in the name of John J. Jones, it was explained to me that this was a part of his "entitles." Most of the students wanted to get an education because they thought it would enable them to earn more money as school-teachers.

Notwithstanding what I have said about them in these respects, I have never seen a more earnest and willing company of young men and women than these students were. They were all willing to learn the right thing as soon as it was shown them what was right. I was determined to start them off on a solid and thorough foundation, so far as their books were concerned. I soon learned that most of them had the merest smattering of the high-sounding things that they had studied. While they could locate the Desert of Sahara or the capital of China on an artificial globe, I found out that the girls could not locate the proper places for the knives and forks on an actual dinner-table, or the places on which the bread and meat should be set.

I had to summon a good deal of courage to take a student who had been studying cube root and "banking and discount," and explain to him that the wisest thing for him to do first was thoroughly master the multiplication table.

The number of pupils increased each week, until by the end of the first month there were nearly fifty. Many of them, however, said that, as they could remain only for two or three months, they wanted to enter a high class and get a diploma the first year if possible.

At the end of the first six weeks a new and rare face entered the school as a co-teacher. This was Miss Olivia A. Davidson, who later became my wife. Miss Davidson was born in Ohio, and received her preparatory education in the public schools of that state. When little more than a girl, she heard of the need of teachers in the South. She went to the state of Mississippi and began teaching there. Later she taught in the city of Memphis. While teaching in Mississippi, one of her pupils became ill with smallpox. Every one in the community was so frightened that no one would nurse the boy. Miss Davidson closed her school and remained by the bedside of the boy night and day until he recovered. While she was at her Ohio home on her vacation, the worst epidemic of yellow fever broke out in Memphis, Tenn., that perhaps has ever occurred in the South. When she heard of this, she at once telegraphed the Mayor of Memphis, offering her services as a yellow-fever nurse, although she had never had the disease.

Miss Davidon's experience in the South showed her that the people needed something more than mere book-learning. She heard of the Hampton system of education, and decided that this was what she wanted in order to prepare herself for better work in the South. The attention of Mrs. Mary Hemenway, of Boston, was attracted to her rare ability. Through Mrs. Hemenway's kindness and generosity, Miss Davidson, after graduating at Hampton, received an opportunity to complete a two years' course of training at the Massachusetts State Normal School at Framingham.

Before she went to Framingham, some one suggested to Miss Davidson that, since she was so very light in colour, she might find it more comfortable not to be known as a coloured women in this school in Massachusetts. She at once replied that under no circumstances and for no considerations would she consent to deceive any one in regard to her racial identity.

Soon after her graduation from the Framingham institution, Miss Davidson came to Tuskegee, bringing into the school many valuable and fresh ideas as to the best methods of teaching, as well as a rare moral character and a life of unselfishness that I think has seldom been equalled. No single individual did more toward laying the foundations of the Tuskegee Institute so as to insure the successful work that has been done there than Olivia A. Davidson.

Miss Davidson and I began consulting as to the future of the school from the first. The students were making progress in learning books and in developing their minds; but it became apparent at once that, if we were to make any permanent impression upon those who had come to us for training we must do something besides teach them mere books. The students had come from homes where they had had no opportunities for lessons which would teach them how to care for their bodies. With few exceptions, the homes in Tuskegee in which the students boarded were but little improvement upon those from which they had come. We wanted to teach the students how to bathe; how to care for their teeth and clothing. We wanted to teach them what to eat, and how to eat it properly, and how to care for their rooms. Aside from this, we wanted to give them such a practical knowledge of some one industry, together with the spirit of industry, thrift, and economy, that they would be sure of knowing how to make a living after they had left us. We wanted to teach them to study actual things instead of mere books alone.

We found that the most of our students came from the country districts, where agriculture in some form or other was the main dependence of the people. We learned that about eighty-five per cent of the coloured people in the Gulf states depended upon agriculture for their living. Since this was true, we wanted to be careful not to educate our students out of sympathy with agricultural life, so that they would be attracted from the country to the cities, and yield to the temptation of trying to live by their wits. We wanted to give them such an education as would fit a large proportion of them to be teachers, and at the same time cause them to return to the plantation districts and show the people there how to put new energy and new ideas into farming, as well as into the intellectual and moral and religious life of the people.

All these ideas and needs crowded themselves upon us with a seriousness that seemed well-nigh overwhelming. What were we to do? We had only the little old shanty and the abandoned church which the good coloured people of the town of Tuskegee had kindly loaned us for the accommodation of the classes. The number of students was increasing daily. The more we saw of them, and the more we travelled through the country districts, the more we saw that our efforts were reaching, to only a partial degree, the actual needs of the people whom we wanted to lift up through the medium of the students whom we should educate and send out as leaders.

The more we talked with the students, who were then coming to us from several parts of the state, the more we found that the chief ambition among a large proportion of them was to get an education so that they would not have to work any longer with their hands.

This is illustrated by a story told of a coloured man in Alabama, who, one hot day in July, while he was at work in a cotton-field, suddenly stopped, and, looking toward the skies, said: "O Lawd, de cotton am so grassy, de work am so hard, and the sun am so hot dat I b'lieve dis darky am called to preach!"

About three months after the opening of the school, and at the time when we were in the greatest anxiety about our work, there came into market for sale an old and abandoned plantation which was situated about a mile from the town of Tuskegee. The mansion house—or "big house," as it would have been called—which had been occupied by the owners during slavery, had been burned. After making a careful examination of the place, it seemed to be just the location that we wanted in order to make our work effective and permanent.

But how were we to get it? The price asked for it was very little—only five hundred dollars—but we had no money, and we were strangers in the town and had no credit. The owner of the land agreed to let us occupy the place if we could make a payment of two hundred and fifty dollars down, with the understanding that the remaining two hundred and fifty dollars must be paid within a year. Although five hundred dollars was cheap for the land, it was a large sum when one did not have any part of it.

In the midst of the difficulty I summoned a great deal of courage and wrote to my friend General J.F.B. Marshall, the Treasurer of the Hampton Institute, putting the situation before him and beseeching him to lend me the two hundred and fifty dollars on my own personal responsibility. Within a few days a reply came to the effect that he had no authority to lend me the money belonging to the Hampton Institute, but that he would gladly lend me the amount needed from his own personal funds.

I confess that the securing of this money in this way was a great surprise to me, as well as a source of gratification. Up to that time I never had had in my possession so much money as one hundred dollars at a time, and the loan which I had asked General Marshall for seemed a tremendously large sum to me. The fact of my being responsible for the repaying of such a large amount of money weighed very heavily upon me.

I lost no time in getting ready to move the school on to the new farm. At the time we occupied the place there were standing upon it a cabin, formerly used as a dining room, an old kitchen, a stable, and an old hen-house. Within a few weeks we had all of these structures in use. The stable was repaired and used as a recitation-room, and very presently the hen-house was utilized for the same purpose.

I recall that one morning, when I told an old coloured man who lived near, and who sometimes helped me, that our school had grown so large that it would be necessary for us to use the hen-house for school purposes, and that I wanted him to help me give it a thorough cleaning out the next day, he replied, in the most earnest manner: "What you mean, boss? You sholy ain't gwine clean out de hen-house in de day-time?"

Nearly all the work of getting the new location ready for school purposes was done by the students after school was over in the afternoon. As soon as we got the cabins in condition to be used, I determined to clear up some land so that we could plant a crop. When I explained my plan to the young men, I noticed that they did not seem to take to it very kindly.

It was hard for them to see the connection between clearing land and an education. Besides, many of them had been school-teachers, and they questioned whether or not clearing land would be in keeping with their dignity. In order to relieve them from any embarrassment, each afternoon after school I took my axe and led the way to the woods. When they saw that I was not afraid or ashamed to work, they began to assist with more enthusiasm. We kept at the work each afternoon, until we had cleared about twenty acres and had planted a crop.

In the meantime Miss Davidson was devising plans to repay the loan. Her first effort was made by holding festivals, or "suppers." She made a personal canvass among the white and coloured families in the town of Tuskegee, and got them to agree to give something, like a cake, a chicken, bread, or pies, that could be sold at the festival. Of course the coloured people were glad to give anything that they could spare, but I want to add that Miss Davidson did not apply to a single white family, so far as I now remember, that failed to donate something; and in many ways the white families showed their interest in the school.

Several of these festivals were held, and quite a little sum of money was raised. A canvass was also made among the people of both races for direct gifts of money, and most of those applied to gave small sums. It was often pathetic to note the gifts of the older coloured people, most of whom had spent their best days in slavery. Sometimes they would give five cents, sometimes twenty-five cents. Sometimes the contribution was a quilt, or a quantity of sugarcane. I recall one old coloured women who was about seventy years of age, who came to see me when we were raising money to pay for the farm. She hobbled into the room where I was, leaning on a cane. She was clad in rags; but they were clean. She said: "Mr. Washin'ton, God knows I spent de bes' days of my life in slavery. God knows I's ignorant an' poor; but," she added, "I knows what you an' Miss Davidson is tryin' to do. I knows you is tryin' to make better men an' better women for de coloured race. I ain't got no money, but I wants you to take dese six eggs, what I's been savin' up, an' I wants you to put dese six eggs into the eddication of dese boys an' gals."

Since the work at Tuskegee started, it has been my privilege to receive many gifts for the benefit of the institution, but never any, I think, that touched me so deeply as this one.

Chapter 9. Anxious Days And Sleepless Nights

The coming of Christmas, that first year of our residence in Alabama, gave us an opportunity to get a farther insight into the real life of the people. The first thing that reminded us that Christmas had arrived was the "foreday" visits of scores of children rapping at our doors, asking for "Chris'mus gifts! Chris'mus gifts!" Between the hours of two o'clock and five o'clock in the morning I presume that we must have had a half-hundred such calls. This custom prevails throughout this portion of the South to-day.

During the days of slavery it was a custom quite generally observed throughout all the Southern states to give the coloured people a week of holiday at Christmas, or to allow the holiday to continue as long as the "yule log" lasted. The male members of the race, and often the female members, were expected to get drunk. We found that for a whole week the coloured people in and around Tuskegee dropped work the day before Christmas, and that it was difficult for any one to perform any service from the time they stopped work until after the New Year. Persons who at other times did not use strong drink thought it quite the proper thing to indulge in it rather freely during the Christmas week. There was a widespread hilarity, and a free use of guns, pistols, and gunpowder generally. The sacredness of the season seemed to have been almost wholly lost sight of.

During this first Christmas vacation I went some distance from the town to visit the people on one of the large plantations. In their poverty and ignorance it was pathetic to see their attempts to get joy out of the season that in most parts of the country is so sacred and so dear to the heart. In one cabin I notice that all that the five children had to remind them of the coming of Christ was a single bunch of firecrackers, which they had divided among them. In another cabin, where there were at least a half-dozen persons, they had only ten cents' worth of ginger-cakes, which had been bought in the store the day before. In another family they had only a few pieces of sugarcane. In still another cabin I found nothing but a new jug of cheap, mean whiskey, which the husband and wife were making free use of, notwithstanding the fact that the husband was one of the local ministers. In a few instances I found that the people had gotten hold of some bright-coloured cards that had been designed for advertising purposes, and were making the most of these. In other homes some member of the family had bought a new pistol. In the majority of cases there was nothing to be seen in the cabin to remind one of the coming of the Saviour, except that the people had ceased work in the fields and were lounging about their homes. At night, during Christmas week, they usually had what they called a "frolic," in some cabin on the plantation. That meant a kind of rough dance, where there was likely to be a good deal of whiskey used, and where there might be some shooting or cutting with razors.

While I was making this Christmas visit I met an old coloured man who was one of the numerous local preachers, who tried to convince me, from the experience Adam had in the Garden of Eden, that God had cursed all labour, and that, therefore, it was a sin for any man to work. For that reason this man sought to do as little work as possible. He seemed at that time to be supremely happy, because he was living, as he expressed it, through one week that was free from sin.

In the school we made a special effort to teach our students the meaning of Christmas, and to give them lessons in its proper observance. In this we have been successful to a degree that makes me feel safe in saying that the season now has a new meaning, not only through all that immediate region, but, in a measure, wherever our graduates have gone.

At the present time one of the most satisfactory features of the Christmas and Thanksgiving season at Tuskegee is the unselfish and beautiful way in which our graduates and students spend their time in administering to the comfort and happiness of others, especially the unfortunate. Not long ago some of our young men spent a holiday in rebuilding a cabin for a helpless coloured women who was about seventy-five years old. At another time I remember that I made it known in chapel, one night, that a very poor student was suffering from cold, because he needed a coat. The next morning two coats were sent to my office for him.

I have referred to the disposition on the part of the white people in the town of Tuskegee and vicinity to help the school. From the first, I resolved to make the school a real part of the community in which it was located. I was determined that no one should have the feeling that it was a foreign institution, dropped down in the midst of the people, for which they had no responsibility and in which they had no interest. I noticed that the very fact that they had been asking to contribute toward the purchase of the land made them begin to feel as if it was going to be their school, to a large degree. I noted that just in proportion as we made the white people feel that the institution was a part of the life of the community, and that, while we wanted to make friends in Boston, for example, we also wanted to make white friends in Tuskegee, and that we wanted to make the school of real service to all the people, their attitude toward the school became favourable.

Perhaps I might add right here, what I hope to demonstrate later, that, so far as I know, the Tuskegee school at the present time has no warmer and more enthusiastic friends anywhere than it has among the white citizens of Tuskegee and throughout the state of Alabama and the entire South. From the first, I have advised our people in the South to make friends in every straightforward, manly way with their next-door neighbour, whether he be a black man or a white man. I have also advised them, where no principle is at stake, to consult the interests of their local communities, and to advise with their friends in regard to their voting.

For several months the work of securing the money with which to pay for the farm went on without ceasing. At the end of three months enough was secured to repay the loan of two hundred and fifty dollars to General Marshall, and within two months more we had secured the entire five hundred dollars and had received a deed of the one hundred acres of land. This gave us a great deal of satisfaction. It was not only a source of satisfaction to secure a permanent location for the school, but it was equally satisfactory to know that the greater part of the money with which it was paid for had been gotten from the white and coloured people in the town of Tuskegee. The most of this money was obtained by holding festivals and concerts, and from small individual donations.

Our next effort was in the direction of increasing the cultivation of the land, so as to secure some return from it, and at the same time give the students training in agriculture. All the industries at Tuskegee have been started in natural and logical order, growing out of the needs of a community settlement. We began with farming, because we wanted something to eat.

Many of the students, also, were able to remain in school but a few weeks at a time, because they had so little money with which to pay their board. Thus another object which made it desirable to get an industrial system started was in order to make it available as a means of helping the students to earn money enough so that they might be able to remain in school during the nine months' session of the school year.

The first animal that the school came into possession of was an old blind horse given us by one of the white citizens of Tuskegee. Perhaps I may add here that at the present time the school owns over two hundred horses, colts, mules, cows, calves, and oxen, and about seven hundred hogs and pigs, as well as a large number of sheep and goats.

The school was constantly growing in numbers, so much so that, after we had got the farm paid for, the cultivation of the land begun, and the old cabins which we had found on the place somewhat repaired, we turned our attention toward providing a large, substantial building. After having given a good deal of thought to the subject, we finally had the plans drawn for a building that was estimated to cost about six thousand dollars. This seemed to us a tremendous sum, but we knew that the school must go backward or forward, and that our work would mean little unless we could get hold of the students in their home life.

One incident which occurred about this time gave me a great deal of satisfaction as well as surprise. When it became known in the town that we were discussing the plans for a new, large building, a Southern white man who was operating a sawmill not far from Tuskegee came to me and said that he would gladly put all the lumber necessary to erect the building on the grounds, with no other guarantee for payment than my word that it would be paid for when we secured some money. I told the man frankly that at the time we did not have in our hands one dollar of the money needed.

Notwithstanding this, he insisted on being allowed to put the lumber on the grounds. After we had secured some portion of the money we permitted him to do this.

Miss Davidson again began the work of securing in various ways small contributions for the new building from the white and coloured people in and near Tuskegee. I think I never saw a community of people so happy over anything as were the coloured people over the prospect of this new building. One day, when we were holding a meeting to secure funds for its erection, an old, ante-bellum coloured man came a distance of twelve miles and brought in his ox-cart a large hog. When the meeting was in progress, he rose in the midst of the company and said that he had no money which he could give, but he had raised two fine hogs, and that he had brought one of them as a contribution toward the expenses of the building. He closed his announcement by saying: "Any nigger that's got any love for his race, or any respect for himself, will bring a hog to the next meeting." Quite a number of men in the community also volunteered to give several days' work, each, toward the erection of the building.

After we had secured all the help that we could in Tuskegee, Miss Davidson decided to go North for the purpose of securing additional funds. For weeks she visited individuals and spoke in churches and before Sunday schools and other organizations. She found this work quite trying, and often embarrassing. The school was not known, but she was not long in winning her way into the confidence of the best people in the North.

The first gift from any Northern person was received from a New York lady whom Miss Davidson met on the boat that was bringing her North. They fell into a conversation, and the Northern lady became so much interested in the effort being made at Tuskegee that before they parted Miss Davidson was handed a check for fifty dollars. For some time before our marriage, and also after it, Miss Davidson kept up the work of securing money in the North and in the South by interesting people by personal visits and through correspondence. At the same time she kept in close touch with the work at Tuskegee, as lady principal and classroom teacher. In addition to this, she worked among the older people in and near Tuskegee, and taught a Sunday school class in the town. She was never very strong, but never seemed happy unless she was giving all of her strength to the cause which she loved. Often, at night, after spending the day in going from door to door trying to interest persons in the work at Tuskegee, she would be so exhausted that she could not undress herself. A lady upon whom she called, in Boston, afterward told me that at one time when Miss Davidson called her to see and send up her card the lady was detained a little before she could see Miss Davidson, and when she entered the parlour she found Miss Davidson so exhausted that she had fallen asleep.

While putting up our first building, which was named Porter Hall, after Mr. A.H. Porter, of Brooklyn, N.Y., who gave a generous sum toward its erection, the need for money became acute. I had given one of our creditors a promise that upon a certain day he should be paid four hundred dollars. On the morning of that day we did not have a dollar. The mail arrived at the school at ten o'clock, and in this mail there was a check sent by Miss Davidson for exactly four hundred dollars. I could relate many instances of almost the same character. This four hundred dollars was given by two ladies in Boston. Two years later, when the work at Tuskegee had grown considerably, and when we were in the midst of a season when we were so much in need of money that the future looked doubtful and gloomy, the same two Boston ladies sent us six thousand dollars. Words cannot describe our surprise, or the encouragement that the gift brought to us. Perhaps I might add here that for fourteen years these same friends have sent us six thousand dollars a year.

As soon as the plans were drawn for the new building, the students began digging out the earth where the foundations were to be laid, working after the regular classes were over. They had not fully outgrown the idea that it was hardly the proper thing for them to use their hands, since they had come there, as one of them expressed it, "to be educated, and not to work." Gradually, though, I noted with satisfaction that a sentiment in favour of work was gaining ground. After a few weeks of hard work the foundations were ready, and a day was appointed for the laying of the corner-stone.

When it is considered that the laying of this corner-stone took place in the heart of the South, in the "Black Belt," in the centre of that part of our country that was most devoted to slavery; that at that time slavery had been abolished only about sixteen years; that only sixteen years before no Negro could be taught from books without the teacher receiving the condemnation of the law or of public sentiment—when all this is considered, the scene that was witnessed on that spring day at Tuskegee was a remarkable one. I believe there are few places in the world where it could have taken place.

The principal address was delivered by the Hon. Waddy Thompson, the Superintendent of Education for the county. About the corner-stone were gathered the teachers, the students, their parents and friends, the county officials—who were white—and all the leading white men in that vicinity, together with many of the black men and women whom the same white people but a few years before had held a title to as property. The members of both races were anxious to exercise the privilege of placing under the corner-stone some momento.

Before the building was completed we passed through some very trying seasons. More than once our hearts were made to bleed, as it were, because bills were falling due that we did not have the money to meet. Perhaps no one who has not gone through the experience, month after month, of trying to erect buildings and provide equipment for a school when no one knew where the money was to come from, can properly appreciate the difficulties under which we laboured. During the first years at Tuskegee I recall that night after night I would roll and toss on my bed, without sleep, because of the anxiety and uncertainty which we were in regarding money. I knew that, in a large degree, we were trying an experiment—that of testing whether or not it was possible for Negroes to build up and control the affairs of a large education institution. I knew that if we failed it would injure the whole race. I knew that the presumption was against us. I knew that in the case of white people beginning such an enterprise it would be taken for granted that they were going to succeed, but in our case I felt that people would be surprised if we succeeded. All this made a burden which pressed down on us, sometimes, it seemed, at the rate of a thousand pounds to the square inch.

In all our difficulties and anxieties, however, I never went to a white or a black person in the town of Tuskegee for any assistance that was in their power to render, without being helped according to their means. More than a dozen times, when bills figuring up into the hundreds of dollars were falling due, I applied to the white men of Tuskegee for small loans, often borrowing small amounts from as many as a half-dozen persons, to meet our obligations. One thing I was determined to do from the first, and that was to keep the credit of the school high; and this, I think I can say without boasting, we have done all through these years.

I shall always remember a bit of advice given me by Mr. George W. Campbell, the white man to whom I have referred to as the one who induced General Armstrong to send me to Tuskegee. Soon after I entered upon the work Mr. Campbell said to me, in his fatherly way: "Washington, always remember that credit is capital."

At one time when we were in the greatest distress for money that we ever experienced, I placed the situation frankly before General Armstrong. Without hesitation he gave me his personal check for all the money which he had saved for his own use. This was not the only time that General Armstrong helped Tuskegee in this way. I do not think I have ever made this fact public before.

During the summer of 1882, at the end of the first year's work of the school, I was married to Miss Fannie N. Smith, of Malden, W. Va. We began keeping house in Tuskegee early in the fall. This made a home for our teachers, who now had been increase to four in number. My wife was also a graduate of the Hampton Institute. After earnest and constant work in the interests of the school, together with her housekeeping duties, my wife passed away in May, 1884. One child, Portia M. Washington, was born during our marriage.

From the first, my wife most earnestly devoted her thoughts and time to the work of the school, and was completely one with me in every interest and ambition. She passed away, however, before she had an opportunity of seeing what the school was designed to be.

Chapter 10. A Harder Task Than Making Bricks Without Straw

From the very beginning, at Tuskegee, I was determined to have the students do not only the agricultural and domestic work, but to have them erect their own buildings. My plan was to have them, while performing this service, taught the latest and best methods of labour, so that the school would not only get the benefit of their efforts, but the students themselves would be taught to see not only utility in labour, but beauty and dignity; would be taught, in fact, how to lift labour up from mere drudgery and toil, and would learn to love work for its own sake. My plan was not to teach them to work in the old way, but to show them how to make the forces of nature—air, water, steam, electricity, horse-power—assist them in their labour.

At first many advised against the experiment of having the buildings erected by the labour of the students, but I was determined to stick to it. I told those who doubted the wisdom of the plan that I knew that our first buildings would not be so comfortable or so complete in their finish as buildings erected by the experienced hands of outside workmen, but that in the teaching of civilization, self-help, and self-reliance, the erection of buildings by the students themselves would more than compensate for any lack of comfort or fine finish.

I further told those who doubted the wisdom of this plan, that the majority of our students came to us in poverty, from the cabins of the cotton, sugar, and rice plantations of the South, and that while I knew it would please the students very much to place them at once in finely constructed buildings, I felt that it would be following out a more natural process of development to teach them how to construct their own buildings. Mistakes I knew would be made, but these mistakes would teach us valuable lessons for the future.

During the now nineteen years' existence of the Tuskegee school, the plan of having the buildings erected by student labour has been adhered to. In this time forty buildings, counting small and large, have been built, and all except four are almost wholly the product of student labour. As an additional result, hundreds of men are now scattered throughout the South who received their knowledge of mechanics while being taught how to erect these buildings. Skill and knowledge are now handed down from one set of students to another in this way, until at the present time a building of any description or size can be constructed wholly by our instructors and students, from the drawing of the plans to the putting in of the electric fixtures, without going off the grounds for a single workman.

Not a few times, when a new student has been led into the temptation of marring the looks of some building by leadpencil marks or by the cuts of a jack-knife, I have heard an old student remind him: "Don't do that. That is our building. I helped put it up."

In the early days of the school I think my most trying experience was in the matter of brickmaking. As soon as we got the farm work reasonably well started, we directed our next efforts toward the industry of making bricks. We needed these for use in connection with the erection of our own buildings; but there was also another reason for establishing this industry. There was no brickyard in the town, and in addition to our own needs there was a demand for bricks in the general market.

I had always sympathized with the "Children of Israel," in their task of "making bricks without straw," but ours was the task of making bricks with no money and no experience.

In the first place, the work was hard and dirty, and it was difficult to get the students to help. When it came to brickmaking, their distaste for manual labour in connection with book education became especially manifest. It was not a pleasant task for one to stand in the mud-pit for hours, with the mud up to his knees. More than one man became disgusted and left the school.

We tried several locations before we opened up a pit that furnished brick clay. I had always supposed that brickmaking was very simple, but I soon found out by bitter experience that it required special skill and knowledge, particularly in the burning of the bricks. After a good deal of effort we moulded about twenty-five thousand bricks, and put them into a kiln to be burned. This kiln turned out to be a failure, because it was not properly constructed or properly burned. We began at once, however, on a second kiln. This, for some reason, also proved a failure. The failure of this kiln made it still more difficult to get the students to take part in the work. Several of the teachers, however, who had been trained in the industries at Hampton, volunteered their services, and in some way we succeeded in getting a third kiln ready for burning. The burning of a kiln required about a week. Toward the latter part of the week, when it seemed as if we were going to have a good many thousand bricks in a few hours, in the middle of the night the kiln fell. For the third time we had failed.

The failure of this last kiln left me without a single dollar with which to make another experiment. Most of the teachers advised the abandoning of the effort to make bricks. In the midst of my troubles I thought of a watch which had come into my possession years before. I took the watch to the city of Montgomery, which was not far distant, and placed it in a pawn-shop. I secured cash upon it to the amount of fifteen dollars, with which to renew the brickmaking experiment. I returned to Tuskegee, and, with the help of the fifteen dollars, rallied our rather demoralized and discouraged forces and began a fourth attempt to make bricks. This time, I am glad to say, we were successful. Before I got hold of any money, the time-limit on my watch had expired, and I have never seen it since; but I have never regretted the loss of it.

Brickmaking has now become such an important industry at the school that last season our students manufactured twelve hundred thousand of first-class bricks, of a quality suitable to be sold in any market. Aside from this, scores of young men have mastered the brickmaking trade—both the making of bricks by hand and by machinery—and are now engaged in this industry in many parts of the South.

The making of these bricks taught me an important lesson in regard to the relations of the two races in the South. Many white people who had had no contact with the school, and perhaps no sympathy with it, came to us to buy bricks because they found out that ours were good bricks. They discovered that we were supplying a real want in the community.

The making of these bricks caused many of the white residents of the neighbourhood to begin to feel that the education of the Negro was not making him worthless, but that in educating our students we were adding something to the wealth and comfort of the community. As the people of the neighbourhood came to us to buy bricks, we got acquainted with them; they traded with us and we with them. Our business interests became intermingled. We had something which they wanted; they had something which we wanted. This, in a large measure, helped to lay the foundation for the pleasant relations that have continued to exist between us and the white people in that section, and which now extend throughout the South.

Wherever one of our brickmakers has gone in the South, we find that he has something to contribute to the well-being of the community into which he has gone; something that has made the community feel that, in a degree, it is indebted to him, and perhaps, to a certain extent, dependent upon him. In this way pleasant relations between the races have been simulated.

My experience is that there is something in human nature which always makes an individual recognize and reward merit, no matter under what colour of skin merit is found. I have found, too, that it is the visible, the tangible, that goes a long ways in softening prejudices. The actual sight of a first-class house that a Negro has built is ten times more potent than pages of discussion about a house that he ought to build, or perhaps could build.

The same principle of industrial education has been carried out in the building of our own wagons, carts, and buggies, from the first. We now own and use on our farm and about the school dozens of these vehicles, and every one of them has been built by the hands of the students. Aside from this, we help supply the local market with these vehicles. The supplying of them to the people in the community has had the same effect as the supplying of bricks, and the man who learns at Tuskegee to build and repair wagons and carts is regarded as a benefactor by both races in the community where he goes. The people with whom he lives and works are going to think twice before they part with such a man.

The individual who can do something that the world wants done will, in the end, make his way regardless of race. One man may go into a community prepared to supply the people there with an analysis of Greek sentences. The community may not at the time be prepared for, or feel the need of, Greek analysis, but it may feel its need of bricks and houses and wagons. If the man can supply the need for those, then, it will lead eventually to a demand for the first product, and with the demand will come the ability to appreciate it and to profit by it.

About the time that we succeeded in burning our first kiln of bricks we began facing in an emphasized form the objection of the students to being taught to work. By this time it had gotten to be pretty well advertised throughout the state that every student who came to Tuskegee, no matter what his financial ability might be, must learn some industry. Quite a number of letters came from parents protesting against their children engaging in labour while they were in the school. Other parents came to the school to protest in person. Most of the new students brought a written or a verbal request from their parents to the effect that they wanted their children taught nothing but books. The more books, the larger they were, and the longer the titles printed upon them, the better pleased the students and their parents seemed to be.

I gave little heed to these protests, except that I lost no opportunity to go into as many parts of the state as I could, for the purpose of speaking to the parents, and showing them the value of industrial education. Besides, I talked to the students constantly on the subject. Notwithstanding the unpopularity of industrial work, the school continued to increase in numbers to such an extent that by the middle of the second year there was an attendance of about one hundred and fifty, representing almost all parts of the state of Alabama, and including a few from other states.

In the summer of 1882 Miss Davidson and I both went North and engaged in the work of raising funds for the completion of our new building. On my way North I stopped in New York to try to get a letter of recommendation from an officer of a missionary organization who had become somewhat acquainted with me a few years previous. This man not only refused to give me the letter, but advised me most earnestly to go back home at once, and not make any attempt to get money, for he was quite sure that I would never get more than enough to pay my travelling expenses. I thanked him for his advice, and proceeded on my journey.

The first place I went to in the North, was Northampton, Mass., where

I spent nearly a half-day in looking for a coloured family with whom I could board, never dreaming that any hotel would admit me. I was greatly surprised when I found that I would have no trouble in being accommodated at a hotel.

We were successful in getting money enough so that on Thanksgiving Day of that year we held our first service in the chapel of Porter Hall, although the building was not completed.

In looking about for some one to preach the Thanksgiving sermon, I found one of the rarest men that it has ever been my privilege to know. This was the Rev. Robert C. Bedford, a white man from Wisconsin, who was then pastor of a little coloured Congregational church in Montgomery, Ala. Before going to Montgomery to look for some one to preach this sermon I had never heard of Mr. Bedford. He had never heard of me. He gladly consented to come to Tuskegee and hold the Thanksgiving service. It was the first service of the kind that the coloured people there had ever observed, and what a deep interest they manifested in it! The sight of the new building made it a day of Thanksgiving for them never to be forgotten.

Mr. Bedford consented to become one of the trustees of the school, and in that capacity, and as a worker for it, he has been connected with it for eighteen years. During this time he has borne the school upon his heart night and day, and is never so happy as when he is performing some service, no matter how humble, for it. He completely obliterates himself in everything, and looks only for permission to serve where service is most disagreeable, and where others would not be attracted. In all my relations with him he has seemed to me to approach as nearly to the spirit of the Master as almost any man I ever met.

A little later there came into the service of the school another man, quite young at the time, and fresh from Hampton, without whose service the school never could have become what it is. This was Mr. Warren Logan, who now for seventeen years has been the treasurer of the Institute, and the acting principal during my absence. He has always shown a degree of unselfishness and an amount of business tact, coupled with a clear judgment, that has kept the school in good condition no matter how long I have been absent from it. During all the financial stress through which the school has passed, his patience and faith in our ultimate success have not left him.

As soon as our first building was near enough to completion so that we could occupy a portion of it—which was near the middle of the second year of the school—we opened a boarding department. Students had begun coming from quite a distance, and in such increasing numbers that we felt more and more that we were merely skimming over the surface, in that we were not getting hold of the students in their home life.

We had nothing but the students and their appetites with which to begin a boarding department. No provision had been made in the new building for a kitchen and dining room; but we discovered that by digging out a large amount of earth from under the building we could make a partially lighted basement room that could be used for a kitchen and dining room. Again I called on the students to volunteer for work, this time to assist in digging out the basement. This they did, and in a few weeks we had a place to cook and eat in, although it was very rough and uncomfortable. Any one seeing the place now would never believe that it was once used for a dining room.

The most serious problem, though, was to get the boarding department started off in running order, with nothing to do with in the way of furniture, and with no money with which to buy anything. The merchants in the town would let us have what food we wanted on credit. In fact, in those earlier years I was constantly embarrassed because people seemed to have more faith in me than I had in myself. It was pretty hard to cook, however, without stoves, and awkward to eat without dishes. At first the cooking was done out-of-doors, in the old-fashioned, primitive style, in pots and skillets placed over a fire. Some of the carpenters' benches that had been used in the construction of the building were utilized for tables. As for dishes, there were too few to make it worth while to spend time in describing them.

No one connected with the boarding department seemed to have any idea that meals must be served at certain fixed and regular hours, and this was a source of great worry. Everything was so out of joint and so inconvenient that I feel safe in saying that for the first two weeks something was wrong at every meal. Either the meat was not done or had been burnt, or the salt had been left out of the bread, or the tea had been forgotten.

Early one morning I was standing near the dining-room door listening to the complaints of the students. The complaints that morning were especially emphatic and numerous, because the whole breakfast had been a failure. One of the girls who had failed to get any breakfast came out and went to the well to draw some water to drink and take the place of the breakfast which she had not been able to get. When she reached the well, she found that the rope was broken and that she could get no water. She turned from the well and said, in the most discouraged tone, not knowing that I was where I could hear her, "We can't even get water to drink at this school." I think no one remark ever came so near discouraging me as that one.

At another time, when Mr. Bedford—whom I have already spoken of as one of our trustees, and a devoted friend of the institution—was visiting the school, he was given a bedroom immediately over the dining room. Early in the morning he was awakened by a rather animated discussion between two boys in the dining room below. The discussion was over the question as to whose turn it was to use the coffee-cup that morning. One boy won the case by proving that for three mornings he had not had an opportunity to use the cup at all.

But gradually, with patience and hard work, we brought order out of chaos, just as will be true of any problem if we stick to it with patience and wisdom and earnest effort.

As I look back now over that part of our struggle, I am glad to see that we had it. I am glad that we endured all those discomforts and inconveniences. I am glad that our students had to dig out the place for their kitchen and dining room. I am glad that our first boarding-place was in the dismal, ill-lighted, and damp basement. Had we started in a fine, attractive, convenient room, I fear we would have "lost our heads" and become "stuck up." It means a great deal, I think, to start off on a foundation which one has made for one's self.

When our old students return to Tuskegee now, as they often do, and go into our large, beautiful, well-ventilated, and well-lighted dining room, and see tempting, well-cooked food—largely grown by the students themselves—and see tables, neat tablecloths and napkins, and vases of flowers upon the tables, and hear singing birds, and note that each meal is served exactly upon the minute, with no disorder, and with almost no complaint coming from the hundreds that now fill our dining room, they, too, often say to me that they are glad that we started as we did, and built ourselves up year by year, by a slow and natural process of growth.

⊡ ⊡ ⊡

Chapter 11. Making Their Beds Before They Could Lie On Them

A little later in the history of the school we had a visit from General J.F.B. Marshall, the Treasurer of the Hampton Institute, who had had faith enough to lend us the first two hundred and fifty dollars with which to make a payment down on the farm. He remained with us a week, and made a careful inspection of everything. He seemed well pleased with our progress, and wrote back interesting and encouraging reports to Hampton. A little later Miss Mary F. Mackie, the teacher who had given me the "sweeping" examination when I entered Hampton, came to see us, and still later General Armstrong himself came.

At the time of the visits of these Hampton friends the number of teachers at Tuskegee had increased considerably, and the most of the new teachers were graduates of the Hampton Institute. We gave our Hampton friends, especially General Armstrong, a cordial welcome. They were all surprised and pleased at the rapid progress that the school had made within so short a time. The coloured people from miles around came to the school to get a look at General Armstrong, about whom they had heard so much. The General was not only welcomed by the members of my own race, but by the Southern white people as well.

This first visit which General Armstrong made to Tuskegee gave me an opportunity to get an insight into his character such as I had not before had. I refer to his interest in the Southern white people. Before this I had had the thought that General Armstrong, having fought the Southern white man, rather cherished a feeling of bitterness toward the white South, and was interested in helping only the coloured man there. But this visit convinced me that I did not know the greatness and the generosity of the man. I soon learned, by his visits to the Southern white people, and from his conversations with them, that he was as anxious about the prosperity and the happiness of the white race as the black. He cherished no bitterness against the South, and was happy when an opportunity offered for manifesting his sympathy. In all my acquaintance with General Armstrong I never heard him speak, in public or in private, a single bitter word against the white man in the South. From his example in this respect I learned the lesson that great men cultivate love, and that only little men cherish a spirit of hatred. I learned that assistance given to the weak makes the one who gives it strong; and that oppression of the unfortunate makes one weak.

It is now long ago that I learned this lesson from General Armstrong, and resolved that I would permit no man, no matter what his colour might be, to narrow and degrade my soul by making me hate him. With God's help, I believe that I have completely rid myself of any ill feeling toward the Southern white man for any wrong that he may have inflicted upon my race. I am made to feel just as happy now when I am rendering service to Southern white men as when the service is rendered to a member of my own race. I pity from the bottom of my heart any individual who is so unfortunate as to get into the habit of holding race prejudice.

The more I consider the subject, the more strongly I am convinced that the most harmful effect of the practice to which the people in certain sections of the South have felt themselves compelled to resort, in order to get rid of the force of the Negroes' ballot, is not wholly in the wrong done to the Negro, but in the permanent injury to the morals of the white man. The wrong to the Negro is temporary, but to the morals of the white man the injury is permanent. I have noted time and time again that when an individual perjures himself in order to break the force of the black man's ballot, he soon learns to practise dishonesty in other relations of life, not only where the Negro is concerned, but equally so where a white man is concerned. The white man who begins by cheating a Negro usually ends by cheating a white man. The white man who begins to break the law by lynching a Negro soon yields to the temptation to lynch a white man. All this, it seems to me, makes it important that the whole Nation lend a hand in trying to lift the burden of ignorance from the South.

Another thing that is becoming more apparent each year in the development of education in the South is the influence of General Armstrong's idea of education; and this not upon the blacks alone, but upon the whites also. At the present time there is almost no Southern state that is not putting forth efforts in the direction of securing industrial education for its white boys and girls, and in most cases it is easy to trace the history of these efforts back to General Armstrong.

Soon after the opening of our humble boarding department students began coming to us in still larger numbers. For weeks we not only had to contend with the difficulty of providing board, with no money, but also with that of providing sleeping accommodations. For this purpose we rented a number of cabins near the school. These cabins were in a dilapidated condition, and during the winter months the students who occupied them necessarily suffered from the cold. We charge the students eight dollars a month—all they were able to pay—for their board. This included, besides board, room, fuel, and washing. We also gave the students credit on their board bills for all the work which they did for the school which was of any value to the institution. The cost of tuition, which was fifty dollars a year for each student, we had to secure then, as now, wherever we could.

This small charge in cash gave us no capital with which to start a boarding department. The weather during the second winter of our work was very cold. We were not able to provide enough bed-clothes to keep the students warm. In fact, for some time we were not able to provide, except in a few cases, bedsteads and mattresses of any kind. During the coldest nights I was so troubled about the discomfort of the students that I could not sleep myself. I recall that on several occasions I went in the middle of the night to the shanties occupied by the young men, for the purpose of confronting them. Often I found some of them sitting huddled around a fire, with the one blanket which we had been able to provide wrapped around them, trying in this way to keep warm. During the whole night some of them did not attempt to lie down. One morning, when the night previous had been unusually cold, I asked those of the students in the chapel who thought that they had been frostbitten during the night to raise their hands. Three hands went up. Notwithstanding these experiences, there was almost no complaining on the part of the students. They knew that we were doing the best that we could for them. They were happy in the privilege of being permitted to enjoy any kind of opportunity that would enable them to improve their condition. They were constantly asking what they might do to lighten the burdens of the teachers.

I have heard it stated more than once, both in the North and in the South, that coloured people would not obey and respect each other when one member of the race is placed in a position of authority over others. In regard to this general belief and these statements, I can say that during the nineteen years of my experience at Tuskegee I never, either by word or act, have been treated with disrespect by any student or officer connected with the institution. On the other hand, I am constantly embarrassed by the many acts of thoughtful kindness. The students do not seem to want to see me carry a large book or a satchel or any kind of a burden through the grounds. In such cases more than one always offers to relieve me. I almost never go out of my office when the rain is falling that some student does not come to my side with an umbrella and ask to be allowed to hold it over me.

While writing upon this subject, it is a pleasure for me to add that in all my contact with the white people of the South I have never received a single personal insult. The white people in and near Tuskegee, to an especial degree, seem to count it as a privilege to show me all the respect within their power, and often go out of their way to do this.

Not very long ago I was making a journey between Dallas (Texas) and Houston. In some way it became known in advance that I was on the train. At nearly every station at which the train stopped, numbers of white people, including in most cases of the officials of the town, came aboard and introduced themselves and thanked me heartily for the work that I was trying to do for the South.

On another occasion, when I was making a trip from Augusta, Georgia, to Atlanta, being rather tired from much travel, I rode in a Pullman sleeper. When I went into the car, I found there two ladies from Boston whom I knew well. These good ladies were perfectly ignorant, it seems, of the customs of the South, and in the goodness of their hearts insisted that I take a seat with them in their section. After some hesitation I consented. I had been there but a few minutes when one of them, without my knowledge, ordered supper to be served for the three of us. This embarrassed me still further. The car was full of Southern white men, most of whom had their eyes on our party. When I found that supper had been ordered, I tried to contrive some excuse that would permit me to leave the section, but the ladies insisted that I must eat with them. I finally settled back in my seat with a sigh, and said to myself, "I am in for it now, sure."

To add further to the embarrassment of the situation, soon after the supper was placed on the table one of the ladies remembered that she had in her satchel a special kind of tea which she wished served, and as she said she felt quite sure the porter did not know how to brew it properly, she insisted upon getting up and preparing and serving it herself. At last the meal was over; and it seemed the longest one that I had ever eaten. When we were through, I decided to get myself out of the embarrassing situation and go to the smoking-room, where most of the men were by that time, to see how the land lay. In the meantime, however, it had become known in some way throughout the car who I was. When I went into the smoking-room I was never more surprised in my life than when each man, nearly every one of them a citizen of Georgia, came up and introduced himself to me and thanked me earnestly for the work that I was trying to do for the whole South. This was not flattery, because each one of these individuals knew that he had nothing to gain by trying to flatter me.

From the first I have sought to impress the students with the idea that Tuskegee is not my institution, or that of the officers, but that it is their institution, and that they have as much interest in it as any of the trustees or instructors. I have further sought to have them feel that I am at the institution as their friend and adviser, and not as their overseer. It has been my aim to have them speak with directness and frankness about anything that concerns the life of the school. Two or three times a year I ask the students to write me a letter criticising or making complaints or suggestions about anything connected with the institution. When this is not done, I have them meet me in the chapel for a heart-to-heart talk about the conduct of the school. There are no meetings with our students that I enjoy more than these, and none are more helpful to me in planning for the future. These meetings, it seems to me, enable me to get at the very heart of all that concerns the school. Few things help an individual more than to place responsibility upon him, and to let him know that you trust him. When I have read of labour troubles between employers and employees, I have often thought that many strikes and similar disturbances might be avoided if the employers would cultivate the habit of getting nearer to their employees, of consulting and advising with them, and letting them feel that the interests of the two are the same. Every individual responds to confidence, and this is not more true of any race than of the Negroes.

Let them once understand that you are unselfishly interested in them, and you can lead them to any extent.

It was my aim from the first at Tuskegee to not only have the buildings erected by the students themselves, but to have them make their own furniture as far as was possible. I now marvel at the patience of the students while sleeping upon the floor while waiting for some kind of a bedstead to be constructed, or at their sleeping without any kind of a mattress while waiting for something that looked like a mattress to be made.

In the early days we had very few students who had been used to handling carpenters' tools, and the bedsteads made by the students then were very rough and very weak. Not unfrequently when I went into the students' rooms in the morning I would find at least two bedsteads lying about on the floor. The problem of providing mattresses was a difficult one to solve. We finally mastered this, however, by getting some cheap cloth and sewing pieces of this together as to make large bags. These bags we filled with the pine straw—or, as it is sometimes called, pine needles—which we secured from the forests near by. I am glad to say that the industry of mattress-making has grown steadily since then, and has been improved to such an extent that at the present time it is an important branch of the work which is taught systematically to a number of our girls, and that the mattresses that now come out of the mattress-shop at Tuskegee are about as good as those bought in the average store. For some time after the opening of the boarding department we had no chairs in the students' bedrooms or in the dining rooms. Instead of chairs we used stools which the students constructed by nailing together three pieces of rough board. As a rule, the furniture in the students' rooms during the early days of the school consisted of a bed, some stools, and sometimes a rough table made by the students. The plan of having the students make the furniture is still followed, but the number of pieces in a room has been increased, and the workmanship has so improved that little fault can be found with the articles now. One thing that I have always insisted upon at Tuskegee is that everywhere there should be absolute cleanliness. Over and over again the students were reminded in those first years—and are reminded now—that people would excuse us for our poverty, for our lack of comforts and conveniences, but that they would not excuse us for dirt.

Another thing that has been insisted upon at the school is the use of the tooth-brush. "The gospel of the tooth-brush," as General Armstrong used to call it, is part of our creed at Tuskegee. No student is permitted to retain who does not keep and use a tooth-brush. Several times, in recent years, students have come to us who brought with them almost no other article except a tooth-brush. They had heard from the lips of other students about our insisting upon the use of this, and so, to make a good impression, they brought at least a tooth-brush with them. I remember that one morning, not long ago, I went with the lady principal on her usual morning tour of inspection of the girls' rooms. We found one room that contained three girls who had recently arrived at the school. When I asked them if they had tooth-brushes, one of the girls replied, pointing to a brush: "Yes, sir. That is our brush. We bought it together, yesterday." It did not take them long to learn a different lesson.

It has been interesting to note the effect that the use of the tooth-brush has had in bringing about a higher degree of civilization among the students. With few exceptions, I have noticed that, if we can get a student to the point where, when the first or second tooth-brush disappears, he of his own motion buys another, I have not been disappointed in the future of that individual. Absolute cleanliness of the body has been insisted upon from the first. The students have been taught to bathe as regularly as to take their meals. This lesson we began teaching before we had anything in the shape of a bath-house. Most of the students came from plantation districts, and often we had to teach them how to sleep at night; that is, whether between the two sheets—after we got to the point where we could provide them two sheets—or under both of them. Naturally I found it difficult to teach them to sleep between two sheets when we were able to supply but one. The importance of the use of the night-gown received the same attention.

For a long time one of the most difficult tasks was to teach the students that all the buttons were to be kept on their clothes, and that there must be no torn places or grease-spots. This lesson, I am pleased to be able to say, has been so thoroughly learned and so faithfully handed down from year to year by one set of students to another that often at the present time, when the students march out of the chapel in the evening and their dress is inspected, as it is every night, not one button is found to be missing.

Chapter 12. Raising Money

When we opened our boarding department, we provided rooms in the attic of Porter Hall, our first building, for a number of girls. But the number of students, of both sexes, continued to increase. We could find rooms outside the school grounds for many of the young men, but the girls we did not care to expose in this way. Very soon the problem of providing more rooms for the girls, as well as a larger boarding department for all the students, grew serious. As a result, we finally decided to undertake the construction of a still larger building—a building that would contain rooms for the girls and boarding accommodations for all.

After having had a preliminary sketch of the needed building made, we found that it would cost about ten thousand dollars. We had no money whatever with which to begin; still we decided to give the needed building a name. We knew we could name it, even though we were in doubt about our ability to secure the means for its construction. We decided to call the proposed building Alabama Hall, in honour of the state in which we were labouring. Again Miss Davidson began making efforts to enlist the interest and help of the coloured and white people in and near Tuskegee. They responded willingly, in proportion to their means. The students, as in the case of our first building, Porter Hall, began digging out the dirt in order to allow the laying of the foundations.

When we seemed at the end of our resources, so far as securing money was concerned, something occurred which showed the greatness of General Armstrong—something which proved how far he was above the ordinary individual. When we were in the midst of great anxiety as to where and how we were to get funds for the new building, I received a telegram from General Armstrong asking me if I could spend a month travelling with him through the North, and asking me, if I could do so, to come to

Hampton at once. Of course I accepted General Armstrong's invitation, and went to Hampton immediately. On arriving there I found that the General had decided to take a quartette of singers through the North, and hold meetings for a month in important cities, at which meetings he and I were to speak. Imagine my surprise when the General told me, further, that these meetings were to be held, not in the interests of Hampton, but in the interests of Tuskegee, and that the Hampton Institute was to be responsible for all the expenses.

Although he never told me so in so many words, I found that General Armstrong took this method of introducing me to the people of the North, as well as for the sake of securing some immediate funds to be used in the erection of Alabama Hall. A weak and narrow man would have reasoned that all the money which came to Tuskegee in this way would be just so much taken from the Hampton Institute; but none of these selfish or short-sighted feelings ever entered the breast of General Armstrong. He was too big to be little, too good to be mean. He knew that the people in the North who gave money gave it for the purpose of helping the whole cause of Negro civilization, and not merely for the advancement of any one school. The General knew, too, that the way to strengthen Hampton was to make it a centre of unselfish power in the working out of the whole Southern problem.

In regard to the addresses which I was to make in the North, I recall just one piece of advice which the General gave me. He said: "Give them an idea for every word." I think it would be hard to improve upon this advice; and it might be made to apply to all public speaking. From that time to the present I have always tried to keep his advice in mind.

Meetings were held in New York, Brooklyn, Boston, Philadelphia, and other large cities, and at all of these meetings General Armstrong pleased, together with myself, for help, not for Hampton, but for Tuskegee. At these meetings an especial effort was made to secure help for the building of Alabama Hall, as well as to introduce the school to the attention of the general public. In both these respects the meetings proved successful.

After that kindly introduction I began going North alone to secure funds. During the last fifteen years I have been compelled to spend a large proportion of my time away from the school, in an effort to secure money to provide for the growing needs of the institution. In my efforts to get funds I have had some experiences that may be of interest to my readers. Time and time again I have been asked, by people who are trying to secure money for philanthropic purposes, what rule or rules I followed to secure the interest and help of people who were able to contribute money to worthy objects. As far as the science of what is called begging can be reduced to rules, I would say that I have had but two rules. First, always to do my whole duty regarding making our work known to individuals and organizations; and, second, not to worry about the results. This second rule has been the hardest for me to live up to. When bills are on the eve of falling due, with not a dollar in hand with which to meet them, it is pretty difficult to learn not to worry, although I think I am learning more and more each year that all worry simply consumes, and to no purpose, just so much physical and mental strength that might otherwise be given to effective work. After considerable experience in coming into contact with wealthy and noted men, I have observed that those who have accomplished the greatest results are those who "keep under the body"; are those who never grow excited or lose self-control, but are always calm, self-possessed, patient, and polite. I think that President William McKinley is the best example of a man of this class that I have ever seen.

In order to be successful in any kind of undertaking, I think the main thing is for one to grow to the point where he completely forgets himself; that is, to lose himself in a great cause. In proportion as one loses himself in the way, in the same degree does he get the highest happiness out of his work.

My experience in getting money for Tuskegee has taught me to have no patience with those people who are always condemning the rich because they are rich, and because they do not give more to objects of charity. In the first place, those who are guilty of such sweeping criticisms do not know how many people would be made poor, and how much suffering would result, if wealthy people were to part all at once with any large proportion of their wealth in a way to disorganize and cripple great business enterprises. Then very few persons have any idea of the large number of applications for help that rich people are constantly being flooded with. I know wealthy people who receive as much as twenty calls a day for help. More than once when I have gone into the offices of rich men, I have found half a dozen persons waiting to see them, and all come for the same purpose, that of securing money. And all these calls in person, to say nothing of the applications received through the mails. Very few people have any idea of the amount of money given away by persons who never permit their names to be known. I have often heard persons condemned for not giving away money, who, to my own knowledge, were giving away thousands of dollars every year so quietly that the world knew nothing about it.

As an example of this, there are two ladies in New York, whose names rarely appear in print, but who, in a quiet way, have given us the means with which to erect three large and important buildings during the last eight years. Besides the gift of these buildings, they have made other generous donations to the school. And they not only help Tuskegee, but they are constantly seeking opportunities to help other worthy causes.

Although it has been my privilege to be the medium through which a good many hundred thousand dollars have been received for the work at Tuskegee, I have always avoided what the world calls "begging." I often tell people that I have never "begged" any money, and that I am not a "beggar." My experience and observation have convinced me that persistent asking outright for money from the rich does not, as a rule, secure help. I have usually proceeded on the principle that persons who possess sense enough to earn money have sense enough to know how to give it away, and that the mere making known of the facts regarding Tuskegee, and especially the facts regarding the work of the graduates, has been more effective than outright begging. I think that the presentation of facts, on a high, dignified plane, is all the begging that most rich people care for.

While the work of going from door to door and from office to office is hard, disagreeable, and costly in bodily strength, yet it has some compensations. Such work gives one a rare opportunity to study human nature. It also has its compensations in giving one an opportunity to meet some of the best people in the world—to be more correct, I think I should say the best people in the world. When one takes a broad survey of the country, he will find that the most useful and influential people in it are those who take the deepest interest in institutions that exist for the purpose of making the world better.

At one time, when I was in Boston, I called at the door of a rather wealthy lady, and was admitted to the vestibule and sent up my card. While I was waiting for an answer, her husband came in, and asked me in the most abrupt manner what I wanted. When I tried to explain the object of my call, he became still more ungentlemanly in his words and manner, and finally grew so excited that I left the house without waiting for a reply from the lady. A few blocks from that house I called to see a gentleman who received me in the most cordial manner. He wrote me his check for a generous sum, and then, before I had had an opportunity to thank him, said: "I am so grateful to you, Mr. Washington, for giving me the opportunity to help a good cause. It is a privilege to have a share in it. We in Boston are constantly indebted to you for doing our work." My experience in securing money convinces me that the first type of man is growing more rare all the time, and that the latter type is increasing; that is, that, more and more, rich people are coming to regard men and women who apply to them for help for worthy objects, not as beggars, but as agents for doing their work.

In the city of Boston I have rarely called upon an individual for funds that I have not been thanked for calling, usually before I could get an opportunity to thank the donor for the money. In that city the donors seem to feel, in a large degree, that an honour is being conferred upon them in their being permitted to give. Nowhere else have I met with, in so large a measure, this fine and Christlike spirit as in the city of Boston, although there are many notable instances of it outside that city. I repeat my belief that the world is growing in the direction of giving. I repeat that the main rule by which I have been guided in collecting money is to do my full duty in regard to giving people who have money an opportunity for help.

In the early years of the Tuskegee school I walked the streets or travelled country roads in the North for days and days without receiving a dollar. Often as it happened, when during the week I had been disappointed in not getting a cent from the very individuals from whom I most expected help, and when I was almost broken down and discouraged, that generous help has come from some one who I had had little idea would give at all.

I recall that on one occasion I obtained information that led me to believe that a gentleman who lived about two miles out in the country from Stamford, Conn., might become interested in our efforts at Tuskegee if our conditions and needs were presented to him. On an unusually cold and stormy day I walked the two miles to see him. After some difficulty

I succeeded in securing an interview with him. He listened with some degree of interest to what I had to say, but did not give me anything. I could not help having the feeling that, in a measure, the three hours that I had spent in seeing him had been thrown away. Still, I had followed my usual rule of doing my duty. If I had not seen him, I should have felt unhappy over neglect of duty.

Two years after this visit a letter came to Tuskegee from this man, which read like this: "Enclosed I send you a New York draft for ten thousand dollars, to be used in furtherance of your work. I had placed this sum in my will for your school, but deem it wiser to give it to you while I live. I recall with pleasure your visit to me two years ago."

I can hardly imagine any occurrence which could have given me more genuine satisfaction than the receipt of this draft. It was by far the largest single donation which up to that time the school had ever received. It came at a time when an unusually long period had passed since we had received any money. We were in great distress because of lack of funds, and the nervous strain was tremendous. It is difficult for me to think of any situation that is more trying on the nerves than that of conducting a large institution, with heavy obligations to meet, without knowing where the money is to come from to meet these obligations from month to month.

In our case I felt a double responsibility, and this made the anxiety all the more intense. If the institution had been officered by white persons, and had failed, it would have injured the cause of Negro education; but I knew that the failure of our institution, officered by Negroes, would not only mean the loss of a school, but would cause people, in a large degree, to lose faith in the ability of the entire race. The receipt of this draft for ten thousand dollars, under all these circumstances, partially lifted a burden that had been pressing down upon me for days.

From the beginning of our work to the present I have always had the feeling, and lose no opportunity to impress our teachers with the same idea, that the school will always be supported in proportion as the inside of the institution is kept clean and pure and wholesome.

The first time I ever saw the late Collis P. Huntington, the great railroad man, he gave me two dollars for our school. The last time I saw him, which was a few months before he died, he gave me fifty thousand dollars toward our endowment fund. Between these two gifts there were others of generous proportions which came every year from both Mr. and Mrs. Huntington.

Some people may say that it was Tuskegee's good luck that brought to us this gift of fifty thousand dollars. No, it was not luck. It was hard work. Nothing ever comes to me, that is worth having, except as the result of hard work. When Mr. Huntington gave me the first two dollars, I did not blame him for not giving me more, but made up my mind that I was going to convince him by tangible results that we were worthy of larger gifts. For a dozen years I made a strong effort to convince Mr. Huntington of the value of our work. I noted that just in proportion as the usefulness of the school grew, his donations increased. Never did I meet an individual who took a more kindly and sympathetic interest in our school than did Mr. Huntington. He not only gave money to us, but took time in which to advise me, as a father would a son, about the general conduct of the school.

More than once I have found myself in some pretty tight places while collecting money in the North. The following incident I have never related but once before, for the reason that I feared that people would not believe it. One morning I found myself in Providence, Rhode Island, without a cent of money with which to buy breakfast. In crossing the street to see a lady from whom I hoped to get some money, I found a bright new twenty-five-cent piece in the middle of the street track. I not only had this twenty-five cents for my breakfast, but within a few minutes I had a donation from the lady on whom I had started to call.

At one of our Commencements I was bold enough to invite the Rev. E. Winchester Donald, D.D., rector of Trinity Church, Boston, to preach the Commencement sermon. As we then had no room large enough to accommodate all who would be present, the place of meeting was under a large improvised arbour, built partly of brush and partly of rough boards.

Soon after Dr. Donald had begun speaking, the rain came down in torrents, and he had to stop, while someone held an umbrella over him.

The boldness of what I had done never dawned upon me until I saw the picture made by the rector of Trinity Church standing before that large audience under an old umbrella, waiting for the rain to cease so that he could go on with his address.

It was not very long before the rain ceased and Dr. Donald finished his sermon; and an excellent sermon it was, too, in spite of the weather. After he had gone to his room, and had gotten the wet threads of his clothes dry, Dr. Donald ventured the remark that a large chapel at Tuskegee would not be out of place. The next day a letter came from two ladies who were then travelling in Italy, saying that they had decided to give us the money for such a chapel as we needed.

A short time ago we received twenty thousand dollars from Mr. Andrew Carnegie, to be used for the purpose of erecting a new library building. Our first library and reading-room were in a corner of a shanty, and the whole thing occupied a space about five by twelve feet. It required ten years of work before I was able to secure Mr. Carnegie's interest and help. The first time I saw him, ten years ago, he seemed to take but little interest in our school, but I was determined to show him that we were worthy of his help. After ten years of hard work I wrote him a letter reading as follows:

December 15, 1900.

Mr. Andrew Carnegie, 5 W. Fifty-first St., New York.

Dear Sir: Complying with the request which you made of me when I saw you at your residence a few days ago, I now submit in writing an appeal for a library building for our institution.

We have 1100 students, 86 officers and instructors, together with their families, and about 200 coloured people living near the school, all of whom would make use of the library building.

We have over 12,000 books, periodicals, etc., gifts from our friends, but we have no suitable place for them, and we have no suitable reading-room.

Our graduates go to work in every section of the South, and whatever knowledge might be obtained in the library would serve to assist in the elevation of the whole Negro race.

Such a building as we need could be erected for about $20,000. All of the work for the building, such as brickmaking, brick-masonry, carpentry, blacksmithing, etc., would be done by the students. The money which you would give would not only supply the building, but the erection of the building would give a large number of students an opportunity to learn the building trades, and the students would use the money paid to them to keep themselves in school. I do not believe that a similar amount of money often could be made go so far in uplifting a whole race.

If you wish further information, I shall be glad to furnish it.

Yours truly,

Booker T. Washington, Principal.

The next mail brought back the following reply: "I will be very glad to pay the bills for the library building as they are incurred, to the extent of twenty thousand dollars, and I am glad of this opportunity to show the interest I have in your noble work."

I have found that strict business methods go a long way in securing the interest of rich people. It has been my constant aim at Tuskegee to carry out, in our financial and other operations, such business methods as would be approved of by any New York banking house.

I have spoken of several large gifts to the school; but by far the greater proportion of the money that has built up the institution has come in the form of small donations from persons of moderate means. It is upon these small gifts, which carry with them the interest of hundreds of donors, that any philanthropic work must depend largely for its support. In my efforts to get money I have often been surprised at the patience and deep interest of the ministers, who are besieged on every hand and at all hours of the day for help. If no other consideration had convinced me of the value of the Christian life, the Christlike work which the Church of all denominations in America has done during the last thirty-five years for the elevation of the black man would have made me a Christian. In a large degree it has been the pennies, the nickels, and the dimes which have come from the Sunday-schools, the Christian Endeavour societies, and the missionary societies, as well as from the church proper, that have helped to elevate the Negro at so rapid a rate.

This speaking of small gifts reminds me to say that very few Tuskegee graduates fail to send us an annual contribution. These contributions range from twenty-five cents up to ten dollars.

Soon after beginning our third year's work we were surprised to receive money from three special sources, and up to the present time we have continued to receive help from them. First, the State Legislature of Alabama increased its annual appropriation from two thousand dollars to three thousand dollars; I might add that still later it increased this sum to four thousand five hundred dollars a year. The effort to secure this increase was led by the Hon. M.F. Foster, the member of the Legislature from Tuskegee. Second, we received one thousand dollars from the John F. Slater Fund. Our work seemed to please the trustees of this fund, as they soon began increasing their annual grant. This has been added to from time to time until at present we receive eleven thousand dollars annually from the Fund. The other help to which I have referred came in the shape of an allowance from the Peabody Fund. This was at first five hundred dollars, but it has since been increased to fifteen hundred dollars.

The effort to secure help from the Slater and Peabody Funds brought me into contact with two rare men—men who have had much to do in shaping the policy for the education of the Negro.

I refer to the Hon. J.L.M. Curry, of Washington, who is the general agent for these two funds, and Mr. Morris K. Jessup, of New York. Dr. Curry is a native of the South, an ex-Confederate soldier, yet I do not believe there is any man in the country who is more deeply interested in the highest welfare of the Negro than Dr. Curry, or one who is more free from race prejudice.

He enjoys the unique distinction of possessing to an equal degree the confidence of the black man and the Southern white man. I shall never forget the first time I met him. It was in Richmond, Va., where he was then living.

I had heard much about him. When I first went into his presence, trembling because of my youth and inexperience, he took me by the hand so cordially, and spoke such encouraging words, and gave me such helpful advice regarding the proper course to pursue, that I came to know him then, as I have known him ever since, as a high example of one who is constantly and unselfishly at work for the betterment of humanity.

Mr. Morris K. Jessup, the treasurer of the Slater Fund, I refer to because I know of no man of wealth and large and complicated business responsibilities who gives not only money but his time and thought to the subject of the proper method of elevating the Negro to the extent that is true of Mr. Jessup.

It is very largely through this effort and influence that during the last few years the subject of industrial education has assumed the importance that it has, and been placed on its present footing.

Chapter 13. Two Thousand Miles For A Five-Minute Speech

Soon after the opening of our boarding department, quite a number of students who evidently were worthy, but who were so poor that they did not have any money to pay even the small charges at the school, began applying for admission. This class was composed of both men and women. It was a great trial to refuse admission to these applicants, and in 1884 we established a night-school to accommodate a few of them.

The night-school was organized on a plan similar to the one which I had helped to establish at Hampton. At first it was composed of about a dozen students. They were admitted to the night-school only when they had no money with which to pay any part of their board in the regular day-school. It was further required that they must work for ten hours during the day at some trade or industry, and study academic branches for two hours during the evening. This was the requirement for the first one or two years of their stay. They were to be paid something above the cost of their board, with the understanding that all of their earnings, except a very small part, were to be reserved in the school's treasury, to be used for paying their board in the regular day-school after they had entered that department. The night-school, started in this manner, has grown until there are at present four hundred and fifty-seven students enrolled in it alone.

There could hardly be a more severe test of a student's worth than this branch of the Institute's work. It is largely because it furnishes such a good opportunity to test the backbone of a student that I place such high value upon our night-school. Any one who is willing to work ten hours a day at the brick-yard, or in the laundry, through one or two years, in order that he or she may have the privilege of studying academic branches for two hours in the evening, has enough bottom to warrant being further educated.

After the student has left the night-school he enters the day-school, where he takes academic branches four days in a week, and works at his trade two days. Besides this he usually works at his trade during the three summer months. As a rule, after a student has succeeded in going through the night-school test, he finds a way to finish the regular course in industrial and academic training. No student, no matter how much money he may be able to command, is permitted to go through school without doing manual labour. In fact, the industrial work is now as popular as the academic branches. Some of the most successful men and women who have graduated from the institution obtained their start in the night-school.

While a great deal of stress is laid upon the industrial side of the work at Tuskegee, we do not neglect or overlook in any degree the religious and spiritual side. The school is strictly undenominational, but it is thoroughly Christian, and the spiritual training of the students is not neglected. Our preaching service, prayer-meetings, Sunday-school, Christian Endeavour Society, Young Men's Christian Association, and various missionary organizations, testify to this.

In 1885, Miss Olivia Davidson, to whom I have already referred as being largely responsible for the success of the school during its early history, and I were married. During our married life she continued to divide her time and strength between our home and the work for the school. She not only continued to work in the school at Tuskegee, but also kept up her habit of going North to secure funds. In 1889 she died, after four years of happy married life and eight years of hard and happy work for the school. She literally wore herself out in her never ceasing efforts in behalf of the work that she so dearly loved. During our married life there were born to us two bright, beautiful boys, Booker Taliaferro and Ernest Davidson. The older of these, Booker, has already mastered the brick-maker's trade at Tuskegee.

I have often been asked how I began the practice of public speaking. In answer I would say that I never planned to give any large part of my life to speaking in public. I have always had more of an ambition to do things than merely to talk about doing them. It seems that when I went North with General Armstrong to speak at the series of public meetings to which I have referred, the President of the National Educational Association, the Hon. Thomas W. Bicknell, was present at one of those meetings and heard me speak. A few days afterward he sent me an invitation to deliver an address at the next meeting of the Educational Association. This meeting was to be held in Madison, Wis. I accepted the invitation. This was, in a sense, the beginning of my public-speaking career.

On the evening that I spoke before the Association there must have been not far from four thousand persons present. Without my knowing it, there were a large number of people present from Alabama, and some from the town of Tuskegee. These white people afterward frankly told me that they went to this meeting expecting to hear the South roundly abused, but were pleasantly surprised to find that there was no word of abuse in my address. On the contrary, the South was given credit for all the praiseworthy things that it had done. A white lady who was teacher in a college in Tuskegee wrote back to the local paper that she was gratified, as well as surprised, to note the credit which I gave the white people of Tuskegee for their help in getting the school started. This address at Madison was the first that I had delivered that in any large measure dealt with the general problem of the races. Those who heard it seemed to be pleased with what I said and with the general position that I took.

When I first came to Tuskegee, I determined that I would make it my home, that I would take as much pride in the right actions of the people of the town as any white man could do, and that I would, at the same time, deplore the wrong-doing of the people as much as any white man. I determined never to say anything in a public address in the North that I would not be willing to say in the South. I early learned that it is a hard matter to convert an individual by abusing him, and that this is more often accomplished by giving credit for all the praiseworthy actions performed than by calling attention alone to all the evil done.

While pursuing this policy I have not failed, at the proper time and in the proper manner, to call attention, in no uncertain terms, to the wrongs which any part of the South has been guilty of. I have found that there is a large element in the South that is quick to respond to straightforward, honest criticism of any wrong policy. As a rule, the place to criticise the South, when criticism is necessary, is in the South—not in Boston. A

Boston man who came to Alabama to criticise Boston would not effect so much good, I think, as one who had his word of criticism to say in Boston.

In this address at Madison I took the ground that the policy to be pursued with references to the races was, by every honourable means, to bring them together and to encourage the cultivation of friendly relations, instead of doing that which would embitter. I further contended that, in relation to his vote, the Negro should more and more consider the interests of the community in which he lived, rather than seek alone to please some one who lived a thousand miles away from him and from his interests.

In this address I said that the whole future of the Negro rested largely upon the question as to whether or not he should make himself, through his skill, intelligence, and character, of such undeniable value to the community in which he lived that the community could not dispense with his presence. I said that any individual who learned to do something better than anybody else—learned to do a common thing in an uncommon manner—had solved his problem, regardless of the colour of his skin, and that in proportion as the Negro learned to produce what other people wanted and must have, in the same proportion would he be respected.

I spoke of an instance where one of our graduates had produced two hundred and sixty-six bushels of sweet potatoes from an acre of ground, in a community where the average production had been only forty-nine bushels to the acre. He had been able to do this by reason of his knowledge of the chemistry of the soil and by his knowledge of improved methods of agriculture. The white farmers in the neighbourhood respected him, and came to him for ideas regarding the raising of sweet potatoes. These white farmers honoured and respected him because he, by his skill and knowledge, had added something to the wealth and the comfort of the community in which he lived. I explained that my theory of education for the Negro would not, for example, confine him for all time to farm life—to the production of the best and the most sweet potatoes—but that, if he succeeded in this line of industry, he could lay the foundations upon which his children and grand-children could grow to higher and more important things in life.

Such, in brief, were some of the views I advocated in this first address dealing with the broad question of the relations of the two races, and since that time I have not found any reason for changing my views on any important point.

In my early life I used to cherish a feeling of ill will toward any one who spoke in bitter terms against the Negro, or who advocated measures that tended to oppress the black man or take from him opportunities for growth in the most complete manner. Now, whenever I hear any one advocating measures that are meant to curtail the development of another, I pity the individual who would do this. I know that the one who makes this mistake does so because of his own lack of opportunity for the highest kind of growth. I pity him because I know that he is trying to stop the progress of the world, and because I know that in time the development and the ceaseless advance of humanity will make him ashamed of his weak and narrow position. One might as well try to stop the progress of a mighty railroad train by throwing his body across the track, as to try to stop the growth of the world in the direction of giving mankind more intelligence, more culture, more skill, more liberty, and in the direction of extending more sympathy and more brotherly kindness.

The address which I delivered at Madison, before the National Educational Association, gave me a rather wide introduction in the North, and soon after that opportunities began offering themselves for me to address audiences there.

I was anxious, however, that the way might also be opened for me to speak directly to a representative Southern white audience. A partial opportunity of this kind, one that seemed to me might serve as an entering wedge, presented itself in 1893, when the international meeting of Christian Workers was held at Atlanta, Ga. When this invitation came to me, I had engagements in Boston that seemed to make it impossible for me to speak in Atlanta. Still, after looking over my list of dates and places carefully, I found that I could take a train from Boston that would get me into Atlanta about thirty minutes before my address was to be delivered, and that I could remain in that city before taking another train for Boston. My invitation to speak in Atlanta stipulated that I was to confine my address to five minutes. The question, then, was whether or not I could put enough into a five-minute address to make it worth while for me to make such a trip.

I knew that the audience would be largely composed of the most influential class of white men and women, and that it would be a rare opportunity for me to let them know what we were trying to do at Tuskegee, as well as to speak to them about the relations of the races. So I decided to make the trip. I spoke for five minutes to an audience of two thousand people, composed mostly of Southern and Northern whites. What I said seemed to be received with favour and enthusiasm. The Atlanta papers of the next day commented in friendly terms on my address, and a good deal was said about it in different parts of the country. I felt that I had in some degree accomplished my object—that of getting a hearing from the dominant class of the South.

The demands made upon me for public addresses continued to increase, coming in about equal numbers from my own people and from Northern whites. I gave as much time to these addresses as I could spare from the immediate work at Tuskegee. Most of the addresses in the North were made for the direct purpose of getting funds with which to support the school. Those delivered before the coloured people had for their main object the impressing upon them the importance of industrial and technical education in addition to academic and religious training.

I now come to that one of the incidents in my life which seems to have excited the greatest amount of interest, and which perhaps went further than anything else in giving me a reputation that in a sense might be called National. I refer to the address which I delivered at the opening of the Atlanta Cotton states and International Exposition, at Atlanta, Ga., September 18, 1895.

So much has been said and written about this incident, and so many questions have been asked me concerning the address, that perhaps I may be excused for taking up the matter with some detail. The five-minute address in Atlanta, which I came from Boston to deliver, was possibly the prime cause for an opportunity being given me to make the second address there. In the spring of 1895 I received a telegram from prominent citizens in Atlanta asking me to accompany a committee from that city to Washington for the purpose of appearing before a committee of Congress in the interest of securing Government help for the Exposition. The committee was composed of about twenty-five of the most prominent and most influential white men of Georgia. All the members of this committee were white men except Bishop Grant, Bishop Gaines, and myself. The Mayor and several other city and state officials spoke before the committee. They were followed by the two coloured bishops. My name was the last on the list of speakers. I had never before appeared before such a committee, nor had I ever delivered any address in the capital of the Nation. I had many misgivings as to what I ought to say, and as to the impression that my address would make. While I cannot recall in detail what I said, I remember that I tried to impress upon the committee, with all the earnestness and plainness of any language that I could command, that if Congress wanted to do something which would assist in ridding the South of the race question and making friends between the two races, it should, in every proper way, encourage the material and intellectual growth of both races. I said that the Atlanta Exposition would present an opportunity for both races to show what advance they had made since freedom, and would at the same time afford encouragement to them to make still greater progress.

I tried to emphasize the fact that while the Negro should not be deprived by unfair means of the franchise, political agitation alone would not save him, and that back of the ballot he must have property, industry, skill, economy, intelligence, and character, and that no race without these elements could permanently succeed. I said that in granting the appropriation Congress could do something that would prove to be of real and lasting value to both races, and that it was the first great opportunity of the kind that had been presented since the close of the Civil War.

I spoke for fifteen or twenty minutes, and was surprised at the close of my address to receive the hearty congratulations of the Georgia committee and of the members of Congress who were present. The Committee was unanimous in making a favourable report, and in a few days the bill passed Congress. With the passing of this bill the success of the Atlanta Exposition was assured.

Soon after this trip to Washington the directors of the Exposition decided that it would be a fitting recognition of the coloured race to erect a large and attractive building which should be devoted wholly to showing the progress of the Negro since freedom. It was further decided to have the building designed and erected wholly by Negro mechanics. This plan was carried out. In design, beauty, and general finish the Negro Building was equal to the others on the grounds.

After it was decided to have a separate Negro exhibit, the question arose as to who should take care of it. The officials of the Exposition were anxious that I should assume this responsibility, but I declined to do so, on the plea that the work at Tuskegee at that time demanded my time and strength. Largely at my suggestion, Mr. I. Garland Penn, of Lynchburg, Va., was selected to be at the head of the Negro department. I gave him all the aid that I could. The Negro exhibit, as a whole, was large and creditable. The two exhibits in this department which attracted the greatest amount of attention were those from the Hampton Institute and the Tuskegee Institute. The people who seemed to be the most surprised, as well as pleased, at what they saw in the Negro Building were the Southern white people.

As the day for the opening of the Exposition drew near, the Board of Directors began preparing the programme for the opening exercises. In the discussion from day to day of the various features of this programme, the question came up as to the advisability of putting a member of the Negro race on for one of the opening addresses, since the Negroes had been asked to take such a prominent part in the Exposition. It was argued, further, that such recognition would mark the good feeling prevailing between the two races. Of course there were those who were opposed to any such recognition of the rights of the Negro, but the Board of Directors, composed of men who represented the best and most progressive element in the South, had their way, and voted to invite a black man to speak on the opening day. The next thing was to decide upon the person who was thus to represent the Negro race. After the question had been canvassed for several days, the directors voted unanimously to ask me to deliver one of the opening-day addresses, and in a few days after that I received the official invitation.

The receiving of this invitation brought to me a sense of responsibility that it would be hard for any one not placed in my position to appreciate. What were my feelings when this invitation came to me? I remembered that I had been a slave; that my early years had been spent in the lowest depths of poverty and ignorance, and that I had had little opportunity to prepare me for such a responsibility as this. It was only a few years before that time that any white man in the audience might have claimed me as his slave; and it was easily possible that some of my former owners might be present to hear me speak.

I knew, too, that this was the first time in the entire history of the Negro that a member of my race had been asked to speak from the same platform with white Southern men and women on any important National occasion. I was asked now to speak to an audience composed of the wealth and culture of the white South, the representatives of my former masters. I knew, too, that while the greater part of my audience would be composed of Southern people, yet there would be present a large number of Northern whites, as well as a great many men and women of my own race.

I was determined to say nothing that I did not feel from the bottom of my heart to be true and right. When the invitation came to me, there was not one word of intimation as to what I should say or as to what I should omit. In this I felt that the Board of Directors had paid a tribute to me. They knew that by one sentence I could have blasted, in a large degree, the success of the Exposition. I was also painfully conscious of the fact that, while I must be true to my own race in my utterances, I had it in my power to make such an ill-timed address as would result in preventing any similar invitation being extended to a black man again for years to come. I was equally determined to be true to the North, as well as to the best element of the white South, in what I had to say.

The papers, North and South, had taken up the discussion of my coming speech, and as the time for it drew near this discussion became more and more widespread. Not a few of the Southern white papers were unfriendly to the idea of my speaking. From my own race I received many suggestions as to what I ought to say. I prepared myself as best I could for the address, but as the eighteenth of September drew nearer, the heavier my heart became, and the more I feared that my effort would prove a failure and a disappointment.

The invitation had come at a time when I was very busy with my school work, as it was the beginning of our school year. After preparing my address, I went through it, as I usually do with those utterances which I consider particularly important, with Mrs. Washington, and she approved of what I intended to say. On the sixteenth of September, the day before I was to start for Atlanta, so many of the Tuskegee teachers expressed a desire to hear my address that I consented to read it to them in a body. When I had done so, and had heard their criticisms and comments, I felt somewhat relieved, since they seemed to think well of what I had to say.

On the morning of September 17, together with Mrs. Washington and my three children, I started for Atlanta. I felt a good deal as I suppose a man feels when he is on his way to the gallows. In passing through the town of Tuskegee I met a white farmer who lived some distance out in the country. In a jesting manner this man said: "Washington, you have spoken before the Northern white people, the Negroes in the South, and to us country white people in the South; but Atlanta, to-morrow, you will have before you the Northern whites, the Southern whites, and the Negroes all together. I am afraid that you have got yourself in a tight place." This farmer diagnosed the situation correctly, but his frank words did not add anything to my comfort.

In the course of the journey from Tuskegee to Atlanta both coloured and white people came to the train to point me out, and discussed with perfect freedom, in my hearings, what was going to take place the next day. We were met by a committee in Atlanta. Almost the first thing that I heard when I got off the train in that city was an expression something like this, from an old coloured man near by: "Dat's de man of my race what's gwine to make a speech at de Exposition to-morrow. I'se sho' gwine to hear him."

Atlanta was literally packed, at the time, with people from all parts of the country, and with representatives of foreign governments, as well as with military and civic organizations. The afternoon papers had forecasts of the next day's proceedings in flaring headlines. All this tended to add to my burden. I did not sleep much that night. The next morning, before day, I went carefully over what I planned to say. I also kneeled down and asked God's blessing upon my effort. Right here, perhaps, I ought to add that I make it a rule never to go before an audience, on any occasion, without asking the blessing of God upon what I want to say.

I always make it a rule to make especial preparation for each separate address. No two audiences are exactly alike. It is my aim to reach and talk to the heart of each individual audience, taking it into my confidence very much as I would a person. When I am speaking to an audience, I care little for how what I am saying is going to sound in the newspapers, or to another audience, or to an individual. At the time, the audience before me absorbs all my sympathy, thought, and energy.

Early in the morning a committee called to escort me to my place in the procession which was to march to the Exposition grounds. In this procession were prominent coloured citizens in carriages, as well as several Negro military organizations.

I noted that the Exposition officials seemed to go out of their way to see that all of the coloured people in the procession were properly placed and properly treated. The procession was about three hours in reaching the Exposition grounds, and during all of this time the sun was shining down upon us disagreeably hot.

When we reached the grounds, the heat, together with my nervous anxiety, made me feel as if I were about ready to collapse, and to feel that my address was not going to be a success. When I entered the audience-room, I found it packed with humanity from bottom to top, and there were thousands outside who could not get in.

The room was very large, and well suited to public speaking. When I entered the room, there were vigorous cheers from the coloured portion of the audience, and faint cheers from some of the white people.

I had been told, while I had been in Atlanta, that while many white people were going to be present to hear me speak, simply out of curiosity, and that others who would be present would be in full sympathy with me, there was a still larger element of the audience which would consist of those who were going to be present for the purpose of hearing me make a fool of myself, or, at least, of hearing me say some foolish thing so that they could say to the officials who had invited me to speak, "I told you so!"

One of the trustees of the Tuskegee Institute, as well as my personal friend, Mr. William H. Baldwin, Jr. was at the time General Manager of the Southern Railroad, and happened to be in Atlanta on that day. He was so nervous about the kind of reception that I would have, and the effect that my speech would produce, that he could not persuade himself to go into the building, but walked back and forth in the grounds outside until the opening exercises were over.

Chapter 14. The Atlanta Exposition Address

The Atlanta Exposition, at which I had been asked to make an address as a representative of the Negro race, as stated in the last chapter, was opened with a short address from Governor Bullock. After other interesting exercises, including an invocation from Bishop Nelson, of Georgia, a dedicatory ode by Albert Howell, Jr., and addresses by the President of the Exposition and Mrs. Joseph Thompson, the President of the Woman's Board, Governor Bullock introduce me with the words, "We have with us to-day a representative of Negro enterprise and Negro civilization."

When I arose to speak, there was considerable cheering, especially from the coloured people. As I remember it now, the thing that was uppermost in my mind was the desire to say something that would cement the friendship of the races and bring about hearty cooperation between them. So far as my outward surroundings were concerned, the only thing that I recall distinctly now is that when I got up, I saw thousands of eyes looking intently into my face. The following is the address which I delivered:—

Mr. President and Gentlemen of the Board of Directors and Citizens.

One-third of the population of the South is of the Negro race. No enterprise seeking the material, civil, or moral welfare of this section can disregard this element of our population and reach the highest success. I but convey to you, Mr. President and Directors, the sentiment of the masses of my race when I say that in no way have the value and manhood of the American Negro been more fittingly and generously recognized than by the managers of this magnificent Exposition at every stage of its progress. It is a recognition that will do more to cement the friendship of the two races than any occurrence since the dawn of our freedom.

Not only this, but the opportunity here afforded will awaken among us a new era of industrial progress. Ignorant and inexperienced, it is not strange that in the first years of our new life we began at the top instead of at the bottom; that a seat in Congress or the state legislature was more sought than real estate or industrial skill; that the political convention or stump speaking had more attractions than starting a dairy farm or truck garden.

A ship lost at sea for many days suddenly sighted a friendly vessel. From the mast of the unfortunate vessel was seen a signal, "Water, water; we die of thirst!" The answer from the friendly vessel at once came back, "Cast down your bucket where you are." A second time the signal, "Water, water; send us water!" ran up from the distressed vessel, and was answered, "Cast down your bucket where you are." And a third and fourth signal for water was answered, "Cast down your bucket where you are." The captain of the distressed vessel, at last heading the injunction, cast down his bucket, and it came up full of fresh, sparkling water from the mouth of the Amazon River. To those of my race who depend on bettering their condition in a foreign land or who underestimate the importance of cultivating friendly relations with the Southern white man, who is their next-door neighbour, I would say: "Cast down your bucket where you are"—cast it down in making friends in every manly way of the people of all races by whom we are surrounded.

Cast it down in agriculture, mechanics, in commerce, in domestic service, and in the professions. And in this connection it is well to bear in mind that whatever other sins the South may be called to bear, when it comes to business, pure and simple, it is in the South that the Negro is given a man's chance in the commercial world, and in nothing is this Exposition more eloquent than in emphasizing this chance. Our greatest danger is that in the great leap from slavery to freedom we may overlook the fact that the masses of us are to live by the productions of our hands, and fail to keep in mind that we shall prosper in proportion as we learn to dignify and glorify common labour and put brains and skill into the common occupations of life; shall prosper in proportion as we learn to draw the line between the superficial and the substantial, the ornamental gewgaws of life and the useful. No race can prosper till it learns that there is as much dignity in tilling a field as in writing a poem. It is at the bottom of life we must begin, and not at the top. Nor should we permit our grievances to overshadow our opportunities.

To those of the white race who look to the incoming of those of foreign birth and strange tongue and habits of the prosperity of the South, were I permitted I would repeat what I say to my own race: "Cast down your bucket where you are." Cast it down among the eight millions of Negroes whose habits you know, whose fidelity and love you have tested in days when to have proved treacherous meant the ruin of your firesides. Cast down your bucket among these people who have, without strikes and labour wars, tilled your fields, cleared your forests, builded your railroads and cities, and brought forth treasures from the bowels of the earth, and helped make possible this magnificent representation of the progress of the South. Casting down your bucket among my people, helping and encouraging them as you are doing on these grounds, and to education of head, hand, and heart, you will find that they will buy your surplus land, make blossom the waste places in your fields, and run your factories. While doing this, you can be sure in the future, as in the past, that you and your families will be surrounded by the most patient, faithful, law-abiding, and unresentful people that the world has seen. As we have proved our loyalty to you in the past, nursing your children, watching by the sick-bed of your mothers and fathers, and often following them with tear-dimmed eyes to their graves, so in the future, in our humble way, we shall stand by you with a devotion that no foreigner can approach, ready to lay down our lives, if need be, in defence of yours, interlacing our industrial, commercial, civil, and religious life with yours in a way that shall make the interests of both races one. In all things that are purely social we can be as separate as the fingers, yet one as the hand in all things essential to mutual progress.

There is no defence or security for any of us except in the highest intelligence and development of all. If anywhere there are efforts tending to curtail the fullest growth of the Negro, let these efforts be turned into stimulating, encouraging, and making him the most useful and intelligent citizen. Effort or means so invested will pay a thousand per cent interest. These efforts will be twice blessed—"blessing him that gives and him that takes."

There is no escape through law of man or God from the inevitable:—

The laws of changeless justice bind

Oppressor with oppressed;

And close as sin and suffering joined

We march to fate abreast.

Nearly sixteen millions of hands will aid you in pulling the load upward, or they will pull against you the load downward. We shall constitute one-third and more of the ignorance and crime of the South, or one-third its intelligence and progress; we shall contribute one-third to the business and industrial prosperity of the South, or we shall prove a veritable body of death, stagnating, depressing, retarding every effort to advance the body politic.

Gentlemen of the Exposition, as we present to you our humble effort at an exhibition of our progress, you must not expect overmuch. Starting thirty years ago with ownership here and there in a few quilts and pumpkins and chickens (gathered from miscellaneous sources), remember the path that has led from these to the inventions and production of agricultural implements, buggies, steam-engines, newspapers, books, statuary, carving, paintings, the management of drug-stores and banks, has not been trodden without contact with thorns and thistles. While we take pride in what we exhibit as a result of our independent efforts, we do not for a moment forget that our part in this exhibition would fall far short of your expectations but for the constant help that has come to our education life, not only from the Southern states, but especially from Northern philanthropists, who have made their gifts a constant stream of blessing and encouragement.

The wisest among my race understand that the agitation of questions of social equality is the extremest folly, and that progress in the enjoyment of all the privileges that will come to us must be the result of severe and constant struggle rather than of artificial forcing. No race that has anything to contribute to the markets of the world is long in any degree ostracized. It is important and right that all privileges of the law be ours, but it is vastly more important that we be prepared for the exercises of these privileges. The opportunity to earn a dollar in a factory just now is worth infinitely more than the opportunity to spend a dollar in an opera-house.

In conclusion, may I repeat that nothing in thirty years has given us more hope and encouragement, and drawn us so near to you of the white race, as this opportunity offered by the Exposition; and here bending, as it were, over the altar that represents the results of the struggles of your race and mine, both starting practically empty-handed three decades ago, I pledge that in your effort to work out the great and intricate problem which God has laid at the doors of the South, you shall have at all times the patient, sympathetic help of my race; only let this be constantly in mind, that, while from representations in these buildings of the product of field, of forest, of mine, of factory, letters, and art, much good will come, yet far above and beyond material benefits will be that higher good, that, let us pray God, will come, in a blotting out of sectional differences and racial animosities and suspicions, in a determination to administer absolute justice, in a willing obedience among all classes to the mandates of law. This, this, coupled with our material prosperity, will bring into our beloved South a new heaven and a new earth.

The first thing that I remember, after I had finished speaking, was that Governor Bullock rushed across the platform and took me by the hand, and that others did the same. I received so many and such hearty congratulations that I found it difficult to get out of the building. I did not appreciate to any degree, however, the impression which my address seemed to have made, until the next morning, when I went into the business part of the city. As soon as I was recognized, I was surprised to find myself pointed out and surrounded by a crowd of men who wished to shake hands with me. This was kept up on every street on to which I went, to an extent which embarrassed me so much that I went back to my boarding-place. The next morning I returned to Tuskegee. At the station in Atlanta, and at almost all of the stations at which the train stopped between that city and Tuskegee, I found a crowd of people anxious to shake hands with me.

The papers in all parts of the United States published the address in full, and for months afterward there were complimentary editorial references to it. Mr. Clark Howell, the editor of the Atlanta Constitution, telegraphed to a New York paper, among other words, the following, "I do not exaggerate when I say that Professor Booker T. Washington's address yesterday was one of the most notable speeches, both as to character and as to the warmth of its reception, ever delivered to a Southern audience.

The address was a revelation. The whole speech is a platform upon which blacks and whites can stand with full justice to each other."

The Boston Transcript said editorially: "The speech of Booker T. Washington at the Atlanta Exposition, this week, seems to have dwarfed all the other proceedings and the Exposition itself. The sensation that it has caused in the press has never been equalled."

I very soon began receiving all kinds of propositions from lecture bureaus, and editors of magazines and papers, to take the lecture platform, and to write articles. One lecture bureau offered me fifty thousand dollars, or two hundred dollars a night and expenses, if I would place my services at its disposal for a given period. To all these communications I replied that my life-work was at Tuskegee; and that whenever I spoke it must be in the interests of Tuskegee school and my race, and that I would enter into no arrangements that seemed to place a mere commercial value upon my services.

Some days after its delivery I sent a copy of my address to the President of the United States, the Hon. Grover Cleveland. I received from him the following autograph reply:—

Gray Gables, Buzzard's Bay, Mass.,

October 6, 1895.

Booker T. Washington, Esq.:

My Dear Sir: I thank you for sending me a copy of your address delivered at the Atlanta Exposition.

I thank you with much enthusiasm for making the address. I have read it with intense interest, and I think the Exposition would be fully justified if it did not do more than furnish the opportunity for its delivery. Your words cannot fail to delight and encourage all who wish well for your race; and if our coloured fellow-citizens do not from your utterances gather new hope and form new determinations to gain every valuable advantage offered them by their citizenship, it will be strange indeed.

Yours very truly,

Grover Cleveland.

Later I met Mr. Cleveland, for the first time, when, as President, he visited the Atlanta Exposition. At the request of myself and others he consented to spend an hour in the Negro Building, for the purpose of inspecting the Negro exhibit and of giving the coloured people in attendance an opportunity to shake hands with him. As soon as I met Mr. Cleveland I became impressed with his simplicity, greatness, and rugged honesty. I have met him many times since then, both at public functions and at his private residence in Princeton, and the more I see of him the more I admire him. When he visited the Negro Building in Atlanta he seemed to give himself up wholly, for that hour, to the coloured people. He seemed to be as careful to shake hands with some old coloured "auntie" clad partially in rags, and to take as much pleasure in doing so, as if he were greeting some millionaire. Many of the coloured people took advantage of the occasion to get him to write his name in a book or on a slip of paper. He was as careful and patient in doing this as if he were putting his signature to some great state document.

Mr. Cleveland has not only shown his friendship for me in many personal ways, but has always consented to do anything I have asked of him for our school. This he has done, whether it was to make a personal donation or to use his influence in securing the donations of others. Judging from my personal acquaintance with Mr. Cleveland, I do not believe that he is conscious of possessing any colour prejudice. He is too great for that. In my contact with people I find that, as a rule, it is only the little, narrow people who live for themselves, who never read good books, who do not travel, who never open up their souls in a way to permit them to come into contact with other souls—with the great outside world. No man whose vision is bounded by colour can come into contact with what is highest and best in the world. In meeting men, in many places, I have found that the happiest people are those who do the most for others; the most miserable are those who do the least. I have also found that few things, if any, are capable of making one so blind and narrow as race prejudice. I often say to our students, in the course of my talks to them on Sunday evenings in the chapel, that the longer I live and the more experience I have of the world, the more I am convinced that, after all, the one thing that is most worth living for—and dying for, if need be—is the opportunity of making some one else more happy and more useful.

The coloured people and the coloured newspapers at first seemed to be greatly pleased with the character of my Atlanta address, as well as with its reception. But after the first burst of enthusiasm began to die away, and the coloured people began reading the speech in cold type, some of them seemed to feel that they had been hypnotized. They seemed to feel that I had been too liberal in my remarks toward the Southern whites, and that I had not spoken out strongly enough for what they termed the "rights" of my race. For a while there was a reaction, so far as a certain element of my own race was concerned, but later these reactionary ones seemed to have been won over to my way of believing and acting.

While speaking of changes in public sentiment, I recall that about ten years after the school at Tuskegee was established, I had an experience that I shall never forget. Dr. Lyman Abbott, then the pastor of Plymouth Church, and also editor of the Outlook (then the Christian Union), asked me to write a letter for his paper giving my opinion of the exact condition, mental and moral, of the coloured ministers in the South, as based upon my observations. I wrote the letter, giving the exact facts as I conceived them to be. The picture painted was a rather black one—or, since I am black, shall I say "white"? It could not be otherwise with a race but a few years out of slavery, a race which had not had time or opportunity to produce a competent ministry.

What I said soon reached every Negro minister in the country, I think, and the letters of condemnation which I received from them were not few. I think that for a year after the publication of this article every association and every conference or religious body of any kind, of my race, that met, did not fail before adjourning to pass a resolution condemning me, or calling upon me to retract or modify what I had said. Many of these organizations went so far in their resolutions as to advise parents to cease sending their children to Tuskegee. One association even appointed a "missionary" whose duty it was to warn the people against sending their children to Tuskegee. This missionary had a son in the school, and I noticed that, whatever the "missionary" might have said or done with regard to others, he was careful not to take his son away from the institution. Many of the coloured papers, especially those that were the organs of religious bodies, joined in the general chorus of condemnation or demands for retraction.

During the whole time of the excitement, and through all the criticism, I did not utter a word of explanation or retraction. I knew that I was right, and that time and the sober second thought of the people would vindicate me. It was not long before the bishops and other church leaders began to make careful investigation of the conditions of the ministry, and they found out that I was right. In fact, the oldest and most influential bishop in one branch of the Methodist Church said that my words were far too mild. Very soon public sentiment began making itself felt, in demanding a purifying of the ministry. While this is not yet complete by any means, I think I may say, without egotism, and I have been told by many of our most influential ministers, that my words had much to do with starting a demand for the placing of a higher type of men in the pulpit. I have had the satisfaction of having many who once condemned me thank me heartily for my frank words.

The change of the attitude of the Negro ministry, so far as regards myself, is so complete that at the present time I have no warmer friends among any class than I have among the clergymen. The improvement in the character and life of the Negro ministers is one of the most gratifying evidences of the progress of the race. My experience with them, as well as other events in my life, convince me that the thing to do, when one feels sure that he has said or done the right thing, and is condemned, is to stand still and keep quiet. If he is right, time will show it.

In the midst of the discussion which was going on concerning my Atlanta speech, I received the letter which I give below, from Dr. Gilman, the President of Johns Hopkins University, who had been made chairman of the judges of award in connection with the Atlanta Exposition:—

Johns Hopkins University, Baltimore,

President's Office, September 30, 1895.

Dear Mr. Washington: Would it be agreeable to you to be one of the Judges of Award in the Department of Education at Atlanta? If so, I shall be glad to place your name upon the list. A line by telegraph will be welcomed.

Yours very truly,

D.C. Gilman

I think I was even more surprised to receive this invitation than I had been to receive the invitation to speak at the opening of the Exposition. It was to be a part of my duty, as one of the jurors, to pass not only upon the exhibits of the coloured schools, but also upon those of the white schools. I accepted the position, and spent a month in Atlanta in performance of the duties which it entailed. The board of jurors was a large one, containing in all of sixty members. It was about equally divided between Southern white people and Northern white people. Among them were college presidents, leading scientists and men of letters, and specialists in many subjects. When the group of jurors to which I was assigned met for organization, Mr. Thomas Nelson Page, who was one of the number, moved that I be made secretary of that division, and the motion was unanimously adopted. Nearly half of our division were Southern people. In performing my duties in the inspection of the exhibits of white schools I was in every case treated with respect, and at the close of our labours I parted from my associates with regret.

I am often asked to express myself more freely than I do upon the political condition and the political future of my race. These recollections of my experience in Atlanta give me the opportunity to do so briefly. My own belief is, although I have never before said so in so many words, that the time will come when the Negro in the South will be accorded all the political rights which his ability, character, and material possessions entitle him to. I think, though, that the opportunity to freely exercise such political rights will not come in any large degree through outside or artificial forcing, but will be accorded to the Negro by the Southern white people themselves, and that they will protect him in the exercise of those rights. Just as soon as the South gets over the old feeling that it is being forced by "foreigners," or "aliens," to do something which it does not want to do, I believe that the change in the direction that I have indicated is going to begin. In fact, there are indications that it is already beginning in a slight degree.

Let me illustrate my meaning. Suppose that some months before the opening of the Atlanta Exposition there had been a general demand from the press and public platform outside the South that a Negro be given a place on the opening programme, and that a Negro be placed upon the board of jurors of award. Would any such recognition of the race have taken place? I do not think so. The Atlanta officials went as far as they did because they felt it to be a pleasure, as well as a duty, to reward what they considered merit in the Negro race. Say what we will, there is something in human nature which we cannot blot out, which makes one man, in the end, recognize and reward merit in another, regardless of colour or race.

I believe it is the duty of the Negro—as the greater part of the race is already doing—to deport himself modestly in regard to political claims, depending upon the slow but sure influences that proceed from the possession of property, intelligence, and high character for the full recognition of his political rights. I think that the according of the full exercise of political rights is going to be a matter of natural, slow growth, not an over-night, gourd-vine affair. I do not believe that the Negro should cease voting, for a man cannot learn the exercise of self-government by ceasing to vote, any more than a boy can learn to swim by keeping out of the water, but I do believe that in his voting he should more and more be influenced by those of intelligence and character who are his next-door neighbours.

I know coloured men who, through the encouragement, help, and advice of Southern white people, have accumulated thousands of dollars' worth of property, but who, at the same time, would never think of going to those same persons for advice concerning the casting of their ballots. This, it seems to me, is unwise and unreasonable, and should cease. In saying this I do not mean that the Negro should truckle, or not vote from principle, for the instant he ceases to vote from principle he loses the confidence and respect of the Southern white man even.

I do not believe that any state should make a law that permits an ignorant and poverty-stricken white man to vote, and prevents a black man in the same condition from voting. Such a law is not only unjust, but it will react, as all unjust laws do, in time; for the effect of such a law is to encourage the Negro to secure education and property, and at the same time it encourages the white man to remain in ignorance and poverty. I believe that in time, through the operation of intelligence and friendly race relations, all cheating at the ballot-box in the South will cease. It will become apparent that the white man who begins by cheating a Negro out of his ballot soon learns to cheat a white man out of his, and that the man who does this ends his career of dishonesty by the theft of property or by some equally serious crime. In my opinion, the time will come when the South will encourage all of its citizens to vote. It will see that it pays better, from every standpoint, to have healthy, vigorous life than to have that political stagnation which always results when one-half of the population has no share and no interest in the Government.

As a rule, I believe in universal, free suffrage, but I believe that in the South we are confronted with peculiar conditions that justify the protection of the ballot in many of the states, for a while at least, either by an education test, a property test, or by both combined; but whatever tests are required, they should be made to apply with equal and exact justice to both races.

Chapter 15. The Secret Of Success In Public Speaking

As to how my address at Atlanta was received by the audience in the Exposition building, I think I prefer to let Mr. James Creelman, the noted war correspondent, tell. Mr. Creelman was present, and telegraphed the following account to the New York World:—

Atlanta, September 18.

While President Cleveland was waiting at Gray Gables to-day, to send the electric spark that started the machinery of the Atlanta Exposition, a Negro Moses stood before a great audience of white people and delivered an oration that marks a new epoch in the history of the South; and a body of Negro troops marched in a procession with the citizen soldiery of Georgia and Louisiana. The whole city is thrilling to-night with a realization of the extraordinary significance of these two unprecedented events. Nothing has happened since Henry Grady's immortal speech before the New England society in New York that indicates so profoundly the spirit of the New South, except, perhaps, the opening of the Exposition itself.

When Professor Booker T. Washington, Principal of an industrial school for coloured people in Tuskegee, Ala. stood on the platform of the Auditorium, with the sun shining over the heads of his auditors into his eyes, and with his whole face lit up with the fire of prophecy, Clark Howell, the successor of Henry Grady, said to me, "That man's speech is the beginning of a moral revolution in America."

It is the first time that a Negro has made a speech in the South on any important occasion before an audience composed of white men and women. It electrified the audience, and the response was as if it had come from the throat of a whirlwind.

Mrs. Thompson had hardly taken her seat when all eyes were turned on a tall tawny Negro sitting in the front row of the platform. It was Professor Booker T. Washington, President of the Tuskegee (Alabama) Normal and Industrial Institute, who must rank from this time forth as the foremost man of his race in America. Gilmore's Band played the "Star-Spangled Banner," and the audience cheered. The tune changed to "Dixie" and the audience roared with shrill "hi-yis." Again the music changed, this time to "Yankee Doodle," and the clamour lessened.

All this time the eyes of the thousands present looked straight at the Negro orator. A strange thing was to happen. A black man was to speak for his people, with none to interrupt him. As Professor Washington strode to the edge of the stage, the low, descending sun shot fiery rays through the windows into his face. A great shout greeted him. He turned his head to avoid the blinding light, and moved about the platform for relief. Then he turned his wonderful countenance to the sun without a blink of the eyelids, and began to talk.

There was a remarkable figure; tall, bony, straight as a Sioux chief, high forehead, straight nose, heavy jaws, and strong, determined mouth, with big white teeth, piercing eyes, and a commanding manner. The sinews stood out on his bronzed neck, and his muscular right arm swung high in the air, with a lead-pencil grasped in the clinched brown fist. His big feet were planted squarely, with the heels together and the toes turned out. His voice range out clear and true, and he paused impressively as he made each point. Within ten minutes the multitude was in an uproar of enthusiasm— handkerchiefs were waved, canes were flourished, hats were tossed in the air. The fairest women of Georgia stood up and cheered. It was as if the orator had bewitched them.

And when he held his dusky hand high above his head, with the fingers stretched wide apart, and said to the white people of the South on behalf of his race, "In all things that are purely social we can be as separate as the fingers, yet one as the hand in all things essential to mutual progress," the great wave of sound dashed itself against the walls, and the whole audience was on its feet in a delirium of applause, and I thought at that moment of the night when Henry Grady stood among the curling wreaths of tobacco-smoke in Delmonico's banquet-hall and said, "I am a Cavalier among Roundheads."

I have heard the great orators of many countries, but not even Gladstone himself could have pleased a cause with most consummate power than did this angular Negro, standing in a nimbus of sunshine, surrounded by the men who once fought to keep his race in bondage. The roar might swell ever so high, but the expression of his earnest face never changed.

A ragged, ebony giant, squatted on the floor in one of the aisles, watched the orator with burning eyes and tremulous face until the supreme burst of applause came, and then the tears ran down his face. Most of the Negroes in the audience were crying, perhaps without knowing just why.

At the close of the speech Governor Bullock rushed across the stage and seized the orator's hand. Another shout greeted this demonstration, and for a few minutes the two men stood facing each other, hand in hand.

So far as I could spare the time from the immediate work at Tuskegee, after my Atlanta address, I accepted some of the invitations to speak in public which came to me, especially those that would take me into territory where I thought it would pay to plead the cause of my race, but I always did this with the understanding that I was to be free to talk about my life-work and the needs of my people. I also had it understood that I was not to speak in the capacity of a professional lecturer, or for mere commercial gain.

In my efforts on the public platform I never have been able to understand why people come to hear me speak. This question I never can rid myself of. Time and time again, as I have stood in the street in front of a building and have seen men and women passing in large numbers into the audience room where I was to speak, I have felt ashamed that I should be the cause of people—as it seemed to me—wasting a valuable hour of their time. Some years ago I was to deliver an address before a literary society in Madison, Wis. An hour before the time set for me to speak, a fierce snow-storm began, and continued for several hours. I made up my mind that there would be no audience, and that I should not have to speak, but, as a matter of duty, I went to the church, and found it packed with people. The surprise gave me a shock that I did not recover from during the whole evening.

People often ask me if I feel nervous before speaking, or else they suggest that, since I speak often, they suppose that I get used to it. In answer to this question I have to say that I always suffer intensely from nervousness before speaking. More than once, just before I was to make an important address, this nervous strain has been so great that I have resolved never again to speak in public. I not only feel nervous before speaking, but after I have finished I usually feel a sense of regret, because it seems to me as if I had left out of my address the main thing and the best thing that I had meant to say.

There is a great compensation, though, for this preliminary nervous suffering, that comes to me after I have been speaking for about ten minutes, and have come to feel that I have really mastered my audience, and that we have gotten into full and complete sympathy with each other. It seems to me that there is rarely such a combination of mental and physical delight in any effort as that which comes to a public speaker when he feels that he has a great audience completely within his control. There is a thread of sympathy and oneness that connects a public speaker with his audience, that is just as strong as though it was something tangible and visible. If in an audience of a thousand people there is one person who is not in sympathy with my views, or is inclined to be doubtful, cold, or critical, I can pick him out. When I have found him I usually go straight at him, and it is a great satisfaction to watch the process of his thawing out. I find that the most effective medicine for such individuals is administered at first in the form of a story, although I never tell an anecdote simply for the sake of telling one. That kind of thing, I think, is empty and hollow, and an audience soon finds it out.

I believe that one always does himself and his audience an injustice when he speaks merely for the sake of speaking. I do not believe that one should speak unless, deep down in his heart, he feels convinced that he has a message to deliver. When one feels, from the bottom of his feet to the top of his head, that he has something to say that is going to help some individual or some cause, then let him say it; and in delivering his message I do not believe that many of the artificial rules of elocution can, under such circumstances, help him very much. Although there are certain things, such as pauses, breathing, and pitch of voice, that are very important, none of these can take the place of soul in an address. When I have an address to deliver, I like to forget all about the rules for the proper use of the English language, and all about rhetoric and that sort of thing, and I like to make the audience forget all about these things, too.

Nothing tends to throw me off my balance so quickly, when I am speaking, as to have some one leave the room. To prevent this, I make up my mind, as a rule, that I will try to make my address so interesting, will try to state so many interesting facts one after another, that no one can leave. The average audience, I have come to believe, wants facts rather than generalities or sermonizing. Most people, I think, are able to draw proper conclusions if they are given the facts in an interesting form on which to base them.

As to the kind of audience that I like best to talk to, I would put at the top of the list an organization of strong, wide-awake, business men, such, for example, as is found in Boston, New York, Chicago, and Buffalo. I have found no other audience so quick to see a point, and so responsive. Within the last few years I have had the privilege of speaking before most of the leading organizations of this kind in the large cities of the United States. The best time to get hold of an organization of business men is after a good dinner, although I think that one of the worst instruments of torture that was ever invented is the custom which makes it necessary for a speaker to sit through a fourteen-course dinner, every minute of the time feeling sure that his speech is going to prove a dismal failure and disappointment.

I rarely take part in one of these long dinners that I do not wish that I could put myself back in the little cabin where I was a slave boy, and again go through the experience there—one that I shall never forget—of getting molasses to eat once a week from the "big house." Our usual diet on the plantation was corn bread and pork, but on Sunday morning my mother was permitted to bring down a little molasses from the "big house" for her three children, and when it was received how I did wish that every day was Sunday! I would get my tin plate and hold it up for the sweet morsel, but I would always shut my eyes while the molasses was being poured out into the plate, with the hope that when I opened them I would be surprised to see how much I had got. When I opened my eyes I would tip the plate in one direction and another, so as to make the molasses spread all over it, in the full belief that there would be more of it and that it would last longer if spread out in this way. So strong are my childish impressions of those Sunday morning feasts that it would be pretty hard for any one to convince me that there is not more molasses on a plate when it is spread all over the plate than when it occupies a little corner—if there is a corner in a plate. At any rate, I have never believed in "cornering" syrup. My share of the syrup was usually about two tablespoonfuls, and those two spoonfuls of molasses were much more enjoyable to me than is a fourteen-course dinner after which I am to speak.

Next to a company of business men, I prefer to speak to an audience of Southern people, of either race, together or taken separately. Their enthusiasm and responsiveness are a constant delight. The "amens" and "dat's de truf" that come spontaneously from the coloured individuals are calculated to spur any speaker on to his best efforts. I think that next in order of preference I would place a college audience. It has been my privilege to deliver addresses at many of our leading colleges including Harvard, Yale, Williams, Amherst, Fisk University, the University of Pennsylvania, Wellesley, the University of Michigan, Trinity College in North Carolina, and many others.

It has been a matter of deep interest to me to note the number of people who have come to shake hands with me after an address, who say that this is the first time they have ever called a Negro "Mister."

When speaking directly in the interests of the Tuskegee Institute, I usually arrange, some time in advance, a series of meetings in important centres. This takes me before churches, Sunday-schools, Christian Endeavour Societies, and men's and women's clubs. When doing this I sometimes speak before as many as four organizations in a single day.

Three years ago, at the suggestion of Mr. Morris K. Jessup, of New York, and Dr. J.L.M. Curry, the general agent of the fund, the trustees of the John F. Slater Fund voted a sum of money to be used in paying the expenses of Mrs. Washington and myself while holding a series of meetings among the coloured people in the large centres of Negro population, especially in the large cities of the ex-slaveholding states. Each year during the last three years we have devoted some weeks to this work. The plan that we have followed has been for me to speak in the morning to the ministers, teachers, and professional men. In the afternoon Mrs. Washington would speak to the women alone, and in the evening I spoke to a large mass-meeting. In almost every case the meetings have been attended not only by the coloured people in large numbers, but by the white people. In Chattanooga, Tenn., for example, there was present at the mass-meeting an audience of not less than three thousand persons, and I was informed that eight hundred of these were white. I have done no work that I really enjoyed more than this, or that I think has accomplished more good.

These meetings have given Mrs. Washington and myself an opportunity to get first-hand, accurate information as to the real condition of the race, by seeing the people in their homes, their churches, their Sunday-schools, and their places of work, as well as in the prisons and dens of crime. These meetings also gave us an opportunity to see the relations that exist between the races. I never feel so hopeful about the race as I do after being engaged in a series of these meetings. I know that on such occasions there is much that comes to the surface that is superficial and deceptive, but I have had experience enough not to be deceived by mere signs and fleeting enthusiasms. I have taken pains to go to the bottom of things and get facts, in a cold, business-like manner.

I have seen the statement made lately, by one who claims to know what he is talking about, that, taking the whole Negro race into account, ninety per cent of the Negro women are not virtuous. There never was a baser falsehood uttered concerning a race, or a statement made that was less capable of being proved by actual facts.

No one can come into contact with the race for twenty years, as I have done in the heart of the South, without being convinced that the race is constantly making slow but sure progress materially, educationally, and morally. One might take up the life of the worst element in New York City, for example, and prove almost anything he wanted to prove concerning the white man, but all will agree that this is not a fair test.

Early in the year 1897 I received a letter inviting me to deliver an address at the dedication of the Robert Gould Shaw monument in Boston. I accepted the invitation. It is not necessary for me, I am sure, to explain who Robert Gould Shaw was, and what he did. The monument to his memory stands near the head of the Boston Common, facing the State House. It is counted to be the most perfect piece of art of the kind to be found in the country.

The exercises connected with the dedication were held in Music Hall, in Boston, and the great hall was packed from top to bottom with one of the most distinguished audiences that ever assembled in the city. Among those present were more persons representing the famous old anti-slavery element that it is likely will ever be brought together in the country again. The late Hon. Roger Wolcott, then Governor of Massachusetts, was the presiding officer, and on the platform with him were many other officials and hundreds of distinguished men. A report of the meeting which appeared in the Boston Transcript will describe it better than any words of mine could do:—

The core and kernel of yesterday's great noon meeting, in honour of the Brotherhood of Man, in Music Hall, was the superb address of the Negro President of Tuskegee. "Booker T. Washington received his Harvard A.M. last June, the first of his race," said Governor Wolcott, "to receive an honorary degree from the oldest university in the land, and this for the wise leadership of his people." When Mr. Washington rose in the flag-filled, enthusiasm-warmed, patriotic, and glowing atmosphere of Music Hall, people felt keenly that here was the civic justification of the old abolition spirit of Massachusetts; in his person the proof of her ancient and indomitable faith; in his strong thought and rich oratory, the crown and glory of the old war days of suffering and strife. The scene was full of historic beauty and deep significance. "Cold" Boston was alive with the fire that is always hot in her heart for righteousness and truth. Rows and rows of people who are seldom seen at any public function, whole families of those who are certain to be out of town on a holiday, crowded the place to overflowing. The city was at her birthright fte in the persons of hundreds of her best citizens, men and women whose names and lives stand for the virtues that make for honourable civic pride.

Battle-music had filled the air. Ovation after ovation, applause warm and prolonged, had greeted the officers and friends of Colonel Shaw, the sculptor, St. Gaudens, the memorial Committee, the Governor and his staff, and the Negro soldiers of the Fifty-fourth Massachusetts as they came upon the platform or entered the hall. Colonel Henry Lee, of Governor Andrew's old staff, had made a noble, simple presentation speech for the committee, paying tribute to Mr. John M. Forbes, in whose stead he served. Governor Wolcott had made his short, memorable speech, saying, "Fort Wagner marked an epoch in the history of a race, and called it into manhood." Mayor Quincy had received the monument for the city of Boston. The story of Colonel Shaw and his black regiment had been told in gallant words, and then, after the singing of

Mine eyes have seen the glory

Of the coming of the Lord,

Booker Washington arose. It was, of course, just the moment for him. The multitude, shaken out of its usual symphony-concert calm, quivered with an excitement that was not suppressed. A dozen times it had sprung to its feet to cheer and wave and hurrah, as one person. When this man of culture and voice and power, as well as a dark skin, began, and uttered the names of Stearns and of Andrew, feeling began to mount. You could see tears glisten in the eyes of soldiers and civilians. When the orator turned to the coloured soldiers on the platform, to the colour-bearer of Fort Wagner, who smilingly bore still the flag he had never lowered even when wounded, and said, "To you, to the scarred and scattered remnants of the Fifty-fourth, who, with empty sleeve and wanting leg, have honoured this occasion with your presence, to you, your commander is not dead. Though Boston erected no monument and history recorded no story, in you and in the loyal race which you represent, Robert Gould Shaw would have a monument which time could not wear away," then came the climax of the emotion of the day and the hour. It was Roger Wolcott, as well as the Governor of Massachusetts, the individual representative of the people's sympathy as well as the chief magistrate, who had sprung first to his feet and cried, "Three cheers to Booker T. Washington!"

Among those on the platform was Sergeant William H. Carney, of New Bedford, Mass., the brave coloured officer who was the colour-bearer at Fort Wagner and held the American flag. In spite of the fact that a large part of his regiment was killed, he escaped, and exclaimed, after the battle was over, "The old flag never touched the ground."

This flag Sergeant Carney held in his hands as he sat on the platform, and when I turned to address the survivors of the coloured regiment who were present, and referred to Sergeant Carney, he rose, as if by instinct, and raised the flag. It has been my privilege to witness a good many satisfactory and rather sensational demonstrations in connection with some of my public addresses, but in dramatic effect I have never seen or experienced anything which equalled this. For a number of minutes the audience seemed to entirely lose control of itself.

In the general rejoicing throughout the country which followed the close of the Spanish-American war, peace celebrations were arranged in several of the large cities. I was asked by President William R. Harper, of the University of Chicago, who was chairman of the committee of invitations for the celebration to be held in the city of Chicago, to deliver one of the addresses at the celebration there. I accepted the invitation, and delivered two addresses there during the Jubilee week. The first of these, and the principal one, was given in the Auditorium, on the evening of Sunday, October 16. This was the largest audience that I have ever addressed, in any part of the country; and besides speaking in the main Auditorium, I also addressed, that same evening, two overflow audiences in other parts of the city.

It was said that there were sixteen thousand persons in the Auditorium, and it seemed to me as if there were as many more on the outside trying to get in. It was impossible for any one to get near the entrance without the aid of a policeman. President William McKinley attended this meeting, as did also the members of his Cabinet, many foreign ministers, and a large number of army and navy officers, many of whom had distinguished themselves in the war which had just closed. The speakers, besides myself, on Sunday evening, were Rabbi Emil G. Hirsch, Father Thomas P. Hodnett, and Dr. John H. Barrows.

The Chicago Times-Herald, in describing the meeting, said of my address:—

He pictured the Negro choosing slavery rather than extinction; recalled Crispus Attucks shedding his blood at the beginning of the American Revolution, that white Americans might be free, while black Americans remained in slavery; rehearsed the conduct of the Negroes with Jackson at New Orleans; drew a vivid and pathetic picture of the Southern slaves protecting and supporting the families of their masters while the latter were fighting to perpetuate black slavery; recounted the bravery of coloured troops at Port Hudson and Forts Wagner and Pillow, and praised the heroism of the black regiments that stormed El Caney and Santiago to give freedom to the enslaved people of Cuba, forgetting, for the time being, the unjust discrimination that law and custom make against them in their own country.

In all of these things, the speaker declared, his race had chosen the better part. And then he made his eloquent appeal to the consciences of the white Americans: "When you have gotten the full story of the heroic conduct of the Negro in the Spanish-American war, have heard it from the lips of Northern soldier and Southern soldier, from ex-abolitionist and ex-masters, then decide within yourselves whether a race that is thus willing to die for its country should not be given the highest opportunity to live for its country."

The part of the speech which seems to arouse the wildest and most sensational enthusiasm was that in which I thanked the President for his recognition of the Negro in his appointments during the Spanish-American war. The President was sitting in a box at the right of the stage. When I addressed him I turned toward the box, and as I finished the sentence thanking him for his generosity, the whole audience rose and cheered again and again, waving handkerchiefs and hats and canes, until the President arose in the box and bowed his acknowledgements. At that the enthusiasm broke out again, and the demonstration was almost indescribable.

One portion of my address at Chicago seemed to have been misunderstood by the Southern press, and some of the Southern papers took occasion to criticise me rather strongly. These criticisms continued for several weeks, until I finally received a letter from the editor of the Age-Herald, published in Birmingham, Ala., asking me if I would say just what I meant by this part of the address. I replied to him in a letter which seemed to satisfy my critics. In this letter I said that I had made it a rule never to say before a Northern audience anything that I would not say before an audience in the South. I said that I did not think it was necessary for me to go into extended explanations; if my seventeen years of work in the heart of the South had not been explanation enough, I did not see how words could explain. I said that I made the same plea that I had made in my address at Atlanta, for the blotting out of race prejudice in "commercial and civil relations." I said that what is termed social recognition was a question which I never discussed, and then I quoted from my Atlanta address what I had said there in regard to that subject.

In meeting crowds of people at public gatherings, there is one type of individual that I dread. I mean the crank. I have become so accustomed to these people now that I can pick them out at a distance when I see them elbowing their way up to me. The average crank has a long beard, poorly cared for, a lean, narrow face, and wears a black coat. The front of his vest and coat are slick with grease, and his trousers bag at the knees.

In Chicago, after I had spoken at a meeting, I met one of these fellows. They usually have some process for curing all of the ills of the world at once. This Chicago specimen had a patent process by which he said Indian corn could be kept through a period of three or four years, and he felt sure that if the Negro race in the South would, as a whole, adopt his process, it would settle the whole race question. It mattered nothing that I tried to convince him that our present problem was to teach the Negroes how to produce enough corn to last them through one year. Another Chicago crank had a scheme by which he wanted me to join him in an effort to close up all the National banks in the country. If that was done, he felt sure it would put the Negro on his feet.

The number of people who stand ready to consume one's time, to no purpose, is almost countless. At one time I spoke before a large audience in Boston in the evening. The next morning I was awakened by having a card brought to my room, and with it a message that some one was anxious to see me. Thinking that it must be something very important, I dressed hastily and went down. When I reached the hotel office I found a blank and innocent-looking individual waiting for me, who coolly remarked: "I heard you talk at a meeting last night. I rather liked your talk, and so I came in this morning to hear you talk some more."

I am often asked how it is possible for me to superintend the work at Tuskegee and at the same time be so much away from the school. In partial answer to this I would say that I think I have learned, in some degree at least, to disregard the old maxim which says, "Do not get others to do that which you can do yourself." My motto, on the other hand, is, "Do not do that which others can do as well."

One of the most encouraging signs in connection with the Tuskegee school is found in the fact that the organization is so thorough that the daily work of the school is not dependent upon the presence of any one individual. The whole executive force, including instructors and clerks, now numbers eighty-six. This force is so organized and subdivided that the machinery of the school goes on day by day like clockwork. Most of our teachers have been connected with the institutions for a number of years, and are as much interested in it as I am. In my absence, Mr. Warren Logan, the treasurer, who has been at the school seventeen years, is the executive. He is efficiently supported by Mrs. Washington, and by my faithful secretary, Mr. Emmett J. Scott, who handles the bulk of my correspondence and keeps me in daily touch with the life of the school, and who also keeps me informed of whatever takes place in the South that concerns the race. I owe more to his tact, wisdom, and hard work than I can describe.

The main executive work of the school, whether I am at Tuskegee or not, centres in what we call the executive council. This council meets twice a week, and is composed of the nine persons who are at the head of the nine departments of the school. For example: Mrs. B.K. Bruce, the Lady Principal, the widow of the late ex-senator Bruce, is a member of the council, and represents in it all that pertains to the life of the girls at the school. In addition to the executive council there is a financial committee of six, that meets every week and decides upon the expenditures for the week. Once a month, and sometimes oftener, there is a general meeting of all the instructors. Aside from these there are innumerable smaller meetings, such as that of the instructors in the Phelps Hall Bible Training School, or of the instructors in the agricultural department.

In order that I may keep in constant touch with the life of the institution, I have a system of reports so arranged that a record of the school's work reaches me every day of the year, no matter in what part of the country I am. I know by these reports even what students are excused from school, and why they are excused—whether for reasons of ill health or otherwise. Through the medium of these reports I know each day what the income of the school in money is; I know how many gallons of milk and how many pounds of butter come from the dairy; what the bill of fare for the teachers and students is; whether a certain kind of meat was boiled or baked, and whether certain vegetables served in the dining room were bought from a store or procured from our own farm. Human nature I find to be very much the same the world over, and it is sometimes not hard to yield to the temptation to go to a barrel of rice that has come from the store—with the grain all prepared to go in the pot—rather than to take the time and trouble to go to the field and dig and wash one's own sweet potatoes, which might be prepared in a manner to take the place of the rice.

I am often asked how, in the midst of so much work, a large part of which is for the public, I can find time for any rest or recreation, and what kind of recreation or sports I am fond of. This is rather a difficult question to answer. I have a strong feeling that every individual owes it to himself, and to the cause which he is serving, to keep a vigorous, healthy body, with the nerves steady and strong, prepared for great efforts and prepared for disappointments and trying positions. As far as I can, I make it a rule to plan for each day's work—not merely to go through with the same routine of daily duties, but to get rid of the routine work as early in the day as possible, and then to enter upon some new or advance work. I make it a rule to clear my desk every day, before leaving my office, of all correspondence and memoranda, so that on the morrow I can begin a new day of work. I make it a rule never to let my work drive me, but to so master it, and keep it in such complete control, and to keep so far ahead of it, that I will be the master instead of the servant. There is a physical and mental and spiritual enjoyment that comes from a consciousness of being the absolute master of one's work, in all its details, that is very satisfactory and inspiring. My experience teaches me that, if one learns to follow this plan, he gets a freshness of body and vigour of mind out of work that goes a long way toward keeping him strong and healthy. I believe that when one can grow to the point where he loves his work, this gives him a kind of strength that is most valuable.

When I begin my work in the morning, I expect to have a successful and pleasant day of it, but at the same time I prepare myself for unpleasant and unexpected hard places. I prepared myself to hear that one of our school buildings is on fire, or has burned, or that some disagreeable accident has occurred, or that some one has abused me in a public address or printed article, for something that I have done or omitted to do, or for something that he had heard that I had said—probably something that I had never thought of saying.

In nineteen years of continuous work I have taken but one vacation. That was two years ago, when some of my friends put the money into my hands and forced Mrs. Washington and myself to spend three months in Europe. I have said that I believe it is the duty of every one to keep his body in good condition. I try to look after the little ills, with the idea that if I take care of the little ills the big ones will not come. When I find myself unable to sleep well, I know that something is wrong. If I find any part of my system the least weak, and not performing its duty, I consult a good physician. The ability to sleep well, at any time and in any place, I find of great advantage. I have so trained myself that I can lie down for a nap of fifteen or twenty minutes, and get up refreshed in body and mind.

I have said that I make it a rule to finish up each day's work before leaving it. There is, perhaps, one exception to this. When I have an unusually difficult question to decide—one that appeals strongly to the emotions—I find it a safe rule to sleep over it for a night, or to wait until I have had an opportunity to talk it over with my wife and friends.

As to my reading; the most time I get for solid reading is when I am on the cars. Newspapers are to me a constant source of delight and recreation. The only trouble is that I read too many of them. Fiction I care little for.

Frequently I have to almost force myself to read a novel that is on every one's lips. The kind of reading that I have the greatest fondness for is biography. I like to be sure that I am reading about a real man or a real thing. I think I do not go too far when I say that I have read nearly every book and magazine article that has been written about Abraham Lincoln. In literature he is my patron saint.

Out of the twelve months in a year I suppose that, on an average, I spend six months away from Tuskegee. While my being absent from the school so much unquestionably has its disadvantages, yet there are at the same time some compensations. The change of work brings a certain kind of rest. I enjoy a ride of a long distance on the cars, when I am permitted to ride where I can be comfortable. I get rest on the cars, except when the inevitable individual who seems to be on every train approaches me with the now familiar phrase: "Isn't this Booker Washington? I want to introduce myself to you." Absence from the school enables me to lose sight of the unimportant details of the work, and study it in a broader and more comprehensive manner than I could do on the grounds. This absence also brings me into contact with the best work being done in educational lines, and into contact with the best educators in the land.

But, after all this is said, the time when I get the most solid rest and recreation is when I can be at Tuskegee, and, after our evening meal is over, can sit down, as is our custom, with my wife and Portia and Baker and Davidson, my three children, and read a story, or each take turns in telling a story. To me there is nothing on earth equal to that, although what is nearly equal to it is to go with them for an hour or more, as we like to do on Sunday afternoons, into the woods, where we can live for a while near the heart of nature, where no one can disturb or vex us, surrounded by pure air, the trees, the shrubbery, the flowers, and the sweet fragrance that springs from a hundred plants, enjoying the chirp of the crickets and the songs of the birds. This is solid rest.

My garden, also, what little time I can be at Tuskegee, is another source of rest and enjoyment. Somehow I like, as often as possible, to touch nature, not something that is artificial or an imitation, but the real thing. When I can leave my office in time so that I can spend thirty or forty minutes in spading the ground, in planting seeds, in digging about the plants, I feel that I am coming into contact with something that is giving me strength for the many duties and hard places that await me out in the big world. I pity the man or woman who has never learned to enjoy nature and to get strength and inspiration out of it.

Aside from the large number of fowls and animals kept by the school, I keep individually a number of pigs and fowls of the best grades, and in raising these I take a great deal of pleasure. I think the pig is my favourite animal. Few things are more satisfactory to me than a high-grade Berkshire or Poland China pig.

Games I care little for. I have never seen a game of football. In cards I do not know one card from another. A game of old-fashioned marbles with my two boys, once in a while, is all I care for in this direction. I suppose I would care for games now if I had had any time in my youth to give to them, but that was not possible.

Chapter 16. Europe

In 1893 I was married to Miss Margaret James Murray, a native of Mississippi, and a graduate of Fisk University, in Nashville, Tenn., who had come to Tuskegee as a teacher several years before, and at the time we were married was filling the position of Lady Principal. Not only is Mrs. Washington completely one with me in the work directly connected with the school, relieving me of many burdens and perplexities, but aside from her work on the school grounds, she carries on a mothers' meeting in the town of Tuskegee, and a plantation work among the women, children, and men who live in a settlement connected with a large plantation about eight miles from Tuskegee. Both the mothers' meeting and the plantation work are carried on, not only with a view to helping those who are directly reached, but also for the purpose of furnishing object-lessons in these two kinds of work that may be followed by our students when they go out into the world for their own life-work.

Aside from these two enterprises, Mrs. Washington is also largely responsible for a woman's club at the school which brings together, twice a month, the women who live on the school grounds and those who live near, for the discussion of some important topic. She is also the President of what is known as the Federation of Southern Coloured Women's Clubs, and is Chairman of the Executive Committee of the National Federation of Coloured Women's Clubs.

Portia, the oldest of my three children, has learned dressmaking. She has unusual ability in instrumental music. Aside from her studies at Tuskegee, she has already begun to teach there.

Booker Taliaferro is my next oldest child. Young as he is, he has already nearly mastered the brickmason's trade. He began working at this trade when he was quite small, dividing his time between this and class work;

and he has developed great skill in the trade and a fondness for it. He says that he is going to be an architect and brickmason. One of the most satisfactory letters that I have ever received from any one came to me from Booker last summer. When I left home for the summer, I told him that he must work at his trade half of each day, and that the other half of the day he could spend as he pleased. When I had been away from home two weeks, I received the following letter from him:

Tuskegee, Alabama.

My dear Papa: Before you left home you told me to work at my trade half of each day. I like my work so much that I want to work at my trade all day. Besides, I want to earn all the money I can, so that when I go to another school I shall have money to pay my expenses.

Your son,

Booker.

My youngest child, Ernest Davidson Washington, says that he is going to be a physician. In addition to going to school, where he studies books and has manual training, he regularly spends a portion of his time in the office of our resident physician, and has already learned to do many of the duties which pertain to a doctor's office.

The thing in my life which brings me the keenest regret is that my work in connection with public affairs keeps me for so much of the time away from my family, where, of all places in the world, I delight to be. I always envy the individual whose life-work is so laid that he can spend his evenings at home. I have sometimes thought that people who have this rare privilege do not appreciate it as they should. It is such a rest and relief to get away from crowds of people, and handshaking, and travelling, to get home, even if it be for but a very brief while.

Another thing at Tuskegee out of which I get a great deal of pleasure and satisfaction is in the meeting with our students, and teachers, and their families, in the chapel for devotional exercises every evening at half-past eight, the last thing before retiring for the night. It is an inspiring sight when one stands on the platform there and sees before him eleven or twelve hundred earnest young men and women; and one cannot but feel that it is a privilege to help to guide them to a higher and more useful life.

In the spring of 1899 there came to me what I might describe as almost the greatest surprise of my life. Some good ladies in Boston arranged a public meeting in the interests of Tuskegee, to be held in the Hollis Street Theatre. This meeting was attended by large numbers of the best people of Boston, of both races. Bishop Lawrence presided. In addition to an address made by myself, Mr. Paul Lawrence Dunbar read from his poems, and Dr. W.E.B. Du Bois read an original sketch.

Some of those who attended this meeting noticed that I seemed unusually tired, and some little time after the close of the meeting, one of the ladies who had been interested in it asked me in a casual way if I had ever been to Europe. I replied that I never had. She asked me if I had ever thought of going, and I told her no; that it was something entirely beyond me. This conversation soon passed out of my mind, but a few days afterward I was informed that some friends in Boston, including Mr. Francis J. Garrison, had raised a sum of money sufficient to pay all the expenses of Mrs. Washington and myself during a three or four months' trip to Europe. It was added with emphasis that we must go. A year previous to this Mr. Garrison had attempted to get me to promise to go to Europe for a summer's rest, with the understanding that he would be responsible for raising the money among his friends for the expenses of the trip. At that time such a journey seemed so entirely foreign to anything that I should ever be able to undertake that I did confess I did not give the matter very serious attention; but later Mr. Garrison joined his efforts to those of the ladies whom I have mentioned, and when their plans were made known to me Mr. Garrison not only had the route mapped out, but had, I believe, selected the steamer upon which we were to sail.

The whole thing was so sudden and so unexpected that I was completely taken off my feet. I had been at work steadily for eighteen years in connection with Tuskegee, and I had never thought of anything else but ending my life in that way. Each day the school seemed to depend upon me more largely for its daily expenses, and I told these Boston friends that, while I thanked them sincerely for their thoughtfulness and generosity, I could not go to Europe, for the reason that the school could not live financially while I was absent. They then informed me that Mr. Henry L. Higginson, and some other good friends who I know do not want their names made public, were then raising a sum of money which would be sufficient to keep the school in operation while I was away. At this point

I was compelled to surrender. Every avenue of escape had been closed.

Deep down in my heart the whole thing seemed more like a dream than like reality, and for a long time it was difficult for me to make myself believe that I was actually going to Europe. I had been born and largely reared in the lowest depths of slavery, ignorance, and poverty. In my childhood I had suffered for want of a place to sleep, for lack of food, clothing, and shelter. I had not had the privilege of sitting down to a dining-table until I was quite well grown. Luxuries had always seemed to me to be something meant for white people, not for my race. I had always regarded Europe, and London, and Paris, much as I regarded heaven. And now could it be that I was actually going to Europe? Such thoughts as these were constantly with me.

Two other thoughts troubled me a good deal. I feared that people who heard that Mrs. Washington and I were going to Europe might not know all the circumstances, and might get the idea that we had become, as some might say, "stuck up," and were trying to "show off." I recalled that from my youth I had heard it said that too often, when people of my race reached any degree of success, they were inclined to unduly exalt themselves; to try and ape the wealthy, and in so doing to lose their heads. The fear that people might think this of us haunted me a good deal. Then, too, I could not see how my conscience would permit me to spare the time from my work and be happy. It seemed mean and selfish in me to be taking a vacation while others were at work, and while there was so much that needed to be done. From the time I could remember, I had always been at work, and I did not see how I could spend three or four months in doing nothing. The fact was that I did not know how to take a vacation.

Mrs. Washington had much the same difficulty in getting away, but she was anxious to go because she thought that I needed the rest. There were many important National questions bearing upon the life of the race which were being agitated at that time, and this made it all the harder for us to decide to go. We finally gave our Boston friends our promise that we would go, and then they insisted that the date of our departure be set as soon as possible.

So we decided upon May 10. My good friend Mr. Garrison kindly took charge of all the details necessary for the success of the trip, and he, as well as other friends, gave us a great number of letters of introduction to people in France and England, and made other arrangements for our comfort and convenience abroad. Good-bys were said at Tuskegee, and we were in New York May 9, ready to sail the next day. Our daughter Portia, who was then studying in South Framingham, Mass., came to New York to see us off. Mr. Scott, my secretary, came with me to New York, in order that I might clear up the last bit of business before I left. Other friends also came to New York to see us off. Just before we went on board the steamer another pleasant surprise came to us in the form of a letter from two generous ladies, stating that they had decided to give us the money with which to erect a new building to be used in properly housing all our industries for girls at Tuskegee.

We were to sail on the Friesland, of the Red Star Line, and a beautiful vessel she was. We went on board just before noon, the hour of sailing. I had never before been on board a large ocean steamer, and the feeling which took possession of me when I found myself there is rather hard to describe. It was a feeling, I think, of awe mingled with delight. We were agreeably surprised to find that the captain, as well as several of the other officers, not only knew who we were, but was expecting us and gave us a pleasant greeting. There were several passengers whom we knew, including Senator Sewell, of New Jersey, and Edward Marshall, the newspaper correspondent. I had just a little fear that we would not be treated civilly by some of the passengers. This fear was based upon what I had heard other people of my race, who had crossed the ocean, say about unpleasant experiences in crossing the ocean in American vessels. But in our case, from the captain down to the most humble servant, we were treated with the greatest kindness. Nor was this kindness confined to those who were connected with the steamer; it was shown by all the passengers also. There were not a few Southern men and women on board, and they were as cordial as those from other parts of the country.

As soon as the last good-bys were said, and the steamer had cut loose from the wharf, the load of care, anxiety, and responsibility which I had carried for eighteen years began to lift itself from my shoulders at the rate, it seemed to me, of a pound a minute. It was the first time in all those years that I had felt, even in a measure, free from care; and my feeling of relief it is hard to describe on paper. Added to this was the delightful anticipation of being in Europe soon. It all seemed more like a dream than like a reality.

Mr. Garrison had thoughtfully arranged to have us have one of the most comfortable rooms on the ship. The second or third day out I began to sleep, and I think that I slept at the rate of fifteen hours a day during the remainder of the ten days' passage. Then it was that I began to understand how tired I really was. These long sleeps I kept up for a month after we landed on the other side. It was such an unusual feeling to wake up in the morning and realize that I had no engagements; did not have to take a train at a certain hour; did not have an appointment to meet some one, or to make an address, at a certain hour. How different all this was from the experiences that I have been through when travelling, when I have sometimes slept in three different beds in a single night!

When Sunday came, the captain invited me to conduct the religious services, but, not being a minister, I declined. The passengers, however, began making requests that I deliver an address to them in the dining-saloon some time during the voyage, and this I consented to do. Senator Sewell presided at this meeting. After ten days of delightful weather, during which I was not seasick for a day, we landed at the interesting old city of Antwerp, in Belgium.

The next day after we landed happened to be one of those numberless holidays which the people of those countries are in the habit of observing. It was a bright, beautiful day. Our room in the hotel faced the main public square, and the sights there—the people coming in from the country with all kinds of beautiful flowers to sell, the women coming in with their dogs drawing large, brightly polished cans filled with milk, the people streaming into the cathedral—filled me with a sense of newness that I had never before experienced.

After spending some time in Antwerp, we were invited to go with a part of a half-dozen persons on a trip through Holland. This party included Edward Marshall and some American artists who had come over on the same steamer with us. We accepted the invitation, and enjoyed the trip greatly. I think it was all the more interesting and instructive because we went for most of the way on one of the slow, old-fashioned canal-boats. This gave us an opportunity of seeing and studying the real life of the people in the country districts. We went in this way as far as Rotterdam, and later went to The Hague, where the Peace Conference was then in session, and where we were kindly received by the American representatives.

The thing that impressed itself most on me in Holland was the thoroughness of the agriculture and the excellence of the Holstein cattle. I never knew, before visiting Holland, how much it was possible for people to get out of a small plot of ground. It seemed to me that absolutely no land was wasted. It was worth a trip to Holland, too, just to get a sight of three or four hundred fine Holstein cows grazing in one of those intensely green fields.

From Holland we went to Belgium, and made a hasty trip through that country, stopping at Brussels, where we visited the battlefield of Waterloo. From Belgium we went direct to Paris, where we found that Mr. Theodore Stanton, the son of Mrs. Elizabeth Cady Stanton, had kindly provided accommodations for us. We had barely got settled in Paris before an invitation came to me from the University Club of Paris to be its guest at a banquet which was soon to be given. The other guests were ex-President Benjamin Harrison and Archbishop Ireland, who were in Paris at the time. The American Ambassador, General Horace Porter, presided at the banquet. My address on this occasion seemed to give satisfaction to those who heard it. General Harrison kindly devoted a large portion of his remarks at dinner to myself and to the influence of the work at Tuskegee on the American race question. After my address at this banquet other invitations came to me, but I declined the most of them, knowing that if I accepted them all, the object of my visit would be defeated. I did, however, consent to deliver an address in the American chapel the following Sunday morning, and at this meeting General Harrison, General Porter, and other distinguished Americans were present.

Later we received a formal call from the American Ambassador, and were invited to attend a reception at his residence. At this reception we met many Americans, among them Justices Fuller and Harlan, of the United States Supreme Court. During our entire stay of a month in Paris, both the American Ambassador and his wife, as well as several other Americans, were very kind to us.

While in Paris we saw a good deal of the now famous American Negro painter, Mr. Henry O. Tanner, whom we had formerly known in America. It was very satisfactory to find how well known Mr. Tanner was in the field of art, and to note the high standing which all classes accorded to him. When we told some Americans that we were going to the Luxembourg

Palace to see a painting by an American Negro, it was hard to convince them that a Negro had been thus honoured. I do not believe that they were really convinced of the fact until they saw the picture for themselves. My acquaintance with Mr. Tanner reenforced in my mind the truth which I am constantly trying to impress upon our students at Tuskegee—and on our people throughout the country, as far as I can reach them with my voice— that any man, regardless of colour, will be recognized and rewarded just in proportion as he learns to do something well—learns to do it better than some one else—however humble the thing may be. As I have said, I believe that my race will succeed in proportion as it learns to do a common thing in an uncommon manner; learns to do a thing so thoroughly that no one can improve upon what it has done; learns to make its services of indispensable value. This was the spirit that inspired me in my first effort at Hampton, when I was given the opportunity to sweep and dust that schoolroom. In a degree I felt that my whole future life depended upon the thoroughness with which I cleaned that room, and I was determined to do it so well that no one could find any fault with the job. Few people ever stopped, I found, when looking at his pictures, to inquire whether Mr. Tanner was a Negro painter, a French painter, or a German painter. They simply knew that he was able to produce something which the world wanted—a great painting—and the matter of his colour did not enter into their minds. When a Negro girl learns to cook, to wash dishes, to sew, or write a book, or a Negro boy learns to groom horses, or to grow sweet potatoes, or to produce butter, or to build a house, or to be able to practise medicine, as well or better than some one else, they will be rewarded regardless of race or colour. In the long run, the world is going to have the best, and any difference in race, religion, or previous history will not long keep the world from what it wants.

I think that the whole future of my race hinges on the question as to whether or not it can make itself of such indispensable value that the people in the town and the state where we reside will feel that our presence is necessary to the happiness and well-being of the community. No man who continues to add something to the material, intellectual, and moral well-being of the place in which he lives is long left without proper reward. This is a great human law which cannot be permanently nullified.

The love of pleasure and excitement which seems in a large measure to possess the French people impressed itself upon me. I think they are more noted in this respect than is true of the people of my own race. In point of morality and moral earnestness I do not believe that the French are ahead of my own race in America. Severe competition and the great stress of life have led them to learn to do things more thoroughly and to exercise greater economy; but time, I think, will bring my race to the same point. In the matter of truth and high honour I do not believe that the average Frenchman is ahead of the American Negro; while so far as mercy and kindness to dumb animals go, I believe that my race is far ahead. In fact, when I left France, I had more faith in the future of the black man in America than I had ever possessed.

From Paris we went to London, and reached there early in July, just about the height of the London social season. Parliament was in session, and there was a great deal of gaiety. Mr. Garrison and other friends had provided us with a large number of letters of introduction, and they had also sent letters to other persons in different parts of the United Kingdom, apprising these people of our coming. Very soon after reaching London we were flooded with invitations to attend all manner of social functions, and a great many invitations came to me asking that I deliver public addresses. The most of these invitations I declined, for the reason that I wanted to rest. Neither were we able to accept more than a small proportion of the other invitations. The Rev. Dr. Brooke Herford and Mrs. Herford, whom I had known in Boston, consulted with the American Ambassador, the Hon. Joseph Choate, and arranged for me to speak at a public meeting to be held in Essex Hall. Mr. Choate kindly consented to preside. The meeting was largely attended. There were many distinguished persons present, among them several members of Parliament, including Mr. James Bryce, who spoke at the meeting. What the American Ambassador said in introducing me, as well as a synopsis of what I said, was widely published in England and in the American papers at the time. Dr. and Mrs. Herford gave Mrs. Washington and myself a reception, at which we had the privilege of meeting some of the best people in England. Throughout our stay in London Ambassador Choate was most kind and attentive to us. At the Ambassador's reception I met, for the first time, Mark Twain.

We were the guests several times of Mrs. T. Fisher Unwin, the daughter of the English statesman, Richard Cobden. It seemed as if both Mr. and Mrs. Unwin could not do enough for our comfort and happiness. Later, for nearly a week, we were the guests of the daughter of John Bright, now

Mrs. Clark, of Street, England. Both Mr. and Mrs. Clark, with their daughter, visited us at Tuskegee the next year. In Birmingham, England, we were the guests for several days of Mr. Joseph Sturge, whose father was a great abolitionist and friend of Whittier and Garrison. It was a great privilege to meet throughout England those who had known and honoured the late William Lloyd Garrison, the Hon. Frederick Douglass, and other abolitionists. The English abolitionists with whom we came in contact never seemed to tire of talking about these two Americans. Before going to England I had had no proper conception of the deep interest displayed by the abolitionists of England in the cause of freedom, nor did I realize the amount of substantial help given by them.

In Bristol, England, both Mrs. Washington and I spoke at the Women's Liberal Club. I was also the principal speaker at the Commencement exercises of the Royal College for the Blind. These exercises were held in the Crystal Palace, and the presiding officer was the late Duke of Westminster, who was said to be, I believe, the richest man in England, if not in the world. The Duke, as well as his wife and their daughter, seemed to be pleased with what I said, and thanked me heartily. Through the kindness of Lady Aberdeen, my wife and I were enabled to go with a party of those who were attending the International Congress of Women, then in session in London, to see Queen Victoria, at Windsor Castle, where, afterward, we were all the guests of her Majesty at tea. In our party was Miss Susan B. Anthony, and I was deeply impressed with the fact that one did not often get an opportunity to see, during the same hour, two women so remarkable in different ways as Susan B. Anthony and Queen Victoria.

In the House of Commons, which we visited several times, we met Sir Henry M. Stanley. I talked with him about Africa and its relation to the American Negro, and after my interview with him I became more convinced than ever that there was no hope of the American Negro's improving his condition by emigrating to Africa.

On various occasions Mrs. Washington and I were the guests of Englishmen in their country homes, where, I think, one sees the Englishman at his best. In one thing, at least, I feel sure that the English are ahead of Americans, and that is, that they have learned how to get more out of life. The home life of the English seems to me to be about as perfect as anything can be. Everything moves like clockwork. I was impressed, too, with the deference that the servants show to their "masters" and "mistresses,"—terms which I suppose would not be tolerated in America. The English servant expects, as a rule, to be nothing but a servant, and so he perfects himself in the art to a degree that no class of servants in America has yet reached. In our country the servant expects to become, in a few years, a "master" himself. Which system is preferable? I will not venture an answer.

Another thing that impressed itself upon me throughout England was the high regard that all classes have for law and order, and the ease and thoroughness with which everything is done. The Englishmen, I found, took plenty of time for eating, as for everything else. I am not sure if, in the long run, they do not accomplish as much or more than rushing, nervous Americans do.

My visit to England gave me a higher regard for the nobility than I had had. I had no idea that they were so generally loved and respected by the classes, nor had I any correct conception of how much time and money they spent in works of philanthropy, and how much real heart they put into this work. My impression had been that they merely spent money freely and had a "good time."

It was hard for me to get accustomed to speaking to English audiences. The average Englishman is so serious, and is so tremendously in earnest about everything, that when I told a story that would have made an American audience roar with laughter, the Englishmen simply looked me straight in the face without even cracking a smile.

When the Englishman takes you into his heart and friendship, he binds you there as with cords of steel, and I do not believe that there are many other friendships that are so lasting or so satisfactory. Perhaps I can illustrate this point in no better way than by relating the following incident. Mrs. Washington and I were invited to attend a reception given by the Duke and Duchess of Sutherland, at Stafford House—said to be the finest house in London; I may add that I believe the Duchess of Sutherland is said to be the most beautiful woman in England. There must have been at least three hundred persons at this reception. Twice during the evening the Duchess sought us out for a conversation, and she asked me to write her when we got home, and tell her more about the work at Tuskegee. This I did. When Christmas came we were surprised and delighted to receive her photograph with her autograph on it. The correspondence has continued, and we now feel that in the Duchess of Sutherland we have one of our warmest friends.

After three months in Europe we sailed from Southampton in the steamship St. Louis. On this steamer there was a fine library that had been presented to the ship by the citizens of St. Louis, Mo. In this library I found a life of Frederick Douglass, which I began reading. I became especially interested in Mr. Douglass's description of the way he was treated on shipboard during his first or second visit to England. In this description he told how he was not permitted to enter the cabin, but had to confine himself to the deck of the ship. A few minutes after I had finished reading this description I was waited on by a committee of ladies and gentlemen with the request that I deliver an address at a concert which was to begin the following evening. And yet there are people who are bold enough to say that race feeling in America is not growing less intense! At this concert the Hon. Benjamin B. Odell, Jr., the present governor of New York, presided. I was never given a more cordial hearing anywhere. A large proportion of the passengers were Southern people. After the concert some of the passengers proposed that a subscription be raised to help the work at Tuskegee, and the money to support several scholarships was the result.

While we were in Paris I was very pleasantly surprised to receive the following invitation from the citizens of West Virginia and of the city near which I had spent my boyhood days:—

Charleston, W. Va., May 16, 1899.

Professor Booker T. Washington, Paris, France:

Dear Sir: Many of the best citizens of West Virginia have united in liberal expressions of admiration and praise of your worth and work, and desire that on your return from Europe you should favour them with your presence and with the inspiration of your words. We must sincerely indorse this move, and on behalf of the citizens of Charleston extend to your our most cordial invitation to have you come to us, that we may honour you who have done so much by your life and work to honour us.

We are,

Very truly yours,

The Common Council of the City of Charleston,

By W. Herman Smith, Mayor.

This invitation from the City Council of Charleston was accompanied by the following:—

Professor Booker T. Washington, Paris, France:

Dear Sir: We, the citizens of Charleston and West Virginia, desire to express our pride in you and the splendid career that you have thus far accomplished, and ask that we be permitted to show our pride and interest in a substantial way.

Your recent visit to your old home in our midst awoke within us the keenest regret that we were not permitted to hear you and render some substantial aid to your work, before you left for Europe.

In view of the foregoing, we earnestly invite you to share the hospitality of our city upon your return from Europe, and give us the opportunity to hear you and put ourselves in touch with your work in a way that will be most gratifying to yourself, and that we may receive the inspiration of your words and presence.

An early reply to this invitation, with an indication of the time you may reach our city, will greatly oblige,

Yours very respectfully,

The Charleston Daily Gazette, The Daily Mail-Tribune; G.W. Atkinson, Governor; E.L. Boggs, Secretary to Governor; Wm. M.O. Dawson, Secretary of State; L.M. La Follette, Auditor; J.R. Trotter, Superintendent of Schools; E.W. Wilson, ex-Governor; W.A. MacCorkle, ex-Governor; John Q. Dickinson, President Kanawha Valley Bank; L. Prichard, President Charleston National Bank; Geo. S. Couch, President Kanawha National Bank; Ed. Reid, Cashier Kanawha National Bank; Geo. S. Laidley, Superintended City Schools; L.E. McWhorter, President Board of Education; Chas. K. Payne, wholesale merchant; and many others.

This invitation, coming as it did from the City Council, the state officers, and all the substantial citizens of both races of the community where I had spent my boyhood, and from which I had gone a few years before, unknown, in poverty and ignorance, in quest of an education, not only surprised me, but almost unmanned me. I could not understand what I had done to deserve it all.

I accepted the invitation, and at the appointed day was met at the railway station at Charleston by a committee headed by ex-Governor W.A. MacCorkle, and composed of men of both races. The public reception was held in the Opera-House at Charleston. The Governor of the state, the Hon. George W. Atkinson, presided, and an address of welcome was made by ex-Governor MacCorkle. A prominent part in the reception was taken by the coloured citizens. The Opera-House was filled with citizens of both races, and among the white people were many for whom I had worked when I was a boy. The next day Governor and Mrs. Atkinson gave me a public reception at the State House, which was attended by all classes.

Not long after this the coloured people in Atlanta, Georgia, gave me a reception at which the Governor of the state presided, and a similar reception was given me in New Orleans, which was presided over by the Mayor of the city. Invitations came from many other places which I was not able to accept.

Chapter 17. Last Words

Before going to Europe some events came into my life which were great surprises to me. In fact, my whole life has largely been one of surprises. I believe that any man's life will be filled with constant, unexpected encouragements of this kind if he makes up his mind to do his level best each day of his life—that is, tries to make each day reach as nearly as possible the high-water mark of pure, unselfish, useful living. I pity the man, black or white, who has never experienced the joy and satisfaction that come to one by reason of an effort to assist in making some one else more useful and more happy.

Six months before he died, and nearly a year after he had been stricken with paralysis, General Armstrong expressed a wish to visit Tuskegee again before he passed away. Notwithstanding the fact that he had lost the use of his limbs to such an extent that he was practically helpless, his wish was gratified, and he was brought to Tuskegee. The owners of the Tuskegee Railroad, white men living in the town, offered to run a special train, without cost, out of the main station—Chehaw, five miles away—to meet him. He arrived on the school grounds about nine o'clock in the evening. Some one had suggested that we give the General a "pine-knot torchlight reception." This plan was carried out, and the moment that his carriage entered the school grounds he began passing between two lines of lighted and waving "fat pine" wood knots held by over a thousand students and teachers. The whole thing was so novel and surprising that the General was completely overcome with happiness. He remained a guest in my home for nearly two months, and, although almost wholly without the use of voice or limb, he spent nearly every hour in devising ways and means to help the South. Time and time again he said to me, during this visit, that it was not only the duty of the country to assist in elevating the Negro of the South, but the poor white man as well. At the end of his visit I resolved anew to devote myself more earnestly than ever to the cause which was so near his heart. I said that if a man in his condition was willing to think, work, and act, I should not be wanting in furthering in every possible way the wish of his heart.

The death of General Armstrong, a few weeks later, gave me the privilege of getting acquainted with one of the finest, most unselfish, and most attractive men that I have ever come in contact with. I refer to the Rev. Dr. Hollis B. Frissell, now the Principal of the Hampton Institute, and General Armstrong's successor. Under the clear, strong, and almost perfect leadership of Dr. Frissell, Hampton has had a career of prosperity and usefulness that is all that the General could have wished for. It seems to be the constant effort of Dr. Frissell to hide his own great personality behind that of General Armstrong—to make himself of "no reputation" for the sake of the cause.

More than once I have been asked what was the greatest surprise that ever came to me. I have little hesitation in answering that question. It was the following letter, which came to me one Sunday morning when I was sitting on the veranda of my home at Tuskegee, surrounded by my wife and three children:—

Harvard University, Cambridge, May 28, 1896.

President Booker T. Washington,

My Dear Sir: Harvard University desired to confer on you at the approaching Commencement an honorary degree; but it is our custom to confer degrees only on gentlemen who are present. Our Commencement occurs this year on June 24, and your presence would be desirable from about noon till about five o'clock in the afternoon. Would it be possible for you to be in Cambridge on that day?

Believe me, with great regard,

Very truly yours,

Charles W. Eliot.

This was a recognition that had never in the slightest manner entered into my mind, and it was hard for me to realize that I was to be honoured by a degree from the oldest and most renowned university in America. As I sat upon my veranda, with this letter in my hand, tears came into my eyes. My whole former life—my life as a slave on the plantation, my work in the coal- mine, the times when I was without food and clothing, when I made my bed under a sidewalk, my struggles for an education, the trying days I had had at Tuskegee, days when I did not know where to turn for a dollar to continue the work there, the ostracism and sometimes oppression of my race,—all this passed before me and nearly overcame me.

I had never sought or cared for what the world calls fame. I have always looked upon fame as something to be used in accomplishing good. I have often said to my friends that if I can use whatever prominence may have come to me as an instrument with which to do good, I am content to have it. I care for it only as a means to be used for doing good, just as wealth may be used. The more I come into contact with wealthy people, the more I believe that they are growing in the direction of looking upon their money simply as an instrument which God has placed in their hand for doing good with. I never go to the office of Mr. John D. Rockefeller, who more than once has been generous to Tuskegee, without being reminded of this. The close, careful, and minute investigation that he always makes in order to be sure that every dollar that he gives will do the most good—an investigation that is just as searching as if he were investing money in a business enterprise— convinces me that the growth in this direction is most encouraging.

At nine o'clock, on the morning of June 24, I met President Eliot, the Board of Overseers of Harvard University, and the other guests, at the designated place on the university grounds, for the purpose of being escorted to Sanders Theatre, where the Commencement exercises were to be held and degrees conferred. Among others invited to be present for the purpose of receiving a degree at this time were General Nelson A. Miles, Dr. Bell, the inventor of the Bell telephone, Bishop Vincent, and the Rev. Minot J. Savage. We were placed in line immediately behind the President and the Board of Overseers, and directly afterward the Governor of Massachusetts, escorted by the Lancers, arrived and took his place in the line of march by the side of President Eliot. In the line there were also various other officers and professors, clad in cap and gown. In this order we marched to Sanders Theatre, where, after the usual Commencement exercises, came the conferring of the honorary degrees. This, it seems, is always considered the most interesting feature at Harvard. It is not known, until the individuals appear, upon whom the honorary degrees are to be conferred, and those receiving these honours are cheered by the students and others in proportion to their popularity. During the conferring of the degrees excitement and enthusiasm are at the highest pitch.

When my name was called, I rose, and President Eliot, in beautiful and strong English, conferred upon me the degree of Master of Arts. After these exercises were over, those who had received honorary degrees were invited to lunch with the President. After the lunch we were formed in line again, and were escorted by the Marshal of the day, who that year happened to be Bishop William Lawrence, through the grounds, where, at different points, those who had been honoured were called by name and received the Harvard yell. This march ended at Memorial Hall, where the alumni dinner was served. To see over a thousand strong men, representing all that is best in State, Church, business, and education, with the glow and enthusiasm of college loyalty and college pride,—which has, I think, a peculiar Harvard flavour,—is a sight that does not easily fade from memory.

Among the speakers after dinner were President Eliot, Governor Roger Wolcott, General Miles, Dr. Minot J. Savage, the Hon. Henry Cabot Lodge, and myself. When I was called upon, I said, among other things:—

It would in some measure relieve my embarrassment if I could, even in a slight degree, feel myself worthy of the great honour which you do me to-day. Why you have called me from the Black Belt of the South, from among my humble people, to share in the honours of this occasion, is not for me to explain; and yet it may not be inappropriate for me to suggest that it seems to me that one of the most vital questions that touch our American life is how to bring the strong, wealthy, and learned into helpful touch with the poorest, most ignorant, and humblest, and at the same time make one appreciate the vitalizing, strengthening influence of the other. How shall we make the mansion on yon Beacon Street feel and see the need of the spirits in the lowliest cabin in Alabama cotton-fields or Louisiana sugar-bottoms? This problem Harvard University is solving, not by bringing itself down, but by bringing the masses up.

If my life in the past has meant anything in the lifting up of my people and the bringing about of better relations between your race and mine, I assure you from this day it will mean doubly more. In the economy of God there is but one standard by which an individual can succeed—there is but one for a race. This country demands that every race shall measure itself by the American standard. By it a race must rise or fall, succeed or fail, and in the last analysis mere sentiment counts for little.

During the next half-century and more, my race must continue passing through the severe American crucible. We are to be tested in our patience, our forbearance, our perseverance, our power to endure wrong, to withstand temptations, to economize, to acquire and use skill; in our ability to compete, to succeed in commerce, to disregard the superficial for the real, the appearance for the substance, to be great and yet small, learned and yet simple, high and yet the servant of all.

As this was the first time that a New England university had conferred an honorary degree upon a Negro, it was the occasion of much newspaper comment throughout the country. A correspondent of a New York Paper said:—

When the name of Booker T. Washington was called, and he arose to acknowledge and accept, there was such an outburst of applause as greeted no other name except that of the popular soldier patriot, General Miles. The applause was not studied and stiff, sympathetic and condoling; it was enthusiasm and admiration. Every part of the audience from pit to gallery joined in, and a glow covered the cheeks of those around me, proving sincere appreciation of the rising struggle of an ex-slave and the work he has accomplished for his race.

A Boston paper said, editorially:—

In conferring the honorary degree of Master of Arts upon the Principal of Tuskegee Institute, Harvard University has honoured itself as well as the object of this distinction. The work which Professor Booker T. Washington has accomplished for the education, good citizenship, and popular enlightenment in his chosen field of labour in the South entitles him to rank with our national benefactors. The university which can claim him on its list of sons, whether in regular course or honoris causa, may be proud.

It has been mentioned that Mr. Washington is the first of his race to receive an honorary degree from a New England university. This, in itself, is a distinction. But the degree was not conferred because Mr. Washington is a coloured man, or because he was born in slavery, but because he has shown, by his work for the elevation of the people of the Black Belt of the South, a genius and a broad humanity which count for greatness in any man, whether his skin be white or black.

Another Boston paper said:—

It is Harvard which, first among New England colleges, confers an honorary degree upon a black man. No one who has followed the history of Tuskegee and its work can fail to admire the courage, persistence, and splendid common sense of Booker T. Washington.

Well may Harvard honour the ex-slave, the value of whose services, alike to his race and country, only the future can estimate.

The correspondent of the New York Times wrote:—

All the speeches were enthusiastically received, but the coloured man carried off the oratorical honours, and the applause which broke out when he had finished was vociferous and long-continued.

Soon after I began work at Tuskegee I formed a resolution, in the secret of my heart, that I would try to build up a school that would be of so much service to the country that the President of the United States would one day come to see it. This was, I confess, rather a bold resolution, and for a number of years I kept it hidden in my own thoughts, not daring to share it with any one.

In November, 1897, I made the first move in this direction, and that was in securing a visit from a member of President McKinley's Cabinet, the Hon. James Wilson, Secretary of Agriculture. He came to deliver an address at the formal opening of the Slater-Armstrong Agricultural Building, our first large building to be used for the purpose of giving training to our students in agriculture and kindred branches.

In the fall of 1898 I heard that President McKinley was likely to visit Atlanta, Georgia, for the purpose of taking part in the Peace Jubilee exercises to be held there to commemorate the successful close of the Spanish-American war. At this time I had been hard at work, together with our teachers, for eighteen years, trying to build up a school that we thought would be of service to the Nation, and I determined to make a direct effort to secure a visit from the President and his Cabinet. I went to Washington, and I was not long in the city before I found my way to the White House. When I got there I found the waiting rooms full of people, and my heart began to sink, for I feared there would not be much chance of my seeing the President that day, if at all. But, at any rate, I got an opportunity to see Mr. J. Addison Porter, the secretary to the President, and explained to him my mission. Mr. Porter kindly sent my card directly to the President, and in a few minutes word came from Mr. McKinley that he would see me.

How any man can see so many people of all kinds, with all kinds of errands, and do so much hard work, and still keep himself calm, patient, and fresh for each visitor in the way that President McKinley does, I cannot understand. When I saw the President he kindly thanked me for the work which we were doing at Tuskegee for the interests of the country. I then told him, briefly, the object of my visit. I impressed upon him the fact that a visit from the Chief Executive of the Nation would not only encourage our students and teachers, but would help the entire race. He seemed interested, but did not make a promise to go to Tuskegee, for the reason that his plans about going to Atlanta were not then fully made; but he asked me to call the matter to his attention a few weeks later.

By the middle of the following month the President had definitely decided to attend the Peace Jubilee at Atlanta. I went to Washington again and saw him, with a view of getting him to extend his trip to Tuskegee. On this second visit Mr. Charles W. Hare, a prominent white citizen of Tuskegee, kindly volunteered to accompany me, to reenforce my invitation with one from the white people of Tuskegee and the vicinity.

Just previous to my going to Washington the second time, the country had been excited, and the coloured people greatly depressed, because of several severe race riots which had occurred at different points in the South. As soon as I saw the President, I perceived that his heart was greatly burdened by reason of these race disturbances. Although there were many people waiting to see him, he detained me for some time, discussing the condition and prospects of the race. He remarked several times that he was determined to show his interest and faith in the race, not merely in words, but by acts. When I told him that I thought that at that time scarcely anything would go farther in giving hope and encouragement to the race than the fact that the President of the Nation would be willing to travel one hundred and forty miles out of his way to spend a day at a Negro institution, he seemed deeply impressed.

While I was with the President, a white citizen of Atlanta, a Democrat and an ex-slaveholder, came into the room, and the President asked his opinion as to the wisdom of his going to Tuskegee. Without hesitation the Atlanta man replied that it was the proper thing for him to do. This opinion was reenforced by that friend of the race, Dr. J.L.M. Curry. The President promised that he would visit our school on the 16th of December.

When it became known that the President was going to visit our school, the white citizens of the town of Tuskegee—a mile distant from the school— were as much pleased as were our students and teachers. The white people of this town, including both men and women, began arranging to decorate the town, and to form themselves into committees for the purpose of cooperating with the officers of our school in order that the distinguished visitor might have a fitting reception. I think I never realized before this how much the white people of Tuskegee and vicinity thought of our institution. During the days when we were preparing for the President's reception, dozens of these people came to me and said that, while they did not want to push themselves into prominence, if there was anything they could do to help, or to relieve me personally, I had but to intimate it and they would be only too glad to assist. In fact, the thing that touched me almost as deeply as the visit of the President itself was the deep pride which all classes of citizens in Alabama seemed to take in our work.

The morning of December 16th brought to the little city of Tuskegee such a crowd as it had never seen before. With the President came Mrs. McKinley and all of the Cabinet officers but one; and most of them brought their wives or some members of their families. Several prominent generals came, including General Shafter and General Joseph Wheeler, who were recently returned from the Spanish-American war. There was also a host of newspaper correspondents. The Alabama Legislature was in session in Montgomery at this time. This body passed a resolution to adjourn for the purpose of visiting Tuskegee. Just before the arrival of the President's party the Legislature arrived, headed by the governor and other state officials.

The citizens of Tuskegee had decorated the town from the station to the school in a generous manner. In order to economize in the matter of time, we arranged to have the whole school pass in review before the President. Each student carried a stalk of sugar-cane with some open bolls of cotton fastened to the end of it. Following the students the work of all departments of the school passed in review, displayed on "floats" drawn by horses, mules, and oxen. On these floats we tried to exhibit not only the present work of the school, but to show the contrasts between the old methods of doing things and the new. As an example, we showed the old method of dairying in contrast with the improved methods, the old methods of tilling the soil in contrast with the new, the old methods of cooking and housekeeping in contrast with the new. These floats consumed an hour and a half of time in passing.

In his address in our large, new chapel, which the students had recently completed, the President said, among other things:—

To meet you under such pleasant auspices and to have the opportunity of a personal observation of your work is indeed most gratifying. The Tuskegee Normal and Industrial Institute is ideal in its conception, and has already a large and growing reputation in the country, and is not unknown abroad. I congratulate all who are associated in this undertaking for the good work which it is doing in the education of its students to lead lives of honour and usefulness, thus exalting the race for which it was established.

Nowhere, I think, could a more delightful location have been chosen for this unique educational experiment, which has attracted the attention and won the support even of conservative philanthropists in all sections of the country.

To speak of Tuskegee without paying special tribute to Booker T. Washington's genius and perseverance would be impossible. The inception of this noble enterprise was his, and he deserves high credit for it. His was the enthusiasm and enterprise which made its steady progress possible and established in the institution its present high standard of accomplishment. He has won a worthy reputation as one of the great leaders of his race, widely known and much respected at home and abroad as an accomplished educator, a great orator, and a true philanthropist.

The Hon. John D. Long, the Secretary of the Navy, said in part:—

I cannot make a speech to-day. My heart is too full—full of hope, admiration, and pride for my countrymen of both sections and both colours. I am filled with gratitude and admiration for your work, and from this time forward I shall have absolute confidence in your progress and in the solution of the problem in which you are engaged.

The problem, I say, has been solved. A picture has been presented to-day which should be put upon canvas with the pictures of Washington and Lincoln, and transmitted to future time and generations—a picture which the press of the country should spread broadcast over the land, a most dramatic picture, and that picture is this: The President of the United States standing on this platform; on one side the Governor of Alabama, on the other, completing the trinity, a representative of a race only a few years ago in bondage, the coloured President of the Tuskegee Normal and Industrial Institute.

God bless the President under whose majesty such a scene as that is presented to the American people. God bless the state of Alabama, which is showing that it can deal with this problem for itself. God bless the orator, philanthropist, and disciple of the Great Master—who, if he were on earth, would be doing the same work—Booker T. Washington.

Postmaster General Smith closed the address which he made with these words:—

We have witnessed many spectacles within the last few days. We have seen the magnificent grandeur and the magnificent achievements of one of the great metropolitan cities of the South. We have seen heroes of the war pass by in procession. We have seen floral parades. But I am sure my colleagues will agree with me in saying that we have witnessed no spectacle more impressive and more encouraging, more inspiring for our future, than that which we have witnessed here this morning.

Some days after the President returned to Washington I received the letter which follows:—

Executive Mansion, Washington, Dec. 23, 1899.

Dear Sir: By this mail I take pleasure in sending you engrossed copies of the souvenir of the visit of the President to your institution. These sheets bear the autographs of the President and the members of the Cabinet who accompanied him on the trip. Let me take this opportunity of congratulating you most heartily and sincerely upon the great success of the exercises provided for and entertainment furnished us under your auspices during our visit to Tuskegee. Every feature of the programme was perfectly executed and was viewed or participated in with the heartiest satisfaction by every visitor present. The unique exhibition which you gave of your pupils engaged in their industrial vocations was not only artistic but thoroughly impressive. The tribute paid by the President and his Cabinet to your work was none too high, and forms a most encouraging augury, I think, for the future prosperity of your institution. I cannot close without assuring you that the modesty shown by yourself in the exercises was most favourably commented upon by all the members of our party.

With best wishes for the continued advance of your most useful and patriotic undertaking, kind personal regards, and the compliments of the season, believe me, always,

Very sincerely yours,

John Addison Porter,

Secretary to the President.

To President Booker T. Washington, Tuskegee Normal and Industrial Institute, Tuskegee, Ala.

Twenty years have now passed since I made the first humble effort at Tuskegee, in a broken-down shanty and an old hen-house, without owning a dollar's worth of property, and with but one teacher and thirty students. At the present time the institution owns twenty-three hundred acres of land, one thousand of which are under cultivation each year, entirely by student labour. There are now upon the grounds, counting large and small, sixty-six buildings; and all except four of these have been almost wholly erected by the labour of our students. While the students are at work upon the land and in erecting buildings, they are taught, by competent instructors, the latest methods of agriculture and the trades connected with building.

There are in constant operation at the school, in connection with thorough academic and religious training, thirty industrial departments. All of these teach industries at which our men and women can find immediate employment as soon as they leave the institution. The only difficulty now is that the demand for our graduates from both white and black people in the South is so great that we cannot supply more than one-half the persons for whom applications come to us. Neither have we the buildings nor the money for current expenses to enable us to admit to the school more than one-half the young men and women who apply to us for admission.

In our industrial teaching we keep three things in mind: first, that the student shall be so educated that he shall be enabled to meet conditions as they exist now, in the part of the South where he lives—in a word, to be able to do the thing which the world wants done; second, that every student who graduates from the school shall have enough skill, coupled with intelligence and moral character, to enable him to make a living for himself and others; third, to send every graduate out feeling and knowing that labour is dignified and beautiful—to make each one love labour instead of trying to escape it. In addition to the agricultural training which we give to young men, and the training given to our girls in all the usual domestic employments, we now train a number of girls in agriculture each year. These girls are taught gardening, fruit-growing, dairying, bee-culture, and poultry-raising.

While the institution is in no sense denominational, we have a department known as the Phelps Hall Bible Training School, in which a number of students are prepared for the ministry and other forms of Christian work, especially work in the country districts. What is equally important, each one of the students works half of each day at some industry, in order to get skill and the love of work, so that when he goes out from the institution he is prepared to set the people with whom he goes to labour a proper example in the matter of industry.

The value of our property is now over $700,000. If we add to this our endowment fund, which at present is $1,000,000, the value of the total property is now $1,700,000. Aside from the need for more buildings and for money for current expenses, the endowment fund should be increased to at least $3,000,000. The annual current expenses are now about $150,000. The greater part of this I collect each year by going from door to door and from house to house. All of our property is free from mortgage, and is deeded to an undenominational board of trustees who have the control of the institution.

From thirty students the number has grown to fourteen hundred, coming from twenty-seven states and territories, from Africa, Cuba, Porto Rico, Jamaica, and other foreign countries. In our departments there are one hundred and ten officers and instructors; and if we add the families of our instructors, we have a constant population upon our grounds of not far from seventeen hundred people.

I have often been asked how we keep so large a body of people together, and at the same time keep them out of mischief. There are two answers: that the men and women who come to us for an education are in earnest; and that everybody is kept busy. The following outline of our daily work will testify to this:—

5 a.m., rising bell; 5.50 a.m., warning breakfast bell; 6 a.m., breakfast bell; 6.20 a.m., breakfast over; 6.20 to 6.50 a.m., rooms are cleaned; 6.50, work bell; 7.30, morning study hours; 8.20, morning school bell; 8.25, inspection of young men's toilet in ranks; 8.40, devotional exercises in chapel; 8.55, "five minutes with the daily news;" 9 a.m., class work begins; 12, class work closes; 12.15 p.m., dinner; 1 p.m., work bell; 1.30 p.m., class work begins; 3.30 p.m., class work ends; 5.30 p.m., bell to "knock off" work; 6 p.m., supper; 7.10 p.m., evening prayers; 7.30 p.m., evening study hours; 8.45 p.m., evening study hour closes; 9.20 p.m., warning retiring bell; 9.30 p.m., retiring bell.

We try to keep constantly in mind the fact that the worth of the school is to be judged by its graduates. Counting those who have finished the full course, together with those who have taken enough training to enable them to do reasonably good work, we can safely say that at least six thousand men and women from Tuskegee are now at work in different parts of the South; men and women who, by their own example or by direct efforts, are showing the masses of our race now to improve their material, educational, and moral and religious life. What is equally important, they are exhibiting a degree of common sense and self-control which is causing better relations to exist between the races, and is causing the Southern white man to learn to believe in the value of educating the men and women of my race. Aside from this, there is the influence that is constantly being exerted through the mothers' meeting and the plantation work conducted by Mrs. Washington.

Wherever our graduates go, the changes which soon begin to appear in the buying of land, improving homes, saving money, in education, and in high moral characters are remarkable. Whole communities are fast being revolutionized through the instrumentality of these men and women.

Ten years ago I organized at Tuskegee the first Negro Conference. This is an annual gathering which now brings to the school eight or nine hundred representative men and women of the race, who come to spend a day in finding out what the actual industrial, mental, and moral conditions of the people are, and in forming plans for improvement. Out from this central Negro Conference at Tuskegee have grown numerous state and local conferences which are doing the same kind of work. As a result of the influence of these gatherings, one delegate reported at the last annual meeting that ten families in his community had bought and paid for homes.

On the day following the annual Negro Conference, there is the "Workers' Conference." This is composed of officers and teachers who are engaged in educational work in the larger institutions in the South. The Negro Conference furnishes a rare opportunity for these workers to study the real condition of the rank and file of the people.

In the summer of 1900, with the assistance of such prominent coloured men as Mr. T. Thomas Fortune, who has always upheld my hands in every effort, I organized the National Negro Business League, which held its first meeting in Boston, and brought together for the first time a large number of the coloured men who are engaged in various lines of trade or business in different parts of the United States. Thirty states were represented at our first meeting. Out of this national meeting grew state and local business leagues.

In addition to looking after the executive side of the work at Tuskegee, and raising the greater part of the money for the support of the school, I cannot seem to escape the duty of answering at least a part of the calls which come to me unsought to address Southern white audiences and audiences of my own race, as well as frequent gatherings in the North. As to how much of my time is spent in this way, the following clipping from a Buffalo (N.Y.) paper will tell. This has reference to an occasion when I spoke before the National Educational Association in that city.

Booker T. Washington, the foremost educator among the coloured people of the world, was a very busy man from the time he arrived in the city the other night from the West and registered at the Iroquois. He had hardly removed the stains of travel when it was time to partake of supper. Then he held a public levee in the parlours of the Iroquois until eight o'clock. During that time he was greeted by over two hundred eminent teachers and educators from all parts of the United States. Shortly after eight o'clock he was driven in a carriage to Music Hall, and in one hour and a half he made two ringing addresses, to as many as five thousand people, on Negro education. Then Mr. Washington was taken in charge by a delegation of coloured citizens, headed by the Rev. Mr. Watkins, and hustled off to a small informal reception, arranged in honour of the visitor by the people of his race.

Nor can I, in addition to making these addresses, escape the duty of calling the attention of the South and of the country in general, through the medium of the press, to matters that pertain to the interests of both races. This, for example, I have done in regard to the evil habit of lynching. When the Louisiana State Constitutional Convention was in session, I wrote an open letter to that body pleading for justice for the race. In all such efforts I have received warm and hearty support from the Southern newspapers, as well as from those in all other parts of the country.

Despite superficial and temporary signs which might lead one to entertain a contrary opinion, there was never a time when I felt more hopeful for the race than I do at the present. The great human law that in the end recognizes and rewards merit is everlasting and universal. The outside world does not know, neither can it appreciate, the struggle that is constantly going on in the hearts of both the Southern white people and their former slaves to free themselves from racial prejudice; and while both races are thus struggling they should have the sympathy, the support, and the forbearance of the rest of the world.

As I write the closing words of this autobiography I find myself—not by design—in the city of Richmond, Virginia: the city which only a few decades ago was the capital of the Southern Confederacy, and where, about twenty-five years ago, because of my poverty I slept night after night under a sidewalk.

This time I am in Richmond as the guest of the coloured people of the city; and came at their request to deliver an address last night to both races in the Academy of Music, the largest and finest audience room in the city. This was the first time that the coloured people had ever been permitted to use this hall.

The day before I came, the City Council passed a vote to attend the meeting in a body to hear me speak. The state Legislature, including the House of Delegates and the Senate, also passed a unanimous vote to attend in a body. In the presence of hundreds of coloured people, many distinguished white citizens, the City Council, the state Legislature, and state officials, I delivered my message, which was one of hope and cheer; and from the bottom of my heart I thanked both races for this welcome back to the state that gave me birth.

THE SOULS OF BLACK FOLK

William Edward Burghardt Du Bois

SANAGE
PUBLISHING HOUSE

William Edward Burghardt Du Bois (February 23, 1868 – August 27, 1963) was an American sociologist, socialist, historian, civil rights activist, Pan-Africanist, author, writer and editor.

Throughout his lifetime, he wore the hats of an author, writer, editor, civil rights activist, historian, and sociologist. He was the first African-America to earn a doctoral degree at Harvard University and was one of the founders of the National Association for the Advancement of Colored People (NAACP).

THE FORETHOUGHT

Herein lie buried many things which if read with patience may show the strange meaning of being black here at the dawning of the Twentieth Century. This meaning is not without interest to you, Gentle Reader; for the problem of the Twentieth Century is the problem of the color line. I pray you, then, receive my little book in all charity, studying my words with me, forgiving mistake and foible for sake of the faith and passion that is in me, and seeking the grain of truth hidden there.

I have sought here to sketch, in vague, uncertain outline, the spiritual world in which ten thousand thousand Americans live and strive. First, in two chapters I have tried to show what Emancipation meant to them, and what was its aftermath. In a third chapter I have pointed out the slow rise of personal leadership, and criticized candidly the leader who bears the chief burden of his race to-day. Then, in two other chapters I have sketched in swift outline the two worlds within and without the Veil, and thus have come to the central problem of training men for life. Venturing now into deeper detail, I have in two chapters studied the struggles of the massed millions of the black peasantry, and in another have sought to make clear the present relations of the sons of master and man. Leaving, then, the white world, I have stepped within the Veil, raising it that you may view faintly its deeper recesses,—the meaning of its religion, the passion of its human sorrow, and the struggle of its greater souls. All this I have ended with a tale twice told but seldom written, and a chapter of song.

Some of these thoughts of mine have seen the light before in other guise. For kindly consenting to their republication here, in altered and extended form, I must thank the publishers of the Atlantic Monthly, The World's Work, the Dial, The New World, and the Annals of the American Academy of Political and Social Science. Before each chapter, as now printed, stands a bar of the Sorrow Songs,—some echo of haunting melody from the only American music which welled up from black souls in the dark past. And, finally, need I add that I who speak here am bone of the bone and flesh of the flesh of them that live within the Veil?

W.E.B Du B.

ATLANTA, GA., FEB. 1, 1903.

1. OF OUR SPIRITUAL STRIVINGS

O water, voice of my heart, crying in the sand,
All night long crying with a mournful cry,
As I lie and listen, and cannot understand
The voice of my heart in my side or the voice of the sea,
O water, crying for rest, is it I, is it I?
All night long the water is crying to me.

Unresting water, there shall never be rest
Till the last moon droop and the last tide fail,
And the fire of the end begin to burn in the west;
And the heart shall be weary and wonder and cry like the
sea, All life long crying without avail,
As the water all night long is crying to me.

ARTHUR SYMONS.

Between me and the other world there is ever an unasked question: unasked by some through feelings of delicacy; by others through the difficulty of rightly framing it. All, nevertheless, flutter round it. They approach me in a half-hesitant sort of way, eye me curiously or compassionately, and then, instead of saying directly, How does it feel to be a problem? they say, I know an excellent colored man in my town; or, I fought at Mechanicsville; or, Do not these Southern outrages make your blood boil? At these I smile, or am interested, or reduce the boiling to a simmer, as the occasion may require. To the real question, How does it feel to be a problem? I answer seldom a word.

And yet, being a problem is a strange experience,—peculiar even for one who has never been anything else, save perhaps in babyhood and in Europe. It is in the early days of rollicking boyhood that the revelation first bursts upon one, all in a day, as it were. I remember well when the shadow swept across me. I was a little thing, away up in the hills of New England, where the dark Housatonic winds between Hoosac and Taghkanic to the sea. In a wee wooden schoolhouse, something put it into the boys' and girls' heads to buy gorgeous visiting-cards—ten cents a package—and exchange. The exchange was merry, till one girl, a tall newcomer, refused my card,— refused it peremptorily, with a glance. Then it dawned upon me with a certain suddenness that I was different from the others; or like, mayhap, in heart and life and longing, but shut out from their world by a vast veil. I had thereafter no desire to tear down that veil, to creep through; I held all beyond it in common contempt, and lived above it in a region of blue sky and great wandering shadows. That sky was bluest when I could beat my mates at examination-time, or beat them at a foot-race, or even beat their stringy heads. Alas, with the years all this fine contempt began to fade; for the words I longed for, and all their dazzling opportunities, were theirs, not mine. But they should not keep these prizes, I said; some, all, I would wrest from them. Just how I would do it I could never decide: by reading law, by healing the sick, by telling the wonderful tales that swam in my head,— some way. With other black boys the strife was not so fiercely sunny: their youth shrunk into tasteless sycophancy, or into silent hatred of the pale world about them and mocking distrust of everything white; or wasted itself in a bitter cry, Why did God make me an outcast and a stranger in mine own house? The shades of the prison-house closed round about us all: walls strait and stubborn to the whitest, but relentlessly narrow, tall, and unscalable to sons of night who must plod darkly on in resignation, or beat unavailing palms against the stone, or steadily, half hopelessly, watch the streak of blue above.

After the Egyptian and Indian, the Greek and Roman, the Teuton and Mongolian, the Negro is a sort of seventh son, born with a veil, and gifted with second-sight in this American world,—a world which yields him no true self-consciousness, but only lets him see himself through the revelation of the other world. It is a peculiar sensation, this double-consciousness, this sense of always looking at one's self through the eyes of others, of measuring one's soul by the tape of a world that looks on in amused contempt and pity. One ever feels his twoness,—an American, a Negro; two souls, two thoughts, two unreconciled strivings; two warring ideals in one dark body, whose dogged strength alone keeps it from being torn asunder.

The history of the American Negro is the history of this strife,—this longing to attain self-conscious manhood, to merge his double self into a better and truer self. In this merging he wishes neither of the older selves to be lost. He would not Africanize America, for America has too much to teach the world and Africa. He would not bleach his Negro soul in a flood of white Americanism, for he knows that Negro blood has a message for the world. He simply wishes to make it possible for a man to be both a Negro and an American, without being cursed and spit upon by his fellows, without having the doors of Opportunity closed roughly in his face.

This, then, is the end of his striving: to be a co-worker in the kingdom of culture, to escape both death and isolation, to husband and use his best powers and his latent genius. These powers of body and mind have in the past been strangely wasted, dispersed, or forgotten. The shadow of a mighty Negro past flits through the tale of Ethiopia the Shadowy and of Egypt the Sphinx. Through history, the powers of single black men flash here and there like falling stars, and die sometimes before the world has rightly gauged their brightness. Here in America, in the few days since Emancipation, the black man's turning hither and thither in hesitant and doubtful striving has often made his very strength to lose effectiveness, to seem like absence of power, like weakness. And yet it is not weakness,—it is the contradiction of double aims. The double-aimed struggle of the black artisan—on the one hand to escape white contempt for a nation of mere hewers of wood and drawers of water, and on the other hand to plough and nail and dig for a poverty-stricken horde—could only result in making him a poor craftsman, for he had but half a heart in either cause. By the poverty and ignorance of his people, the Negro minister or doctor was tempted toward quackery and demagogy; and by the criticism of the other world, toward ideals that made him ashamed of his lowly tasks. The would-be black savant was confronted by the paradox that the knowledge his people needed was a twice-told tale to his white neighbors, while the knowledge which would teach the white world was Greek to his own flesh and blood. The innate love of harmony and beauty that set the ruder souls of his people a-dancing and a-singing raised but confusion and doubt in the soul of the black artist; for the beauty revealed to him was the soul-beauty of a race which his larger audience despised, and he could not articulate the message of another people. This waste of double aims, this seeking to satisfy two unreconciled ideals, has wrought sad havoc with the courage and faith and deeds of ten thousand thousand people,—has sent them often wooing false gods and invoking false means of salvation, and at times has even seemed about to make them ashamed of themselves.

Away back in the days of bondage they thought to see in one divine event the end of all doubt and disappointment; few men ever worshipped Freedom with half such unquestioning faith as did the American Negro for two centuries. To him, so far as he thought and dreamed, slavery was indeed the sum of all villainies, the cause of all sorrow, the root of all prejudice; Emancipation was the key to a promised land of sweeter beauty than ever stretched before the eyes of wearied Israelites. In song and exhortation swelled one refrain—Liberty; in his tears and curses the God he implored had Freedom in his right hand. At last it came,—suddenly, fearfully, like a dream. With one wild carnival of blood and passion came the message in his own plaintive cadences:—

"Shout, O children!

Shout, you're free!

For God has bought your liberty!"

Years have passed away since then,—ten, twenty, forty; forty years of national life, forty years of renewal and development, and yet the swarthy spectre sits in its accustomed seat at the Nation's feast. In vain do we cry to this our vastest social problem:—

"Take any shape but that, and my firm

nerves Shall never tremble!"

The Nation has not yet found peace from its sins; the freedman has not yet found in freedom his promised land. Whatever of good may have come in these years of change, the shadow of a deep disappointment rests upon the Negro people,—a disappointment all the more bitter because the unattained ideal was unbounded save by the simple ignorance of a lowly people.

The first decade was merely a prolongation of the vain search for freedom, the boon that seemed ever barely to elude their grasp,—like a tantalizing will-o'-the-wisp, maddening and misleading the headless host. The holocaust of war, the terrors of the Ku-Klux Klan, the lies of carpet-baggers, the disorganization of industry, and the contradictory advice of friends and foes, left the bewildered serf with no new watchword beyond the old cry for freedom. As the time flew, however, he began to grasp a new idea. The ideal of liberty demanded for its attainment powerful means, and these the Fifteenth Amendment gave him. The ballot, which before he had looked upon as a visible sign of freedom, he now regarded as the chief means of gaining and perfecting the liberty with which war had partially endowed him. And why not? Had not votes made war and emancipated millions? Had not votes enfranchised the freedmen? Was anything impossible to a power that had done all this? A million black men started with renewed zeal to vote themselves into the kingdom. So the decade flew away, the revolution of 1876 came, and left the half-free serf weary, wondering, but still inspired. Slowly but steadily, in the following years, a new vision began gradually to replace the dream of political power,—a powerful movement, the rise of another ideal to guide the unguided, another pillar of fire by night after a clouded day. It was the ideal of "book-learning"; the curiosity, born of compulsory ignorance, to know and test the power of the cabalistic letters of the white man, the longing to know. Here at last seemed to have been discovered the mountain path to Canaan; longer than the highway of Emancipation and law, steep and rugged, but straight, leading to heights high enough to overlook life.

Up the new path the advance guard toiled, slowly, heavily, doggedly; only those who have watched and guided the faltering feet, the misty minds, the dull understandings, of the dark pupils of these schools know how faithfully, how piteously, this people strove to learn. It was weary work. The cold statistician wrote down the inches of progress here and there, noted also where here and there a foot had slipped or some one had fallen. To the tired climbers, the horizon was ever dark, the mists were often cold, the Canaan was always dim and far away. If, however, the vistas disclosed as yet no goal, no resting-place, little but flattery and criticism, the journey at least gave leisure for reflection and self-examination; it changed the child of Emancipation to the youth with dawning self-consciousness, self-realization, self-respect. In those sombre forests of his striving his own soul rose before him, and he saw himself,—darkly as through a veil; and yet he saw in himself some faint revelation of his power, of his mission. He began to have a dim feeling that, to attain his place in the world, he must be himself, and not another. For the first time he sought to analyze the burden he bore upon his back, that dead-weight of social degradation partially masked behind a half-named Negro problem. He felt his poverty; without a cent, without a home, without land, tools, or savings, he had entered into competition with rich, landed, skilled neighbors. To be a poor man is hard, but to be a poor race in a land of dollars is the very bottom of hardships. He felt the weight of his ignorance,—not simply of letters, but of life, of business, of the humanities; the accumulated sloth and shirking and awkwardness of decades and centuries shackled his hands and feet. Nor was his burden all poverty and ignorance. The red stain of bastardy, which two centuries of systematic legal defilement of Negro women had stamped upon his race, meant not only the loss of ancient African chastity, but also the hereditary weight of a mass of corruption from white adulterers, threatening almost the obliteration of the Negro home.

A people thus handicapped ought not to be asked to race with the world, but rather allowed to give all its time and thought to its own social problems. But alas! while sociologists gleefully count his bastards and his prostitutes, the very soul of the toiling, sweating black man is darkened by the shadow of a vast despair. Men call the shadow prejudice, and learnedly explain it as the natural defence of culture against barbarism, learning against ignorance, purity against crime, the "higher" against the "lower" races. To which the Negro cries Amen! and swears that to so much of this strange prejudice as is founded on just homage to civilization, culture, righteousness, and progress, he humbly bows and meekly does obeisance. But before that nameless prejudice that leaps beyond all this he stands helpless, dismayed, and well-nigh speechless; before that personal disrespect and mockery, the ridicule and systematic humiliation, the distortion of fact and wanton license of fancy, the cynical ignoring of the better and the boisterous welcoming of the worse, the all-pervading desire to inculcate disdain for everything black, from Toussaint to the devil,— before this there rises a sickening despair that would disarm and discourage any nation save that black host to whom "discouragement" is an unwritten word.

But the facing of so vast a prejudice could not but bring the inevitable self-questioning, self-disparagement, and lowering of ideals which ever accompany repression and breed in an atmosphere of contempt and hate. Whisperings and portents came home upon the four winds: Lo! we are diseased and dying, cried the dark hosts; we cannot write, our voting is vain; what need of education, since we must always cook and serve? And the Nation echoed and enforced this self-criticism, saying: Be content to be servants, and nothing more; what need of higher culture for half-men? Away with the black man's ballot, by force or fraud,—and behold the suicide of a race! Nevertheless, out of the evil came something of good,—the more careful adjustment of education to real life, the clearer perception of the Negroes' social responsibilities, and the sobering realization of the meaning of progress.

So dawned the time of Sturm und Drang: storm and stress to-day rocks our little boat on the mad waters of the world-sea; there is within and without the sound of conflict, the burning of body and rending of soul; inspiration strives with doubt, and faith with vain questionings. The bright ideals of the past,—physical freedom, political power, the training of brains and the training of hands,—all these in turn have waxed and waned, until even the last grows dim and overcast. Are they all wrong,—all false? No, not that, but each alone was over-simple and incomplete,—the dreams of a credulous race-childhood, or the fond imaginings of the other world which does not know and does not want to know our power. To be really true, all these ideals must be melted and welded into one. The training of the schools we need to-day more than ever,—the training of deft hands, quick eyes and ears, and above all the broader, deeper, higher culture of gifted minds and pure hearts. The power of the ballot we need in sheer self-defence,—else what shall save us from a second slavery? Freedom, too, the long-sought, we still seek,—the freedom of life and limb, the freedom to work and think, the freedom to love and aspire. Work, culture, liberty,—all these we need, not singly but together, not successively but together, each growing and aiding each, and all striving toward that vaster ideal that swims before the Negro people, the ideal of human brotherhood, gained through the unifying ideal of Race; the ideal of fostering and developing the traits and talents of the

Negro, not in opposition to or contempt for other races, but rather in large conformity to the greater ideals of the American Republic, in order that some day on American soil two world-races may give each to each those characteristics both so sadly lack. We the darker ones come even now not altogether empty-handed: there are to-day no truer exponents of the pure human spirit of the Declaration of Independence than the American Negroes; there is no true American music but the wild sweet melodies of the Negro slave; the American fairy tales and folklore are Indian and African; and, all in all, we black men seem the sole oasis of simple faith and reverence in a dusty desert of dollars and smartness. Will America be poorer if she replace her brutal dyspeptic blundering with light-hearted but determined Negro humility? or her coarse and cruel wit with loving jovial good-humor? or her vulgar music with the soul of the Sorrow Songs?

Merely a concrete test of the underlying principles of the great republic is the Negro Problem, and the spiritual striving of the freedmen's sons is the travail of souls whose burden is almost beyond the measure of their strength, but who bear it in the name of an historic race, in the name of this the land of their fathers' fathers, and in the name of human opportunity.

And now what I have briefly sketched in large outline let me on coming pages tell again in many ways, with loving emphasis and deeper detail, that men may listen to the striving in the souls of black folk.

2. OF THE DAWN OF FREEDOM

Careless seems the great Avenger;
History's lessons but record
One death-grapple in the darkness
'Twixt old systems and the Word;
Truth forever on the scaffold,
Wrong forever on the throne;
Yet that scaffold sways the future,
And behind the dim unknown
Standeth God within the shadow
Keeping watch above His own.

LOWELL.

The problem of the twentieth century is the problem of the color-line,—the relation of the darker to the lighter races of men in Asia and Africa, in America and the islands of the sea. It was a phase of this problem that caused the Civil War; and however much they who marched South and North in 1861 may have fixed on the technical points, of union and local autonomy as a shibboleth, all nevertheless knew, as we know, that the question of Negro slavery was the real cause of the conflict. Curious it was, too, how this deeper question ever forced itself to the surface despite effort and disclaimer. No sooner had Northern armies touched Southern soil than this old question, newly guised, sprang from the earth,—What shall be done with Negroes? Peremptory military commands this way and that, could not answer the query; the Emancipation Proclamation seemed but to broaden and intensify the difficulties; and the War Amendments made the Negro problems of to-day.

It is the aim of this essay to study the period of history from 1861 to 1872 so far as it relates to the American Negro. In effect, this tale of the dawn of Freedom is an account of that government of men called the Freedmen's Bureau,—one of the most singular and interesting of the attempts made by a great nation to grapple with vast problems of race and social condition.

The war has naught to do with slaves, cried Congress, the President, and the Nation; and yet no sooner had the armies, East and West, penetrated Virginia and Tennessee than fugitive slaves appeared within their lines. They came at night, when the flickering camp-fires shone like vast unsteady stars along the black horizon: old men and thin, with gray and tufted hair; women with frightened eyes, dragging whimpering hungry children; men and girls, stalwart and gaunt,—a horde of starving vagabonds, homeless, helpless, and pitiable, in their dark distress. Two methods of treating these newcomers seemed equally logical to opposite sorts of minds. Ben Butler, in Virginia, quickly declared slave property contraband of war, and put the fugitives to work; while Fremont, in Missouri, declared the slaves free under martial law. Butler's action was approved, but Fremont's was hastily countermanded, and his successor, Halleck, saw things differently. "Hereafter," he commanded, "no slaves should be allowed to come into your lines at all; if any come without your knowledge, when owners call for them deliver them." Such a policy was difficult to enforce; some of the black refugees declared themselves freemen, others showed that their masters had deserted them, and still others were captured with forts and plantations. Evidently, too, slaves were a source of strength to the Confederacy, and were being used as laborers and producers. "They constitute a military resource," wrote Secretary Cameron, late in 1861; "and being such, that they should not be turned over to the enemy is too plain to discuss." So gradually the tone of the army chiefs changed; Congress forbade the rendition of fugitives, and Butler's "contrabands" were welcomed as military laborers. This complicated rather than solved the problem, for now the scattering fugitives became a steady stream, which flowed faster as the armies marched.

Then the long-headed man with care-chiselled face who sat in the White House saw the inevitable, and emancipated the slaves of rebels on New Year's, 1863. A month later Congress called earnestly for the Negro soldiers whom the act of July, 1862, had half grudgingly allowed to enlist.

Thus the barriers were levelled and the deed was done. The stream of fugitives swelled to a flood, and anxious army officers kept inquiring: "What must be done with slaves, arriving almost daily? Are we to find food and shelter for women and children?"

It was a Pierce of Boston who pointed out the way, and thus became in a sense the founder of the Freedmen's Bureau. He was a firm friend of Secretary Chase; and when, in 1861, the care of slaves and abandoned lands devolved upon the Treasury officials, Pierce was specially detailed from the ranks to study the conditions. First, he cared for the refugees at Fortress Monroe; and then, after Sherman had captured Hilton Head, Pierce was sent there to found his Port Royal experiment of making free workingmen out of slaves. Before his experiment was barely started, however, the problem of the fugitives had assumed such proportions that it was taken from the hands of the over-burdened Treasury Department and given to the army officials. Already centres of massed freedmen were forming at Fortress Monroe, Washington, New Orleans, Vicksburg and Corinth, Columbus, Ky., and Cairo, Ill., as well as at Port Royal. Army chaplains found here new and fruitful fields; "superintendents of contrabands" multiplied, and some attempt at systematic work was made by enlisting the able-bodied men and giving work to the others.

Then came the Freedmen's Aid societies, born of the touching appeals from Pierce and from these other centres of distress. There was the American Missionary Association, sprung from the Amistad, and now full-grown for work; the various church organizations, the National Freedmen's Relief Association, the American Freedmen's Union, the Western Freedmen's Aid Commission,—in all fifty or more active organizations, which sent clothes, money, school-books, and teachers southward. All they did was needed, for the destitution of the freedmen was often reported as "too appalling for belief," and the situation was daily growing worse rather than better.

And daily, too, it seemed more plain that this was no ordinary matter of temporary relief, but a national crisis; for here loomed a labor problem of vast dimensions. Masses of Negroes stood idle, or, if they worked spasmodically, were never sure of pay; and if perchance they received pay, squandered the new thing thoughtlessly. In these and other ways were camp-life and the new liberty demoralizing the freedmen. The broader economic organization thus clearly demanded sprang up here and there as accident and local conditions determined. Here it was that Pierce's Port Royal plan of leased plantations and guided workmen pointed out the rough way. In Washington the military governor, at the urgent appeal of the superintendent, opened confiscated estates to the cultivation of the fugitives, and there in the shadow of the dome gathered black farm villages. General Dix gave over estates to the freedmen of Fortress Monroe, and so on, South and West. The government and benevolent societies furnished the means of cultivation, and the Negro turned again slowly to work. The systems of control, thus started, rapidly grew, here and there, into strange little governments, like that of General Banks in Louisiana, with its ninety thousand black subjects, its fifty thousand guided laborers, and its annual budget of one hundred thousand dollars and more. It made out four thousand pay-rolls a year, registered all freedmen, inquired into grievances and redressed them, laid and collected taxes, and established a system of public schools. So, too, Colonel Eaton, the superintendent of Tennessee and Arkansas, ruled over one hundred thousand freedmen, leased and cultivated seven thousand acres of cotton land, and fed ten thousand paupers a year. In South Carolina was General Saxton, with his deep interest in black folk. He succeeded Pierce and the Treasury officials, and sold forfeited estates, leased abandoned plantations, encouraged schools, and received from Sherman, after that terribly picturesque march to the sea, thousands of the wretched camp followers.

Three characteristic things one might have seen in Sherman's raid through Georgia, which threw the new situation in shadowy relief: the Conqueror, the Conquered, and the Negro. Some see all significance in the grim front of the destroyer, and some in the bitter sufferers of the Lost Cause. But to me neither soldier nor fugitive speaks with so deep a meaning as that dark human cloud that clung like remorse on the rear of those swift columns, swelling at times to half their size, almost engulfing and choking them. In vain were they ordered back, in vain were bridges hewn from beneath their feet; on they trudged and writhed and surged, until they rolled into Savannah, a starved and naked horde of tens of thousands. There too came the characteristic military remedy: "The islands from Charleston south, the abandoned rice-fields along the rivers for thirty miles back from the sea, and the country bordering the St. John's River, Florida, are reserved and set apart for the settlement of Negroes now made free by act of war." So read the celebrated "Field-order Number Fifteen."

All these experiments, orders, and systems were bound to attract and perplex the government and the nation. Directly after the Emancipation Proclamation, Representative Eliot had introduced a bill creating a Bureau of Emancipation; but it was never reported. The following June a committee of inquiry, appointed by the Secretary of War, reported in favor of a temporary bureau for the "improvement, protection, and employment of refugee freedmen," on much the same lines as were afterwards followed. Petitions came in to President Lincoln from distinguished citizens and organizations, strongly urging a comprehensive and unified plan of dealing with the freedmen, under a bureau which should be "charged with the study of plans and execution of measures for easily guiding, and in every way judiciously and humanely aiding, the passage of our emancipated and yet to be emancipated blacks from the old condition of forced labor to their new state of voluntary industry."

Some half-hearted steps were taken to accomplish this, in part, by putting the whole matter again in charge of the special Treasury agents. Laws of 1863 and 1864 directed them to take charge of and lease abandoned lands for periods not exceeding twelve months, and to "provide in such leases, or otherwise, for the employment and general welfare" of the freedmen. Most of the army officers greeted this as a welcome relief from perplexing "Negro affairs," and Secretary Fessenden, July 29, 1864, issued an excellent system of regulations, which were afterward closely followed by General Howard. Under Treasury agents, large quantities of land were leased in the Mississippi Valley, and many Negroes were employed; but in August, 1864, the new regulations were suspended for reasons of "public policy," and the army was again in control.

Meanwhile Congress had turned its attention to the subject; and in March the House passed a bill by a majority of two establishing a Bureau for Freedmen in the War Department. Charles Sumner, who had charge of the bill in the Senate, argued that freedmen and abandoned lands ought to be under the same department, and reported a substitute for the House bill attaching the Bureau to the Treasury Department. This bill passed, but too late for action by the House. The debates wandered over the whole policy of the administration and the general question of slavery, without touching very closely the specific merits of the measure in hand. Then the national election took place; and the administration, with a vote of renewed confidence from the country, addressed itself to the matter more seriously. A conference between the two branches of Congress agreed upon a carefully drawn measure which contained the chief provisions of Sumner's bill, but made the proposed organization a department independent of both the War and the Treasury officials. The bill was conservative, giving the new department "general superintendence of all freedmen." Its purpose was to "establish regulations" for them, protect them, lease them lands, adjust their wages, and appear in civil and military courts as their "next friend." There were many limitations attached to the powers thus granted, and the organization was made permanent. Nevertheless, the Senate defeated the bill, and a new conference committee was appointed. This committee reported a new bill, February 28, which was whirled through just as the session closed, and became the act of 1865 establishing in the War Department a "Bureau of Refugees, Freedmen, and Abandoned Lands."

This last compromise was a hasty bit of legislation, vague and uncertain in outline. A Bureau was created, "to continue during the present War of Rebellion, and for one year thereafter," to which was given "the supervision and management of all abandoned lands and the control of all subjects relating to refugees and freedmen," under "such rules and regulations as may be presented by the head of the Bureau and approved by the President." A Commissioner, appointed by the President and Senate, was to control the Bureau, with an office force not exceeding ten clerks. The President might also appoint assistant commissioners in the seceded States, and to all these offices military officials might be detailed at regular pay. The Secretary of War could issue rations, clothing, and fuel to the destitute, and all abandoned property was placed in the hands of the Bureau for eventual lease and sale to ex-slaves in forty-acre parcels.

Thus did the United States government definitely assume charge of the emancipated Negro as the ward of the nation. It was a tremendous undertaking. Here at a stroke of the pen was erected a government of millions of men,—and not ordinary men either, but black men emasculated by a peculiarly complete system of slavery, centuries old; and now, suddenly, violently, they come into a new birthright, at a time of war and passion, in the midst of the stricken and embittered population of their former masters. Any man might well have hesitated to assume charge of such a work, with vast responsibilities, indefinite powers, and limited resources. Probably no one but a soldier would have answered such a call promptly; and, indeed, no one but a soldier could be called, for Congress had appropriated no money for salaries and expenses.

Less than a month after the weary Emancipator passed to his rest, his successor assigned Major-Gen. Oliver O. Howard to duty as Commissioner of the new Bureau. He was a Maine man, then only thirty-five years of age. He had marched with Sherman to the sea, had fought well at Gettysburg, and but the year before had been assigned to the command of the Department of Tennessee. An honest man, with too much faith in human nature, little aptitude for business and intricate detail, he had had large opportunity of becoming acquainted at first hand with much of the work before him. And of that work it has been truly said that "no approximately correct history of civilization can ever be written which does not throw out in bold relief, as one of the great landmarks of political and social progress, the organization and administration of the Freedmen's Bureau."

On May 12, 1865, Howard was appointed; and he assumed the duties of his office promptly on the 15th, and began examining the field of work. A curious mess he looked upon: little despotisms, communistic experiments, slavery, peonage, business speculations, organized charity, unorganized almsgiving,—all reeling on under the guise of helping the freedmen, and all enshrined in the smoke and blood of the war and the cursing and silence of angry men. On May 19 the new government—for a government it really was—issued its constitution; commissioners were to be appointed in each of the seceded states, who were to take charge of "all subjects relating to refugees and freedmen," and all relief and rations were to be given by their consent alone. The Bureau invited continued cooperation with benevolent societies, and declared: "It will be the object of all commissioners to introduce practicable systems of compensated labor," and to establish schools. Forthwith nine assistant commissioners were appointed. They were to hasten to their fields of work; seek gradually to close relief establishments, and make the destitute self-supporting; act as courts of law where there were no courts, or where Negroes were not recognized in them as free; establish the institution of marriage among ex-slaves, and keep records; see that freedmen were free to choose their employers, and help in making fair contracts for them; and finally, the circular said: "Simple good faith, for which we hope on all hands for those concerned in the passing away of slavery, will especially relieve the assistant commissioners in the discharge of their duties toward the freedmen, as well as promote the general welfare."

No sooner was the work thus started, and the general system and local organization in some measure begun, than two grave difficulties appeared which changed largely the theory and outcome of Bureau work. First, there were the abandoned lands of the South. It had long been the more or less definitely expressed theory of the North that all the chief problems of Emancipation might be settled by establishing the slaves on the forfeited lands of their masters,—a sort of poetic justice, said some. But this poetry done into solemn prose meant either wholesale confiscation of private property in the South, or vast appropriations. Now Congress had not appropriated a cent, and no sooner did the proclamations of general amnesty appear than the eight hundred thousand acres of abandoned lands in the hands of the Freedmen's Bureau melted quickly away. The second difficulty lay in perfecting the local organization of the Bureau throughout the wide field of work. Making a new machine and sending out officials of duly ascertained fitness for a great work of social reform is no child's task; but this task was even harder, for a new central organization had to be fitted on a heterogeneous and confused but already existing system of relief and control of ex-slaves; and the agents available for this work must be sought for in an army still busy with war operations,—men in the very nature of the case ill fitted for delicate social work,—or among the questionable camp followers of an invading host. Thus, after a year's work, vigorously as it was pushed, the problem looked even more difficult to grasp and solve than at the beginning. Nevertheless, three things that year's work did, well worth the doing: it relieved a vast amount of physical suffering; it transported seven thousand fugitives from congested centres back to the farm; and, best of all, it inaugurated the crusade of the New England schoolma'am.

The annals of this Ninth Crusade are yet to be written,—the tale of a mission that seemed to our age far more quixotic than the quest of St. Louis seemed to his. Behind the mists of ruin and rapine waved the calico dresses of women who dared, and after the hoarse mouthings of the field guns rang the rhythm of the alphabet. Rich and poor they were, serious and curious. Bereaved now of a father, now of a brother, now of more than these, they came seeking a life work in planting New England schoolhouses among the white and black of the South. They did their work well. In that first year they taught one hundred thousand souls, and more.

Evidently, Congress must soon legislate again on the hastily organized Bureau, which had so quickly grown into wide significance and vast possibilities. An institution such as that was well-nigh as difficult to end as to begin. Early in 1866 Congress took up the matter, when Senator Trumbull, of Illinois, introduced a bill to extend the Bureau and enlarge its powers. This measure received, at the hands of Congress, far more thorough discussion and attention than its predecessor. The war cloud had thinned enough to allow a clearer conception of the work of Emancipation. The champions of the bill argued that the strengthening of the Freedmen's Bureau was still a military necessity; that it was needed for the proper carrying out of the Thirteenth Amendment, and was a work of sheer justice to the ex-slave, at a trifling cost to the government. The opponents of the measure declared that the war was over, and the necessity for war measures past; that the Bureau, by reason of its extraordinary powers, was clearly unconstitutional in time of peace, and was destined to irritate the South and pauperize the freedmen, at a final cost of possibly hundreds of millions. These two arguments were unanswered, and indeed unanswerable: the one that the extraordinary powers of the Bureau threatened the civil rights of all citizens; and the other that the government must have power to do what manifestly must be done, and that present abandonment of the freedmen meant their practical reenslavement. The bill which finally passed enlarged and made permanent the Freedmen's Bureau. It was promptly vetoed by President Johnson as "unconstitutional," "unnecessary," and "extrajudicial," and failed of passage over the veto. Meantime, however, the breach between Congress and the President began to broaden, and a modified form of the lost bill was finally passed over the President's second veto, July 16.

The act of 1866 gave the Freedmen's Bureau its final form,—the form by which it will be known to posterity and judged of men. It extended the existence of the Bureau to July, 1868; it authorized additional assistant commissioners, the retention of army officers mustered out of regular service, the sale of certain forfeited lands to freedmen on nominal terms, the sale of Confederate public property for Negro schools, and a wider field of judicial interpretation and cognizance. The government of the unreconstructed South was thus put very largely in the hands of the Freedmen's Bureau, especially as in many cases the departmental military commander was now made also assistant commissioner. It was thus that the Freedmen's Bureau became a full-fledged government of men. It made laws, executed them and interpreted them; it laid and collected taxes, defined and punished crime, maintained and used military force, and dictated such measures as it thought necessary and proper for the accomplishment of its varied ends. Naturally, all these powers were not exercised continuously nor to their fullest extent; and yet, as General Howard has said, "scarcely any subject that has to be legislated upon in civil society failed, at one time or another, to demand the action of this singular Bureau."

To understand and criticise intelligently so vast a work, one must not forget an instant the drift of things in the later sixties. Lee had surrendered, Lincoln was dead, and Johnson and Congress were at loggerheads; the Thirteenth Amendment was adopted, the Fourteenth pending, and the Fifteenth declared in force in 1870. Guerrilla raiding, the ever-present flickering after-flame of war, was spending its forces against the Negroes, and all the Southern land was awakening as from some wild dream to poverty and social revolution. In a time of perfect calm, amid willing neighbors and streaming wealth, the social uplifting of four million slaves to an assured and self-sustaining place in the body politic and economic would have been a herculean task; but when to the inherent difficulties of so delicate and nice a social operation were added the spite and hate of conflict, the hell of war; when suspicion and cruelty were rife, and gaunt Hunger wept beside Bereavement,—in such a case, the work of any instrument of social regeneration was in large part foredoomed to failure. The very name of the Bureau stood for a thing in the South which for two centuries and better men had refused even to argue,—that life amid free Negroes was simply unthinkable, the maddest of experiments.

The agents that the Bureau could command varied all the way from unselfish philanthropists to narrow-minded busybodies and thieves; and even though it be true that the average was far better than the worst, it was the occasional fly that helped spoil the ointment.

Then amid all crouched the freed slave, bewildered between friend and foe. He had emerged from slavery,—not the worst slavery in the world, not a slavery that made all life unbearable, rather a slavery that had here and there something of kindliness, fidelity, and happiness,—but withal slavery, which, so far as human aspiration and desert were concerned, classed the black man and the ox together. And the Negro knew full well that, whatever their deeper convictions may have been, Southern men had fought with desperate energy to perpetuate this slavery under which the black masses, with half-articulate thought, had writhed and shivered. They welcomed freedom with a cry. They shrank from the master who still strove for their chains; they fled to the friends that had freed them, even though those friends stood ready to use them as a club for driving the recalcitrant South back into loyalty. So the cleft between the white and black South grew. Idle to say it never should have been; it was as inevitable as its results were pitiable. Curiously incongruous elements were left arrayed against each other,—the North, the government, the carpet-bagger, and the slave, here; and there, all the South that was white, whether gentleman or vagabond, honest man or rascal, lawless murderer or martyr to duty.

Thus it is doubly difficult to write of this period calmly, so intense was the feeling, so mighty the human passions that swayed and blinded men. Amid it all, two figures ever stand to typify that day to coming ages,—the one, a gray-haired gentleman, whose fathers had quit themselves like men, whose sons lay in nameless graves; who bowed to the evil of slavery because its abolition threatened untold ill to all; who stood at last, in the evening of life, a blighted, ruined form, with hate in his eyes;—and the other, a form hovering dark and mother-like, her awful face black with the mists of centuries, had aforetime quailed at that white master's command, had bent in love over the cradles of his sons and daughters, and closed in death the sunken eyes of his wife,—aye, too, at his behest had laid herself low to his lust, and borne a tawny man-child to the world, only to see her dark boy's limbs scattered to the winds by midnight marauders riding after "damned Niggers." These were the saddest sights of that woful day; and no man clasped the hands of these two passing figures of the present-past; but, hating, they went to their long home, and, hating, their children's children live today.

Here, then, was the field of work for the Freedmen's Bureau; and since, with some hesitation, it was continued by the act of 1868 until 1869, let us look upon four years of its work as a whole. There were, in 1868, nine hundred Bureau officials scattered from Washington to Texas, ruling, directly and indirectly, many millions of men. The deeds of these rulers fall mainly under seven heads: the relief of physical suffering, the overseeing of the beginnings of free labor, the buying and selling of land, the establishment of schools, the paying of bounties, the administration of justice, and the financiering of all these activities.

Up to June, 1869, over half a million patients had been treated by Bureau physicians and surgeons, and sixty hospitals and asylums had been in operation. In fifty months twenty-one million free rations were distributed at a cost of over four million dollars. Next came the difficult question of labor. First, thirty thousand black men were transported from the refuges and relief stations back to the farms, back to the critical trial of a new way of working. Plain instructions went out from Washington: the laborers must be free to choose their employers, no fixed rate of wages was prescribed, and there was to be no peonage or forced labor. So far, so good; but where local agents differed toto caelo in capacity and character, where the personnel was continually changing, the outcome was necessarily varied. The largest element of success lay in the fact that the majority of the freedmen were willing, even eager, to work. So labor contracts were written,—fifty thousand in a single State,—laborers advised, wages guaranteed, and employers supplied. In truth, the organization became a vast labor bureau,—not perfect, indeed, notably defective here and there, but on the whole successful beyond the dreams of thoughtful men. The two great obstacles which confronted the officials were the tyrant and the idler,—the slaveholder who was determined to perpetuate slavery under another name; and, the freedman who regarded freedom as perpetual rest,—the Devil and the Deep Sea.

In the work of establishing the Negroes as peasant proprietors, the Bureau was from the first handicapped and at last absolutely checked. Something was done, and larger things were planned; abandoned lands were leased so long as they remained in the hands of the Bureau, and a total revenue of nearly half a million dollars derived from black tenants. Some other lands to which the nation had gained title were sold on easy terms, and public lands were opened for settlement to the very few freedmen who had tools and capital. But the vision of "forty acres and a mule"—the righteous and reasonable ambition to become a landholder, which the nation had all but categorically promised the freedmen—was destined in most cases to bitter disappointment. And those men of marvellous hindsight who are today seeking to preach the Negro back to the present peonage of the soil know well, or ought to know, that the opportunity of binding the Negro peasant willingly to the soil was lost on that day when the Commissioner of the Freedmen's Bureau had to go to South Carolina and tell the weeping freedmen, after their years of toil, that their land was not theirs, that there was a mistake—somewhere. If by 1874 the Georgia Negro alone owned three hundred and fifty thousand acres of land, it was by grace of his thrift rather than by bounty of the government.

The greatest success of the Freedmen's Bureau lay in the planting of the free school among Negroes, and the idea of free elementary education among all classes in the South. It not only called the school-mistresses through the benevolent agencies and built them schoolhouses, but it helped discover and support such apostles of human culture as Edmund Ware, Samuel Armstrong, and Erastus Cravath. The opposition to Negro education in the South was at first bitter, and showed itself in ashes, insult, and blood; for the South believed an educated Negro to be a dangerous Negro. And the South was not wholly wrong; for education among all kinds of men always has had, and always will have, an element of danger and revolution, of dissatisfaction and discontent. Nevertheless, men strive to know. Perhaps some inkling of this paradox, even in the unquiet days of the Bureau, helped the bayonets allay an opposition to human training which still to-day lies smouldering in the South, but not flaming. Fisk, Atlanta, Howard, and Hampton were founded in these days, and six million dollars were expended for educational work, seven hundred and fifty thousand dollars of which the freedmen themselves gave of their poverty.

Such contributions, together with the buying of land and various other enterprises, showed that the ex-slave was handling some free capital already. The chief initial source of this was labor in the army, and his pay and bounty as a soldier. Payments to Negro soldiers were at first complicated by the ignorance of the recipients, and the fact that the quotas of colored regiments from Northern States were largely filled by recruits from the South, unknown to their fellow soldiers. Consequently, payments were accompanied by such frauds that Congress, by joint resolution in 1867, put the whole matter in the hands of the Freedmen's Bureau. In two years six million dollars was thus distributed to five thousand claimants, and in the end the sum exceeded eight million dollars. Even in this system fraud was frequent; but still the work put needed capital in the hands of practical paupers, and some, at least, was well spent.

The most perplexing and least successful part of the Bureau's work lay in the exercise of its judicial functions. The regular Bureau court consisted of one representative of the employer, one of the Negro, and one of the Bureau. If the Bureau could have maintained a perfectly judicial attitude, this arrangement would have been ideal, and must in time have gained confidence; but the nature of its other activities and the character of its personnel prejudiced the Bureau in favor of the black litigants, and led without doubt to much injustice and annoyance. On the other hand, to leave the Negro in the hands of Southern courts was impossible. In a distracted land where slavery had hardly fallen, to keep the strong from wanton abuse of the weak, and the weak from gloating insolently over the half-shorn strength of the strong, was a thankless, hopeless task. The former masters of the land were peremptorily ordered about, seized, and imprisoned, and punished over and again, with scant courtesy from army officers. The former slaves were intimidated, beaten, raped, and butchered by angry and revengeful men. Bureau courts tended to become centres simply for punishing whites, while the regular civil courts tended to become solely institutions for perpetuating the slavery of blacks. Almost every law and method ingenuity could devise was employed by the legislatures to reduce the Negroes to serfdom,—to make them the slaves of the State, if not of individual owners; while the Bureau officials too often were found striving to put the "bottom rail on top," and gave the freedmen a power and independence which they could not yet use. It is all well enough for us of another generation to wax wise with advice to those who bore the burden in the heat of the day. It is full easy now to see that the man who lost home, fortune, and family at a stroke, and saw his land ruled by "mules and niggers," was really benefited by the passing of slavery. It is not difficult now to say to the young freedman, cheated and cuffed about who has seen his father's head beaten to a jelly and his own mother namelessly assaulted, that the meek shall inherit the earth. Above all, nothing is more convenient than to heap on the Freedmen's Bureau all the evils of that evil day, and damn it utterly for every mistake and blunder that was made.

All this is easy, but it is neither sensible nor just. Someone had blundered, but that was long before Oliver Howard was born; there was criminal aggression and heedless neglect, but without some system of control there would have been far more than there was. Had that control been from within, the Negro would have been re-enslaved, to all intents and purposes. Coming as the control did from without, perfect men and methods would have bettered all things; and even with imperfect agents and questionable methods, the work accomplished was not undeserving of commendation.

Such was the dawn of Freedom; such was the work of the Freedmen's Bureau, which, summed up in brief, may be epitomized thus: for some fifteen million dollars, beside the sums spent before 1865, and the dole of benevolent societies, this Bureau set going a system of free labor, established a beginning of peasant proprietorship, secured the recognition of black freedmen before courts of law, and founded the free common school in the South. On the other hand, it failed to begin the establishment of good-will between ex-masters and freedmen, to guard its work wholly from paternalistic methods which discouraged self-reliance, and to carry out to any considerable extent its implied promises to furnish the freedmen with land. Its successes were the result of hard work, supplemented by the aid of philanthropists and the eager striving of black men. Its failures were the result of bad local agents, the inherent difficulties of the work, and national neglect.

Such an institution, from its wide powers, great responsibilities, large control of moneys, and generally conspicuous position, was naturally open to repeated and bitter attack. It sustained a searching Congressional investigation at the instance of Fernando Wood in 1870. Its archives and few remaining functions were with blunt discourtesy transferred from Howard's control, in his absence, to the supervision of Secretary of War Belknap in 1872, on the Secretary's recommendation. Finally, in consequence of grave intimations of wrong-doing made by the Secretary and his subordinates, General Howard was court-martialed in 1874. In both of these trials the Commissioner of the Freedmen's Bureau was officially exonerated from any wilful misdoing, and his work commended. Nevertheless, many unpleasant things were brought to light,—the methods of transacting the business of the Bureau were faulty; several cases of defalcation were proved, and other frauds strongly suspected; there were some business transactions which savored of dangerous speculation, if not dishonesty; and around it all lay the smirch of the Freedmen's Bank.

Morally and practically, the Freedmen's Bank was part of the Freedmen's Bureau, although it had no legal connection with it. With the prestige of the government back of it, and a directing board of unusual respectability and national reputation, this banking institution had made a remarkable start in the development of that thrift among black folk which slavery had kept them from knowing. Then in one sad day came the crash,—all the hard-earned dollars of the freedmen disappeared; but that was the least of the loss,—all the faith in saving went too, and much of the faith in men; and that was a loss that a Nation which to-day sneers at Negro shiftlessness has never yet made good. Not even ten additional years of slavery could have done so much to throttle the thrift of the freedmen as the mismanagement and bankruptcy of the series of savings banks chartered by the Nation for their especial aid. Where all the blame should rest, it is hard to say; whether the Bureau and the Bank died chiefly by reason of the blows of its selfish friends or the dark machinations of its foes, perhaps even time will never reveal, for here lies unwritten history.

Of the foes without the Bureau, the bitterest were those who attacked not so much its conduct or policy under the law as the necessity for any such institution at all. Such attacks came primarily from the Border States and the South; and they were summed up by Senator Davis, of Kentucky, when he moved to entitle the act of 1866 a bill "to promote strife and conflict between the white and black races ... by a grant of unconstitutional power." The argument gathered tremendous strength South and North; but its very strength was its weakness. For, argued the plain common-sense of the nation, if it is unconstitutional, unpractical, and futile for the nation to stand guardian over its helpless wards, then there is left but one alternative,—to make those wards their own guardians by arming them with the ballot. Moreover, the path of the practical politician pointed the same way; for, argued this opportunist, if we cannot peacefully reconstruct the South with white votes, we certainly can with black votes. So justice and force joined hands.

The alternative thus offered the nation was not between full and restricted Negro suffrage; else every sensible man, black and white, would easily have chosen the latter. It was rather a choice between suffrage and slavery, after endless blood and gold had flowed to sweep human bondage away. Not a single Southern legislature stood ready to admit a Negro, under any conditions, to the polls; not a single Southern legislature believed free Negro labor was possible without a system of restrictions that took all its freedom away; there was scarcely a white man in the South who did not honestly regard Emancipation as a crime, and its practical nullification as a duty. In such a situation, the granting of the ballot to the black man was a necessity, the very least a guilty nation could grant a wronged race, and the only method of compelling the South to accept the results of the war. Thus Negro suffrage ended a civil war by beginning a race feud. And some felt gratitude toward the race thus sacrificed in its swaddling clothes on the altar of national integrity; and some felt and feel only indifference and contempt.

Had political exigencies been less pressing, the opposition to government guardianship of Negroes less bitter, and the attachment to the slave system less strong, the social seer can well imagine a far better policy,—a permanent Freedmen's Bureau, with a national system of Negro schools; a carefully supervised employment and labor office; a system of impartial protection before the regular courts; and such institutions for social betterment as savings-banks, land and building associations, and social settlements. All this vast expenditure of money and brains might have formed a great school of prospective citizenship, and solved in a way we have not yet solved the most perplexing and persistent of the Negro problems.

That such an institution was unthinkable in 1870 was due in part to certain acts of the Freedmen's Bureau itself. It came to regard its work as merely temporary, and Negro suffrage as a final answer to all present perplexities. The political ambition of many of its agents and proteges led it far afield into questionable activities, until the South, nursing its own deep prejudices, came easily to ignore all the good deeds of the Bureau and hate its very name with perfect hatred. So the Freedmen's Bureau died, and its child was the Fifteenth Amendment.

The passing of a great human institution before its work is done, like the untimely passing of a single soul, but leaves a legacy of striving for other men. The legacy of the Freedmen's Bureau is the heavy heritage of this generation. To-day, when new and vaster problems are destined to strain every fibre of the national mind and soul, would it not be well to count this legacy honestly and carefully? For this much all men know: despite compromise, war, and struggle, the Negro is not free. In the backwoods of the Gulf States, for miles and miles, he may not leave the plantation of his birth; in well-nigh the whole rural South the black farmers are peons, bound by law and custom to an economic slavery, from which the only escape is death or the penitentiary. In the most cultured sections and cities of the South the Negroes are a segregated servile caste, with restricted rights and privileges. Before the courts, both in law and custom, they stand on a different and peculiar basis. Taxation without representation is the rule of their political life. And the result of all this is, and in nature must have been, lawlessness and crime. That is the large legacy of the Freedmen's Bureau, the work it did not do because it could not.

I have seen a land right merry with the sun, where children sing, and rolling hills lie like passioned women wanton with harvest. And there in the King's Highways sat and sits a figure veiled and bowed, by which the traveller's footsteps hasten as they go. On the tainted air broods fear. Three centuries' thought has been the raising and unveiling of that bowed human heart, and now behold a century new for the duty and the deed. The problem of the Twentieth Century is the problem of the color-line.

3. OF MR. BOOKER T. WASHINGTON AND OTHERS

From birth till death enslaved; in word, in deed, unmanned!

******

Hereditary bondsmen! Know ye not

Who would be free themselves must strike the blow?

BYRON.

Easily the most striking thing in the history of the American Negro since 1876 is the ascendancy of Mr. Booker T. Washington. It began at the time when war memories and ideals were rapidly passing; a day of astonishing commercial development was dawning; a sense of doubt and hesitation overtook the freedmen's sons,—then it was that his leading began. Mr. Washington came, with a simple definite programme, at the psychological moment when the nation was a little ashamed of having bestowed so much sentiment on Negroes, and was concentrating its energies on Dollars. His programme of industrial education, conciliation of the South, and submission and silence as to civil and political rights, was not wholly original; the Free Negroes from 1830 up to war-time had striven to build industrial schools, and the American Missionary Association had from the first taught various trades; and Price and others had sought a way of honorable alliance with the best of the Southerners. But Mr. Washington first indissolubly linked these things; he put enthusiasm, unlimited energy, and perfect faith into his programme, and changed it from a by-path into a veritable Way of Life. And the tale of the methods by which he did this is a fascinating study of human life.

It startled the nation to hear a Negro advocating such a programme after many decades of bitter complaint; it startled and won the applause of the South, it interested and won the admiration of the North; and after a confused murmur of protest, it silenced if it did not convert the Negroes themselves.

To gain the sympathy and cooperation of the various elements comprising the white South was Mr. Washington's first task; and this, at the time Tuskegee was founded, seemed, for a black man, well-nigh impossible. And yet ten years later it was done in the word spoken at Atlanta: "In all things purely social we can be as separate as the five fingers, and yet one as the hand in all things essential to mutual progress." This "Atlanta Compromise" is by all odds the most notable thing in Mr. Washington's career. The South interpreted it in different ways: the radicals received it as a complete surrender of the demand for civil and political equality; the conservatives, as a generously conceived working basis for mutual understanding. So both approved it, and to-day its author is certainly the most distinguished Southerner since Jefferson Davis, and the one with the largest personal following.

Next to this achievement comes Mr. Washington's work in gaining place and consideration in the North. Others less shrewd and tactful had formerly essayed to sit on these two stools and had fallen between them; but as Mr. Washington knew the heart of the South from birth and training, so by singular insight he intuitively grasped the spirit of the age which was dominating the North. And so thoroughly did he learn the speech and thought of triumphant commercialism, and the ideals of material prosperity, that the picture of a lone black boy poring over a French grammar amid the weeds and dirt of a neglected home soon seemed to him the acme of absurdities. One wonders what Socrates and St. Francis of Assisi would say to this.

And yet this very singleness of vision and thorough oneness with his age is a mark of the successful man. It is as though Nature must needs make men narrow in order to give them force. So Mr. Washington's cult has gained unquestioning followers, his work has wonderfully prospered, his friends are legion, and his enemies are confounded. To-day he stands as the one recognized spokesman of his ten million fellows, and one of the most notable figures in a nation of seventy millions. One hesitates, therefore, to criticise a life which, beginning with so little, has done so much. And yet the time is come when one may speak in all sincerity and utter courtesy of the mistakes and shortcomings of Mr. Washington's career, as well as of his triumphs, without being thought captious or envious, and without forgetting that it is easier to do ill than well in the world.

The criticism that has hitherto met Mr. Washington has not always been of this broad character. In the South especially has he had to walk warily to avoid the harshest judgments,—and naturally so, for he is dealing with the one subject of deepest sensitiveness to that section. Twice—once when at the Chicago celebration of the Spanish-American War he alluded to the color-prejudice that is "eating away the vitals of the South," and once when he dined with President Roosevelt—has the resulting Southern criticism been violent enough to threaten seriously his popularity. In the North the feeling has several times forced itself into words, that Mr. Washington's counsels of submission overlooked certain elements of true manhood, and that his educational programme was unnecessarily narrow. Usually, however, such criticism has not found open expression, although, too, the spiritual sons of the Abolitionists have not been prepared to acknowledge that the schools founded before Tuskegee, by men of broad ideals and self-sacrificing spirit, were wholly failures or worthy of ridicule. While, then, criticism has not failed to follow Mr. Washington, yet the prevailing public opinion of the land has been but too willing to deliver the solution of a wearisome problem into his hands, and say, "If that is all you and your race ask, take it."

Among his own people, however, Mr. Washington has encountered the strongest and most lasting opposition, amounting at times to bitterness, and even today continuing strong and insistent even though largely silenced in outward expression by the public opinion of the nation. Some of this opposition is, of course, mere envy; the disappointment of displaced demagogues and the spite of narrow minds. But aside from this, there is among educated and thoughtful colored men in all parts of the land a feeling of deep regret, sorrow, and apprehension at the wide currency and ascendancy which some of Mr. Washington's theories have gained. These same men admire his sincerity of purpose, and are willing to forgive much to honest endeavor which is doing something worth the doing. They cooperate with Mr. Washington as far as they conscientiously can; and, indeed, it is no ordinary tribute to this man's tact and power that, steering as he must between so many diverse interests and opinions, he so largely retains the respect of all.

But the hushing of the criticism of honest opponents is a dangerous thing. It leads some of the best of the critics to unfortunate silence and paralysis of effort, and others to burst into speech so passionately and intemperately as to lose listeners. Honest and earnest criticism from those whose interests are most nearly touched,—criticism of writers by readers,—this is the soul of democracy and the safeguard of modern society. If the best of the American Negroes receive by outer pressure a leader whom they had not recognized before, manifestly there is here a certain palpable gain. Yet there is also irreparable loss,—a loss of that peculiarly valuable education which a group receives when by search and criticism it finds and commissions its own leaders. The way in which this is done is at once the most elementary and the nicest problem of social growth. History is but the record of such group-leadership; and yet how infinitely changeful is its type and character! And of all types and kinds, what can be more instructive than the leadership of a group within a group?—that curious double movement where real progress may be negative and actual advance be relative retrogression. All this is the social student's inspiration and despair.

Now in the past the American Negro has had instructive experience in the choosing of group leaders, founding thus a peculiar dynasty which in the light of present conditions is worth while studying. When sticks and stones and beasts form the sole environment of a people, their attitude is largely one of determined opposition to and conquest of natural forces. But when to earth and brute is added an environment of men and ideas, then the attitude of the imprisoned group may take three main forms,—a feeling of revolt and revenge; an attempt to adjust all thought and action to the will of the greater group; or, finally, a determined effort at self-realization and self-development despite environing opinion. The influence of all of these attitudes at various times can be traced in the history of the American Negro, and in the evolution of his successive leaders.

Before 1750, while the fire of African freedom still burned in the veins of the slaves, there was in all leadership or attempted leadership but the one motive of revolt and revenge,—typified in the terrible Maroons, the

Danish blacks, and Cato of Stono, and veiling all the Americas in fear of insurrection. The liberalizing tendencies of the latter half of the eighteenth century brought, along with kindlier relations between black and white, thoughts of ultimate adjustment and assimilation. Such aspiration was especially voiced in the earnest songs of Phyllis, in the martyrdom of Attucks, the fighting of Salem and Poor, the intellectual accomplishments of Banneker and Derham, and the political demands of the Cuffes.

Stern financial and social stress after the war cooled much of the previous humanitarian ardor. The disappointment and impatience of the Negroes at the persistence of slavery and serfdom voiced itself in two movements. The slaves in the South, aroused undoubtedly by vague rumors of the Haytian revolt, made three fierce attempts at insurrection,—in 1800 under Gabriel in Virginia, in 1822 under Vesey in Carolina, and in 1831 again in Virginia under the terrible Nat Turner. In the Free States, on the other hand, a new and curious attempt at self-development was made. In Philadelphia and New York color-prescription led to a withdrawal of Negro communicants from white churches and the formation of a peculiar socio-religious institution among the Negroes known as the African Church,—an organization still living and controlling in its various branches over a million of men.

Walker's wild appeal against the trend of the times showed how the world was changing after the coming of the cotton-gin. By 1830 slavery seemed hopelessly fastened on the South, and the slaves thoroughly cowed into submission. The free Negroes of the North, inspired by the mulatto immigrants from the West Indies, began to change the basis of their demands; they recognized the slavery of slaves, but insisted that they themselves were freemen, and sought assimilation and amalgamation with the nation on the same terms with other men. Thus, Forten and Purvis of Philadelphia, Shad of Wilmington, Du Bois of New Haven, Barbadoes of Boston, and others, strove singly and together as men, they said, not as slaves; as "people of color," not as "Negroes." The trend of the times, however, refused them recognition save in individual and exceptional cases, considered them as one with all the despised blacks, and they soon found themselves striving to keep even the rights they formerly had of voting and working and moving as freemen. Schemes of migration and colonization arose among them; but these they refused to entertain, and they eventually turned to the Abolition movement as a final refuge.

Here, led by Remond, Nell, Wells-Brown, and Douglass, a new period of self-assertion and self-development dawned. To be sure, ultimate freedom and assimilation was the ideal before the leaders, but the assertion of the manhood rights of the Negro by himself was the main reliance, and John Brown's raid was the extreme of its logic. After the war and emancipation, the great form of Frederick Douglass, the greatest of American Negro leaders, still led the host. Self-assertion, especially in political lines, was the main programme, and behind Douglass came Elliot, Bruce, and Langston, and the Reconstruction politicians, and, less conspicuous but of greater social significance, Alexander Crummell and Bishop Daniel Payne.

Then came the Revolution of 1876, the suppression of the Negro votes, the changing and shifting of ideals, and the seeking of new lights in the great night. Douglass, in his old age, still bravely stood for the ideals of his early manhood,—ultimate assimilation through self-assertion, and on no other terms. For a time Price arose as a new leader, destined, it seemed, not to give up, but to re-state the old ideals in a form less repugnant to the white South. But he passed away in his prime. Then came the new leader. Nearly all the former ones had become leaders by the silent suffrage of their fellows, had sought to lead their own people alone, and were usually, save Douglass, little known outside their race. But Booker T. Washington arose as essentially the leader not of one race but of two,—a compromiser between the South, the North, and the Negro. Naturally the Negroes resented, at first bitterly, signs of compromise which surrendered their civil and political rights, even though this was to be exchanged for larger chances of economic development. The rich and dominating North, however, was not only weary of the race problem, but was investing largely in Southern enterprises, and welcomed any method of peaceful cooperation. Thus, by national opinion, the Negroes began to recognize Mr. Washington's leadership; and the voice of criticism was hushed.

Mr. Washington represents in Negro thought the old attitude of adjustment and submission; but adjustment at such a peculiar time as to make his programme unique. This is an age of unusual economic development, and Mr. Washington's programme naturally takes an economic cast, becoming a gospel of Work and Money to such an extent as apparently almost completely to overshadow the higher aims of life. Moreover, this is an age when the more advanced races are coming in closer contact with the less developed races, and the race-feeling is therefore intensified; and Mr. Washington's programme practically accepts the alleged inferiority of the Negro races. Again, in our own land, the reaction from the sentiment of war time has given impetus to race-prejudice against Negroes, and Mr. Washington withdraws many of the high demands of Negroes as men and American citizens. In other periods of intensified prejudice all the Negro's tendency to self-assertion has been called forth; at this period a policy of submission is advocated. In the history of nearly all other races and peoples the doctrine preached at such crises has been that manly self-respect is worth more than lands and houses, and that a people who voluntarily surrender such respect, or cease striving for it, are not worth civilizing.

In answer to this, it has been claimed that the Negro can survive only through submission. Mr. Washington distinctly asks that black people give up, at least for the present, three things,—

First, political power,

Second, insistence on civil rights,

Third, higher education of Negro youth,—and concentrate all their energies on industrial education, and accumulation of wealth, and the conciliation of the South. This policy has been courageously and insistently advocated for over fifteen years, and has been triumphant for perhaps ten years. As a result of this tender of the palm-branch, what has been the return? In these years there have occurred:

1. The disfranchisement of the Negro.

2. The legal creation of a distinct status of civil inferiority for the Negro.

3. The steady withdrawal of aid from institutions for the higher training of the Negro.

These movements are not, to be sure, direct results of Mr. Washington's teachings; but his propaganda has, without a shadow of doubt, helped their speedier accomplishment. The question then comes: Is it possible, and probable, that nine millions of men can make effective progress in economic lines if they are deprived of political rights, made a servile caste, and allowed only the most meagre chance for developing their exceptional men? If history and reason give any distinct answer to these questions, it is an emphatic NO. And Mr. Washington thus faces the triple paradox of his career:

1. He is striving nobly to make Negro artisans business men and property-owners; but it is utterly impossible, under modern competitive methods, for workingmen and property-owners to defend their rights and exist without the right of suffrage.

2. He insists on thrift and self-respect, but at the same time counsels a silent submission to civic inferiority such as is bound to sap the manhood of any race in the long run.

3. He advocates common-school and industrial training, and depreciates institutions of higher learning; but neither the Negro common-schools, nor Tuskegee itself, could remain open a day were it not for teachers trained in Negro colleges, or trained by their graduates.

This triple paradox in Mr. Washington's position is the object of criticism by two classes of colored Americans. One class is spiritually descended from Toussaint the Savior, through Gabriel, Vesey, and Turner, and they represent the attitude of revolt and revenge; they hate the white South blindly and distrust the white race generally, and so far as they agree on definite action, think that the Negro's only hope lies in emigration beyond the borders of the United States. And yet, by the irony of fate, nothing has more effectually made this programme seem hopeless than the recent course of the United States toward weaker and darker peoples in the West Indies, Hawaii, and the Philippines,—for where in the world may we go and be safe from lying and brute force?

The other class of Negroes who cannot agree with Mr. Washington has hitherto said little aloud. They deprecate the sight of scattered counsels, of internal disagreement; and especially they dislike making their just criticism of a useful and earnest man an excuse for a general discharge of venom from small-minded opponents. Nevertheless, the questions involved are so fundamental and serious that it is difficult to see how men like the Grimkes, Kelly Miller, J. W. E. Bowen, and other representatives of this group, can much longer be silent. Such men feel in conscience bound to ask of this nation three things:

1. The right to vote.

2. Civic equality.

3. The education of youth according to ability. They acknowledge Mr. Washington's invaluable service in counselling patience and courtesy in such demands; they do not ask that ignorant black men vote when ignorant whites are debarred, or that any reasonable restrictions in the suffrage should not be applied; they know that the low social level of the mass of the race is responsible for much discrimination against it, but they also know, and the nation knows, that relentless color-prejudice is more often a cause than a result of the Negro's degradation; they seek the abatement of this relic of barbarism, and not its systematic encouragement and pampering by all agencies of social power from the Associated Press to the Church of Christ. They advocate, with Mr. Washington, a broad system of Negro common schools supplemented by thorough industrial training; but they are surprised that a man of Mr. Washington's insight cannot see that no such educational system ever has rested or can rest on any other basis than that of the well-equipped college and university, and they insist that there is a demand for a few such institutions throughout the South to train the best of the Negro youth as teachers, professional men, and leaders.

This group of men honor Mr. Washington for his attitude of conciliation toward the white South; they accept the "Atlanta Compromise" in its broadest interpretation; they recognize, with him, many signs of promise, many men of high purpose and fair judgment, in this section; they know that no easy task has been laid upon a region already tottering under heavy burdens. But, nevertheless, they insist that the way to truth and right lies in straightforward honesty, not in indiscriminate flattery; in praising those of the South who do well and criticising uncompromisingly those who do ill; in taking advantage of the opportunities at hand and urging their fellows to do the same, but at the same time in remembering that only a firm adherence to their higher ideals and aspirations will ever keep those ideals within the realm of possibility. They do not expect that the free right to vote, to enjoy civic rights, and to be educated, will come in a moment; they do not expect to see the bias and prejudices of years disappear at the blast of a trumpet; but they are absolutely certain that the way for a people to gain their reasonable rights is not by voluntarily throwing them away and insisting that they do not want them; that the way for a people to gain respect is not by continually belittling and ridiculing themselves; that, on the contrary, Negroes must insist continually, in season and out of season, that voting is necessary to modern manhood, that color discrimination is barbarism, and that black boys need education as well as white boys.

In failing thus to state plainly and unequivocally the legitimate demands of their people, even at the cost of opposing an honored leader, the thinking classes of American Negroes would shirk a heavy responsibility,—a responsibility to themselves, a responsibility to the struggling masses, a responsibility to the darker races of men whose future depends so largely on this American experiment, but especially a responsibility to this nation,— this common Fatherland. It is wrong to encourage a man or a people in evil-doing; it is wrong to aid and abet a national crime simply because it is unpopular not to do so. The growing spirit of kindliness and reconciliation between the North and South after the frightful difference of a generation ago ought to be a source of deep congratulation to all, and especially to those whose mistreatment caused the war; but if that reconciliation is to be marked by the industrial slavery and civic death of those same black men, with permanent legislation into a position of inferiority, then those black men, if they are really men, are called upon by every consideration of patriotism and loyalty to oppose such a course by all civilized methods, even though such opposition involves disagreement with Mr. Booker T. Washington. We have no right to sit silently by while the inevitable seeds are sown for a harvest of disaster to our children, black and white.

First, it is the duty of black men to judge the South discriminatingly. The present generation of Southerners are not responsible for the past, and they should not be blindly hated or blamed for it. Furthermore, to no class is the indiscriminate endorsement of the recent course of the South toward Negroes more nauseating than to the best thought of the South. The South is not "solid"; it is a land in the ferment of social change, wherein forces of all kinds are fighting for supremacy; and to praise the ill the South is today perpetrating is just as wrong as to condemn the good. Discriminating and broad-minded criticism is what the South needs,— needs it for the sake of her own white sons and daughters, and for the insurance of robust, healthy mental and moral development.

Today even the attitude of the Southern whites toward the blacks is not, as so many assume, in all cases the same; the ignorant Southerner hates the Negro, the workingmen fear his competition, the money-makers wish to use him as a laborer, some of the educated see a menace in his upward development, while others—usually the sons of the masters—wish to help him to rise. National opinion has enabled this last class to maintain the Negro common schools, and to protect the Negro partially in property, life, and limb. Through the pressure of the money-makers, the Negro is in danger of being reduced to semi-slavery, especially in the country districts; the workingmen, and those of the educated who fear the Negro, have united to disfranchise him, and some have urged his deportation; while the passions of the ignorant are easily aroused to lynch and abuse any black man. To praise this intricate whirl of thought and prejudice is nonsense; to inveigh indiscriminately against "the South" is unjust; but to use the same breath in praising Governor Aycock, exposing Senator Morgan, arguing with Mr. Thomas Nelson Page, and denouncing Senator Ben Tillman, is not only sane, but the imperative duty of thinking black men.

It would be unjust to Mr. Washington not to acknowledge that in several instances he has opposed movements in the South which were unjust to the Negro; he sent memorials to the Louisiana and Alabama constitutional conventions, he has spoken against lynching, and in other ways has openly or silently set his influence against sinister schemes and unfortunate happenings. Notwithstanding this, it is equally true to assert that on the whole the distinct impression left by Mr. Washington's propaganda is, first, that the South is justified in its present attitude toward the Negro because of the Negro's degradation; secondly, that the prime cause of the Negro's failure to rise more quickly is his wrong education in the past; and, thirdly, that his future rise depends primarily on his own efforts. Each of these propositions is a dangerous half-truth. The supplementary truths must never be lost sight of: first, slavery and race-prejudice are potent if not sufficient causes of the Negro's position; second, industrial and common-school training were necessarily slow in planting because they had to await the black teachers trained by higher institutions,—it being extremely doubtful if any essentially different development was possible, and certainly a Tuskegee was unthinkable before 1880; and, third, while it is a great truth to say that the Negro must strive and strive mightily to help himself, it is equally true that unless his striving be not simply seconded, but rather aroused and encouraged, by the initiative of the richer and wiser environing group, he cannot hope for great success.

In his failure to realize and impress this last point, Mr. Washington is especially to be criticised. His doctrine has tended to make the whites, North and South, shift the burden of the Negro problem to the Negro's shoulders and stand aside as critical and rather pessimistic spectators; when in fact the burden belongs to the nation, and the hands of none of us are clean if we bend not our energies to righting these great wrongs.

The South ought to be led, by candid and honest criticism, to assert her better self and do her full duty to the race she has cruelly wronged and is still wronging. The North—her co-partner in guilt—cannot salve her conscience by plastering it with gold. We cannot settle this problem by diplomacy and suaveness, by "policy" alone. If worse come to worst, can the moral fibre of this country survive the slow throttling and murder of nine millions of men?

The black men of America have a duty to perform, a duty stern and delicate,—a forward movement to oppose a part of the work of their greatest leader. So far as Mr. Washington preaches Thrift, Patience, and Industrial Training for the masses, we must hold up his hands and strive with him, rejoicing in his honors and glorying in the strength of this Joshua called of God and of man to lead the headless host. But so far as Mr. Washington apologizes for injustice, North or South, does not rightly value the privilege and duty of voting, belittles the emasculating effects of caste distinctions, and opposes the higher training and ambition of our brighter minds,—so far as he, the South, or the Nation, does this,—we must unceasingly and firmly oppose them. By every civilized and peaceful method we must strive for the rights which the world accords to men, clinging unwaveringly to those great words which the sons of the Fathers would fain forget: "We hold these truths to be self-evident: That all men are created equal; that they are endowed by their Creator with certain unalienable rights; that among these are life, liberty, and the pursuit of happiness.

4. OF THE MEANING OF PROGRESS

Willst Du Deine Macht verkunden,
Wahle sie die frei von Sunden,
Steh'n in Deinem ew'gen Haus!
Deine Geister sende aus!
Die Unsterblichen, die Reinen,
Die nicht fuhlen, die nicht weinen!
Nicht die zarte Jungfrau wahle,
Nicht der Hirtin weiche Seele!

SCHILLER.

Once upon a time I taught school in the hills of Tennessee, where the broad dark vale of the Mississippi begins to roll and crumple to greet the Alleghanies. I was a Fisk student then, and all Fisk men thought that Tennessee—beyond the Veil—was theirs alone, and in vacation time they sallied forth in lusty bands to meet the county school-commissioners. Young and happy, I too went, and I shall not soon forget that summer, seventeen years ago.

First, there was a Teachers' Institute at the county-seat; and there distinguished guests of the superintendent taught the teachers fractions and spelling and other mysteries,—white teachers in the morning, Negroes at night. A picnic now and then, and a supper, and the rough world was softened by laughter and song. I remember how— But I wander.

There came a day when all the teachers left the Institute and began the hunt for schools. I learn from hearsay (for my mother was mortally afraid of firearms) that the hunting of ducks and bears and men is wonderfully interesting, but I am sure that the man who has never hunted a country school has something to learn of the pleasures of the chase. I see now the white, hot roads lazily rise and fall and wind before me under the burning July sun; I feel the deep weariness of heart and limb as ten, eight, six miles stretch relentlessly ahead; I feel my heart sink heavily as I hear again and again, "Got a teacher? Yes." So I walked on and on—horses were too expensive—until I had wandered beyond railways, beyond stage lines, to a land of "varmints" and rattlesnakes, where the coming of a stranger was an event, and men lived and died in the shadow of one blue hill.

Sprinkled over hill and dale lay cabins and farmhouses, shut out from the world by the forests and the rolling hills toward the east. There I found at last a little school. Josie told me of it; she was a thin, homely girl of twenty, with a dark-brown face and thick, hard hair. I had crossed the stream at Watertown, and rested under the great willows; then I had gone to the little cabin in the lot where Josie was resting on her way to town. The gaunt farmer made me welcome, and Josie, hearing my errand, told me anxiously that they wanted a school over the hill; that but once since the war had a teacher been there; that she herself longed to learn,—and thus she ran on, talking fast and loud, with much earnestness and energy.

Next morning I crossed the tall round hill, lingered to look at the blue and yellow mountains stretching toward the Carolinas, then plunged into the wood, and came out at Josie's home. It was a dull frame cottage with four rooms, perched just below the brow of the hill, amid peach-trees. The father was a quiet, simple soul, calmly ignorant, with no touch of vulgarity. The mother was different,—strong, bustling, and energetic, with a quick, restless tongue, and an ambition to live "like folks." There was a crowd of children. Two boys had gone away. There remained two growing girls; a shy midget of eight; John, tall, awkward, and eighteen; Jim, younger, quicker, and better looking; and two babies of indefinite age. Then there was Josie herself. She seemed to be the centre of the family: always busy at service, or at home, or berry-picking; a little nervous and inclined to scold, like her mother, yet faithful, too, like her father. She had about her a certain fineness, the shadow of an unconscious moral heroism that would willingly give all of life to make life broader, deeper, and fuller for her and hers. I saw much of this family afterwards, and grew to love them for their honest efforts to be decent and comfortable, and for their knowledge of their own ignorance. There was with them no affectation. The mother would scold the father for being so "easy"; Josie would roundly berate the boys for carelessness; and all knew that it was a hard thing to dig a living out of a rocky side-hill.

I secured the school. I remember the day I rode horseback out to the commissioner's house with a pleasant young white fellow who wanted the white school. The road ran down the bed of a stream; the sun laughed and the water jingled, and we rode on. "Come in," said the commissioner,—"come in. Have a seat. Yes, that certificate will do. Stay to dinner. What do you want a month?" "Oh," thought I, "this is lucky"; but even then fell the awful shadow of the Veil, for they ate first, then I—alone.

The schoolhouse was a log hut, where Colonel Wheeler used to shelter his corn. It sat in a lot behind a rail fence and thorn bushes, near the sweetest of springs. There was an entrance where a door once was, and within, a massive rickety fireplace; great chinks between the logs served as windows. Furniture was scarce. A pale blackboard crouched in the corner. My desk was made of three boards, reinforced at critical points, and my chair, borrowed from the landlady, had to be returned every night. Seats for the children—these puzzled me much. I was haunted by a New England vision of neat little desks and chairs, but, alas! the reality was rough plank benches without backs, and at times without legs. They had the one virtue of making naps dangerous,—possibly fatal, for the floor was not to be trusted.

It was a hot morning late in July when the school opened. I trembled when I heard the patter of little feet down the dusty road, and saw the growing row of dark solemn faces and bright eager eyes facing me. First came Josie and her brothers and sisters. The longing to know, to be a student in the great school at Nashville, hovered like a star above this child-woman amid her work and worry, and she studied doggedly. There were the Dowells from their farm over toward Alexandria,—Fanny, with her smooth black face and wondering eyes; Martha, brown and dull; the pretty girl-wife of a brother, and the younger brood.

There were the Burkes,—two brown and yellow lads, and a tiny haughty-eyed girl. Fat Reuben's little chubby girl came, with golden face and old-gold hair, faithful and solemn. 'Thenie was on hand early,—a jolly, ugly, good-hearted girl, who slyly dipped snuff and looked after her little bow-legged brother. When her mother could spare her, 'Tildy came,—a midnight beauty, with starry eyes and tapering limbs; and her brother, correspondingly homely. And then the big boys,—the hulking Lawrences; the lazy Neills, unfathered sons of mother and daughter; Hickman, with a stoop in his shoulders; and the rest.

There they sat, nearly thirty of them, on the rough benches, their faces shading from a pale cream to a deep brown, the little feet bare and swinging, the eyes full of expectation, with here and there a twinkle of mischief, and the hands grasping Webster's blue-black spelling-book. I loved my school, and the fine faith the children had in the wisdom of their teacher was truly marvellous. We read and spelled together, wrote a little, picked flowers, sang, and listened to stories of the world beyond the hill. At times the school would dwindle away, and I would start out. I would visit Mun Eddings, who lived in two very dirty rooms, and ask why little Lugene, whose flaming face seemed ever ablaze with the dark-red hair uncombed, was absent all last week, or why I missed so often the inimitable rags of Mack and Ed. Then the father, who worked Colonel Wheeler's farm on shares, would tell me how the crops needed the boys; and the thin, slovenly mother, whose face was pretty when washed, assured me that Lugene must mind the baby. "But we'll start them again next week." When the Lawrences stopped, I knew that the doubts of the old folks about book-learning had conquered again, and so, toiling up the hill, and getting as far into the cabin as possible, I put Cicero "pro Archia Poeta" into the simplest English with local applications, and usually convinced them—for a week or so.

On Friday nights I often went home with some of the children,—sometimes to Doc Burke's farm. He was a great, loud, thin Black, ever working, and trying to buy the seventy-five acres of hill and dale where he lived; but people said that he would surely fail, and the "white folks would get it all." His wife was a magnificent Amazon, with saffron face and shining hair, uncorseted and barefooted, and the children were strong and beautiful. They lived in a one-and-a-half-room cabin in the hollow of the farm, near the spring. The front room was full of great fat white beds, scrupulously neat; and there were bad chromos on the walls, and a tired centre-table. In the tiny back kitchen I was often invited to "take out and help" myself to fried chicken and wheat biscuit, "meat" and corn pone, string-beans and berries. At first I used to be a little alarmed at the approach of bedtime in the one lone bedroom, but embarrassment was very deftly avoided. First, all the children nodded and slept, and were stowed away in one great pile of goose feathers; next, the mother and the father discreetly slipped away to the kitchen while I went to bed; then, blowing out the dim light, they retired in the dark. In the morning all were up and away before I thought of awaking. Across the road, where fat Reuben lived, they all went outdoors while the teacher retired, because they did not boast the luxury of a kitchen.

I liked to stay with the Dowells, for they had four rooms and plenty of good country fare. Uncle Bird had a small, rough farm, all woods and hills, miles from the big road; but he was full of tales,—he preached now and then,— and with his children, berries, horses, and wheat he was happy and prosperous. Often, to keep the peace, I must go where life was less lovely; for instance, 'Tildy's mother was incorrigibly dirty, Reuben's larder was limited seriously, and herds of untamed insects wandered over the Eddingses' beds. Best of all I loved to go to Josie's, and sit on the porch, eating peaches, while the mother bustled and talked: how Josie had bought the sewing-machine; how Josie worked at service in winter, but that four dollars a month was "mighty little" wages; how Josie longed to go away to school, but that it "looked like" they never could get far enough ahead to let her; how the crops failed and the well was yet unfinished; and, finally, how "mean" some of the white folks were.

For two summers I lived in this little world; it was dull and humdrum. The girls looked at the hill in wistful longing, and the boys fretted and haunted Alexandria. Alexandria was "town,"—a straggling, lazy village of houses, churches, and shops, and an aristocracy of Toms, Dicks, and Captains. Cuddled on the hill to the north was the village of the colored folks, who lived in three- or four-room unpainted cottages, some neat and homelike, and some dirty. The dwellings were scattered rather aimlessly, but they centred about the twin temples of the hamlet, the Methodist, and the Hard-Shell Baptist churches. These, in turn, leaned gingerly on a sad-colored schoolhouse. Hither my little world wended its crooked way on Sunday to meet other worlds, and gossip, and wonder, and make the weekly sacrifice with frenzied priest at the altar of the "old-time religion." Then the soft melody and mighty cadences of Negro song fluttered and thundered.

I have called my tiny community a world, and so its isolation made it; and yet there was among us but a half-awakened common consciousness, sprung from common joy and grief, at burial, birth, or wedding; from a common hardship in poverty, poor land, and low wages; and, above all, from the sight of the Veil that hung between us and Opportunity. All this caused us to think some thoughts together; but these, when ripe for speech, were spoken in various languages. Those whose eyes twenty-five and more years before had seen "the glory of the coming of the Lord," saw in every present hindrance or help a dark fatalism bound to bring all things right in His own good time. The mass of those to whom slavery was a dim recollection of childhood found the world a puzzling thing: it asked little of them, and they answered with little, and yet it ridiculed their offering. Such a paradox they could not understand, and therefore sank into listless indifference, or shiftlessness, or reckless bravado. There were, however, some—such as Josie, Jim, and Ben—to whom War, Hell, and Slavery were but childhood tales, whose young appetites had been whetted to an edge by school and story and half-awakened thought. Ill could they be content, born without and beyond the World. And their weak wings beat against their barriers,— barriers of caste, of youth, of life; at last, in dangerous moments, against everything that opposed even a whim.

The ten years that follow youth, the years when first the realization comes that life is leading somewhere,—these were the years that passed after I left my little school. When they were past, I came by chance once more to the walls of Fisk University, to the halls of the chapel of melody. As I lingered there in the joy and pain of meeting old school-friends, there swept over me a sudden longing to pass again beyond the blue hill, and to see the homes and the school of other days, and to learn how life had gone with my school-children; and I went.

Josie was dead, and the gray-haired mother said simply, "We've had a heap of trouble since you've been away." I had feared for Jim. With a cultured parentage and a social caste to uphold him, he might have made a venturesome merchant or a West Point cadet. But here he was, angry with life and reckless; and when Fanner Durham charged him with stealing wheat, the old man had to ride fast to escape the stones which the furious fool hurled after him. They told Jim to run away; but he would not run, and the constable came that afternoon. It grieved Josie, and great awkward John walked nine miles every day to see his little brother through the bars of Lebanon jail. At last the two came back together in the dark night. The mother cooked supper, and Josie emptied her purse, and the boys stole away. Josie grew thin and silent, yet worked the more. The hill became steep for the quiet old father, and with the boys away there was little to do in the valley. Josie helped them to sell the old farm, and they moved nearer town. Brother Dennis, the carpenter, built a new house with six rooms; Josie toiled a year in Nashville, and brought back ninety dollars to furnish the house and change it to a home.

When the spring came, and the birds twittered, and the stream ran proud and full, little sister Lizzie, bold and thoughtless, flushed with the passion of youth, bestowed herself on the tempter, and brought home a nameless child. Josie shivered and worked on, with the vision of schooldays all fled, with a face wan and tired,—worked until, on a summer's day, some one married another; then Josie crept to her mother like a hurt child, and slept— and sleeps.

I paused to scent the breeze as I entered the valley. The Lawrences have gone,—father and son forever,—and the other son lazily digs in the earth to live. A new young widow rents out their cabin to fat Reuben. Reuben is a Baptist preacher now, but I fear as lazy as ever, though his cabin has three rooms; and little Ella has grown into a bouncing woman, and is ploughing corn on the hot hillside. There are babies a-plenty, and one half-witted girl. Across the valley is a house I did not know before, and there I found, rocking one baby and expecting another, one of my schoolgirls, a daughter of Uncle Bird Dowell. She looked somewhat worried with her new duties, but soon bristled into pride over her neat cabin and the tale of her thrifty husband, and the horse and cow, and the farm they were planning to buy.

My log schoolhouse was gone. In its place stood Progress; and Progress, I understand, is necessarily ugly. The crazy foundation stones still marked the former site of my poor little cabin, and not far away, on six weary boulders, perched a jaunty board house, perhaps twenty by thirty feet, with three windows and a door that locked. Some of the window-glass was broken, and part of an old iron stove lay mournfully under the house. I peeped through the window half reverently, and found things that were more familiar. The blackboard had grown by about two feet, and the seats were still without backs. The county owns the lot now, I hear, and every year there is a session of school. As I sat by the spring and looked on the Old and the New I felt glad, very glad, and yet—

After two long drinks I started on. There was the great double log-house on the corner. I remembered the broken, blighted family that used to live there. The strong, hard face of the mother, with its wilderness of hair, rose before me. She had driven her husband away, and while I taught school a strange man lived there, big and jovial, and people talked. I felt sure that Ben and 'Tildy would come to naught from such a home. But this is an odd world; for Ben is a busy farmer in Smith County, "doing well, too," they say, and he had cared for little 'Tildy until last spring, when a lover married her. A hard life the lad had led, toiling for meat, and laughed at because he was homely and crooked. There was Sam Carlon, an impudent old skinflint, who had definite notions about "niggers," and hired Ben a summer and would not pay him. Then the hungry boy gathered his sacks together, and in broad daylight went into Carlon's corn; and when the hard-fisted farmer set upon him, the angry boy flew at him like a beast. Doc Burke saved a murder and a lynching that day.

The story reminded me again of the Burkes, and an impatience seized me to know who won in the battle, Doc or the seventy-five acres. For it is a hard thing to make a farm out of nothing, even in fifteen years. So I hurried on, thinking of the Burkes. They used to have a certain magnificent barbarism about them that I liked. They were never vulgar, never immoral, but rather rough and primitive, with an unconventionality that spent itself in loud guffaws, slaps on the back, and naps in the corner. I hurried by the cottage of the misborn Neill boys. It was empty, and they were grown into fat, lazy farm-hands. I saw the home of the Hickmans, but Albert, with his stooping shoulders, had passed from the world. Then I came to the Burkes' gate and peered through; the enclosure looked rough and untrimmed, and yet there were the same fences around the old farm save to the left, where lay twenty-five other acres. And lo! the cabin in the hollow had climbed the hill and swollen to a half-finished six-room cottage.

The Burkes held a hundred acres, but they were still in debt. Indeed, the gaunt father who toiled night and day would scarcely be happy out of debt, being so used to it. Some day he must stop, for his massive frame is showing decline. The mother wore shoes, but the lion-like physique of other days was broken. The children had grown up. Rob, the image of his father, was loud and rough with laughter. Birdie, my school baby of six, had grown to a picture of maiden beauty, tall and tawny. "Edgar is gone," said the mother, with head half bowed,—"gone to work in Nashville; he and his father couldn't agree."

Little Doc, the boy born since the time of my school, took me horseback down the creek next morning toward Farmer Dowell's. The road and the stream were battling for mastery, and the stream had the better of it. We splashed and waded, and the merry boy, perched behind me, chattered and laughed. He showed me where Simon Thompson had bought a bit of ground and a home; but his daughter Lana, a plump, brown, slow girl, was not there. She had married a man and a farm twenty miles away. We wound on down the stream till we came to a gate that I did not recognize, but the boy insisted that it was "Uncle Bird's." The farm was fat with the growing crop. In that little valley was a strange stillness as I rode up; for death and marriage had stolen youth and left age and childhood there. We sat and talked that night after the chores were done. Uncle Bird was grayer, and his eyes did not see so well, but he was still jovial. We talked of the acres bought,—one hundred and twenty-five,—of the new guest-chamber added, of Martha's marrying. Then we talked of death: Fanny and Fred were gone; a shadow hung over the other daughter, and when it lifted she was to go to Nashville to school. At last we spoke of the neighbors, and as night fell, Uncle Bird told me how, on a night like that, 'Thenie came wandering back to her home over yonder, to escape the blows of her husband. And next morning she died in the home that her little bow-legged brother, working and saving, had bought for their widowed mother.

My journey was done, and behind me lay hill and dale, and Life and Death. How shall man measure Progress there where the dark-faced Josie lies? How many heartfuls of sorrow shall balance a bushel of wheat? How hard a thing is life to the lowly, and yet how human and real! And all this life and love and strife and failure,—is it the twilight of nightfall or the flush of some faint-dawning day?

Thus sadly musing, I rode to Nashville in the Jim Crow car

5. OF THE WINGS OF ATALANTA

O black boy of Atlanta!
But half was spoken;
The slave's chains and the master's
Alike are broken;
The one curse of the races
Held both in tether;
They are rising—all are rising—
The black and white together.

WHITTIER.

South of the North, yet north of the South, lies the City of a Hundred Hills, peering out from the shadows of the past into the promise of the future. I have seen her in the morning, when the first flush of day had half-roused her; she lay gray and still on the crimson soil of Georgia; then the blue smoke began to curl from her chimneys, the tinkle of bell and scream of whistle broke the silence, the rattle and roar of busy life slowly gathered and swelled, until the seething whirl of the city seemed a strange thing in a sleepy land.

Once, they say, even Atlanta slept dull and drowsy at the foot-hills of the Alleghanies, until the iron baptism of war awakened her with its sullen waters, aroused and maddened her, and left her listening to the sea. And the sea cried to the hills and the hills answered the sea, till the city rose like a widow and cast away her weeds, and toiled for her daily bread; toiled steadily, toiled cunningly,—perhaps with some bitterness, with a touch, of reclame,—and yet with real earnestness, and real sweat.

It is a hard thing to live haunted by the ghost of an untrue dream; to see the wide vision of empire fade into real ashes and dirt; to feel the pang of the conquered, and yet know that with all the Bad that fell on one black day, something was vanquished that deserved to live, something killed that in justice had not dared to die; to know that with the Right that triumphed, triumphed something of Wrong, something sordid and mean, something less than the broadest and best. All this is bitter hard; and many a man and city and people have found in it excuse for sulking, and brooding, and listless waiting.

Such are not men of the sturdier make; they of Atlanta turned resolutely toward the future; and that future held aloft vistas of purple and gold:—Atlanta, Queen of the cotton kingdom; Atlanta, Gateway to the Land of the Sun; Atlanta, the new Lachesis, spinner of web and woof for the world. So the city crowned her hundred hills with factories, and stored her shops with cunning handiwork, and stretched long iron ways to greet the busy Mercury in his coming. And the Nation talked of her striving.

Perhaps Atlanta was not christened for the winged maiden of dull Boeotia; you know the tale,—how swarthy Atalanta, tall and wild, would marry only him who out-raced her; and how the wily Hippomenes laid three apples of gold in the way. She fled like a shadow, paused, startled over the first apple, but even as he stretched his hand, fled again; hovered over the second, then, slipping from his hot grasp, flew over river, vale, and hill; but as she lingered over the third, his arms fell round her, and looking on each other, the blazing passion of their love profaned the sanctuary of Love, and they were cursed. If Atlanta be not named for Atalanta, she ought to have been.

Atalanta is not the first or the last maiden whom greed of gold has led to defile the temple of Love; and not maids alone, but men in the race of life, sink from the high and generous ideals of youth to the gambler's code of the Bourse; and in all our Nation's striving is not the Gospel of Work befouled by the Gospel of Pay? So common is this that one-half think it normal; so unquestioned, that we almost fear to question if the end of racing is not gold, if the aim of man is not rightly to be rich. And if this is the fault of America, how dire a danger lies before a new land and a new city, lest Atlanta, stooping for mere gold, shall find that gold accursed!

It was no maiden's idle whim that started this hard racing; a fearful wilderness lay about the feet of that city after the War,—feudalism, poverty, the rise of the Third Estate, serfdom, the re-birth of Law and Order, and above and between all, the Veil of Race. How heavy a journey for weary feet! what wings must Atalanta have to flit over all this hollow and hill, through sour wood and sullen water, and by the red waste of sun-baked clay! How fleet must Atalanta be if she will not be tempted by gold to profane the Sanctuary!

The Sanctuary of our fathers has, to be sure, few Gods,—some sneer, "all too few." There is the thrifty Mercury of New England, Pluto of the North, and Ceres of the West; and there, too, is the half-forgotten Apollo of the South, under whose aegis the maiden ran,—and as she ran she forgot him, even as there in Boeotia Venus was forgot. She forgot the old ideal of the Southern gentleman,—that new-world heir of the grace and courtliness of patrician, knight, and noble; forgot his honor with his foibles, his kindliness with his carelessness, and stooped to apples of gold,—to men busier and sharper, thriftier and more unscrupulous. Golden apples are beautiful—I remember the lawless days of boyhood, when orchards in crimson and gold tempted me over fence and field—and, too, the merchant who has dethroned the planter is no despicable parvenu. Work and wealth are the mighty levers to lift this old new land; thrift and toil and saving are the highways to new hopes and new possibilities; and yet the warning is needed lest the wily Hippomenes tempt Atalanta to thinking that golden apples are the goal of racing, and not mere incidents by the way.

Atlanta must not lead the South to dream of material prosperity as the touchstone of all success; already the fatal might of this idea is beginning to spread; it is replacing the finer type of Southerner with vulgar money-getters; it is burying the sweeter beauties of Southern life beneath pretence and ostentation. For every social ill the panacea of Wealth has been urged,—wealth to overthrow the remains of the slave feudalism; wealth to raise the "cracker" Third Estate; wealth to employ the black serfs, and the prospect of wealth to keep them working; wealth as the end and aim of politics, and as the legal tender for law and order; and, finally, instead of Truth, Beauty, and Goodness, wealth as the ideal of the Public School.

Not only is this true in the world which Atlanta typifies, but it is threatening to be true of a world beneath and beyond that world,—the Black World beyond the Veil. Today it makes little difference to Atlanta, to the South, what the Negro thinks or dreams or wills. In the soul-life of the land he is to-day, and naturally will long remain, unthought of, half forgotten; and yet when he does come to think and will and do for himself,—and let no man dream that day will never come,—then the part he plays will not be one of sudden learning, but words and thoughts he has been taught to lisp in his race-childhood. To-day the ferment of his striving toward self-realization is to the strife of the white world like a wheel within a wheel: beyond the Veil are smaller but like problems of ideals, of leaders and the led, of serfdom, of poverty, of order and subordination, and, through all, the Veil of Race. Few know of these problems, few who know notice them; and yet there they are, awaiting student, artist, and seer,—a field for somebody sometime to discover. Hither has the temptation of Hippomenes penetrated; already in this smaller world, which now indirectly and anon directly must influence the larger for good or ill, the habit is forming of interpreting the world in dollars. The old leaders of Negro opinion, in the little groups where there is a Negro social consciousness, are being replaced by new; neither the black preacher nor the black teacher leads as he did two decades ago. Into their places are pushing the farmers and gardeners, the well-paid porters and artisans, the business-men,—all those with property and money. And with all this change, so curiously parallel to that of the Other-world, goes too the same inevitable change in ideals. The South laments to-day the slow, steady disappearance of a certain type of Negro,—the faithful, courteous slave of other days, with his incorruptible honesty and dignified humility. He is passing away just as surely as the old type of Southern gentleman is passing, and from not dissimilar causes,—the sudden transformation of a fair far-off ideal of Freedom into the hard reality of bread-winning and the consequent deification of Bread.

In the Black World, the Preacher and Teacher embodied once the ideals of this people—the strife for another and a juster world, the vague dream of righteousness, the mystery of knowing; but to-day the danger is that these ideals, with their simple beauty and weird inspiration, will suddenly sink to a question of cash and a lust for gold. Here stands this black young Atalanta, girding herself for the race that must be run; and if her eyes be still toward the hills and sky as in the days of old, then we may look for noble running; but what if some ruthless or wily or even thoughtless Hippomenes lay golden apples before her? What if the Negro people be wooed from a strife for righteousness, from a love of knowing, to regard dollars as the be-all and end-all of life? What if to the Mammonism of America be added the rising Mammonism of the re-born South, and the Mammonism of this South be reinforced by the budding Mammonism of its half-wakened black millions? Whither, then, is the new-world quest of Goodness and Beauty and Truth gone glimmering? Must this, and that fair flower of Freedom which, despite the jeers of latter-day striplings, sprung from our fathers' blood, must that too degenerate into a dusty quest of gold,—into lawless lust with Hippomenes?

The hundred hills of Atlanta are not all crowned with factories. On one, toward the west, the setting sun throws three buildings in bold relief against the sky. The beauty of the group lies in its simple unity:—a broad lawn of green rising from the red street and mingled roses and peaches; north and south, two plain and stately halls; and in the midst, half hidden in ivy, a larger building, boldly graceful, sparingly decorated, and with one low spire. It is a restful group, —one never looks for more; it is all here, all intelligible. There I live, and there I hear from day to day the low hum of restful life. In winter's twilight, when the red sun glows, I can see the dark figures pass between the halls to the music of the night-bell. In the morning, when the sun is golden, the clang of the day-bell brings the hurry and laughter of three hundred young hearts from hall and street, and from the busy city below,— children all dark and heavy-haired,—to join their clear young voices in the music of the morning sacrifice. In a half-dozen class-rooms they gather then,—here to follow the love-song of Dido, here to listen to the tale of Troy divine; there to wander among the stars, there to wander among men and nations,—and elsewhere other well-worn ways of knowing this queer world. Nothing new, no time-saving devices,—simply old time-glorified methods of delving for Truth, and searching out the hidden beauties of life, and learning the good of living. The riddle of existence is the college curriculum that was laid before the Pharaohs, that was taught in the groves by Plato, that formed the trivium and quadrivium, and is to-day laid before the freedmen's sons by Atlanta University. And this course of study will not change; its methods will grow more deft and effectual, its content richer by toil of scholar and sight of seer; but the true college will ever have one goal,—not to earn meat, but to know the end and aim of that life which meat nourishes.

The vision of life that rises before these dark eyes has in it nothing mean or selfish. Not at Oxford or at Leipsic, not at Yale or Columbia, is there an air of higher resolve or more unfettered striving; the determination to realize for men, both black and white, the broadest possibilities of life, to seek the better and the best, to spread with their own hands the Gospel of Sacrifice,—all this is the burden of their talk and dream. Here, amid a wide desert of caste and proscription, amid the heart-hurting slights and jars and vagaries of a deep race-dislike, lies this green oasis, where hot anger cools, and the bitterness of disappointment is sweetened by the springs and breezes of Parnassus; and here men may lie and listen, and learn of a future fuller than the past, and hear the voice of Time:

"Entbehren sollst du, sollst entbehren."

They made their mistakes, those who planted Fisk and Howard and Atlanta before the smoke of battle had lifted; they made their mistakes, but those mistakes were not the things at which we lately laughed somewhat uproariously. They were right when they sought to found a new educational system upon the University: where, forsooth, shall we ground knowledge save on the broadest and deepest knowledge? The roots of the tree, rather than the leaves, are the sources of its life; and from the dawn of history, from Academus to Cambridge, the culture of the University has been the broad foundation-stone on which is built the kindergarten's A B C.

But these builders did make a mistake in minimizing the gravity of the problem before them; in thinking it a matter of years and decades; in therefore building quickly and laying their foundation carelessly, and lowering the standard of knowing, until they had scattered haphazard through the South some dozen poorly equipped high schools and miscalled them universities. They forgot, too, just as their successors are forgetting, the rule of inequality:—that of the million black youth, some were fitted to know and some to dig; that some had the talent and capacity of university men, and some the talent and capacity of blacksmiths; and that true training meant neither that all should be college men nor all artisans, but that the one should be made a missionary of culture to an untaught people, and the other a free workman among serfs. And to seek to make the blacksmith a scholar is almost as silly as the more modern scheme of making the scholar a blacksmith; almost, but not quite.

The function of the university is not simply to teach bread-winning, or to furnish teachers for the public schools or to be a centre of polite society; it is, above all, to be the organ of that fine adjustment between real life and the growing knowledge of life, an adjustment which forms the secret of civilization. Such an institution the South of to-day sorely needs. She has religion, earnest, bigoted:—religion that on both sides the Veil often omits the sixth, seventh, and eighth commandments, but substitutes a dozen supplementary ones. She has, as Atlanta shows, growing thrift and love of toil; but she lacks that broad knowledge of what the world knows and knew of human living and doing, which she may apply to the thousand problems of real life to-day confronting her. The need of the South is knowledge and culture,—not in dainty limited quantity, as before the war, but in broad busy abundance in the world of work; and until she has this, not all the Apples of Hesperides, be they golden and bejewelled, can save her from the curse of the Boeotian lovers.

The Wings of Atalanta are the coming universities of the South. They alone can bear the maiden past the temptation of golden fruit. They will not guide her flying feet away from the cotton and gold; for—ah, thoughtful Hippomenes!—do not the apples lie in the very Way of Life? But they will guide her over and beyond them, and leave her kneeling in the Sanctuary of Truth and Freedom and broad Humanity, virgin and undefiled. Sadly did the Old South err in human education, despising the education of the masses, and niggardly in the support of colleges. Her ancient university foundations dwindled and withered under the foul breath of slavery; and even since the war they have fought a failing fight for life in the tainted air of social unrest and commercial selfishness, stunted by the death of criticism, and starving for lack of broadly cultured men. And if this is the white South's need and danger, how much heavier the danger and need of the freedmen's sons! how pressing here the need of broad ideals and true culture, the conservation of soul from sordid aims and petty passions! Let us build the Southern university—William and Mary, Trinity, Georgia, Texas, Tulane, Vanderbilt, and the others—fit to live; let us build, too, the Negro universities:—Fisk, whose foundation was ever broad; Howard, at the heart of the Nation; Atlanta at Atlanta, whose ideal of scholarship has been held above the temptation of numbers. Why not here, and perhaps elsewhere, plant deeply and for all time centres of learning and living, colleges that yearly would send into the life of the South a few white men and a few black men of broad culture, catholic tolerance, and trained ability, joining their hands to other hands, and giving to this squabble of the Races a decent and dignified peace?

Patience, Humility, Manners, and Taste, common schools and kindergartens, industrial and technical schools, literature and tolerance,—all these spring from knowledge and culture, the children of the university. So must men and nations build, not otherwise, not upside down.

Teach workers to work,—a wise saying; wise when applied to German boys and American girls; wiser when said of Negro boys, for they have less knowledge of working and none to teach them. Teach thinkers to think,—a needed knowledge in a day of loose and careless logic; and they whose lot is gravest must have the carefulest training to think aright. If these things are so, how foolish to ask what is the best education for one or seven or sixty million souls! shall we teach them trades, or train them in liberal arts? Neither and both: teach the workers to work and the thinkers to think; make carpenters of carpenters, and philosophers of philosophers, and fops of fools. Nor can we pause here. We are training not isolated men but a living group of men,—nay, a group within a group. And the final product of our training must be neither a psychologist nor a brickmason, but a man. And to make men, we must have ideals, broad, pure, and inspiring ends of living,— not sordid money-getting, not apples of gold. The worker must work for the glory of his handiwork, not simply for pay; the thinker must think for truth, not for fame. And all this is gained only by human strife and longing; by ceaseless training and education; by founding Right on righteousness and Truth on the unhampered search for Truth; by founding the common school on the university, and the industrial school on the common school; and weaving thus a system, not a distortion, and bringing a birth, not an abortion.

When night falls on the City of a Hundred Hills, a wind gathers itself from the seas and comes murmuring westward. And at its bidding, the smoke of the drowsy factories sweeps down upon the mighty city and covers it like a pall, while yonder at the University the stars twinkle above Stone Hall. And they say that yon gray mist is the tunic of Atalanta pausing over her golden apples. Fly, my maiden, fly, for yonder comes Hippomenes!

6. OF THE TRAINING OF BLACK MEN

Why, if the Soul can fling the Dust aside,
And naked on the Air of Heaven ride,
Were't not a Shame—were't not a Shame for him
In this clay carcase crippled to abide?

OMAR KHAYYAM (FITZGERALD).

From the shimmering swirl of waters where many, many thoughts ago the slave-ship first saw the square tower of Jamestown, have flowed down to our day three streams of thinking: one swollen from the larger world here and overseas, saying, the multiplying of human wants in culture-lands calls for the world-wide cooperation of men in satisfying them. Hence arises a new human unity, pulling the ends of earth nearer, and all men, black, yellow, and white. The larger humanity strives to feel in this contact of living Nations and sleeping hordes a thrill of new life in the world, crying, "If the contact of Life and Sleep be Death, shame on such Life." To be sure, behind this thought lurks the afterthought of force and dominion,—the making of brown men to delve when the temptation of beads and red calico cloys.

The second thought streaming from the death-ship and the curving river is the thought of the older South,—the sincere and passionate belief that somewhere between men and cattle, God created a tertium quid, and called it a Negro,—a clownish, simple creature, at times even lovable within its limitations, but straitly foreordained to walk within the Veil. To be sure, behind the thought lurks the afterthought,—some of them with favoring chance might become men, but in sheer self-defence we dare not let them, and we build about them walls so high, and hang between them and the light a veil so thick, that they shall not even think of breaking through.

And last of all there trickles down that third and darker thought,—the thought of the things themselves, the confused, half-conscious mutter of men who are black and whitened, crying "Liberty, Freedom, Opportunity—vouchsafe to us, O boastful World, the chance of living men!" To be sure, behind the thought lurks the afterthought,—suppose, after all, the World is right and we are less than men? Suppose this mad impulse within is all wrong, some mock mirage from the untrue?

So here we stand among thoughts of human unity, even through conquest and slavery; the inferiority of black men, even if forced by fraud; a shriek in the night for the freedom of men who themselves are not yet sure of their right to demand it. This is the tangle of thought and afterthought wherein we are called to solve the problem of training men for life.

Behind all its curiousness, so attractive alike to sage and dilettante, lie its dim dangers, throwing across us shadows at once grotesque and awful. Plain it is to us that what the world seeks through desert and wild we have within our threshold,—a stalwart laboring force, suited to the semi-tropics; if, deaf to the voice of the Zeitgeist, we refuse to use and develop these men, we risk poverty and loss. If, on the other hand, seized by the brutal afterthought, we debauch the race thus caught in our talons, selfishly sucking their blood and brains in the future as in the past, what shall save us from national decadence? Only that saner selfishness, which Education teaches, can find the rights of all in the whirl of work.

Again, we may decry the color-prejudice of the South, yet it remains a heavy fact. Such curious kinks of the human mind exist and must be reckoned with soberly. They cannot be laughed away, nor always successfully stormed at, nor easily abolished by act of legislature. And yet they must not be encouraged by being let alone. They must be recognized as facts, but unpleasant facts; things that stand in the way of civilization and religion and common decency. They can be met in but one way,—by the breadth and broadening of human reason, by catholicity of taste and culture. And so, too, the native ambition and aspiration of men, even though they be black, backward, and ungraceful, must not lightly be dealt with. To stimulate wildly weak and untrained minds is to play with mighty fires; to flout their striving idly is to welcome a harvest of brutish crime and shameless lethargy in our very laps. The guiding of thought and the deft coordination of deed is at once the path of honor and humanity.

And so, in this great question of reconciling three vast and partially contradictory streams of thought, the one panacea of Education leaps to the lips of all:—such human training as will best use the labor of all men without enslaving or brutalizing; such training as will give us poise to encourage the prejudices that bulwark society, and to stamp out those that in sheer barbarity deafen us to the wail of prisoned souls within the Veil, and the mounting fury of shackled men.

But when we have vaguely said that Education will set this tangle straight, what have we uttered but a truism? Training for life teaches living; but what training for the profitable living together of black men and white? A hundred and fifty years ago our task would have seemed easier. Then Dr. Johnson blandly assured us that education was needful solely for the embellishments of life, and was useless for ordinary vermin. To-day we have climbed to heights where we would open at least the outer courts of knowledge to all, display its treasures to many, and select the few to whom its mystery of Truth is revealed, not wholly by birth or the accidents of the stock market, but at least in part according to deftness and aim, talent and character. This programme, however, we are sorely puzzled in carrying out through that part of the land where the blight of slavery fell hardest, and where we are dealing with two backward peoples. To make here in human education that ever necessary combination of the permanent and the contingent—of the ideal and the practical in workable equilibrium—has been there, as it ever must be in every age and place, a matter of infinite experiment and frequent mistakes.

In rough approximation we may point out four varying decades of work in Southern education since the Civil War. From the close of the war until 1876, was the period of uncertain groping and temporary relief. There were army schools, mission schools, and schools of the Freedmen's Bureau in chaotic disarrangement seeking system and co-operation. Then followed ten years of constructive definite effort toward the building of complete school systems in the South. Normal schools and colleges were founded for the freedmen, and teachers trained there to man the public schools. There was the inevitable tendency of war to underestimate the prejudices of the master and the ignorance of the slave, and all seemed clear sailing out of the wreckage of the storm. Meantime, starting in this decade yet especially developing from 1885 to 1895, began the industrial revolution of the South. The land saw glimpses of a new destiny and the stirring of new ideals. The educational system striving to complete itself saw new obstacles and a field of work ever broader and deeper. The Negro colleges, hurriedly founded, were inadequately equipped, illogically distributed, and of varying efficiency and grade; the normal and high schools were doing little more than common-school work, and the common schools were training but a third of the children who ought to be in them, and training these too often poorly. At the same time the white South, by reason of its sudden conversion from the slavery ideal, by so much the more became set and strengthened in its racial prejudice, and crystallized it into harsh law and harsher custom; while the marvellous pushing forward of the poor white daily threatened to take even bread and butter from the mouths of the heavily handicapped sons of the freedmen. In the midst, then, of the larger problem of Negro education sprang up the more practical question of work, the inevitable economic quandary that faces a people in the transition from slavery to freedom, and especially those who make that change amid hate and prejudice, lawlessness and ruthless competition.

The industrial school springing to notice in this decade, but coming to full recognition in the decade beginning with 1895, was the proffered answer to this combined educational and economic crisis, and an answer of singular wisdom and timeliness. From the very first in nearly all the schools some attention had been given to training in handiwork, but now was this training first raised to a dignity that brought it in direct touch with the South's magnificent industrial development, and given an emphasis which reminded black folk that before the Temple of Knowledge swing the Gates of Toil.

Yet after all they are but gates, and when turning our eyes from the temporary and the contingent in the Negro problem to the broader question of the permanent uplifting and civilization of black men in America, we have a right to inquire, as this enthusiasm for material advancement mounts to its height, if after all the industrial school is the final and sufficient answer in the training of the Negro race; and to ask gently, but in all sincerity, the ever-recurring query of the ages, Is not life more than meat, and the body more than raiment? And men ask this to-day all the more eagerly because of sinister signs in recent educational movements. The tendency is here, born of slavery and quickened to renewed life by the crazy imperialism of the day, to regard human beings as among the material resources of a land to be trained with an eye single to future dividends. Race-prejudices, which keep brown and black men in their "places," we are coming to regard as useful allies with such a theory, no matter how much they may dull the ambition and sicken the hearts of struggling human beings. And above all, we daily hear that an education that encourages aspiration, that sets the loftiest of ideals and seeks as an end culture and character rather than bread-winning, is the privilege of white men and the danger and delusion of black.

Especially has criticism been directed against the former educational efforts to aid the Negro. In the four periods I have mentioned, we find first, boundless, planless enthusiasm and sacrifice; then the preparation of teachers for a vast public-school system; then the launching and expansion of that school system amid increasing difficulties; and finally the training of workmen for the new and growing industries. This development has been sharply ridiculed as a logical anomaly and flat reversal of nature. Soothly we have been told that first industrial and manual training should have taught the Negro to work, then simple schools should have taught him to read and write, and finally, after years, high and normal schools could have completed the system, as intelligence and wealth demanded.

That a system logically so complete was historically impossible, it needs but a little thought to prove. Progress in human affairs is more often a pull than a push, a surging forward of the exceptional man, and the lifting of his duller brethren slowly and painfully to his vantage-ground. Thus it was no accident that gave birth to universities centuries before the common schools, that made fair Harvard the first flower of our wilderness. So in the South: the mass of the freedmen at the end of the war lacked the intelligence so necessary to modern workingmen. They must first have the common school to teach them to read, write, and cipher; and they must have higher schools to teach teachers for the common schools. The white teachers who flocked South went to establish such a common-school system. Few held the idea of founding colleges; most of them at first would have laughed at the idea. But they faced, as all men since them have faced, that central paradox of the South,—the social separation of the races. At that time it was the sudden volcanic rupture of nearly all relations between black and white, in work and government and family life. Since then a new adjustment of relations in economic and political affairs has grown up,—an adjustment subtle and difficult to grasp, yet singularly ingenious, which leaves still that frightful chasm at the color-line across which men pass at their peril. Thus, then and now, there stand in the South two separate worlds; and separate not simply in the higher realms of social intercourse, but also in church and school, on railway and street-car, in hotels and theatres, in streets and city sections, in books and newspapers, in asylums and jails, in hospitals and graveyards. There is still enough of contact for large economic and group cooperation, but the separation is so thorough and deep that it absolutely precludes for the present between the races anything like that sympathetic and effective group-training and leadership of the one by the other, such as the American Negro and all backward peoples must have for effectual progress.

This the missionaries of '68 soon saw; and if effective industrial and trade schools were impracticable before the establishment of a common-school system, just as certainly no adequate common schools could be founded until there were teachers to teach them. Southern whites would not teach them; Northern whites in sufficient numbers could not be had. If the Negro was to learn, he must teach himself, and the most effective help that could be given him was the establishment of schools to train Negro teachers. This conclusion was slowly but surely reached by every student of the situation until simultaneously, in widely separated regions, without consultation or systematic plan, there arose a series of institutions designed to furnish teachers for the untaught. Above the sneers of critics at the obvious defects of this procedure must ever stand its one crushing rejoinder: in a single generation they put thirty thousand black teachers in the South; they wiped out the illiteracy of the majority of the black people of the land, and they made Tuskegee possible.

Such higher training-schools tended naturally to deepen broader development: at first they were common and grammar schools, then some became high schools. And finally, by 1900, some thirty-four had one year or more of studies of college grade. This development was reached with different degrees of speed in different institutions: Hampton is still a high school, while Fisk University started her college in 1871, and Spelman

Seminary about 1896. In all cases the aim was identical,—to maintain the standards of the lower training by giving teachers and leaders the best practicable training; and above all, to furnish the black world with adequate standards of human culture and lofty ideals of life. It was not enough that the teachers of teachers should be trained in technical normal methods; they must also, so far as possible, be broad-minded, cultured men and women, to scatter civilization among a people whose ignorance was not simply of letters, but of life itself.

It can thus be seen that the work of education in the South began with higher institutions of training, which threw off as their foliage common schools, and later industrial schools, and at the same time strove to shoot their roots ever deeper toward college and university training. That this was an inevitable and necessary development, sooner or later, goes without saying; but there has been, and still is, a question in many minds if the natural growth was not forced, and if the higher training was not either overdone or done with cheap and unsound methods. Among white Southerners this feeling is widespread and positive. A prominent Southern journal voiced this in a recent editorial.

"The experiment that has been made to give the colored students classical training has not been satisfactory. Even though many were able to pursue the course, most of them did so in a parrot-like way, learning what was taught, but not seeming to appropriate the truth and import of their instruction, and graduating without sensible aim or valuable occupation for their future. The whole scheme has proved a waste of time, efforts, and the money of the state."

While most fair-minded men would recognize this as extreme and overdrawn, still without doubt many are asking, Are there a sufficient number of Negroes ready for college training to warrant the undertaking? Are not too many students prematurely forced into this work? Does it not have the effect of dissatisfying the young Negro with his environment? And do these graduates succeed in real life? Such natural questions cannot be evaded, nor on the other hand must a Nation naturally skeptical as to Negro ability assume an unfavorable answer without careful inquiry and patient openness to conviction. We must not forget that most Americans answer all queries regarding the Negro a priori, and that the least that human courtesy can do is to listen to evidence.

The advocates of the higher education of the Negro would be the last to deny the incompleteness and glaring defects of the present system: too many institutions have attempted to do college work, the work in some cases has not been thoroughly done, and quantity rather than quality has sometimes been sought. But all this can be said of higher education throughout the land; it is the almost inevitable incident of educational growth, and leaves the deeper question of the legitimate demand for the higher training of Negroes untouched. And this latter question can be settled in but one way,—by a first-hand study of the facts. If we leave out of view all institutions which have not actually graduated students from a course higher than that of a New England high school, even though they be called colleges; if then we take the thirty-four remaining institutions, we may clear up many misapprehensions by asking searchingly, What kind of institutions are they? what do they teach? and what sort of men do they graduate?

And first we may say that this type of college, including Atlanta, Fisk, and Howard, Wilberforce and Claflin, Shaw, and the rest, is peculiar, almost unique. Through the shining trees that whisper before me as I write, I catch glimpses of a boulder of New England granite, covering a grave, which graduates of Atlanta University have placed there,—

"GRATEFUL MEMORY OF THEIR FORMER TEACHER AND FRIEND AND OF THE UNSELFISH LIFE HE LIVED, AND THE NOBLE WORK HE WROUGHT; THAT THEY, THEIR CHILDREN, AND THEIR CHILDREN'S CHILDREN MIGHT BE BLESSED."

This was the gift of New England to the freed Negro: not alms, but a friend; not cash, but character. It was not and is not money these seething millions want, but love and sympathy, the pulse of hearts beating with red blood;—a gift which to-day only their own kindred and race can bring to the masses, but which once saintly souls brought to their favored children in the crusade of the sixties, that finest thing in American history, and one of the few things untainted by sordid greed and cheap vainglory. The teachers in these institutions came not to keep the Negroes in their place, but to raise them out of the defilement of the places where slavery had wallowed them. The colleges they founded were social settlements;

homes where the best of the sons of the freedmen came in close and sympathetic touch with the best traditions of New England. They lived and ate together, studied and worked, hoped and harkened in the dawning light. In actual formal content their curriculum was doubtless old-fashioned, but in educational power it was supreme, for it was the contact of living souls.

From such schools about two thousand Negroes have gone forth with the bachelor's degree. The number in itself is enough to put at rest the argument that too large a proportion of Negroes are receiving higher training. If the ratio to population of all Negro students throughout the land, in both college and secondary training, be counted, Commissioner Harris assures us "it must be increased to five times its present average" to equal the average of the land.

Fifty years ago the ability of Negro students in any appreciable numbers to master a modern college course would have been difficult to prove. To-day it is proved by the fact that four hundred Negroes, many of whom have been reported as brilliant students, have received the bachelor's degree from Harvard, Yale, Oberlin, and seventy other leading colleges. Here we have, then, nearly twenty-five hundred Negro graduates, of whom the crucial query must be made, How far did their training fit them for life? It is of course extremely difficult to collect satisfactory data on such a point,—difficult to reach the men, to get trustworthy testimony, and to gauge that testimony by any generally acceptable criterion of success. In 1900, the Conference at Atlanta University undertook to study these graduates, and published the results. First they sought to know what these graduates were doing, and succeeded in getting answers from nearly two-thirds of the living. The direct testimony was in almost all cases corroborated by the reports of the colleges where they graduated, so that in the main the reports were worthy of credence. Fifty-three per cent of these graduates were teachers,—presidents of institutions, heads of normal schools, principals of city school-systems, and the like. Seventeen per cent were clergymen; another seventeen per cent were in the professions, chiefly as physicians. Over six per cent were merchants, farmers, and artisans, and four per cent were in the government civil-service. Granting even that a considerable proportion of the third unheard from are unsuccessful, this is a record of usefulness. Personally I know many hundreds of these graduates, and have corresponded with more than a thousand; through others I have followed carefully the life-work of scores; I have taught some of them and some of the pupils whom they have taught, lived in homes which they have builded, and looked at life through their eyes. Comparing them as a class with my fellow students in New England and in Europe, I cannot hesitate in saying that nowhere have I met men and women with a broader spirit of helpfulness, with deeper devotion to their life-work, or with more consecrated determination to succeed in the face of bitter difficulties than among Negro college-bred men. They have, to be sure, their proportion of ne'er-do-wells, their pedants and lettered fools, but they have a surprisingly small proportion of them; they have not that culture of manner which we instinctively associate with university men, forgetting that in reality it is the heritage from cultured homes, and that no people a generation removed from slavery can escape a certain unpleasant rawness and gaucherie, despite the best of training.

With all their larger vision and deeper sensibility, these men have usually been conservative, careful leaders. They have seldom been agitators, have withstood the temptation to head the mob, and have worked steadily and faithfully in a thousand communities in the South. As teachers, they have given the South a commendable system of city schools and large numbers of private normal-schools and academies. Colored college-bred men have worked side by side with white college graduates at Hampton; almost from the beginning the backbone of Tuskegee's teaching force has been formed of graduates from Fisk and Atlanta. And to-day the institute is filled with college graduates, from the energetic wife of the principal down to the teacher of agriculture, including nearly half of the executive council and a majority of the heads of departments. In the professions, college men are slowly but surely leavening the Negro church, are healing and preventing the devastations of disease, and beginning to furnish legal protection for the liberty and property of the toiling masses. All this is needful work. Who would do it if Negroes did not? How could Negroes do it if they were not trained carefully for it? If white people need colleges to furnish teachers, ministers, lawyers, and doctors, do black people need nothing of the sort?

If it is true that there are an appreciable number of Negro youth in the land capable by character and talent to receive that higher training, the end of which is culture, and if the two and a half thousand who have had something of this training in the past have in the main proved themselves useful to their race and generation, the question then comes, What place in the future development of the South ought the Negro college and college-bred man to occupy? That the present social separation and acute race-sensitiveness must eventually yield to the influences of culture, as the South grows civilized, is clear. But such transformation calls for singular wisdom and patience. If, while the healing of this vast sore is progressing, the races are to live for many years side by side, united in economic effort, obeying a common government, sensitive to mutual thought and feeling, yet subtly and silently separate in many matters of deeper human intimacy,—if this unusual and dangerous development is to progress amid peace and order, mutual respect and growing intelligence, it will call for social surgery at once the delicatest and nicest in modern history. It will demand broad-minded, upright men, both white and black, and in its final accomplishment American civilization will triumph. So far as white men are concerned, this fact is to-day being recognized in the South, and a happy renaissance of university education seems imminent. But the very voices that cry hail to this good work are, strange to relate, largely silent or antagonistic to the higher education of the Negro.

Strange to relate! for this is certain, no secure civilization can be built in the South with the Negro as an ignorant, turbulent proletariat. Suppose we seek to remedy this by making them laborers and nothing more: they are not fools, they have tasted of the Tree of Life, and they will not cease to think, will not cease attempting to read the riddle of the world. By taking away their best equipped teachers and leaders, by slamming the door of opportunity in the faces of their bolder and brighter minds, will you make them satisfied with their lot? or will you not rather transfer their leading from the hands of men taught to think to the hands of untrained demagogues? We ought not to forget that despite the pressure of poverty, and despite the active discouragement and even ridicule of friends, the demand for higher training steadily increases among Negro youth: there were, in the years from 1875 to 1880, 22 Negro graduates from Northern colleges; from 1885 to 1890 there were 43, and from 1895 to 1900, nearly 100 graduates. From Southern Negro colleges there were, in the same three periods, 143, 413, and over 500 graduates. Here, then, is the plain thirst for training; by refusing to give this Talented Tenth the key to knowledge, can any sane man imagine that they will lightly lay aside their yearning and contentedly become hewers of wood and drawers of water?

No. The dangerously clear logic of the Negro's position will more and more loudly assert itself in that day when increasing wealth and more intricate social organization preclude the South from being, as it so largely is, simply an armed camp for intimidating black folk. Such waste of energy cannot be spared if the South is to catch up with civilization. And as the black third of the land grows in thrift and skill, unless skilfully guided in its larger philosophy, it must more and more brood over the red past and the creeping, crooked present, until it grasps a gospel of revolt and revenge and throws its new-found energies athwart the current of advance. Even to-day the masses of the Negroes see all too clearly the anomalies of their position and the moral crookedness of yours. You may marshal strong indictments against them, but their counter-cries, lacking though they be in formal logic, have burning truths within them which you may not wholly ignore, O Southern Gentlemen! If you deplore their presence here, they ask, Who brought us? When you cry, Deliver us from the vision of intermarriage, they answer that legal marriage is infinitely better than systematic concubinage and prostitution. And if in just fury you accuse their vagabonds of violating women, they also in fury quite as just may reply: The rape which your gentlemen have done against helpless black women in defiance of your own laws is written on the foreheads of two millions of mulattoes, and written in ineffaceable blood. And finally, when you fasten crime upon this race as its peculiar trait, they answer that slavery was the arch-crime, and lynching and lawlessness its twin abortions; that color and race are not crimes, and yet it is they which in this land receive most unceasing condemnation, North, East, South, and West.

I will not say such arguments are wholly justified,—I will not insist that there is no other side to the shield; but I do say that of the nine millions of Negroes in this nation, there is scarcely one out of the cradle to whom these arguments do not daily present themselves in the guise of terrible truth. I insist that the question of the future is how best to keep these millions from brooding over the wrongs of the past and the difficulties of the present, so that all their energies may be bent toward a cheerful striving and cooperation with their white neighbors toward a larger, juster, and fuller future. That one wise method of doing this lies in the closer knitting of the Negro to the great industrial possibilities of the South is a great truth. And this the common schools and the manual training and trade schools are working to accomplish. But these alone are not enough. The foundations of knowledge in this race, as in others, must be sunk deep in the college and university if we would build a solid, permanent structure. Internal problems of social advance must inevitably come, —problems of work and wages, of families and homes, of morals and the true valuing of the things of life; and all these and other inevitable problems of civilization the Negro must meet and solve largely for himself, by reason of his isolation; and can there be any possible solution other than by study and thought and an appeal to the rich experience of the past? Is there not, with such a group and in such a crisis, infinitely more danger to be apprehended from half-trained minds and shallow thinking than from over-education and over-refinement? Surely we have wit enough to found a Negro college so manned and equipped as to steer successfully between the dilettante and the fool. We shall hardly induce black men to believe that if their stomachs be full, it matters little about their brains. They already dimly perceive that the paths of peace winding between honest toil and dignified manhood call for the guidance of skilled thinkers, the loving, reverent comradeship between the black lowly and the black men emancipated by training and culture.

The function of the Negro college, then, is clear: it must maintain the standards of popular education, it must seek the social regeneration of the Negro, and it must help in the solution of problems of race contact and cooperation. And finally, beyond all this, it must develop men. Above our modern socialism, and out of the worship of the mass, must persist and evolve that higher individualism which the centres of culture protect; there must come a loftier respect for the sovereign human soul that seeks to know itself and the world about it; that seeks a freedom for expansion and self-development; that will love and hate and labor in its own way, untrammeled alike by old and new. Such souls aforetime have inspired and guided worlds, and if we be not wholly bewitched by our Rhinegold, they shall again. Herein the longing of black men must have respect: the rich and bitter depth of their experience, the unknown treasures of their inner life, the strange rendings of nature they have seen, may give the world new points of view and make their loving, living, and doing precious to all human hearts. And to themselves in these the days that try their souls, the chance to soar in the dim blue air above the smoke is to their finer spirits boon and guerdon for what they lose on earth by being black.

I sit with Shakespeare and he winces not. Across the color line I move arm in arm with Balzac and Dumas, where smiling men and welcoming women glide in gilded halls. From out the caves of evening that swing between the strong-limbed earth and the tracery of the stars, I summon Aristotle and Aurelius and what soul I will, and they come all graciously with no scorn nor condescension. So, wed with Truth, I dwell above the Veil. Is this the life you grudge us, O knightly America? Is this the life you long to change into the dull red hideousness of Georgia? Are you so afraid lest peering from this high Pisgah, between Philistine and Amalekite, we sight the Promised Land?

7. OF THE BLACK BELT

I am black but comely, O ye daughters of Jerusalem, As the tents of Kedar, as the curtains of Solomon. Look not upon me, because I am black, Because the sun hath looked upon me: My mother's children were angry with me;

They made me the keeper of the vineyards;

But mine own vineyard have I not kept.

THE SONG OF SOLOMON.

Out of the North the train thundered, and we woke to see the crimson soil of Georgia stretching away bare and monotonous right and left. Here and there lay straggling, unlovely villages, and lean men loafed leisurely at the depots; then again came the stretch of pines and clay. Yet we did not nod, nor weary of the scene; for this is historic ground. Right across our track, three hundred and sixty years ago, wandered the cavalcade of Hernando de Soto, looking for gold and the Great Sea; and he and his foot-sore captives disappeared yonder in the grim forests to the west. Here sits Atlanta, the city of a hundred hills, with something Western, something Southern, and something quite its own, in its busy life. Just this side Atlanta is the land of the Cherokees and to the southwest, not far from where Sam Hose was crucified, you may stand on a spot which is to-day the centre of the Negro problem,—the centre of those nine million men who are America's dark heritage from slavery and the slave-trade.

Not only is Georgia thus the geographical focus of our Negro population, but in many other respects, both now and yesterday, the Negro problems have seemed to be centered in this State. No other State in the Union can count a million Negroes among its citizens,—a population as large as the slave population of the whole Union in 1800; no other State fought so long and strenuously to gather this host of Africans. Oglethorpe thought slavery against law and gospel; but the circumstances which gave Georgia its first inhabitants were not calculated to furnish citizens over-nice in their ideas about rum and slaves. Despite the prohibitions of the trustees, these Georgians, like some of their descendants, proceeded to take the law into their own hands; and so pliant were the judges, and so flagrant the smuggling, and so earnest were the prayers of Whitefield, that by the middle of the eighteenth century all restrictions were swept away, and the slave-trade went merrily on for fifty years and more.

Down in Darien, where the Delegal riots took place some summers ago, there used to come a strong protest against slavery from the Scotch Highlanders; and the Moravians of Ebenezer did not like the system. But not till the Haytian Terror of Toussaint was the trade in men even checked; while the national statute of 1808 did not suffice to stop it. How the Africans poured in!—fifty thousand between 1790 and 1810, and then, from Virginia and from smugglers, two thousand a year for many years more. So the thirty thousand Negroes of Georgia in 1790 doubled in a decade,—were over a hundred thousand in 1810, had reached two hundred thousand in 1820, and half a million at the time of the war. Thus like a snake the black population writhed upward.

But we must hasten on our journey. This that we pass as we near Atlanta is the ancient land of the Cherokees,—that brave Indian nation which strove so long for its fatherland, until Fate and the United States Government drove them beyond the Mississippi. If you wish to ride with me you must come into the "Jim Crow Car." There will be no objection,—already four other white men, and a little white girl with her nurse, are in there. Usually the races are mixed in there; but the white coach is all white. Of course this car is not so good as the other, but it is fairly clean and comfortable. The discomfort lies chiefly in the hearts of those four black men yonder—and in mine.

We rumble south in quite a business-like way. The bare red clay and pines of Northern Georgia begin to disappear, and in their place appears a rich rolling land, luxuriant, and here and there well tilled. This is the land of the Creek Indians; and a hard time the Georgians had to seize it. The towns grow more frequent and more interesting, and brand-new cotton mills rise on every side. Below Macon the world grows darker; for now we approach the Black Belt,—that strange land of shadows, at which even slaves paled in the past, and whence come now only faint and half-intelligible murmurs to the world beyond. The "Jim Crow Car" grows larger and a shade better; three rough field-hands and two or three white loafers accompany us, and the newsboy still spreads his wares at one end. The sun is setting, but we can see the great cotton country as we enter it,—the soil now dark and fertile, now thin and gray, with fruit-trees and dilapidated buildings,—all the way to Albany.

At Albany, in the heart of the Black Belt, we stop. Two hundred miles south of Atlanta, two hundred miles west of the Atlantic, and one hundred miles north of the Great Gulf lies Dougherty County, with ten thousand Negroes and two thousand whites. The Flint River winds down from Andersonville, and, turning suddenly at Albany, the county-seat, hurries on to join the Chattahoochee and the sea. Andrew Jackson knew the Flint well, and marched across it once to avenge the Indian Massacre at Fort Mims. That was in 1814, not long before the battle of New Orleans; and by the Creek treaty that followed this campaign, all Dougherty County, and much other rich land, was ceded to Georgia. Still, settlers fought shy of this land, for the Indians were all about, and they were unpleasant neighbors in those days. The panic of 1837, which Jackson bequeathed to Van Buren, turned the planters from the impoverished lands of Virginia, the Carolinas, and east Georgia, toward the West. The Indians were removed to Indian Territory, and settlers poured into these coveted lands to retrieve their broken fortunes. For a radius of a hundred miles about Albany, stretched a great fertile land, luxuriant with forests of pine, oak, ash, hickory, and poplar; hot with the sun and damp with the rich black swamp-land; and here the corner-stone of the Cotton Kingdom was laid.

Albany is to-day a wide-streeted, placid, Southern town, with a broad sweep of stores and saloons, and flanking rows of homes,—whites usually to the north, and blacks to the south. Six days in the week the town looks decidedly too small for itself, and takes frequent and prolonged naps. But on Saturday suddenly the whole county disgorges itself upon the place, and a perfect flood of black peasantry pours through the streets, fills the stores, blocks the sidewalks, chokes the thoroughfares, and takes full possession of the town. They are black, sturdy, uncouth country folk, good-natured and simple, talkative to a degree, and yet far more silent and brooding than the crowds of the Rhine-pfalz, or Naples, or Cracow. They drink considerable quantities of whiskey, but do not get very drunk;

they talk and laugh loudly at times, but seldom quarrel or fight. They walk up and down the streets, meet and gossip with friends, stare at the shop windows, buy coffee, cheap candy, and clothes, and at dusk drive home—happy? well no, not exactly happy, but much happier than as though they had not come.

Thus Albany is a real capital,—a typical Southern county town, the centre of the life of ten thousand souls; their point of contact with the outer world, their centre of news and gossip, their market for buying and selling, borrowing and lending, their fountain of justice and law. Once upon a time we knew country life so well and city life so little, that we illustrated city life as that of a closely crowded country district. Now the world has well-nigh forgotten what the country is, and we must imagine a little city of black people scattered far and wide over three hundred lonesome square miles of land, without train or trolley, in the midst of cotton and corn, and wide patches of sand and gloomy soil.

It gets pretty hot in Southern Georgia in July,—a sort of dull, determined heat that seems quite independent of the sun; so it took us some days to muster courage enough to leave the porch and venture out on the long country roads, that we might see this unknown world. Finally we started. It was about ten in the morning, bright with a faint breeze, and we jogged leisurely southward in the valley of the Flint. We passed the scattered box-like cabins of the brickyard hands, and the long tenement-row facetiously called "The Ark," and were soon in the open country, and on the confines of the great plantations of other days. There is the "Joe Fields place"; a rough old fellow was he, and had killed many a "nigger" in his day. Twelve miles his plantation used to run,—a regular barony. It is nearly all gone now; only straggling bits belong to the family, and the rest has passed to Jews and Negroes. Even the bits which are left are heavily mortgaged, and, like the rest of the land, tilled by tenants. Here is one of them now,—a tall brown man, a hard worker and a hard drinker, illiterate, but versed in farmlore, as his nodding crops declare. This distressingly new board house is his, and he has just moved out of yonder moss-grown cabin with its one square room.

From the curtains in Benton's house, down the road, a dark comely face is staring at the strangers; for passing carriages are not every-day occurrences here. Benton is an intelligent yellow man with a good-sized family, and manages a plantation blasted by the war and now the broken staff of the widow. He might be well-to-do, they say; but he carouses too much in Albany. And the half-desolate spirit of neglect born of the very soil seems to have settled on these acres. In times past there were cotton-gins and machinery here; but they have rotted away.

The whole land seems forlorn and forsaken. Here are the remnants of the vast plantations of the Sheldons, the Pellots, and the Rensons; but the souls of them are passed. The houses lie in half ruin, or have wholly disappeared; the fences have flown, and the families are wandering in the world. Strange vicissitudes have met these whilom masters. Yonder stretch the wide acres of Bildad Reasor; he died in war-time, but the upstart overseer hastened to wed the widow. Then he went, and his neighbors too, and now only the black tenant remains; but the shadow-hand of the master's grand-nephew or cousin or creditor stretches out of the gray distance to collect the rack-rent remorselessly, and so the land is uncared-for and poor. Only black tenants can stand such a system, and they only because they must. Ten miles we have ridden to-day and have seen no white face.

A resistless feeling of depression falls slowly upon us, despite the gaudy sunshine and the green cottonfields. This, then, is the Cotton Kingdom,—the shadow of a marvellous dream. And where is the King? Perhaps this is he,—the sweating ploughman, tilling his eighty acres with two lean mules, and fighting a hard battle with debt. So we sit musing, until, as we turn a corner on the sandy road, there comes a fairer scene suddenly in view,—a neat cottage snugly ensconced by the road, and near it a little store. A tall bronzed man rises from the porch as we hail him, and comes out to our carriage. He is six feet in height, with a sober face that smiles gravely. He walks too straight to be a tenant,—yes, he owns two hundred and forty acres. "The land is run down since the boom-days of eighteen hundred and fifty," he explains, and cotton is low. Three black tenants live on his place, and in his little store he keeps a small stock of tobacco, snuff, soap, and soda, for the neighborhood. Here is his gin-house with new machinery just installed. Three hundred bales of cotton went through it last year. Two children he has sent away to school. Yes, he says sadly, he is getting on, but cotton is down to four cents; I know how Debt sits staring at him.

Wherever the King may be, the parks and palaces of the Cotton Kingdom have not wholly disappeared. We plunge even now into great groves of oak and towering pine, with an undergrowth of myrtle and shrubbery. This was the "home-house" of the Thompsons,—slave-barons who drove their coach and four in the merry past. All is silence now, and ashes, and tangled weeds. The owner put his whole fortune into the rising cotton industry of the fifties, and with the falling prices of the eighties he packed up and stole away. Yonder is another grove, with unkempt lawn, great magnolias, and grass-grown paths. The Big House stands in half-ruin, its great front door staring blankly at the street, and the back part grotesquely restored for its black tenant. A shabby, well-built Negro he is, unlucky and irresolute. He digs hard to pay rent to the white girl who owns the remnant of the place. She married a policeman, and lives in Savannah.

Now and again we come to churches. Here is one now,—Shepherd's, they call it,—a great whitewashed barn of a thing, perched on stilts of stone, and looking for all the world as though it were just resting here a moment and might be expected to waddle off down the road at almost any time. And yet it is the centre of a hundred cabin homes; and sometimes, of a Sunday, five hundred persons from far and near gather here and talk and eat and sing. There is a schoolhouse near,—a very airy, empty shed; but even this is an improvement, for usually the school is held in the church. The churches vary from log-huts to those like Shepherd's, and the schools from nothing to this little house that sits demurely on the county line. It is a tiny plank-house, perhaps ten by twenty, and has within a double row of rough unplaned benches, resting mostly on legs, sometimes on boxes. Opposite the door is a square home-made desk. In one corner are the ruins of a stove, and in the other a dim blackboard. It is the cheerfulest schoolhouse I have seen in Dougherty, save in town. Back of the schoolhouse is a lodgehouse two stories high and not quite finished. Societies meet there,—societies "to care for the sick and bury the dead"; and these societies grow and flourish.

We had come to the boundaries of Dougherty, and were about to turn west along the county-line, when all these sights were pointed out to us by a kindly old man, black, white-haired, and seventy. Forty-five years he had lived here, and now supports himself and his old wife by the help of the steer tethered yonder and the charity of his black neighbors. He shows us the farm of the Hills just across the county line in Baker,—a widow and two strapping sons, who raised ten bales (one need not add "cotton" down here) last year. There are fences and pigs and cows, and the soft-voiced, velvet-skinned young Memnon, who sauntered half-bashfully over to greet the strangers, is proud of his home. We turn now to the west along the county line. Great dismantled trunks of pines tower above the green cottonfields, cracking their naked gnarled fingers toward the border of living forest beyond. There is little beauty in this region, only a sort of crude abandon that suggests power,—a naked grandeur, as it were. The houses are bare and straight; there are no hammocks or easy-chairs, and few flowers. So when, as here at Rawdon's, one sees a vine clinging to a little porch, and home-like windows peeping over the fences, one takes a long breath. I think I never before quite realized the place of the Fence in civilization. This is the Land of the Unfenced, where crouch on either hand scores of ugly one-room cabins, cheerless and dirty. Here lies the Negro problem in its naked dirt and penury. And here are no fences. But now and then the crisscross rails or straight palings break into view, and then we know a touch of culture is near. Of course Harrison Gohagen,—a quiet yellow man, young, smooth-faced, and diligent,—of course he is lord of some hundred acres, and we expect to see a vision of well-kept rooms and fat beds and laughing children. For has he not fine fences? And those over yonder, why should they build fences on the rack-rented land? It will only increase their rent.

On we wind, through sand and pines and glimpses of old plantations, till there creeps into sight a cluster of buildings,—wood and brick, mills and houses, and scattered cabins. It seemed quite a village. As it came nearer and nearer, however, the aspect changed: the buildings were rotten, the bricks were falling out, the mills were silent, and the store was closed. Only in the cabins appeared now and then a bit of lazy life. I could imagine the place under some weird spell, and was half-minded to search out the princess. An old ragged black man, honest, simple, and improvident, told us the tale. The Wizard of the North—the Capitalist—had rushed down in the seventies to woo this coy dark soil. He bought a square mile or more, and for a time the field-hands sang, the gins groaned, and the mills buzzed. Then came a change. The agent's son embezzled the funds and ran off with them. Then the agent himself disappeared. Finally the new agent stole even the books, and the company in wrath closed its business and its houses, refused to sell, and let houses and furniture and machinery rust and rot. So the Waters-Loring plantation was stilled by the spell of dishonesty, and stands like some gaunt rebuke to a scarred land.

Somehow that plantation ended our day's journey; for I could not shake off the influence of that silent scene. Back toward town we glided, past the straight and thread-like pines, past a dark tree-dotted pond where the air was heavy with a dead sweet perfume. White slender-legged curlews flitted by us, and the garnet blooms of the cotton looked gay against the green and purple stalks. A peasant girl was hoeing in the field, white-turbaned and black-limbed. All this we saw, but the spell still lay upon us.

How curious a land is this,—how full of untold story, of tragedy and laughter, and the rich legacy of human life; shadowed with a tragic past, and big with future promise! This is the Black Belt of Georgia. Dougherty County is the west end of the Black Belt, and men once called it the Egypt of the Confederacy. It is full of historic interest. First there is the Swamp, to the west, where the Chickasawhatchee flows sullenly southward. The shadow of an old plantation lies at its edge, forlorn and dark. Then comes the pool; pendent gray moss and brackish waters appear, and forests filled with wildfowl. In one place the wood is on fire, smouldering in dull red anger; but nobody minds. Then the swamp grows beautiful; a raised road, built by chained Negro convicts, dips down into it, and forms a way walled and almost covered in living green. Spreading trees spring from a prodigal luxuriance of undergrowth; great dark green shadows fade into the black background, until all is one mass of tangled semi-tropical foliage, marvellous in its weird savage splendor. Once we crossed a black silent stream, where the sad trees and writhing creepers, all glinting fiery yellow and green, seemed like some vast cathedral,—some green Milan builded of wildwood. And as I crossed, I seemed to see again that fierce tragedy of seventy years ago. Osceola, the Indian-Negro chieftain, had risen in the swamps of Florida, vowing vengeance. His war-cry reached the red Creeks of Dougherty, and their war-cry rang from the Chattahoochee to the sea. Men and women and children fled and fell before them as they swept into Dougherty. In yonder shadows a dark and hideously painted warrior glided stealthily on,—another and another, until three hundred had crept into the treacherous swamp. Then the false slime closing about them called the white men from the east. Waist-deep, they fought beneath the tall trees, until the war-cry was hushed and the Indians glided back into the west. Small wonder the wood is red.

Then came the black slaves. Day after day the clank of chained feet marching from Virginia and Carolina to Georgia was heard in these rich swamp lands. Day after day the songs of the callous, the wail of the motherless, and the muttered curses of the wretched echoed from the Flint to the Chickasawhatchee, until by 1860 there had risen in West Dougherty perhaps the richest slave kingdom the modern world ever knew. A hundred and fifty barons commanded the labor of nearly six thousand Negroes, held sway over farms with ninety thousand acres tilled land, valued even in times of cheap soil at three millions of dollars. Twenty thousand bales of ginned cotton went yearly to England, New and Old; and men that came there bankrupt made money and grew rich. In a single decade the cotton output increased four-fold and the value of lands was tripled. It was the heyday of the nouveau riche, and a life of careless extravagance among the masters. Four and six bobtailed thoroughbreds rolled their coaches to town; open hospitality and gay entertainment were the rule. Parks and groves were laid out, rich with flower and vine, and in the midst stood the low wide-halled "big house," with its porch and columns and great fireplaces.

And yet with all this there was something sordid, something forced,—a certain feverish unrest and recklessness; for was not all this show and tinsel built upon a groan? "This land was a little Hell," said a ragged, brown, and grave-faced man to me. We were seated near a roadside blacksmith shop, and behind was the bare ruin of some master's home. "I've seen niggers drop dead in the furrow, but they were kicked aside, and the plough never stopped. Down in the guard-house, there's where the blood ran."

With such foundations a kingdom must in time sway and fall. The masters moved to Macon and Augusta, and left only the irresponsible overseers on the land. And the result is such ruin as this, the Lloyd "home-place":—great waving oaks, a spread of lawn, myrtles and chestnuts, all ragged and wild; a solitary gate-post standing where once was a castle entrance; an old rusty anvil lying amid rotting bellows and wood in the ruins of a blacksmith shop; a wide rambling old mansion, brown and dingy, filled now with the grandchildren of the slaves who once waited on its tables; while the family of the master has dwindled to two lone women, who live in Macon and feed hungrily off the remnants of an earldom. So we ride on, past phantom gates and falling homes,—past the once flourishing farms of the Smiths, the Gandys, and the Lagores,—and find all dilapidated and half ruined, even there where a solitary white woman, a relic of other days, sits alone in state among miles of Negroes and rides to town in her ancient coach each day.

This was indeed the Egypt of the Confederacy,—the rich granary whence potatoes and corn and cotton poured out to the famished and ragged Confederate troops as they battled for a cause lost long before 1861. Sheltered and secure, it became the place of refuge for families, wealth, and slaves. Yet even then the hard ruthless rape of the land began to tell. The red-clay sub-soil already had begun to peer above the loam. The harder the slaves were driven the more careless and fatal was their farming. Then came the revolution of war and Emancipation, the bewilderment of Reconstruction,—and now, what is the Egypt of the Confederacy, and what meaning has it for the nation's weal or woe?

It is a land of rapid contrasts and of curiously mingled hope and pain. Here sits a pretty blue-eyed quadroon hiding her bare feet; she was married only last week, and yonder in the field is her dark young husband, hoeing to support her, at thirty cents a day without board. Across the way is Gatesby, brown and tall, lord of two thousand acres shrewdly won and held. There is a store conducted by his black son, a blacksmith shop, and a ginnery. Five miles below here is a town owned and controlled by one white New Englander. He owns almost a Rhode Island county, with thousands of acres and hundreds of black laborers. Their cabins look better than most, and the farm, with machinery and fertilizers, is much more business-like than any in the county, although the manager drives hard bargains in wages. When now we turn and look five miles above, there on the edge of town are five houses of prostitutes,—two of blacks and three of whites; and in one of the houses of the whites a worthless black boy was harbored too openly two years ago; so he was hanged for rape. And here, too, is the high whitewashed fence of the "stockade," as the county prison is called; the white folks say it is ever full of black criminals,—the black folks say that only colored boys are sent to jail, and they not because they are guilty, but because the State needs criminals to eke out its income by their forced labor.

Immigrants are heirs of the slave baron in Dougherty; and as we ride westward, by wide stretching cornfields and stubby orchards of peach and pear, we see on all sides within the circle of dark forest a Land of Canaan. Here and there are tales of projects for money-getting, born in the swift days of Reconstruction,—"improvement" companies, wine companies, mills and factories; most failed, and foreigners fell heir. It is a beautiful land, this Dougherty, west of the Flint. The forests are wonderful, the solemn pines have disappeared, and this is the "Oakey Woods," with its wealth of hickories, beeches, oaks and palmettos. But a pall of debt hangs over the beautiful land; the merchants are in debt to the wholesalers, the planters are in debt to the merchants, the tenants owe the planters, and laborers bow and bend beneath the burden of it all. Here and there a man has raised his head above these murky waters. We passed one fenced stock-farm with grass and grazing cattle, that looked very home-like after endless corn and cotton. Here and there are black free-holders: there is the gaunt dull-black Jackson, with his hundred acres. "I says, 'Look up! If you don't look up you can't get up,'" remarks Jackson, philosophically. And he's gotten up. Dark Carter's neat barns would do credit to New England. His master helped him to get a start, but when the black man died last fall the master's sons immediately laid claim to the estate. "And them white folks will get it, too," said my yellow gossip.

I turn from these well-tended acres with a comfortable feeling that the Negro is rising. Even then, however, the fields, as we proceed, begin to redden and the trees disappear. Rows of old cabins appear filled with renters and laborers,—cheerless, bare, and dirty, for the most part, although here and there the very age and decay makes the scene picturesque. A young black fellow greets us. He is twenty-two, and just married. Until last year he had good luck renting; then cotton fell, and the sheriff seized and sold all he had. So he moved here, where the rent is higher, the land poorer, and the owner inflexible; he rents a forty-dollar mule for twenty dollars a year. Poor lad!—a slave at twenty-two. This plantation, owned now by a foreigner, was a part of the famous Bolton estate. After the war it was for many years worked by gangs of Negro convicts,—and black convicts then were even more plentiful than now; it was a way of making Negroes work, and the question of guilt was a minor one. Hard tales of cruelty and mistreatment of the chained freemen are told, but the county authorities were deaf until the free-labor market was nearly ruined by wholesale migration. Then they took the convicts from the plantations, but not until one of the fairest regions of the "Oakey Woods" had been ruined and ravished into a red waste, out of which only a Yankee or an immigrant could squeeze more blood from debt-cursed tenants.

No wonder that Luke Black, slow, dull, and discouraged, shuffles to our carriage and talks hopelessly. Why should he strive? Every year finds him deeper in debt. How strange that Georgia, the world-heralded refuge of poor debtors, should bind her own to sloth and misfortune as ruthlessly as ever England did! The poor land groans with its birth-pains, and brings forth scarcely a hundred pounds of cotton to the acre, where fifty years ago it yielded eight times as much. Of his meagre yield the tenant pays from a quarter to a third in rent, and most of the rest in interest on food and supplies bought on credit. Twenty years yonder sunken-cheeked, old black man has labored under that system, and now, turned day-laborer, is supporting his wife and boarding himself on his wages of a dollar and a half a week, received only part of the year.

The Bolton convict farm formerly included the neighboring plantation. Here it was that the convicts were lodged in the great log prison still standing. A dismal place it still remains, with rows of ugly huts filled with surly ignorant tenants. "What rent do you pay here?" I inquired. "I don't know,—what is it, Sam?" "All we make," answered Sam. It is a depressing place,—bare, unshaded, with no charm of past association, only a memory of forced human toil,—now, then, and before the war. They are not happy, these black men whom we meet throughout this region. There is little of the joyous abandon and playfulness which we are wont to associate with the plantation Negro. At best, the natural good-nature is edged with complaint or has changed into sullenness and gloom. And now and then it blazes forth in veiled but hot anger. I remember one big red-eyed black whom we met by the roadside. Forty-five years he had labored on this farm, beginning with nothing, and still having nothing. To be sure, he had given four children a common-school training, and perhaps if the new fence-law had not allowed unfenced crops in West Dougherty he might have raised a little stock and kept ahead. As it is, he is hopelessly in debt, disappointed, and embittered. He stopped us to inquire after the black boy in Albany, whom it was said a policeman had shot and killed for loud talking on the sidewalk. And then he said slowly:

"Let a white man touch me, and he dies; I don't boast this,—I don't say it around loud, or before the children,—but I mean it. I've seen them whip my father and my old mother in them cotton-rows till the blood ran; by—" and we passed on.

Now Sears, whom we met next lolling under the chubby oak-trees, was of quite different fibre. Happy?—Well, yes; he laughed and flipped pebbles, and thought the world was as it was. He had worked here twelve years and has nothing but a mortgaged mule. Children? Yes, seven; but they hadn't been to school this year,—couldn't afford books and clothes, and couldn't spare their work. There go part of them to the fields now,—three big boys astride mules, and a strapping girl with bare brown legs. Careless ignorance and laziness here, fierce hate and vindictiveness there;—these are the extremes of the Negro problem which we met that day, and we scarce knew which we preferred.

Here and there we meet distinct characters quite out of the ordinary. One came out of a piece of newly cleared ground, making a wide detour to avoid the snakes. He was an old, hollow-cheeked man, with a drawn and characterful brown face. He had a sort of self-contained quaintness and rough humor impossible to describe; a certain cynical earnestness that puzzled one. "The niggers were jealous of me over on the other place," he said, "and so me and the old woman begged this piece of woods, and I cleared it up myself. Made nothing for two years, but I reckon I've got a crop now." The cotton looked tall and rich, and we praised it. He curtsied low, and then bowed almost to the ground, with an imperturbable gravity that seemed almost suspicious. Then he continued, "My mule died last week,"— a calamity in this land equal to a devastating fire in town,—"but a white man loaned me another." Then he added, eyeing us, "Oh, I gets along with white folks." We turned the conversation. "Bears? deer?" he answered, "well, I should say there were," and he let fly a string of brave oaths, as he told hunting-tales of the swamp. We left him standing still in the middle of the road looking after us, and yet apparently not noticing us.

The Whistle place, which includes his bit of land, was bought soon after the war by an English syndicate, the "Dixie Cotton and Corn Company." A marvellous deal of style their factor put on, with his servants and coach-and-six; so much so that the concern soon landed in inextricable bankruptcy. Nobody lives in the old house now, but a man comes each winter out of the North and collects his high rents. I know not which are the more touching,— such old empty houses, or the homes of the masters' sons. Sad and bitter tales lie hidden back of those white doors,—tales of poverty, of struggle, of disappointment. A revolution such as that of '63 is a terrible thing; they that rose rich in the morning often slept in paupers' beds. Beggars and vulgar speculators rose to rule over them, and their children went astray. See yonder sad-colored house, with its cabins and fences and glad crops! It is not glad within; last month the prodigal son of the struggling father wrote home from the city for money. Money! Where was it to come from? And so the son rose in the night and killed his baby, and killed his wife, and shot himself dead. And the world passed on.

I remember wheeling around a bend in the road beside a graceful bit of forest and a singing brook. A long low house faced us, with porch and flying pillars, great oaken door, and a broad lawn shining in the evening sun. But the window-panes were gone, the pillars were worm-eaten, and the moss- grown roof was falling in. Half curiously I peered through the unhinged door, and saw where, on the wall across the hall, was written in once gay letters a faded "Welcome."

Quite a contrast to the southwestern part of Dougherty County is the northwest. Soberly timbered in oak and pine, it has none of that half-tropical luxuriance of the southwest. Then, too, there are fewer signs of a romantic past, and more of systematic modern land-grabbing and money-getting. White people are more in evidence here, and farmer and hired labor replace to some extent the absentee landlord and rack-rented tenant. The crops have neither the luxuriance of the richer land nor the signs of neglect so often seen, and there were fences and meadows here and there. Most of this land was poor, and beneath the notice of the slave-baron, before the war. Since then his poor relations and foreign immigrants have seized it. The returns of the farmer are too small to allow much for wages, and yet he will not sell off small farms. There is the Negro Sanford; he has worked fourteen years as overseer on the Ladson place, and "paid out enough for fertilizers to have bought a farm," but the owner will not sell off a few acres.

Two children—a boy and a girl—are hoeing sturdily in the fields on the farm where Corliss works. He is smooth-faced and brown, and is fencing up his pigs. He used to run a successful cotton-gin, but the Cotton Seed Oil Trust has forced the price of ginning so low that he says it hardly pays him. He points out a stately old house over the way as the home of "Pa Willis." We eagerly ride over, for "Pa Willis" was the tall and powerful black Moses who led the Negroes for a generation, and led them well. He was a Baptist preacher, and when he died, two thousand black people followed him to the grave; and now they preach his funeral sermon each year. His widow lives here,—a weazened, sharp-featured little woman, who curtsied quaintly as we greeted her. Further on lives Jack Delson, the most prosperous Negro farmer in the county. It is a joy to meet him,—a great broad-shouldered, handsome black man, intelligent and jovial. Six hundred and fifty acres he owns, and has eleven black tenants. A neat and tidy home nestled in a flower-garden, and a little store stands beside it.

We pass the Munson place, where a plucky white widow is renting and struggling; and the eleven hundred acres of the Sennet plantation, with its Negro overseer. Then the character of the farms begins to change. Nearly all the lands belong to Russian Jews; the overseers are white, and the cabins are bare board-houses scattered here and there. The rents are high, and day-laborers and "contract" hands abound. It is a keen, hard struggle for living here, and few have time to talk. Tired with the long ride, we gladly drive into Gillonsville. It is a silent cluster of farmhouses standing on the crossroads, with one of its stores closed and the other kept by a Negro preacher. They tell great tales of busy times at Gillonsville before all the railroads came to Albany; now it is chiefly a memory. Riding down the street, we stop at the preacher's and seat ourselves before the door. It was one of those scenes one cannot soon forget:—a wide, low, little house, whose motherly roof reached over and sheltered a snug little porch. There we sat, after the long hot drive, drinking cool water,—the talkative little storekeeper who is my daily companion; the silent old black woman patching pantaloons and saying never a word; the ragged picture of helpless misfortune who called in just to see the preacher; and finally the neat matronly preacher's wife, plump, yellow, and intelligent. "Own land?" said the wife; "well, only this house." Then she added quietly. "We did buy seven hundred acres across up yonder, and paid for it; but they cheated us out of it. Sells was the owner." "Sells!" echoed the ragged misfortune, who was leaning against the balustrade and listening, "he's a regular cheat. I worked for him thirty-seven days this spring, and he paid me in cardboard checks which were to be cashed at the end of the month. But he never cashed them,—kept putting me off. Then the sheriff came and took my mule and corn and furniture—" "Furniture? But furniture is exempt from seizure by law." "Well, he took it just the same," said the hard-faced man.

8. OF THE QUEST OF THE GOLDEN FLEECE

But the Brute said in his breast, "Till the mills I grind
have ceased,
The riches shall be dust of dust, dry ashes be the feast!

"On the strong and cunning few
Cynic favors I will strew;
I will stuff their maw with overplus until their spirit dies;
From the patient and the low

I will take the joys they know;
They shall hunger after vanities and still an-hungered go.
Madness shall be on the people, ghastly jealousies arise;
Brother's blood shall cry on brother up the dead and empty skies.

WILLIAM VAUGHN MOODY.

Have you ever seen a cotton-field white with harvest,—its golden fleece hovering above the black earth like a silvery cloud edged with dark green, its bold white signals waving like the foam of billows from Carolina to Texas across that Black and human Sea? I have sometimes half suspected that here the winged ram Chrysomallus left that Fleece after which Jason and his Argonauts went vaguely wandering into the shadowy East three thousand years ago; and certainly one might frame a pretty and not far-fetched analogy of witchery and dragons' teeth, and blood and armed men, between the ancient and the modern quest of the Golden Fleece in the Black Sea.

And now the golden fleece is found; not only found, but, in its birthplace, woven. For the hum of the cotton-mills is the newest and most significant thing in the New South to-day. All through the Carolinas and Georgia, away down to Mexico, rise these gaunt red buildings, bare and homely, and yet so busy and noisy withal that they scarce seem to belong to the slow and sleepy land. Perhaps they sprang from dragons' teeth. So the Cotton Kingdom still lives; the world still bows beneath her sceptre. Even the markets that once defied the parvenu have crept one by one across the seas, and then slowly and reluctantly, but surely, have started toward the Black Belt.

To be sure, there are those who wag their heads knowingly and tell us that the capital of the Cotton Kingdom has moved from the Black to the White Belt,—that the Negro of to-day raises not more than half of the cotton crop. Such men forget that the cotton crop has doubled, and more than doubled, since the era of slavery, and that, even granting their contention, the Negro is still supreme in a Cotton Kingdom larger than that on which the Confederacy builded its hopes. So the Negro forms to-day one of the chief figures in a great world-industry; and this, for its own sake, and in the light of historic interest, makes the field-hands of the cotton country worth studying.

We seldom study the condition of the Negro to-day honestly and carefully. It is so much easier to assume that we know it all. Or perhaps, having already reached conclusions in our own minds, we are loth to have them disturbed by facts. And yet how little we really know of these millions,—of their daily lives and longings, of their homely joys and sorrows, of their real shortcomings and the meaning of their crimes! All this we can only learn by intimate contact with the masses, and not by wholesale arguments covering millions separate in time and space, and differing widely in training and culture. To-day, then, my reader, let us turn our faces to the Black Belt of Georgia and seek simply to know the condition of the black farm-laborers of one county there.

Here in 1890 lived ten thousand Negroes and two thousand whites. The country is rich, yet the people are poor. The keynote of the Black Belt is debt; not commercial credit, but debt in the sense of continued inability on the part of the mass of the population to make income cover expense. This is the direct heritage of the South from the wasteful economies of the slave regime; but it was emphasized and brought to a crisis by the Emancipation of the slaves. In 1860, Dougherty County had six thousand slaves, worth at least two and a half millions of dollars; its farms were estimated at three millions,—making five and a half millions of property, the value of which depended largely on the slave system, and on the speculative demand for land once marvellously rich but already partially devitalized by careless and exhaustive culture. The war then meant a financial crash; in place of the five and a half millions of 1860, there remained in 1870 only farms valued at less than two millions. With this came increased competition in cotton culture from the rich lands of Texas; a steady fall in the normal price of cotton followed, from about fourteen cents a pound in 1860 until it reached four cents in 1898. Such a financial revolution was it that involved the owners of the cotton-belt in debt. And if things went ill with the master, how fared it with the man?

The plantations of Dougherty County in slavery days were not as imposing and aristocratic as those of Virginia. The Big House was smaller and usually one-storied, and sat very near the slave cabins. Sometimes these cabins stretched off on either side like wings; sometimes only on one side, forming a double row, or edging the road that turned into the plantation from the main thoroughfare. The form and disposition of the laborers' cabins throughout the Black Belt is to-day the same as in slavery days. Some live in the self-same cabins, others in cabins rebuilt on the sites of the old. All are sprinkled in little groups over the face of the land, centering about some dilapidated Big House where the head-tenant or agent lives. The general character and arrangement of these dwellings remains on the whole unaltered. There were in the county, outside the corporate town of Albany, about fifteen hundred Negro families in 1898. Out of all these, only a single family occupied a house with seven rooms; only fourteen have five rooms or more. The mass live in one- and two-room homes.

The size and arrangements of a people's homes are no unfair index of their condition. If, then, we inquire more carefully into these Negro homes, we find much that is unsatisfactory. All over the face of the land is the one-room cabin,—now standing in the shadow of the Big House, now staring at the dusty road, now rising dark and sombre amid the green of the cotton-fields. It is nearly always old and bare, built of rough boards, and neither plastered nor ceiled. Light and ventilation are supplied by the single door and by the square hole in the wall with its wooden shutter. There is no glass, porch, or ornamentation without. Within is a fireplace, black and smoky, and usually unsteady with age. A bed or two, a table, a wooden chest, and a few chairs compose the furniture; while a stray show-bill or a newspaper makes up the decorations for the walls. Now and then one may find such a cabin kept scrupulously neat, with merry steaming fireplaces and hospitable door; but the majority are dirty and dilapidated, smelling of eating and sleeping, poorly ventilated, and anything but homes.

Above all, the cabins are crowded. We have come to associate crowding with homes in cities almost exclusively. This is primarily because we have so little accurate knowledge of country life. Here in Dougherty County one may find families of eight and ten occupying one or two rooms, and for every ten rooms of house accommodation for the Negroes there are twenty-five persons. The worst tenement abominations of New York do not have above twenty-two persons for every ten rooms. Of course, one small, close room in a city, without a yard, is in many respects worse than the larger single country room. In other respects it is better; it has glass windows, a decent chimney, and a trustworthy floor. The single great advantage of the Negro peasant is that he may spend most of his life outside his hovel, in the open fields.

There are four chief causes of these wretched homes: First, long custom born of slavery has assigned such homes to Negroes; white laborers would be offered better accommodations, and might, for that and similar reasons, give better work. Secondly, the Negroes, used to such accommodations, do not as a rule demand better; they do not know what better houses mean. Thirdly, the landlords as a class have not yet come to realize that it is a good business investment to raise the standard of living among labor by slow and judicious methods; that a Negro laborer who demands three rooms and fifty cents a day would give more efficient work and leave a larger profit than a discouraged toiler herding his family in one room and working for thirty cents. Lastly, among such conditions of life there are few incentives to make the laborer become a better farmer. If he is ambitious, he moves to town or tries other labor; as a tenant-farmer his outlook is almost hopeless, and following it as a makeshift, he takes the house that is given him without protest.

In such homes, then, these Negro peasants live. The families are both small and large; there are many single tenants,—widows and bachelors, and remnants of broken groups. The system of labor and the size of the houses both tend to the breaking up of family groups: the grown children go away as contract hands or migrate to town, the sister goes into service; and so one finds many families with hosts of babies, and many newly married couples, but comparatively few families with half-grown and grown sons and daughters. The average size of Negro families has undoubtedly decreased since the war, primarily from economic stress. In Russia over a third of the bridegrooms and over half the brides are under twenty; the same was true of the antebellum Negroes. Today, however, very few of the boys and less than a fifth of the Negro girls under twenty are married. The young men marry between the ages of twenty-five and thirty-five; the young women between twenty and thirty. Such postponement is due to the difficulty of earning sufficient to rear and support a family; and it undoubtedly leads, in the country districts, to sexual immorality. The form of this immorality, however, is very seldom that of prostitution, and less frequently that of illegitimacy than one would imagine. Rather, it takes the form of separation and desertion after a family group has been formed. The number of separated persons is thirty-five to the thousand,—a very large number. It would of course be unfair to compare this number with divorce statistics, for many of these separated women are in reality widowed, were the truth known, and in other cases the separation is not permanent. Nevertheless, here lies the seat of greatest moral danger. There is little or no prostitution among these Negroes, and over three-fourths of the families, as found by house-to-house investigation, deserve to be classed as decent people with considerable regard for female chastity. To be sure, the ideas of the mass would not suit New England, and there are many loose habits and notions. Yet the rate of illegitimacy is undoubtedly lower than in Austria or Italy, and the women as a class are modest. The plague-spot in sexual relations is easy marriage and easy separation. This is no sudden development, nor the fruit of Emancipation. It is the plain heritage from slavery. In those days Sam, with his master's consent, "took up" with Mary. No ceremony was necessary, and in the busy life of the great plantations of the Black Belt it was usually dispensed with. If now the master needed Sam's work in another plantation or in another part of the same plantation, or if he took a notion to sell the slave, Sam's married life with Mary was usually unceremoniously broken, and then it was clearly to the master's interest to have both of them take new mates. This widespread custom of two centuries has not been eradicated in thirty years. To-day Sam's grandson "takes up" with a woman without license or ceremony; they live together decently and honestly, and are, to all intents and purposes, man and wife. Sometimes these unions are never broken until death; but in too many cases family quarrels, a roving spirit, a rival suitor, or perhaps more frequently the hopeless battle to support a family, lead to separation, and a broken household is the result. The Negro church has done much to stop this practice, and now most marriage ceremonies are performed by the pastors. Nevertheless, the evil is still deep seated, and only a general raising of the standard of living will finally cure it.

Looking now at the county black population as a whole, it is fair to characterize it as poor and ignorant. Perhaps ten per cent compose the well-to-do and the best of the laborers, while at least nine per cent are thoroughly lewd and vicious. The rest, over eighty per cent, are poor and ignorant, fairly honest and well meaning, plodding, and to a degree shiftless, with some but not great sexual looseness. Such class lines are by no means fixed; they vary, one might almost say, with the price of cotton. The degree of ignorance cannot easily be expressed. We may say, for instance, that nearly two-thirds of them cannot read or write. This but partially expresses the fact. They are ignorant of the world about them, of modern economic organization, of the function of government, of individual worth and possibilities,—of nearly all those things which slavery in self-defence had to keep them from learning. Much that the white boy imbibes from his earliest social atmosphere forms the puzzling problems of the black boy's mature years. America is not another word for Opportunity to all her sons.

It is easy for us to lose ourselves in details in endeavoring to grasp and comprehend the real condition of a mass of human beings. We often forget that each unit in the mass is a throbbing human soul. Ignorant it may be, and poverty stricken, black and curious in limb and ways and thought; and yet it loves and hates, it toils and tires, it laughs and weeps its bitter tears, and looks in vague and awful longing at the grim horizon of its life,—all this, even as you and I. These black thousands are not in reality lazy; they are improvident and careless; they insist on breaking the monotony of toil with a glimpse at the great town-world on Saturday;

they have their loafers and their rascals; but the great mass of them work continuously and faithfully for a return, and under circumstances that would call forth equal voluntary effort from few if any other modern laboring class. Over eighty-eight per cent of them—men, women, and children—are farmers. Indeed, this is almost the only industry. Most of the children get their schooling after the "crops are laid by," and very few there are that stay in school after the spring work has begun. Child-labor is to be found here in some of its worst phases, as fostering ignorance and stunting physical development. With the grown men of the county there is little variety in work: thirteen hundred are farmers, and two hundred are laborers, teamsters, etc., including twenty-four artisans, ten merchants, twenty-one preachers, and four teachers. This narrowness of life reaches its maximum among the women: thirteen hundred and fifty of these are farm laborers, one hundred are servants and washerwomen, leaving sixty-five housewives, eight teachers, and six seamstresses.

Among this people there is no leisure class. We often forget that in the United States over half the youth and adults are not in the world earning incomes, but are making homes, learning of the world, or resting after the heat of the strife. But here ninety-six per cent are toiling; no one with leisure to turn the bare and cheerless cabin into a home, no old folks to sit beside the fire and hand down traditions of the past; little of careless happy childhood and dreaming youth. The dull monotony of daily toil is broken only by the gayety of the thoughtless and the Saturday trip to town. The toil, like all farm toil, is monotonous, and here there are little machinery and few tools to relieve its burdensome drudgery. But with all this, it is work in the pure open air, and this is something in a day when fresh air is scarce.

The land on the whole is still fertile, despite long abuse. For nine or ten months in succession the crops will come if asked: garden vegetables in April, grain in May, melons in June and July, hay in August, sweet potatoes in September, and cotton from then to Christmas. And yet on two-thirds of the land there is but one crop, and that leaves the toilers in debt. Why is this?

Away down the Baysan road, where the broad flat fields are flanked by great oak forests, is a plantation; many thousands of acres it used to run, here and there, and beyond the great wood. Thirteen hundred human beings here obeyed the call of one,—were his in body, and largely in soul. One of them lives there yet,—a short, stocky man, his dull-brown face seamed and drawn, and his tightly curled hair gray-white. The crops? Just tolerable, he said; just tolerable. Getting on? No—he wasn't getting on at all. Smith of Albany "furnishes" him, and his rent is eight hundred pounds of cotton. Can't make anything at that. Why didn't he buy land! Humph! Takes money to buy land. And he turns away. Free! The most piteous thing amid all the black ruin of war-time, amid the broken fortunes of the masters, the blighted hopes of mothers and maidens, and the fall of an empire,—the most piteous thing amid all this was the black freedman who threw down his hoe because the world called him free. What did such a mockery of freedom mean? Not a cent of money, not an inch of land, not a mouthful of victuals,—not even ownership of the rags on his back. Free! On Saturday, once or twice a month, the old master, before the war, used to dole out bacon and meal to his Negroes. And after the first flush of freedom wore off, and his true helplessness dawned on the freedman, he came back and picked up his hoe, and old master still doled out his bacon and meal. The legal form of service was theoretically far different; in practice, task-work or "cropping" was substituted for daily toil in gangs; and the slave gradually became a metayer, or tenant on shares, in name, but a laborer with indeterminate wages in fact.

Still the price of cotton fell, and gradually the landlords deserted their plantations, and the reign of the merchant began. The merchant of the Black Belt is a curious institution,—part banker, part landlord, part banker, and part despot. His store, which used most frequently to stand at the cross-roads and become the centre of a weekly village, has now moved to town; and thither the Negro tenant follows him. The merchant keeps everything,—clothes and shoes, coffee and sugar, pork and meal, canned and dried goods, wagons and ploughs, seed and fertilizer,—and what he has not in stock he can give you an order for at the store across the way. Here, then, comes the tenant, Sam Scott, after he has contracted with some absent landlord's agent for hiring forty acres of land; he fingers his hat nervously until the merchant finishes his morning chat with Colonel Saunders, and calls out, "Well, Sam, what do you want?" Sam wants him to "furnish" him,—i.e., to advance him food and clothing for the year, and perhaps seed and tools, until his crop is raised and sold. If Sam seems a favorable subject, he and the merchant go to a lawyer, and

Sam executes a chattel mortgage on his mule and wagon in return for seed and a week's rations. As soon as the green cotton-leaves appear above the ground, another mortgage is given on the "crop." Every Saturday, or at longer intervals, Sam calls upon the merchant for his "rations"; a family of five usually gets about thirty pounds of fat side-pork and a couple of bushels of cornmeal a month. Besides this, clothing and shoes must be furnished; if Sam or his family is sick, there are orders on the druggist and doctor; if the mule wants shoeing, an order on the blacksmith, etc. If Sam is a hard worker and crops promise well, he is often encouraged to buy more,—sugar, extra clothes, perhaps a buggy. But he is seldom encouraged to save. When cotton rose to ten cents last fall, the shrewd merchants of Dougherty County sold a thousand buggies in one season, mostly to black men.

The security offered for such transactions—a crop and chattel mortgage—may at first seem slight. And, indeed, the merchants tell many a true tale of shiftlessness and cheating; of cotton picked at night, mules disappearing, and tenants absconding. But on the whole the merchant of the Black Belt is the most prosperous man in the section. So skilfully and so closely has he drawn the bonds of the law about the tenant, that the black man has often simply to choose between pauperism and crime; he "waives" all homestead exemptions in his contract; he cannot touch his own mortgaged crop, which the laws put almost in the full control of the land-owner and of the merchant. When the crop is growing the merchant watches it like a hawk; as soon as it is ready for market he takes possession of it, sells it, pays the landowner his rent, subtracts his bill for supplies, and if, as sometimes happens, there is anything left, he hands it over to the black serf for his Christmas celebration.

The direct result of this system is an all-cotton scheme of agriculture and the continued bankruptcy of the tenant. The currency of the Black Belt is cotton. It is a crop always salable for ready money, not usually subject to great yearly fluctuations in price, and one which the Negroes know how to raise. The landlord therefore demands his rent in cotton, and the merchant will accept mortgages on no other crop. There is no use asking the black tenant, then, to diversify his crops,—he cannot under this system. Moreover, the system is bound to bankrupt the tenant. I remember once meeting a little one-mule wagon on the River road. A young black fellow sat in it driving listlessly, his elbows on his knees. His dark-faced wife sat beside him, stolid, silent.

"Hello!" cried my driver,—he has a most imprudent way of addressing these people, though they seem used to it,—"what have you got there?"

"Meat and meal," answered the man, stopping. The meat lay uncovered in the bottom of the wagon,—a great thin side of fat pork covered with salt; the meal was in a white bushel bag.

"What did you pay for that meat?"

"Ten cents a pound." It could have been bought for six or seven cents cash.

"And the meal?"

"Two dollars." One dollar and ten cents is the cash price in town. Here was a man paying five dollars for goods which he could have bought for three dollars cash, and raised for one dollar or one dollar and a half.

Yet it is not wholly his fault. The Negro farmer started behind,—started in debt. This was not his choosing, but the crime of this happy-go-lucky nation which goes blundering along with its Reconstruction tragedies, its Spanish war interludes and Philippine matinees, just as though God really were dead. Once in debt, it is no easy matter for a whole race to emerge.

In the year of low-priced cotton, 1898, out of three hundred tenant families one hundred and seventy-five ended their year's work in debt to the extent of fourteen thousand dollars; fifty cleared nothing, and the remaining seventy-five made a total profit of sixteen hundred dollars. The net indebtedness of the black tenant families of the whole county must have been at least sixty thousand dollars. In a more prosperous year the situation is far better; but on the average the majority of tenants end the year even, or in debt, which means that they work for board and clothes. Such an economic organization is radically wrong. Whose is the blame?

The underlying causes of this situation are complicated but discernible. And one of the chief, outside the carelessness of the nation in letting the slave start with nothing, is the widespread opinion among the merchants and employers of the Black Belt that only by the slavery of debt can the Negro be kept at work. Without doubt, some pressure was necessary at the beginning of the free-labor system to keep the listless and lazy at work; and even to-day the mass of the Negro laborers need stricter guardianship than most Northern laborers. Behind this honest and widespread opinion dishonesty and cheating of the ignorant laborers have a good chance to take refuge. And to all this must be added the obvious fact that a slave ancestry and a system of unrequited toil has not improved the efficiency or temper of the mass of black laborers. Nor is this peculiar to Sambo; it has in history been just as true of John and Hans, of Jacques and Pat, of all ground-down peasantries. Such is the situation of the mass of the Negroes in the Black Belt to-day; and they are thinking about it. Crime, and a cheap and dangerous socialism, are the inevitable results of this pondering. I see now that ragged black man sitting on a log, aimlessly whittling a stick. He muttered to me with the murmur of many ages, when he said: "White man sit down whole year; Nigger work day and night and make crop; Nigger hardly gits bread and meat; white man sittin' down gits all. It's wrong." And what do the better classes of Negroes do to improve their situation? One of two things: if any way possible, they buy land; if not, they migrate to town. Just as centuries ago it was no easy thing for the serf to escape into the freedom of town-life, even so to-day there are hindrances laid in the way of county laborers. In considerable parts of all the Gulf States, and especially in Mississippi, Louisiana, and Arkansas, the Negroes on the plantations in the back-country districts are still held at forced labor practically without wages. Especially is this true in districts where the farmers are composed of the more ignorant class of poor whites, and the Negroes are beyond the reach of schools and intercourse with their advancing fellows. If such a peon should run away, the sheriff, elected by white suffrage, can usually be depended on to catch the fugitive, return him, and ask no questions. If he escape to another county, a charge of petty thieving, easily true, can be depended upon to secure his return. Even if some unduly officious person insist upon a trial, neighborly comity will probably make his conviction sure, and then the labor due the county can easily be bought by the master. Such a system is impossible in the more civilized parts of the South, or near the large towns and cities; but in those vast stretches of land beyond the telegraph and the newspaper the spirit of the Thirteenth Amendment is sadly broken. This represents the lowest economic depths of the black American peasant; and in a study of the rise and condition of the Negro freeholder we must trace his economic progress from the modern serfdom.

Even in the better-ordered country districts of the South the free movement of agricultural laborers is hindered by the migration-agent laws. The "Associated Press" recently informed the world of the arrest of a young white man in Southern Georgia who represented the "Atlantic Naval Supplies Company," and who "was caught in the act of enticing hands from the turpentine farm of Mr. John Greer." The crime for which this young man was arrested is taxed five hundred dollars for each county in which the employment agent proposes to gather laborers for work outside the State. Thus the Negroes' ignorance of the labor-market outside his own vicinity is increased rather than diminished by the laws of nearly every Southern State.

Similar to such measures is the unwritten law of the back districts and small towns of the South, that the character of all Negroes unknown to the mass of the community must be vouched for by some white man. This is really a revival of the old Roman idea of the patron under whose protection the new-made freedman was put. In many instances this system has been of great good to the Negro, and very often under the protection and guidance of the former master's family, or other white friends, the freedman progressed in wealth and morality. But the same system has in other cases resulted in the refusal of whole communities to recognize the right of a Negro to change his habitation and to be master of his own fortunes. A black stranger in Baker County, Georgia, for instance, is liable to be stopped anywhere on the public highway and made to state his business to the satisfaction of any white interrogator. If he fails to give a suitable answer, or seems too independent or "sassy," he may be arrested or summarily driven away.

Thus it is that in the country districts of the South, by written or unwritten law, peonage, hindrances to the migration of labor, and a system of white patronage exists over large areas. Besides this, the chance for lawless oppression and illegal exactions is vastly greater in the country than in the city, and nearly all the more serious race disturbances of the last decade have arisen from disputes in the count between master and man,—as, for instance, the Sam Hose affair. As a result of such a situation, there arose, first, the Black Belt; and, second, the Migration to Town. The Black Belt was not, as many assumed, a movement toward fields of labor under more genial climatic conditions; it was primarily a huddling for self-protection,—a massing of the black population for mutual defence in order to secure the peace and tranquillity necessary to economic advance. This movement took place between Emancipation and 1880, and only partially accomplished the desired results. The rush to town since 1880 is the counter-movement of men disappointed in the economic opportunities of the Black Belt.

In Dougherty County, Georgia, one can see easily the results of this experiment in huddling for protection. Only ten per cent of the adult population was born in the county, and yet the blacks outnumber the whites four or five to one. There is undoubtedly a security to the blacks in their very numbers,—a personal freedom from arbitrary treatment, which makes hundreds of laborers cling to Dougherty in spite of low wages and economic distress. But a change is coming, and slowly but surely even here the agricultural laborers are drifting to town and leaving the broad acres behind. Why is this? Why do not the Negroes become land-owners, and build up the black landed peasantry, which has for a generation and more been the dream of philanthropist and statesman?

To the car-window sociologist, to the man who seeks to understand and know the South by devoting the few leisure hours of a holiday trip to unravelling the snarl of centuries,—to such men very often the whole trouble with the black field-hand may be summed up by Aunt Ophelia's word, "Shiftless!" They have noted repeatedly scenes like one I saw last summer. We were riding along the highroad to town at the close of a long hot day. A couple of young black fellows passed us in a muleteam, with several bushels of loose corn in the ear. One was driving, listlessly bent forward, his elbows on his knees,—a happy-go-lucky, careless picture of irresponsibility. The other was fast asleep in the bottom of the wagon. As we passed we noticed an ear of corn fall from the wagon. They never saw it,—not they. A rod farther on we noted another ear on the ground; and between that creeping mule and town we counted twenty-six ears of corn. Shiftless? Yes, the personification of shiftlessness. And yet follow those boys: they are not lazy; to-morrow morning they'll be up with the sun; they work hard when they do work, and they work willingly. They have no sordid, selfish, money-getting ways, but rather a fine disdain for mere cash. They'll loaf before your face and work behind your back with good-natured honesty. They'll steal a watermelon, and hand you back your lost purse intact. Their great defect as laborers lies in their lack of incentive beyond the mere pleasure of physical exertion. They are careless because they have not found that it pays to be careful; they are improvident because the improvident ones of their acquaintance get on about as well as the provident. Above all, they cannot see why they should take unusual pains to make the white man's land better, or to fatten his mule, or save his corn. On the other hand, the white land-owner argues that any attempt to improve these laborers by increased responsibility, or higher wages, or better homes, or land of their own, would be sure to result in failure. He shows his Northern visitor the scarred and wretched land; the ruined mansions, the worn-out soil and mortgaged acres, and says, This is Negro freedom!

Now it happens that both master and man have just enough argument on their respective sides to make it difficult for them to understand each other. The Negro dimly personifies in the white man all his ills and misfortunes; if he is poor, it is because the white man seizes the fruit of his toil; if he is ignorant, it is because the white man gives him neither time nor facilities to learn; and, indeed, if any misfortune happens to him, it is because of some hidden machinations of "white folks." On the other hand, the masters and the masters' sons have never been able to see why the Negro, instead of settling down to be day-laborers for bread and clothes, are infected with a silly desire to rise in the world, and why they are sulky, dissatisfied, and careless, where their fathers were happy and dumb and faithful. "Why, you niggers have an easier time than I do," said a puzzled Albany merchant to his black customer. "Yes," he replied, "and so does yo' hogs."

Taking, then, the dissatisfied and shiftless field-hand as a starting-point, let us inquire how the black thousands of Dougherty have struggled from him up toward their ideal, and what that ideal is. All social struggle is evidenced by the rise, first of economic, then of social classes, among a homogeneous population. To-day the following economic classes are plainly differentiated among these Negroes.

A "submerged tenth" of croppers, with a few paupers; forty per cent who are metayers and thirty-nine per cent of semi-metayers and wage-laborers. There are left five per cent of money-renters and six per cent of freeholders,—the "Upper Ten" of the land. The croppers are entirely without capital, even in the limited sense of food or money to keep them from seed-time to harvest. All they furnish is their labor; the land-owner furnishes land, stock, tools, seed, and house; and at the end of the year the laborer gets from a third to a half of the crop. Out of his share, however, comes pay and interest for food and clothing advanced him during the year. Thus we have a laborer without capital and without wages, and an employer whose capital is largely his employees' wages. It is an unsatisfactory arrangement, both for hirer and hired, and is usually in vogue on poor land with hard-pressed owners.

Above the croppers come the great mass of the black population who work the land on their own responsibility, paying rent in cotton and supported by the crop-mortgage system. After the war this system was attractive to the freedmen on account of its larger freedom and its possibility for making a surplus. But with the carrying out of the crop-lien system, the deterioration of the land, and the slavery of debt, the position of the metayers has sunk to a dead level of practically unrewarded toil. Formerly all tenants had some capital, and often considerable; but absentee landlordism, rising rack-rent, and failing cotton have stripped them well-nigh of all, and probably not over half of them to-day own their mules. The change from cropper to tenant was accomplished by fixing the rent. If, now, the rent fixed was reasonable, this was an incentive to the tenant to strive. On the other hand, if the rent was too high, or if the land deteriorated, the result was to discourage and check the efforts of the black peasantry. There is no doubt that the latter case is true; that in Dougherty County every economic advantage of the price of cotton in market and of the strivings of the tenant has been taken advantage of by the landlords and merchants, and swallowed up in rent and interest. If cotton rose in price, the rent rose even higher; if cotton fell, the rent remained or followed reluctantly. If the tenant worked hard and raised a large crop, his rent was raised the next year; if that year the crop failed, his corn was confiscated and his mule sold for debt. There were, of course, exceptions to this,—cases of personal kindness and forbearance; but in the vast majority of cases the rule was to extract the uttermost farthing from the mass of the black farm laborers.

The average metayer pays from twenty to thirty per cent of his crop in rent. The result of such rack-rent can only be evil,—abuse and neglect of the soil, deterioration in the character of the laborers, and a widespread sense of injustice. "Wherever the country is poor," cried Arthur Young, "it is in the hands of metayers," and "their condition is more wretched than that of day-laborers." He was talking of Italy a century ago; but he might have been talking of Dougherty County to-day. And especially is that true to-day which he declares was true in France before the Revolution: "The metayers are considered as little better than menial servants, removable at pleasure, and obliged to conform in all things to the will of the landlords." On this low plane half the black population of Dougherty County—perhaps more than half the black millions of this land—are to-day struggling.

A degree above these we may place those laborers who receive money wages for their work. Some receive a house with perhaps a garden-spot; then supplies of food and clothing are advanced, and certain fixed wages are given at the end of the year, varying from thirty to sixty dollars, out of which the supplies must be paid for, with interest. About eighteen per cent of the population belong to this class of semi-metayers, while twenty-two per cent are laborers paid by the month or year, and are either "furnished" by their own savings or perhaps more usually by some merchant who takes his chances of payment. Such laborers receive from thirty-five to fifty cents a day during the working season. They are usually young unmarried persons, some being women; and when they marry they sink to the class of metayers, or, more seldom, become renters.

The renters for fixed money rentals are the first of the emerging classes, and form five per cent of the families. The sole advantage of this small class is their freedom to choose their crops, and the increased responsibility which comes through having money transactions. While some of the renters differ little in condition from the metayers, yet on the whole they are more intelligent and responsible persons, and are the ones who eventually become land-owners. Their better character and greater shrewdness enable them to gain, perhaps to demand, better terms in rents; rented farms, varying from forty to a hundred acres, bear an average rental of about fifty-four dollars a year. The men who conduct such farms do not long remain renters; either they sink to metayers, or with a successful series of harvests rise to be land-owners.

In 1870 the tax-books of Dougherty report no Negroes as landholders. If there were any such at that time,—and there may have been a few,—their land was probably held in the name of some white patron,—a method not uncommon during slavery. In 1875 ownership of land had begun with seven hundred and fifty acres; ten years later this had increased to over sixty-five hundred acres, to nine thousand acres in 1890 and ten thousand in 1900. The total assessed property has in this same period risen from eighty thousand dollars in 1875 to two hundred and forty thousand dollars in 1900.

Two circumstances complicate this development and make it in some respects difficult to be sure of the real tendencies; they are the panic of 1893, and the low price of cotton in 1898. Besides this, the system of assessing property in the country districts of Georgia is somewhat antiquated and of uncertain statistical value; there are no assessors, and each man makes a sworn return to a tax-receiver. Thus public opinion plays a large part, and the returns vary strangely from year to year. Certainly these figures show the small amount of accumulated capital among the Negroes, and the consequent large dependence of their property on temporary prosperity. They have little to tide over a few years of economic depression, and are at the mercy of the cotton-market far more than the whites. And thus the land-owners, despite their marvellous efforts, are really a transient class, continually being depleted by those who fall back into the class of renters or metayers, and augmented by newcomers from the masses. Of one hundred land-owners in 1898, half had bought their land since 1893, a fourth between 1890 and 1893, a fifth between 1884 and 1890, and the rest between 1870 and 1884. In all, one hundred and eighty-five Negroes have owned land in this county since 1875.

If all the black land-owners who had ever held land here had kept it or left it in the hands of black men, the Negroes would have owned nearer thirty thousand acres than the fifteen thousand they now hold. And yet these fifteen thousand acres are a creditable showing,—a proof of no little weight of the worth and ability of the Negro people. If they had been given an economic start at Emancipation, if they had been in an enlightened and rich community which really desired their best good, then we might perhaps call such a result small or even insignificant. But for a few thousand poor ignorant field-hands, in the face of poverty, a falling market, and social stress, to save and capitalize two hundred thousand dollars in a generation has meant a tremendous effort. The rise of a nation, the pressing forward of a social class, means a bitter struggle, a hard and soul-sickening battle with the world such as few of the more favored classes know or appreciate.

Out of the hard economic conditions of this portion of the Black Belt, only six per cent of the population have succeeded in emerging into peasant proprietorship; and these are not all firmly fixed, but grow and shrink in number with the wavering of the cotton-market. Fully ninety-four per cent have struggled for land and failed, and half of them sit in hopeless serfdom. For these there is one other avenue of escape toward which they have turned in increasing numbers, namely, migration to town. A glance at the distribution of land among the black owners curiously reveals this fact. In 1898 the holdings were as follows: Under forty acres, forty-nine families; forty to two hundred and fifty acres, seventeen families; two hundred and fifty to one thousand acres, thirteen families; one thousand or more acres, two families. Now in 1890 there were forty-four holdings, but only nine of these were under forty acres. The great increase of holdings, then, has come in the buying of small homesteads near town, where their owners really share in the town life; this is a part of the rush to town. And for every land- owner who has thus hurried away from the narrow and hard conditions of country life, how many field-hands, how many tenants, how many ruined renters, have joined that long procession? Is it not strange compensation? The sin of the country districts is visited on the town, and the social sores of city life to-day may, here in Dougherty County, and perhaps in many places near and far, look for their final healing without the city walls.

9. OF THE SONS OF MASTER AND MAN

Life treads on life, and heart on heart;
We press too close in church and mart
To keep a dream or grave apart.

MRS. BROWNING.

The world-old phenomenon of the contact of diverse races of men is to have new exemplification during the new century. Indeed, the characteristic of our age is the contact of European civilization with the world's undeveloped peoples. Whatever we may say of the results of such contact in the past, it certainly forms a chapter in human action not pleasant to look back upon. War, murder, slavery, extermination, and debauchery,—this has again and again been the result of carrying civilization and the blessed gospel to the isles of the sea and the heathen without the law. Nor does it altogether satisfy the conscience of the modern world to be told complacently that all this has been right and proper, the fated triumph of strength over weakness, of righteousness over evil, of superiors over inferiors. It would certainly be soothing if one could readily believe all this; and yet there are too many ugly facts for everything to be thus easily explained away. We feel and know that there are many delicate differences in race psychology, numberless changes that our crude social measurements are not yet able to follow minutely, which explain much of history and social development. At the same time, too, we know that these considerations have never adequately explained or excused the triumph of brute force and cunning over weakness and innocence.

It is, then, the strife of all honorable men of the twentieth century to see that in the future competition of races the survival of the fittest shall mean the triumph of the good, the beautiful, and the true; that we may be able to preserve for future civilization all that is really fine and noble and strong, and not continue to put a premium on greed and impudence and cruelty. To bring this hope to fruition, we are compelled daily to turn more and more to a conscientious study of the phenomena of race-contact,—to a study frank and fair, and not falsified and colored by our wishes or our fears. And we have in the South as fine a field for such a study as the world affords,—a field, to be sure, which the average American scientist deems somewhat beneath his dignity, and which the average man who is not a scientist knows all about, but nevertheless a line of study which by reason of the enormous race complications with which God seems about to punish this nation must increasingly claim our sober attention, study, and thought, we must ask, what are the actual relations of whites and blacks in the South? and we must be answered, not by apology or fault-finding, but by a plain, unvarnished tale.

In the civilized life of to-day the contact of men and their relations to each other fall in a few main lines of action and communication: there is, first, the physical proximity of home and dwelling-places, the way in which neighborhoods group themselves, and the contiguity of neighborhoods. Secondly, and in our age chiefest, there are the economic relations,—the methods by which individuals cooperate for earning a living, for the mutual satisfaction of wants, for the production of wealth. Next, there are the political relations, the cooperation in social control, in group government, in laying and paying the burden of taxation. In the fourth place there are the less tangible but highly important forms of intellectual contact and commerce, the interchange of ideas through conversation and conference, through periodicals and libraries; and, above all, the gradual formation for each community of that curious tertium quid which we call public opinion. Closely allied with this come the various forms of social contact in everyday life, in travel, in theatres, in house gatherings, in marrying and giving in marriage. Finally, there are the varying forms of religious enterprise, of moral teaching and benevolent endeavor. These are the principal ways in which men living in the same communities are brought into contact with each other. It is my present task, therefore, to indicate, from my point of view, how the black race in the South meet and mingle with the whites in these matters of everyday life.

First, as to physical dwelling. It is usually possible to draw in nearly every Southern community a physical color-line on the map, on the one side of which whites dwell and on the other Negroes. The winding and intricacy of the geographical color-line varies, of course, in different communities. I know some towns where a straight line drawn through the middle of the main street separates nine-tenths of the whites from nine-tenths of the blacks. In other towns the older settlement of whites has been encircled by a broad band of blacks; in still other cases little settlements or nuclei of blacks have sprung up amid surrounding whites. Usually in cities each street has its distinctive color, and only now and then do the colors meet in close proximity. Even in the country something of this segregation is manifest in the smaller areas, and of course in the larger phenomena of the Black Belt.

All this segregation by color is largely independent of that natural clustering by social grades common to all communities. A Negro slum may be in dangerous proximity to a white residence quarter, while it is quite common to find a white slum planted in the heart of a respectable Negro district. One thing, however, seldom occurs: the best of the whites and the best of the Negroes almost never live in anything like close proximity. It thus happens that in nearly every Southern town and city, both whites and blacks see commonly the worst of each other. This is a vast change from the situation in the past, when, through the close contact of master and house-servant in the patriarchal big house, one found the best of both races in close contact and sympathy, while at the same time the squalor and dull round of toil among the field-hands was removed from the sight and hearing of the family. One can easily see how a person who saw slavery thus from his father's parlors, and sees freedom on the streets of a great city, fails to grasp or comprehend the whole of the new picture. On the other hand, the settled belief of the mass of the Negroes that the Southern white people do not have the black man's best interests at heart has been intensified in later years by this continual daily contact of the better class of blacks with the worst representatives of the white race.

Coming now to the economic relations of the races, we are on ground made familiar by study, much discussion, and no little philanthropic effort. And yet with all this there are many essential elements in the cooperation of

Negroes and whites for work and wealth that are too readily overlooked or not thoroughly understood. The average American can easily conceive of a rich land awaiting development and filled with black laborers. To him the Southern problem is simply that of making efficient workingmen out of this material, by giving them the requisite technical skill and the help of invested capital. The problem, however, is by no means as simple as this, from the obvious fact that these workingmen have been trained for centuries as slaves. They exhibit, therefore, all the advantages and defects of such training; they are willing and good-natured, but not self-reliant, provident, or careful. If now the economic development of the South is to be pushed to the verge of exploitation, as seems probable, then we have a mass of workingmen thrown into relentless competition with the workingmen of the world, but handicapped by a training the very opposite to that of the modern self-reliant democratic laborer. What the black laborer needs is careful personal guidance, group leadership of men with hearts in their bosoms, to train them to foresight, carefulness, and honesty. Nor does it require any fine-spun theories of racial differences to prove the necessity of such group training after the brains of the race have been knocked out by two hundred and fifty years of assiduous education in submission, carelessness, and stealing. After Emancipation, it was the plain duty of some one to assume this group leadership and training of the Negro laborer. I will not stop here to inquire whose duty it was—whether that of the white ex-master who had profited by unpaid toil, or the Northern philanthropist whose persistence brought on the crisis, or the National Government whose edict freed the bondmen; I will not stop to ask whose duty it was, but I insist it was the duty of some one to see that these workingmen were not left alone and unguided, without capital, without land, without skill, without economic organization, without even the bald protection of law, order, and decency,—left in a great land, not to settle down to slow and careful internal development, but destined to be thrown almost immediately into relentless and sharp competition with the best of modern workingmen under an economic system where every participant is fighting for himself, and too often utterly regardless of the rights or welfare of his neighbor.

For we must never forget that the economic system of the South to-day which has succeeded the old regime is not the same system as that of the old industrial North, of England, or of France, with their trade-unions, their restrictive laws, their written and unwritten commercial customs, and their long experience. It is, rather, a copy of that England of the early nineteenth century, before the factory acts,—the England that wrung pity from thinkers and fired the wrath of Carlyle. The rod of empire that passed from the hands of Southern gentlemen in 1865, partly by force, partly by their own petulance, has never returned to them. Rather it has passed to those men who have come to take charge of the industrial exploitation of the New South,—the sons of poor whites fired with a new thirst for wealth and power, thrifty and avaricious Yankees, and unscrupulous immigrants. Into the hands of these men the Southern laborers, white and black, have fallen; and this to their sorrow. For the laborers as such, there is in these new captains of industry neither love nor hate, neither sympathy nor romance; it is a cold question of dollars and dividends. Under such a system all labor is bound to suffer. Even the white laborers are not yet intelligent, thrifty, and well trained enough to maintain themselves against the powerful inroads of organized capital. The results among them, even, are long hours of toil, low wages, child labor, and lack of protection against usury and cheating. But among the black laborers all this is aggravated, first, by a race prejudice which varies from a doubt and distrust among the best element of whites to a frenzied hatred among the worst; and, secondly, it is aggravated, as I have said before, by the wretched economic heritage of the freedmen from slavery. With this training it is difficult for the freedman to learn to grasp the opportunities already opened to him, and the new opportunities are seldom given him, but go by favor to the whites.

Left by the best elements of the South with little protection or oversight, he has been made in law and custom the victim of the worst and most unscrupulous men in each community. The crop-lien system which is depopulating the fields of the South is not simply the result of shiftlessness on the part of Negroes, but is also the result of cunningly devised laws as to mortgages, liens, and misdemeanors, which can be made by conscienceless men to entrap and snare the unwary until escape is impossible, further toil a farce, and protest a crime. I have seen, in the Black Belt of Georgia, an ignorant, honest Negro buy and pay for a farm in installments three separate times, and then in the face of law and decency the enterprising American who sold it to him pocketed the money and deed and left the black man landless, to labor on his own land at thirty cents a day. I have seen a black farmer fall in debt to a white storekeeper, and that storekeeper go to his farm and strip it of every single marketable article,—mules, ploughs, stored crops, tools, furniture, bedding, clocks, looking-glass,—and all this without a sheriff or officer, in the face of the law for homestead exemptions, and without rendering to a single responsible person any account or reckoning. And such proceedings can happen, and will happen, in any community where a class of ignorant toilers are placed by custom and race-prejudice beyond the pale of sympathy and race-brotherhood. So long as the best elements of a community do not feel in duty bound to protect and train and care for the weaker members of their group, they leave them to be preyed upon by these swindlers and rascals.

This unfortunate economic situation does not mean the hindrance of all advance in the black South, or the absence of a class of black landlords and mechanics who, in spite of disadvantages, are accumulating property and making good citizens. But it does mean that this class is not nearly so large as a fairer economic system might easily make it, that those who survive in the competition are handicapped so as to accomplish much less than they deserve to, and that, above all, the personnel of the successful class is left to chance and accident, and not to any intelligent culling or reasonable methods of selection. As a remedy for this, there is but one possible procedure. We must accept some of the race prejudice in the South as a fact,—deplorable in its intensity, unfortunate in results, and dangerous for the future, but nevertheless a hard fact which only time can efface. We cannot hope, then, in this generation, or for several generations, that the mass of the whites can be brought to assume that close sympathetic and self-sacrificing leadership of the blacks which their present situation so eloquently demands. Such leadership, such social teaching and example, must come from the blacks themselves. For some time men doubted as to whether the Negro could develop such leaders; but to-day no one seriously disputes the capability of individual Negroes to assimilate the culture and common sense of modern civilization, and to pass it on, to some extent at least, to their fellows. If this is true, then here is the path out of the economic situation, and here is the imperative demand for trained Negro leaders of character and intelligence,—men of skill, men of light and leading, college-bred men, black captains of industry, and missionaries of culture; men who thoroughly comprehend and know modern civilization, and can take hold of Negro communities and raise and train them by force of precept and example, deep sympathy, and the inspiration of common blood and ideals. But if such men are to be effective they must have some power,—they must be backed by the best public opinion of these communities, and able to wield for their objects and aims such weapons as the experience of the world has taught are indispensable to human progress.

Of such weapons the greatest, perhaps, in the modern world is the power of the ballot; and this brings me to a consideration of the third form of contact between whites and blacks in the South,—political activity.

In the attitude of the American mind toward Negro suffrage can be traced with unusual accuracy the prevalent conceptions of government. In the fifties we were near enough the echoes of the French Revolution to believe pretty thoroughly in universal suffrage. We argued, as we thought then rather logically, that no social class was so good, so true, and so disinterested as to be trusted wholly with the political destiny of its neighbors; that in every state the best arbiters of their own welfare are the persons directly affected; consequently that it is only by arming every hand with a ballot,—with the right to have a voice in the policy of the state,—that the greatest good to the greatest number could be attained. To be sure, there were objections to these arguments, but we thought we had answered them tersely and convincingly; if some one complained of the ignorance of voters, we answered, "Educate them." If another complained of their venality, we replied, "Disfranchise them or put them in jail." And, finally, to the men who feared demagogues and the natural perversity of some human beings we insisted that time and bitter experience would teach the most hardheaded. It was at this time that the question of Negro suffrage in the South was raised. Here was a defenceless people suddenly made free. How were they to be protected from those who did not believe in their freedom and were determined to thwart it? Not by force, said the North; not by government guardianship, said the South; then by the ballot, the sole and legitimate defence of a free people, said the Common Sense of the Nation. No one thought, at the time, that the ex-slaves could use the ballot intelligently or very effectively; but they did think that the possession of so great power by a great class in the nation would compel their fellows to educate this class to its intelligent use.

Meantime, new thoughts came to the nation: the inevitable period of moral retrogression and political trickery that ever follows in the wake of war overtook us. So flagrant became the political scandals that reputable men began to leave politics alone, and politics consequently became disreputable. Men began to pride themselves on having nothing to do with their own government, and to agree tacitly with those who regarded public office as a private perquisite. In this state of mind it became easy to wink at the suppression of the Negro vote in the South, and to advise self-respecting Negroes to leave politics entirely alone. The decent and reputable citizens of the North who neglected their own civic duties grew hilarious over the exaggerated importance with which the Negro regarded the franchise. Thus it easily happened that more and more the better class of Negroes followed the advice from abroad and the pressure from home, and took no further interest in politics, leaving to the careless and the venal of their race the exercise of their rights as voters. The black vote that still remained was not trained and educated, but further debauched by open and unblushing bribery, or force and fraud; until the Negro voter was thoroughly inoculated with the idea that politics was a method of private gain by disreputable means.

And finally, now, to-day, when we are awakening to the fact that the perpetuity of republican institutions on this continent depends on the purification of the ballot, the civic training of voters, and the raising of voting to the plane of a solemn duty which a patriotic citizen neglects to his peril and to the peril of his children's children,—in this day, when we are striving for a renaissance of civic virtue, what are we going to say to the black voter of the South? Are we going to tell him still that politics is a disreputable and useless form of human activity? Are we going to induce the best class of Negroes to take less and less interest in government, and to give up their right to take such an interest, without a protest? I am not saying a word against all legitimate efforts to purge the ballot of ignorance, pauperism, and crime. But few have pretended that the present movement for disfranchisement in the South is for such a purpose; it has been plainly and frankly declared in nearly every case that the object of the disfranchising laws is the elimination of the black man from politics.

Now, is this a minor matter which has no influence on the main question of the industrial and intellectual development of the Negro? Can we establish a mass of black laborers and artisans and landholders in the South who, by law and public opinion, have absolutely no voice in shaping the laws under which they live and work? Can the modern organization of industry, assuming as it does free democratic government and the power and ability of the laboring classes to compel respect for their welfare,—can this system be carried out in the South when half its laboring force is voiceless in the public councils and powerless in its own defence? To-day the black man of the South has almost nothing to say as to how much he shall be taxed, or how those taxes shall be expended; as to who shall execute the laws, and how they shall do it; as to who shall make the laws, and how they shall be made. It is pitiable that frantic efforts must be made at critical times to get law-makers in some States even to listen to the respectful presentation of the black man's side of a current controversy. Daily the Negro is coming more and more to look upon law and justice, not as protecting safeguards, but as sources of humiliation and oppression. The laws are made by men who have little interest in him; they are executed by men who have absolutely no motive for treating the black people with courtesy or consideration; and, finally, the accused law-breaker is tried, not by his peers, but too often by men who would rather punish ten innocent Negroes than let one guilty one escape.

I should be the last one to deny the patent weaknesses and shortcomings of the Negro people; I should be the last to withhold sympathy from the white South in its efforts to solve its intricate social problems. I freely acknowledged that it is possible, and sometimes best, that a partially undeveloped people should be ruled by the best of their stronger and better neighbors for their own good, until such time as they can start and fight the world's battles alone. I have already pointed out how sorely in need of such economic and spiritual guidance the emancipated Negro was, and I am quite willing to admit that if the representatives of the best white Southern public opinion were the ruling and guiding powers in the South to-day the conditions indicated would be fairly well fulfilled. But the point I have insisted upon and now emphasize again, is that the best opinion of the South to-day is not the ruling opinion. That to leave the Negro helpless and without a ballot to-day is to leave him not to the guidance of the best, but rather to the exploitation and debauchment of the worst; that this is no truer of the South than of the North,—of the North than of Europe: in any land, in any country under modern free competition, to lay any class of weak and despised people, be they white, black, or blue, at the political mercy of their stronger, richer, and more resourceful fellows, is a temptation which human nature seldom has withstood and seldom will withstand.

Moreover, the political status of the Negro in the South is closely connected with the question of Negro crime. There can be no doubt that crime among Negroes has sensibly increased in the last thirty years, and that there has appeared in the slums of great cities a distinct criminal class among the blacks. In explaining this unfortunate development, we must note two things: (1) that the inevitable result of Emancipation was to increase crime and criminals, and (2) that the police system of the South was primarily designed to control slaves. As to the first point, we must not forget that under a strict slave system there can scarcely be such a thing as crime. But when these variously constituted human particles are suddenly thrown broadcast on the sea of life, some swim, some sink, and some hang suspended, to be forced up or down by the chance currents of a busy hurrying world. So great an economic and social revolution as swept the South in '63 meant a weeding out among the Negroes of the incompetents and vicious, the beginning of a differentiation of social grades. Now a rising group of people are not lifted bodily from the ground like an inert solid mass, but rather stretch upward like a living plant with its roots still clinging in the mould. The appearance, therefore, of the Negro criminal was a phenomenon to be awaited; and while it causes anxiety, it should not occasion surprise.

Here again the hope for the future depended peculiarly on careful and delicate dealing with these criminals. Their offences at first were those of laziness, carelessness, and impulse, rather than of malignity or ungoverned viciousness. Such misdemeanors needed discriminating treatment, firm but reformatory, with no hint of injustice, and full proof of guilt. For such dealing with criminals, white or black, the South had no machinery, no adequate jails or reformatories; its police system was arranged to deal with blacks alone, and tacitly assumed that every white man was ipso facto a member of that police. Thus grew up a double system of justice, which erred on the white side by undue leniency and the practical immunity of red-handed criminals, and erred on the black side by undue severity, injustice, and lack of discrimination. For, as I have said, the police system of the South was originally designed to keep track of all Negroes, not simply of criminals; and when the Negroes were freed and the whole South was convinced of the impossibility of free Negro labor, the first and almost universal device was to use the courts as a means of reenslaving the blacks. It was not then a question of crime, but rather one of color, that settled a man's conviction on almost any charge. Thus Negroes came to look upon courts as instruments of injustice and oppression, and upon those convicted in them as martyrs and victims.

When, now, the real Negro criminal appeared, and instead of petty stealing and vagrancy we began to have highway robbery, burglary, murder, and rape, there was a curious effect on both sides the color-line: the Negroes refused to believe the evidence of white witnesses or the fairness of white juries, so that the greatest deterrent to crime, the public opinion of one's own social caste, was lost, and the criminal was looked upon as crucified rather than hanged. On the other hand, the whites, used to being careless as to the guilt or innocence of accused Negroes, were swept in moments of passion beyond law, reason, and decency. Such a situation is bound to increase crime, and has increased it. To natural viciousness and vagrancy are being daily added motives of revolt and revenge which stir up all the latent savagery of both races and make peaceful attention to economic development often impossible.

But the chief problem in any community cursed with crime is not the punishment of the criminals, but the preventing of the young from being trained to crime. And here again the peculiar conditions of the South have prevented proper precautions. I have seen twelve-year-old boys working in chains on the public streets of Atlanta, directly in front of the schools, in company with old and hardened criminals; and this indiscriminate mingling of men and women and children makes the chain-gangs perfect schools of crime and debauchery. The struggle for reformatories, which has gone on in Virginia, Georgia, and other States, is the one encouraging sign of the awakening of some communities to the suicidal results of this policy.

It is the public schools, however, which can be made, outside the homes, the greatest means of training decent self-respecting citizens. We have been so hotly engaged recently in discussing trade-schools and the higher education that the pitiable plight of the public-school system in the South has almost dropped from view. Of every five dollars spent for public education in the State of Georgia, the white schools get four dollars and the Negro one dollar; and even then the white public-school system, save in the cities, is bad and cries for reform. If this is true of the whites, what of the blacks? I am becoming more and more convinced, as I look upon the system of common-school training in the South, that the national government must soon step in and aid popular education in some way. To-day it has been only by the most strenuous efforts on the part of the thinking men of the South that the Negro's share of the school fund has not been cut down to a pittance in some half-dozen States; and that movement not only is not dead, but in many communities is gaining strength. What in the name of reason does this nation expect of a people, poorly trained and hard pressed in severe economic competition, without political rights, and with ludicrously inadequate common-school facilities? What can it expect but crime and listlessness, offset here and there by the dogged struggles of the fortunate and more determined who are themselves buoyed by the hope that in due time the country will come to its senses?

I have thus far sought to make clear the physical, economic, and political relations of the Negroes and whites in the South, as I have conceived them, including, for the reasons set forth, crime and education. But after all that has been said on these more tangible matters of human contact, there still remains a part essential to a proper description of the South which it is difficult to describe or fix in terms easily understood by strangers. It is, in fine, the atmosphere of the land, the thought and feeling, the thousand and one little actions which go to make up life. In any community or nation it is these little things which are most elusive to the grasp and yet most essential to any clear conception of the group life taken as a whole. What is thus true of all communities is peculiarly true of the South, where, outside of written history and outside of printed law, there has been going on for a generation as deep a storm and stress of human souls, as intense a ferment of feeling, as intricate a writhing of spirit, as ever a people experienced. Within and without the sombre veil of color vast social forces have been at work,— efforts for human betterment, movements toward disintegration and despair, tragedies and comedies in social and economic life, and a swaying and lifting and sinking of human hearts which have made this land a land of mingled sorrow and joy, of change and excitement and unrest.

The centre of this spiritual turmoil has ever been the millions of black freedmen and their sons, whose destiny is so fatefully bound up with that of the nation. And yet the casual observer visiting the South sees at first little of this. He notes the growing frequency of dark faces as he rides along,— but otherwise the days slip lazily on, the sun shines, and this little world seems as happy and contented as other worlds he has visited. Indeed, on the question of questions—the Negro problem—he hears so little that there almost seems to be a conspiracy of silence; the morning papers seldom mention it, and then usually in a far-fetched academic way, and indeed almost every one seems to forget and ignore the darker half of the land, until the astonished visitor is inclined to ask if after all there IS any problem here. But if he lingers long enough there comes the awakening: perhaps in a sudden whirl of passion which leaves him gasping at its bitter intensity; more likely in a gradually dawning sense of things he had not at first noticed. Slowly but surely his eyes begin to catch the shadows of the color-line: here he meets crowds of Negroes and whites; then he is suddenly aware that he cannot discover a single dark face; or again at the close of a day's wandering he may find himself in some strange assembly, where all faces are tinged brown or black, and where he has the vague, uncomfortable feeling of the stranger. He realizes at last that silently, resistlessly, the world about flows by him in two great streams: they ripple on in the same sunshine, they approach and mingle their waters in seeming carelessness,—then they divide and flow wide apart. It is done quietly; no mistakes are made, or if one occurs, the swift arm of the law and of public opinion swings down for a moment, as when the other day a black man and a white woman were arrested for talking together on Whitehall Street in Atlanta.

Now if one notices carefully one will see that between these two worlds, despite much physical contact and daily intermingling, there is almost no community of intellectual life or point of transference where the thoughts and feelings of one race can come into direct contact and sympathy with the thoughts and feelings of the other. Before and directly after the war, when all the best of the Negroes were domestic servants in the best of the white families, there were bonds of intimacy, affection, and sometimes blood relationship, between the races. They lived in the same home, shared in the family life, often attended the same church, and talked and conversed with each other. But the increasing civilization of the Negro since then has naturally meant the development of higher classes: there are increasing numbers of ministers, teachers, physicians, merchants, mechanics, and independent farmers, who by nature and training are the aristocracy and leaders of the blacks. Between them, however, and the best element of the whites, there is little or no intellectual commerce. They go to separate churches, they live in separate sections, they are strictly separated in all public gatherings, they travel separately, and they are beginning to read different papers and books. To most libraries, lectures, concerts, and museums, Negroes are either not admitted at all, or on terms peculiarly galling to the pride of the very classes who might otherwise be attracted. The daily paper chronicles the doings of the black world from afar with no great regard for accuracy; and so on, throughout the category of means for intellectual communication,—schools, conferences, efforts for social betterment, and the like,—it is usually true that the very representatives of the two races, who for mutual benefit and the welfare of the land ought to be in complete understanding and sympathy, are so far strangers that one side thinks all whites are narrow and prejudiced, and the other thinks educated Negroes dangerous and insolent. Moreover, in a land where the tyranny of public opinion and the intolerance of criticism is for obvious historical reasons so strong as in the South, such a situation is extremely difficult to correct. The white man, as well as the Negro, is bound and barred by the color-line, and many a scheme of friendliness and philanthropy, of broad-minded sympathy and generous fellowship between the two has dropped still-born because some busybody has forced the color-question to the front and brought the tremendous force of unwritten law against the innovators.

It is hardly necessary for me to add very much in regard to the social contact between the races. Nothing has come to replace that finer sympathy and love between some masters and house servants which the radical and more uncompromising drawing of the color-line in recent years has caused almost completely to disappear. In a world where it means so much to take a man by the hand and sit beside him, to look frankly into his eyes and feel his heart beating with red blood; in a world where a social cigar or a cup of tea together means more than legislative halls and magazine articles and speeches,—one can imagine the consequences of the almost utter absence of such social amenities between estranged races, whose separation extends even to parks and streetcars.

Here there can be none of that social going down to the people,—the opening of heart and hand of the best to the worst, in generous acknowledgment of a common humanity and a common destiny. On the other hand, in matters of simple almsgiving, where there can be no question of social contact, and in the succor of the aged and sick, the South, as if stirred by a feeling of its unfortunate limitations, is generous to a fault. The black beggar is never turned away without a good deal more than a crust, and a call for help for the unfortunate meets quick response. I remember, one cold winter, in Atlanta, when I refrained from contributing to a public relief fund lest Negroes should be discriminated against, I afterward inquired of a friend: "Were any black people receiving aid?" "Why," said he, "they were all black."

And yet this does not touch the kernel of the problem. Human advancement is not a mere question of almsgiving, but rather of sympathy and cooperation among classes who would scorn charity. And here is a land where, in the higher walks of life, in all the higher striving for the good and noble and true, the color-line comes to separate natural friends and coworkers; while at the bottom of the social group, in the saloon, the gambling-hell, and the brothel, that same line wavers and disappears.

I have sought to paint an average picture of real relations between the sons of master and man in the South. I have not glossed over matters for policy's sake, for I fear we have already gone too far in that sort of thing. On the other hand, I have sincerely sought to let no unfair exaggerations creep in. I do not doubt that in some Southern communities conditions are better than those I have indicated; while I am no less certain that in other communities they are far worse.

Nor does the paradox and danger of this situation fail to interest and perplex the best conscience of the South. Deeply religious and intensely democratic as are the mass of the whites, they feel acutely the false position in which the Negro problems place them. Such an essentially honest-hearted and generous people cannot cite the caste-levelling precepts of Christianity, or believe in equality of opportunity for all men, without coming to feel more and more with each generation that the present drawing of the color-line is a flat contradiction to their beliefs and professions. But just as often as they come to this point, the present social condition of the Negro stands as a menace and a portent before even the most open-minded: if there were nothing to charge against the Negro but his blackness or other physical peculiarities, they argue, the problem would be comparatively simple; but what can we say to his ignorance, shiftlessness, poverty, and crime? can a self-respecting group hold anything but the least possible fellowship with such persons and survive? and shall we let a mawkish sentiment sweep away the culture of our fathers or the hope of our children? The argument so put is of great strength, but it is not a whit stronger than the argument of thinking Negroes: granted, they reply, that the condition of our masses is bad; there is certainly on the one hand adequate historical cause for this, and unmistakable evidence that no small number have, in spite of tremendous disadvantages, risen to the level of American civilization. And when, by proscription and prejudice, these same Negroes are classed with and treated like the lowest of their people, simply because they are Negroes, such a policy not only discourages thrift and intelligence among black men, but puts a direct premium on the very things you complain of,—inefficiency and crime. Draw lines of crime, of incompetency, of vice, as tightly and uncompromisingly as you will, for these things must be proscribed; but a color-line not only does not accomplish this purpose, but thwarts it.

In the face of two such arguments, the future of the South depends on the ability of the representatives of these opposing views to see and appreciate and sympathize with each other's position,—for the Negro to realize more deeply than he does at present the need of uplifting the masses of his people, for the white people to realize more vividly than they have yet done the deadening and disastrous effect of a color-prejudice that classes Phillis Wheatley and Sam Hose in the same despised class.

It is not enough for the Negroes to declare that color-prejudice is the sole cause of their social condition, nor for the white South to reply that their social condition is the main cause of prejudice. They both act as reciprocal cause and effect, and a change in neither alone will bring the desired effect. Both must change, or neither can improve to any great extent. The Negro cannot stand the present reactionary tendencies and unreasoning drawing of the color-line indefinitely without discouragement and retrogression. And the condition of the Negro is ever the excuse for further discrimination. Only by a union of intelligence and sympathy across the color-line in this critical period of the Republic shall justice and right triumph,

"That mind and soul according well,
May make one music as before,
But vaster."

10. OF THE FAITH OF THE FATHERS

Dim face of Beauty haunting all the world,
Fair face of Beauty all too fair to see,
Where the lost stars adown the heavens are hurled,—

There, there alone for thee
May white peace be.

Beauty, sad face of Beauty, Mystery, Wonder,
What are these dreams to foolish babbling men
Who cry with little noises 'neath the thunder

Of Ages ground to sand,
To a little sand.

FIONA MACLEOD.

It was out in the country, far from home, far from my foster home, on a dark Sunday night. The road wandered from our rambling log-house up the stony bed of a creek, past wheat and corn, until we could hear dimly across the fields a rhythmic cadence of song,—soft, thrilling, powerful, that swelled and died sorrowfully in our ears. I was a country schoolteacher then, fresh from the East, and had never seen a Southern Negro revival. To be sure, we in Berkshire were not perhaps as stiff and formal as they in Suffolk of olden time; yet we were very quiet and subdued, and I know not what would have happened those clear Sabbath mornings had some one punctuated the sermon with a wild scream, or interrupted the long prayer with a loud Amen! And so most striking to me, as I approached the village and the little plain church perched aloft, was the air of intense excitement that possessed that mass of black folk. A sort of suppressed terror hung in the air and seemed to seize us,—a pythian madness, a demoniac possession, that lent terrible reality to song and word. The black and massive form of the preacher swayed and quivered as the words crowded to his lips and flew at us in singular eloquence. The people moaned and fluttered, and then the gaunt-cheeked brown woman beside me suddenly leaped straight into the air and shrieked like a lost soul, while round about came wail and groan and outcry, and a scene of human passion such as I had never conceived before.

Those who have not thus witnessed the frenzy of a Negro revival in the untouched backwoods of the South can but dimly realize the religious feeling of the slave; as described, such scenes appear grotesque and funny, but as seen they are awful. Three things characterized this religion of the slave,—the Preacher, the Music, and the Frenzy. The Preacher is the most unique personality developed by the Negro on American soil. A leader, a politician, an orator, a "boss," an intriguer, an idealist,—all these he is, and ever, too, the centre of a group of men, now twenty, now a thousand in number. The combination of a certain adroitness with deep-seated earnestness, of tact with consummate ability, gave him his preeminence, and helps him maintain it. The type, of course, varies according to time and place, from the West Indies in the sixteenth century to New England in the nineteenth, and from the Mississippi bottoms to cities like New Orleans or New York.

The Music of Negro religion is that plaintive rhythmic melody, with its touching minor cadences, which, despite caricature and defilement, still remains the most original and beautiful expression of human life and longing yet born on American soil. Sprung from the African forests, where its counterpart can still be heard, it was adapted, changed, and intensified by the tragic soul-life of the slave, until, under the stress of law and whip, it became the one true expression of a people's sorrow, despair, and hope.

Finally the Frenzy of "Shouting," when the Spirit of the Lord passed by, and, seizing the devotee, made him mad with supernatural joy, was the last essential of Negro religion and the one more devoutly believed in than all the rest. It varied in expression from the silent rapt countenance or the low murmur and moan to the mad abandon of physical fervor,—

the stamping, shrieking, and shouting, the rushing to and fro and wild waving of arms, the weeping and laughing, the vision and the trance. All this is nothing new in the world, but old as religion, as Delphi and Endor. And so firm a hold did it have on the Negro, that many generations firmly believed that without this visible manifestation of the God there could be no true communion with the Invisible.

These were the characteristics of Negro religious life as developed up to the time of Emancipation. Since under the peculiar circumstances of the black man's environment they were the one expression of his higher life, they are of deep interest to the student of his development, both socially and psychologically. Numerous are the attractive lines of inquiry that here group themselves. What did slavery mean to the African savage? What was his attitude toward the World and Life? What seemed to him good and evil,— God and Devil? Whither went his longings and strivings, and wherefore were his heart-burnings and disappointments? Answers to such questions can come only from a study of Negro religion as a development, through its gradual changes from the heathenism of the Gold Coast to the institutional Negro church of Chicago.

Moreover, the religious growth of millions of men, even though they be slaves, cannot be without potent influence upon their contemporaries. The Methodists and Baptists of America owe much of their condition to the silent but potent influence of their millions of Negro converts. Especially is this noticeable in the South, where theology and religious philosophy are on this account a long way behind the North, and where the religion of the poor whites is a plain copy of Negro thought and methods. The mass of "gospel" hymns which has swept through American churches and well-nigh ruined our sense of song consists largely of debased imitations of Negro melodies made by ears that caught the jingle but not the music, the body but not the soul, of the Jubilee songs. It is thus clear that the study of Negro religion is not only a vital part of the history of the Negro in America, but no uninteresting part of American history.

The Negro church of to-day is the social centre of Negro life in the United States, and the most characteristic expression of African character. Take a typical church in a small Virginia town: it is the "First Baptist"—a roomy brick edifice seating five hundred or more persons, tastefully finished in Georgia pine, with a carpet, a small organ, and stained-glass windows.

Underneath is a large assembly room with benches. This building is the central club-house of a community of a thousand or more Negroes. Various organizations meet here,—the church proper, the Sunday-school, two or three insurance societies, women's societies, secret societies, and mass meetings of various kinds. Entertainments, suppers, and lectures are held beside the five or six regular weekly religious services. Considerable sums of money are collected and expended here, employment is found for the idle, strangers are introduced, news is disseminated and charity distributed. At the same time this social, intellectual, and economic centre is a religious centre of great power. Depravity, Sin, Redemption, Heaven, Hell, and Damnation are preached twice a Sunday after the crops are laid by; and few indeed of the community have the hardihood to withstand conversion. Back of this more formal religion, the Church often stands as a real conserver of morals, a strengthener of family life, and the final authority on what is Good and Right.

Thus one can see in the Negro church to-day, reproduced in microcosm, all the great world from which the Negro is cut off by color-prejudice and social condition. In the great city churches the same tendency is noticeable and in many respects emphasized. A great church like the Bethel of Philadelphia has over eleven hundred members, an edifice seating fifteen hundred persons and valued at one hundred thousand dollars, an annual budget of five thousand dollars, and a government consisting of a pastor with several assisting local preachers, an executive and legislative board, financial boards and tax collectors; general church meetings for making laws; sub-divided groups led by class leaders, a company of militia, and twenty-four auxiliary societies. The activity of a church like this is immense and far-reaching, and the bishops who preside over these organizations throughout the land are among the most powerful Negro rulers in the world.

Such churches are really governments of men, and consequently a little investigation reveals the curious fact that, in the South, at least, practically every American Negro is a church member. Some, to be sure, are not regularly enrolled, and a few do not habitually attend services; but, practically, a proscribed people must have a social centre, and that centre for this people is the Negro church. The census of 1890 showed nearly twenty-four thousand Negro churches in the country, with a total enrolled membership of over two and a half millions, or ten actual church members to every twenty-eight persons, and in some Southern States one in every two persons. Besides these there is the large number who, while not enrolled as members, attend and take part in many of the activities of the church. There is an organized Negro church for every sixty black families in the nation, and in some States for every forty families, owning, on an average, a thousand dollars' worth of property each, or nearly twenty-six million dollars in all.

Such, then, is the large development of the Negro church since Emancipation. The question now is, What have been the successive steps of this social history and what are the present tendencies? First, we must realize that no such institution as the Negro church could rear itself without definite historical foundations. These foundations we can find if we remember that the social history of the Negro did not start in America. He was brought from a definite social environment,—the polygamous clan life under the headship of the chief and the potent influence of the priest. His religion was nature-worship, with profound belief in invisible surrounding influences, good and bad, and his worship was through incantation and sacrifice. The first rude change in this life was the slave ship and the West Indian sugar-fields. The plantation organization replaced the clan and tribe, and the white master replaced the chief with far greater and more despotic powers. Forced and long-continued toil became the rule of life, the old ties of blood relationship and kinship disappeared, and instead of the family appeared a new polygamy and polyandry, which, in some cases, almost reached promiscuity. It was a terrific social revolution, and yet some traces were retained of the former group life, and the chief remaining institution was the Priest or Medicine-man. He early appeared on the plantation and found his function as the healer of the sick, the interpreter of the Unknown, the comforter of the sorrowing, the supernatural avenger of wrong, and the one who rudely but picturesquely expressed the longing, disappointment, and resentment of a stolen and oppressed people. Thus, as bard, physician, judge, and priest, within the narrow limits allowed by the slave system, rose the Negro preacher, and under him the first church was not at first by any means Christian nor definitely organized; rather it was an adaptation and mingling of heathen rites among the members of each plantation, and roughly designated as Voodooism. Association with the masters, missionary effort and motives of expediency gave these rites an early veneer of Christianity, and after the lapse of many generations the Negro church became Christian.

Two characteristic things must be noticed in regard to the church. First, it became almost entirely Baptist and Methodist in faith; secondly, as a social institution it antedated by many decades the monogamic Negro home. From the very circumstances of its beginning, the church was confined to the plantation, and consisted primarily of a series of disconnected units; although, later on, some freedom of movement was allowed, still this geographical limitation was always important and was one cause of the spread of the decentralized and democratic Baptist faith among the slaves. At the same time, the visible rite of baptism appealed strongly to their mystic temperament. To-day the Baptist Church is still largest in membership among Negroes, and has a million and a half communicants. Next in popularity came the churches organized in connection with the white neighboring churches, chiefly Baptist and Methodist, with a few Episcopalian and others. The Methodists still form the second greatest denomination, with nearly a million members. The faith of these two leading denominations was more suited to the slave church from the prominence they gave to religious feeling and fervor. The Negro membership in other denominations has always been small and relatively unimportant, although the Episcopalians and Presbyterians are gaining among the more intelligent classes to-day, and the Catholic Church is making headway in certain sections. After Emancipation, and still earlier in the North, the Negro churches largely severed such affiliations as they had had with the white churches, either by choice or by compulsion. The Baptist churches became independent, but the Methodists were compelled early to unite for purposes of episcopal government. This gave rise to the great African Methodist Church, the greatest Negro organization in the world, to the Zion Church and the Colored Methodist, and to the black conferences and churches in this and other denominations.

The second fact noted, namely, that the Negro church antedates the Negro home, leads to an explanation of much that is paradoxical in this communistic institution and in the morals of its members. But especially it leads us to regard this institution as peculiarly the expression of the inner ethical life of a people in a sense seldom true elsewhere. Let us turn, then, from the outer physical development of the church to the more important inner ethical life of the people who compose it. The Negro has already been pointed out many times as a religious animal,—a being of that deep emotional nature which turns instinctively toward the supernatural. Endowed with a rich tropical imagination and a keen, delicate appreciation of Nature, the transplanted African lived in a world animate with gods and devils, elves and witches; full of strange influences,—of Good to be implored, of Evil to be propitiated. Slavery, then, was to him the dark triumph of Evil over him. All the hateful powers of the Under-world were striving against him, and a spirit of revolt and revenge filled his heart. He called up all the resources of heathenism to aid,—exorcism and witch-craft, the mysterious Obi worship with its barbarious rites, spells, and blood-sacrifice even, now and then, of human victims. Weird midnight orgies and mystic conjurations were invoked, the witch-woman and the voodoo-priest became the centre of Negro group life, and that vein of vague superstition which characterizes the unlettered Negro even to-day was deepened and strengthened.

In spite, however, of such success as that of the fierce Maroons, the Danish blacks, and others, the spirit of revolt gradually died away under the untiring energy and superior strength of the slave masters. By the middle of the eighteenth century the black slave had sunk, with hushed murmurs, to his place at the bottom of a new economic system, and was unconsciously ripe for a new philosophy of life. Nothing suited his condition then better than the doctrines of passive submission embodied in the newly learned Christianity. Slave masters early realized this, and cheerfully aided religious propaganda within certain bounds. The long system of repression and degradation of the Negro tended to emphasize the elements of his character which made him a valuable chattel: courtesy became humility, moral strength degenerated into submission, and the exquisite native appreciation of the beautiful became an infinite capacity for dumb suffering. The Negro, losing the joy of this world, eagerly seized upon the offered conceptions of the next; the avenging Spirit of the Lord enjoining patience in this world, under sorrow and tribulation until the Great Day when He should lead His dark children home,—this became his comforting dream. His preacher repeated the prophecy, and his bards sang,—

"Children, we all shall be free
When the Lord shall appear!"

This deep religious fatalism, painted so beautifully in "Uncle Tom," came soon to breed, as all fatalistic faiths will, the sensualist side by side with the martyr. Under the lax moral life of the plantation, where marriage was a farce, laziness a virtue, and property a theft, a religion of resignation and submission degenerated easily, in less strenuous minds, into a philosophy of indulgence and crime. Many of the worst characteristics of the Negro masses of to-day had their seed in this period of the slave's ethical growth. Here it was that the Home was ruined under the very shadow of the Church, white and black; here habits of shiftlessness took root, and sullen hopelessness replaced hopeful strife.

With the beginning of the abolition movement and the gradual growth of a class of free Negroes came a change. We often neglect the influence of the freedman before the war, because of the paucity of his numbers and the small weight he had in the history of the nation. But we must not forget that his chief influence was internal,—was exerted on the black world; and that there he was the ethical and social leader. Huddled as he was in a few centres like Philadelphia, New York, and New Orleans, the masses of the freedmen sank into poverty and listlessness; but not all of them. The free Negro leader early arose and his chief characteristic was intense earnestness and deep feeling on the slavery question. Freedom became to him a real thing and not a dream. His religion became darker and more intense, and into his ethics crept a note of revenge, into his songs a day of reckoning close at hand. The "Coming of the Lord" swept this side of Death, and came to be a thing to be hoped for in this day. Through fugitive slaves and irrepressible discussion this desire for freedom seized the black millions still in bondage, and became their one ideal of life. The black bards caught new notes, and sometimes even dared to sing,—

"O Freedom, O Freedom, O Freedom over me!
Before I'll be a slave
I'll be buried in my grave,
And go home to my Lord
And be free."

For fifty years Negro religion thus transformed itself and identified itself with the dream of Abolition, until that which was a radical fad in the white North and an anarchistic plot in the white South had become a religion to the black world. Thus, when Emancipation finally came, it seemed to the freedman a literal Coming of the Lord. His fervid imagination was stirred as never before, by the tramp of armies, the blood and dust of battle, and the wail and whirl of social upheaval. He stood dumb and motionless before the whirlwind: what had he to do with it? Was it not the Lord's doing, and marvellous in his eyes? Joyed and bewildered with what came, he stood awaiting new wonders till the inevitable Age of Reaction swept over the nation and brought the crisis of to-day.

It is difficult to explain clearly the present critical stage of Negro religion. First, we must remember that living as the blacks do in close contact with a great modern nation, and sharing, although imperfectly, the soul-life of that nation, they must necessarily be affected more or less directly by all the religious and ethical forces that are to-day moving the United States. These questions and movements are, however, overshadowed and dwarfed by the (to them) all-important question of their civil, political, and economic status. They must perpetually discuss the "Negro Problem,"—must live, move, and have their being in it, and interpret all else in its light or darkness. With this come, too, peculiar problems of their inner life,—of the status of women, the maintenance of Home, the training of children, the accumulation of wealth, and the prevention of crime. All this must mean a time of intense ethical ferment, of religious heart-searching and intellectual unrest. From the double life every American Negro must live, as a Negro and as an American, as swept on by the current of the nineteenth while yet struggling in the eddies of the fifteenth century,—from this must arise a painful self-consciousness, an almost morbid sense of personality and a moral hesitancy which is fatal to self-confidence. The worlds within and without the Veil of Color are changing, and changing rapidly, but not at the same rate, not in the same way; and this must produce a peculiar wrenching of the soul, a peculiar sense of doubt and bewilderment. Such a double life, with double thoughts, double duties, and double social classes, must give rise to double words and double ideals, and tempt the mind to pretence or revolt, to hypocrisy or radicalism.

In some such doubtful words and phrases can one perhaps most clearly picture the peculiar ethical paradox that faces the Negro of to-day and is tingeing and changing his religious life. Feeling that his rights and his dearest ideals are being trampled upon, that the public conscience is ever more deaf to his righteous appeal, and that all the reactionary forces of prejudice, greed, and revenge are daily gaining new strength and fresh allies, the Negro faces no enviable dilemma. Conscious of his impotence, and pessimistic, he often becomes bitter and vindictive; and his religion, instead of a worship, is a complaint and a curse, a wail rather than a hope, a sneer rather than a faith. On the other hand, another type of mind, shrewder and keener and more tortuous too, sees in the very strength of the anti-Negro movement its patent weaknesses, and with Jesuitic casuistry is deterred by no ethical considerations in the endeavor to turn this weakness to the black man's strength. Thus we have two great and hardly reconcilable streams of thought and ethical strivings; the danger of the one lies in anarchy, that of the other in hypocrisy. The one type of Negro stands almost ready to curse God and die, and the other is too often found a traitor to right and a coward before force; the one is wedded to ideals remote, whimsical, perhaps impossible of realization; the other forgets that life is more than meat and the body more than raiment. But, after all, is not this simply the writhing of the age translated into black,—the triumph of the Lie which today, with its false culture, faces the hideousness of the anarchist assassin?

To-day the two groups of Negroes, the one in the North, the other in the South, represent these divergent ethical tendencies, the first tending toward radicalism, the other toward hypocritical compromise. It is no idle regret with which the white South mourns the loss of the old-time Negro,— the frank, honest, simple old servant who stood for the earlier religious age of submission and humility. With all his laziness and lack of many elements of true manhood, he was at least open-hearted, faithful, and sincere. To-day he is gone, but who is to blame for his going? Is it not those very persons who mourn for him? Is it not the tendency, born of Reconstruction and Reaction, to found a society on lawlessness and deception, to tamper with the moral fibre of a naturally honest and straightforward people until the whites threaten to become ungovernable tyrants and the blacks criminals and hypocrites? Deception is the natural defence of the weak against the strong, and the South used it for many years against its conquerors; to-day it must be prepared to see its black proletariat turn that same two-edged weapon against itself. And how natural this is! The death of Denmark Vesey and Nat Turner proved long since to the Negro the present hopelessness of physical defence. Political defence is becoming less and less available, and economic defence is still only partially effective. But there is a patent defence at hand,—the defence of deception and flattery, of cajoling and lying. It is the same defence which peasants of the Middle Age used and which left its stamp on their character for centuries. To-day the young Negro of the South who would succeed cannot be frank and outspoken, honest and self-assertive, but rather he is daily tempted to be silent and wary, politic and sly; he must flatter and be pleasant, endure petty insults with a smile, shut his eyes to wrong; in too many cases he sees positive personal advantage in deception and lying. His real thoughts, his real aspirations, must be guarded in whispers; he must not criticise, he must not complain. Patience, humility, and adroitness must, in these growing black youth, replace impulse, manliness, and courage. With this sacrifice there is an economic opening, and perhaps peace and some prosperity. Without this there is riot, migration, or crime. Nor is this situation peculiar to the Southern United States, is it not rather the only method by which undeveloped races have gained the right to share modern culture? The price of culture is a Lie.

On the other hand, in the North the tendency is to emphasize the radicalism of the Negro. Driven from his birthright in the South by a situation at which every fibre of his more outspoken and assertive nature revolts, he finds himself in a land where he can scarcely earn a decent living amid the harsh competition and the color discrimination. At the same time, through schools and periodicals, discussions and lectures, he is intellectually quickened and awakened. The soul, long pent up and dwarfed, suddenly expands in new-found freedom. What wonder that every tendency is to excess,—radical complaint, radical remedies, bitter denunciation or angry silence. Some sink, some rise. The criminal and the sensualist leave the church for the gambling-hell and the brothel, and fill the slums of Chicago and Baltimore; the better classes segregate themselves from the group-life of both white and black, and form an aristocracy, cultured but pessimistic, whose bitter criticism stings while it points out no way of escape. They despise the submission and subserviency of the Southern Negroes, but offer no other means by which a poor and oppressed minority can exist side by side with its masters. Feeling deeply and keenly the tendencies and opportunities of the age in which they live, their souls are bitter at the fate which drops the Veil between; and the very fact that this bitterness is natural and justifiable only serves to intensify it and make it more maddening.

Between the two extreme types of ethical attitude which I have thus sought to make clear wavers the mass of the millions of Negroes, North and South; and their religious life and activity partake of this social conflict within their ranks. Their churches are differentiating,—now into groups of cold, fashionable devotees, in no way distinguishable from similar white groups save in color of skin; now into large social and business institutions catering to the desire for information and amusement of their members, warily avoiding unpleasant questions both within and without the black world, and preaching in effect if not in word: Dum vivimus, vivamus.

But back of this still broods silently the deep religious feeling of the real Negro heart, the stirring, unguided might of powerful human souls who have lost the guiding star of the past and seek in the great night a new religious ideal. Some day the Awakening will come, when the pent-up vigor of ten million souls shall sweep irresistibly toward the Goal, out of the Valley of the Shadow of Death, where all that makes life worth living—Liberty, Justice, and Right—is marked "For White People Only."

11. OF THE PASSING OF THE FIRST-BORN

O sister, sister, thy first-begotten,
The hands that cling and the feet that follow,
The voice of the child's blood crying yet,
WHO HATH REMEMBERED ME? WHO HATH FORGOTTEN?
Thou hast forgotten, O summer swallow,
But the world shall end when I forget.

SWINBURNE.

"Unto you a child is born," sang the bit of yellow paper that fluttered into my room one brown October morning. Then the fear of fatherhood mingled wildly with the joy of creation; I wondered how it looked and how it felt— what were its eyes, and how its hair curled and crumpled itself. And I thought in awe of her,—she who had slept with Death to tear a man-child from underneath her heart, while I was unconsciously wandering. I fled to my wife and child, repeating the while to myself half wonderingly, "Wife and child? Wife and child?"—fled fast and faster than boat and steam-car, and yet must ever impatiently await them; away from the hard-voiced city, away from the flickering sea into my own Berkshire Hills that sit all sadly guarding the gates of Massachusetts.

Up the stairs I ran to the wan mother and whimpering babe, to the sanctuary on whose altar a life at my bidding had offered itself to win a life, and won. What is this tiny formless thing, this newborn wail from an unknown world,—all head and voice? I handle it curiously, and watch perplexed its winking, breathing, and sneezing. I did not love it then; it seemed a ludicrous thing to love; but her I loved, my girl-mother, she whom now I saw unfolding like the glory of the morning—the transfigured woman. Through her I came to love the wee thing, as it grew strong; as its little soul unfolded itself in twitter and cry and half-formed word, and as its eyes caught the gleam and flash of life. How beautiful he was, with his olive- tinted flesh and dark gold ringlets, his eyes of mingled blue and brown, his perfect little limbs, and the soft voluptuous roll which the blood of Africa had moulded into his features! I held him in my arms, after we had sped far away from our Southern home,—held him, and glanced at the hot red soil of Georgia and the breathless city of a hundred hills, and felt a vague unrest. Why was his hair tinted with gold? An evil omen was golden hair in my life. Why had not the brown of his eyes crushed out and killed the blue?—for brown were his father's eyes, and his father's father's. And thus in the Land of the Color-line I saw, as it fell across my baby, the shadow of the Veil.

Within the Veil was he born, said I; and there within shall he live,—a Negro and a Negro's son. Holding in that little head—ah, bitterly!—he unbowed pride of a hunted race, clinging with that tiny dimpled hand—ah, wearily!— to a hope not hopeless but unhopeful, and seeing with those bright wondering eyes that peer into my soul a land whose freedom is to us a mockery and whose liberty a lie. I saw the shadow of the Veil as it passed over my baby, I saw the cold city towering above the blood-red land. I held my face beside his little cheek, showed him the star-children and the twinkling lights as they began to flash, and stilled with an even-song the unvoiced terror of my life.

So sturdy and masterful he grew, so filled with bubbling life, so tremulous with the unspoken wisdom of a life but eighteen months distant from the All-life,—we were not far from worshipping this revelation of the divine, my wife and I. Her own life builded and moulded itself upon the child; he tinged her every dream and idealized her every effort. No hands but hers must touch and garnish those little limbs; no dress or frill must touch them that had not wearied her fingers; no voice but hers could coax him off to Dreamland, and she and he together spoke some soft and unknown tongue and in it held communion. I too mused above his little white bed; saw the strength of my own arm stretched onward through the ages through the newer strength of his; saw the dream of my black fathers stagger a step onward in the wild phantasm of the world; heard in his baby voice the voice of the Prophet that was to rise within the Veil.

And so we dreamed and loved and planned by fall and winter, and the full flush of the long Southern spring, till the hot winds rolled from the fetid Gulf, till the roses shivered and the still stern sun quivered its awful light over the hills of Atlanta. And then one night the little feet pattered wearily to the wee white bed, and the tiny hands trembled; and a warm flushed face tossed on the pillow, and we knew baby was sick. Ten days he lay there,—a swift week and three endless days, wasting, wasting away. Cheerily the mother nursed him the first days, and laughed into the little eyes that smiled again. Tenderly then she hovered round him, till the smile fled away and Fear crouched beside the little bed.

Then the day ended not, and night was a dreamless terror, and joy and sleep slipped away. I hear now that Voice at midnight calling me from dull and dreamless trance,—crying, "The Shadow of Death! The Shadow of Death!" Out into the starlight I crept, to rouse the gray physician,—the Shadow of Death, the Shadow of Death. The hours trembled on; the night listened; the ghastly dawn glided like a tired thing across the lamplight. Then we two alone looked upon the child as he turned toward us with great eyes, and stretched his stringlike hands,—the Shadow of Death! And we spoke no word, and turned away.

He died at eventide, when the sun lay like a brooding sorrow above the western hills, veiling its face; when the winds spoke not, and the trees, the great green trees he loved, stood motionless. I saw his breath beat quicker and quicker, pause, and then his little soul leapt like a star that travels in the night and left a world of darkness in its train. The day changed not; the same tall trees peeped in at the windows, the same green grass glinted in the setting sun. Only in the chamber of death writhed the world's most piteous thing—a childless mother.

I shirk not. I long for work. I pant for a life full of striving. I am no coward, to shrink before the rugged rush of the storm, nor even quail before the awful shadow of the Veil. But hearken, O Death! Is not this my life hard enough,— is not that dull land that stretches its sneering web about me cold enough,—is not all the world beyond these four little walls pitiless enough, but that thou must needs enter here,—thou, O Death? About my head the thundering storm beat like a heartless voice, and the crazy forest pulsed with the curses of the weak; but what cared I, within my home beside my wife and baby boy? Wast thou so jealous of one little coign of happiness that thou must needs enter there,—thou, O Death?

A perfect life was his, all joy and love, with tears to make it brighter,—sweet as a summer's day beside the Housatonic. The world loved him; the women kissed his curls, the men looked gravely into his wonderful eyes, and the children hovered and fluttered about him. I can see him now, changing like the sky from sparkling laughter to darkening frowns, and then to wondering thoughtfulness as he watched the world. He knew no color-line, poor dear—and the Veil, though it shadowed him, had not yet darkened half his sun. He loved the white matron, he loved his black nurse; and in his little world walked souls alone, uncolored and unclothed. I—yea, all men—are larger and purer by the infinite breadth of that one little life. She who in simple clearness of vision sees beyond the stars said when he had flown, "He will be happy There; he ever loved beautiful things." And I, far more ignorant, and blind by the web of mine own weaving, sit alone winding words and muttering, "If still he be, and he be There, and there be a There, let him be happy, O Fate!"

Blithe was the morning of his burial, with bird and song and sweet-smelling flowers. The trees whispered to the grass, but the children sat with hushed faces. And yet it seemed a ghostly unreal day,—the wraith of Life. We seemed to rumble down an unknown street behind a little white bundle of posies, with the shadow of a song in our ears. The busy city dinned about us; they did not say much, those pale-faced hurrying men and women; they did not say much,—they only glanced and said, "Niggers!"

We could not lay him in the ground there in Georgia, for the earth there is strangely red; so we bore him away to the northward, with his flowers and his little folded hands. In vain, in vain!—for where, O God! beneath thy broad blue sky shall my dark baby rest in peace,—where Reverence dwells, and Goodness, and a Freedom that is free?

All that day and all that night there sat an awful gladness in my heart,—nay, blame me not if I see the world thus darkly through the Veil,—and my soul whispers ever to me saying, "Not dead, not dead, but escaped; not bond, but free." No bitter meanness now shall sicken his baby heart till it die a living death, no taunt shall madden his happy boyhood. Fool that I was to think or wish that this little soul should grow choked and deformed within the Veil! I might have known that yonder deep unworldly look that ever and anon floated past his eyes was peering far beyond this narrow Now. In the poise of his little curl-crowned head did there not sit all that wild pride of being which his father had hardly crushed in his own heart? For what, forsooth, shall a Negro want with pride amid the studied humiliations of fifty million fellows? Well sped, my boy, before the world had dubbed your ambition insolence, had held your ideals unattainable, and taught you to cringe and bow. Better far this nameless void that stops my life than a sea of sorrow for you.

Idle words; he might have borne his burden more bravely than we,—aye, and found it lighter too, some day; for surely, surely this is not the end. Surely there shall yet dawn some mighty morning to lift the Veil and set the prisoned free. Not for me,—I shall die in my bonds,—but for fresh young souls who have not known the night and waken to the morning; a morning when men ask of the workman, not "Is he white?" but "Can he work?" When men ask artists, not "Are they black?" but "Do they know?" Some morning this may be, long, long years to come. But now there wails, on that dark shore within the Veil, the same deep voice, THOU SHALT FOREGO! And all have I foregone at that command, and with small complaint,—all save that fair young form that lies so coldly wed with death in the nest I had builded.

If one must have gone, why not I? Why may I not rest me from this restlessness and sleep from this wide waking? Was not the world's alembic, Time, in his young hands, and is not my time waning? Are there so many workers in the vineyard that the fair promise of this little body could lightly be tossed away? The wretched of my race that line the alleys of the nation sit fatherless and unmothered; but Love sat beside his cradle, and in his ear Wisdom waited to speak. Perhaps now he knows the All-love, and needs not to be wise. Sleep, then, child,—sleep till I sleep and waken to a baby voice and the ceaseless patter of little feet—above the Veil.

12. OF ALEXANDER CRUMMELL

Then from the Dawn it seemed there came, but faint
As from beyond the limit of the world,
Like the last echo born of a great cry,
Sounds, as if some fair city were one voice
Around a king returning from his wars.

TENNYSON.

This is the story of a human heart,—the tale of a black boy who many long years ago began to struggle with life that he might know the world and know himself. Three temptations he met on those dark dunes that lay gray and dismal before the wonder-eyes of the child: the temptation of Hate, that stood out against the red dawn; the temptation of Despair, that darkened noonday; and the temptation of Doubt, that ever steals along with twilight. Above all, you must hear of the vales he crossed,—the Valley of Humiliation and the Valley of the Shadow of Death.

I saw Alexander Crummell first at a Wilberforce commencement season, amid its bustle and crush. Tall, frail, and black he stood, with simple dignity and an unmistakable air of good breeding. I talked with him apart, where the storming of the lusty young orators could not harm us. I spoke to him politely, then curiously, then eagerly, as I began to feel the fineness of his character,—his calm courtesy, the sweetness of his strength, and his fair blending of the hope and truth of life. Instinctively I bowed before this man, as one bows before the prophets of the world. Some seer he seemed, that came not from the crimson Past or the gray To-come, but from the pulsing Now,—that mocking world which seemed to me at once so light and dark, so splendid and sordid. Fourscore years had he wandered in this same world of mine, within the Veil.

He was born with the Missouri Compromise and lay a-dying amid the echoes of Manila and El Caney: stirring times for living, times dark to look back upon, darker to look forward to. The black-faced lad that paused over his mud and marbles seventy years ago saw puzzling vistas as he looked down the world. The slave-ship still groaned across the Atlantic, faint cries burdened the Southern breeze, and the great black father whispered mad tales of cruelty into those young ears. From the low doorway the mother silently watched her boy at play, and at nightfall sought him eagerly lest the shadows bear him away to the land of slaves.

So his young mind worked and winced and shaped curiously a vision of Life; and in the midst of that vision ever stood one dark figure alone,—ever with the hard, thick countenance of that bitter father, and a form that fell in vast and shapeless folds. Thus the temptation of Hate grew and shadowed the growing child,—gliding stealthily into his laughter, fading into his play, and seizing his dreams by day and night with rough, rude turbulence. So the black boy asked of sky and sun and flower the never-answered Why? and loved, as he grew, neither the world nor the world's rough ways.

Strange temptation for a child, you may think; and yet in this wide land to-day a thousand thousand dark children brood before this same temptation, and feel its cold and shuddering arms. For them, perhaps, some one will some day lift the Veil,—will come tenderly and cheerily into those sad little lives and brush the brooding hate away, just as Beriah Green strode in upon the life of Alexander Crummell. And before the bluff, kind-hearted man the shadow seemed less dark. Beriah Green had a school in Oneida County, New York, with a score of mischievous boys. "I'm going to bring a black boy here to educate," said Beriah Green, as only a crank and an abolitionist would have dared to say. "Oho!" laughed the boys. "Ye-es," said his wife; and Alexander came. Once before, the black boy had sought a school, had travelled, cold and hungry, four hundred miles up into free New Hampshire, to Canaan. But the godly farmers hitched ninety yoke of oxen to the abolition schoolhouse and dragged it into the middle of the swamp. The black boy trudged away.

The nineteenth was the first century of human sympathy,—the age when half wonderingly we began to descry in others that transfigured spark of divinity which we call Myself; when clodhoppers and peasants, and tramps and thieves, and millionaires and—sometimes—Negroes, became throbbing souls whose warm pulsing life touched us so nearly that we half gasped with surprise, crying, "Thou too! Hast Thou seen Sorrow and the dull waters of Hopelessness? Hast Thou known Life?" And then all helplessly we peered into those Other-worlds, and wailed, "O World of Worlds, how shall man make you one?"

So in that little Oneida school there came to those schoolboys a revelation of thought and longing beneath one black skin, of which they had not dreamed before. And to the lonely boy came a new dawn of sympathy and inspiration. The shadowy, formless thing—the temptation of Hate, that hovered between him and the world—grew fainter and less sinister. It did not wholly fade away, but diffused itself and lingered thick at the edges. Through it the child now first saw the blue and gold of life,—the sun-swept road that ran 'twixt heaven and earth until in one far-off wan wavering line they met and kissed. A vision of life came to the growing boy,—mystic, wonderful. He raised his head, stretched himself, breathed deep of the fresh new air. Yonder, behind the forests, he heard strange sounds; then glinting through the trees he saw, far, far away, the bronzed hosts of a nation calling,—calling faintly, calling loudly. He heard the hateful clank of their chains; he felt them cringe and grovel, and there rose within him a protest and a prophecy. And he girded himself to walk down the world.

A voice and vision called him to be a priest,—a seer to lead the uncalled out of the house of bondage. He saw the headless host turn toward him like the whirling of mad waters,—he stretched forth his hands eagerly, and then, even as he stretched them, suddenly there swept across the vision the temptation of Despair.

They were not wicked men,—the problem of life is not the problem of the wicked,—they were calm, good men, Bishops of the Apostolic Church of God, and strove toward righteousness. They said slowly, "It is all very natural—it is even commendable; but the General Theological Seminary of the Episcopal Church cannot admit a Negro." And when that thin, half-grotesque figure still haunted their doors, they put their hands kindly, half sorrowfully, on his shoulders, and said, "Now,—of course, we—we know how YOU feel about it; but you see it is impossible,—that is—well—it is premature. Sometime, we trust—sincerely trust—all such distinctions will fade away; but now the world is as it is."

This was the temptation of Despair; and the young man fought it doggedly. Like some grave shadow he flitted by those halls, pleading, arguing, half angrily demanding admittance, until there came the final NO: until men hustled the disturber away, marked him as foolish, unreasonable, and injudicious, a vain rebel against God's law. And then from that Vision Splendid all the glory faded slowly away, and left an earth gray and stern rolling on beneath a dark despair. Even the kind hands that stretched themselves toward him from out the depths of that dull morning seemed but parts of the purple shadows. He saw them coldly, and asked, "Why should I strive by special grace when the way of the world is closed to me?" All gently yet, the hands urged him on,—the hands of young John Jay, that daring father's daring son; the hands of the good folk of Boston, that free city. And yet, with a way to the priesthood of the Church open at last before him, the cloud lingered there; and even when in old St. Paul's the venerable Bishop raised his white arms above the Negro deacon—even then the burden had not lifted from that heart, for there had passed a glory from the earth.

And yet the fire through which Alexander Crummell went did not burn in vain. Slowly and more soberly he took up again his plan of life. More critically he studied the situation. Deep down below the slavery and servitude of the Negro people he saw their fatal weaknesses, which long years of mistreatment had emphasized. The dearth of strong moral character, of unbending righteousness, he felt, was their great shortcoming, and here he would begin. He would gather the best of his people into some little Episcopal chapel and there lead, teach, and inspire them, till the leaven spread, till the children grew, till the world hearkened, till—till—and then across his dream gleamed some faint after-glow of that first fair vision of youth—only an after-glow, for there had passed a glory from the earth.

One day—it was in 1842, and the springtide was struggling merrily with the May winds of New England—he stood at last in his own chapel in Providence, a priest of the Church. The days sped by, and the dark young clergyman labored; he wrote his sermons carefully; he intoned his prayers with a soft, earnest voice; he haunted the streets and accosted the wayfarers; he visited the sick, and knelt beside the dying. He worked and toiled, week by week, day by day, month by month. And yet month by month the congregation dwindled, week by week the hollow walls echoed more sharply, day by day the calls came fewer and fewer, and day by day the third temptation sat clearer and still more clearly within the Veil; a temptation, as it were, bland and smiling, with just a shade of mockery in its smooth tones. First it came casually, in the cadence of a voice: "Oh, colored folks? Yes." Or perhaps more definitely: "What do you EXPECT?" In voice and gesture lay the doubt—the temptation of Doubt. How he hated it, and stormed at it furiously! "Of course they are capable," he cried; "of course they can learn and strive and achieve—" and "Of course," added the temptation softly, "they do nothing of the sort." Of all the three temptations, this one struck the deepest. Hate? He had outgrown so childish a thing. Despair? He had steeled his right arm against it, and fought it with the vigor of determination. But to doubt the worth of his life-work,—to doubt the destiny and capability of the race his soul loved because it was his; to find listless squalor instead of eager endeavor; to hear his own lips whispering, "They do not care; they cannot know; they are dumb driven cattle,—why cast your pearls before swine?"—this, this seemed more than man could bear; and he closed the door, and sank upon the steps of the chancel, and cast his robe upon the floor and writhed.

The evening sunbeams had set the dust to dancing in the gloomy chapel when he arose. He folded his vestments, put away the hymn-books, and closed the great Bible. He stepped out into the twilight, looked back upon the narrow little pulpit with a weary smile, and locked the door. Then he walked briskly to the Bishop, and told the Bishop what the Bishop already knew. "I have failed," he said simply. And gaining courage by the confession, he added: "What I need is a larger constituency. There are comparatively few Negroes here, and perhaps they are not of the best. I must go where the field is wider, and try again." So the Bishop sent him to Philadelphia, with a letter to Bishop Onderdonk.

Bishop Onderdonk lived at the head of six white steps,—corpulent, red-faced, and the author of several thrilling tracts on Apostolic Succession. It was after dinner, and the Bishop had settled himself for a pleasant season of contemplation, when the bell must needs ring, and there must burst in upon the Bishop a letter and a thin, ungainly Negro. Bishop Onderdonk read the letter hastily and frowned. Fortunately, his mind was already clear on this point; and he cleared his brow and looked at Crummell. Then he said, slowly and impressively: "I will receive you into this diocese on one condition: no Negro priest can sit in my church convention, and no Negro church must ask for representation there."

I sometimes fancy I can see that tableau: the frail black figure, nervously twitching his hat before the massive abdomen of Bishop Onderdonk; his threadbare coat thrown against the dark woodwork of the bookcases, where Fox's "Lives of the Martyrs" nestled happily beside "The Whole Duty of Man." I seem to see the wide eyes of the Negro wander past the Bishop's broadcloth to where the swinging glass doors of the cabinet glow in the sunlight. A little blue fly is trying to cross the yawning keyhole. He marches briskly up to it, peers into the chasm in a surprised sort of way, and rubs his feelers reflectively; then he essays its depths, and, finding it bottomless, draws back again. The dark-faced priest finds himself wondering if the fly too has faced its Valley of Humiliation, and if it will plunge into it,—when lo! it spreads its tiny wings and buzzes merrily across, leaving the watcher wingless and alone.

Then the full weight of his burden fell upon him. The rich walls wheeled away, and before him lay the cold rough moor winding on through life, cut in twain by one thick granite ridge,—here, the Valley of Humiliation; yonder, the Valley of the Shadow of Death. And I know not which be darker,—no, not I. But this I know: in yonder Vale of the Humble stand to-day a million swarthy men, who willingly would

". . . bear the whips and scorns of time,
The oppressor's wrong, the proud man's contumely,
The pangs of despised love, the law's delay,
The insolence of office, and the spurns
That patient merit of the unworthy takes,"—

all this and more would they bear did they but know that this were sacrifice and not a meaner thing. So surged the thought within that lone black breast. The Bishop cleared his throat suggestively; then, recollecting that there was really nothing to say, considerately said nothing, only sat tapping his foot impatiently. But Alexander Crummell said, slowly and heavily: "I will never enter your diocese on such terms." And saying this, he turned and passed into the Valley of the Shadow of Death. You might have noted only the physical dying, the shattered frame and hacking cough; but in that soul lay deeper death than that. He found a chapel in New York,—the church of his father; he labored for it in poverty and starvation, scorned by his fellow priests. Half in despair, he wandered across the sea, a beggar with outstretched hands. Englishmen clasped them,—Wilberforce and Stanley, Thirwell and Ingles, and even Froude and Macaulay; Sir Benjamin Brodie bade him rest awhile at Queen's College in Cambridge, and there he lingered, struggling for health of body and mind, until he took his degree in '53. Restless still, and unsatisfied, he turned toward Africa, and for long years, amid the spawn of the slave-smugglers, sought a new heaven and a new earth.

So the man groped for light; all this was not Life,—it was the world-wandering of a soul in search of itself, the striving of one who vainly sought his place in the world, ever haunted by the shadow of a death that is more than death,—the passing of a soul that has missed its duty. Twenty years he wandered,—twenty years and more; and yet the hard rasping question kept gnawing within him, "What, in God's name, am I on earth for?" In the narrow New York parish his soul seemed cramped and smothered. In the fine old air of the English University he heard the millions wailing over the sea. In the wild fever-cursed swamps of West Africa he stood helpless and alone.

You will not wonder at his weird pilgrimage,—you who in the swift whirl of living, amid its cold paradox and marvellous vision, have fronted life and asked its riddle face to face. And if you find that riddle hard to read, remember that yonder black boy finds it just a little harder; if it is difficult for you to find and face your duty, it is a shade more difficult for him; if your heart sickens in the blood and dust of battle, remember that to him the dust is thicker and the battle fiercer. No wonder the wanderers fall! No wonder we point to thief and murderer, and haunting prostitute, and the never-ending throng of unhearsed dead! The Valley of the Shadow of Death gives few of its pilgrims back to the world.

But Alexander Crummell it gave back. Out of the temptation of Hate, and burned by the fire of Despair, triumphant over Doubt, and steeled by Sacrifice against Humiliation, he turned at last home across the waters, humble and strong, gentle and determined. He bent to all the gibes and prejudices, to all hatred and discrimination, with that rare courtesy which is the armor of pure souls. He fought among his own, the low, the grasping, and the wicked, with that unbending righteousness which is the sword of the just. He never faltered, he seldom complained; he simply worked, inspiring the young, rebuking the old, helping the weak, guiding the strong.

So he grew, and brought within his wide influence all that was best of those who walk within the Veil. They who live without knew not nor dreamed of that full power within, that mighty inspiration which the dull gauze of caste decreed that most men should not know. And now that he is gone, I sweep the Veil away and cry, Lo! the soul to whose dear memory I bring this little tribute. I can see his face still, dark and heavy-lined beneath his snowy hair; lighting and shading, now with inspiration for the future, now in innocent pain at some human wickedness, now with sorrow at some hard memory from the past. The more I met Alexander Crummell, the more I felt how much that world was losing which knew so little of him. In another age he might have sat among the elders of the land in purple-bordered toga; in another country mothers might have sung him to the cradles.

He did his work,—he did it nobly and well; and yet I sorrow that here he worked alone, with so little human sympathy. His name to-day, in this broad land, means little, and comes to fifty million ears laden with no incense of memory or emulation. And herein lies the tragedy of the age: not that men are poor,—all men know something of poverty; not that men are wicked,— who is good? not that men are ignorant,—what is Truth? Nay, but that men know so little of men.

He sat one morning gazing toward the sea. He smiled and said, "The gate is rusty on the hinges." That night at starrise a wind came moaning out of the west to blow the gate ajar, and then the soul I loved fled like a flame across the Seas, and in its seat sat Death.

I wonder where he is to-day? I wonder if in that dim world beyond, as he came gliding in, there rose on some wan throne a King,—a dark and pierced Jew, who knows the writhings of the earthly damned, saying, as he laid those heart-wrung talents down, "Well done!" while round about the morning stars sat singing.

13. OF THE COMING OF JOHN

What bring they 'neath the midnight,
Beside the River-sea?
They bring the human heart wherein
No nightly calm can be;
That droppeth never with the wind,
Nor drieth with the dew;
O calm it, God; thy calm is broad
To cover spirits too.

The river floweth on.

MRS. BROWNING.

Carlisle Street runs westward from the centre of Johnstown, across a great black bridge, down a hill and up again, by little shops and meat-markets, past single-storied homes, until suddenly it stops against a wide green lawn. It is a broad, restful place, with two large buildings outlined against the west. When at evening the winds come swelling from the east, and the great pall of the city's smoke hangs wearily above the valley, then the red west glows like a dreamland down Carlisle Street, and, at the tolling of the supper-bell, throws the passing forms of students in dark silhouette against the sky. Tall and black, they move slowly by, and seem in the sinister light to flit before the city like dim warning ghosts. Perhaps they are; for this is Wells Institute, and these black students have few dealings with the white city below.

And if you will notice, night after night, there is one dark form that ever hurries last and late toward the twinkling lights of Swain Hall,—for Jones is never on time. A long, straggling fellow he is, brown and hard-haired, who seems to be growing straight out of his clothes, and walks with a half-apologetic roll. He used perpetually to set the quiet dining-room into waves of merriment, as he stole to his place after the bell had tapped for prayers; he seemed so perfectly awkward. And yet one glance at his face made one forgive him much,—that broad, good-natured smile in which lay no bit of art or artifice, but seemed just bubbling good-nature and genuine satisfaction with the world.

He came to us from Altamaha, away down there beneath the gnarled oaks of Southeastern Georgia, where the sea croons to the sands and the sands listen till they sink half drowned beneath the waters, rising only here and there in long, low islands. The white folk of Altamaha voted John a good boy,—fine plough-hand, good in the rice-fields, handy everywhere, and always good-natured and respectful. But they shook their heads when his mother wanted to send him off to school. "It'll spoil him,—ruin him," they said; and they talked as though they knew. But full half the black folk followed him proudly to the station, and carried his queer little trunk and many bundles. And there they shook and shook hands, and the girls kissed him shyly and the boys clapped him on the back. So the train came, and he pinched his little sister lovingly, and put his great arms about his mother's neck, and then was away with a puff and a roar into the great yellow world that flamed and flared about the doubtful pilgrim. Up the coast they hurried, past the squares and palmettos of Savannah, through the cotton-fields and through the weary night, to Millville, and came with the morning to the noise and bustle of Johnstown.

And they that stood behind, that morning in Altamaha, and watched the train as it noisily bore playmate and brother and son away to the world, had thereafter one ever-recurring word,—"When John comes." Then what parties were to be, and what speakings in the churches; what new furniture in the front room,—perhaps even a new front room; and there would be a new schoolhouse, with John as teacher; and then perhaps a big wedding; all this and more—when John comes. But the white people shook their heads.

At first he was coming at Christmas-time,—but the vacation proved too short; and then, the next summer,—but times were hard and schooling costly, and so, instead, he worked in Johnstown. And so it drifted to the next summer, and the next,—till playmates scattered, and mother grew gray, and sister went up to the Judge's kitchen to work. And still the legend lingered,—"When John comes."

Up at the Judge's they rather liked this refrain; for they too had a John—a fair-haired, smooth-faced boy, who had played many a long summer's day to its close with his darker namesake. "Yes, sir! John is at Princeton, sir," said the broad-shouldered gray-haired Judge every morning as he marched down to the post-office. "Showing the Yankees what a Southern gentleman can do," he added; and strode home again with his letters and papers. Up at the great pillared house they lingered long over the Princeton letter,—the Judge and his frail wife, his sister and growing daughters. "It'll make a man of him," said the Judge, "college is the place." And then he asked the shy little waitress, "Well, Jennie, how's your John?" and added reflectively, "Too bad, too bad your mother sent him off—it will spoil him." And the waitress wondered.

Thus in the far-away Southern village the world lay waiting, half consciously, the coming of two young men, and dreamed in an inarticulate way of new things that would be done and new thoughts that all would think. And yet it was singular that few thought of two Johns,—for the black folk thought of one John, and he was black; and the white folk thought of another John, and he was white. And neither world thought the other world's thought, save with a vague unrest.

Up in Johnstown, at the Institute, we were long puzzled at the case of John Jones. For a long time the clay seemed unfit for any sort of moulding. He was loud and boisterous, always laughing and singing, and never able to work consecutively at anything. He did not know how to study; he had no idea of thoroughness; and with his tardiness, carelessness, and appalling good-humor, we were sore perplexed. One night we sat in faculty-meeting, worried and serious; for Jones was in trouble again. This last escapade was too much, and so we solemnly voted "that Jones, on account of repeated disorder and inattention to work, be suspended for the rest of the term."

It seemed to us that the first time life ever struck Jones as a really serious thing was when the Dean told him he must leave school. He stared at the gray-haired man blankly, with great eyes. "Why,—why," he faltered, "but—I haven't graduated!" Then the Dean slowly and clearly explained, reminding him of the tardiness and the carelessness, of the poor lessons and neglected work, of the noise and disorder, until the fellow hung his head in confusion.

Then he said quickly, "But you won't tell mammy and sister,—you won't write mammy, now will you? For if you won't I'll go out into the city and work, and come back next term and show you something." So the Dean promised faithfully, and John shouldered his little trunk, giving neither word nor look to the giggling boys, and walked down Carlisle Street to the great city, with sober eyes and a set and serious face.

Perhaps we imagined it, but someway it seemed to us that the serious look that crept over his boyish face that afternoon never left it again. When he came back to us he went to work with all his rugged strength. It was a hard struggle, for things did not come easily to him,—few crowding memories of early life and teaching came to help him on his new way; but all the world toward which he strove was of his own building, and he builded slow and hard. As the light dawned lingeringly on his new creations, he sat rapt and silent before the vision, or wandered alone over the green campus peering through and beyond the world of men into a world of thought. And the thoughts at times puzzled him sorely; he could not see just why the circle was not square, and carried it out fifty-six decimal places one midnight,— would have gone further, indeed, had not the matron rapped for lights out. He caught terrible colds lying on his back in the meadows of nights, trying to think out the solar system; he had grave doubts as to the ethics of the Fall of Rome, and strongly suspected the Germans of being thieves and rascals, despite his textbooks; he pondered long over every new Greek word, and wondered why this meant that and why it couldn't mean something else, and how it must have felt to think all things in Greek. So he thought and puzzled along for himself,—pausing perplexed where others skipped merrily, and walking steadily through the difficulties where the rest stopped and surrendered.

Thus he grew in body and soul, and with him his clothes seemed to grow and arrange themselves; coat sleeves got longer, cuffs appeared, and collars got less soiled. Now and then his boots shone, and a new dignity crept into his walk. And we who saw daily a new thoughtfulness growing in his eyes began to expect something of this plodding boy. Thus he passed out of the preparatory school into college, and we who watched him felt four more years of change, which almost transformed the tall, grave man who bowed to us commencement morning. He had left his queer thought-world and come back to a world of motion and of men. He looked now for the first time sharply about him, and wondered he had seen so little before. He grew slowly to feel almost for the first time the Veil that lay between him and the white world; he first noticed now the oppression that had not seemed oppression before, differences that erstwhile seemed natural, restraints and slights that in his boyhood days had gone unnoticed or been greeted with a laugh. He felt angry now when men did not call him "Mister," he clenched his hands at the "Jim Crow" cars, and chafed at the color-line that hemmed in him and his. A tinge of sarcasm crept into his speech, and a vague bitterness into his life; and he sat long hours wondering and planning a way around these crooked things. Daily he found himself shrinking from the choked and narrow life of his native town. And yet he always planned to go back to Altamaha,—always planned to work there. Still, more and more as the day approached he hesitated with a nameless dread; and even the day after graduation he seized with eagerness the offer of the Dean to send him North with the quartette during the summer vacation, to sing for the Institute. A breath of air before the plunge, he said to himself in half apology.

It was a bright September afternoon, and the streets of New York were brilliant with moving men. They reminded John of the sea, as he sat in the square and watched them, so changelessly changing, so bright and dark, so grave and gay. He scanned their rich and faultless clothes, the way they carried their hands, the shape of their hats; he peered into the hurrying carriages. Then, leaning back with a sigh, he said, "This is the World." The notion suddenly seized him to see where the world was going; since many of the richer and brighter seemed hurrying all one way. So when a tall, light-haired young man and a little talkative lady came by, he rose half hesitatingly and followed them. Up the street they went, past stores and gay shops, across a broad square, until with a hundred others they entered the high portal of a great building.

He was pushed toward the ticket-office with the others, and felt in his pocket for the new five-dollar bill he had hoarded. There seemed really no time for hesitation, so he drew it bravely out, passed it to the busy clerk, and received simply a ticket but no change. When at last he realized that he had paid five dollars to enter he knew not what, he stood stockstill amazed. "Be careful," said a low voice behind him; "you must not lynch the colored gentleman simply because he's in your way," and a girl looked up roguishly into the eyes of her fair-haired escort. A shade of annoyance passed over the escort's face. "You WILL not understand us at the South," he said half impatiently, as if continuing an argument. "With all your professions, one never sees in the North so cordial and intimate relations between white and black as are everyday occurrences with us. Why, I remember my closest playfellow in boyhood was a little Negro named after me, and surely no two,—WELL!" The man stopped short and flushed to the roots of his hair, for there directly beside his reserved orchestra chairs sat the Negro he had stumbled over in the hallway. He hesitated and grew pale with anger, called the usher and gave him his card, with a few peremptory words, and slowly sat down. The lady deftly changed the subject.

All this John did not see, for he sat in a half-daze minding the scene about him; the delicate beauty of the hall, the faint perfume, the moving myriad of men, the rich clothing and low hum of talking seemed all a part of a world so different from his, so strangely more beautiful than anything he had known, that he sat in dreamland, and started when, after a hush, rose high and clear the music of Lohengrin's swan. The infinite beauty of the wail lingered and swept through every muscle of his frame, and put it all a-tune. He closed his eyes and grasped the elbows of the chair, touching unwittingly the lady's arm. And the lady drew away. A deep longing swelled in all his heart to rise with that clear music out of the dirt and dust of that low life that held him prisoned and befouled. If he could only live up in the free air where birds sang and setting suns had no touch of blood! Who had called him to be the slave and butt of all? And if he had called, what right had he to call when a world like this lay open before men?

Then the movement changed, and fuller, mightier harmony swelled away. He looked thoughtfully across the hall, and wondered why the beautiful gray-haired woman looked so listless, and what the little man could be whispering about. He would not like to be listless and idle, he thought, for he felt with the music the movement of power within him. If he but had some master-work, some life-service, hard,—aye, bitter hard, but without the cringing and sickening servility, without the cruel hurt that hardened his heart and soul. When at last a soft sorrow crept across the violins, there came to him the vision of a far-off home, the great eyes of his sister, and the dark drawn face of his mother. And his heart sank below the waters, even as the sea-sand sinks by the shores of Altamaha, only to be lifted aloft again with that last ethereal wail of the swan that quivered and faded away into the sky.

It left John sitting so silent and rapt that he did not for some time notice the usher tapping him lightly on the shoulder and saying politely, "Will you step this way, please, sir?" A little surprised, he arose quickly at the last tap, and, turning to leave his seat, looked full into the face of the fair-haired young man. For the first time the young man recognized his dark boyhood playmate, and John knew that it was the Judge's son. The White John started, lifted his hand, and then froze into his chair; the black John smiled lightly, then grimly, and followed the usher down the aisle. The manager was sorry, very, very sorry,—but he explained that some mistake had been made in selling the gentleman a seat already disposed of; he would refund the money, of course,—and indeed felt the matter keenly, and so forth, and—before he had finished John was gone, walking hurriedly across the square and down the broad streets, and as he passed the park he buttoned his coat and said, "John Jones, you're a natural-born fool." Then he went to his lodgings and wrote a letter, and tore it up; he wrote another, and threw it in the fire. Then he seized a scrap of paper and wrote: "Dear Mother and Sister—I am coming—John."

"Perhaps," said John, as he settled himself on the train, "perhaps I am to blame myself in struggling against my manifest destiny simply because it looks hard and unpleasant. Here is my duty to Altamaha plain before me; perhaps they'll let me help settle the Negro problems there,—perhaps they won't. 'I will go in to the King, which is not according to the law; and if I perish, I perish.'" And then he mused and dreamed, and planned a life-work; and the train flew south.

Down in Altamaha, after seven long years, all the world knew John was coming. The homes were scrubbed and scoured,—above all, one; the gardens and yards had an unwonted trimness, and Jennie bought a new gingham. With some finesse and negotiation, all the dark Methodists and Presbyterians were induced to join in a monster welcome at the Baptist Church; and as the day drew near, warm discussions arose on every corner as to the exact extent and nature of John's accomplishments. It was noontide on a gray and cloudy day when he came. The black town flocked to the depot, with a little of the white at the edges,—a happy throng, with "Good-mawnings" and "Howdys" and laughing and joking and jostling. Mother sat yonder in the window watching; but sister Jennie stood on the platform, nervously fingering her dress, tall and lithe, with soft brown skin and loving eyes peering from out a tangled wilderness of hair. John rose gloomily as the train stopped, for he was thinking of the "Jim Crow" car; he stepped to the platform, and paused: a little dingy station, a black crowd gaudy and dirty, a half-mile of dilapidated shanties along a straggling ditch of mud. An overwhelming sense of the sordidness and narrowness of it all seized him; he looked in vain for his mother, kissed coldly the tall, strange girl who called him brother, spoke a short, dry word here and there; then, lingering neither for handshaking nor gossip, started silently up the street, raising his hat merely to the last eager old aunty, to her open-mouthed astonishment. The people were distinctly bewildered. This silent, cold man,—was this John? Where was his smile and hearty hand-grasp? "'Peared kind o' down in the mouf," said the Methodist preacher thoughtfully. "Seemed monstus stuck up," complained a Baptist sister. But the white postmaster from the edge of the crowd expressed the opinion of his folks plainly. "That damn Nigger," said he, as he shouldered the mail and arranged his tobacco, "has gone North and got plum full o' fool notions; but they won't work in Altamaha." And the crowd melted away.

The meeting of welcome at the Baptist Church was a failure. Rain spoiled the barbecue, and thunder turned the milk in the ice-cream. When the speaking came at night, the house was crowded to overflowing. The three preachers had especially prepared themselves, but somehow John's manner seemed to throw a blanket over everything,—he seemed so cold and preoccupied, and had so strange an air of restraint that the Methodist brother could not warm up to his theme and elicited not a single "Amen"; the Presbyterian prayer was but feebly responded to, and even the Baptist preacher, though he wakened faint enthusiasm, got so mixed up in his favorite sentence that he had to close it by stopping fully fifteen minutes sooner than he meant. The people moved uneasily in their seats as John rose to reply. He spoke slowly and methodically. The age, he said, demanded new ideas; we were far different from those men of the seventeenth and eighteenth centuries,—with broader ideas of human brotherhood and destiny. Then he spoke of the rise of charity and popular education, and particularly of the spread of wealth and work. The question was, then, he added reflectively, looking at the low discolored ceiling, what part the Negroes of this land would take in the striving of the new century. He sketched in vague outline the new Industrial School that might rise among these pines, he spoke in detail of the charitable and philanthropic work that might be organized, of money that might be saved for banks and business. Finally he urged unity, and deprecated especially religious and denominational bickering. "To-day," he said, with a smile, "the world cares little whether a man be Baptist or Methodist, or indeed a churchman at all, so long as he is good and true. What difference does it make whether a man be baptized in river or washbowl, or not at all? Let's leave all that littleness, and look higher." Then, thinking of nothing else, he slowly sat down. A painful hush seized that crowded mass. Little had they understood of what he said, for he spoke an unknown tongue, save the last word about baptism; that they knew, and they sat very still while the clock ticked. Then at last a low suppressed snarl came from the Amen corner, and an old bent man arose, walked over the seats, and climbed straight up into the pulpit. He was wrinkled and black, with scant gray and tufted hair; his voice and hands shook as with palsy; but on his face lay the intense rapt look of the religious fanatic. He seized the Bible with his rough, huge hands; twice he raised it inarticulate, and then fairly burst into words, with rude and awful eloquence. He quivered, swayed, and bent; then rose aloft in perfect majesty, till the people moaned and wept, wailed and shouted, and a wild shrieking arose from the corners where all the pent-up feeling of the hour gathered itself and rushed into the air. John never knew clearly what the old man said; he only felt himself held up to scorn and scathing denunciation for trampling on the true Religion, and he realized with amazement that all unknowingly he had put rough, rude hands on something this little world held sacred. He arose silently, and passed out into the night. Down toward the sea he went, in the fitful starlight, half conscious of the girl who followed timidly after him. When at last he stood upon the bluff, he turned to his little sister and looked upon her sorrowfully, remembering with sudden pain how little thought he had given her. He put his arm about her and let her passion of tears spend itself on his shoulder.

Long they stood together, peering over the gray unresting water.

"John," she said, "does it make every one—unhappy when they study and learn lots of things?"

He paused and smiled. "I am afraid it does," he said.

"And, John, are you glad you studied?" "Yes," came the answer, slowly but positively.

She watched the flickering lights upon the sea, and said thoughtfully, "I wish I was unhappy,—and—and," putting both arms about his neck, "I think I am, a little, John."

It was several days later that John walked up to the Judge's house to ask for the privilege of teaching the Negro school. The Judge himself met him at the front door, stared a little hard at him, and said brusquely, "Go 'round to the kitchen door, John, and wait." Sitting on the kitchen steps, John stared at the corn, thoroughly perplexed. What on earth had come over him? Every step he made offended some one. He had come to save his people, and before he left the depot he had hurt them. He sought to teach them at the church, and had outraged their deepest feelings. He had schooled himself to be respectful to the Judge, and then blundered into his front door. And all the time he had meant right,—and yet, and yet, somehow he found it so hard and strange to fit his old surroundings again, to find his place in the world about him. He could not remember that he used to have any difficulty in the past, when life was glad and gay. The world seemed smooth and easy then. Perhaps,—but his sister came to the kitchen door just then and said the Judge awaited him.

The Judge sat in the dining-room amid his morning's mail, and he did not ask John to sit down. He plunged squarely into the business. "You've come for the school, I suppose. Well John, I want to speak to you plainly. You know I'm a friend to your people. I've helped you and your family, and would have done more if you hadn't got the notion of going off. Now I like the colored people, and sympathize with all their reasonable aspirations; but you and I both know, John, that in this country the Negro must remain subordinate, and can never expect to be the equal of white men. In their place, your people can be honest and respectful; and God knows, I'll do what I can to help them. But when they want to reverse nature, and rule white men, and marry white women, and sit in my parlor, then, by God! we'll hold them under if we have to lynch every Nigger in the land. Now,

John, the question is, are you, with your education and Northern notions, going to accept the situation and teach the darkies to be faithful servants and laborers as your fathers were,—I knew your father, John, he belonged to my brother, and he was a good Nigger. Well—well, are you going to be like him, or are you going to try to put fool ideas of rising and equality into these folks' heads, and make them discontented and unhappy?"

"I am going to accept the situation, Judge Henderson," answered John, with a brevity that did not escape the keen old man. He hesitated a moment, and then said shortly, "Very well,—we'll try you awhile. Good-morning."

It was a full month after the opening of the Negro school that the other John came home, tall, gay, and headstrong. The mother wept, the sisters sang. The whole white town was glad. A proud man was the Judge, and it was a goodly sight to see the two swinging down Main Street together. And yet all did not go smoothly between them, for the younger man could not and did not veil his contempt for the little town, and plainly had his heart set on New York. Now the one cherished ambition of the Judge was to see his son mayor of Altamaha, representative to the legislature, and—who could say?—governor of Georgia. So the argument often waxed hot between them. "Good heavens, father," the younger man would say after dinner, as he lighted a cigar and stood by the fireplace, "you surely don't expect a young fellow like me to settle down permanently in this—this God-forgotten town with nothing but mud and Negroes?" "I did," the Judge would answer laconically; and on this particular day it seemed from the gathering scowl that he was about to add something more emphatic, but neighbors had already begun to drop in to admire his son, and the conversation drifted.

"Heah that John is livenin' things up at the darky school," volunteered the postmaster, after a pause.

"What now?" asked the Judge, sharply.

"Oh, nothin' in particulah,—just his almighty air and uppish ways. B'lieve I did heah somethin' about his givin' talks on the French Revolution, equality, and such like. He's what I call a dangerous Nigger."

"Have you heard him say anything out of the way?"

"Why, no,—but Sally, our girl, told my wife a lot of rot. Then, too, I don't need to heah: a Nigger what won't say 'sir' to a white man, or—"

"Who is this John?" interrupted the son.

"Why, it's little black John, Peggy's son,—your old playfellow."

The young man's face flushed angrily, and then he laughed.

"Oh," said he, "it's the darky that tried to force himself into a seat beside the lady I was escorting—"

But Judge Henderson waited to hear no more. He had been nettled all day, and now at this he rose with a half-smothered oath, took his hat and cane, and walked straight to the schoolhouse.

For John, it had been a long, hard pull to get things started in the rickety old shanty that sheltered his school. The Negroes were rent into factions for and against him, the parents were careless, the children irregular and dirty, and books, pencils, and slates largely missing. Nevertheless, he struggled hopefully on, and seemed to see at last some glimmering of dawn. The attendance was larger and the children were a shade cleaner this week. Even the booby class in reading showed a little comforting progress. So John settled himself with renewed patience this afternoon.

"Now, Mandy," he said cheerfully, "that's better; but you mustn't chop your words up so: 'If—the-man—goes.' Why, your little brother even wouldn't tell a story that way, now would he?"

"Naw, suh, he cain't talk."

"All right; now let's try again: 'If the man—'

"John!"

The whole school started in surprise, and the teacher half arose, as the red, angry face of the Judge appeared in the open doorway.

"John, this school is closed. You children can go home and get to work. The white people of Altamaha are not spending their money on black folks to have their heads crammed with impudence and lies. Clear out! I'll lock the door myself."

Up at the great pillared house the tall young son wandered aimlessly about after his father's abrupt departure. In the house there was little to interest him; the books were old and stale, the local newspaper flat, and the women had retired with headaches and sewing. He tried a nap, but it was too warm. So he sauntered out into the fields, complaining disconsolately, "Good Lord! how long will this imprisonment last!" He was not a bad fellow,—just a little spoiled and self-indulgent, and as headstrong as his proud father. He seemed a young man pleasant to look upon, as he sat on the great black stump at the edge of the pines idly swinging his legs and smoking. "Why, there isn't even a girl worth getting up a respectable flirtation with," he growled. Just then his eye caught a tall, willowy figure hurrying toward him on the narrow path. He looked with interest at first, and then burst into a laugh as he said, "Well, I declare, if it isn't Jennie, the little brown kitchen-maid! Why, I never noticed before what a trim little body she is. Hello, Jennie! Why, you haven't kissed me since I came home," he said gaily. The young girl stared at him in surprise and confusion,—faltered something inarticulate, and attempted to pass. But a wilful mood had seized the young idler, and he caught at her arm. Frightened, she slipped by; and half mischievously he turned and ran after her through the tall pines.

Yonder, toward the sea, at the end of the path, came John slowly, with his head down. He had turned wearily homeward from the schoolhouse; then, thinking to shield his mother from the blow, started to meet his sister as she came from work and break the news of his dismissal to her. "I'll go away," he said slowly; "I'll go away and find work, and send for them. I cannot live here longer." And then the fierce, buried anger surged up into his throat. He waved his arms and hurried wildly up the path. The great brown sea lay silent. The air scarce breathed. The dying day bathed the twisted oaks and mighty pines in black and gold. There came from the wind no warning, not a whisper from the cloudless sky. There was only a black man hurrying on with an ache in his heart, seeing neither sun nor sea, but starting as from a dream at the frightened cry that woke the pines, to see his dark sister struggling in the arms of a tall and fair-haired man.

He said not a word, but, seizing a fallen limb, struck him with all the pent-up hatred of his great black arm, and the body lay white and still beneath the pines, all bathed in sunshine and in blood. John looked at it dreamily, then walked back to the house briskly, and said in a soft voice, "Mammy, I'm going away—I'm going to be free."

She gazed at him dimly and faltered, "No'th, honey, is yo' gwine No'th agin?"

He looked out where the North Star glistened pale above the waters, and said, "Yes, mammy, I'm going—North."

Then, without another word, he went out into the narrow lane, up by the straight pines, to the same winding path, and seated himself on the great black stump, looking at the blood where the body had lain. Yonder in the gray past he had played with that dead boy, romping together under the solemn trees. The night deepened; he thought of the boys at Johnstown. He wondered how Brown had turned out, and Carey? And Jones,—Jones? Why, he was Jones, and he wondered what they would all say when they knew, when they knew, in that great long dining-room with its hundreds of merry eyes. Then as the sheen of the starlight stole over him, he thought of the gilded ceiling of that vast concert hall, heard stealing toward him the faint sweet music of the swan. Hark! was it music, or the hurry and shouting of men? Yes, surely! Clear and high the faint sweet melody rose and fluttered like a living thing, so that the very earth trembled as with the tramp of horses and murmur of angry men. He leaned back and smiled toward the sea, whence rose the strange melody, away from the dark shadows where lay the noise of horses galloping, galloping on. With an effort he roused himself, bent forward, and looked steadily down the pathway, softly humming the "Song of the Bride,"—

"Freudig gefuhrt, ziehet dahin."

Amid the trees in the dim morning twilight he watched their shadows dancing and heard their horses thundering toward him, until at last they came sweeping like a storm, and he saw in front that haggard white-haired man, whose eyes flashed red with fury. Oh, how he pitied him,—pitied him,—and wondered if he had the coiling twisted rope. Then, as the storm burst round him, he rose slowly to his feet and turned his closed eyes toward the Sea.

And the world whistled in his ears.

14. OF THE SORROW SONGS

I walk through the churchyard
To lay this body down;
I know moon-rise, I know star-rise;
I walk in the moonlight, I walk in the starlight;
I'll lie in the grave and stretch out my arms,
I'll go to judgment in the evening of the day,
And my soul and thy soul shall meet that day,
When I lay this body down.

NEGRO SONG.

They that walked in darkness sang songs in the olden days—Sorrow Songs—for they were weary at heart. And so before each thought that I have written in this book I have set a phrase, a haunting echo of these weird old songs in which the soul of the black slave spoke to men. Ever since I was a child these songs have stirred me strangely. They came out of the South unknown to me, one by one, and yet at once I knew them as of me and of mine. Then in after years when I came to Nashville I saw the great temple builded of these songs towering over the pale city. To me Jubilee Hall seemed ever made of the songs themselves, and its bricks were red with the blood and dust of toil. Out of them rose for me morning, noon, and night, bursts of wonderful melody, full of the voices of my brothers and sisters, full of the voices of the past.

Little of beauty has America given the world save the rude grandeur God himself stamped on her bosom; the human spirit in this new world has expressed itself in vigor and ingenuity rather than in beauty. And so by fateful chance the Negro folk-song—the rhythmic cry of the slave—stands to-day not simply as the sole American music, but as the most beautiful expression of human experience born this side the seas. It has been neglected, it has been, and is, half despised, and above all it has been persistently mistaken and misunderstood; but notwithstanding, it still remains as the singular spiritual heritage of the nation and the greatest gift of the Negro people.

Away back in the thirties the melody of these slave songs stirred the nation, but the songs were soon half forgotten. Some, like "Near the lake where drooped the willow," passed into current airs and their source was forgotten; others were caricatured on the "minstrel" stage and their memory died away. Then in war-time came the singular Port Royal experiment after the capture of Hilton Head, and perhaps for the first time the North met the Southern slave face to face and heart to heart with no third witness. The Sea Islands of the Carolinas, where they met, were filled with a black folk of primitive type, touched and moulded less by the world about them than any others outside the Black Belt. Their appearance was uncouth, their language funny, but their hearts were human and their singing stirred men with a mighty power. Thomas Wentworth Higginson hastened to tell of these songs, and Miss McKim and others urged upon the world their rare beauty. But the world listened only half credulously until the Fisk Jubilee Singers sang the slave songs so deeply into the world's heart that it can never wholly forget them again.

There was once a blacksmith's son born at Cadiz, New York, who in the changes of time taught school in Ohio and helped defend Cincinnati from Kirby Smith. Then he fought at Chancellorsville and Gettysburg and finally served in the Freedmen's Bureau at Nashville. Here he formed a Sunday-school class of black children in 1866, and sang with them and taught them to sing. And then they taught him to sing, and when once the glory of the Jubilee songs passed into the soul of George L. White, he knew his life-work was to let those Negroes sing to the world as they had sung to him. So in 1871 the pilgrimage of the Fisk Jubilee Singers began. North to Cincinnati they rode,—four half-clothed black boys and five girl-women,—led by a man with a cause and a purpose. They stopped at Wilberforce, the oldest of Negro schools, where a black bishop blessed them. Then they went, fighting cold and starvation, shut out of hotels, and cheerfully sneered at, ever northward; and ever the magic of their song kept thrilling hearts, until a burst of applause in the Congregational Council at Oberlin revealed them to the world. They came to New York and Henry Ward Beecher dared to welcome them, even though the metropolitan dailies sneered at his "Nigger Minstrels." So their songs conquered till they sang across the land and across the sea, before Queen and Kaiser, in Scotland and Ireland, Holland and Switzerland. Seven years they sang, and brought back a hundred and fifty thousand dollars to found Fisk University.

Since their day they have been imitated—sometimes well, by the singers of Hampton and Atlanta, sometimes ill, by straggling quartettes. Caricature has sought again to spoil the quaint beauty of the music, and has filled the air with many debased melodies which vulgar ears scarce know from the real. But the true Negro folk-song still lives in the hearts of those who have heard them truly sung and in the hearts of the Negro people.

What are these songs, and what do they mean? I know little of music and can say nothing in technical phrase, but I know something of men, and knowing them, I know that these songs are the articulate message of the slave to the world. They tell us in these eager days that life was joyous to the black slave, careless and happy. I can easily believe this of some, of many. But not all the past South, though it rose from the dead, can gainsay the heart-touching witness of these songs. They are the music of an unhappy people, of the children of disappointment; they tell of death and suffering and unvoiced longing toward a truer world, of misty wanderings and hidden ways.

The songs are indeed the siftings of centuries; the music is far more ancient than the words, and in it we can trace here and there signs of development. My grandfather's grandmother was seized by an evil Dutch trader two centuries ago; and coming to the valleys of the Hudson and Housatonic, black, little, and lithe, she shivered and shrank in the harsh north winds, looked longingly at the hills, and often crooned a heathen melody to the child between her knees, thus:

Do ba-na co-ba, ge-ne me, ge-ne me!
Do ba-na co-ba, ge-ne me, ge-ne me!

Ben d' nu-li, nu-li, nu-li, ben d' le.

The child sang it to his children and they to their children's children, and so two hundred years it has travelled down to us and we sing it to our children, knowing as little as our fathers what its words may mean, but knowing well the meaning of its music.

This was primitive African music; it may be seen in larger form in the strange chant which heralds "The Coming of John":

"You may bury me in the East,
You may bury me in the West,
But I'll hear the trumpet sound in that morning,"

—the voice of exile.

Ten master songs, more or less, one may pluck from the forest of melody-songs of undoubted Negro origin and wide popular currency, and songs peculiarly characteristic of the slave. One of these I have just mentioned. Another whose strains begin this book is "Nobody knows the trouble I've seen." When, struck with a sudden poverty, the United States refused to fulfill its promises of land to the freedmen, a brigadier-general went down to the Sea Islands to carry the news. An old woman on the outskirts of the throng began singing this song; all the mass joined with her, swaying. And the soldier wept.

The third song is the cradle-song of death which all men know,-"Swing low, sweet chariot,"—whose bars begin the life story of "Alexander Crummell." Then there is the song of many waters, "Roll, Jordan, roll," a mighty chorus with minor cadences. There were many songs of the fugitive like that which opens "The Wings of Atalanta," and the more familiar "Been a-listening." The seventh is the song of the End and the Beginning—"My Lord, what a mourning! when the stars begin to fall"; a strain of this is placed before "The Dawn of Freedom." The song of groping—"My way's cloudy"—begins "The Meaning of Progress"; the ninth is the song of this chapter—"Wrestlin' Jacob, the day is a-breaking,"—a paean of hopeful strife. The last master song is the song of songs—"Steal away,"—sprung from "The Faith of the Fathers."

There are many others of the Negro folk-songs as striking and characteristic as these, as, for instance, the three strains in the third, eighth, and ninth chapters; and others I am sure could easily make a selection on more scientific principles. There are, too, songs that seem to be a step removed from the more primitive types: there is the maze-like medley, "Bright sparkles," one phrase of which heads "The Black Belt"; the Easter carol, "Dust, dust and ashes"; the dirge, "My mother's took her flight and gone home"; and that burst of melody hovering over "The Passing of the First-Born"—"I hope my mother will be there in that beautiful world on high."

These represent a third step in the development of the slave song, of which "You may bury me in the East" is the first, and songs like "March on" (chapter six) and "Steal away" are the second. The first is African music, the second Afro-American, while the third is a blending of Negro music with the music heard in the foster land. The result is still distinctively Negro and the method of blending original, but the elements are both Negro and Caucasian. One might go further and find a fourth step in this development, where the songs of white America have been distinctively influenced by the slave songs or have incorporated whole phrases of Negro melody, as "Swanee River" and "Old Black Joe." Side by side, too, with the growth has gone the debasements and imitations—the Negro "minstrel" songs, many of the "gospel" hymns, and some of the contemporary "coon" songs,—a mass of music in which the novice may easily lose himself and never find the real Negro melodies.

In these songs, I have said, the slave spoke to the world. Such a message is naturally veiled and half articulate. Words and music have lost each other and new and cant phrases of a dimly understood theology have displaced the older sentiment. Once in a while we catch a strange word of an unknown tongue, as the "Mighty Myo," which figures as a river of death; more often slight words or mere doggerel are joined to music of singular sweetness. Purely secular songs are few in number, partly because many of them were turned into hymns by a change of words, partly because the frolics were seldom heard by the stranger, and the music less often caught.

Of nearly all the songs, however, the music is distinctly sorrowful. The ten master songs I have mentioned tell in word and music of trouble and exile, of strife and hiding; they grope toward some unseen power and sigh for rest in the End.

The words that are left to us are not without interest, and, cleared of evident dross, they conceal much of real poetry and meaning beneath conventional theology and unmeaning rhapsody. Like all primitive folk, the slave stood near to Nature's heart. Life was a "rough and rolling sea" like the brown Atlantic of the Sea Islands; the "Wilderness" was the home of God, and the "lonesome valley" led to the way of life. "Winter'll soon be over," was the picture of life and death to a tropical imagination. The sudden wild thunderstorms of the South awed and impressed the Negroes,—at times the rumbling seemed to them "mournful," at times imperious:

"My Lord calls me,
He calls me by the thunder,
The trumpet sounds it in my soul."

The monotonous toil and exposure is painted in many words. One sees the ploughmen in the hot, moist furrow, singing:

"Dere's no rain to wet you,
Dere's no sun to burn you,
Oh, push along, believer,
I want to go home."

The bowed and bent old man cries, with thrice-repeated wail:
"O Lord, keep me from sinking down,"
and he rebukes the devil of doubt who can whisper:
"Jesus is dead and God's gone away."

Yet the soul-hunger is there, the restlessness of the savage, the wail of the wanderer, and the plaint is put in one little phrase:

My soul wants something that's new, that's new

Over the inner thoughts of the slaves and their relations one with another the shadow of fear ever hung, so that we get but glimpses here and there, and also with them, eloquent omissions and silences. Mother and child are sung, but seldom father; fugitive and weary wanderer call for pity and affection, but there is little of wooing and wedding; the rocks and the mountains are well known, but home is unknown. Strange blending of love and helplessness sings through the refrain:

"Yonder's my ole mudder,
Been waggin' at de hill so long;
'Bout time she cross over,
Git home bime-by."

Elsewhere comes the cry of the "motherless" and the "Farewell, farewell, my only child."

Love-songs are scarce and fall into two categories—the frivolous and light, and the sad. Of deep successful love there is ominous silence, and in one of the oldest of these songs there is a depth of history and meaning:

Poor Ro-sy, poor gal; Poor Ro-sy,
poor gal; Ro-sy break my poor heart,
Heav'n shall-a-be my home.

A black woman said of the song, "It can't be sung without a full heart and a troubled sperrit." The same voice sings here that sings in the German folk-song:

"Jetz Geh i' an's brunele, trink' aber net."

Of death the Negro showed little fear, but talked of it familiarly and even fondly as simply a crossing of the waters, perhaps—who knows?—back to his ancient forests again. Later days transfigured his fatalism, and amid the dust and dirt the toiler sang:

"Dust, dust and ashes, fly over my grave,
But the Lord shall bear my spirit home."

The things evidently borrowed from the surrounding world undergo characteristic change when they enter the mouth of the slave. Especially is this true of Bible phrases. "Weep, O captive daughter of Zion," is quaintly turned into "Zion, weep-a-low," and the wheels of Ezekiel are turned every way in the mystic dreaming of the slave, till he says:

There's a little wheel a-turnin' in-a-my heart."

As in olden time, the words of these hymns were improvised by some leading minstrel of the religious band. The circumstances of the gathering, however, the rhythm of the songs, and the limitations of allowable thought, confined the poetry for the most part to single or double lines, and they seldom were expanded to quatrains or longer tales, although there are some few examples of sustained efforts, chiefly paraphrases of the Bible. Three short series of verses have always attracted me,—the one that heads this chapter, of one line of which Thomas Wentworth Higginson has fittingly said, "Never, it seems to me, since man first lived and suffered was his infinite longing for peace uttered more plaintively." The second and third are descriptions of the Last Judgment,—the one a late improvisation, with some traces of outside influence:

"Oh, the stars in the elements are falling,
And the moon drips away into blood,
And the ransomed of the Lord are returning unto
God, Blessed be the name of the Lord."

And the other earlier and homelier picture from the low coast lands:

"Michael, haul the boat ashore,
Then you'll hear the horn they blow,
Then you'll hear the trumpet sound,
Trumpet sound the world around,
Trumpet sound for rich and poor,
Trumpet sound the Jubilee,
Trumpet sound for you and me."

Through all the sorrow of the Sorrow Songs there breathes a hope—a faith in the ultimate justice of things. The minor cadences of despair change often to triumph and calm confidence. Sometimes it is faith in life, sometimes a faith in death, sometimes assurance of boundless justice in some fair world beyond. But whichever it is, the meaning is always clear: that sometime, somewhere, men will judge men by their souls and not by their skins. Is such a hope justified? Do the Sorrow Songs sing true?

The silently growing assumption of this age is that the probation of races is past, and that the backward races of to-day are of proven inefficiency and not worth the saving. Such an assumption is the arrogance of peoples irreverent toward Time and ignorant of the deeds of men. A thousand years ago such an assumption, easily possible, would have made it difficult for the Teuton to prove his right to life. Two thousand years ago such dogmatism, readily welcome, would have scouted the idea of blond races ever leading civilization. So wofully unorganized is sociological knowledge that the meaning of progress, the meaning of "swift" and "slow" in human doing, and the limits of human perfectability, are veiled, unanswered sphinxes on the shores of science. Why should AEschylus have sung two thousand years before Shakespeare was born? Why has civilization flourished in Europe, and flickered, flamed, and died in Africa? So long as the world stands meekly dumb before such questions, shall this nation proclaim its ignorance and unhallowed prejudices by denying freedom of opportunity to those who brought the Sorrow Songs to the Seats of the Mighty?

Your country? How came it yours? Before the Pilgrims landed we were here. Here we have brought our three gifts and mingled them with yours: a gift of story and song—soft, stirring melody in an ill-harmonized and unmelodious land; the gift of sweat and brawn to beat back the wilderness, conquer the soil, and lay the foundations of this vast economic empire two hundred years earlier than your weak hands could have done it; the third, a gift of the Spirit. Around us the history of the land has centred for thrice a hundred years; out of the nation's heart we have called all that was best to throttle and subdue all that was worst; fire and blood, prayer and sacrifice, have billowed over this people, and they have found peace only in the altars of the God of Right. Nor has our gift of the Spirit been merely passive. Actively we have woven ourselves with the very warp and woof of this nation,—we fought their battles, shared their sorrow, mingled our blood with theirs, and generation after generation have pleaded with a headstrong, careless people to despise not Justice, Mercy, and Truth, lest the nation be smitten with a curse. Our song, our toil, our cheer, and warning have been given to this nation in blood-brotherhood. Are not these gifts worth the giving? Is not this work and striving? Would America have been America without her Negro people?

Even so is the hope that sang in the songs of my fathers well sung. If somewhere in this whirl and chaos of things there dwells Eternal Good, pitiful yet masterful, then anon in His good time America shall rend the Veil and the prisoned shall go free. Free, free as the sunshine trickling down the morning into these high windows of mine, free as yonder fresh young voices welling up to me from the caverns of brick and mortar below—swelling with song, instinct with life, tremulous treble and darkening bass. My children, my little children, are singing to the sunshine, and thus they sing:

Let us cheer the wea-ry trav-el-ler,
Cheer the wea-ry trav-el-ler, Let us
cheer the wea-ry trav-el-ler
A-long the heav-en-ly way.

And the traveller girds himself, and sets his face toward the Morning, and goes his way.

THE AFTERTHOUGHT

Hear my cry, O God the Reader; vouchsafe that this my book fall not still-born into the world wilderness. Let there spring, Gentle One, from out its leaves vigor of thought and thoughtful deed to reap the harvest wonderful. Let the ears of a guilty people tingle with truth, and seventy millions sigh for the righteousness which exalteth nations, in this drear day when human brotherhood is mockery and a snare. Thus in Thy good time may infinite reason turn the tangle straight, and these crooked marks on a fragile leaf be not indeed.

Narrative of the Life of FREDERICK DOUGLASS

FREDERICK DOUGLASS

SANAGE
PUBLISHING HOUSE

Frederick Douglass (February 1818 – February 20, 1895) was an American social reformer, abolitionist, orator, writer, and statesman. After escaping from slavery in Maryland, he became a national leader of the abolitionist movement in Massachusetts and New York, becoming famous for his oratoryand incisive antislavery writings. Accordingly, he was described by abolitionists in his time as a living counter-example to slaveholders' arguments that slaves lacked the intellectual capacity to function as independent American citizens.

PREFACE.

IN the month of August, 1841, I attended an anti-slavery convention in Nantucket, at which it was my happiness to become acquainted with FREDERICK DOUGLASS, the writer of the following Narrative. He was a stranger to nearly every member of that body; but, having recently made his escape from the southern prison-house of bondage, and feeling his curiosity excited to ascertain the principles and measures of the abolitionists,—o f whom he had heard a somewhat vague description while he was a slave,—h e was induced to give his attendance, on the occasion alluded to, though at that time a resident in New Bedford.

Fortunate, most fortunate occurrence!— fortunate for the millions of his manacled brethren, yet panting for deliverance from their awful thraldom!— fortunate for the cause of negro emancipation, and of universal liberty!— fortunate for the land of his birth, which he has already done so much to save and bless!— fortunate for a large circle of friends and acquaintances, whose sympathy and affection he has strongly secured by the many sufferings he has endured, by his virtuous traits of character, by his ever-abiding remembrance of those who are in bonds, as being bound with them!— fortunate for the multitudes, in various parts of our republic, whose minds he has enlightened on the subject of slavery, and who have been melted to tears by his pathos, or roused to virtuous indignation by his stirring eloquence against the enslavers of men!— fortunate for himself, as it at once brought him into the field of public usefulness, " gave the world assurance of a MAN," quickened the slumbering energies of his soul, and consecrated him to the great work of breaking the rod of the oppressor, and letting the oppressed go free!

I shall never forget his first speech at the convention— the extraordinary emotion it excited in my own mind— the powerful impression it created upon a crowded auditory, completely taken by surprise— the applause which followed from the beginning to the end of his felicitous remarks. I think I never hated slavery so intensely as at that moment; certainly, my perception of the enormous outrage which is inflicted by it, on the godlike nature of its victims, was rendered far more clear than ever. There stood one, in physical proportion and stature commanding and exact— in intellect richly endowed— in natural eloquence a prodigy— in soul manifestly " created but a little lower than the angels" — yet a slave, ay, a fugitive slave,— trembling for his safety, hardly daring to believe that on the American soil, a single white person could be found who would befriend him at all hazards, for the love of God and humanity! Capable of high attainments as an intellectual and moral being— needing nothing but a comparatively small amount of cultivation to make him an ornament to society and a blessing to his race— by the law of the land, by the voice of the people, by the terms of the slave code, he was only a piece of property, a beast of burden, a chattel personal, nevertheless!

A beloved friend from New Bedford prevailed on Mr. DOUGLASS to address the convention. He came forward to the platform with a hesitancy and embarrassment, necessarily the attendants of a sensitive mind in such a novel position. After apologizing for his ignorance, and reminding the audience that slavery was a poor school for the human intellect and heart, he proceeded to narrate some of the facts in his own history as a slave, and in the course of his speech gave utterance to many noble thoughts and thrilling reflections. As soon as he had taken his seat, filled with hope and admiration, I rose, and declared that PATRICK HENRY, of revolutionary fame, never made a speech more eloquent in the cause of liberty, than the one we had just listened to from the lips of that hunted fugitive. So I believed at that time— such is my belief now. I reminded the audience of the peril which surrounded this self-emancipated young man at the North,— even in Massachusetts, on the soil of the Pilgrim Fathers, among the descendants of revolutionary sires; and I appealed to them, whether they would ever allow him to be carried back into slavery,— law or no law, constitution or no constitution. The response was unanimous and in thunder-tones— " NO!" " Will you succor and protect him as a brother-man— a resident of the old Bay State?" " YES!" shouted the whole mass, with an energy so startling, that the ruthless tyrants south of Mason and Dixon's line might almost have heard the mighty burst of feeling, and recognized it as the pledge of an invincible determination, on the part of those who gave it, never to betray him that wanders, but to hide the outcast, and firmly to abide the consequences.

It was at once deeply impressed upon my mind, that, if Mr. DOUGLASS could be persuaded to consecrate his time and talents to the promotion of the anti-slavery enterprise, a powerful impetus would be given to it, and a stunning blow at the same time inflicted on northern prejudice against a colored complexion. I therefore endeavored to instil hope and courage into his mind, in order that he might dare to engage in a vocation so anomalous and responsible for a person in his situation; and I was seconded in this effort by warm-hearted friends, especially by the late General Agent of the Massachusetts Anti-Slavery Society, Mr. JOHN A. COLLINS, whose judgment in this instance entirely coincided with my own. At first, he could give no encouragement; with unfeigned diffidence, he expressed his conviction that he was not adequate to the performance of so great a task; the path marked out was wholly an untrodden one; he was sincerely apprehensive that he should do more harm than good. After much deliberation, however, he consented to make a trial; and ever since that period, he has acted as a lecturing agent, under the auspices either of the American or the Massachusetts Anti-Slavery Society. In labors he has been most abundant; and his success in combating prejudice, in gaining proselytes, in agitating the public mind, has far surpassed the most sanguine expectations that were raised at the commencement of his brilliant career. He has borne himself with gentleness and meekness, yet with true manliness of character. As a public speaker, he excels in pathos, wit, comparison, imitation, strength of reasoning, and fluency of language. There is in him that union of head and heart, which is indispensable to an enlightenment of the heads and a winning of the hearts of others. May his strength continue to be equal to his day! May he continue to " grow in grace, and in the knowledge of God," that he may be increasingly serviceable in the cause of bleeding humanity, whether at home or abroad!

It is certainly a very remarkable fact, that one of the most efficient advocates of the slave population, now before the public, is a fugitive slave, in the person of FREDERICK DOUGLASS; and that the free colored population of the United States are as ably represented by one of their own number, in the person of CHARLES LENOX REMOND, whose eloquent appeals have extorted the highest applause of multitudes on both sides of the Atlantic. Let the calumniators of the colored race despise themselves for their baseness and illiberality of spirit, and henceforth cease to talk of the natural inferiority of those who require nothing but time and opportunity to attain to the highest point of human excellence.

It may, perhaps, be fairly questioned, whether any other portion of the population of the earth could have endured the privations, sufferings and horrors of slavery, without having become more degraded in the scale of humanity than the slaves of African descent. Nothing has been left undone to cripple their intellects, darken their minds, debase their moral nature, obliterate all traces of their relationship to mankind; and yet how wonderfully they have sustained the mighty load of a most frightful bondage, under which they have been groaning for centuries! To illustrate the effect of slavery on the white man,— to show that he has no powers of endurance, in such a condition, superior to those of his black brother,— DANIEL O'CONNELL, the distinguished advocate of universal emancipation, and the mightiest champion of prostrate but not conquered Ireland, relates the following anecdote in a speech delivered by him in the Conciliation Hall, Dublin, before the Loyal National Repeal Association, March 31, 1845. " No matter," said Mr. O'CONNELL, " under what specious term it may disguise itself, slavery is still hideous. *It has a natural, an inevitable tendency to brutalize every noble faculty of man.* An American sailor, who was cast away on the shore of Africa, where he was kept in slavery for three years, was, at the expiration of that period, found to be imbruted and stultified— he had lost all reasoning power; and having forgotten his native language, could only utter some savage gibberish between Arabic and English, which nobody could understand, and which even he himself found difficulty in pronouncing. So much for the humanizing influence of THE DOMESTIC INSTITUTION!" Admitting this to have been an extraordinary case of mental deterioration, it proves at least that the white slave can sink as low in the scale of humanity as the black one.

Mr. DOUGLASS has very properly chosen to write his own Narrative, in his own style, and according to the best of his ability, rather than to employ some one else. It is, therefore, entirely his own production; and, considering how long and dark was the career he had to run as a slave,— how few have been his opportunities to improve his mind since he broke his iron fetters,— it is, in my judgment, highly creditable to his head and heart. He who can peruse it without a tearful eye, a heaving breast, an afflicted spirit,— without being filled with an unutterable abhorrence of slavery and all its abettors, and animated with a determination to seek the immediate overthrow of that execrable system,— without trembling for the fate of this country in the hands of a righteous God, who is ever on the side of the oppressed, and whose arm is not shortened that it cannot save,— must have a flinty heart, and be qualified to act the part of a trafficker " in slaves and the souls of men." I am confident that it is essentially true in all its statements; that nothing has been set down in malice, nothing exaggerated, nothing drawn from the imagination; that it comes short of the reality, rather than overstates a single fact in regard to SLAVERY AS IT IS. The experience of FREDERICK DOUGLASS, as a slave, was not a peculiar one; his lot was not especially a hard one; his case may be regarded as a very fair specimen of the treatment of slaves in Maryland, in which State it is conceded that they are better fed and less cruelly treated than in Georgia, Alabama, or Louisiana. Many have suffered incomparably more, while very few on the plantations have suffered less, than himself. Yet how deplorable was his situation! what terrible chastisements were inflicted upon his person! what still more shocking outrages were perpetrated upon his mind! with all his noble powers and sublime aspirations, how like a brute was he treated, even by those professing to have the same mind in them that was in Christ Jesus! to what dreadful liabilities was he continually subjected! how destitute of friendly counsel and aid, even in his greatest extremities! how heavy was the midnight of woe which shrouded in blackness the last ray of hope, and filled the future with terror and gloom! what longings after freedom took possession of his breast, and how his misery augmented, in proportion as he grew reflective and intelligent,— thus demonstrating that a happy slave is an extinct man! how he thought, reasoned, felt, under the lash of the driver, with the chains upon his limbs! what perils he encountered in his endeavors to escape from his horrible doom! and how signal have been his deliverance and preservation in the midst of a nation of pitiless enemies!

This Narrative contains many affecting incidents, many passages of great eloquence and power; but I think the most thrilling one of them all is the description DOUGLASS gives of his feelings, as he stood soliloquizing respecting his fate, and the chances of his one day being a freeman, on the banks of the Chesapeake Bay—v iewing the receding vessels as they flew with their white wings before the breeze, and apostrophizing them as animated by the living spirit of freedom. Who can read that passage, and be insensible to its pathos and sublimity? Compressed into it is a whole Alexandrian library of thought, feeling, and sentiment— all that can, all that need be urged, in the form of expostulation, entreaty, rebuke, against that crime of crimes,— making man the property of his fellow-man! O, how accursed is that system, which entombs the godlike mind of man, defaces the divine image, reduces those who by creation were crowned with glory and honor to a level with four-footed beasts, and exalts the dealer in human flesh above all that is called God! Why should its existence be prolonged one hour? Is it not evil, only evil, and that continually? What does its presence imply but the absence of all fear of God, all regard for man, on the part of the people of the United States? Heaven speed its eternal overthrow!

So profoundly ignorant of the nature of slavery are many persons, that they are stubbornly incredulous whenever they read or listen to any recital of the cruelties which are daily inflicted on its victims. They do not deny that the slaves are held as property; but that terrible fact seems to convey to their minds no idea of injustice, exposure to outrage, or savage barbarity. Tell them of cruel scourgings, of mutilations and brandings, of scenes of pollution and blood, of the banishment of all light and knowledge, and they affect to be greatly indignant at such enormous exaggerations, such wholesale misstatements, such abominable libels on the character of the southern planters! As if all these direful outrages were not the natural results of slavery! As if it were less cruel to reduce a human being to the condition of a thing, than to give him a severe flagellation, or to deprive him of necessary food and clothing! As if whips, chains, thumb-screws, paddles, bloodhounds, overseers, drivers, patrols, were not all indispensable to keep the slaves down, and to give protection to their ruthless oppressors! As if, when the marriage institution is abolished, concubinage, adultery, and incest, must not necessarily abound; when all the rights of humanity are annihilated, any barrier remains to protect the victim from the fury of the spoiler; when absolute power is assumed over life and liberty, it will not be wielded with destructive sway! Skeptics of this character abound in society. In some few instances, their incredulity arises from a want of reflection; but, generally, it indicates a hatred of the light, a desire to shield slavery from the assaults of its foes, a contempt of the colored race, whether bond or free. Such will try to discredit the shocking tales of slaveholding cruelty which are recorded in this truthful

Narrative; but they will labor in vain. Mr. DOUGLASS has frankly disclosed the place of his birth, the names of those who claimed ownership in his body and soul, and the names also of those who committed the crimes which he has alleged against them. His statements, therefore, may easily be disproved, if they are untrue.

In the course of his Narrative, he relates two instances of murderous cruelty,— in one of which a planter deliberately shot a slave belonging to a neighboring plantation, who had unintentionally gotten within his lordly domain in quest of fish; and in the other, an overseer blew out the brains of a slave who had fled to a stream of water to escape a bloody scourging. Mr. DOUGLASS states that in neither of these instances was any thing done by way of legal arrest or judicial investigation. The Baltimore American, of March 17, 1845, relates a similar case of atrocity, perpetrated with similar impunity— as follows:— " *Shooting a slave.*— We learn, upon the authority of a letter from Charles county, Maryland, received by a gentleman of this city, that a young man, named Matthews, a nephew of General Matthews, and whose father, it is believed, holds an office at Washington, killed one of the slaves upon his father's farm by shooting him. The letter states that young Matthews had been left in charge of the farm; that he gave an order to the servant, which was disobeyed, when he proceeded to the house, *obtained a gun, and, returning, shot the servant*. He immediately, the letter continues, fled to his father's residence, where he still remains unmolested." — Let it never be forgotten, that no slaveholder or overseer can be convicted of any outrage perpetrated on the person of a slave, however diabolical it may be, on the testimony of colored witnesses, whether bond or free. By the slave code, they are adjudged to be as incompetent to testify against a white man, as though they were indeed a part of the brute creation. Hence, there is no legal protection in fact, whatever there may be in form, for the slave population; and any amount of cruelty may be inflicted on them with impunity.

Is it possible for the human mind to conceive of a more horrible state of society?

The effect of a religious profession on the conduct of southern masters is vividly described in the following Narrative, and shown to be any thing but salutary. In the nature of the case, it must be in the highest degree pernicious. The testimony of Mr. DOUGLASS, on this point, is sustained by a cloud of witnesses, whose veracity is unimpeachable. " A slaveholder's profession of Christianity is a palpable imposture. He is a felon of the highest grade. He is a man-stealer. It is of no importance what you put in the other scale."

Reader! are you with the man-stealers in sympathy and purpose, or on the side of their down-trodden victims? If with the former, then are you the foe of God and man. If with the latter, what are you prepared to do and dare in their behalf? Be faithful, be vigilant, be untiring in your efforts to break every yoke, and let the oppressed go free. Come what may— cost what it may— inscribe on the banner which you unfurl to the breeze, as your religious and political motto— " NO COMPROMISE WITH SLAVERY! NO UNION WITH SLAVEHOLDERS!"

WM. LLOYD GARRISON.

BOSTON, *May* 1, 1845.

Letter

From Wendell Phillips, Esq.

BOSTON, *April* 22, 1845.

My Dear Friend:

You remember the old fable of "The Man and the Lion," where the lion complained that he should not be so misrepresented "when the lions wrote history."

I am glad the time has come when the "lions write history." We have been left long enough to gather the character of slavery from the involuntary evidence of the masters. One might, indeed, rest sufficiently satisfied with what, it is evident, must be, in general, the results of such a relation, without seeking farther to find whether they have followed in every instance. Indeed, those who stare at the half-peck of corn a week, and love to count the lashes on the slave's back, are seldom the " stuff" out of which reformers and abolitionists are to be made. I remember that, in 1838, many were waiting for the results of the West India experiment, before they could come into our ranks. Those " results" have come long ago; but, alas! few of that number have come with them, as converts. A man must be disposed to judge of emancipation by other tests than whether it has increased the produce of sugar,— and to hate slavery for other reasons than because it starves men and whips women,—b efore he is ready to lay the first stone of his anti-slavery life.

I was glad to learn, in your story, how early the most neglected of God's children waken to a sense of their rights, and of the injustice done them. Experience is a keen teacher; and long before you had mastered your A B

C, or knew where the " white sails" of the Chesapeake were bound, you began, I see, to gauge the wretchedness of the slave, not by his hunger and want, not by his lashes and toil, but by the cruel and blighting death which gathers over his soul.

In connection with this, there is one circumstance which makes your recollections peculiarly valuable, and renders your early insight the more remarkable. You come from that part of the country where we are told slavery appears with its fairest features. Let us hear, then, what it is at its best estate—g aze on its bright side, if it has one; and then imagination may task her powers to add dark lines to the picture, as she travels southward to that (for the colored man) Valley of the Shadow of Death, where the Mississippi sweeps along.

Again, we have known you long, and can put the most entire confidence in your truth, candor, and sincerity. Every one who has heard you speak has felt, and, I am confident, every one who reads your book will feel, persuaded that you give them a fair specimen of the whole truth. No one-sided portrait,— no wholesale complaints,—bu t strict justice done, whenever individual kindliness has neutralized, for a moment, the deadly system with which it was strangely allied. You have been with us, too, some years, and can fairly compare the twilight of rights, which your race enjoy at the North, with that " noon of night" under which they labor south of Mason and Dixon's line. Tell us whether, after all, the half-free colored man of Massachusetts is worse off than the pampered slave of the rice swamps!

In reading your life, no one can say that we have unfairly picked out some rare specimens of cruelty. We know that the bitter drops, which even you have drained from the cup, are no incidental aggravations, no individual ills, but such as must mingle always and necessarily in the lot of every slave. They are the essential ingredients, not the occasional results, of the system.

After all, I shall read your book with trembling for you. Some years ago, when you were beginning to tell me your real name and birthplace, you may remember I stopped you, and preferred to remain ignorant of all. With the exception of a vague description, so I continued, till the other day, when you read me your memoirs. I hardly knew, at the time, whether to thank you or not for the sight of them, when I reflected that it was still dangerous, in Massachusetts, for honest men to tell their names! They say the fathers, in 1776, signed the Declaration of Independence with the halter about their necks. You, too, publish your declaration of freedom with danger compassing you around. In all the broad lands which the Constitution of the United States overshadows, there is no single spot,— ho wever narrow or desolate,— where a fugitive slave can plant himself and say, " I am safe." The whole armory of Northern Law has no shield for you. I am free to say that, in your place, I should throw the MS. into the fire.

You, perhaps, may tell your story in safety, endeared as you are to so many warm hearts by rare gifts, and a still rarer devotion of them to the service of others. But it will be owing only to your labors, and the fearless efforts of those who, trampling the laws and Constitution of the country under their feet, are determined that they will " hide the outcast," a nd that their hearths shall be, spite of the law, an asylum for the oppressed, if, some time or other, the humblest may stand in our streets, and bear witness in safety against the cruelties of which he has been the victim.

Yet it is sad to think, that these very throbbing hearts which welcome your story, and form your best safeguard in telling it, are all beating contrary to the " statute in such case made and provided." Go on, my dear friend, till you, and those who, like you, have been saved, so as by fire, from the dark prison-house, shall stereotype these free, illegal pulses into statutes; and New England, cutting loose from a blood-stained Union, shall glory in being the house of refuge for the oppressed;— till we no longer merely " *hide* the outcast," or make a merit of standing idly by while he is hunted in our midst; but, consecrating anew the soil of the Pilgrims as an asylum for the oppressed, proclaim our *welcome* to the slave so loudly, that the tones shall reach every hut in the Carolinas, and make the broken-hearted bondman leap up at the thought of old Massachusetts.

God speed the day!

Till then, and ever,

Yours truly,

WENDELL PHILLIPS.

FREDERICK DOUGLASS.

Chapter I.

I WAS born in Tuckahoe, near Hillsborough, and about twelve miles from Easton, in Talbot county, Maryland. I have no accurate knowledge of my age, never having seen any authentic record containing it. By far the larger part of the slaves know as little of their ages as horses know of theirs, and it is the wish of most masters within my knowledge to keep their slaves thus ignorant. I do not remember to have ever met a slave who could tell of his birthday. They seldom come nearer to it than planting-time, harvest-time, cherry-time, spring-time, or fall-time. A want of information concerning my own was a source of unhappiness to me even during childhood. The white children could tell their ages. I could not tell why I ought to be deprived of the same privilege. I was not allowed to make any inquiries of my master concerning it. He deemed all such inquiries on the part of a slave improper and impertinent, and evidence of a restless spirit. The nearest estimate I can give makes me now between twenty-seven and twenty-eight years of age. I come to this, from hearing my master say, some time during 1835, I was about seventeen years old.

My mother was named Harriet Bailey. She was the daughter of Isaac and Betsey Bailey, both colored, and quite dark. My mother was of a darker complexion than either my grandmother or grandfather.

My father was a white man. He was admitted to be such by all I ever heard speak of my parentage. The opinion was also whispered that my master was my father; but of the correctness of this opinion, I know nothing; the means of knowing was withheld from me. My mother and I were separated when I was but an infant—b efore I knew her as my mother. It is a common custom, in the part of Maryland from which I ran away, to part children from their mothers at a very early age. Frequently, before the child has reached its twelfth month, its mother is taken from it, and hired out on some farm a considerable distance off, and the child is placed under the care of an old woman, too old for field labor. For what this separation is done, I do not know, unless it be to hinder the development of the child's affection toward its mother, and to blunt and destroy the natural affection of the mother for the child. This is the inevitable result.

I never saw my mother, to know her as such, more than four or five times in my life; and each of these times was very short in duration, and at night. She was hired by a Mr. Stewart, who lived about twelve miles from my home. She made her journeys to see me in the night, travelling the whole distance on foot, after the performance of her day's work. She was a field hand, and a whipping is the penalty of not being in the field at sunrise, unless a slave has special permission from his or her master to the contrary— a permission which they seldom get, and one that gives to him that gives it the proud name of being a kind master. I do not recollect of ever seeing my mother by the light of day. She was with me in the night. She would lie down with me, and get me to sleep, but long before I waked she was gone. Very little communication ever took place between us. Death soon ended what little we could have while she lived, and with it her hardships and suffering. She died when I was about seven years old, on one of my master's farms, near Lee's Mill. I was not allowed to be present during her illness, at her death, or burial. She was gone long before I knew any thing about it. Never having enjoyed, to any considerable extent, her soothing presence, her tender and watchful care, I received the tidings of her death with much the same emotions I should have probably felt at the death of a stranger.

Called thus suddenly away, she left me without the slightest intimation of who my father was. The whisper that my master was my father, may or may not be true; and, true or false, it is of but little consequence to my purpose whilst the fact remains, in all its glaring odiousness, that slaveholders have ordained, and by law established, that the children of slave women shall in all cases follow the condition of their mothers; and this is done too obviously to administer to their own lusts, and make a gratification of their wicked desires profitable as well as pleasurable; for by this cunning arrangement, the slaveholder, in cases not a few, sustains to his slaves the double relation of master and father.

I know of such cases; and it is worthy of remark that such slaves invariably suffer greater hardships, and have more to contend with, than others. They are, in the first place, a constant offence to their mistress. She is ever disposed to find fault with them; they can seldom do any thing to please her; she is never better pleased than when she sees them under the lash, especially when she suspects her husband of showing to his mulatto children favors which he withholds from his black slaves. The master is frequently compelled to sell this class of his slaves, out of deference to the feelings of his white wife; and, cruel as the deed may strike any one to be, for a man to sell his own children to human flesh-mongers, it is often the dictate of humanity for him to do so; for, unless he does this, he must not only whip them himself, but must stand by and see one white son tie up his brother, of but few shades darker complexion than himself, and ply the gory lash to his naked back; and if he lisp one word of disapproval, it is set down to his parental partiality, and only makes a bad matter worse, both for himself and the slave whom he would protect and defend.

Every year brings with it multitudes of this class of slaves. It was doubtless in consequence of a knowledge of this fact, that one great statesman of the south predicted the downfall of slavery by the inevitable laws of population. Whether this prophecy is ever fulfilled or not, it is nevertheless plain that a very different-looking class of people are springing up at the south, and are now held in slavery, from those originally brought to this country from Africa; and if their increase do no other good, it will do away the force of the argument, that God cursed Ham, and therefore American slavery is right. If the lineal descendants of Ham are alone to be scripturally enslaved, it is certain that slavery at the south must soon become unscriptural; for thousands are ushered into the world, annually, who, like myself, owe their existence to white fathers, and those fathers most frequently their own masters.

I have had two masters. My first master's name was Anthony. I do not remember his first name. He was generally called Captain Anthony— a title which, I presume, he acquired by sailing a craft on the Chesapeake Bay. He was not considered a rich slaveholder. He owned two or three farms, and about thirty slaves. His farms and slaves were under the care of an overseer. The overseer's name was Plummer. Mr. Plummer was a miserable drunkard, a profane swearer, and a savage monster. He always went armed with a cowskin and a heavy cudgel. I have known him to cut and slash the women's heads so horribly, that even master would be enraged at his cruelty, and would threaten to whip him if he did not mind himself. Master, however, was not a humane slaveholder. It required extraordinary barbarity on the part of an overseer to affect him. He was a cruel man, hardened by a long life of slaveholding. He would at times seem to take great pleasure in whipping a slave. I have often been awakened at the dawn of day by the most heart-rending shrieks of an own aunt of mine, whom he used to tie up to a joist, and whip upon her naked back till she was literally covered with blood. No words, no tears, no prayers, from his gory victim, seemed to move his iron heart from its bloody purpose. The louder she screamed, the harder he whipped; and where the blood ran fastest, there he whipped longest. He would whip her to make her scream, and whip her to make her hush; and not until overcome by fatigue, would he cease to swing the blood-clotted cowskin. I remember the first time I ever witnessed this horrible exhibition. I was quite a child, but I well remember it. I never shall forget it whilst I remember any thing. It was the first of a long series of such outrages, of which I was doomed to be a witness and a participant. It struck me with awful force. It was the blood-stained gate, the entrance to the hell of slavery, through which I was about to pass. It was a most terrible spectacle. I wish I could commit to paper the feelings with which I beheld it.

This occurrence took place very soon after I went to live with my old master, and under the following circumstances. Aunt Hester went out one night,— where or for what I do not know,— and happened to be absent when my master desired her presence. He had ordered her not to go out evenings, and warned her that she must never let him catch her in company with a young man, who was paying attention to her belonging to Colonel Lloyd. The young man's name was Ned Roberts, generally called Lloyd's Ned. Why master was so careful of her, may be safely left to conjecture. She was a woman of noble form, and of graceful proportions, having very few equals, and fewer superiors, in personal appearance, among the colored or white women of our neighborhood.

Aunt Hester had not only disobeyed his orders in going out, but had been found in company with Lloyd' s Ned; which circumstance, I found, from what he said while whipping her, was the chief offence. Had he been a man of pure morals himself, he might have been thought interested in protecting the innocence of my aunt; but those who knew him will not suspect him of any such virtue. Before he commenced whipping Aunt

Hester, he took her into the kitchen, and stripped her from neck to waist, leaving her neck, shoulders, and back, entirely naked. He then told her to cross her hands, calling her at the same time a d— —d b— —h . After crossing her hands, he tied them with a strong rope, and led her to a stool under a large hook in the joist, put in for the purpose. He made her get upon the stool, and tied her hands to the hook. She now stood fair for his infernal purpose. Her arms were stretched up at their full length, so that she stood upon the ends of her toes. He then said to her, " Now, you d— —d b—— h, I'll learn you how to disobey my orders!" and after rolling up his sleeves, he commenced to lay on the heavy cowskin, and soon the warm, red blood (amid heart-rending shrieks from her, and horrid oaths from him) came dripping to the floor. I was so terrified and horror-stricken at the sight, that I hid myself in a closet, and dared not venture out till long after the bloody transaction was over. I expected it would be my turn next. It was all new to me. I had never seen any thing like it before. I had always lived with my grandmother on the outskirts of the plantation, where she was put to raise the children of the younger women. I had therefore been, until now, out of the way of the bloody scenes that often occurred on the plantation.

CHAPTER II.

MY master's family consisted of two sons, Andrew and Richard; one daughter, Lucretia, and her husband, Captain Thomas Auld. They lived in one house, upon the home plantation of Colonel Edward Lloyd. My master was Colonel Lloyd's clerk and superintendent. He was what might be called the overseer of the overseers. I spent two years of childhood on this plantation in my old master's family. It was here that I witnessed the bloody transaction recorded in the first chapter; and as I received my first impressions of slavery on this plantation, I will give some description of it, and of slavery as it there existed. The plantation is about twelve miles north of Easton, in Talbot county, and is situated on the border of Miles River. The principal products raised upon it were tobacco, corn, and wheat. These were raised in great abundance; so that, with the products of this and the other farms belonging to him, he was able to keep in almost constant employment a large sloop, in carrying them to market at Baltimore. This sloop was named Sally Lloyd, in honor of one of the colonel's daughters. My master's son-in-law, Captain Auld, was master of the vessel; she was otherwise manned by the colonel's own slaves. Their names were Peter, Isaac, Rich, and Jake. These were esteemed very highly by the other slaves, and looked upon as the privileged ones of the plantation; for it was no small affair, in the eyes of the slaves, to be allowed to see Baltimore.

Colonel Lloyd kept from three to four hundred slaves on his home plantation, and owned a large number more on the neighboring farms belonging to him. The names of the farms nearest to the home plantation were Wye Town and New Design. " Wye Town" was under the overseership of a man named Noah Willis. New Design was under the overseership of a Mr. Townsend. The overseers of these, and all the rest of the farms, numbering over twenty, received advice and direction from the managers of the home plantation. This was the great business place. It was the seat of government for the whole twenty farms. All disputes among the overseers were settled here. If a slave was convicted of any high misdemeanor, became unmanageable, or evinced a determination to run away, he was brought immediately here, severely whipped, put on board the sloop, carried to Baltimore, and sold to Austin Woolfolk, or some other slave-trader, as a warning to the slaves remaining.

Here, too, the slaves of all the other farms received their monthly allowance of food, and their yearly clothing. The men and women slaves received, as their monthly allowance of food, eight pounds of pork, or its equivalent in fish, and one bushel of corn meal. Their yearly clothing consisted of two coarse linen shirts, one pair of linen trousers, like the shirts, one jacket, one pair of trousers for winter, made of coarse negro cloth, one pair of stockings, and one pair of shoes; the whole of which could not have cost more than seven dollars. The allowance of the slave children was given to their mothers, or the old women having the care of them. The children unable to work in the field had neither shoes, stockings, jackets, nor trousers, given to them; their clothing consisted of two coarse linen shirts per year. When these failed them, they went naked until the next allowance-day. Children from seven to ten years old, of both sexes, almost naked, might be seen at all seasons of the year.

There were no beds given the slaves, unless one coarse blanket be considered such, and none but the men and women had these. This, however, is not considered a very great privation. They find less difficulty from the want of beds, than from the want of time to sleep; for when their day's work in the field is done, the most of them having their washing, mending, and cooking to do, and having few or none of the ordinary facilities for doing either of these, very many of their sleeping hours are consumed in preparing for the field the coming day; and when this is done, old and young, male and female, married and single, drop down side by side, on one common bed,— the cold, damp floor,— each covering himself or herself with their miserable blankets; and here they sleep till they are summoned to the field by the driver's horn. At the sound of this, all must rise, and be off to the field. There must be no halting; every one must be at his or her post; and woe betides them who hear not this morning summons to the field; for if they are not awakened by the sense of hearing, they are by the sense of feeling: no age nor sex finds any favor. Mr. Severe, the overseer, used to stand by the door of the quarter, armed with a large hickory stick and heavy cowskin, ready to whip any one who was so unfortunate as not to hear, or, from any other cause, was prevented from being ready to start for the field at the sound of the horn.

Mr. Severe was rightly named: he was a cruel man. I have seen him whip a woman, causing the blood to run half an hour at the time; and this, too, in the midst of her crying children, pleading for their mother's release. He seemed to take pleasure in manifesting his fiendish barbarity. Added to his cruelty, he was a profane swearer. It was enough to chill the blood and stiffen the hair of an ordinary man to hear him talk. Scarce a sentence escaped him but that was commenced or concluded by some horrid oath. The field was the place to witness his cruelty and profanity. His presence made it both the field of blood and of blasphemy. From the rising till the going down of the sun, he was cursing, raving, cutting, and slashing among the slaves of the field, in the most frightful manner. His career was short. He died very soon after I went to Colonel Lloyd's; and he died as he lived, uttering, with his dying groans, bitter curses and horrid oaths. His death was regarded by the slaves as the result of a merciful providence.

Mr. Severe's place was filled by a Mr. Hopkins. He was a very different man. He was less cruel, less profane, and made less noise, than Mr. Severe. His course was characterized by no extraordinary demonstrations of cruelty. He whipped, but seemed to take no pleasure in it. He was called by the slaves a good overseer.

The home plantation of Colonel Lloyd wore the appearance of a country village. All the mechanical operations for all the farms were performed here. The shoemaking and mending, the blacksmithing, cartwrighting, coopering, weaving, and grain-grinding, were all performed by the slaves on the home plantation. The whole place wore a business-like aspect very unlike the neighboring farms. The number of houses, too, conspired to give it advantage over the neighboring farms. It was called by the slaves the Great House Farm. Few privileges were esteemed higher, by the slaves of the out-farms, than that of being selected to do errands at the Great House Farm. It was associated in their minds with greatness. A representative could not be prouder of his election to a seat in the American Congress, than a slave on one of the out-farms would be of for this office sought as diligently to please their overseers, as the of seekers in the political parties seek to please and deceive the people. same traits of character might be seen in Colonel Lloyd's slaves, as seen in the slaves of the political parties.

The slaves selected to go to the Great House Farm, for the mon allowance for themselves and their fellow-slaves, were peculi enthusiastic. While on their way, they would make the dense old wo for miles around, reverberate with their wild songs, revealing at once highest joy and the deepest sadness. They would compose and sin they went along, consulting neither time nor tune. The thought that c up, came out— if not in the word, in the sound;— and as frequent the one as in the other. They would sometimes sing the most path sentiment in the most rapturous tone, and the most rapturous sentin in the most pathetic tone. Into all of their songs they would manag weave something of the Great House Farm. Especially would they do when leaving home. They would then sing most exultingly the follov words:—

"I am going away to the Great House Farm!
O, yea! O, yea! O!"

This they would sing, as a chorus, to words which to many w seem unmeaning jargon, but which, nevertheless, were full of mea to themselves. I have sometimes thought that the mere hearing of th songs would do more to impress some minds with the horrible chara of slavery, than the reading of whole volumes of philosophy on the sub could do.

I did not, when a slave, understand the deep meaning of those r and apparently incoherent songs. I was myself within the circle; so th neither saw nor heard as those without might see and hear. They tc tale of woe which was then altogether beyond my feeble comprehens they were tones loud, long, and deep; they breathed the prayer complaint of souls boiling over with the bitterest anguish. Every tone was a testimony against slavery, and a prayer to God for deliverance from chains. The hearing of those wild notes always depressed my spirit, and filled me with ineffable sadness. I have frequently found myself in tears while hearing them. The mere recurrence to those songs, even now, afflicts me; and while I am writing these lines, an expression of feeling has already found its way down my cheek. To those songs I trace my first glimmering conception of the dehumanizing character of slavery. I can never get rid of that conception. Those songs still follow me, to deepen my hatred of slavery, and quicken my sympathies for my brethren in bonds. If any one wishes to be impressed with the soul-killing effects of slavery, let him go to Colonel Lloyd's plantation, and, on allowance-day, place himself in the deep pine woods, and there let him, in silence, analyze the sounds that shall pass through the chambers of his soul,— and if he is not thus impressed, it will only be because " there is no flesh in his obdurate heart."

I have often been utterly astonished, since I came to the north, to find persons who could speak of the singing, among slaves, as evidence of their contentment and happiness. It is impossible to conceive of a greater mistake. Slaves sing most when they are most unhappy. The songs of the slave represent the sorrows of his heart; and he is relieved by them, only as an aching heart is relieved by its tears. At least, such is my experience. I have often sung to drown my sorrow, but seldom to express my happiness. Crying for joy, and singing for joy, were alike uncommon to me while in the jaws of slavery. The singing of a man cast away upon a desolate island might be as appropriately considered as evidence of contentment and happiness, as the singing of a slave; the songs of the one and of the other are prompted by the same emotion.

Chapter III.

COLONEL LLOYD kept a large and finely cultivated garden, which afforded almost constant employment for four men, besides the chief gardener, (Mr. M'Durmond.) This garden was probably the greatest attraction of the place. During the summer months, people came from far and near— from Baltimore, Easton, and Annapolis— to see it. It abounded in fruits of almost every description, from the hardy apple of the north to the delicate orange of the south. This garden was not the least source of trouble on the plantation. Its excellent fruit was quite a temptation to the hungry swarms of boys, as well as the older slaves, belonging to the colonel, few of whom had the virtue or the vice to resist it. Scarcely a day passed, during the summer, but that some slave had to take the lash for stealing fruit. The colonel had to resort to all kinds of stratagems to keep his slaves out of the garden. The last and most successful one was that of tarring his fence all around; after which, if a slave was caught with any tar upon his person, it was deemed sufficient proof that he had either been into the garden, or had tried to get in. In either case, he was severely whipped by the chief gardener. This plan worked well; the slaves became as fearful of tar as of the lash. They seemed to realize the impossibility of touching tar without being defiled.

The colonel also kept a splendid riding equipage. His stable and carriage-house presented the appearance of some of our large city livery establishments. His horses were of the finest form and noblest blood. His carriage-house contained three splendid coaches, three or four gigs, besides dearborns and barouches of the most fashionable style.

This establishment was under the care of two slaves—o ld Barney and young Barney— father and son. To attend to this establishment was their sole work. But it was by no means an easy employment; for in nothing was

Colonel Lloyd more particular than in the management of his horses. The slightest inattention to these was unpardonable, and was visited upon those, under whose care they were placed, with the severest punishment; no excuse could shield them, if the colonel only suspected any want of attention to his horses— a supposition which he frequently indulged, and one which, of course, made the office of old and young Barney a very trying one. They never knew when they were safe from punishment. They were frequently whipped when least deserving, and escaped whipping when most deserving it. Every thing depended upon the looks of the horses, and the state of Colonel Lloyd's own mind when his horses were brought to him for use. If a horse did not move fast enough, or hold his head high enough, it was owing to some fault of his keepers. It was painful to stand near the stable-door, and hear the various complaints against the keepers when a horse was taken out for use. " This horse has not had proper attention. He has not been sufficiently rubbed and curried, or he has not been properly fed; his food was too wet or too dry; he got it too soon or too late; he was too hot or too cold; he had too much hay, and not enough of grain; or he had too much grain, and not enough of hay; instead of old Barney's attending to the horse, he had very improperly left it to his son." To all these complaints, no matter how unjust, the slave must answer never a word. Colonel Lloyd could not brook any contradiction from a slave. When he spoke, a slave must stand, listen, and tremble; and such was literally the case. I have seen Colonel Lloyd make old Barney, a man between fifty and sixty years of age, uncover his bald head, kneel down upon the cold, damp ground, and receive upon his naked and toil-worn shoulders more than thirty lashes at the time. Colonel Lloyd had three sons— Edward, Murray, and Daniel,— and three sons-in-law, Mr. Winder, Mr. Nicholson, and Mr. Lowndes. All of these lived at the Great House Farm, and enjoyed the luxury of whipping the servants when they pleased, from old Barney down to William Wilkes, the coach-driver. I have seen Winder make one of the house-servants stand off from him a suitable distance to be touched with the end of his whip, and at every stroke raise great ridges upon his back.

To describe the wealth of Colonel Lloyd would be almost equal to describing the riches of Job. He kept from ten to fifteen house-servants. He was said to own a thousand slaves, and I think this estimate quite within the truth. Colonel Lloyd owned so many that he did not know them when he saw them; nor did all the slaves of the out-farms know him. It is reported of him, that, while riding along the road one day, he met a colored man, and addressed him in the usual manner of speaking to colored people on the public highways of the south: " Well, boy, whom do you belong to?" " To Colonel Lloyd," replied the slave. " Well, does the colonel treat you well?" " No, sir," was the ready reply. " What, does he work you too hard?" " Yes, sir."

" Well, don't he give you enough to eat?" " Yes, sir, he gives me enough, such as it is."

The colonel, after ascertaining where the slave belonged, rode on; the man also went on about his business, not dreaming that he had been conversing with his master. He thought, said, and heard nothing more of the matter, until two or three weeks afterwards. The poor man was then informed by his overseer that, for having found fault with his master, he was now to be sold to a Georgia trader. He was immediately chained and handcuffed; and thus, without a moment's warning, he was snatched away, and forever sundered, from his family and friends, by a hand more unrelenting than death. This is the penalty of telling the truth, of telling the simple truth, in answer to a series of plain questions.

It is partly in consequence of such facts, that slaves, when inquired of as to their condition and the character of their masters, almost universally say they are contented, and that their masters are kind. The slaveholders have been known to send in spies among their slaves, to ascertain their views and feelings in regard to their condition. The frequency of this has had the effect to establish among the slaves the maxim, that a still tongue makes a wise head. They suppress the truth rather than take the consequences of telling it, and in so doing prove themselves a part of the human family. If they have any thing to say of their masters, it is generally in their masters' favor, especially when speaking to an untried man. I have been frequently asked, when a slave, if I had a kind master, and do not remember ever to have given a negative answer; nor did I, in pursuing this course, consider myself as uttering what was absolutely false; for I always measured the kindness of my master by the standard of kindness set up among slaveholders around us. Moreover, slaves are like other people, and imbibe prejudices quite common to others. They think their own better than that of others. Many, under the influence of this prejudice, think their own masters are better than the masters of other slaves; and this, too, in some cases, when the very reverse is true. Indeed, it is not uncommon for slaves even to fall out and quarrel among themselves about the relative goodness of their masters, each contending for the superior goodness of his own over that of the others. At the very same time, they mutually execrate their masters when viewed separately. It was so on our plantation. When Colonel Lloyd's slaves met the slaves of Jacob Jepson, they seldom parted without a quarrel about their masters; Colonel Lloyd's slaves contending that he was the richest, and Mr. Jepson's slaves that he was the smartest, and most of a man. Colonel Lloyd's slaves would boast his ability to buy and sell Jacob Jepson. Mr. Jepson's slaves would boast his ability to whip Colonel Lloyd. These quarrels would almost always end in a fight between the parties, and those that whipped were supposed to have gained the point at issue. They seemed to think that the greatness of their masters was transferable to themselves. It was considered as being bad enough to be a slave; but to be a poor man's slave was deemed a disgrace indeed!

Chapter IV.

MR. HOPKINS remained but a short time in the office of overseer. Why his career was so short, I do not know, but suppose he lacked the necessary severity to suit Colonel Lloyd. Mr. Hopkins was succeeded by Mr. Austin Gore, a man possessing, in an eminent degree, all those traits of character indispensable to what is called a first-rate overseer. Mr. Gore had served Colonel Lloyd, in the capacity of overseer, upon one of the out-farms, and had shown himself worthy of the high station of overseer upon the home or Great House Farm.

Mr. Gore was proud, ambitious, and persevering. He was artful, cruel, and obdurate. He was just the man for such a place, and it was just the place for such a man. It afforded scope for the full exercise of all his powers, and he seemed to be perfectly at home in it. He was one of those who could torture the slightest look, word, or gesture, on the part of the slave, into impudence, and would treat it accordingly. There must be no answering back to him; no explanation was allowed a slave, showing himself to have been wrongfully accused. Mr. Gore acted fully up to the maxim laid down by slaveholders,— " It is better that a dozen slaves should suffer under the lash, than that the overseer should be convicted, in the presence of the slaves, of having been at fault." No matter how innocent a slave might be— it availed him nothing, when accused by Mr. Gore of any misdemeanor. To be accused was to be convicted, and to be convicted was to be punished; the one always following the other with immutable certainty. To escape punishment was to escape accusation; and few slaves had the fortune to do either, under the overseership of Mr. Gore. He was just proud enough to demand the most debasing homage of the slave, and quite servile enough to crouch, himself, at the feet of the master. He was ambitious enough to be contented with nothing short of the highest rank of overseers, and persevering enough to reach the height of his ambition. He was cruel enough to inflict the severest punishment, artful enough to descend to the lowest trickery, and obdurate enough to be insensible to the voice of a reproving conscience. He was, of all the overseers, the most dreaded by the slaves. His presence was painful; his eye flashed confusion; and seldom was his sharp, shrill voice heard, without producing horror and trembling in their ranks.

Mr. Gore was a grave man, and, though a young man, he indulged in no jokes, said no funny words, seldom smiled. His words were in perfect keeping with his looks, and his looks were in perfect keeping with his words. Overseers will sometimes indulge in a witty word, even with the slaves; not so with Mr. Gore. He spoke but to command, and commanded but to be obeyed; he dealt sparingly with his words, and bountifully with his whip, never using the former where the latter would answer as well. When he whipped, he seemed to do so from a sense of duty, and feared no consequences. He did nothing reluctantly, no matter how disagreeable; always at his post, never inconsistent. He never promised but to fulfil. He was, in a word, a man of the most inflexible firmness and stone-like coolness.

His savage barbarity was equalled only by the consummate coolness with which he committed the grossest and most savage deeds upon the slaves under his charge. Mr. Gore once undertook to whip one of Colonel Lloyd's slaves, by the name of Demby. He had given Demby but few stripes, when, to get rid of the scourging, he ran and plunged himself into a creek, and stood there at the depth of his shoulders, refusing to come out. Mr. Gore told him that he would give him three calls, and that, if he did not come out at the third call, he would shoot him. The first call was given. Demby made no response, but stood his ground. The second and third calls were given with the same result. Mr. Gore then, without consultation or deliberation with any one, not even giving Demby an additional call, raised his musket to his face, taking deadly aim at his standing victim, and in an instant poor Demby was no more. His mangled body sank out of sight, and blood and brains marked the water where he had stood.

A thrill of horror flashed through every soul upon the plantation, excepting Mr. Gore. He alone seemed cool and collected. He was asked by Colonel Lloyd and my old master, why he resorted to this extraordinary expedient. His reply was, (as well as I can remember,) that Demby had become unmanageable. He was setting a dangerous example to the other slaves,—on e which, if suffered to pass without some such demonstration on his part, would finally lead to the total subversion of all rule and order upon the plantation. He argued that if one slave refused to be corrected, and escaped with his life, the other slaves would soon copy the example; the result of which would be, the freedom of the slaves, and the enslavement of the whites. Mr. Gore's defence was satisfactory. He was continued in his station as overseer upon the home plantation. His fame as an overseer went abroad. His horrid crime was not even submitted to judicial investigation. It was committed in the presence of slaves, and they of course could neither institute a suit, nor testify against him; and thus the guilty perpetrator of one of the bloodiest and most foul murders goes unwhipped of justice, and uncensured by the community in which he lives. Mr. Gore lived in St. Michael's, Talbot county, Maryland, when I left there; and if he is still alive, he very probably lives there now; and if so, he is now, as he was then, as highly esteemed and as much respected as though his guilty soul had not been stained with his brother's blood.

I speak advisedly when I say this,— that killing a slave, or any colored person, in Talbot county, Maryland, is not treated as a crime, either by the courts or the community. Mr. Thomas Lanman, of St. Michael's, killed two slaves, one of whom he killed with a hatchet, by knocking his brains out. He used to boast of the commission of the awful and bloody deed. I have heard him do so laughingly, saying, among other things, that he was the only benefactor of his country in the company, and that when others would do as much as he had done, we should be relieved of " the d— —d niggers."

The wife of Mr. Giles Hicks, living but a short distance from where I used to live, murdered my wife's cousin, a young girl between fifteen and sixteen years of age, mangling her person in the most horrible manner, breaking her nose and breastbone with a stick, so that the poor girl expired in a few hours afterward. She was immediately buried, but had not been in her untimely grave but a few hours before she was taken up and examined by the coroner, who decided that she had come to her death by severe beating. The offence for which this girl was thus murdered was this:— She had been set that night to mind Mrs. Hicks's baby, and during the night she fell asleep, and the baby cried. She, having lost her rest for several nights previous, did not hear the crying. They were both in the room with Mrs. Hicks. Mrs. Hicks, finding the girl slow to move, jumped from her bed, seized an oak stick of wood by the fireplace, and with it broke the girl's nose and breastbone, and thus ended her life. I will not say that this most horrid murder produced no sensation in the community. It did produce sensation, but not enough to bring the murderess to punishment. There was a warrant issued for her arrest, but it was never served. Thus she escaped not only punishment, but even the pain of being arraigned before a court for her horrid crime.

Whilst I am detailing bloody deeds which took place during my stay on Colonel Lloyd's plantation, I will briefly narrate another, which occurred about the same time as the murder of Demby by Mr. Gore.

Colonel Lloyd's slaves were in the habit of spending a part of their nights and Sundays in fishing for oysters, and in this way made up the deficiency of their scanty allowance. An old man belonging to Colonel Lloyd, while thus engaged, happened to get beyond the limits of Colonel Lloyd's, and on the premises of Mr. Beal Bondly. At this trespass, Mr. Bondly took offence, and with his musket came down to the shore, and blew its deadly contents into the poor old man.

Mr. Bondly came over to see Colonel Lloyd the next day, whether to pay him for his property, or to justify himself in what he had done, I know not. At any rate, this whole fiendish transaction was soon hushed up. There was very little said about it at all, and nothing done. It was a common saying, even among little white boys, that it was worth a half-cent to kill a " nigger," and a half-cent to bury one.

Chapter V.

AS to my own treatment while I lived on Colonel Lloyd's plantation, it was very similar to that of the other slave children. I was not old enough to work in the field, and there being little else than field work to do, I had a great deal of leisure time. The most I had to do was to drive up the cows at evening, keep the fowls out of the garden, keep the front yard clean, and run of errands for my old master's daughter, Mrs. Lucretia Auld. The most of my leisure time I spent in helping Master Daniel Lloyd in finding his birds, after he had shot them. My connection with Master Daniel was of some advantage to me. He became quite attached to me, and was a sort of protector of me. He would not allow the older boys to impose upon me, and would divide his cakes with me.

I was seldom whipped by my old master, and suffered little from any thing else than hunger and cold. I suffered much from hunger, but much more from cold. In hottest summer and coldest winter, I was kept almost naked— no shoes, no stockings, no jacket, no trousers, nothing on but a coarse tow linen shirt, reaching only to my knees. I had no bed. I must have perished with cold, but that, the coldest nights, I used to steal a bag which was used for carrying corn to the mill. I would crawl into this bag, and there sleep on the cold, damp, clay floor, with my head in and feet out. My feet have been so cracked with the frost, that the pen with which I am writing might be laid in the gashes.

We were not regularly allowanced. Our food was coarse corn meal boiled. This was called *mush*. It was put into a large wooden tray or trough, and set down upon the ground. The children were then called, like so many pigs, and like so many pigs they would come and devour the mush; some with oyster-shells, others with pieces of shingle, some with naked hands, and none with spoons. He that ate fastest got most; he that was strongest secured the best place; and few left the trough satisfied.

I was probably between seven and eight years old when I left Colonel Lloyd's plantation. I left it with joy. I shall never forget the ecstasy with which I received the intelligence that my old master (Anthony) had determined to let me go to Baltimore, to live with Mr. Hugh Auld, brother to my old master's son-in-law, Captain Thomas Auld. I received this information about three days before my departure. They were three of the happiest days I ever enjoyed. I spent the most part of all these three days in the creek, washing off the plantation scurf, and preparing myself for my departure.

The pride of appearance which this would indicate was not my own. I spent the time in washing, not so much because I wished to, but because Mrs. Lucretia had told me I must get all the dead skin off my feet and knees before I could go to Baltimore; for the people in Baltimore were very cleanly, and would laugh at me if I looked dirty. Besides, she was going to give me a pair of trousers, which I should not put on unless I got all the dirt off me. The thought of owning a pair of trousers was great indeed! It was almost a sufficient motive, not only to make me take off what would be called by pig-drovers the mange, but the skin itself. I went at it in good earnest, working for the first time with the hope of reward.

The ties that ordinarily bind children to their homes were all suspended in my case. I found no severe trial in my departure. My home was charmless; it was not home to me; on parting from it, I could not feel that I was leaving any thing which I could have enjoyed by staying. My mother was dead, my grandmother lived far off, so that I seldom saw her. I had two sisters and one brother, that lived in the same house with me; but the early separation of us from our mother had well nigh blotted the fact of our relationship from our memories. I looked for home elsewhere, and was confident of finding none which I should relish less than the one which I was leaving. If, however, I found in my new home hardship, hunger, whipping, and nakedness, I had the consolation that I should not have escaped any one of them by staying. Having already had more than a taste of them in the house of my old master, and having endured them there, I very naturally inferred my ability to endure them elsewhere, and especially at Baltimore; for I had something of the feeling about Baltimore that is expressed in the proverb, that " being hanged in England is preferable to dying a natural death in Ireland." I had the strongest desire to see Baltimore. Cousin

Tom, though not fluent in speech, had inspired me with that desire by his eloquent description of the place. I could never point out any thing at the Great House, no matter how beautiful or powerful, but that he had seen something at Baltimore far exceeding, both in beauty and strength, the object which I pointed out to him. Even the Great House itself, with all its pictures, was far inferior to many buildings in Baltimore. So strong was my desire, that I thought a gratification of it would fully compensate for whatever loss of comforts I should sustain by the exchange. I left without a regret, and with the highest hopes of future happiness.

We sailed out of Miles River for Baltimore on a Saturday morning. I remember only the day of the week, for at that time I had no knowledge of the days of the month, nor the months of the year. On setting sail, I walked aft, and gave to Colonel Lloyd's plantation what I hoped would be the last look. I then placed myself in the bows of the sloop, and there spent the remainder of the day in looking ahead, interesting myself in what was in the distance rather than in things near by or behind.

In the afternoon of that day, we reached Annapolis, the capital of the State. We stopped but a few moments, so that I had no time to go on shore. It was the first large town that I had ever seen, and though it would look small compared with some of our New England factory villages, I thought it a wonderful place for its size— more imposing even than the Great House Farm!

We arrived at Baltimore early on Sunday morning, landing at Smith's Wharf, not far from Bowley's Wharf. We had on board the sloop a large flock of sheep; and after aiding in driving them to the slaughterhouse of Mr. Curtis on Louden Slater's Hill, I was conducted by Rich, one of the hands belonging on board of the sloop, to my new home in Alliciana Street, near Mr. Gardner' s ship-yard, on Fells Point.

Mr. and Mrs. Auld were both at home, and met me at the door with their little son Thomas, to take care of whom I had been given. And here I saw what I had never seen before; it was a white face beaming with the most kindly emotions; it was the face of my new mistress, Sophia Auld. I wish I could describe the rapture that flashed through my soul as I beheld it. It was a new and strange sight to me, brightening up my pathway with the light of happiness. Little Thomas was told, there was his Freddy,—and I was told to take care of little Thomas; and thus I entered upon the duties of my new home with the most cheering prospect ahead.

I look upon my departure from Colonel Lloyd's plantation as one of the most interesting events of my life. It is possible, and even quite probable, that but for the mere circumstance of being removed from that plantation to Baltimore, I should have to-day, instead of being here seated by my own table, in the enjoyment of freedom and the happiness of home, writing this Narrative, been confined in the galling chains of slavery. Going to live at Baltimore laid the foundation, and opened the gateway, to all my subsequent prosperity. I have ever regarded it as the first plain manifestation of that kind providence which has ever since attended me, and marked my life with so many favors. I regarded the selection of myself as being somewhat remarkable. There were a number of slave children that might have been sent from the plantation to Baltimore. There were those younger, those older, and those of the same age. I was chosen from among them all, and was the first, last, and only choice.

I may be deemed superstitious, and even egotistical, in regarding this event as a special interposition of divine Providence in my favor. But I should be false to the earliest sentiments of my soul, if I suppressed the opinion. I prefer to be true to myself, even at the hazard of incurring the ridicule of others, rather than to be false, and incur my own abhorrence. From my earliest recollection, I date the entertainment of a deep conviction that slavery would not always be able to hold me within its foul embrace; and in the darkest hours of my career in slavery, this living word of faith and spirit of hope departed not from me, but remained like ministering angels to cheer me through the gloom. This good spirit was from God, and to him I offer thanksgiving and praise.

Chapter VI.

MY new mistress proved to be all she appeared when I first met her at the door,— a woman of the kindest heart and finest feelings. She had never had a slave under her control previously to myself, and prior to her marriage she had been dependent upon her own industry for a living. She was by trade a weaver; and by constant application to her business, she had been in a good degree preserved from the blighting and dehumanizing effects of slavery. I was utterly astonished at her goodness. I scarcely knew how to behave towards her. She was entirely unlike any other white woman I had ever seen. I could not approach her as I was accustomed to approach other white ladies. My early instruction was all out of place. The crouching servility, usually so acceptable a quality in a slave, did not answer when manifested toward her. Her favor was not gained by it; she seemed to be disturbed by it. She did not deem it impudent or unmannerly for a slave to look her in the face. The meanest slave was put fully at ease in her presence, and none left without feeling better for having seen her. Her face was made of heavenly smiles, and her voice of tranquil music.

But, alas! this kind heart had but a short time to remain such. The fatal poison of irresponsible power was already in her hands, and soon commenced its infernal work. That cheerful eye, under the influence of slavery, soon became red with rage; that voice, made all of sweet accord, changed to one of harsh and horrid discord; and that angelic face gave place to that of a demon.

Very soon after I went to live with Mr. and Mrs. Auld, she very kindly commenced to teach me the A, B, C. After I had learned this, she assisted me in learning to spell words of three or four letters. Just at this point of my progress, Mr. Auld found out what was going on, and at once forbade Mrs. Auld to instruct me further, telling her, among other things, that it was unlawful, as well as unsafe, to teach a slave to read. To use his own words, further, he said, " If you give a nigger an inch, he will take an ell. A nigger should know nothing but to obey his master— to do as he is told to do. Learning would spoil the best nigger in the world. Now," said he, " if you teach that nigger (speaking of myself) how to read, there would be no keeping him. It would forever unfit him to be a slave. He would at once become unmanageable, and of no value to his master. As to himself, it could do him no good, but a great deal of harm. It would make him discontented and unhappy." These words sank deep into my heart, stirred up sentiments within that lay slumbering, and called into existence an entirely new train of thought. It was a new and special revelation, explaining dark and mysterious things, with which my youthful understanding had struggled, but struggled in vain. I now understood what had been to me a most perplexing difficulty— to wit, the white man's power to enslave the black man. It was a grand achievement, and I prized it highly. From that moment, I understood the pathway from slavery to freedom. It was just what I wanted, and I got it at a time when I the least expected it. Whilst I was saddened by the thought of losing the aid of my kind mistress, I was gladdened by the invaluable instruction which, by the merest accident, I had gained from my master. Though conscious of the difficulty of learning without a teacher, I set out with high hope, and a fixed purpose, at whatever cost of trouble, to learn how to read. The very decided manner with which he spoke, and strove to impress his wife with the evil consequences of giving me instruction, served to convince me that he was deeply sensible of the truths he was uttering. It gave me the best assurance that I might rely with the utmost confidence on the results which, he said, would flow from teaching me to read. What he most dreaded, that I most desired. What he most loved, that I most hated. That which to him was a great evil, to be carefully shunned, was to me a great good, to be diligently sought; and the argument which he so warmly urged, against my learning to read, only served to inspire me with a desire and determination to learn. In learning to read, I owe almost as much to the bitter opposition of my master, as to the kindly aid of my mistress. I acknowledge the benefit of both.

I had resided but a short time in Baltimore before I observed a marked difference, in the treatment of slaves, from that which I had witnessed in the country. A city slave is almost a freeman, compared with a slave on the plantation. He is much better fed and clothed, and enjoys privileges altogether unknown to the slave on the plantation. There is a vestige of decency, a sense of shame, that does much to curb and check those outbreaks of atrocious cruelty so commonly enacted upon the plantation. He is a desperate slaveholder, who will shock the humanity of his non-slaveholding neighbors with the cries of his lacerated slave. Few are willing to incur the odium attaching to the reputation of being a cruel master; and above all things, they would not be known as not giving a slave enough to eat. Every city slaveholder is anxious to have it known of him, that he feeds his slaves well; and it is due to them to say, that most of them do give their slaves enough to eat. There are, however, some painful exceptions to this rule. Directly opposite to us, on Philpot Street, lived Mr. Thomas Hamilton. He owned two slaves. Their names were Henrietta and Mary. Henrietta was about twenty-two years of age, Mary was about fourteen; and of all the mangled and emaciated creatures I ever looked upon, these two were the most so. His heart must be harder than stone, that could look upon these unmoved. The head, neck, and shoulders of Mary were literally cut to pieces. I have frequently felt her head, and found it nearly covered with festering sores, caused by the lash of her cruel mistress. I do not know that her master ever whipped her, but I have been an eye-witness to the cruelty of Mrs. Hamilton. I used to be in Mr. Hamilton's house nearly every day. Mrs. Hamilton used to sit in a large chair in the middle of the room, with a heavy cowskin always by her side, and scarce an hour passed during the day but was marked by the blood of one of these slaves. The girls seldom passed her without her saying, " Move faster, you *black gip*!" a t the same time giving them a blow with the cowskin over the head or shoulders, often drawing the blood. She would then say, " Take that, you *black gip!*" — continuing, " If you don't move faster, I'll move you!" Added to the cruel lashings to which these slaves were subjected, they were kept nearly half-starved. They seldom knew what it was to eat a full meal. I have seen Mary contending with the pigs for the offal thrown into the street. So much was Mary kicked and cut to pieces, that she was oftener called " *pecked*" than by her name.

CHAPTER VII.

I LIVED in Master Hugh' s family about seven years. During this time, I succeeded in learning to read and write. In accomplishing this, I was compelled to resort to various stratagems. I had no regular teacher. My mistress, who had kindly commenced to instruct me, had, in compliance with the advice and direction of her husband, not only ceased to instruct, but had set her face against my being instructed by any one else. It is due, however, to my mistress to say of her, that she did not adopt this course of treatment immediately. She at first lacked the depravity indispensable to shutting me up in mental darkness. It was at least necessary for her to have some training in the exercise of irresponsible power, to make her equal to the task of treating me as though I were a brute.

My mistress was, as I have said, a kind and tender-hearted woman; and in the simplicity of her soul she commenced, when I first went to live with her, to treat me as she supposed one human being ought to treat another. In entering upon the duties of a slaveholder, she did not seem to perceive that I sustained to her the relation of a mere chattel, and that for her to treat me as a human being was not only wrong, but dangerously so. Slavery proved as injurious to her as it did to me. When I went there, she was a pious, warm, and tender-hearted woman. There was no sorrow or suffering for which she had not a tear. She had bread for the hungry, clothes for the naked, and comfort for every mourner that came within her reach. Slavery soon proved its ability to divest her of these heavenly qualities. Under its influence, the tender heart became stone, and the lamblike disposition gave way to one of tiger-like fierceness. The first step in her downward course was in her ceasing to instruct me. She now commenced to practise her husband's precepts. She finally became even more violent in her opposition than her husband himself. She was not satisfied with simply doing as well as he had commanded; she seemed anxious to do better. Nothing seemed to make her more angry than to see me with a newspaper. She seemed to think that here lay the danger. I have had her rush at me with a face made all up of fury, and snatch from me a newspaper, in a manner that fully revealed her apprehension. She was an apt woman; and a little experience soon demonstrated, to her satisfaction, that education and slavery were incompatible with each other.

From this time I was most narrowly watched. If I was in a separate room any considerable length of time, I was sure to be suspected of having a book, and was at once called to give an account of myself. All this, however, was too late. The first step had been taken. Mistress, in teaching me the alphabet, had given me the *inch*, and no precaution could prevent me from taking the *ell*.

The plan which I adopted, and the one by which I was most successful, was that of making friends of all the little white boys whom I met in the street. As many of these as I could, I converted into teachers. With their kindly aid, obtained at different times and in different places, I finally succeeded in learning to read. When I was sent of errands, I always took my book with me, and by going one part of my errand quickly, I found time to get a lesson before my return. I used also to carry bread with me, enough of which was always in the house, and to which I was always welcome; for I was much better off in this regard than many of the poor white children in our neighborhood. This bread I used to bestow upon the hungry little urchins, who, in return, would give me that more valuable bread of knowledge. I am strongly tempted to give the names of two or three of those little boys, as a testimonial of the gratitude and affection I bear them; but prudence forbids;—no t that it would injure me, but it might embarrass them; for it is almost an unpardonable offence to teach slaves to read in this Christian country. It is enough to say of the dear little fellows, that they lived on Philpot Street, very near Durgin and Bailey's ship-yard. I used to talk this matter of slavery over with them. I would sometimes say to them, I wished I could be as free as they would be when they got to be men. " You will be free as soon as you are twenty-one, *but I am a slave for life*! Have not I as good a right to be free as you have?" These words used to trouble them; they would express for me the liveliest sympathy, and console me with the hope that something would occur by which I might be free.

I was now about twelve years old, and the thought of being a *slave for life* began to bear heavily upon my heart. Just about this time, I got hold of a book entitled " The Columbian Orator." Every opportunity I got, I used to read this book. Among much of other interesting matter, I found in it a dialogue between a master and his slave. The slave was represented as having run away from his master three times. The dialogue represented the conversation which took place between them, when the slave was retaken the third time. In this dialogue, the whole argument in behalf of slavery was brought forward by the master, all of which was disposed of by the slave. The slave was made to say some very smart as well as impressive things in reply to his master— things which had the desired though unexpected effect; for the conversation resulted in the voluntary emancipation of the slave on the part of the master.

In the same book, I met with one of Sheridan' s mighty speeches on and in behalf of Catholic emancipation. These were choice documents to me. I read them over and over again with unabated interest. They gave tongue to interesting thoughts of my own soul, which had frequently flashed through my mind, and died away for want of utterance. The moral which I gained from the dialogue was the power of truth over the conscience of even a slaveholder. What I got from Sheridan was a bold denunciation of slavery, and a powerful vindication of human rights. The reading of these documents enabled me to utter my thoughts, and to meet the arguments brought forward to sustain slavery; but while they relieved me of one difficulty, they brought on another even more painful than the one of which I was relieved. The more I read, the more I was led to abhor and detest my enslavers. I could regard them in no other light than a band of successful robbers, who had left their homes, and gone to Africa, and stolen us from our homes, and in a strange land reduced us to slavery. I loathed them as being the meanest as well as the most wicked of men. As I read and contemplated the subject, behold! that very discontentment which Master Hugh had predicted would follow my learning to read had already come, to torment and sting my soul to unutterable anguish. As I writhed under it, I would at times feel that learning to read had been a curse rather than a blessing. It had given me a view of my wretched condition, without the remedy. It opened my eyes to the horrible pit, but to no ladder upon which to get out. In moments of agony, I envied my fellow-slaves for their stupidity. I have often wished myself a beast. I preferred the condition of the meanest reptile to my own. Any thing, no matter what, to get rid of thinking! It was this everlasting thinking of my condition that tormented me. There was no getting rid of it. It was pressed upon me by every object within sight or hearing, animate or inanimate. The silver trump of freedom had roused my soul to eternal wakefulness. Freedom now appeared, to disappear no more forever. It was heard in every sound, and seen in every thing. It was ever present to torment me with a sense of my wretched condition. I saw nothing without seeing it, I heard nothing without hearing it, and felt nothing without feeling it. It looked from every star, it smiled in every calm, breathed in every wind, and moved in every storm.

I often found myself regretting my own existence, and wishing myself dead; and but for the hope of being free, I have no doubt but that I should have killed myself, or done something for which I should have been killed. While in this state of mind, I was eager to hear any one speak of slavery. I was a ready listener. Every little while, I could hear something about the abolitionists. It was some time before I found what the word meant. It was always used in such connections as to make it an interesting word to me. If a slave ran away and succeeded in getting clear, or if a slave killed his master, set fire to a barn, or did any thing very wrong in the mind of a slaveholder, it was spoken of as the fruit of *abolition*. Hearing the word in this connection very often, I set about learning what it meant. The dictionary afforded me little or no help. I found it was " the act of abolishing;" but then I did not know what was to be abolished. Here I was perplexed. I did not dare to ask any one about its meaning, for I was satisfied that it was something they wanted me to know very little about. After a patient waiting, I got one of our city papers, containing an account of the number of petitions from the north, praying for the abolition of slavery in the District of Columbia, and of the slave trade between the States. From this time I understood the words *abolition* and *abolitionist*, and always drew near when that word was spoken, expecting to hear something of importance to myself and fellow-slaves. The light broke in upon me by degrees. I went one day down on the wharf of Mr. Waters; and seeing two Irishmen unloading a scow of stone, I went, unasked, and helped them. When we had finished, one of them came to me and asked me if I were a slave. I told him I was. He asked, " Are ye a slave for life?" I told him that I was. The good Irishman seemed to be deeply affected by the statement. He said to the other that it was a pity so fine a little fellow as myself should be a slave for life. He said it was a shame to hold me. They both advised me to run away to the north; that I should find friends there, and that I should be free. I pretended not to be interested in what they said, and treated them as if I did not understand them; for I feared they might be treacherous. White men have been known to encourage slaves to escape, and then, to get the reward, catch them and return them to their masters. I was afraid that these seemingly good men might use me so; but I nevertheless remembered their advice, and from that time I resolved to run away. I looked forward to a time at which it would be safe for me to escape. I was too young to think of doing so immediately; besides, I wished to learn how to write, as I might have occasion to write my own pass. I consoled myself with the hope that I should one day find a good chance. Meanwhile, I would learn to write.

The idea as to how I might learn to write was suggested to me by being in Durgin and Bailey's ship-yard, and frequently seeing the ship carpenters, after hewing, and getting a piece of timber ready for use, write on the timber the name of that part of the ship for which it was intended. When a piece of timber was intended for the larboard side, it would be marked thus— " L." When a piece was for the starboard side, it would be marked thus— " S." A piece for the larboard side forward, would be marked thus— " L. F." When a piece was for starboard side forward, it would be marked thus— " S. F." For larboard aft, it would be marked thus— " L. A." For starboard aft, it would be marked thus— " S. A." I soon learned the names of these letters, and for what they were intended when placed upon a piece of timber in the ship-yard. I immediately commenced copying them, and in a short time was able to make the four letters named. After that, when I met with any boy who I knew could write, I would tell him I could write as well as he. The next word would be, " I don't believe you. Let me see you try it." I would then make the letters which I had been so fortunate as to learn, and ask him to beat that. In this way I got a good many lessons in writing, which it is quite possible I should never have gotten in any other way. During this time, my copy-book was the board fence, brick wall, and pavement; my pen and ink was a lump of chalk. With these, I learned mainly how to write. I then commenced and continued copying the Italics in Webster's Spelling Book, until I could make them all without looking on the book. By this time, my little Master Thomas had gone to school, and learned how to write, and had written over a number of copy-books. These had been brought home, and shown to some of our near neighbors, and then laid aside. My mistress used to go to class meeting at the Wilk Street meetinghouse every Monday afternoon, and leave me to take care of the house. When left thus, I used to spend the time in writing in the spaces left in Master Thomas's copy-book, copying what he had written. I continued to do this until I could write a hand very similar to that of Master Thomas. Thus, after a long, tedious effort for years, I finally succeeded in learning how to write.

CHAPTER VIII.

IN a very short time after I went to live at Baltimore, my old master's youngest son Richard died; and in about three years and six months after his death, my old master, Captain Anthony, died, leaving only his son, Andrew, and daughter, Lucretia, to share his estate. He died while on a visit to see his daughter at Hillsborough. Cut off thus unexpectedly, he left no will as to the disposal of his property. It was therefore necessary to have a valuation of the property, that it might be equally divided between Mrs. Lucretia and Master Andrew. I was immediately sent for, to be valued with the other property. Here again my feelings rose up in detestation of slavery. I had now a new conception of my degraded condition. Prior to this, I had become, if not insensible to my lot, at least partly so. I left Baltimore with a young heart overborne with sadness, and a soul full of apprehension. I took passage with Captain Rowe, in the schooner Wild Cat, and, after a sail of about twenty-four hours, I found myself near the place of my birth. I had now been absent from it almost, if not quite, five years. I, however, remembered the place very well. I was only about five years old when I left it, to go and live with my old master on Colonel Lloyd's plantation; so that I was now between ten and eleven years old.

We were all ranked together at the valuation. Men and women, old and young, married and single, were ranked with horses, sheep, and swine. There were horses and men, cattle and women, pigs and children, all holding the same rank in the scale of being, and were all subjected to the same narrow examination. Silvery-headed age and sprightly youth, maids and matrons, had to undergo the same indelicate inspection. At this moment, I saw more clearly than ever the brutalizing effects of slavery upon both slave and slaveholder.

After the valuation, then came the division. I have no language to express the high excitement and deep anxiety which were felt among us poor slaves during this time. Our fate for life was now to be decided. We had no more voice in that decision than the brutes among whom we were ranked. A single word from the white men was enough— against all our wishes, prayers, and entreaties— to sunder forever the dearest friends, dearest kindred, and strongest ties known to human beings. In addition to the pain of separation, there was the horrid dread of falling into the hands of Master Andrew. He was known to us all as being a most cruel wretch,— a common drunkard, who had, by his reckless mismanagement and profligate dissipation, already wasted a large portion of his father's property. We all felt that we might as well be sold at once to the Georgia traders, as to pass into his hands; for we knew that that would be our inevitable condition,— a condition held by us all in the utmost horror and dread.

I suffered more anxiety than most of my fellow-slaves. I had known what it was to be kindly treated; they had known nothing of the kind. They had seen little or nothing of the world. They were in very deed men and women of sorrow, and acquainted with grief. Their backs had been made familiar with the bloody lash, so that they had become callous; mine was yet tender; for while at Baltimore I got few whippings, and few slaves could boast of a kinder master and mistress than myself; and the thought of passing out of their hands into those of Master Andrew— a man who, but a few days before, to give me a sample of his bloody disposition, took my little brother by the throat, threw him on the ground, and with the heel of his boot stamped upon his head till the blood gushed from his nose and ears— was well calculated to make me anxious as to my fate. After he had committed this savage outrage upon my brother, he turned to me, and said that was the way he meant to serve me one of these days,— meaning, I suppose, when I came into his possession.

Thanks to a kind Providence, I fell to the portion of Mrs. Lucretia, and was sent immediately back to Baltimore, to live again in the family of Master Hugh. Their joy at my return equalled their sorrow at my departure. It was a glad day to me. I had escaped a worse than lion's jaws. I was absent from Baltimore, for the purpose of valuation and division, just about one month, and it seemed to have been six.

Very soon after my return to Baltimore, my mistress, Lucretia, died, leaving her husband and one child, Amanda; and in a very short time after her death, Master Andrew died. Now all the property of my old master, slaves included, was in the hands of strangers,— strangers who had had nothing to do with accumulating it. Not a slave was left free. All remained slaves, from the youngest to the oldest. If any one thing in my experience, more than another, served to deepen my conviction of the infernal character of slavery, and to fill me with unutterable loathing of slaveholders, it was their base ingratitude to my poor old grandmother. She had served my old master faithfully from youth to old age. She had been the source of all his wealth; she had peopled his plantation with slaves; she had become a great grandmother in his service. She had rocked him in infancy, attended him in childhood, served him through life, and at his death wiped from his icy brow the cold death-sweat, and closed his eyes forever. She was nevertheless left a slave— a slave for life— a slave in the hands of strangers; and in their hands she saw her children, her grandchildren, and her great-grandchildren, divided, like so many sheep, without being gratified with the small privilege of a single word, as to their or her own destiny. And, to cap the climax of their base ingratitude and fiendish barbarity, my grandmother, who was now very old, having outlived my old master and all his children, having seen the beginning and end of all of them, and her present owners finding she was of but little value, her frame already racked with the pains of old age, and complete helplessness fast stealing over her once active limbs, they took her to the woods, built her a little hut, put up a little mud-chimney, and then made her welcome to the privilege of supporting herself there in perfect loneliness; thus virtually turning her out to die! If my poor old grandmother now lives, she lives to suffer in utter loneliness; she lives to remember and mourn over the loss of children, the loss of grandchildren, and the loss of great-grandchildren. They are, in the language of the slave's poet, Whittier,—

" Gone, gone, sold and gone
To the rice swamp dank and lone,
Where the slave-whip ceaseless swings,
Where the noisome insect stings,
Where the fever-demon strews
Poison with the falling dews,
Where the sickly sunbeams glare

Through the hot and misty air:—
Gone, gone, sold and gone
To the rice swamp dank and lone,
From Virginia hills and waters—
Woe is me, my stolen daughters!"

The hearth is desolate. The children, the unconscious children, who once sang and danced in her presence, are gone. She gropes her way, in the darkness of age, for a drink of water. Instead of the voices of her children, she hears by day the moans of the dove, and by night the screams of the hideous owl. All is gloom. The grave is at the door. And now, when weighed down by the pains and aches of old age, when the head inclines to the feet, when the beginning and ending of human existence meet, and helpless infancy and painful old age combine together— at this time, this most needful time, the time for the exercise of that tenderness and affection which children only can exercise towards a declining parent— my poor old grandmother, the devoted mother of twelve children, is left all alone, in yonder little hut, before a few dim embers. She stands— she sits— she staggers— she falls— she groans— she dies— and there are none of her children or grandchildren present, to wipe from her wrinkled brow the cold sweat of death, or to place beneath the sod her fallen remains. Will not a righteous God visit for these things?

In about two years after the death of Mrs. Lucretia, Master Thomas married his second wife. Her name was Rowena Hamilton. She was the eldest daughter of Mr. William Hamilton. Master now lived in St. Michael's. Not long after his marriage, a misunderstanding took place between himself and Master Hugh; and as a means of punishing his brother, he took me from him to live with himself at St. Michael's. Here I underwent another most painful separation. It, however, was not so severe as the one I dreaded at the division of property; for, during this interval, a great change had taken place in Master Hugh and his once kind and affectionate wife. The influence of brandy upon him, and of slavery upon her, had effected a disastrous change in the characters of both; so that, as far as they were concerned, I thought I had little to lose by the change. But it was not to them that I was attached. It was to those little Baltimore boys that I felt the strongest attachment. I had received many good lessons from them, and was still receiving them, and the thought of leaving them was painful indeed. I was leaving, too, without the hope of ever being allowed to return. Master Thomas had said he would never let me return again. The barrier betwixt himself and brother he considered impassable.

I then had to regret that I did not at least make the attempt to carry out my resolution to run away; for the chances of success are tenfold greater from the city than from the country.

I sailed from Baltimore for St. Michael's in the sloop Amanda, Captain Edward Dodson. On my passage, I paid particular attention to the direction which the steamboats took to go to Philadelphia. I found, instead of going down, on reaching North Point they went up the bay, in a north-easterly direction. I deemed this knowledge of the utmost importance. My determination to run away was again revived. I resolved to wait only so long as the offering of a favorable opportunity. When that came, I was determined to be off.

Chapter IX.

I HAVE now reached a period of my life when I can give dates. I left Baltimore, and went to live with Master Thomas Auld, at St. Michael's, in March, 1832. It was now more than seven years since I lived with him in the family of my old master, on Colonel Lloyd's plantation. We of course were now almost entire strangers to each other. He was to me a new master, and I to him a new slave. I was ignorant of his temper and disposition; he was equally so of mine. A very short time, however, brought us into full acquaintance with each other. I was made acquainted with his wife not less than with himself. They were well matched, being equally mean and cruel. I was now, for the first time during a space of more than seven years, made to feel the painful gnawings of hunger— a something which I had not experienced before since I left Colonel Lloyd's plantation. It went hard enough with me then, when I could look back to no period at which I had enjoyed a sufficiency. It was tenfold harder after living in Master Hugh's family, where I had always had enough to eat, and of that which was good. I have said Master Thomas was a mean man. He was so. Not to give a slave enough to eat, is regarded as the most aggravated development of meanness even among slaveholders. The rule is, no matter how coarse the food, only let there be enough of it. This is the theory; and in the part of Maryland from which I came, it is the general practice,— though there are many exceptions. Master Thomas gave us enough of neither coarse nor fine food. There were four slaves of us in the kitchen— my sister Eliza, my aunt Priscilla, Henny, and myself; and we were allowed less than a half of a bushel of corn-meal per week, and very little else, either in the shape of meat or vegetables. It was not enough for us to subsist upon. We were therefore reduced to the wretched necessity of living at the expense of our neighbors. This we did by begging and stealing, whichever came handy in the time of need, the one being considered as legitimate as the other.

A great many times have we poor creatures been nearly perishing with hunger, when food in abundance lay mouldering in the safe and smoke-house, and our pious mistress was aware of the fact; and yet that mistress and her husband would kneel every morning, and pray that God would bless them in basket and store!

Bad as all slaveholders are, we seldom meet one destitute of every element of character commanding respect. My master was one of this rare sort. I do not know of one single noble act ever performed by him. The leading trait in his character was meanness; and if there were any other element in his nature, it was made subject to this. He was mean; and, like most other mean men, he lacked the ability to conceal his meanness. Captain Auld was not born a slaveholder. He had been a poor man, master only of a Bay craft. He came into possession of all his slaves by marriage; and of all men, adopted slaveholders are the worst. He was cruel, but cowardly. He commanded without firmness. In the enforcement of his rules, he was at times rigid, and at times lax. At times, he spoke to his slaves with the firmness of Napoleon and the fury of a demon; at other times, he might well be mistaken for an inquirer who had lost his way. He did nothing of himself. He might have passed for a lion, but for his ears. In all things noble which he attempted, his own meanness shone most conspicuous. His airs, words, and actions, were the airs, words, and actions of born slaveholders, and, being assumed, were awkward enough. He was not even a good imitator. He possessed all the disposition to deceive, but wanted the power. Having no resources within himself, he was compelled to be the copyist of many, and being such, he was forever the victim of inconsistency; and of consequence he was an object of contempt, and was held as such even by his slaves. The luxury of having slaves of his own to wait upon him was something new and unprepared for. He was a slaveholder without the ability to hold slaves. He found himself incapable of managing his slaves either by force, fear, or fraud. We seldom called him " master;" we generally called him " Captain Auld," and were hardly disposed to title him at all. I doubt not that our conduct had much to do with making him appear awkward, and of consequence fretful. Our want of reverence for him must have perplexed him greatly. He wished to have us call him master, but lacked the firmness necessary to command us to do so. His wife used to insist upon our calling him so, but to no purpose. In August, 1832, my master attended a Methodist camp-meeting held in the

Bay-side, Talbot county, and there experienced religion. I indulged a faint hope that his conversion would lead him to emancipate his slaves, and that, if he did not do this, it would, at any rate, make him more kind and humane. I was disappointed in both these respects. It neither made him to be humane to his slaves, nor to emancipate them. If it had any effect on his character, it made him more cruel and hateful in all his ways; for I believe him to have been a much worse man after his conversion than before. Prior to his conversion, he relied upon his own depravity to shield and sustain him in his savage barbarity; but after his conversion, he found religious sanction and support for his slaveholding cruelty. He made the greatest pretensions to piety. His house was the house of prayer. He prayed morning, noon, and night. He very soon distinguished himself among his brethren, and was soon made a class-leader and exhorter. His activity in revivals was great, and he proved himself an instrument in the hands of the church in converting many souls. His house was the preachers' home.

They used to take great pleasure in coming there to put up; for while he starved us, he stuffed them. We have had three or four preachers there at a time. The names of those who used to come most frequently while I lived there, were Mr. Storks, Mr. Ewery, Mr. Humphry, and Mr. Hickey. I have also seen Mr. George Cookman at our house. We slaves loved Mr. Cookman. We believed him to be a good man. We thought him instrumental in getting Mr. Samuel Harrison, a very rich slaveholder, to emancipate his slaves; and by some means got the impression that he was laboring to effect the emancipation of all the slaves. When he was at our house, we were sure to be called in to prayers. When the others were there, we were sometimes called in and sometimes not. Mr. Cookman took more notice of us than either of the other ministers. He could not come among us without betraying his sympathy for us, and, stupid as we were, we had the sagacity to see it.

While I lived with my master in St. Michael's, there was a white young man, a Mr. Wilson, who proposed to keep a Sabbath school for the instruction of such slaves as might be disposed to learn to read the New Testament. We met but three times, when Mr. West and Mr. Fairbanks, both class-leaders, with many others, came upon us with sticks and other missiles, drove us off, and forbade us to meet again. Thus ended our little Sabbath school in the pious town of St. Michael's.

I have said my master found religious sanction for his cruelty. As an example, I will state one of many facts going to prove the charge. I have seen him tie up a lame young woman, and whip her with a heavy cowskin upon her naked shoulders, causing the warm red blood to drip; and, in justification of the bloody deed, he would quote this passage of Scripture— " He that knoweth his master' s will, and doeth it not, shall be beaten with many stripes."

Master would keep this lacerated young woman tied up in this horrid situation four or five hours at a time. I have known him to tie her up early in the morning, and whip her before breakfast; leave her, go to his store, return at dinner, and whip her again, cutting her in the places already made raw with his cruel lash. The secret of master's cruelty toward " Henny" is found in the fact of her being almost helpless. When quite a child, she fell into the fire, and burned herself horribly. Her hands were so burnt that she never got the use of them. She could do very little but bear heavy burdens. She was to master a bill of expense; and as he was a mean man, she was a constant offence to him. He seemed desirous of getting the poor girl out of existence. He gave her away once to his sister; but, being a poor gift, she was not disposed to keep her. Finally, my benevolent master, to use his own words, " set her adrift to take care of herself." Here was a recently-converted man, holding on upon the mother, and at the same time turning out her helpless child, to starve and die! Master Thomas was one of the many pious slaveholders who hold slaves for the very charitable purpose of taking care of them.

My master and myself had quite a number of differences. He found me unsuitable to his purpose. My city life, he said, had had a very pernicious effect upon me. It had almost ruined me for every good purpose, and fitted me for every thing which was bad. One of my greatest faults was that of letting his horse run away, and go down to his father-in-law's farm, which was about five miles from St. Michael's. I would then have to go after it. My reason for this kind of carelessness, or carefulness, was, that I could always get something to eat when I went there. Master William Hamilton, my master's father-in-law, always gave his slaves enough to eat. I never left there hungry, no matter how great the need of my speedy return. Master Thomas at length said he would stand it no longer. I had lived with him nine months, during which time he had given me a number of severe whippings, all to no good purpose. He resolved to put me out, as he said, to be broken; and, for this purpose, he let me for one year to a man named Edward Covey. Mr. Covey was a poor man, a farm-renter. He rented the place upon which he lived, as also the hands with which he tilled it. Mr. Covey had acquired a very high reputation for breaking young slaves, and this reputation was of immense value to him. It enabled him to get his farm tilled with much less expense to himself than he could have had it done without such a reputation. Some slaveholders thought it not much loss to allow Mr. Covey to have their slaves one year, for the sake of the training to which they were subjected, without any other compensation. He could hire young help with great ease, in consequence of this reputation. Added to the natural good qualities of Mr. Covey, he was a professor of religion— a pious soul— a member and a class-leader in the Methodist church. All of this added weight to his reputation as a " nigger-breaker." I was aware of all the facts, having been made acquainted with them by a young man who had lived there. I nevertheless made the change gladly; for I was sure of getting enough to eat, which is not the smallest consideration to a hungry man.

CHAPTER X.

I LEFT Master Thomas's house, and went to live with Mr. Covey, on the 1st of January, 1833. I was now, for the first time in my life, a field hand. In my new employment, I found myself even more awkward than a country boy appeared to be in a large city. I had been at my new home but one week before Mr. Covey gave me a very severe whipping, cutting my back, causing the blood to run, and raising ridges on my flesh as large as my little finger. The details of this affair are as follows: Mr. Covey sent me, very early in the morning of one of our coldest days in the month of January, to the woods, to get a load of wood. He gave me a team of unbroken oxen. He told me which was the in-hand ox, and which the off-hand one. He then tied the end of a large rope around the horns of the in-hand ox, and gave me the other end of it, and told me, if the oxen started to run, that I must hold on upon the rope. I had never driven oxen before, and of course I was very awkward. I, however, succeeded in getting to the edge of the woods with little difficulty; but I had got a very few rods into the woods, when the oxen took fright, and started full tilt, carrying the cart against trees, and over stumps, in the most frightful manner. I expected every moment that my brains would be dashed out against the trees. After running thus for a considerable distance, they finally upset the cart, dashing it with great force against a tree, and threw themselves into a dense thicket. How I escaped death, I do not know. There I was, entirely alone, in a thick wood, in a place new to me. My cart was upset and shattered, my oxen were entangled among the young trees, and there was none to help me. After a long spell of effort, I succeeded in getting my cart righted, my oxen disentangled, and again yoked to the cart. I now proceeded with my team to the place where I had, the day before, been chopping wood, and loaded my cart pretty heavily, thinking in this way to tame my oxen. I then proceeded on my way home. I had now consumed one half of the day. I got out of the woods safely, and now felt out of danger. I stopped my oxen to open the woods gate; and just as I did so, before I could get hold of my ox-rope, the oxen again started, rushed through the gate, catching it between the wheel and the body of the cart, tearing it to pieces, and coming within a few inches of crushing me against the gate-post. Thus twice, in one short day, I escaped death by the merest chance. On my return, I told Mr. Covey what had happened, and how it happened. He ordered me to return to the woods again immediately. I did so, and he followed on after me. Just as I got into the woods, he came up and told me to stop my cart, and that he would teach me how to trifle away my time, and break gates. He then went to a large gum-tree, and with his axe cut three large switches, and, after trimming them up neatly with his pocket-knife, he ordered me to take off my clothes. I made him no answer, but stood with my clothes on. He repeated his order. I still made him no answer, nor did I move to strip myself. Upon this he rushed at me with the fierceness of a tiger, tore off my clothes, and lashed me till he had worn out his switches, cutting me so savagely as to leave the marks visible for a long time after. This whipping was the first of a number just like it, and for similar offences.

I lived with Mr. Covey one year. During the first six months, of that year, scarce a week passed without his whipping me. I was seldom free from a sore back. My awkwardness was almost always his excuse for whipping me. We were worked fully up to the point of endurance. Long before day we were up, our horses fed, and by the first approach of day we were off to the field with our hoes and ploughing teams. Mr. Covey gave us enough to eat, but scarce time to eat it. We were often less than five minutes taking our meals. We were often in the field from the first approach of day till its last lingering ray had left us; and at saving-fodder time, midnight often caught us in the field binding blades.

Covey would be out with us. The way he used to stand it, was this. He would spend the most of his afternoons in bed. He would then come out fresh in the evening, ready to urge us on with his words, example, and frequently with the whip. Mr. Covey was one of the few slaveholders who could and did work with his hands. He was a hard-working man. He knew by himself just what a man or a boy could do. There was no deceiving him. His work went on in his absence almost as well as in his presence; and he had the faculty of making us feel that he was ever present with us. This he did by surprising us. He seldom approached the spot where we were at work openly, if he could do it secretly. He always aimed at taking us by surprise. Such was his cunning, that we used to call him, among ourselves, " the snake." When we were at work in the cornfield, he would sometimes crawl on his hands and knees to avoid detection, and all at once he would rise nearly in our midst, and scream out, " Ha, ha! Come, come! Dash on, dash on!" This being his mode of attack, it was never safe to stop a single minute. His comings were like a thief in the night. He appeared to us as being ever at hand. He was under every tree, behind every stump, in every bush, and at every window, on the plantation. He would sometimes mount his horse, as if bound to St. Michael's, a distance of seven miles, and in half an hour afterwards you would see him coiled up in the corner of the wood-fence, watching every motion of the slaves. He would, for this purpose, leave his horse tied up in the woods. Again, he would sometimes walk up to us, and give us orders as though he was upon the point of starting on a long journey, turn his back upon us, and make as though he was going to the house to get ready; and, before he would get half way thither, he would turn short and crawl into a fence-corner, or behind some tree, and there watch us till the going down of the sun.

Mr. Covey's *forte* consisted in his power to deceive. His life was devoted to planning and perpetrating the grossest deceptions. Every thing he possessed in the shape of learning or religion, he made conform to his disposition to deceive. He seemed to think himself equal to deceiving the Almighty. He would make a short prayer in the morning, and a long prayer at night; and, strange as it may seem, few men would at times appear more devotional than he. The exercises of his family devotions were always commenced with singing; and, as he was a very poor singer himself, the duty of raising the hymn generally came upon me. He would read his hymn, and nod at me to commence. I would at times do so; at others, I would not. My non-compliance would almost always produce much confusion. To show himself independent of me, he would start and stagger through with his hymn in the most discordant manner. In this state of mind, he prayed with more than ordinary spirit. Poor man! such was his disposition, and success at deceiving, I do verily believe that he sometimes deceived himself into the solemn belief, that he was a sincere worshipper of the most high God; and this, too, at a time when he may be said to have been guilty of compelling his woman slave to commit the sin of adultery. The facts in the case are these: Mr. Covey was a poor man; he was just commencing in life; he was only able to buy one slave; and, shocking as is the fact, he bought her, as he said, for a *breeder*. This woman was named Caroline. Mr. Covey bought her from Mr. Thomas Lowe, about six miles from St. Michael's. She was a large, able-bodied woman, about twenty years old. She had already given birth to one child, which proved her to be just what he wanted. After buying her, he hired a married man of Mr. Samuel Harrison, to live with him one year; and him he used to fasten up with her every night! The result was, that, at the end of the year, the miserable woman gave birth to twins. At this result Mr. Covey seemed to be highly pleased, both with the man and the wretched woman. Such was his joy, and that of his wife, that nothing they could do for Caroline during her confinement was too good, or too hard, to be done. The children were regarded as being quite an addition to his wealth.

If at any one time of my life more than another, I was made to drink the bitterest dregs of slavery, that time was during the first six months of my stay with Mr. Covey. We were worked in all weathers. It was never too hot or too cold; it could never rain, blow, hail, or snow, too hard for us to work in the field. Work, work, work, was scarcely more the order of the day than of the night. The longest days were too short for him, and the shortest nights too long for him. I was somewhat unmanageable when I first went there, but a few months of this discipline tamed me. Mr. Covey succeeded in breaking me. I was broken in body, soul, and spirit. My natural elasticity was crushed, my intellect languished, the disposition to read departed, the cheerful spark that lingered about my eye died; the dark night of slavery closed in upon me; and behold a man transformed into a brute!

Sunday was my only leisure time. I spent this in a sort of beast-like stupor, between sleep and wake, under some large tree. At times I would rise up, a flash of energetic freedom would dart through my soul, accompanied with a faint beam of hope, that flickered for a moment, and then vanished. I sank down again, mourning over my wretched condition. I was sometimes prompted to take my life, and that of Covey, but was prevented by a combination of hope and fear. My sufferings on this plantation seem now like a dream rather than a stern reality.

Our house stood within a few rods of the Chesapeake Bay, whose broad bosom was ever white with sails from every quarter of the habitable globe.

Those beautiful vessels, robed in purest white, so delightful to the eye of freemen, were to me so many shrouded ghosts, to terrify and torment me with thoughts of my wretched condition. I have often, in the deep stillness of a summer's Sabbath, stood all alone upon the lofty banks of that noble bay, and traced, with saddened heart and tearful eye, the countless number of sails moving off to the mighty ocean. The sight of these always affected me powerfully. My thoughts would compel utterance; and there, with no audience but the Almighty, I would pour out my soul's complaint, in my rude way, with an apostrophe to the moving multitude of ships:—

" You are loosed from your moorings, and are free; I am fast in my chains, and am a slave! You move merrily before the gentle gale, and I sadly before the bloody whip! You are freedom's swift-winged angels, that fly round the world; I am confined in bands of iron! O that I were free! O, that I were on one of your gallant decks, and under your protecting wing! Alas! betwixt me and you, the turbid waters roll. Go on, go on. O that I could also go! Could I but swim! If I could fly! O, why was I born a man, of whom to make a brute! The glad ship is gone; she hides in the dim distance. I am left in the hottest hell of unending slavery. O God, save me! God, deliver me! Let me be free! Is there any God? Why am I a slave? I will run away. I will not stand it. Get caught, or get clear, I'll try it. I had as well die with ague as the fever. I have only one life to lose. I had as well be killed running as die standing. Only think of it; one hundred miles straight north, and I am free! Try it? Yes! God helping me, I will. It cannot be that I shall live and die a slave. I will take to the water. This very bay shall yet bear me into freedom. The steamboats steered in a north-east course from North Point. I will do the same; and when I get to the head of the bay, I will turn my canoe adrift, and walk straight through Delaware into Pennsylvania. When I get there, I shall not be required to have a pass; I can travel without being disturbed. Let but the first opportunity offer, and, come what will, I am off. Meanwhile, I will try to bear up under the yoke. I am not the only slave in the world. Why should I fret? I can bear as much as any of them. Besides, I am but a boy, and all boys are bound to some one. It may be that my misery in slavery will only increase my happiness when I get free. There is a better day coming."

Thus I used to think, and thus I used to speak to myself; goaded almost to madness at one moment, and at the next reconciling myself to my wretched lot.

I have already intimated that my condition was much worse, during the first six months of my stay at Mr. Covey's, than in the last six. The circumstances leading to the change in Mr. Covey's course toward me form an epoch in my humble history. You have seen how a man was made a slave; you shall see how a slave was made a man. On one of the hottest days of the month of August, 1833, Bill Smith, William Hughes, a slave named Eli, and myself, were engaged in fanning wheat. Hughes was clearing the fanned wheat from before the fan. Eli was turning, Smith was feeding, and I was carrying wheat to the fan. The work was simple, requiring strength rather than intellect; yet, to one entirely unused to such work, it came very hard. About three o'clock of that day, I broke down; my strength failed me; I was seized with a violent aching of the head, attended with extreme dizziness; I trembled in every limb. Finding what was coming, I nerved myself up, feeling it would never do to stop work. I stood as long as I could stagger to the hopper with grain. When I could stand no longer, I fell, and felt as if held down by an immense weight. The fan of course stopped; every one had his own work to do; and no one could do the work of the other, and have his own go on at the same time.

Mr. Covey was at the house, about one hundred yards from the treading-yard where we were fanning. On hearing the fan stop, he left immediately, and came to the spot where we were. He hastily inquired what the matter was. Bill answered that I was sick, and there was no one to bring wheat to the fan. I had by this time crawled away under the side of the post and rail-fence by which the yard was enclosed, hoping to find relief by getting out of the sun. He then asked where I was. He was told by one of the hands. He came to the spot, and, after looking at me awhile, asked me what was the matter. I told him as well as I could, for I scarce had strength to speak. He then gave me a savage kick in the side, and told me to get up. I tried to do so, but fell back in the attempt. He gave me another kick, and again told me to rise. I again tried, and succeeded in gaining my feet; but, stooping to get the tub with which I was feeding the fan, I again staggered and fell. While down in this situation, Mr. Covey took up the hickory slat with which Hughes had been striking off the half-bushel measure, and with it gave me a heavy blow upon the head, making a large wound, and the blood ran freely; and with this again told me to get up. I made no effort to comply, having now made up my mind to let him do his worst. In a short time after receiving this blow, my head grew better. Mr. Covey had now left me to my fate. At this moment I resolved, for the first time, to go to my master, enter a complaint, and ask his protection. In order to do this, I must that afternoon walk seven miles; and this, under the circumstances, was truly a severe undertaking. I was exceedingly feeble; made so as much by the kicks and blows which I received, as by the severe fit of sickness to which I had been subjected. I, however, watched my chance, while Covey was looking in an opposite direction, and started for St. Michael's. I succeeded in getting a considerable distance on my way to the woods, when Covey discovered me, and called after me to come back, threatening what he would do if I did not come. I disregarded both his calls and his threats, and made my way to the woods as fast as my feeble state would allow; and thinking I might be overhauled by him if I kept the road, I walked through the woods, keeping far enough from the road to avoid detection, and near enough to prevent losing my way. I had not gone far before my little strength again failed me. I could go no farther. I fell down, and lay for a considerable time. The blood was yet oozing from the wound on my head. For a time I thought I should bleed to death; and think now that I should have done so, but that the blood so matted my hair as to stop the wound. After lying there about three quarters of an hour, I nerved myself up again, and started on my way, through bogs and briers, barefooted and bareheaded, tearing my feet sometimes at nearly every step; and after a journey of about seven miles, occupying some five hours to perform it, I arrived at master's store. I then presented an appearance enough to affect any but a heart of iron. From the crown of my head to my feet, I was covered with blood. My hair was all clotted with dust and blood; my shirt was stiff with blood. I suppose I looked like a man who had escaped a den of wild beasts, and barely escaped them. In this state I appeared before my master, humbly entreating him to interpose his authority for my protection. I told him all the circumstances as well as I could, and it seemed, as I spoke, at times to affect him. He would then walk the floor, and seek to justify Covey by saying he expected I deserved it. He asked me what I wanted. I told him, to let me get a new home; that as sure as I lived with Mr. Covey again, I should live with but to die with him; that Covey would surely kill me; he was in a fair way for it. Master Thomas ridiculed the idea that there was any danger of Mr. Covey's killing me, and said that he knew Mr. Covey; that he was a good man, and that he could not think of taking me from him; that, should he do so, he would lose the whole year's wages; that I belonged to Mr. Covey for one year, and that I must go back to him, come what might; and that I must not trouble him with any more stories, or that he would himself *get hold of me*. After threatening me thus, he gave me a very large dose of salts, telling me that I might remain in St. Michael's that night, (it being quite late,) but that I must be off back to Mr. Covey's early in the morning; and that if I did not, he would *get hold of me*, which meant that he would whip me. I remained all night, and, according to his orders, I started off to Covey's in the morning, (Saturday morning,) wearied in body and broken in spirit. I got no supper that night, or breakfast that morning. I reached Covey's about nine o'clock; and just as I was getting over the fence that divided Mrs. Kemp's fields from ours, out ran Covey with his cowskin, to give me another whipping. Before he could reach me, I succeeded in getting to the cornfield; and as the corn was very high, it afforded me the means of hiding. He seemed very angry, and searched for me a long time. My behavior was altogether unaccountable. He finally gave up the chase, thinking, I suppose, that I must come home for something to eat; he would give himself no further trouble in looking for me. I spent that day mostly in the woods, having the alternative before me,— to go home and be whipped to death, or stay in the woods and be starved to death. That night, I fell in with Sandy Jenkins, a slave with whom I was somewhat acquainted. Sandy had a free wife who lived about four miles from Mr. Covey's; and it being Saturday, he was on his way to see her. I told him my circumstances, and he very kindly invited me to go home with him. I went home with him, and talked this whole matter over, and got his advice as to what course it was best for me to pursue. I found Sandy an old adviser. He told me, with great solemnity, I must go back to Covey; but that before I went, I must go with him into another part of the woods, where there was a certain root, which, if I would take some of it with me, carrying it *always on my right side*, would render it impossible for Mr. Covey, or any other white man, to whip me. He said he had carried it for years; and since he had done so, he had never received a blow, and never expected to while he carried it. I at first rejected the idea, that the simple carrying of a root in my pocket would have any such effect as he had said, and was not disposed to take it; but Sandy impressed the necessity with much earnestness, telling me it could do no harm, if it did no good. To please him, I at length took the root, and, according to his direction, carried it upon my right side. This was Sunday morning. I immediately started for home; and upon entering the yard gate, out came Mr. Covey on his way to meeting. He spoke to me very kindly, bade me drive the pigs from a lot near by, and passed on towards the church. Now, this singular conduct of Mr. Covey really made me begin to think that there was something in the *root* which Sandy had given me; and had it been on any other day than Sunday, I could have attributed the conduct to no other cause than the influence of that *root*; and as it was, I was half inclined to think the root to be something more than I at first had taken it to be. All went well till Monday morning. On this morning, the virtue of the *root* was fully tested. Long before daylight, I was called to go and rub, curry, and feed, the horses. I obeyed, and was glad to obey. But whilst thus engaged, whilst in the act of throwing down some blades from the loft, Mr. Covey entered the stable with a long rope; and just as I was half out of the loft, he caught hold of my legs, and was about tying me. As soon as I found what he was up to, I gave a sudden spring, and as I did so, he holding to my legs, I was brought sprawling on the stable floor.

Mr. Covey seemed now to think he had me, and could do what he pleased; but at this moment—from whence came the spirit I don't know—I resolved to fight; and, suiting my action to the resolution, I seized Covey hard by the throat; and as I did so, I rose. He held on to me, and I to him. My resistance was so entirely unexpected that Covey seemed taken all aback. He trembled like a leaf. This gave me assurance, and I held him uneasy, causing the blood to run where I touched him with the ends of my fingers. Mr. Covey soon called out to Hughes for help. Hughes came, and, while Covey held me, attempted to tie my right hand. While he was in the act of doing so, I watched my chance, and gave him a heavy kick close under the ribs. This kick fairly sickened Hughes, so that he left me in the hands of Mr. Covey. This kick had the effect of not only weakening Hughes, but Covey also. When he saw Hughes bending over with pain, his courage quailed. He asked me if I meant to persist in my resistance. I told him I did, come what might; that he had used me like a brute for six months, and that I was determined to be used so no longer. With that, he strove to drag me to a stick that was lying just out of the stable door. He meant to knock me down. But just as he was leaning over to get the stick, I seized him with both hands by his collar, and brought him by a sudden snatch to the ground. By this time, Bill came. Covey called upon him for assistance. Bill wanted to know what he could do. Covey said, " Take hold of him, take hold of him!" Bill said his master hired him out to work, and not to help to whip me; so he left Covey and myself to fight our own battle out. We were at it for nearly two hours. Covey at length let me go, puffing and blowing at a great rate, saying that if I had not resisted, he would not have whipped me half so much. The truth was, that he had not whipped me at all. I considered him as getting entirely the worst end of the bargain; for he had drawn no blood from me, but I had from him. The whole six months afterwards, that I spent with Mr. Covey, he never laid the weight of his finger upon me in anger. He would occasionally say, he didn't want to get hold of me again. " No," thought I, " you need not; for you will come off worse than you did before."

This battle with Mr. Covey was the turning-point in my career as a slave. It rekindled the few expiring embers of freedom, and revived within me a sense of my own manhood. It recalled the departed self-confidence, and inspired me again with a determination to be free. The gratification afforded by the triumph was a full compensation for whatever else might follow, even death itself. He only can understand the deep satisfaction which I experienced, who has himself repelled by force the bloody arm of slavery. I felt as I never felt before. It was a glorious resurrection, from the tomb of slavery, to the heaven of freedom. My long-crushed spirit rose, cowardice departed, bold defiance took its place; and I now resolved that, however long I might remain a slave in form, the day had passed forever when I could be a slave in fact. I did not hesitate to let it be known of me, that the white man who expected to succeed in whipping, must also succeed in killing me.

From this time I was never again what might be called fairly whipped, though I remained a slave four years afterwards. I had several fights, but was never whipped.

It was for a long time a matter of surprise to me why Mr. Covey did not immediately have me taken by the constable to the whipping-post, and there regularly whipped for the crime of raising my hand against a white man in defence of myself. And the only explanation I can now think of does not entirely satisfy me; but such as it is, I will give it. Mr. Covey enjoyed the most unbounded reputation for being a first-rate overseer and negro-breaker. It was of considerable importance to him. That reputation was at stake; and had he sent me— a boy about sixteen years old— to the public whipping-post, his reputation would have been lost; so, to save his reputation, he suffered me to go unpunished.

My term of actual service to Mr. Edward Covey ended on Christmas day, 1833. The days between Christmas and New Year's day are allowed as holidays; and, accordingly, we were not required to perform any labor, more than to feed and take care of the stock. This time we regarded as our own, by the grace of our masters; and we therefore used or abused it nearly as we pleased. Those of us who had families at a distance, were generally allowed to spend the whole six days in their society. This time, however, was spent in various ways. The staid, sober, thinking and industrious ones of our number would employ themselves in making corn-brooms, mats, horse-collars, and baskets; and another class of us would spend the time in hunting opossums, hares, and coons. But by far the larger part engaged in such sports and merriments as playing ball, wrestling, running foot-races, fiddling, dancing, and drinking whisky; and this latter mode of spending the time was by far the most agreeable to the feelings of our masters. A slave who would work during the holidays was considered by our masters as scarcely deserving them. He was regarded as one who rejected the favor of his master. It was deemed a disgrace not to get drunk at Christmas; and he was regarded as lazy indeed, who had not provided himself with the necessary means, during the year, to get whisky enough to last him through Christmas.

From what I know of the effect of these holidays upon the slave, I believe them to be among the most effective means in the hands of the slaveholder in keeping down the spirit of insurrection. Were the slaveholders at once to abandon this practice, I have not the slightest doubt it would lead to an immediate insurrection among the slaves. These holidays serve as conductors, or safety-valves, to carry off the rebellious spirit of enslaved humanity. But for these, the slave would be forced up to the wildest desperation; and woe betide the slaveholder, the day he ventures to remove or hinder the operation of those conductors! I warn him that, in such an event, a spirit will go forth in their midst, more to be dreaded than the most appalling earthquake.

The holidays are part and parcel of the gross fraud, wrong, and inhumanity of slavery. They are professedly a custom established by the benevolence of the slaveholders; but I undertake to say, it is the result of selfishness, and one of the grossest frauds committed upon the down-trodden slave. They do not give the slaves this time because they would not like to have their work during its continuance, but because they know it would be unsafe to deprive them of it. This will be seen by the fact, that the slaveholders like to have their slaves spend those days just in such a manner as to make them as glad of their ending as of their beginning. Their object seems to be, to disgust their slaves with freedom, by plunging them into the lowest depths of dissipation. For instance, the slaveholders not only like to see the slave drink of his own accord, but will adopt various plans to make him drunk. One plan is, to make bets on their slaves, as to who can drink the most whisky without getting drunk; and in this way they succeed in getting whole multitudes to drink to excess. Thus, when the slave asks for virtuous freedom, the cunning slaveholder, knowing his ignorance, cheats him with a dose of vicious dissipation, artfully labelled with the name of liberty. The most of us used to drink it down, and the result was just what might be supposed: many of us were led to think that there was little to choose between liberty and slavery. We felt, and very properly too, that we had almost as well be slaves to man as to rum. So, when the holidays ended, we staggered up from the filth of our wallowing, took a long breath, and marched to the field,— feeling, upon the whole, rather glad to go, from what our master had deceived us into a belief was freedom, back to the arms of slavery.

I have said that this mode of treatment is a part of the whole system of fraud and inhumanity of slavery. It is so. The mode here adopted to disgust the slave with freedom, by allowing him to see only the abuse of it, is carried out in other things. For instance, a slave loves molasses; he steals some. His master, in many cases, goes off to town, and buys a large quantity; he returns, takes his whip, and commands the slave to eat the molasses, until the poor fellow is made sick at the very mention of it. The same mode is sometimes adopted to make the slaves refrain from asking for more food than their regular allowance. A slave runs through his allowance, and applies for more. His master is enraged at him; but, not willing to send him off without food, gives him more than is necessary, and compels him to eat it within a given time. Then, if he complains that he cannot eat it, he is said to be satisfied neither full nor fasting, and is whipped for being hard to please! I have an abundance of such illustrations of the same principle, drawn from my own observation, but think the cases I have cited sufficient. The practice is a very common one.

On the first of January, 1834, I left Mr. Covey, and went to live with Mr. William Freeland, who lived about three miles from St. Michael's. I soon found Mr. Freeland a very different man from Mr. Covey. Though not rich, he was what would be called an educated southern gentleman.

Mr. Covey, as I have shown, was a well-trained negro-breaker and slave-driver. The former (slaveholder though he was) seemed to possess some regard for honor, some reverence for justice, and some respect for humanity. The latter seemed totally insensible to all such sentiments. Mr. Freeland had many of the faults peculiar to slaveholders, such as being very passionate and fretful; but I must do him the justice to say, that he was exceedingly free from those degrading vices to which Mr. Covey was constantly addicted. The one was open and frank, and we always knew where to find him. The other was a most artful deceiver, and could be understood only by such as were skilful enough to detect his cunningly-devised frauds. Another advantage I gained in my new master was, he made no pretensions to, or profession of, religion; and this, in my opinion, was truly a great advantage. I assert most unhesitatingly, that the religion of the south is a mere covering for the most horrid crimes,— a justifier of the most appalling barbarity,— a sanctifier of the most hateful frauds,— and a dark shelter under, which the darkest, foulest, grossest, and most infernal deeds of slaveholders find the strongest protection. Were I to be again reduced to the chains of slavery, next to that enslavement, I should regard being the slave of a religious master the greatest calamity that could befall me. For of all slaveholders with whom I have ever met, religious slaveholders are the worst. I have ever found them the meanest and basest, the most cruel and cowardly, of all others. It was my unhappy lot not only to belong to a religious slaveholder, but to live in a community of such religionists. Very near Mr. Freeland lived the Rev. Daniel Weeden, and in the same neighborhood lived the Rev. Rigby Hopkins. These were members and ministers in the Reformed Methodist Church. Mr. Weeden owned, among others, a woman slave, whose name I have forgotten. This woman's back, for weeks, was kept literally raw, made so by the lash of this merciless, *religious* wretch. He used to hire hands. His maxim was, Behave well or behave ill, it is the duty of a master occasionally to whip a slave, to remind him of his master's authority. Such was his theory, and such his practice.

Mr. Hopkins was even worse than Mr. Weeden. His chief boast was his ability to manage slaves. The peculiar feature of his government was that of whipping slaves in advance of deserving it. He always managed to have one or more of his slaves to whip every Monday morning. He did this to alarm their fears, and strike terror into those who escaped. His plan was to whip for the smallest offences, to prevent the commission of large ones.

Mr. Hopkins could always find some excuse for whipping a slave. It would astonish one, unaccustomed to a slaveholding life, to see with what wonderful ease a slaveholder can find things, of which to make occasion to whip a slave. A mere look, word, or motion,— a mistake, accident, or want of power,— are all matters for which a slave may be whipped at any time. Does a slave look dissatisfied? It is said, he has the devil in him, and it must be whipped out. Does he speak loudly when spoken to by his master? Then he is getting high-minded, and should be taken down a button-hole lower. Does he forget to pull off his hat at the approach of a white person? Then he is wanting in reverence, and should be whipped for it. Does he ever venture to vindicate his conduct, when censured for it? Then he is guilty of impudence,—o ne of the greatest crimes of which a slave can be guilty. Does he ever venture to suggest a different mode of doing things from that pointed out by his master? He is indeed presumptuous, and getting above himself; and nothing less than a flogging will do for him. Does he, while ploughing, break a plough,—o r, while hoeing, break a hoe? It is owing to his carelessness, and for it a slave must always be whipped. Mr. Hopkins could always find something of this sort to justify the use of the lash, and he seldom failed to embrace such opportunities. There was not a man in the whole county, with whom the slaves who had the getting their own home, would not prefer to live, rather than with this Rev. Mr. Hopkins. And yet there was not a man any where round, who made higher professions of religion, or was more active in revivals,— more attentive to the class, love-feast, prayer and preaching meetings, or more devotional in his family,— that prayed earlier, later, louder, and longer,— than this same reverend slave-driver, Rigby Hopkins.

But to return to Mr. Freeland, and to my experience while in his employment. He, like Mr. Covey, gave us enough to eat; but, unlike Mr. Covey, he also gave us sufficient time to take our meals. He worked us hard, but always between sunrise and sunset. He required a good deal of work to be done, but gave us good tools with which to work. His farm was large, but he employed hands enough to work it, and with ease, compared with many of his neighbors. My treatment, while in his employment, was heavenly, compared with what I experienced at the hands of Mr. Edward Covey.

Mr. Freeland was himself the owner of but two slaves. Their names were Henry Harris and John Harris. The rest of his hands he hired. These consisted of myself, Sandy Jenkins,* and Handy Caldwell. Henry and John were quite intelligent, and in a very little while after I went there, I succeeded in creating in them a strong desire to learn how to read. This desire soon sprang up in the others also. They very soon mustered up some old spelling-books, and nothing would do but that I must keep a Sabbath school. I agreed to do so, and accordingly devoted my Sundays to teaching these my loved fellow-slaves how to read. Neither of them knew his letters when I went there. Some of the slaves of the neighboring farms found what was going on, and also availed themselves of this little opportunity to learn to read. It was understood, among all who came, that there must be as little display about it as possible. It was necessary to keep our religious masters at St. Michael's unacquainted with the fact, that, instead of spending the Sabbath in wrestling, boxing, and drinking whisky, we were trying to learn how to read the will of God; for they had much rather see us engaged in those degrading sports, than to see us behaving like intellectual, moral, and accountable beings. My blood boils as I think of the bloody manner in which Messrs. Wright Fairbanks and Garrison West, both class-leaders, in connection with many others, rushed in upon us with sticks and stones, and broke up our virtuous little Sabbath school, at St. Michael' s— all calling themselves Christians! humble followers of the Lord Jesus Christ! But I am again digressing.

I held my Sabbath school at the house of a free colored man, whose name I deem it imprudent to mention; for should it be known, it might embarrass him greatly, though the crime of holding the school was committed ten years ago. I had at one time over forty scholars, and those of the right sort, ardently desiring to learn. They were of all ages, though mostly men and women. I look back to those Sundays with an amount of pleasure not to be expressed. They were great days to my soul. The work of instructing my dear fellow-slaves was the sweetest engagement with which I was ever blessed. We loved each other, and to leave them at the close of the Sabbath was a severe cross indeed. When I think that these precious souls are to-day shut up in the prison-house of slavery, my feelings overcome me, and I am almost ready to ask, " Does a righteous

* This is the same man who gave me the roots to prevent my being whipped by Mr. Covey. He was " a clever soul." We used frequently to talk about the fight with Covey, and as often as we did so, he would claim my success as the result of the roots which he gave me. This superstition is very common among the more ignorant slaves. A slave seldom dies but that his death is attributed to trickery.

God govern the universe? and for what does he hold the thunders in his right hand, if not to smite the oppressor, and deliver the spoiled out of the hand of the spoiler?" These dear souls came not to Sabbath school because it was popular to do so, nor did I teach them because it was reputable to be thus engaged. Every moment they spent in that school, they were liable to be taken up, and given thirty-nine lashes. They came because they wished to learn. Their minds had been starved by their cruel masters. They had been shut up in mental darkness. I taught them, because it was the delight of my soul to be doing something that looked like bettering the condition of my race. I kept up my school nearly the whole year I lived with Mr. Freeland; and, beside my Sabbath school, I devoted three evenings in the week, during the winter, to teaching the slaves at home. And I have the happiness to know, that several of those who came to Sabbath school learned how to read; and that one, at least, is now free through my agency.

The year passed off smoothly. It seemed only about half as long as the year which preceded it. I went through it without receiving a single blow. I will give Mr. Freeland the credit of being the best master I ever had, *till I became my own master.* For the ease with which I passed the year, I was, however, somewhat indebted to the society of my fellow-slaves. They were noble souls; they not only possessed loving hearts, but brave ones. We were linked and interlinked with each other. I loved them with a love stronger than any thing I have experienced since. It is sometimes said that we slaves do not love and confide in each other. In answer to this assertion, I can say, I never loved any or confided in any people more than my fellow-slaves, and especially those with whom I lived at Mr. Freeland's. I believe we would have died for each other. We never undertook to do any thing, of any importance, without a mutual consultation. We never moved separately. We were one; and as much so by our tempers and dispositions, as by the mutual hardships to which we were necessarily subjected by our condition as slaves.

At the close of the year 1834, Mr. Freeland again hired me of my master, for the year 1835. But, by this time, I began to want to live *upon free land as well as with Freeland;* and I was no longer content, therefore, to live with him or any other slaveholder. I began, with the commencement of the year, to prepare myself for a final struggle, which should decide my fate one way or the other. My tendency was upward. I was fast approaching manhood, and year after year had passed, and I was still a slave. These thoughts roused me— I must do something. I therefore resolved that 1835 should not pass without witnessing an attempt, on my part, to secure my liberty. But I was not willing to cherish this determination alone. My fellow-slaves were dear to me. I was anxious to have them participate with me in this, my life-giving determination. I therefore, though with great prudence, commenced early to ascertain their views and feelings in regard to their condition, and to imbue their minds with thoughts of freedom. I bent myself to devising ways and means for our escape, and meanwhile strove, on all fitting occasions, to impress them with the gross fraud and inhumanity of slavery. I went first to Henry, next to John, then to the others. I found, in them all, warm hearts and noble spirits. They were ready to hear, and ready to act when a feasible plan should be proposed. This was what I wanted. I talked to them of our want of manhood, if we submitted to our enslavement without at least one noble effort to be free. We met often, and consulted frequently, and told our hopes and fears, recounted the difficulties, real and imagined, which we should be called on to meet. At times we were almost disposed to give up, and try to content ourselves with our wretched lot; at others, we were firm and unbending in our determination to go. Whenever we suggested any plan, there was shrinking— the odds were fearful. Our path was beset with the greatest obstacles; and if we succeeded in gaining the end of it, our right to be free was yet questionable— we were yet liable to be returned to bondage. We could see no spot, this side of the ocean, where we could be free. We knew nothing about Canada.

Our knowledge of the north did not extend farther than New York; and to go there, and be forever harassed with the frightful liability of being returned to slavery— with the certainty of being treated tenfold worse than before— the thought was truly a horrible one, and one which it was not easy to overcome. The case sometimes stood thus: At every gate through which we were to pass, we saw a watchman— at every ferry a guard—o n every bridge a sentinel— and in every wood a patrol. We were hemmed in upon every side. Here were the difficulties, real or imagined— the good to be sought, and the evil to be shunned. On the one hand, there stood slavery, a stern reality, glaring frightfully upon us,— its robes already crimsoned with the blood of millions, and even now feasting itself greedily upon our own flesh. On the other hand, away back in the dim distance, under the flickering light of the north star, behind some craggy hill or snow-covered mountain, stood a doubtful freedom— half frozen—b eckoning us to come and share its hospitality. This in itself was sometimes enough to stagger us; but when we permitted ourselves to survey the road, we were frequently appalled. Upon either side we saw grim death, assuming the most horrid shapes. Now it was starvation, causing us to eat our own flesh;—no w we were contending with the waves, and were drowned;—no w we were overtaken, and torn to pieces by the fangs of the terrible bloodhound. We were stung by scorpions, chased by wild beasts, bitten by snakes, and finally, after having nearly reached the desired spot,—after swimming rivers, encountering wild beasts, sleeping in the woods, suffering hunger and nakedness,— we were overtaken by our pursuers, and, in our resistance, we were shot dead upon the spot! I say, this picture sometimes appalled us, and made us

> " rather bear those ills we had, Than
> fly to others, that we knew not of."

In coming to a fixed determination to run away, we did more than Patrick Henry, when he resolved upon liberty or death. With us it was a doubtful liberty at most, and almost certain death if we failed. For my part, I should prefer death to hopeless bondage.

Sandy, one of our number, gave up the notion, but still encouraged us. Our company then consisted of Henry Harris, John Harris, Henry Bailey, Charles Roberts, and myself. Henry Bailey was my uncle, and belonged to my master. Charles married my aunt: he belonged to my master's father-in-law, Mr. William Hamilton.

The plan we finally concluded upon was, to get a large canoe belonging to Mr. Hamilton, and upon the Saturday night previous to Easter holidays, paddle directly up the Chesapeake Bay. On our arrival at the head of the bay, a distance of seventy or eighty miles from where we lived, it was our purpose to turn our canoe adrift, and follow the guidance of the north star till we got beyond the limits of Maryland. Our reason for taking the water route was, that we were less liable to be suspected as runaways; we hoped to be regarded as fishermen; whereas, if we should take the land route, we should be subjected to interruptions of almost every kind. Any one having a white face, and being so disposed, could stop us, and subject us to examination.

The week before our intended start, I wrote several protections, one for each of us. As well as I can remember, they were in the following words, to wit:—

" THIS is to certify that I, the undersigned, have given the bearer, my servant, full liberty to go to Baltimore, and spend the Easter holidays. Written with mine own hand, &c., 1835.

" WILLIAM HAMILTON
" Near St. Michael's, in Talbot county, Maryland."

We were not going to Baltimore; but, in going up the bay, we went toward Baltimore, and these protections were only intended to protect us while on the bay.

As the time drew near for our departure, our anxiety became more and more intense. It was truly a matter of life and death with us. The strength of our determination was about to be fully tested. At this time, I was very active in explaining every difficulty, removing every doubt, dispelling every fear, and inspiring all with the firmness indispensable to success in our undertaking; assuring them that half was gained the instant we made the move; we had talked long enough; we were now ready to move; if not now, we never should be; and if we did not intend to move now, we had as well fold our arms, sit down, and acknowledge ourselves fit only to be slaves. This, none of us were prepared to acknowledge. Every man stood firm; and at our last meeting, we pledged ourselves afresh, in the most solemn manner, that, at the time appointed, we would certainly start in pursuit of freedom. This was in the middle of the week, at the end of which we were to be off. We went, as usual, to our several fields of labor, but with bosoms highly agitated with thoughts of our truly hazardous undertaking. We tried to conceal our feelings as much as possible; and I think we succeeded very well.

After a painful waiting, the Saturday morning, whose night was to witness our departure, came. I hailed it with joy, bring what of sadness it might. Friday night was a sleepless one for me. I probably felt more anxious than the rest, because I was, by common consent, at the head of the whole affair. The responsibility of success or failure lay heavily upon me. The glory of the one, and the confusion of the other, were alike mine. The first two hours of that morning were such as I never experienced before, and hope never to again. Early in the morning, we went, as usual, to the field. We were spreading manure; and all at once, while thus engaged, I was overwhelmed with an indescribable feeling, in the fulness of which I turned to Sandy, who was near by, and said, " We are betrayed!" " Well," said he, " that thought has this moment struck me." We said no more. I was never more certain of any thing.

The horn was blown as usual, and we went up from the field to the house for breakfast. I went for the form, more than for want of any thing to eat that morning. Just as I got to the house, in looking out at the lane gate, I saw four white men, with two colored men. The white men were on horseback, and the colored ones were walking behind, as if tied. I watched them a few moments till they got up to our lane gate. Here they halted, and tied the colored men to the gate-post. I was not yet certain as to what the matter was. In a few moments, in rode Mr. Hamilton, with a speed betokening great excitement. He came to the door, and inquired if Master William was in. He was told he was at the barn. Mr. Hamilton, without dismounting, rode up to the barn with extraordinary speed. In a few moments, he and Mr. Freeland returned to the house. By this time, the three constables rode up, and in great haste dismounted, tied their horses, and met Master William and Mr. Hamilton returning from the barn; and after talking awhile, they all walked up to the kitchen door. There was no one in the kitchen but myself and John. Henry and Sandy were up at the barn. Mr. Freeland put his head in at the door, and called me by name, saying, there were some gentlemen at the door who wished to see me. I stepped to the door, and inquired what they wanted. They at once seized me, and, without giving me any satisfaction, tied me— lashing my hands closely together. I insisted upon knowing what the matter was. They at length said, that they had learned I had been in a " scrape," and that I was to be examined before my master; and if their information proved false, I should not be hurt.

In a few moments, they succeeded in tying John. They then turned to Henry, who had by this time returned, and commanded him to cross his hands. " I won't!" said Henry, in a firm tone, indicating his readiness to meet the consequences of his refusal. " Won't you?" said Tom Graham, the constable.

" No, I won't!" said Henry, in a still stronger tone. With this, two of the constables pulled out their shining pistols, and swore, by their Creator, that they would make him cross his hands or kill him. Each cocked his pistol, and, with fingers on the trigger, walked up to Henry, saying, at the same time, if he did not cross his hands, they would blow his damned heart out. " Shoot me, shoot me!" said Henry; " you can't kill me but once. Shoot, shoot,— and be damned! *I won't be tied!*" This he said in a tone of loud defiance; and at the same time, with a motion as quick as lightning, he with one single stroke dashed the pistols from the hand of each constable. As he did this, all hands fell upon him, and, after beating him some time, they finally overpowered him, and got him tied.

During the scuffle, I managed, I know not how, to get my pass out, and, without being discovered, put it into the fire. We were all now tied; and just as we were to leave for Easton jail, Betsy Freeland, mother of William Freeland, came to the door with her hands full of biscuits, and divided them between Henry and John. She then delivered herself of a speech, to the following effect:— addressing herself to me, she said, " *You devil! You yellow devil!* it was you that put it into the heads of Henry and John to run away. But for you, you long-legged mulatto devil! Henry nor John would never have thought of such a thing." I made no reply, and was immediately hurried off towards St. Michael's. Just a moment previous to the scuffle with Henry, Mr. Hamilton suggested the propriety of making a search for the protections which he had understood Frederick had written for himself and the rest. But, just at the moment he was about carrying his proposal into effect, his aid was needed in helping to tie Henry; and the excitement attending the scuffle caused them either to forget, or to deem it unsafe, under the circumstances, to search. So we were not yet convicted of the intention to run away.

When we got about half way to St. Michael's, while the constables having us in charge were looking ahead, Henry inquired of me what he should do with his pass. I told him to eat it with his biscuit, and own nothing; and we passed the word around, " *Own nothing;*" and " *Own nothing!*" said we all. Our confidence in each other was unshaken. We were resolved to succeed or fail together, after the calamity had befallen us as much as before. We were now prepared for any thing. We were to be dragged that morning fifteen miles behind horses, and then to be placed in the Easton jail. When we reached St. Michael's, we underwent a sort of examination. We all denied that we ever intended to run away. We did this more to bring out the evidence against us, than from any hope of getting clear of being sold; for, as I have said, we were ready for that. The fact was, we cared but little where we went, so we went together. Our greatest concern was about separation. We dreaded that more than any thing this side of death. We found the evidence against us to be the testimony of one person; our master would not tell who it was; but we came to a unanimous decision among ourselves as to who their informant was. We were sent off to the jail at Easton. When we got there, we were delivered up to the sheriff, Mr. Joseph Graham, and by him placed in jail. Henry, John, and myself, were placed in one room together— Charles, and Henry Bailey, in another. Their object in separating us was to hinder concert.

We had been in jail scarcely twenty minutes, when a swarm of slave traders, and agents for slave traders, flocked into jail to look at us, and to ascertain if we were for sale. Such a set of beings I never saw before! I felt myself surrounded by so many fiends from perdition. A band of pirates never looked more like their father, the devil. They laughed and grinned over us, saying, " Ah, my boys! we have got you, haven't we?" And after taunting us in various ways, they one by one went into an examination of us, with intent to ascertain our value. They would impudently ask us if we would not like to have them for our masters. We would make them no answer, and leave them to find out as best they could. Then they would curse and swear at us, telling us that they could take the devil out of us in a very little while, if we were only in their hands.

While in jail, we found ourselves in much more comfortable quarters than we expected when we went there. We did not get much to eat, nor that which was very good; but we had a good clean room, from the windows of which we could see what was going on in the street, which was very much better than though we had been placed in one of the dark, damp cells. Upon the whole, we got along very well, so far as the jail and its keeper were concerned. Immediately after the holidays were over, contrary to all our expectations, Mr. Hamilton and Mr. Freeland came up to Easton, and took Charles, the two Henrys, and John, out of jail, and carried them home, leaving me alone. I regarded this separation as a final one. It caused me more pain than any thing else in the whole transaction. I was ready for any thing rather than separation. I supposed that they had consulted together, and had decided that, as I was the whole cause of the intention of the others to run away, it was hard to make the innocent suffer with the guilty; and that they had, therefore, concluded to take the others home, and sell me, as a warning to the others that remained. It is due to the noble Henry to say, he seemed almost as reluctant at leaving the prison as at leaving home to come to the prison. But we knew we should, in all probability, be separated, if we were sold; and since he was in their hands, he concluded to go peaceably home.

I was now left to my fate. I was all alone, and within the walls of a stone prison. But a few days before, and I was full of hope. I expected to have been safe in a land of freedom; but now I was covered with gloom, sunk down to the utmost despair. I thought the possibility of freedom was gone. I was kept in this way about one week, at the end of which, Captain Auld, my master, to my surprise and utter astonishment, came up, and took me out, with the intention of sending me, with a gentleman of his acquaintance, into Alabama. But, from some cause or other, he did not send me to Alabama, but concluded to send me back to Baltimore, to live again with his brother Hugh, and to learn a trade.

Thus, after an absence of three years and one month, I was once more permitted to return to my old home at Baltimore. My master sent me away, because there existed against me a very great prejudice in the community, and he feared I might be killed.

In a few weeks after I went to Baltimore, Master Hugh hired me to Mr. William Gardner, an extensive ship-builder, on Fell's Point. I was put there to learn how to calk. It, however, proved a very unfavorable place for the accomplishment of this object. Mr. Gardner was engaged that spring in building two large man-of-war brigs, professedly for the Mexican government. The vessels were to be launched in the July of that year, and in failure thereof, Mr. Gardner was to lose a considerable sum; so that when I entered, all was hurry. There was no time to learn any thing. Every man had to do that which he knew how to do. In entering the shipyard, my orders from Mr. Gardner were, to do whatever the carpenters commanded me to do. This was placing me at the beck and call of about seventy-five men. I was to regard all these as masters. Their word was to be my law. My situation was a most trying one. At times I needed a dozen pair of hands. I was called a dozen ways in the space of a single minute. Three or four voices would strike my ear at the same moment. It was— " Fred., come help me to cant this timber here." — " Fred., come carry this timber yonder." — " Fred., bring that roller here." — " Fred., go get a fresh can of water." — " Fred., come help saw off the end of this timber." — " Fred., go quick, and get the crowbar." — " Fred., hold on the end of this fall." — " Fred., go to the blacksmith's shop, and get a new punch." — " Hurra, Fred.! run and bring me a cold chisel." — " I say, Fred., bear a hand, and get up a fire as quick as lightning under that steam-box." — " Halloo, nigger! come, turn this grindstone." — " Come, come! move, move! and bowse this timber forward." — " I say, darky, blast your eyes, why don't you heat up some pitch?" — " Halloo! halloo! halloo!" (Three voices at the same time.) " Come here!— Go there!— Hold on where you are! Damn you, if you move, I'll knock your brains out!"

This was my school for eight months; and I might have remained there longer, but for a most horrid fight I had with four of the white apprentices, in which my left eye was nearly knocked out, and I was horribly mangled in other respects. The facts in the case were these: Until a very little while after I went there, white and black ship-carpenters worked side by side, and no one seemed to see any impropriety in it. All hands seemed to be very well satisfied. Many of the black carpenters were freemen. Things seemed to be going on very well. All at once, the white carpenters knocked off, and said they would not work with free colored workmen. Their reason for this, as alleged, was, that if free colored carpenters were encouraged, they would soon take the trade into their own hands, and poor white men would be thrown out of employment. They therefore felt called upon at once to put a stop to it. And, taking advantage of Mr. Gardner's necessities, they broke off, swearing they would work no longer, unless he would discharge his black carpenters. Now, though this did not extend to me in form, it did reach me in fact. My fellow-apprentices very soon began to feel it degrading to them to work with me. They began to put on airs, and talk about the " niggers" taking the country, saying we all ought to be killed; and, being encouraged by the journeymen, they commenced making my condition as hard as they could, by hectoring me around, and sometimes striking me. I, of course, kept the vow I made after the fight with Mr. Covey, and struck back again, regardless of consequences; and while I kept them from combining, I succeeded very well; for I could whip the whole of them, taking them separately. They, however, at length combined, and came upon me, armed with sticks, stones, and heavy handspikes. One came in front with a half brick. There was one at each side of me, and one behind me. While I was attending to those in front, and on either side, the one behind ran up with the handspike, and struck me a heavy blow upon the head. It stunned me. I fell, and with this they all ran upon me, and fell to beating me with their fists. I let them lay on for a while, gathering strength. In an instant, I gave a sudden surge, and rose to my hands and knees. Just as I did that, one of their number gave me, with his heavy boot, a powerful kick in the left eye. My eyeball seemed to have burst. When they saw my eye closed, and badly swollen, they left me. With this I seized the handspike, and for a time pursued them. But here the carpenters interfered, and I thought I might as well give it up. It was impossible to stand my hand against so many. All this took place in sight of not less than fifty white ship-carpenters, and not one interposed a friendly word; but some cried, " Kill the damned nigger! Kill him! kill him! He struck a white person." I found my only chance for life was in flight. I succeeded in getting away without an additional blow, and barely so; for to strike a white man is death by Lynch law,— and that was the law in Mr. Gardner's ship-yard; nor is there much of any other out of Mr. Gardner's ship-yard.

I went directly home, and told the story of my wrongs to Master Hugh; and I am happy to say of him, irreligious as he was, his conduct was heavenly, compared with that of his brother Thomas under similar circumstances. He listened attentively to my narration of the circumstances leading to the savage outrage, and gave many proofs of his strong indignation at it. The heart of my once overkind mistress was again melted into pity. My puffed-out eye and blood-covered face moved her to tears. She took a chair by me, washed the blood from my face, and, with a mother's tenderness, bound up my head, covering the wounded eye with a lean piece of fresh beef. It was almost compensation for my suffering to witness, once more, a manifestation of kindness from this, my once affectionate old mistress. Master Hugh was very much enraged. He gave expression to his feelings by pouring out curses upon the heads of those who did the deed. As soon as I got a little the better of my bruises, he took me with him to Esquire Watson's, on Bond Street, to see what could be done about the matter. Mr. Watson inquired who saw the assault committed. Master Hugh told him it was done in Mr. Gardner's ship-yard at midday, where there were a large company of men at work. " As to that," he said, " the deed was done, and there was no question as to who did it." His answer was, he could do nothing in the case, unless some white man would come forward and testify. He could issue no warrant on my word. If I had been killed in the presence of a thousand colored people, their testimony combined would have been insufficient to have arrested one of the murderers. Master Hugh, for once, was compelled to say this state of things was too bad. Of course, it was impossible to get any white man to volunteer his testimony in my behalf, and against the white young men. Even those who may have sympathized with me were not prepared to do this. It required a degree of courage unknown to them to do so; for just at that time, the slightest manifestation of humanity toward a colored person was denounced as abolitionism, and that name subjected its bearer to frightful liabilities. The watchwords of the bloody-minded in that region, and in those days, were, " Damn the abolitionists!" a nd " Damn the niggers!" There was nothing done, and probably nothing would have been done if I had been killed. Such was, and such remains, the state of things in the Christian city of Baltimore.

Master Hugh, finding he could get no redress, refused to let me go back again to Mr. Gardner. He kept me himself, and his wife dressed my wound till I was again restored to health. He then took me into the ship-yard of which he was foreman, in the employment of Mr. Walter Price. There I was immediately set to calking, and very soon learned the art of using my mallet and irons. In the course of one year from the time I left Mr. Gardner's, I was able to command the highest wages given to the most experienced calkers. I was now of some importance to my master. I was bringing him from six to seven dollars per week. I sometimes brought him nine dollars per week: my wages were a dollar and a half a day. After learning how to calk, I sought my own employment, made my own contracts, and collected the money which I earned. My pathway became much more smooth than before; my condition was now much more comfortable. When I could get no calking to do, I did nothing. During these leisure times, those old notions about freedom would steal over me again. When in Mr. Gardner's employment, I was kept in such a perpetual whirl of excitement, I could think of nothing, scarcely, but my life; and in thinking of my life, I almost forgot my liberty. I have observed this in my experience of slavery,— that whenever my condition was improved, instead of its increasing my contentment, it only increased my desire to be free, and set me to thinking of plans to gain my freedom. I have found that, to make a contented slave, it is necessary to make a thoughtless one. It is necessary to darken his moral and mental vision, and, as far as possible, to annihilate the power of reason. He must be able to detect no inconsistencies in slavery; he must be made to feel that slavery is right; and he can be brought to that only when he ceases to be a man.

I was now getting, as I have said, one dollar and fifty cents per day. I contracted for it; I earned it; it was paid to me; it was rightfully my own; yet, upon each returning Saturday night, I was compelled to deliver every cent of that money to Master Hugh. And why? Not because he earned it,—no t because he had any hand in earning it,—no t because I owed it to him,—no r because he possessed the slightest shadow of a right to it; but solely because he had the power to compel me to give it up. The right of the grim-visaged pirate upon the high seas is exactly the same.

CHAPTER XI.

I NOW come to that part of my life during which I planned, and finally succeeded in making, my escape from slavery. But before narrating any of the peculiar circumstances, I deem it proper to make known my intention not to state all the facts connected with the transaction. My reasons for pursuing this course may be understood from the following: First, were I to give a minute statement of all the facts, it is not only possible, but quite probable, that others would thereby be involved in the most embarrassing difficulties. Secondly, such a statement would most undoubtedly induce greater vigilance on the part of slaveholders than has existed heretofore among them; which would, of course, be the means of guarding a door whereby some dear brother bondman might escape his galling chains. I deeply regret the necessity that impels me to suppress any thing of importance connected with my experience in slavery. It would afford me great pleasure indeed, as well as materially add to the interest of my narrative, were I at liberty to gratify a curiosity, which I know exists in the minds of many, by an accurate statement of all the facts pertaining to my most fortunate escape. But I must deprive myself of this pleasure, and the curious of the gratification which such a statement would afford. I would allow myself to suffer under the greatest imputations which evil-minded men might suggest, rather than exculpate myself, and thereby run the hazard of closing the slightest avenue by which a brother slave might clear himself of the chains and fetters of slavery.

I have never approved of the very public manner in which some of our western friends have conducted what they call the *underground railroad,* but which I think, by their open declarations, has been made most emphatically the *upperground railroad*. I honor those good men and women for their noble daring, and applaud them for willingly subjecting themselves to bloody persecution, by openly avowing their participation in the escape of slaves. I, however, can see very little good resulting from such a course, either to themselves or the slaves escaping; while, upon the other hand, I see and feel assured that those open declarations are a positive evil to the slaves remaining, who are seeking to escape. They do nothing towards enlightening the slave, whilst they do much towards enlightening the master. They stimulate him to greater watchfulness, and enhance his power to capture his slave. We owe something to the slave south of the line as well as to those north of it; and in aiding the latter on their way to freedom, we should be careful to do nothing which would be likely to hinder the former from escaping from slavery. I would keep the merciless slaveholder profoundly ignorant of the means of flight adopted by the slave. I would leave him to imagine himself surrounded by myriads of invisible tormentors, ever ready to snatch from his infernal grasp his trembling prey. Let him be left to feel his way in the dark; let darkness commensurate with his crime hover over him; and let him feel that at every step he takes, in pursuit of the flying bondman, he is running the frightful risk of having his hot brains dashed out by an invisible agency. Let us render the tyrant no aid; let us not hold the light by which he can trace the footprints of our flying brother. But enough of this. I will now proceed to the statement of those facts, connected with my escape, for which I am alone responsible, and for which no one can be made to suffer but myself.

In the early part of the year 1838, I became quite restless. I could see no reason why I should, at the end of each week, pour the reward of my toil into the purse of my master. When I carried to him my weekly wages, he would, after counting the money, look me in the face with a robber-like fierceness, and ask, " Is this all?" He was satisfied with nothing less than the last cent. He would, however, when I made him six dollars, sometimes give me six cents, to encourage me. It had the opposite effect. I regarded it as a sort of admission of my right to the whole. The fact that he gave me any part of my wages was proof, to my mind, that he believed me entitled to the whole of them. I always felt worse for having received any thing; for I feared that the giving me a few cents would ease his conscience, and make him feel himself to be a pretty honorable sort of robber. My discontent grew upon me. I was ever on the look-out for means of escape; and, finding no direct means, I determined to try to hire my time, with a view of getting money with which to make my escape. In the spring of 1838, when Master Thomas came to Baltimore to purchase his spring goods, I got an opportunity, and applied to him to allow me to hire my time. He unhesitatingly refused my request, and told me this was another stratagem by which to escape. He told me I could go nowhere but that he could get me; and that, in the event of my running away, he should spare no pains in his efforts to catch me. He exhorted me to content myself, and be obedient. He told me, if I would be happy, I must lay out no plans for the future. He said, if I behaved myself properly, he would take care of me. Indeed, he advised me to complete thoughtlessness of the future, and taught me to depend solely upon him for happiness. He seemed to see fully the pressing necessity of setting aside my intellectual nature, in order to contentment in slavery. But in spite of him, and even in spite of myself, I continued to think, and to think about the injustice of my enslavement, and the means of escape.

About two months after this, I applied to Master Hugh for the privilege of hiring my time. He was not acquainted with the fact that I had applied to Master Thomas, and had been refused. He too, at first, seemed disposed to refuse; but, after some reflection, he granted me the privilege, and proposed the following terms: I was to be allowed all my time, make all contracts with those for whom I worked, and find my own employment; and, in return for this liberty, I was to pay him three dollars at the end of each week; find myself in calking tools, and in board and clothing. My board was two dollars and a half per week. This, with the wear and tear of clothing and calking tools, made my regular expenses about six dollars per week. This amount I was compelled to make up, or relinquish the privilege of hiring my time. Rain or shine, work or no work, at the end of each week the money must be forthcoming, or I must give up my privilege. This arrangement, it will be perceived, was decidedly in my master's favor. It relieved him of all need of looking after me. His money was sure. He received all the benefits of slaveholding without its evils; while I endured all the evils of a slave, and suffered all the care and anxiety of a freeman. I found it a hard bargain. But, hard as it was, I thought it better than the old mode of getting along. It was a step towards freedom to be allowed to bear the responsibilities of a freeman, and I was determined to hold on upon it. I bent myself to the work of making money. I was ready to work at night as well as day, and by the most untiring perseverance and industry, I made enough to meet my expenses, and lay up a little money every week. I went on thus from May till August. Master Hugh then refused to allow me to hire my time longer. The ground for his refusal was a failure on my part, one Saturday night, to pay him for my week's time. This failure was occasioned by my attending a camp meeting about ten miles from Baltimore. During the week, I had entered into an engagement with a number of young friends to start from Baltimore to the camp ground early Saturday evening; and being detained by my employer, I was unable to get down to Master Hugh's without disappointing the company. I knew that Master Hugh was in no special need of the money that night. I therefore decided to go to camp meeting, and upon my return pay him the three dollars. I staid at the camp meeting one day longer than I intended when I left. But as soon as I returned, I called upon him to pay him what he considered his due. I found him very angry; he could scarce restrain his wrath. He said he had a great mind to give me a severe whipping. He wished to know how I dared go out of the city without asking his permission. I told him I hired my time and while I paid him the price which he asked for it, I did not know that I was bound to ask him when and where I should go. This reply troubled him; and, after reflecting a few moments, he turned to me, and said I should hire my time no longer; that the next thing he should know of, I would be running away. Upon the same plea, he told me to bring my tools and clothing home forthwith. I did so; but instead of seeking work, as I had been accustomed to do previously to hiring my time, I spent the whole week without the performance of a single stroke of work. I did this in retaliation. Saturday night, he called upon me as usual for my week's wages. I told him I had no wages; I had done no work that week. Here we were upon the point of coming to blows. He raved, and swore his determination to get hold of me. I did not allow myself a single word; but was resolved, if he laid the weight of his hand upon me, it should be blow for blow. He did not strike me, but told me that he would find me in constant employment in future. I thought the matter over during the next day, Sunday, and finally resolved upon the third day of September, as the day upon which I would make a second attempt to secure my freedom. I now had three weeks during which to prepare for my journey. Early on Monday morning, before Master Hugh had time to make any engagement for me, I went out and got employment of Mr. Butler, at his ship-yard near the drawbridge, upon what is called the City Block, thus making it unnecessary for him to seek employment for me. At the end of the week, I brought him between eight and nine dollars. He seemed very well pleased, and asked why I did not do the same the week before. He little knew what my plans were. My object in working steadily was to remove any suspicion he might entertain of my intent to run away; and in this I succeeded admirably. I suppose he thought I was never better satisfied with my condition than at the very time during which I was planning my escape. The second week passed, and again I carried him my full wages; and so well pleased was he, that he gave me twenty-five cents, (quite a large sum for a slaveholder to give a slave,) and bade me to make a good use of it. I told him I would.

Things went on without very smoothly indeed, but within there was trouble. It is impossible for me to describe my feelings as the time of my contemplated start drew near. I had a number of warm-hearted friends in Baltimore,— friends that I loved almost as I did my life,— and the thought of being separated from them forever was painful beyond expression. It is my opinion that thousands would escape from slavery, who now remain, but for the strong cords of affection that bind them to their friends. The thought of leaving my friends was decidedly the most painful thought with which I had to contend. The love of them was my tender point, and shook my decision more than all things else. Besides the pain of separation, the dread and apprehension of a failure exceeded what I had experienced at my first attempt. The appalling defeat I then sustained returned to torment me. I felt assured that, if I failed in this attempt, my case would be a hopeless one— it would seal my fate as a slave forever. I could not hope to get off with any thing less than the severest punishment, and being placed beyond the means of escape. It required no very vivid imagination to depict the most frightful scenes through which I should have to pass, in case I failed. The wretchedness of slavery, and the blessedness of freedom, were perpetually before me. It was life and death with me. But I remained firm, and, according to my resolution, on the third day of September, 1838, I left my chains, and succeeded in reaching New York without the slightest interruption of any kind. How I did so,— what means I adopted,— what direction I travelled, and by what mode of conveyance,— I must leave unexplained, for the reasons before mentioned.

I have been frequently asked how I felt when I found myself in a free State. I have never been able to answer the question with any satisfaction to myself. It was a moment of the highest excitement I ever experienced. I suppose I felt as one may imagine the unarmed mariner to feel when he is rescued by a friendly man-of-war from the pursuit of a pirate. In writing to a dear friend, immediately after my arrival at New York, I said I felt like one who had escaped a den of hungry lions. This state of mind, however, very soon subsided; and I was again seized with a feeling of great insecurity and loneliness. I was yet liable to be taken back, and subjected to all the tortures of slavery. This in itself was enough to damp the ardor of my enthusiasm. But the loneliness overcame me. There I was in the midst of thousands, and yet a perfect stranger; without home and without friends, in the midst of thousands of my own brethren— children of a common Father, and yet I dared not to unfold to any one of them my sad condition. I was afraid to speak to any one for fear of speaking to the wrong one, and thereby falling into the hands of money-loving kidnappers, whose business it was to lie in wait for the panting fugitive, as the ferocious beasts of the forest lie in wait for their prey. The motto which I adopted when I started from slavery was this— " Trust no man!" I saw in every white man an enemy, and in almost every colored man cause for distrust. It was a most painful situation; and, to understand it, one must needs experience it, or imagine himself in similar circumstances. Let him be a fugitive slave in a strange land— a land given up to be the hunting-ground for slaveholders— whose inhabitants are legalized kidnappers— where he is every moment subjected to the terrible liability of being seized upon by his fellow-men, as the hideous crocodile seizes upon his prey!— I say, let him place himself in my situation— without home or friends— without money or credit— wanting shelter, and no one to give it— wanting bread, and no money to buy it,— and at the same time let him feel that he is pursued by merciless men-hunters, and in total darkness as to what to do, where to go, or where to stay,—p erfectly helpless both as to the means of defence and means of escape,— in the midst of plenty, yet suffering the terrible gnawings of hunger,— in the midst of houses, yet having no home,— among fellow-men, yet feeling as if in the midst of wild beasts, whose greediness to swallow up the trembling and half-famished fugitive is only equalled by that with which the monsters of the deep swallow up the helpless fish upon which they subsist,— I say, let him be placed in this most trying situation,— the situation in which I was placed,— then, and not till then, will he fully appreciate the hardships of, and know how to sympathize with, the toil-worn and whip-scarred fugitive slave.

Thank Heaven, I remained but a short time in this distressed situation. I was relieved from it by the humane hand of Mr. DAVID RUGGLES, whose vigilance, kindness, and perseverance, I shall never forget. I am glad of an opportunity to express, as far as words can, the love and gratitude I bear him. Mr. Ruggles is now afflicted with blindness, and is himself in need of the same kind offices which he was once so forward in the performance of toward others. I had been in New York but a few days, when Mr. Ruggles sought me out, and very kindly took me to his boarding-house at the corner of Church and Lespenard Streets. Mr. Ruggles was then very deeply engaged in the memorable *Darg* case, as well as attending to a number of other fugitive slaves, devising ways and means for their successful escape; and, though watched and hemmed in on almost every side, he seemed to be more than a match for his enemies.

Very soon after I went to Mr. Ruggles, he wished to know of me where I wanted to go; as he deemed it unsafe for me to remain in New York. I told him I was a calker, and should like to go where I could get work. I thought of going to Canada; but he decided against it, and in favor of my going to New Bedford, thinking I should be able to get work there at my trade. At this time, Anna,* my intended wife, came on; for I wrote to her immediately after my arrival at New York, (notwithstanding my homeless, houseless, and helpless condition,) informing her of my successful flight, and wishing her to come on forthwith. In a few days after her arrival, Mr. Ruggles called in the Rev. J. W. C. Pennington, who, in the presence of Mr. Ruggles, Mrs. Michaels, and two or three others, performed the marriage ceremony, and gave us a certificate, of which the following is an exact copy:—

" THIS may certify, that I joined together in holy matrimony Frederick Johnson† and Anna Murray, as man and wife, in the presence of Mr. David Ruggles and Mrs. Michaels.

" JAMES W. C. PENNINGTON.

" *New York, Sept.* 15, 1838."

Upon receiving this certificate, and a five-dollar bill from Mr. Ruggles, I shouldered one part of our baggage, and Anna took up the other, and we set out forthwith to take passage on board of the steamboat John W. Richmond for Newport, on our way to New Bedford. Mr. Ruggles gave me a letter to a Mr. Shaw in Newport, and told me, in case my money did not serve me to New Bedford, to stop in Newport and obtain further assistance; but upon our arrival at Newport, we were so anxious to get to

---

* She was free.

† I had changed my name from Frederick Bailey to that of Johnson.

a place of safety, that, notwithstanding we lacked the necessary money to pay our fare, we decided to take seats in the stage, and promise to pay when we got to New Bedford. We were encouraged to do this by two excellent gentlemen, residents of New Bedford, whose names I afterward ascertained to be Joseph Ricketson and William C. Taber. They seemed at once to understand our circumstances, and gave us such assurance of their friendliness as put us fully at ease in their presence. It was good indeed to meet with such friends, at such a time. Upon reaching New Bedford, we were directed to the house of Mr. Nathan Johnson, by whom we were kindly received, and hospitably provided for. Both Mr. and Mrs. Johnson took a deep and lively interest in our welfare. They proved themselves quite worthy of the name of abolitionists. When the stage-driver found us unable to pay our fare, he held on upon our baggage as security for the debt. I had but to mention the fact to Mr. Johnson, and he forthwith advanced the money.

We now began to feel a degree of safety, and to prepare ourselves for the duties and responsibilities of a life of freedom. On the morning after our arrival at New Bedford, while at the breakfast-table, the question arose as to what name I should be called by. The name given me by my mother was, " Frederick Augustus Washington Bailey." I, however, had dispensed with the two middle names long before I left Maryland so that I was generally known by the name of " Frederick Bailey." I started from Baltimore bearing the name of " Stanley." When I got to New York, I again changed my name to " Frederick Johnson," and thought that would be the last change. But when I got to New Bedford, I found it necessary again to change my name. The reason of this necessity was, that there were so many Johnsons in New Bedford, it was already quite difficult to distinguish between them. I gave Mr. Johnson the privilege of choosing me a name, but told him he must not take from me the name of " Frederick." I must hold on to that, to preserve a sense of my identity. Mr. Johnson had just been reading the " Lady of the Lake," a nd at once suggested that my name be " Douglass." From that time until now I have been called " Frederick Douglass;" and as I am more widely known by that name than by either of the others, I shall continue to use it as my own.

I was quite disappointed at the general appearance of things in New Bedford. The impression which I had received respecting the character and condition of the people of the north, I found to be singularly erroneous. I had very strangely supposed, while in slavery, that few of the comforts, and scarcely any of the luxuries, of life were enjoyed at the north, compared with what were enjoyed by the slaveholders of the south. I probably came to this conclusion from the fact that northern people owned no slaves. I supposed that they were about upon a level with the non-slaveholding population of the south. I knew they were exceedingly poor, and I had been accustomed to regard their poverty as the necessary consequence of their being non-slaveholders. I had somehow imbibed the opinion that, in the absence of slaves, there could be no wealth, and very little refinement. And upon coming to the north, I expected to meet with a rough, hard-handed, and uncultivated population, living in the most Spartan-like simplicity, knowing nothing of the ease, luxury, pomp, and grandeur of southern slaveholders. Such being my conjectures, any one acquainted with the appearance of New Bedford may very readily infer how palpably I must have seen my mistake.

In the afternoon of the day when I reached New Bedford, I visited the wharves, to take a view of the shipping. Here I found myself surrounded with the strongest proofs of wealth. Lying at the wharves, and riding in the stream, I saw many ships of the finest model, in the best order, and of the largest size. Upon the right and left, I was walled in by granite warehouses of the widest dimensions, stowed to their utmost capacity with the necessaries and comforts of life. Added to this, almost every body seemed to be at work, but noiselessly so, compared with what I had been accustomed to in Baltimore. There were no loud songs heard from those engaged in loading and unloading ships. I heard no deep oaths or horrid curses on the laborer. I saw no whipping of men; but all seemed to go smoothly on. Every man appeared to understand his work, and went at it with a sober, yet cheerful earnestness, which betokened the deep interest which he felt in what he was doing, as well as a sense of his own dignity as a man. To me this looked exceedingly strange. From the wharves I strolled around and over the town, gazing with wonder and admiration at the splendid churches, beautiful dwellings, and finely-cultivated gardens; evincing an amount of wealth, comfort, taste, and refinement, such as I had never seen in any part of slaveholding Maryland.

Every thing looked clean, new, and beautiful. I saw few or no dilapidated houses, with poverty-stricken inmates; no half-naked children and barefooted women, such as I had been accustomed to see in Hillsborough,

Easton, St. Michael's, and Baltimore. The people looked more able, stronger, healthier, and happier, than those of Maryland. I was for once made glad by a view of extreme wealth, without being saddened by seeing extreme poverty. But the most astonishing as well as the most interesting thing to me was the condition of the colored people, a great many of whom, like myself, had escaped thither as a refuge from the hunters of men. I found many, who had not been seven years out of their chains, living in finer houses, and evidently enjoying more of the comforts of life, than the average of slaveholders in Maryland. I will venture to assert, that my friend Mr. Nathan Johnson (of whom I can say with a grateful heart, " I was hungry, and he gave me meat; I was thirsty, and he gave me drink; I was a stranger, and he took me in") lived in a neater house; dined at a better table; took, paid for, and read, more newspapers; better understood the moral, religious, and political character of the nation,— than nine tenths of the slaveholders in Talbot county Maryland. Yet Mr. Johnson was a working man. His hands were hardened by toil, and not his alone, but those also of Mrs. Johnson. I found the colored people much more spirited than I had supposed they would be. I found among them a determination to protect each other from the blood-thirsty kidnapper, at all hazards. Soon after my arrival, I was told of a circumstance which illustrated their spirit. A colored man and a fugitive slave were on unfriendly terms. The former was heard to threaten the latter with informing his master of his whereabouts. Straightway a meeting was called among the colored people, under the stereotyped notice, " Business of importance!" The betrayer was invited to attend. The people came at the appointed hour, and organized the meeting by appointing a very religious old gentleman as president, who, I believe, made a prayer, after which he addressed the meeting as follows: " *Friends, we have got him here, and I would recommend that you young men just take him outside the door, and kill him!*" With this, a number of them bolted at him; but they were intercepted by some more timid than themselves, and the betrayer escaped their vengeance, and has not been seen in New Bedford since. I believe there have been no more such threats, and should there be hereafter, I doubt not that death would be the consequence.

I found employment, the third day after my arrival, in stowing a sloop with a load of oil. It was new, dirty, and hard work for me; but I went at it with a glad heart and a willing hand. I was now my own master. It was a happy moment, the rapture of which can be understood only by those who have been slaves. It was the first work, the reward of which was to be entirely my own. There was no Master Hugh standing ready, the moment I earned the money, to rob me of it. I worked that day with a pleasure I had never before experienced. I was at work for myself and newly-married wife. It was to me the starting-point of a new existence. When I got through with that job, I went in pursuit of a job of calking; but such was the strength of prejudice against color, among the white calkers, that they refused to work with me, and of course I could get no employment.* Finding my trade of no immediate benefit, I threw off my calking habiliments, and prepared myself to do any kind of work I could get to do. Mr. Johnson kindly let me have his wood-horse and saw, and I very soon found myself a plenty of work. There was no work too hard— non e too dirty. I was ready to saw wood, shovel coal, carry wood, sweep the chimney, or roll oil casks,— all of which I did for nearly three years in New Bedford, before I became known to the anti-slavery world.

In about four months after I went to New Bedford, there came a young man to me, and inquired if I did not wish to take the " Liberator." I told him I did; but, just having made my escape from slavery, I remarked that I was unable to pay for it then. I, however, finally became a subscriber to it. The paper came, and I read it from week to week with such feelings as it would be quite idle for me to attempt to describe. The paper became my meat and my drink. My soul was set all on fire. Its sympathy for my brethren in bonds— its scathing denunciations of slaveholders— its faithful exposures of slavery— and its powerful attacks upon the upholders of the institution— sent a thrill of joy through my soul, such as I had never felt before!

I had not long been a reader of the " Liberator," before I got a pretty correct idea of the principles, measures and spirit of the anti-slavery reform. I took right hold of the cause. I could do but little; but what I could, I did with a joyful heart, and never felt happier than when in an anti-slavery meeting. I seldom had much to say at the meetings, because what I wanted to say was said so much better by others. But, while attending an anti-slavery convention at Nantucket, on the 11th of August, 1841, I felt strongly moved to speak, and was at the same time much urged to do so by Mr. William C. Coffin, a gentleman who had heard me speak in the

* I am told that colored persons can now get employment at calking in New Bedford— a result of anti-slavery effort.a

colored people's meeting at New Bedford. It was a severe cross, and I took it up reluctantly. The truth was, I felt myself a slave, and the idea of speaking to white people weighed me down. I spoke but a few moments, when I felt a degree of freedom, and said what I desired with considerable ease. From that time until now, I have been engaged in pleading the cause of my brethren— with what success, and with what devotion, I leave those acquainted with my labors to decide.

APPENDIX.

I FIND, since reading over the foregoing Narrative, that I have, in several instances, spoken in such a tone and manner, respecting religion, as may possibly lead those unacquainted with my religious views to suppose me an opponent of all religion. To remove the liability of such misapprehension, I deem it proper to append the following brief explanation. What I have said respecting and against religion, I mean strictly to apply to the *slaveholding religion* of this land, and with no possible reference to Christianity proper; for, between the Christianity of this land, and the Christianity of Christ, I recognize the widest possible difference— so wide, that to receive the one as good, pure, and holy, is of necessity to reject the other as bad, corrupt, and wicked. To be the friend of the one, is of necessity to be the enemy of the other. I love the pure, peaceable, and impartial Christianity of Christ: I therefore hate the corrupt, slaveholding, women-whipping, cradle-plundering, partial and hypocritical Christianity of this land. Indeed, I can see no reason, but the most deceitful one, for calling the religion of this land Christianity. I look upon it as the climax of all misnomers, the boldest of all frauds, and the grossest of all libels. Never was there a clearer case of " stealing the livery of the court of heaven to serve the devil in." I am filled with unutterable loathing when I contemplate the religious pomp and show, together with the horrible inconsistencies, which every where surround me. We have men-stealers for ministers, women-whippers for missionaries, and cradle-plunderers for church members. The man who wields the blood-clotted cowskin during the week fills the pulpit on Sunday, and claims to be a minister of the meek and lowly Jesus. The man who robs me of my earnings at the end of each week meets me as a class-leader on Sunday morning, to show me the way of life, and the path of salvation. He who sells my sister, for purposes of prostitution, stands forth as the pious advocate of purity. He who proclaims it a religious duty to read the Bible denies me the right of learning to read the name of the God who made me. He who is the religious advocate of marriage robs whole millions of its sacred influence, and leaves them to the ravages of wholesale pollution. The warm defender of the sacredness of the family relation is the same that scatters whole families,— sundering husbands and wives, parents and children, sisters and brothers,— leaving the hut vacant, and the hearth desolate. We see the thief preaching against theft, and the adulterer against adultery. We have men sold to build churches, women sold to support the gospel, and babes sold to purchase Bibles for the *poor heathen! all for the glory of God and the good of souls!* The slave auctioneer's bell and the church-going bell chime in with each other, and the bitter cries of the heart-broken slave are drowned in the religious shouts of his pious master. Revivals of religion and revivals in the slave-trade go hand in hand together. The slave prison and the church stand near each other. The clanking of fetters and the rattling of chains in the prison, and the pious psalm and solemn prayer in the church, may be heard at the same time. The dealers in the bodies and souls of men erect their stand in the presence of the pulpit, and they mutually help each other. The dealer gives his blood-stained gold to support the pulpit, and the pulpit, in return, covers his infernal business with the garb of Christianity. Here we have religion and robbery the allies of each other— devils dressed in angels' robes, and hell presenting the semblance of paradise.

" Just God! and these are they,
Who minister at thine altar, God of right!
Men who their hands, with prayer and blessing, lay
On Israel's ark of light.

" What! preach, and kidnap men?
Give thanks, and rob thy own afflicted poor?
Talk of thy glorious liberty, and then
Bolt hard the captive's door?

" What! servants of thy own
Merciful Son, who came to seek and save
The homeless and the outcast, fettering down
The tasked and plundered slave!

" Pilate and Herod friends!
Chief priests and rulers, as of old, combine!

Just God and holy! is that church which lends
Strength to the spoiler thine?"

The Christianity of America is a Christianity, of whose votaries it may be as truly said, as it was of the ancient scribes and Pharisees, " They bind heavy burdens, and grievous to be borne, and lay them on men's shoulders, but they themselves will not move them with one of their fingers. All their works they do for to be seen of men.— They love the uppermost rooms at feasts, and the chief seats in the synagogues, ... and to be called of men, Rabbi, Rabbi.— But woe unto you, scribes and Pharisees, hypocrites! for ye shut up the kingdom of heaven against men; for ye neither go in yourselves, neither suffer ye them that are entering to go in. Ye devour widows' houses, and for a pretence make long prayers; therefore ye shall receive the greater damnation. Ye compass sea and land to make one proselyte, and when he is made, ye make him twofold more the child of hell than yourselves.— Woe unto you, scribes and Pharisees, hypocrites! for ye pay tithe of mint, and anise, and cumin, and have omitted the weightier matters of the law, judgment, mercy, and faith; these ought ye to have done, and not to leave the other undone. Ye blind guides! which strain at a gnat, and swallow a camel. Woe unto you, scribes and Pharisees, hypocrites! for ye make clean the outside of the cup and of the platter; but within, they are full of extortion and excess.— Woe unto you, scribes and Pharisees, hypocrites! for ye are like unto whited sepulchres, which indeed appear beautiful outward, but are within full of dead men's bones, and of all uncleanness. Even so ye also outwardly appear righteous unto men, but within ye are full of hypocrisy and iniquity."

Dark and terrible as is this picture, I hold it to be strictly true of the overwhelming mass of professed Christians in America. They strain at a gnat, and swallow a camel. Could any thing be more true of our churches? They would be shocked at the proposition of fellowshipping a sheep-stealer; and at the same time they hug to their communion a man-stealer, and brand me with being an infidel, if I find fault with them for it. They attend with Pharisaical strictness to the outward forms of religion, and at the same time neglect the weightier matters of the law, judgment, mercy, and faith. They are always ready to sacrifice, but seldom to show mercy. They are they who are represented as professing to love God whom they have not seen, whilst they hate their brother whom they have seen. They love the heathen on the other side of the globe. They can pray for him, pay money to have the Bible put into his hand, and missionaries to instruct him; while they despise and totally neglect the heathen at their own doors.

Such is, very briefly, my view of the religion of this land; and to avoid any misunderstanding, growing out of the use of general terms, I mean by the religion of this land, that which is revealed in the words, deeds, and actions, of those bodies, north and south, calling themselves Christian churches, and yet in union with slaveholders. It is against religion, as presented by these bodies, that I have felt it my duty to testify.

I conclude these remarks by copying the following portrait of the religion of the south, (which is, by communion and fellowship, the religion of the north,) which I soberly affirm is " true to the life," a nd without caricature or the slightest exaggeration. It is said to have been drawn, several years before the present anti-slavery agitation began, by a northern Methodist preacher, who, while residing at the south, had an opportunity to see slaveholding morals, manners, and piety, with his own eyes. " Shall I not visit for these things? saith the Lord. Shall not my soul be avenged on such a nation as this?"

" A PARODY

" Come, saints and sinners, hear me tell
How pious priests whip Jack and Nell,
And women buy and children sell,
And preach all sinners down to hell,
And sing of heavenly union.

" They'll bleat and baa, dona like goats,
Gorge down black sheep, and strain at
motes, Array their backs in fine black coats,
Then seize their negroes by their throats,
And choke, for heavenly union.

" They'll church you if you sip a dram,
And damn you if you steal a lamb;
Yet rob old Tony, Doll, and Sam,
Of human rights, and bread and ham;
Kidnapper's heavenly union.

" They'll loudly talk of Christ's reward,
And bind his image with a cord,
And scold, and swing the lash abhorred,
And sell their brother in the Lord
To handcuffed heavenly union.

" They'll read and sing a sacred song,
And make a prayer both loud and long,
And teach the right and do the wrong,
Hailing the brother, sister throng,
With words of heavenly union.

" We wonder how such saints can sing,
Or praise the Lord upon the wing,
Who roar, and scold, and whip, and sting,
And to their slaves and mammon cling,
In guilty conscience union.

" They'll raise tobacco, corn, and rye,
And drive, and thieve, and cheat, and lie,
And lay up treasures in the sky,
By making switch and cowskin fly,
In hope of heavenly union.

" They'll crack old Tony on the skull,
And preach and roar like Bashan bull,
Or braying ass, of mischief full,
Then seize old Jacob by the wool,
And pull for heavenly union.

" A roaring, ranting, sleek man-thief,
Who lived on mutton, veal, and beef,
Yet never would afford relief
To needy, sable sons of grief,
Was big with heavenly union.

" 'Love not the world,' the preacher said,
And winked his eye, and shook his head;
He seized on Tom, and Dick, and Ned, Cut
short their meat, and clothes, and bread,

Yet still loved heavenly union.

"Another preacher whining spoke
Of One whose heart for sinners broke:
He tied old Nanny to an oak,
And drew the blood at every stroke,
And prayed for heavenly union.

"Two others oped their iron jaws,
And waved their children-stealing paws;
There sat their children in gewgaws;
By stinting negroes' backs and maws,
They kept up heavenly union.

"All good from Jack another takes,
And entertains their flirts and rakes,
Who dress as sleek as glossy snakes,
And cram their mouths with sweetened cakes;
And this goes down for union."

Sincerely and earnestly hoping that this little book may do something toward throwing light on the American slave system, and hastening the glad day of deliverance to the millions of my brethren in bonds— faithfully relying upon the power of truth, love, and justice, for success in my humble efforts— and solemnly pledging myself anew to the sacred cause,— I subscribe myself,

FREDERICK DOUGLASS.

LYNN, *Mass., April* 28, 1845.

THE END.

SOLOMON NORTHUP

TWELVE YEARS A SLAVE

SANAGE
PUBLISHING HOUSE

Solomon Northup (1808 - c. 1864-1875) was an African American carpenter who was born free in Minerva, Essex County, New York, but was bound into slavery later in life for a period of twelve years. He regained his freedom in January 1853.

SOLOMON IN HIS PLANTATION SUIT.

Solomon Northup

"It is a singular coincidence, that Solomon Northup was carried to a plantation in the Red River country - that same region where the scene of Uncle Tom's captivity was laid - and his account of this plantation, and the mode of life there, and some incidents which he describes, form a striking parallel to that history"

Key to Uncle Tom's Cabin, p.174

****

TO

HARRIET BEECHER STOWE,

WHOSE NAME, THROUGHOUT THE WORLD, IS IDENTIFIED WITH

THE GREAT REFORM:

THIS NARRATIVE, AFFORDING ANOTHER

KEY TO UNCLE TOM'S CABIN,

IS RESPECTFULLY DEDICATED.

EPIGRAPH

⊙ ⊙ ⊙

Such dupes are men to custom, and so prone
To reverence what is ancient, and can plead
A course of long observance for its use,
That even servitude, the worst of ills,
Because delivered down from sire to son,
Is kept and guarded as a sacred thing.
But is it fit or can it bear the shock
Of rational discussion, that a man
Compounded and made up, like other men,
Of elements tumultuous, in whom lust
And folly in as ample measure meet,
As in the bosom of the slave he rules,
Should be a despot absolute, and boast
Himself the only freeman of his land?

— Cowper.

EDITOR'S PREFACE

When the editor commenced the preparation of the following narrative, he did not suppose it would reach the size of this volume. In order, however, to present all the facts which have been communicated to him, it has seemed necessary to extend it to its present length.

Many of the statements contained in the following pages are corroborated by abundant evidence—others rest entirely upon Solomon's assertion. That he has adhered strictly to the truth the editor, at least, who has had an opportunity of detecting any contradiction or discrepancy in his statements, is well satisfied. He has invariably repeated the same story without deviating in the slightest particular, and has also carefully perused the manuscript, dictating an alteration wherever the most trivial inaccuracy has appealed.

It was Solomon's fortune, during his captivity, to be owned by several masters. The treatment he received while at the "Pine Woods" shows that among slaveholders there are men of humanity as well of cruelty. Some of them are spoken of with emotions of gratitude—others in a spirit of bitterness. It is believed that the following account of his experience on Bayou Boeuf presents a correct picture of Slavery in all its lights, and shadows, as it now exists in that locality. Unbiased, as he conceives, by any prepossessions or prejudices, the only object of the editor has been to give a faithful history of Solomon Northup's life, as he received it from his lips.

In the accomplishment of that object, he trusts he has succeeded, notwithstanding the numerous faults of style and of expression it may be found to contain.

DAVID WILSON.

WHITEHALL, N. Y., May, 1853.

⊙ ⊙ ⊙

CHAPTER 1. INTRODUCTORY—ANCESTRY—THE NORTHUP FAMILY—BIRTH AND PARENTAGE...

⊙ ⊙ ⊙

Introductory—Ancestry—The Northup Family—Birth And Parentage—Mintus Northup—Marriage With Anne Hampton—Good Resolutions—Champlain Canal— Rafting Excursion To Canada—Farming—The Violin—Cooking—Removal To Saratoga—Parker And Perry—Slaves—And Slavery—The Children—The Beginning Of Sorrow

Having been born a freeman, and for more than thirty years enjoyed the blessings of liberty in a free State–and having at the end of that time been kidnapped and sold into Slavery, where I remained, until happily rescued in the month of January, 1853, after a bondage of twelve years— it has been suggested that an account of my life and fortunes would not be uninteresting to the public.

Since my return to liberty, I have not failed to perceive the increasing interest throughout the Northern States, in regard to the subject of Slavery. Works of fiction, professing to portray its features in their more pleasing as well as more repugnant aspects, have been circulated to an extent unprecedented, and, as I understand, have created a fruitful topic of comment and discussion.

I can speak of Slavery only so far as it came under my own observation—only so far as I have known and experienced it in my own person. My object is, to give a candid and truthful statement of facts, to repeat the story of my life, without exaggeration, leaving it for others to determine, whether even the pages of fiction present a picture of more cruel wrong or a severer bondage.

As far back as I have been able to ascertain, my ancestors on the paternal side were slaves in Rhode Island. They belonged to a family by the name of Northup, one of whom, removing to the State of New York, settled at Hoosic, in Rensselaer county. He brought with him Mintus Northup, my father. On the death of this gentleman, which must have occurred some fifty years ago, my father became free, having been emancipated by a direction in his will.

Henry B. Northup, Esq., of Sandy Hill, a distinguished counselor at law, and the man to whom, under Providence, I am indebted for my present liberty, and my return to the society of my wife and children, is a relative of the family in which my forefathers were thus held to service, and from which they took the name I bear. To this fact may be attributed the persevering interest he has taken in my behalf.

Sometime after my father's liberation, he removed to the town of Minerva, Essex county, N. Y., where I was born, in the month of July, 1808. How long he remained in the latter place I have not the means of definitely ascertaining. From thence he removed to Granville, Washington county, near a place known as Slyborough, where, for some years, he labored on the farm of Clark Northup, also a relative of his old master; from thence he removed to the Alden farm, at Moss Street, a short distance north of the village of Sandy Hill; and from thence to the farm now owned by Russel Pratt, situated on the road leading from Fort Edward to Argyle, where he continued to reside until his death, which took place on the 22d day of November, 1829. He left a widow and two children – myself, and Joseph, an elder brother. The latter is still living in the county of Oswego, near the city of that name; my mother died during the period of my captivity.

Though born a slave, and laboring under the disadvantages to which my unfortunate race is subjected, my father was a man respected for his industry and integrity, as many now living, who well remember him, are ready to testify. His whole life was passed in the peaceful pursuits of agriculture, never seeking employment in those more menial positions, which seem to be especially allotted to the children of Africa. Besides giving us an education surpassing that ordinarily bestowed upon children in our condition, he acquired, by his diligence and economy, a sufficient property qualification to entitle him to the right of suffrage. He was accustomed to speak to us of his early life; and although at all times cherishing the warmest emotions of kindness, and even of affection towards the family, in whose house he had been a bondsman, he nevertheless comprehended the system of Slavery, and dwelt with sorrow on the degradation of his race. He endeavored to imbue our minds with sentiments of morality, and to teach us to place our, trust and confidence in Him who regards the humblest as well as the highest of his creatures. How often since that time has the recollection of his paternal counsels occurred to me, while lying in a slave hut in the distant and sickly regions of Louisiana, smarting with the undeserved wounds which an inhuman master had inflicted, and longing only for the grave which had covered him, to shield me also from the lash of the oppressor. In the church yard at Sandy Hill, an humble stone marks the spot where he reposes, after having worthily performed the duties appertaining to the lowly sphere wherein God had appointed him to walk.

Up to this period I had been principally engaged with my father in the labors of the farm. The leisure hours allowed me were generally either employed over my books, or playing on the violin—an amusement which was the ruling passion of my youth. It has also been the source of consolation since, affording, pleasure to the simple beings with whom my lot was cast, and beguiling my own thoughts, for many hours, from the painful contemplation of my fate.

On Christmas day, 1829, I was married to Anne Hampton, a colored girl then living in the vicinity of our residence. The ceremony was performed at Fort Edward, by Timothy Eddy, Esq., a magistrate of that town, and still a prominent citizen of the place. She had resided a long time at Sandy Hill, with Mr. Baird, proprietor of the Eagle Tavern, and also in the family of Rev. Alexander Proudfit, of Salem. This gentleman for many years had presided over the Presbyterian society at the latter place, and was widely distinguished for his learning and piety. Anne still holds in grateful remembrance the exceeding kindness and the excellent counsels of that good man. She is not able to determine the exact line of her descent, but the blood of three races mingles in her veins. It is difficult to tell whether the red, white, or black predominates. The union of them all, however, in her origin, has given her a singular but pleasing expression, such as is rarely to be seen. Though somewhat resembling, yet she cannot properly be styled a quadroon, a class to which, I have omitted to mention, my mother belonged.

I had just now passed the period of my minority, having reached the age of twenty–one years in the month of July previous. Deprived of the advice and assistance of my father, with a wife dependent upon me for support, I resolved to enter upon a life of industry, and notwithstanding the obstacle of color, and the consciousness of my lowly state, indulged in pleasant dreams of a good time coming, when the possession of some humble habitation, with a few surrounding acres, should reward my labors, and bring me the means of happiness and comfort.

From the time of my marriage to this day the love I have borne my wife has been sincere and unabated, and only those who have felt the glowing tenderness a father cherishes for his offspring, can appreciate my affection for the beloved children which have since been born to us. This much I deem appropriate and necessary to day, in order that those who read these pages, may comprehend the poignancy of those sufferings I have been doomed to bear. Immediately upon our marriage we commenced house–keeping, in the old yellow building then standing at the southern extremity of Fort Edward village, and which has since been transformed into a modern mansion, and lately occupied by Captain Lathrop. It is known as the Fort House. In this building the courts were sometime held after the organization of the county. It was also occupied by Burgoyne in 1777, being situated near the old Fort on the left bank of the Hudson.

During the winter I was employed with others repairing the Champlain Canal, on that section over which William Van Nortwick was superintendent. David McEachron had the immediate charge of the men in whose company I labored. By the time the canal opened in the spring, I was enabled, from the savings of my wages, to purchase a pair of horses, and other things necessarily required in the business of navigation.

Having hired several efficient hands to assist me, I entered into contracts for the transportation of large rafts of timber from Lake Champlain to Troy. Dyer Beckwith and a Mr. Bartemy, of Whitehall, accompanied me on several trips. During the season I became perfectly familiar with the art and mysteries of rafting—a knowledge which afterwards enabled me to render profitable service to a worthy master, and to astonish the simple-witted lumbermen on the banks of the Bayou Boeuf.

In one of my voyages down Lake Champlain, I was induced to make a visit to Canada. Repairing to Montreal, I visited the cathedral and other places of interest in that city, from whence I continued my excursion to Kingston and other towns, obtaining a knowledge of localities, which was also of service to me afterwards, as will appear towards the close of this narrative.

Having completed my contracts on the canal satisfactorily to myself and to my employer, and not wishing to remain idle, now that the navigation of the canal was again suspended, I entered into another contract with Medad Gunn, to cut a large quantity of wood. In this business I was engaged during the winter of 1831–32.

With the return of spring, Anne and myself conceived the project of taking a farm in the neighborhood. I had been accustomed from earliest youth to agricultural labors, and it was an occupation congenial to my tastes. I accordingly entered into arrangements for a part of the old Alden farm, on which my father formerly resided. With one cow, one swine, a yoke of fine oxen I had lately purchased of Lewis Brown, in Hartford, and other personal property and effects, we proceeded to our new home in Kingsbury. That year I planted twenty-five acres of corn, sowed large fields of oats, and commenced farming upon as large a scale as my utmost means would permit. Anne was diligent about the house affairs, while I toiled laboriously in the field.

On this place we continued to reside until 1834. In the winter season I had numerous calls to play on the violin. Wherever the young people assembled to dance, I was almost invariably there. Throughout the surrounding villages my fiddle was notorious. Anne, also, during her long residence at the Eagle Tavern, had become somewhat famous as a cook. During court weeks, and on public occasions, she was employed at high wages in the kitchen at Sherrill's Coffee House.

We always returned home from the performance of these services with money in our pockets, so that, with fiddling, cooking, and farming, we soon found ourselves in the possession of abundance, and, in fact, leading a happy and prosperous life. Well, indeed, would it have been for us had we remained on the farm at Kingsbury, but the time came when the next step was to be taken towards the cruel destiny that awaited me.

In March, 1834, we removed to Saratoga Springs. We occupied a house belonging to Daniel O'Brien, on the north side of Washington street. At that time Isaac Taylor kept a large boarding house, known as Washington Hall, at the north end of Broadway. He employed me to drive a hack, in which capacity I worked for him two years. After this time I was generally employed through the visiting season, as also was Anne, in the United States Hotel, and other public houses of the place. In winter seasons I relied upon my violin, though during the construction of the Troy and Saratoga railroad, I performed many hard days' labor upon it.

I was in the habit, at Saratoga, of purchasing articles necessary for my family at the stores of Mr. Cephas Parker and Mr. William Perry, gentlemen towards whom, for many acts of kindness, I entertained feelings of strong regard. It was for this reason that twelve years afterwards, I caused to be directed to them the letter, which is hereinafter inserted, and which was the means, in the hands of Mr. Northup, of my fortunate deliverance.

While living at the United States Hotel, I frequently met with slaves, who had accompanied their masters from the South. They were always well dressed and well provided for, leading apparently an easy life, with but few of its ordinary troubles to perplex them. Many times they entered into conversation with me on the subject of Slavery. Almost uniformly I found they cherished a secret desire for liberty. Some of them expressed the most ardent anxiety to escape, and consulted me on the best method of effecting it. The fear of punishment, however, which they knew was certain to attend their re–capture and return, in all cases proved sufficient to deter them from the experiment. Having all my life breathed the free air of the North, and conscious that I possessed the same feelings and affections that find a place in the white man's breast; conscious, moreover, of an intelligence equal to that of some men, at least, with a fairer skin. I was too ignorant, perhaps too independent, to conceive how any one could be content to live in the abject condition of a slave. I could not comprehend the justice of that law, or that religion, which upholds or recognizes the principle of Slavery; and never once, I am proud to say, did I fail to counsel any one who came to me, to watch his opportunity, and strike for freedom.

I continued to reside at Saratoga until the spring of 1841. The flattering anticipations which, seven years before, had seduced us from the quiet farm house, on the east side of the Hudson, had not been realized. Though always in comfortable circumstances, we had not prospered. The society and associations at that world–renowned watering place, were not calculated to preserve the simple habits of industry and economy to which I had been accustomed, but, on the contrary, to substitute others in their stead, tending to shiftlessness and extravagance.

At this time we were the parents of three children—Elizabeth, Margaret, and Alonzo. Elizabeth, the eldest, was in her tenth year; Margaret was two years younger, and little Alonzo had just passed his fifth birth–day. They filled our house with gladness. Their young voices were music in our ears. Many an airy castle did their mother and myself build for the little innocents. When not at labor I was always walking with them, clad in their best attire, through the streets and groves of Saratoga. Their presence was my delight, and I clasped them to my bosom with as warm and tender love as if their clouded skins had been as white as snow.

Thus far the history of my life presents nothing whatever unusual—nothing but the common hopes, and loves, and labors of an obscure colored man, making his humble progress in the world. But now I had reached a turning point in my existence—reached the threshold of unutterable wrong, and sorrow, and despair. Now had I approached within the shadow of the cloud, into the thick darkness whereof I was soon to disappear, thenceforward to be hidden from the eyes of all my kindred, and shut out from the sweet light of liberty, for many a weary year.

CHAPTER 2. THE TWO STRANGERS—THE CIRCUS COMPANY...

⊙ ⊙ ⊙

The Two Strangers—The Circus Company—Departure From Saratoga—Ventriloquism And Legerdemain—Journey To New York—Free Papers—Brown And Hamilton—The Haste To Reach The Circus—Arrival In Washington—Funeral Of Harrison—The Sudden Sickness—The Torment Of Thirst—The Receding Light— Insensibility—Chains And Darkness.

ONE morning, towards the latter part of the month of March, 1841, having at that time no particular business to engage my attention, I was walking about the village of Saratoga Springs, thinking to myself where I might obtain some present employment, until the busy season should arrive. Anne, as was her usual custom, had gone over to Sandy Hill, a distance of some twenty miles, to take charge of the Culinary department at Sherrill's Coffee House, during the session of the court. Elizabeth, I think, had accompanied her. Margaret and Alonzo were with their aunt at Saratoga.

On the corner of Congress street and Broadway near the tavern, then, and for aught I know to the contrary, still kept by Mr. Moon, I was met by two gentlemen of respectable appearance, both of whom were entirely unknown to me. I have the impression that they were introduced to me by some one of my acquaintances, but who, I have in vain endeavored to recall, with the remark that I was an expert player on the violin.

At any rate, they immediately entered into conversation on that subject, making numerous inquiries touching my proficiency in that respect. My responses being to all appearances satisfactory, they proposed to engage my services for a short period, stating, at the same time, I was just such a person as their business required. Their names, as they afterwards gave them to me, were Merrill Brown and Abram Hamilton, though whether these were their true appellations, I have strong reasons to doubt. The former was a man apparently forty years of age, somewhat short and thick-set, with a countenance indicating shrewdness and intelligence. He wore a black frock coat and black hat, and said he resided either at Rochester or at Syracuse. The latter was a young man of fair complexion and light eyes, and, I should judge, had not passed the age of twenty-five. He was tall and slender, dressed in a snuff-colored coat, with glossy hat, and vest of elegant pattern. His whole apparel was in the extreme of fashion. His appearance was somewhat effeminate, but prepossessing and there was about him an easy air, that showed he had mingled with the world. They were connected, as they informed me, with a circus company, then in the city of Washington; that they were on their way thither to rejoin it, having left it for a short time to make an excursion northward, for the purpose of seeing the country, and were paying their expenses by an occasional exhibition. They also remarked that they had found much difficulty in procuring music for their entertainments, and that if I would accompany them as far as New-York, they would give me one dollar for each day's services, and three dollars in addition for every night I played at their performances, besides sufficient to pay the expenses of my return from New-York to Saratoga.

I at once accepted the tempting offer, both for the reward it promised, and from a desire to visit the metropolis. They were anxious to leave immediately. Thinking my absence would be brief, I did not deem it necessary to write to Anne whither I had gone; in fact supposing that my return, perhaps, would be as soon as hers. So taking a change of linen and my violin, I was ready to depart. The carriage was brought round—a covered one, drawn by a pair of noble bays, altogether forming an elegant establishment. Their baggage, consisting of three large trunks, was fastened on the rack, and mounting to the driver's seat, while they took their places in the rear, I drove away from Saratoga on the road to Albany, elated with my new position, and happy as I had ever been, on any day in all my life.

We passed through Ballston, and striking the ridge road, as it is called, if my memory correctly serves me, followed it direct to Albany. We reached that city before dark, and stopped at a hotel southward from the Museum. This night I had an opportunity of witnessing one of their performances—the only one, during the whole period I was with them. Hamilton was stationed at the door; I formed the orchestra, while Brown provided the entertainment. It consisted in throwing balls, dancing on the rope, frying pancakes in a hat, causing invisible pigs to squeal, and other like feats of ventriloquism and legerdemain. The audience was extraordinarily sparse, and not of the selectest character at that, and Hamilton's report of the proceeds but a "beggarly account of empty boxes."

Early next morning we renewed our journey. The burden of their conversation now was the expression of an anxiety to reach the circus without delay. They hurried forward, without again stopping to exhibit, and in due course of time, we reached New-York, taking lodgings at a house on the west side of the city, in a street running from Broadway to the river. I supposed my journey was at an end, and expected in a day or two at least, to return to my friends and family at Saratoga. Brown and Hamilton, however, began to importune me to continue with them to Washington. They alleged that immediately on their arrival, now that the summer season was approaching, the circus would set out for the north. They promised me a situation and high wages if I would accompany them. Largely did they expatiate on the advantages that would result to me, and such were the flattering representations they made, that I finally concluded to accept the offer.

The next morning they suggested that, inasmuch as we were about entering a slave State, it would be well, before leaving New-York, to procure free papers. The idea struck me as a prudent one, though I think it would scarcely have occurred to me, had they not proposed it. We proceeded at once to what I understood to be the Custom House. They made oath to certain facts showing I was a free man. A paper was drawn up and handed us, with the direction to take it to the clerk's office. We did so, and the clerk having added something to it, for which he was paid six shillings, we returned again to the Custom House. Some further formalities were gone through with before it was completed, when, paying the officer two dollars, I placed the papers in my pocket, and started with my two friends to our hotel. I thought at the time I must confess, that the papers were scarcely worth the cost of obtaining them— the apprehension of danger to my personal safety never having suggested itself to me in the remotest manner. The clerk, to whom we were directed, I remember, made a memorandum in a large book, which, I presume, is in the office yet. A reference to the entries during the latter part of March, or first of April, 1841, I have no doubt will satisfy the incredulous, at least so far as this particular transaction is concerned.

With the evidence of freedom in my possession, the next day after our arrival in New–York, we crossed the ferry to Jersey City, and took the road to Philadelphia. Here we remained one night, continuing our journey towards Baltimore early in the morning. In due time, we arrived in the latter city, and stopped at a hotel near the railroad depot, either kept by a Mr. Rathbone, or known as the Rathbone House. All the way from New–York, their anxiety to reach the circus seemed to grow more and more intense. We left the carriage at Baltimore, and entering the cars, proceeded to Washington, at which place we arrived just at nightfall, the evening previous to the funeral of General Harrison, and stopped at Gadsby's Hotel, on Pennsylvania Avenue.

After supper they called me to their apartments, and paid me forty–three dollars, a sum greater than my wages amounted to, Which act of generosity was in consequence, they said, of their not having exhibited as often as they had given me to anticipate, during our trip from Saratoga. They moreover informed me that it had been the intention of the circus company to leave Washington the next morning, but that on account of the funeral, they had concluded to remain another day. They were then, as they had been from the time of our first meeting, extremely kind. No opportunity was omitted of addressing me in the language of approbation, while, on the other hand, I was certainly much prepossessed in their favor. I gave them my confidence without reserve, and would freely have trusted them to almost any extent. Their constant conversation and manner towards me—their foresight in suggesting the idea of free papers, and a hundred other little acts, unnecessary to be repeated—all indicated that they were friends indeed, sincerely solicitous for my welfare. I know not but they were. I know not but they were innocent of the great wickedness of which I now believe them guilty. Whether they were accessory to my misfortunes—subtle and inhuman monsters in the shape of men—designedly luring me away from home and family, and liberty, for the sake of gold—those these read these pages will have the same means of determining as myself If they were innocent, my sudden disappearance must have been unaccountable indeed, but revolving in my mind all the attending circumstances, I never yet could indulge, towards them, so charitable a supposition.

After receiving the money from them, of which they appeared to have an abundance, they advised me not to go into the streets that night, inasmuch as I was unacquainted with the customs of the city. Promising to remember their advice, I left them together, and soon after was shown by a colored servant to a sleeping room in the back part of the hotel, on the ground floor. I laid down to rest, thinking of home and wife, and children, and the long distance that stretched between us, until I fell asleep. But no good angel of pity came to my bedside, bidding me to fly— no voice of mercy forewarned me in my dreams of the trials that were just at hand.

The next day there was a great pageant in Washington. The roar of cannon and the tolling of bells filled the air, while many houses were shrouded with crape, and the streets were black with people. As the day advanced, the procession made its appearance, coming slowly through the Avenue, carriage after carriage, in long succession, while thousands upon thousands followed on foot—all moving to the sound of melancholy music. They were bearing the dead body of Harrison to the grave.

From early in the morning, I was constantly in the company of Hamilton and Brown. They were the only persons I knew in Washington. We stood together as the funeral pomp passed by. I remember distinctly how the window glass would break and rattle to the ground, after each report of the cannon they were firing in the burial ground. We went to the Capitol, and walked a long time about the grounds. In the afternoon, they strolled towards the President's House, all the time keeping me near to them, and pointing out various places of interest. As yet, I had seen nothing of the circus. In fact, I had thought of it but little, if at all, amidst the excitement of the day.

My friends, several times during the afternoon, entered drinking saloons, and called for liquor. They were by no means in the habit, however, so far as I knew them, of indulging to excess. On these occasions, after serving themselves, they would pour out a glass and hand it to me. I did not become intoxicated, as may be inferred from what subsequently occurred. Towards evening, and soon after partaking of one of these potations, I began to experience most unpleasant sensations. I felt extremely ill. My head commenced aching—a dull, heavy pain, inexpressibly disagreeable. At the supper table, I was without appetite; the sight and flavor of food was nauseous. About dark the same servant conducted me to the room I had occupied the previous night. Brown and Hamilton advised me to retire, commiserating me kindly, and expressing hopes that I would be better in the morning. Divesting myself of coat and boots merely, I threw myself upon the bed. It was impossible to sleep. The pain in my head continued to increase, until it became almost unbearable. In a short time I became thirsty. My lips were parched. I could think of nothing but water—of lakes and flowing rivers, of brooks where I had stooped to drink, and of the dripping bucket, rising with its cool and overflowing nectar, from the bottom of the well. Towards midnight, as near as I could judge, I arose, unable longer to bear such intensity of thirst. I was a stranger in the house, and knew nothing of its apartments. There was no one up, as

I could observe. Groping about at random, I knew not where, I found the way at last to a kitchen in the basement. Two or three colored servants were moving through it, one of whom, a woman, gave me two glasses of water. It afforded momentary relief, but by the time I had reached my room again, the same burning desire of drink, the same tormenting thirst, had again returned. It was even more torturing than before, as was also the wild pain in my head, if such a thing could be. I was in sore distress—in most excruciating agony! I seemed to stand on the brink of madness! The memory of that night of horrible suffering will follow me to the grave.

In the course of an hour or more after my return from the kitchen, I was conscious of some one entering my room. There seemed to be several—a mingling of various voices,—but how many, or who they were, I cannot tell. Whether Brown and Hamilton were among them, is a mere matter of conjecture. I only remember with any degree of distinctness, that I was told it was necessary to go to a physician and procure medicine, and that pulling on my boots, without coat or hat, I followed them through a long passage-way, or alley, into the open street. It ran out at right angles from Pennsylvania Avenue. On the opposite side there was a light burning in a window. My impression is there were then three persons with me, but it is altogether indefinite and vague, and like the memory of a painful dream. Going towards the light, which I imagined proceeded from a physician's office, and which seemed to recede as I advanced, is the last glimmering recollection I can now recall. From that moment I was insensible. How long I remained in that condition — whether only that night, or many days and nights — I do not know, but when consciousness returned I found myself alone, in utter darkness, and in chains.

The pain in my head had subsided in a measure, but I was very faint and weak. I was sitting upon a low bench, made of rough boards, and without coat or hat. I was hand cuffed. Around my ankles also were a pair of heavy fetters. One end of a chain was fastened to a large ring in the floor, the other to the fetters on my ankles. I tried in vain to stand upon my feet. Waking from such a painful trance, it was some time before I could collect my thoughts. Where was I? What was the meaning of these chains? Where were Brown and Hamilton? What had I done to deserve imprisonment in such a dungeon? I could not comprehend. There was a blank of some indefinite period, preceding my awakening in that lonely place, the events of which the utmost stretch of memory was unable to recall. I listened intently for some sign or sound of life, but nothing broke the oppressive silence, save the clinking of my chains, whenever I chanced to move. I spoke aloud, but the sound of my voice startled me. I felt of my pockets, so far as the fetters would allow—far enough, indeed, to ascertain that I had not only been robbed of liberty, but that my money and free papers were also gone! Then did the idea begin to break upon my mind, at first dim and confused, that I had been kidnapped. But that I thought was incredible. There must have been some misapprehension—some unfortunate mistake. It could not be that a free citizen of New-York, who had wronged no man, nor violated any law, should be dealt with thus inhumanly. The more I contemplated my situation, however, the more I became confirmed in my suspicions. It was a desolate thought, indeed. I felt there was no trust or mercy in unfeeling man, and commending myself to the God of the oppressed, bowed my head upon my fettered hands, and wept most bitterly.

⊙ ⊙ ⊙

CHAPTER 3. PAINFUL MEDITATIONS—JAMES H. BURCH—WILLIAMS' SLAVE PEN...

⊙ ⊙ ⊙

Painful Meditations—James H. Burch—Williams' Slave Pen In Washington—The Lackey, Radrurn—Assert My Freedom—The Anger Of The Trader—The Paddle And Cat-O'—Ninetails—The Whipping—New Acquaintances—Ray, Williams, And Randall—Arrival Of Little Emily And Her Mother In The Pen—Maternal Sorrows— The Story Of Eliza.

SOME three hours elapsed, during which time I remained seated on the low bench, absorbed in painful meditations. At length I heard the crowing of a cock, and soon a distant rumbling sound, as of carriages hurrying through the streets, came to my ears, and I knew that it was day. No ray of light, however, penetrated my prison. Finally, I heard footsteps immediately overhead, as of some one walking to and fro. It occurred to me then that I must be in an underground apartment, and the damp, mouldy odors of the place confirmed the supposition. The noise above continued for at least an hour, when, at last, I heard footsteps approaching from without. A key rattled in the lock—a strong door swung back upon its hinges, admitting a flood of light, and two men entered and stood before me. One of them was a large, powerful man, forty years of age, perhaps, with dark, chestnut-colored hair, slightly interspersed with gray. His face was full, his complexion flush, his features grossly coarse, expressive of nothing but cruelty and cunning. He was about five feet ten inches high, of full habit, and, without prejudice, I must be allowed to say, was a man whose whole appearance was sinister and repugnant. His name was James H. Burch, as I learned afterwards—a well-known slave-dealer in Washington, and then, or lately connected in business, as a partner, with Theophilus Freeman, of New-Orleans. The person who accompanied him was a simple lackey, named Ebenezer Radburn, who acted merely in the capacity of turnkey. Both of these men still live in Washington, or did, at the time of my return through that city from slavery in January last.

The light admitted through the open door enabled me to observe the room in which I was confined. It was about twelve feet square—the walls of solid masonry. The floor was of heavy plank. There was one small window, crossed with great iron bars, with an outside shutter, securely fastened.

An iron-bound door led into an adjoining cell, or vault, wholly destitute of windows, or any means of admitting light. The furniture of the room in which I was, consisted of the wooden bench on which I sat, an old-fashioned, dirty box stove, and besides these, in either cell, there was neither bed, nor blanket, nor any other thing whatever. The door, through which Burch and Radburn entered, led through a small passage, up a flight of steps into a yard, surrounded by a brick wall ten or twelve feet high, immediately in rear of a building of the same width as itself. The yard extended rearward from the house about thirty feet. In one part of the wall there was a strongly ironed door, opening into a narrow, covered passage, leading along one side of the house into the street. The doom of the colored man, upon whom the door leading out of that narrow passage closed, was sealed. The top of the wall supported one end of a roof, which ascended inwards, forming a kind of open shed. Underneath the roof there was a crazy loft all round, where slaves, if so disposed, might sleep at night, or in inclement weather seek shelter from the storm. It was like a farmer's barnyard in most respects, save it was so constructed that the outside world could never see the human cattle that were herded there.

The building to which the yard was attached, was two stories high, fronting on one of the public streets of Washington. Its outside presented only the appearance of a quiet private residence. A stranger looking at it, would never have dreamed of its execrable uses. Strange as it may seem, within plain sight of this same house, looking down from its commanding height upon it, was the Capitol. The voices of patriotic representatives boasting of freedom and equality, and the rattling of the poor slave's chains, almost commingled. A slave pen within the very shadow of the Capitol!

Such is a correct description as it was in 1841, of Williams' slave pen in Washington, in one of the cellars of which I found myself so unaccountably confined.

"Well, my boy, how do you feel now?" said Burch, as he entered through the open door. I replied that I was sick, and inquired the cause of my imprisonment. He answered that I was his slave— that he had bought me, and that he was about to send me to New-Orleans. I asserted, aloud and boldly, that I was a freeman—a resident of Saratoga, where I had a wife and children, who were also free, and that my name was Northup. I complained bitterly of the strange treatment I had received, and threatened, upon my liberation, to have satisfaction for the wrong. He denied that I was free, and with an emphatic oath, declared that I came from Georgia. Again and again I asserted I was no man's slave, and insisted upon his taking off my chains at once. He endeavored to hush me, as if he feared my voice would be overheard. But I would not be silent, and denounced the authors of my imprisonment, whoever they might be, as unmitigated villains. Finding he could not quiet me, he flew into a towering passion. With blasphemous oaths, he called me a black liar, a runaway from Georgia, and every other profane and vulgar epithet that the most indecent fancy could conceive.

During this time Radburn was standing silently by. His business was, to oversee this human, or rather inhuman stable, receiving slaves, feeding, and whipping them, at the rate of two shillings a head per day. Turning to him, Burch ordered the paddle and cat-o'-ninetails to be brought in. He disappeared, and in a few moments returned with these instruments of torture. The paddle, as it is termed in slave-beating parlance, or at least the one with which I first became acquainted, and of which I now speak, was a piece of hard-wood board, eighteen or twenty inches long, moulded to the shape of an old-fashioned pudding stick, or ordinary oar The flattened portion, which was about the size in circumference of two open hands, was bored with a small auger in numerous places. The cat was a large rope of many strands— the strands unraveled, and a knot tied at the extremity of each.

As soon as these formidable whips appeared, I was seized by both of them, and roughly divested of my clothing. My feet, as has been stated, were fastened to the floor. Drawing me over the bench, face downwards, Radburn placed his heavy foot upon the fetters, between my wrists, holding them painfully to the floor. With the paddle, Burch commenced beating me. Blow after blow was inflicted upon my naked body. When his unrelenting arm grew tired, he stopped and asked if I still insisted I was a free man. I did insist upon it, and then the blows were renewed, faster and more energetically, if possible, than before. When again tired, he would repeat the same question, and receiving the same answer, continue his cruel labor. All this time, the incarnate devil was uttering most fiendish oaths. At length the paddle broke, leaving the useless handle in his hand. Still I would not yield. All his brutal blows could not force from my lips the foul lie that I was a slave. Casting madly on the floor the handle of the broken paddle, he seized the rope. This was far more painful than the other. I struggled with all my power, but it was in vain. I prayed for mercy, but my prayer was only answered with imprecations and with stripes. I thought I must die beneath the lashes of the accursed brute. Even now the flesh crawls upon my bones, as I recall the scene. I was all on fire. My sufferings I can compare to nothing else than the burning agonies of hell!

SCENE IN THE SLAVE PEN AT WASHINGTON.

At last I became silent to his repeated questions. I would make no reply. In fact, I was becoming almost unable to speak. Still he plied the lash without stint upon my poor body, until it seemed that the lacerated flesh was stripped from my bones at every stroke. A man with a particle of mercy in his soul would not have beaten even a dog so cruelly. At length Radburn said that it was useless to whip me any more—that I would be sore enough. Thereupon Burch desisted, saying, with an admonitory shake of his fist in my face, and hissing the words through his firm–set teeth, that if ever I dared to utter again that I was entitled to my freedom, that I had been kidnapped, or any thing whatever of the kind, the castigation I had just received was nothing in comparison with what would follow. He swore that he would either conquer or kill me. With these consolatory words, the fetters were taken from my wrists, my feet still remaining fastened to the ring; the shutter of the little barred window, which had been opened, was again closed, and going out, locking the great door behind them, I was left in darkness as before.

In an hour, perhaps two, my heart leaped to my throat, as the key rattled in the door again. I, who had been so lonely, and who had longed so ardently to see some one, I cared not who, now shuddered at the thought of man's approach. A human face was fearful to me, especially a white one. Radburn entered, bringing with him, on a tin plate, a piece of shriveled fried pork, a slice of bread and a cup of water. He asked me how I felt, and remarked that I had received a pretty severe flogging. He remonstrated with me against the propriety of asserting my freedom. In rather a patronizing and confidential manner, he gave it to me as his advice, that the less I said on that subject the better it would be for me. The man evidently endeavored to appear kind—whether touched at the sight of my sad condition, or with the view of silencing, on my part, any further expression of my rights, it is not necessary now to conjecture. He unlocked the festers from my ankles, opened the shutters of the little window, and departed, leaving me again alone.

By this time I had become stiff and sore; my body was covered with blisters, and it was with great pain and difficulty that I could move. From the window I could observe nothing but the roof resting on the adjacent wall. At night I laid down upon the damp, hard floor, without any pillow or covering whatever. Punctually, twice a day, Radburn came in, with his pork, and bread, and water. I had but little appetite, though I was tormented with continual thirst. My wounds would not permit me to remain but a few minutes in any one position; so, sitting, or standing, or moving slowly round, I passed the days and nights. I was heart sick and discouraged. Thoughts of my family, of my wife and children, continually occupied my mind. When sleep overpowered me I dreamed of them— dreamed I was again in Saratoga—that I could see their faces, and hear their voices calling me. Awakening from the pleasant phantasms of sleep to the bitter realities around me, I could but groan and weep. Still my spirit was not broken. I indulged the anticipation of escape, and that speedily. It was impossible, I reasoned, that men could be so unjust as to detain me as a slave, when the truth of my case was known. Burch, ascertaining I was no runaway from Georgia, would certainly let me go. Though suspicions of Brown and Hamilton were not unfrequent, I could not reconcile myself to the idea that they were instrumental to my imprisonment. Surely they would seek me out—they would deliver me from thraldom. Alas! I had not then learned the measure of "man's inhumanity to man," nor to what limitless extent of wickedness he will go for the love of gain.

In the course of several days the outer door was thrown open, allowing me the liberty of the yard. There I found three slaves—one of them a lad of ten years, the others young men of about twenty and twenty-five. I was not long in forming an acquaintance, and learning their names and the particulars of their history.

The eldest was a colored man named Clemens Ray. He had lived in Washington; had driven a hack, and worked in a livery stable there for a long time. He was very intelligent, and fully comprehended his situation. The thought of going south overwhelmed him with grief. Burch had purchased him a few days before, and had placed him there until such time as he was ready to send him to the New-Orleans market. From him I learned for the first time that I was in William's Slave Pen., a place I had never heard of previously. He described to me the uses for which it was designed. I repeated to him the particulars of my unhappy story, but he could only give me the consolation of his sympathy. He also advised me to be silent henceforth on the subject of my freedom for, knowing, the character of Burch, he assured me that it would only be attended with renewed whip-ping. The next eldest was named John Williams. He was raised in Virginia, not far from Washington. Burch had taken him in payment of a debt, and he constantly entertained the hope that his master would redeem him—a hope that was subsequently realized. The lad was a sprightly child, that answered to the name of Randall. Most of the time he was playing about the yard, but occasionally would cry, calling for his mother, and wondering when she would come. His mother's absence seemed to be the great and only grief in his little heart. He was too young to realize his condition, and when the memory of his mother was not in his mind, he amused us with his pleasant pranks.

At night, Ray, Williams, and the boy, slept in the loft of the shed, while I was locked in the cell. Finally we were each provided with blankets, such as are used upon horses—the only bedding I was allowed to have for twelve years afterwards. Ray and Williams asked me many questions about New-York —how colored people were treated there; how they could have homes and families of their own, with none to disturb and oppress them; and Ray, especially, sighed continually for freedom. Such conversations, however, were not in the hearing of Burch, or the keeper Radburn. Aspirations such as these would have brought down the lash upon our backs.

It is necessary in this narrative, in order to present a full and truthful statement of all the principal events in the history of my life, and to portray the institution of Slavery as I have seen and known it, to speak of well-known places, and of many persons who are yet living. I am, and always was, an entire stranger in Washington and its vicinity—aside from Burch and Radburn, knowing no man there, except as I have heard of them through my enslaved companions What I am about to say, if false, can be easily contradicted.

I remained in Williams, slave pen about two weeks. The night previous to my departure a woman was brought in, weeping bitterly, and leading by the hand a little child. They were Randall's mother and half-sister. On meeting them he was overjoyed, clinging to her dress, kissing the child, and exhibiting every demonstration of delight. The mother also clasped him in her arms, embraced him tenderly, and gazed at him fondly through her tears, calling him by many an endearing name.

Emily, the child, was seven or eight years old, of light complexion, and with a face of admirable beauty. Her hair fell in curls around her neck, while the style and richness of her dress, and the neatness of her whole appearance indicated she had been brought up in the midst of wealth. She was a sweet child indeed. The woman also was arrayed in silk, with rings upon her fingers, and golden ornaments suspended from her ears. Her air and manners, the correctness and propriety of her language—all showed evidently, that she had sometime stood above the common level of a slave. She seemed to be amazed at finding herself in such a place as that. It was plainly a sudden and unexpected turn of fortune that had brought her there. Filling the air with her complaining she was hustled, with the children and myself, into the cell. Language can convey but an inadequate impression of the lamentations to which she gave incessant utterance. Throwing herself upon the floor, and encircling the children in her arms, she poured forth such touching words as only maternal love and kindness can suggest. They nestled closely to her, as if there only was there any safety or protection. At last they slept, their heads resting upon her lap. While they slumbered, she smoothed the hair back from their little foreheads, and talked to them all night long. She called them her darlings —her sweet babes—poor innocent things, that knew not the misery they were destined to endure. Soon they would have no mother to comfort them—they would be taken from her. What would become of them? Oh! she could not live away from her little Emmy and her dear boy. They had always been good children, and had such loving ways. It would break her heart, God knew, she said, if they were taken from her; and yet she knew they meant to sell them, and, may be, they would be separated, and could never see each other any more. It was enough to melt heart of stone to listen to the pitiful expressions of that desolate and distracted mother. Her name was Eliza, and this was the story of her life, as she afterwards related it.

She was the slave of a rich man, living in the neighborhood of Washington. She was born, I think she said, on his plantation. Years before, he had fallen into dissipated habits, and quarreled with his wife. In fact, soon after the birth of Randall, they separated. Leaving his wife and daughter in the house they had always occupied, he erected a new one nearby, on the estate. Into this house he brought Eliza; and, on condition of her living with him, she and her children were to be emancipated. She resided with him there nine years, with servants to attend upon her, and provided with every comfort and luxury of life. Emily was his child! Finally, her young mistress, who had always remained with her mother at the homestead, married a Mr. Jacob Brooks. At length, for some cause, (as I gathered from her relation,) beyond Berry's control, a division of his property was made. She and her children fell to the share of Mr. Brooks. During the nine years she had lived with Berry, in consequence of the position she was compelled to occupy, she and Emily had become the object of Mrs. Berry and her daughter's hatred and dislike. Berry himself she represented as a man of naturally a kind heart, who always promised her that she should have her freedom, and who, she had no doubt, would arrant it to her then, if it were only in his power. As soon as they thus came into the possession and control of the daughter, it became very manifest they would not live long together. The sight of Eliza seemed to be odious to Mrs. Brooks; neither could she bear to look upon the child, half-sister, and beautiful as she was!

The day she was led into the pen, Brooks had brought her from the estate into the city, under pretence that the time had come when her free papers were to be executed, in fulfillment of her master's promise. Elated at the prospect of immediate liberty, she decked herself and little Emmy in their best apparel, and accompanied him with a joyful heart. On their arrival in the city, instead of being baptized into the family of freemen, she was delivered to the trader Burch. The paper that was executed was a bill of sale. The hope of years was blasted in a moment. From the hight of most exulting happiness to the utmost depths of wretchedness, she had that day descended. No wonder that she wept, and filled the pen with wailings and expressions of heart-rending woe.

Eliza is now dead. Far up the Red River, where it pours its waters sluggishly through the unhealthy low lands of Louisiana, she rests in the grave at last—the only resting place of the poor slave! How all her fears were realized—how she mourned day and night, and never would be comforted—how, as she predicted, her heart did indeed break, with the burden of maternal sorrow, will be seen as the narrative proceeds.

⊙ ⊙ ⊙

CHAPTER 4. ELIZA'S SORROWS—PREPARATION TO EMBARK—DRIVEN THROUGH...

⊙ ⊙ ⊙

Eliza's Sorrows—Preparation To Embark—Driven Through The Street's Of Washington—Hall, Columbia—The Tomb Of Washington—Clem Ray—The Breakfast On The Steamer—The Happy Birds—Aquia Creek—Fredericksburg—Arrival In Richmond—Goodin And His Slave Pen—Robert, Of Cincinnati—David And His Wife—Mary And Lethe—Clem's Return—His Subsequent Escape To Canada—The Brig Orleans—James H. Burch.

AT intervals during the first night of Eliza's incarceration in the pen, she complained bitterly of Jacob Brook's, her young mistress' husband. She declared that had she been aware of the deception he intended to practice upon her, he never would have brought her there alive. They had chosen the opportunity of getting her away when Master Berry was absent from the plantation. He had always been kind to her. She wished that she could see him; but she knew that even he was unable now to rescue her. Then would she commence weeping again—kissing the sleeping children—talking first to one, then to the other, as they lay in their unconscious slumbers, with their heads upon her lap. So wore the long night away; and when the morning dawned, and night had come again, still she kept mourning on, and would not be consoled.

About midnight following, the cell door opened, and Burch and Radburn entered, with lanterns in their hands. Burch, with an oath, ordered us to roll up our blankets without delay, and get ready to go on board tile boat. He swore we would be left unless we hurried fast. He aroused the children from their slumbers with a rough shake, and said they were d-d sleepy, it appeared. Going out into the yard, he called Clem Ray, ordering him to leave the loft and come into the cell, and bring his blanket with him. When Clem appeared, he placed us side by side, and fastened us together with hand-cuffs—my left hand to his right. John Williams had been taken out a day or two before, his master having redeemed him, greatly to his delight. Clem and I were ordered to march, Eliza and the children following, We were conducted into the yard, from thence into the covered passage, and up a flight of steps through a side door into the upper room, where I had heard the walking to and fro. Its furniture was a stove, a few old chairs, and a long table, covered with papers. It was a white-washed room, without any carpet on the floor, and seemed a sort of office. By one of the windows, I remember, hung a rusty sword, which attracted my attention. Burch's trunk was there. In obedience to his orders, I took hold of one of its handles with my unfettered hand, while he taking hold of the other, we proceeded out of the front door into the street in the same order as we had left the cell.

It was a dark night. All was quiet. I could see lights, or the reflection of them, over towards Pennsylvania Avenue, but there was no one, not even a straggler, to be seen. I was almost resolved to attempt to break away. Had I not been hand-cuffed the attempt would certainly have been made, whatever consequence might have followed. Radburn was in the rear, carrying a large stick, and hurrying up the children as fast as the little ones could walk. So we passed, hand-cuffed and in silence, through the streets of Washington through the Capital of a nation, whose theory of government, we are told, rests on the foundation of man's inalienable right to life, LIBERTY, and the pursuit of happiness! Hail! Columbia, happy land, indeed!

Reaching the steamboat, we were quickly hustled into the hold, among barrels and boxes of freight. A colored servant brought a light, the bell rung, and soon the vessel started down the Potomac, carrying us we knew not where. The bell tolled as we passed the tomb of Washington! Burch, no doubt, with uncovered head, bowed reverently before the sacred ashes of the man who devoted his illustrious life to the liberty of his country.

None of us slept that night but Randall and little Emmy. For the first time Clem Ray was wholly overcome. To him the idea of going south was terrible in the extreme. He was leaving the friends and associations of his youth every thing, that was dear and precious to his heart—in all probability never to return. He and Eliza mingled their tears together, bemoaning their cruel fate. For my own part, difficult as it was, I endeavored to keep up my spirits. I resolved in my mind a hundred plans of escape, and fully determined to make the attempt the first desperate chance that offered. I had by this time become satisfied, however, that my true policy was to say nothing further on the subject of my having been born a freeman. It would but expose me to mal- treatment, and diminish the chances of liberation.

After sunrise in the morning we were called up on deck to breakfast. Burch took our hand-cuffs off, and we sat down to table. He asked Eliza if she would take a dram. She declined, thanking him politely. During the meal we were all silent—not a word passed between us. A mulatto woman who served at table seemed to take an interest in our behalf—told us to cheer up, and not to be so cast down. Breakfast over, the hand-cuffs were restored, and Burch ordered us out on the stern deck. We sat down together on some boxes, still saying nothing in Burch's presence. Occasionally a passenger would walk out to where we were, look at us for a while, then silently return.

It was a very pleasant morning. The fields along the river were covered with verdure, far in advance of what I had been accustomed to see at that season of the year. The sun shone out warmly; the birds were singing in the trees. The happy birds—I envied them. I wished for wings like them, that I might cleave the air to where my birdlings waited vainly for their father's coming, in the cooler region. of the North.

In the forenoon the steamer reached Aquia Creek. There the passengers took stages—Burch and his five slaves occupying one exclusively. He laughed with the children, and at one stopping place went so far as to purchase them a piece of gingerbread. He told me to hold up my head and look smart. That I might, perhaps, get a good master if I behaved myself. I made him no reply. His face was hateful to me, and I could not bear to look upon it. I sat in the corner, cherishing in my heart the hope, not yet extinct, of some day meeting the tyrant on the soil of my native State.

At Fredericksburgh we were transferred from the stage coach to a car, and before dark arrived in Richmond, the chief city of Virginia. At this city we were taken from the cars, and driven through the street to a slave pen, between the railroad depot and the river, kept by a Mr. Goodin. This pen is similar to Williams' in Washington, except it is somewhat larger; and besides, there were two small houses standing at opposite corners within the yard. These houses are usually found within slave yards, being used as rooms for the examination of human chattels by purchasers before concluding a bargain. Unsoundness in a slave, as well as in a horse, detracts materially from his value. If no warranty is given, a close examination is a matter of particular importance to the negro jockey.

We were met at the door of Goodin's yard by that gentleman himself—a short, fat man, with a round, plump face, black hair and whiskers, and a complexion almost as dark as some of his own negroes. He had a hard, stern look, and was perhaps about fifty years of age. Burch and he met with great cordiality. They were evidently old friends. Shaking each other warmly by the hand, Burch remarked he had brought some company, inquired at what time the brig would leave, and was answered that it would probably leave the next day at such an hour. Goodin then turned to me, took hold of my arm, turned me partly round, looked at me sharply with the air of one who considered himself a good judge of property, and as if estimating in his own mind about how much I was worth.

"Well, boy, where did you come from?" Forgetting myself, for a moment, I answered, "From New-York."

"New-York! H—l! what have you been doing up there?" was his astonished interrogatory.

Observing Burch at this moment looking at me with an angry expression that conveyed a meaning it was not difficult to understand, I immediately said, "O, I have only been up that way a piece," in a manner intended to imply that although I might have been as far as New-York, yet I wished it distinctly understood that I did not belong to that free State, nor to any other.

Goodin then turned to Clem, and then to Eliza and the children, examining them severally, and asking various questions. He was pleased with Emily, as was every one who saw the child's sweet countenance. She was not as tidy as when I first beheld her; her hair was now somewhat disheveled; but through its unkempt and soft profusion there still beamed a little face of most surpassing loveliness. "Altogether we were a fair lot—a devilish good lot," he said, enforcing that opinion with more than one emphatic adjective not found in the Christian vocabulary. Thereupon we passed into the yard. Quite a number of slaves, as many as thirty I should say, were moving about, or sitting on benches under the shed. They were all cleanly dressed—the men with hats, the women with handkerchiefs tied about their heads.

Burch and Goodin, after separating from us, walked up the steps at the back part of the main building, and sat down upon the door sill. They entered into conversation, but the subject of it I could not hear. Presently Burch came down into the yard, unfettered me, and led me into one of the small houses.

"You told that man you came from New-York," said he.

I replied, "I told him I had been up as far as New-York, to be sure, but did not tell him I belonged there, nor that I was a freeman. I meant no harm at all, Master Burch. I would not have said it had I thought."

He looked at me a moment as if he was ready to devour me, then turning round went out. In a few minutes he returned. "If ever I hear you say a word about New-York, or about your freedom, I will be the death of you—I will kill you; you may rely on that," he ejaculated fiercely.

I doubt not he understood then better than I did, the danger and the penalty of selling a free man into slavery. He felt the necessity of closing my mouth against the crime he knew he was committing. Of course, my life would not have weighed a feather, in any emergency requiring such a sacrifice. Undoubtedly, he meant precisely what he said.

Under the shed on one side of the yard, there was constructed a rough table, while overhead were sleeping lofts—the same as in the pen at Washington. After partaking at this table of our supper of pork and bread, I was hand-cuffed to a large yellow man, quite stout and fleshy, with a countenance expressive of the utmost melancholy. He was a man of intelligence and information. Chained together, it was not long before we became acquainted with each other's history. His name was Robert. Like myself, he had been born free, and had a wife and two children in Cincinnati. He said he had come south with two men, who had hired him in the city of his residence. Without free papers, he had been seized at Fredericksburgh, placed in confinement, and beaten until he had learned, as I had, the necessity and the policy of silence. He had been in Goodin's pen about three weeks. To this man I became much attached. We could sympathize with, and understand each other. It was with tears and a heavy heart, not many days subsequently, that I saw him die, and looked for the last time upon his lifeless form!

Robert and myself, with Clem, Eliza and her children, slept that night upon our blankets, in one of the small houses in the yard. There were four others, all from the same plantation, who had been sold and were now on their way south, who also occupied it with us. David and his wife, Caroline, both mulattos, were exceedingly affected. They dreaded the thought of being put into the cane and cotton fields; but their greatest source of anxiety was the apprehension of being separated. Mary, a tall, lithe girl, of a most jetty black, was listless and apparently indifferent. Like many of the class, she scarcely knew there was such a word as freedom. Brought up in the ignorance of a brute, she possessed but little more than a brute's intelligence. She was one of those, and there are very many, who fear nothing but their master's lash, and know no further duty than to obey his voice. The other was Lethe. She was of an entirely different character. She had long, straight hair, and bore more the appearance of an Indian than a negro woman. She had sharp and spiteful eyes, and continually gave utterance to the language of hatred and revenge. Her husband had been sold. She knew not where she was. An exchange of masters, she was sure, could not be for the worse. She cared not whither they might carry her. Pointing to the scars upon her face, the desperate creature wished that she might see the day when she could wipe them off in some man's blood!

While we were thus learning the history of each other's wretchedness, Eliza was seated in a corner by herself, singing hymns and praying for her children. Wearied from the loss of so much sleep, I could no longer bear up against the advances of that "sweet restorer," and laying down by the side of Robert, on the floor, soon forgot my troubles, and slept until the dawn of day.

In the morning, having swept the yard, and washed ourselves, under Goodin's superintendence, we were ordered to roll up our blankets, and make ready for the continuance of our journey. Clem Ray was informed that he would go no further, Burch, for some cause, having concluded to carry him back to Washington. He was much rejoiced. Shaking hands, we parted in the slave pen at Richmond, and I have not seen him since. But, much to my surprise, since my return, I learned that he had escaped from bondage, and on his way to the free soil of Canada, lodged one night at the house of my brother-in-law in Saratoga, informing my family of the place and the condition in which he left me.

In the afternoon we were drawn up, two abreast, Robert and myself in advance, and in this order, driven by Burch and Goodin from the yard, through the streets of Richmond to the brig Orleans. She was a vessel of respectable size, full rigged, and freighted principally with tobacco. We were all on board by five o'clock. Burch brought us each a tin cup and a spoon. There were forty of us in the brig, being all, except Clem, that were in the pen.

With a small pocket knife that had not been taken from me, I began cutting the initials of my name upon the tin cup. The others immediately flocked round me, requesting me to mark theirs in a similar manner. In time, I gratified them all, of which they did not appear to be forgetful.

We were all stowed away in the hold at night, and the hatch barred down. We laid on boxes, or where- ever there was room enough to stretch our blankets on the floor.

Burch accompanied us no farther than Richmond, returning from that point to the capital with Clem. Not until the lapse of almost twelve years, to wit, in January last, in the Washington police office, did I set my eyes upon his face again.

James H. Burch was a slave-trader—buying men, women and children at low prices, and selling them at an advance. He was a speculator in human flesh—a disreputable calling—and so considered at the South. For the present he disappears from the scenes recorded in this narrative, but he will appear again before its close, not in the character of a man- whipping tyrant, but as an arrested, cringing criminal in a court of law, that failed to do him justice.

⊙ ⊙ ⊙

CHAPTER 5. ARRIVAL AT NORFOLK—FREDERICK AND MARIA—ARTHUR, THE FREEMAN...

⊙ ⊙ ⊙

Arrival At Norfolk—Frederick And Maria—Arthur, The Freeman Appointed Steward—Jim, Cuffee, And Jenny—The Storm—Bahama Banks—The Calm—The Conspiracy—The Long Boat—The Small-Pox—Death Of Robert—Manning, The Sailor—The Meeting In The Forecastle—The Letter—Arrival At New-Orleans— Arthur's Rescue—Theophilus Freeman, The Consignee—Platt—First Night In The New-Orleans Slave Pen.

AFTER we were all on board, the brig Orleans proceeded down James River. Passing into Chesapeake Bay, we arrived next day opposite the city of Norfolk. While lying at anchor, a lighter approached us from the town, bringing four more slaves. Frederick, a boy of eighteen, had been born a slave, as also had Henry, who was some years older. They had both been house servants in the city. Maria was a rather genteel looting colored girl, with a faultless form, but ignorant and extremely vain. The idea of going to New–Orleans was pleasing to her. She entertained an extravagantly high opinion of her own attractions. Assuming a haughty mien, she declared to her companions, that immediately on our arrival in New–Orleans, she had no doubt, some wealthy single gentleman of good taste would purchase her at once!

But the most prominent of the four, was as a man named Arthur. As the lighter approached, he struggled stoutly with his keepers. It was with main force that he was dragged aboard the brig. He protested, in a loud voice, against the treatment he was receiving, and demanded to be released. His face was swollen, and covered with wounds and bruises, and, indeed, one side of it was a complete raw sore. He was forced, with all haste, down the hatchway into the hold. I caught an outline of his story as he was borne struggling along, of which he afterwards gave me a more full relation, and it was as follows.

He had long resided in the city of Norfolk, and was a free man. He had a family living there, and was a mason by trade. Having been unusually detained, he was returning late one night to his house in the suburbs of the city, when he was attacked by a gang of persons in an unfrequented street. He fought until his strength failed him. Overpowered at last, he was gagged and bound with ropes, and beaten, until he became insensible. For several days they secreted him in the slave pen at Norfolk—a very common establishment, it appears, in the cities of the South. The night before, he had been taken out and put on board the lighter, which, pushing out from shore, had awaited our arrival. For some time he continued his protestations, and was altogether irreconcilable. At length, however, he became silent. He sank into a gloomy and thoughtful mood, and appeared to be counseling with himself. There was in the man's determined face, something that suggested the thought of desperation.

After leaving Norfolk the hand-cuffs were taken off, and during the day we were allowed to remain on deck. The captain selected Robert as his waiter, and I was appointed to superintend the cooking department, and the distribution of food and water. I had three assistants, Jim, Cuffee and Jenny. Jenny's business was to prepare the coffee, which consisted of corn meal scorched in a kettle, boiled and sweetened with molasses. Jim and Cuffee baked the hoe-cake and boiled the bacon.

Standing by a table, formed of a wide board resting on the heads of the barrels, I cut and handed to each a slice of meat and a "dodger" of the bread, and from Jenny's kettle also dipped out for each a cup of the coffee. The use of plates was dispensed with, and their sable fingers took the place of knives and forks. Jim and Cuffee were very demure and attentive to business, somewhat inflated with their situation as second cooks, and without doubt feeling that there was a great responsibility resting on them. I was called steward—a name given me by the captain.

The slaves were fed twice a day, at ten and five o'clock—always receiving the same kind and quantity of fare, and in the same manner as above described. At night we were driven into the hold, and securely fastened down.

Scarcely were we out of sight of land before we were overtaken by a violent storm. The brig rolled and plunged until we feared she would go down. Some were sea-sick, others on their knees praying, while some were fast holding to each other, paralyzed with fear. The sea-sickness rendered the place of our confinement loathsome and disgusting. It would have been a happy thing for most of us—it would have saved the agony of many hundred lashes, and miserable deaths at last—had the compassionate sea snatched us that day from the clutches of remorseless men. The thought of Randall and little Emmy sinking down among the monsters of the deep, is a more pleasant contemplation than to think of them as they are now, perhaps, dragging out lives of unrequited toil.

When in sight of the Bahama Banks, at a place called Old Point Compass, or the Hole in the Wall, we were becalmed three days. There was scarcely a breath of air. The waters of the gulf presented a singularly white appearance, like lime water.

In the order of events, I come now to the relation of an occurrence, which I never call to mind but with sensations of regret. I thank God, who has since permitted me to escape from the thralldom of slavery, that through his merciful interposition I was prevented from imbruing my hands in the blood of his creatures. Let not those who have never been placed in like circumstances, judge me harshly. Until they have been chained and beaten—until they find themselves in the situation I was, borne away from home and family towards a land of bondage—let them refrain from saying what they would not do for liberty. How far I should have been justified in the sight of God and man, it is unnecessary now to speculate upon. It is enough to say that I am able to congratulate myself upon the harmless termination of an affair which threatened, for a time, to be attended with serious results.

Towards evening, on the first day of the calm, Arthur and myself were in the bow of the vessel, seated on the windlass. We were conversing together of the probable destiny that awaited us, and mourning together over our misfortunes. Arthur said, and I agreed with him, that death was far less terrible than the living prospect that was before us. For a long time we talked of our children, our past lives, and of the probabilities of escape. Obtaining possession of the brig was suggested by one of us. We discussed the possibility of our being able, in such an event, to make our way to the harbor of New–York. I knew little of the compass; but the idea of risking the experiment was eagerly entertained. The chances, for and against us, in an encounter with the crew, was canvassed. Who could be relied upon, and who could not, the proper time and manner of the attack, were all talked over and over again. From the moment the plot suggested itself I began to hope. I revolved it constantly in my mind. As difficulty after difficulty arose, some ready conceit was at hand, demonstrating how it could be overcome. While others slept, Arthur and I were maturing, our plans. At length, with much caution, Robert was gradually made acquainted with our intentions. He approved of them at once, and entered into the conspiracy with a zealous spirit. There was not another slave we dared to trust. Brought up in fear and ignorance as they are, it can scarcely be conceived how servilely they will cringe before a white man's look. It was not safe to deposit so bold a secret with any of them, and finally we three resolved to take upon ourselves alone the fearful responsibility of the attempt.

At night, as has been said, we were driven into the hold, and the hatch barred down. How to reach the deck was the first difficulty that presented itself. On the bow of the brig, however I had observed the small boat lying bottom upwards. It occurred to me that by secreting ourselves underneath it, we would not be missed from the crowd, as they were hurried down into the hold at night. I was selected to make the experiment, in order to satisfy ourselves of its feasibility. The next evening, accordingly, after supper, watching my opportunity, I hastily concealed myself beneath it. Lying close upon the deck, I could see what was going on around me, while wholly unperceived myself In the morning, as they came up, I slipped from my hiding place without being observed. The result was entirely satisfactory.

The captain and mate slept in the cabin of the former. From Robert, who had frequent occasion, in his capacity of waiter, to make observations in that quarter we ascertained the exact position of their respective berths. He further informed us that there were always two pistols and a cutlass lying on the table. The crew's cook slept in the cook galley on deck, a sort of vehicle on wheels, that could be moved about as convenience required, while the sailors, numbering only six, either slept in the forecastle, or in hammocks swung among the rigging.

Finally our arrangements were all completed. Arthur and I were to steal silently to the captain's cabin, seize the pistols and cutlass, and as quickly as possible despatch him and the mate. Robert, with a club, was to stand by the door leading from the deck down into the cabin, and, in case of necessity, beat back the sailors, until we could hurry to his assistance. We were to proceed then as circumstances might require. Should the attack be so sudden and successful as to prevent resistance, the hatch was to remain barred down; otherwise the slaves were to be called up, and in the crowd, d, and hurry, and confusion of the time, we resolved to regain our liberty or lose our lives. I was then to assume the unaccustomed place of pilot, and, steering northward, we trusted that some lucky wind might bear us to the soil of freedom.

The mate's name was Biddee, the captain's I cannot now recall, though I rarely ever forget a name once heard. The captain was a small, genteel man, erect and prompt, with a proud bearing, and looked the personification of courage. If he is still living, and these pages should chance to meet his eye, he will learn a fact connected with the voyage of the brig, from Richmond to New-Orleans, in 1841, not entered on his log-book.

We were all prepared, and impatiently waiting an opportunity of putting our designs into execution, when they were frustrated by a sad and unforeseen event. Robert was taken ill. It was soon announced that he had the small-pox. He continued to grow worse, and four days previous to our arrival in New-Orleans he died. One of the sailors sewed him in his blanket, with a large stone from the ballast at his feet, and then laying him on a hatchway, and elevating it with tackles above the railing, the inanimate body of poor Robert was consigned to the white waters of the gulf.

We were all panic-stricken by the appearance of the small-pox. The captain ordered lime to be scattered through the hold, and other prudent precautions to be taken. The death of Robert, however, and the presence of the malady, oppressed me sadly, and I gazed out over the great waste of waters with a spirit that was indeed disconsolate.

An evening or two after Robert's burial, I was leaning on the hatchway near the forecastle, full of desponding thoughts, when a sailor in a kind voice asked me why I was so down-hearted. The tone and manner of the man assured me, and I answered, because I was a freeman, and had been kidnapped. He remarked. that it was enough to make any one down- hearted, and continued to interrogate me until he learned the particulars of my whole history. He was evidently much interested in my behalf, and, in the blunt speech of a sailor, swore he would aid me all he could, if it "split his timbers." I requested him to furnish me pen, ink and paper, in order that I might write to some of my friends. He promised to obtain them—but how I could use them undiscovered was a difficulty. If I could only get into the forecastle while his watch was off, and the other sailors asleep, the thing could be accomplished. The small boat instantly occurred to me. He thought we were not far from the Balize, at the mouth of the Mississippi, and it was necessary that the letter be written soon, or the opportunity would be lost. Accordingly, by arrangement, I managed the next night to secret myself again under the long-boat. His watch was off at twelve. I saw him pass into the forecastle, and in about an hour followed him. He was nodding over a table, half asleep, on which a sickly light was flickering, and on which also was a pen and sheet of paper. As I entered he aroused, beckoned me to a seat beside him, and pointed to the paper. I directed the letter to Henry B. Northup, of Sandy Hill—stating that I had been kidnapped, was then on board the brig Orleans, bound for New-Orleans; that it was then impossible for me to conjecture my ultimate destination, and requesting he would take measures to rescue me. The letter was sealed and directed, and Manning, having read it, promised to deposit it in the New-Orleans post-office. I hastened back to my place under the long-boat, and in the morning, as the slaves came up and were walking round, crept out unnoticed and mingled with them.

My good friend, whose name was John Manning, was an Englishman by birth, and a noble-hearted, generous sailor as ever walked a deck. He had lived in Boston—was a tall, well-built man, about twenty-four years old, with a face somewhat pock-marked, but full of benevolent expression.

Nothing to vary the monotony of our daily life occurred, until we reached New-Orleans. On coming to the levee, and before the vessel was made fast, I saw Manning leap on shore and hurry away into the city. As he started off he looked back over his shoulder significantly, giving me to understand the object of his errand. Presently he returned, and passing close by me, hunched me with his elbow, with a peculiar wink, as much as to say, "it is all right."

The letter, as I have since learned, reached Sandy Hill. Mr. Northup visited Albany and laid it before Governor Seward, but inasmuch as it gave no definite information as to my probable locality, it was not, at that time, deemed advisable to institute measures for my liberation. It was concluded to delay, trusting that a knowledge of where I was might eventually be obtained.

A happy and touching scene was witnessed immediately upon our reaching the levee. Just as Manning left the brig, on his way to the post-office two men came up and called aloud for Arthur. The latter, as he recognized them, was almost crazy with delight. He could hardly be restrained from leaping over the brig's side; and when they met soon after, he grasped them by the hand, and clung to them a long, long time. They were men from Norfolk, who had come on to New-Orleans to rescue him. His kidnappers, they informed him, had been arrested, and were then confined in the Norfolk prison. They conversed a few moments with the captain, and then departed with the rejoicing Arthur.

But in all the crowd that thronged the wharf, there was no one who knew or cared for me. Not one. No familiar voice greeted my ears, nor was there a single face that I had ever seen. Soon Arthur would rejoin his family, and have the satisfaction of seeing his wrongs avenged; my family, alas, should I ever see them more? There was a feeling of utter desolation in my heart, filling it with a despairing and regretful sense, that I had not gone down with Robert to the bottom of the sea.

Very soon traders and consignees came on board. One, a tall, thin-faced man, with light complexion and a little bent, made his appearance, with a paper in his hand. Burch's gang, consisting of myself, Eliza and her children, Harry, Lethe, and some others, who had joined us at Richmond, were consigned to him. This gentleman was Mr. Theophilus Freeman. Reading from his paper, he called, "Platt." No one answered. The name was called again and again, but still there was no reply. Then Lethe was called, then Eliza, then Harry, until the list was finished, each one stepping forward as his or her name was called.

"Captain, where's Platt?" demanded Theophilus Freeman.

The captain was unable to inform him, no one being, on board answering to that name.

"Who shipped *that* nigger?" he again inquired of the captain, pointing to me.

"Burch," replied the captain.

"Your name is Platt—you answer my description. Why don't you come forward?" he demanded of me, in an angry tone.

I informed him that was not my name; that I had never been called by it, but that I had no objection to it as I knew of.

"Well, I will learn you your name," said he; "and so you won't forget it either, by –," he added.

Mr. Theophilus Freeman, by the way, was not a whit behind his partner, Burch, in the matter of blasphemy. On the vessel I had gone by the name of "Steward," and this was the first time I had ever been designated as Platt—the name forwarded by Burch to his consignee. From the vessel I observed the chain–gang at work on the levee. We passed near them as we were driven to Freeman's slave pen. This pen is very similar to Goodin's in Richmond, except the yard was enclosed by plank, standing upright, with ends sharpened, instead of brick walls.

Including us, there were now at least fifty in this pen. Depositing our blankets in one of the small buildings in the yard, and having been called up and fed, we were allowed to saunter about the enclosure until night, when we wrapped our blankets round us and laid down under the shed, or in the loft, or in the open yard, just as each one preferred.

It was but a short time I closed my eyes that night. Thought was busy in my brain. Could it be possible that I was thousands of miles from home—that I had been driven through the streets like a dumb beast— that I had been chained and beaten without mercy—that I was even then herded with a drove of slaves, a slave myself? Were the events of the last few weeks realities indeed?—or was I passing only through the dismal phases of a long, protracted dream? It was no illusion. My cup of sorrow was full to overflowing. Then I lifted up my hands to God, and in the still watches of the night, surrounded by the sleeping forms of my companions, begged for mercy on the poor, forsaken captive. To the Almighty Father of us all—

the freeman and the slave—I poured forth the supplications of a broken spirit, imploring strength from on high to bear up against the burden of my troubles, until the morning light aroused the slumberers, ushering in another day of bondage.

⊙ ⊙ ⊙

CHAPTER 6. FREEMAN'S INDUSTRY—CLEANLINESS AND CLOTHES...

⊙ ⊙ ⊙

Freeman's Industry—Cleanliness And Clothes—Exercising In The Show Room—The Dance—Bob, The Fiddler—Arrival Of Customers—Slaves Examined—The Old Gentleman Of New Orleans—Sale Of David, Caroline And Lethe—Parting Of Randall And Eliza—Small Pox—The Hospital—Recovery And Return To Freeman's Slave Pen—The Purchaser Of Eliza, Harry And Platt—Eliza's Agony On Parting From Little Emily.

The very amiable, pious-hearted Mr. Theophilus Freeman, partner or consignee of James H. Burch, and keeper of the slave pen in New- Orleans, was out among his animals early in the morning. With an occasional kick of the older men and women, and many a sharp crack of the whip about the ears of the younger slaves, it was not long before they were all astir, and wide awake. Mr. Theophilus Freeman bustled about in a very industrious manner, getting his property ready for the sales- room, intending, no doubt, to do that day a rousing business.

In the first place we were required to wash thoroughly, and those with beards, to shave. We were then furnished with a new suit each, cheap, but clean. The men had hat, coat, shirt, pants and shoes; the women frocks of calico, and handkerchiefs to bind about their heads. We were now conducted into a large room in the front part of the building to which the yard was attached, in order to be properly trained, before the admission of customers. The men were arranged on one side of the room, the women on the other. The tallest was placed at the head of the row, then the next tallest, and so on in the order of their respective heights. Emily was at the foot of the line of women. Freeman charged us to remember our places; exhorted us to appear smart and lively, sometimes threatening, and again, holding out various inducements. During the day he exercised us in the art of "looking smart," and of moving to our places with exact precision.

After being fed, in the afternoon, we were again paraded and made to dance. Bob, a colored boy, who had some time belonged to Freeman, played on the violin. Standing near him, I made bold to inquire if he could play the "Virginia Reel." He answered he could not, and asked me if I could play. Replying in the affirmative, he handed me the violin. I struck up a tune, and finished it. Freeman ordered me to continue playing, and seemed well pleased, telling Bob that I far excelled him—a remark that seemed to grieve my musical companion very much.

Next day many customers called to examine Freeman's "new lot." The latter gentleman was very loquacious, dwelling at much length upon our several good points and qualities. He would make us hold up our heads, walk briskly back and forth, while customers would feel of our hands and arms and bodies, turn us about, ask us what we could do, make us open our mouths and show our teeth, precisely as a jockey examines a horse which he is about to barter for or purchase. Sometimes a man or woman was taken back to the small house in the yard, stripped, and inspected more minutely. Scars upon a slave's back were considered evidence of a rebellious or unruly spirit, and hurt his sale.

One old gentleman, who said he wanted a coachman, appeared to take a fancy to me. From his conversation with Burch, I learned he was a resident in the city. I very much desired that he would buy me, because I conceived it would not be difficult to make my escape from New-Orleans on some northern vessel. Freeman asked him fifteen hundred dollars for me. The old gentleman insisted it was too much, as times were very hard. Freeman, however, declared that I was sound and healthy, of a good constitution, and intelligent. He made it a point to enlarge upon my musical attainments. The old gentleman argued quite adroitly that there was nothing extraordinary about the nigger, and finally, to my regret, went out, saying he would call again. During the day, however, a number of sales were made. David and Caroline were purchased together by a Natchez planter. They left us, grinning broadly, and in the most happy state of mind, caused by the fact of their not being separated. Lethe was sold to a planter of Baton Rouge, her eyes flashing with anger as she was led away.

The same man also purchased Randall. The little fellow was made to jump, and run across the floor, and perform many other feats, exhibiting his activity and condition. All the time the trade was going on, Eliza was crying aloud, and wringing her hands. She besought the man not to buy him, unless he also bought herself and Emily. She promised, in that case, to be the most faithful slave that ever lived. The man answered that he could not afford it, and then Eliza burst into a paroxysm of grief, weeping plaintively. Freeman turned round to her, savagely, with his whip in his uplifted hand, ordering her to stop her noise, or he would flog her. He would not have such work—such snivelling; and unless she ceased that minute, he would take her to the yard and give her a hundred lashes. Yes, he would take the nonsense out of her pretty quick—if he didn't, might he be d—d. Eliza shrunk before him, and tried to wipe away her tears, but it was all in vain. She wanted to be with her children, she said, the little time she had to live. All the frowns and threats of Freeman, could not wholly silence the afflicted mother. She kept on begging and beseeching them, most piteously not to separate the three. Over and over again she told them how she loved her boy. A great many times she repeated her former promises—how very faithful and obedient she would be; how hard she would labor day and night, to the last moment of her life, if he would only buy them all together. But it was of no avail; the man could not afford it. The bargain was agreed upon, and Randall must go alone. Then Eliza ran to him; embraced him passionately; kissed him again and again; told him to remember her— all the while her tears falling in the boy's face like rain.

Freeman damned her, calling her a blubbering, bawling wench, and ordered her to go to her place, and behave herself; and be somebody. He swore he wouldn't stand such stuff but a little longer. He would soon give her something to cry about, if she was not mighty careful, and that she might depend upon.

The planter from Baton Rouge, with his new purchases, was ready to depart.

"Don't cry, mama. I will be a good boy. Don't cry," said Randall, looking back, as they passed out of the door.

What has become of the lad, God knows. It was a mournful scene indeed. I would have cried myself if I had dared.

That night, nearly all who came in on the brig Orleans, were taken ill. They complained of violent pain in the head and back. Little Emily—a thing unusual with her—cried constantly. In the morning, a physician was called in, but was unable to determine the nature of our complaint. While examining me, and asking questions touching my symptoms, I gave it as my opinion that it was an attack of smallpox—mentioning the fact of Robert's death as the reason of my belief. It might be so indeed, he thought, and he would send for the head physician of the hospital. Shortly, the head physician came—a small, light-haired man, whom they called Dr. Carr. He pronounced it small-pox, whereupon there was much alarm throughout the yard. Soon after Dr. Carr left, Eliza, Emmy, Harry and myself were put into a hack and driven to the hospital a large white marble building, standing on the outskirts of the city. Harry and I were placed in a room in one of the upper stories. I became very sick. For three days I was entirely blind. While lying in this state one day, Bob came in, saying to Dr. Carr that Freeman had sent him over to inquire how we were getting on. Tell him, said the doctor, that Platt is very bad, but that if he survives until nine o'clock, he may recover.

I expected to die. Though there was little in the prospect before me worth living for, the near approach of death appalled me. I thought I could have been resigned to yield up my life in the bosom of my family, but to expire in the midst of strangers, under such circumstances, was a bitter reflection.

There were a great number in the hospital, of both sexes, and of all ages. In the rear of the building coffins were manufactured. When one died, the bell tolled—a signal to the undertaker to come and bear away the body to the potter's field. Many times, each day and night, the tolling bell sent forth its melancholy voice, announcing another death. But my time had not yet come. The crisis having passed, I began to revive, and at the end of two weeks and two days, returned with Harry to the pen, bearing upon my face the effects of the malady, which to this day continues to disfigure it. Eliza and Emily were also brought back next day in a hack, and again were we paraded in the sales-room, for the inspection and examination of purchasers. I still indulged the hope that the old gentleman in search of a coachman would call again, as he had promised, and purchase me. In that event I felt an abiding confidence that I would soon regain my liberty. Customer after customer entered, but the old gentleman never made his appearance.

At length, one day, while we were in the yard, Freeman came out and ordered us to our places, in the great room. A gentleman was waiting for us as we entered, and inasmuch as he will be often mentioned in the progress of this narrative, a description of his personal appearance, and my estimation of his character, at first sight, may not be out of place.

He was a man above the ordinary height, somewhat bent and stooping forward. He was a good-looking man, and appeared to have reached about the middle age of life. There was nothing repulsive in his presence; but on the other hand, there was something cheerful and attractive in his face, and in his tone of voice. The finer elements were all kindly mingled in his breast, as any one could see. He moved about among us, asking many questions, as to what we could do, and what labor we had been accustomed to; if we thought we would like to live with him, and would be good boys if he would buy us, and other interrogatories of like character.

After some further inspection, and conversation touching prices, he finally offered Freeman one thousand dollars for me, nine hundred for Harry, and seven hundred for Eliza. Whether the small-pox had depreciated our value, or from what cause Freeman had concluded to fall five hundred dollars from the price I was before held at, I cannot say. At any rate, after a little shrewd reflection, he announced his acceptance of the offer.

As soon as Eliza heard it, she was in an agony again. By this time she had become haggard and hollow-eyed with sickness and with sorrow. It would be a relief if I could consistently pass over in silence the scene that now ensued. It recalls memories more mournful and affecting than any language can portray. I have seen mothers kissing for the last time the faces of their dead offspring; I have seen them looking down into the grave, as the earth fell with a dull sound upon their coffins, hiding them from their eyes forever; but never have I seen such an exhibition of intense, unmeasured, and unbounded grief, as when Eliza was parted from her child. She broke from her place in the line of women, and rushing down where Emily was standing, caught her in her arms. The child, sensible of some impending danger, instinctively fastened her hands around her mother's neck, and nestled her little head upon her bosom. Freeman sternly ordered her to be quiet, but she did not heed him. He caught her by the arm and pulled her rudely, but she only clung the closer to the child. Then, with a volley of great oaths, he struck her such a heartless blow, that she staggered backward, and was like to fall.

Oh! how piteously then did she beseech and beg and pray that they might not be separated. Why could they not be purchased together? Why not let her have one of her dear children? "Mercy, mercy, master!" she cried, falling on her knees. "Please, master, buy Emily. I can never work any if she is taken from me; I will die."

SEPERATION OF ELIZA AND HER LAST CHILD.

Freeman interfered again, but, disregarding him, she still plead most earnestly, telling how Randall had been taken from her—how she never him see him again, and now it was too bad—oh, God! it was too bad, too cruel, to take her away from Emily—her pride—her only darling, that could not live, it was so young, without its mother!

Finally, after much more of supplication, the purchaser of Eliza stepped forward, evidently affected, and said to Freeman he would buy Emily, and asked him what her price was.

"What is her *price*? Buy her?" was the responsive interrogatory of Theophilus Freeman. And instantly answering his own inquiry, he added, "I won't sell her. She's not for sale."

The man remarked he was not in need of one so young—that it would be of no profit to him, but since the mother was so fond of her, rather than see them separated, he would pay a reasonable price. But to this humane proposal Freeman was entirely deaf. He would not sell her then on any account whatever. There were heaps and piles of money to be made of her, he said, when she was a few years older. There were men enough in New-Orleans who would give five thousand dollars for such an extra, handsome, fancy piece as Emily would be, rather than not get her. No, no, he would not sell her then. She was a beauty—a picture—a doll—one of the regular bloods—none of your thick-lipped, bullet-headed, cotton-picking niggers—if she was might he be d—d.

When Eliza heard Freeman's determination not to part with Emily, she became absolutely frantic.

"I will *not* go without her. They shall not take her from me," she fairly shrieked, her shrieks commingling with the loud and angry voice of Freeman, commanding her to be silent.

Meantime Harry and myself had been to the yard and returned with our blankets, and were at the front door ready to leave. Our purchaser stood near us, gazing at Eliza with an expression indicative of regret at having bought her at the expense of so much sorrow. We waited some time, when, finally, Freeman, out of patience, tore Emily from her mother by main force, the two clinging to each other with all their might.

"Don't leave me, mama—don't leave me," screamed the child, as its mother was pushed harshly forward; "Don't leave me—come back, mama," she still cried, stretching forth her little arms imploringly. But she cried in vain. Out of the door and into the street we were quickly hurried. Still we could hear her calling to her mother, "Come back—don't leave me—come back, mama," until her infant voice grew faint and still more faint, and gradually died away as distance intervened, and finally was wholly lost.

Eliza never after saw or heard of Emily or Randall. Day nor night, however, were they ever absent from her memory. In the cotton field, in the cabin, always and everywhere, she was talking of them—often to them, as if they were actually present. Only when absorbed in that illusion, or asleep, did she ever have a moment's comfort afterwards.

She was no common slave, as has been said. To a large share of natural intelligence which she possessed, was added a general knowledge and information on most subjects. She had enjoyed opportunities such as are afforded to very few of her oppressed class. She had been lifted up into the regions of a higher life. Freedom—freedom for herself and for her offspring, for many years had been her cloud by day, her pillar of fire by night. In her pilgrimage through the wilderness of bondage, with eyes fixed upon that hope-inspiring beacon, she had at length ascended to "the top of Pisgah," and beheld "the land of promise." In an unexpected moment she was utterly overwhelmed with disappointment and despair. The glorious vision of liberty faded from her sight as they led her away into captivity. Now "she weepeth sore in the night, and tears are on her cheeks, all her friends have dealt treacherously with her, they have become her enemies."

⊙ ⊙ ⊙

CHAPTER 7. THE STEAMBOAT RODOLPH— DEPARTURE FROM NEW-ORLEANS...

⊙ ⊙ ⊙

The Steamboat Rodolph—Departure From New-Orleans—William Ford—Arrival At Alexandria, On Red River—Resolutions—The Great Pine Woods—Wild Cattle— Martin's Summer Residence—The Texas Road—Arrival At Master Ford's—Rose— Mistress Ford—Sally, And Her Children—John, The Cook—Walter, Sam, And Antony—The Mills On Indian Creek—Sabbath Days—Sam's Conversion—The Profit Of Kindness—Rafting—Adam Taydem, The Little White Man—Cascalla And His Tribe—The Indian Ball—John Tibeats—The Storm Approaching.

ON leaving, the New–Orleans slave pen, Harry and I followed our new master through the streets, while Eliza, crying and turning back, was forced along by Freeman and his minions, until we found ourselves on board the steamboat Rodolph, then lying at the levee. In the course of half an hour we were moving briskly up the Mississippi, bound for some point on Red River. There were quite a number of slaves on board beside ourselves, just purchased in the New–Orleans market. I remember a Mr. Kelsow, who was said to be a well known and extensive planter, had in charge a gang of women.

Our master's name was William Ford. He resided then in the "Great Pine Woods," in the parish of Avoyelles, situated on the right bank of Red River, in the heart of Louisiana. He is now a Baptist preacher. Throughout the whole parish of Avoyelles, and especially along both shores of Bayou Boeuf, where he is more intimately known, he is accounted by his fellow-citizens as a worthy minister of God. In many northern minds, perhaps, the idea of a man holding his brother man in servitude, and the traffic in human flesh, may seem altogether incompatible with their conceptions of a moral or religious life. From descriptions of such men as Burch and Freeman, and others hereinafter mentioned, they are led to despise and execrate the whole class of slaveholders, indiscriminately. But I was sometime his slave, and had an opportunity of learning well his character and disposition, and it is but simple justice to him when I say, in my opinion, there never was a more kind, noble, candid, Christian man than William Ford. The influences and associations that had always surrounded him, blinded him to the inherent wrong at the bottom of the system of Slavery. He never doubted the moral right of one man holding another in subjection. Looking through the same medium with his fathers before him, he saw things in the same light. Brought up under other circumstances and other influences, his notions would undoubtedly have been different. Nevertheless, he was a model master, walking uprightly, according to the light of his understanding, and fortunate was the slave who came to his possession. Were all men such as he, Slavery would be deprived of more than half its bitterness.

We were two days and three nights on board the steamboat Rodolph, during which time nothing of particular interest occurred. I was now known as Platt, the name given me by Burch, and by which I was designated through the whole period of my servitude. Eliza was sold by the name of "Dradey." She was so distinguished in the conveyance to Ford, now on record in the recorder's office in New-Orleans.

On our passage I was constantly reflecting on my situation, and consulting with myself on the best course to pursue in order to effect my ultimate escape. Sometimes, not only then, but afterwards, I was almost on the point of disclosing fully to Ford the facts of my history. I am inclined now to the opinion it would have resulted in my benefit. This course was often considered, but through fear of its miscarriage, never put into execution, until eventually my transfer and his pecuniary embarrassments rendered it evidently unsafe. Afterwards, under other masters, unlike William Ford, I knew well enough the slightest knowledge of my real character would consign me at once to the remoter depths of Slavery. I was too costly a chattel to be lost, and was well aware that I would be taken farther on, into some by–place, over the Texan border, perhaps, and sold; that I would be disposed of as the thief disposes of his stolen horse, if my right to freedom was even whispered. So I resolved to lock the secret closely in my heart—never to utter one word or syllable as to who or what I was —trusting in Providence and my own shrewdness for deliverance.

At length we left the steamboat Rodolph at a place called Alexandria, several hundred miles from New–Orleans. It is a small town on the southern shore of Red River. Having remained there over night, we entered the morning train of cars, and were soon at Bayou Lamourie, a still smaller place, distant eighteen miles from Alexandria. At that time it was the termination of the railroad. Ford's plantation was situated on the Texas road, twelve miles from Lamourie, in the Great Pine Woods. This distance, it was announced to us, must be traveled on foot, there being public conveyances no farther. Accordingly we all set out in the company of Ford. It was an excessively hot day. Harry, Eliza, and myself were yet weak, and the bottoms of our feet w were very tender from the effects of the small–pox. We proceeded slowly, Ford telling us to take our time and sit down and rest whenever we desired—a privilege that was taken advantage of quite frequently. After leaving, Lamourie and crossing two plantations, one belonging to Mr. Carnell, the other to a Mr. Flint, we reached the Pine Woods, a wilderness that stretches to the Sabine River.

The whole country about Red River is low and marshy. The Pine Woods, as they are called, is comparatively upland, with frequent small intervals, however, running through them. This upland is covered with numerous trees—the white oak, the chincopin, resembling chestnut, but principally the yellow pine. They are of great size, running up sixty feet, and perfectly straight. The woods were full of cattle, very shy and wild, dashing away in herds, with a loud snuff, at our approach. Some of them were marked or branded, the rest appeared to be in their wild and untamed state. They are much smaller than northern breeds, and the peculiarity about them that most attracted my attention was their horns. They stand out from the sides of the head precisely straight, like two iron spikes.

At noon we reached a cleared piece of ground containing three or four acres. Upon it was a small, unpainted, wooden house, a corn crib, or, as we would say, a barn, and a log kitchen, standing about a rod from the house. It was the summer residence of Mr. Martin. Rich planters, having large establishments on Bayou Boeuf, are accustomed to spend the warmer season in these woods. Here they find clear water and delightful shades. In fact, these retreats are to the planters of that section of the country what Newport and Saratoga are to the wealthier inhabitants of northern cities.

We were sent around into the kitchen, and supplied with sweet potatoes, corn–bread, and bacon, while Master Ford dined with Martin in the house. There were several slaves about the premises. Martin came out and took a look at us, asking Ford the price of each, if we were green hands, and so forth, and making inquiries in relation to the slave market generally

After a long rest we set forth again, following the Texas road, which had the appearance of being very rarely traveled. For five miles we passed through continuous woods without observing a single habitation. At length, just as the sun was sinking in the west, we entered another opening, containing some twelve or fifteen acres.

In this opening stood a house much larger than Mr. Martin's. It was two stories high, with a piazza in front. In the rear of it was also a log kitchen, poultry house, corncribs, and several negro cabins. Near the house was a peach orchard, and gardens of orange and pomegranate trees. The space was entirely surrounded by woods, and covered with a carpet of rich, rank verdure. It was a quiet, lonely, pleasant place —literally a green spot in the wilderness. It was the residence of my master, William Ford.

As we approached, a yellow girl—her name was Rose—was standing on the piazza. Going to the door, she called her mistress, who presently came running out to meet her lord. She kissed him, and laughingly demanded if he had bought "those niggers." Ford said he had, and told us to go round to Sally's cabin and rest ourselves. Turning the corner of the house, we discovered Sally washing—her two baby children near her, rolling on the grass. They jumped up and toddled towards us, looked at us a moment like a brace of rabbits, then ran back to their mother as if afraid of us.

Sally conducted us into the cabin, told us to lay down our bundles and be seated, for she was sure that we were tired. Just then John, the cook, a boy some sixteen years of age, and blacker than any crow, came running in, looked steadily in our faces, then turning round, without saying as much as "how d'ye do," ran back to the kitchen, laughing loudly, as if our coming was a great joke indeed.

Much wearied with our walk, as soon as it was dark, Harry and I wrapped our blankets round us, and laid down upon the cabin floor. My thoughts, as usual, wandered back to my wife and children. The consciousness of my real situation; the hopelessness of any effort to escape through the wide forests of Avoyelles, pressed heavily upon me, yet my heart was at home in Saratoga.

I was awakened early in the morning by the voice of Master Ford, calling Rose. She hastened into the house to dress the children, Sally to the field to milk the cows, while John was busy in the kitchen preparing breakfast. In the meantime Harry and I were strolling about the yard, looking at our new quarters. Just after breakfast a colored man, driving three yoke of oxen, attached to a wagon load of lumber, drove into the opening. He was a slave of Ford's, named Walton, the husband of Rose. By the way, Rose was a native of Washington, and had been brought from thence five years before. She had never seen Eliza, but she had heard of Berry, and they knew the same streets, and the same people, either personally, or by reputation. They became fast friends immediately, and talked a great deal together of old times, and of friends they had left behind.

Ford was at that time a wealthy man. Besides his seat in the Pine Woods, he owned a large lumbering establishment on Indian Creek, four miles distant, and also, in his wife's right, an extensive plantation and many slaves on Bayou Boeuf.

Walton had come with his load of lumber from the mills on Indian Creek. Ford directed us to return with him, saying he would follow us as soon as possible. Before leaving, Mistress Ford called me into the storeroom, and handed me, as it is there termed, a tin bucket of molasses for Harry and myself.

Eliza was still ringing her hands and deploring the loss of her children. Ford tried as much as possible to console her—told her she need not work very hard; that she might remain with Rose, and assist the madam in the house affairs.

Riding with Walton in the wagon, Harry and I became quite well acquainted with him long before reaching Indian Creek. He was a "born thrall" of Ford's, and spoke kindly and affectionately of him, as a child would speak of his own father. In answer to his inquiries from whence I came, I told him from Washington. Of that city, he had heard much from his wife, Rose, and all the way plied me with many extravagant and absurd questions.

On reaching the mills at Indian Creek, we found two more of Ford's slaves, Sam and Antony. Sam, also, was a Washingtonian, having been brought out in the same gang with Rose. He had worked on a farm near Georgetown. Antony was a blacksmith, from Kentucky, who had been in his present master's service about ten years. Sam knew Burch, and when informed that he was the trader who had sent me on from Washington, it was remarkable how well we agreed upon the subject of his superlative rascality. He had forwarded Sam, also.

On Ford's arrival at the mill, we were employed in piling lumber, and chopping logs, which occupation we continued during the remainder of the summer.

We usually spent our Sabbaths at the opening, on which days our master would gather all his slaves about him, and read and expound the Scriptures. He sought to inculcate in our minds feelings of kindness towards each other, of dependence upon God— setting forth the rewards promised unto those who lead an upright and prayerful life. Seated in the doorway of his house, surrounded by his man-servants and his maid-servants, who looked earnestly into the good man's face, he spoke of the loving kindness of the Creator, and of the life that is to come. Often did the voice of prayer ascend from his lips to heaven, the only sound that broke the solitude of the place.

In the course of the summer Sam became deeply convicted, his mind dwelling intensely on the subject of religion. His mistress gave him a Bible, which he carried with him to his work. Whatever leisure time was allowed him, he spent in perusing it, though it was only with great difficulty that he could master any part of it. I often read to him, a favor which he well repaid me by many expressions of gratitude. Sam's piety was frequently observed by white men who came to the mill, and the remark it most generally provoked was, that a man like Ford, who allowed his slaves to have Bibles, was "not fit to own a nigger."

He, however, lost nothing by his kindness. It is a fact I have more than once observed, that those who treated their slaves most leniently, were rewarded by the greatest amount of labor. I know it from my own experience. It was a source of pleasure to surprise Master Ford with a greater day's work than was required, while, under subsequent masters, there was no prompter to extra effort but the overseer's lash.

It was the desire of Ford's approving voice that suggested to me an idea that resulted to his profit. The lumber we were manufacturing was contracted to be delivered at Lamourie. It had hitherto been transported by land, and was an important item of expense. Indian Creek, upon which the mills were situated, was a narrow but deep stream emptying into Bayou Boeuf. In some places it was not more than twelve feet wide, and much obstructed with trunks of trees. Bayou Boeuf was connected with Bayou Lamourie. I ascertained the distance from the mills to the point on the latter bayou, where our lumber was to be delivered, was but a few miles less by land than by water. Provided the creek could be made navigable for rafts, it occurred to me that the expense of transportation would be materially diminished.

Adam Taydem, a little white man who had been a soldier in Florida, and had strolled into that distant region, was foreman and superintendent of the mills. He scouted the idea; but Ford, when I laid it before him, received it favorably, and permitted me to try the experiment.

Having removed the obstructions, I made up a narrow raft, consisting of twelve cribs. At this business I think I was quite skillful, not having forgotten my experience years before on the Champlain canal. I labored hard, being extremely anxious to succeed, both from a desire to please my master, and to show Adam Taydem, that my scheme was not such a visionary one as he incessantly pronounced it. One hand could manage three cribs. I took charge of the forward three, and commenced poling down the creek. In due time we entered the first bayou, and finally reached our destination in a shorter period of time than I had anticipated.

The arrival of the raft at Lamourie created a sensation, while Mr. Ford loaded me with commendation. On all sides I heard Ford's Platt pronounced the "smartest nigger in the Pine Woods"—in fact I was the Fulton of Indian Creek. I was not insensible to the praise bestowed upon me, and enjoyed, especially, my triumph over Taydem, whose half-malicious ridicule had stung my pride. From this time the entire control of bringing the lumber to Lamourie was placed in my hands until the contract was fulfilled.

Indian Creek, in its whole length, flows through a magnificent forest. There dwells on its shore a tribe of Indians, a remnant of the Chickasaws or Chickopees, if I remember rightly. They live in simple huts, ten or twelve feet square, constructed of pine poles and covered with bark. They subsist principally on the flesh of the deer, the coon, and opossum, all of which are plenty in these woods. Sometimes they exchange venison for a little corn and whisky with the planters on the bayous. Their usual dress is buckskin breeches and calico hunting shirts of fantastic colors, buttoned from belt to chin. They wear brass rings on their wrists, and in their ears and noses. The dress of the squaws is very similar. They are fond of dogs and horses—owning many of the latter, of a small, tough breed—and are skillful riders. Their bridles, girths and saddles were made of raw skins of animals; their stirrups of a certain kind of wood. Mounted astride their ponies, men and women, I have seen them dash out into the woods at the utmost of their speed, following narrow winding paths, and dodging trees, in a manner that eclipsed the most miraculous feats of civilized equestrianism. Circling away in various directions, the forest echoing and re-echoing with their whoops, they would presently return at the same dashing, headlong speed with which they started. Their village was on Indian Creek, known as Indian Castle, but their range extended to the Sabine River. Occasionally a tribe from Texas would come over on a visit, and then there was indeed a carnival in the "Great Pine Woods." Chief of the tribe was Cascalla; second in rank, John Baltese, his son-in-law; with both of whom, as with many others of the tribe, I became acquainted during my frequent voyages down the creek with rafts. Sam and myself would often visit them when the day's task w as done. They were obedient to the chief; the word of Cascalla was their law. They were a rude but harmless people, and enjoyed their wild mode of life. They had little fancy for the open country, the cleared lands on the shores of the bayous, but preferred to hide themselves within the shadows of the forest. They worshiped the Great Spirit, loved whisky, and were happy.

On one occasion I was present at a dance, when a roving herd from Texas had encamped in their village. The entire carcass of a deer was roasting before a large fire, which threw its light a long distance among the trees under which they were assembled. When they had formed in a ring, men and squaws alternately, a sort of Indian fiddle set up an indescribable tune. It was a continuous, melancholy kind of wavy sound, with the slightest possible variation. At the first note, if indeed there was more than one note in the whole tune, they circled around, trotting after each other, and giving utterance to a guttural, sing–song noise, equally as nondescript as the music of the fiddle. At the end of the third circuit, they would stop suddenly, whoop as if their lungs would crack, then break from the ring, forming in couples, man and squaw, each jumping backwards as far as possible from the other, then forwards—which graceful feat having been twice or thrice accomplished, they would form in a ring, and go trotting round again. The best dancer appeared to be considered the one who could whoop the loudest, jump the farthest, and utter the most excruciating noise. At intervals, one or more would leave the dancing circle, and going to the fire, cut from the roasting carcass a slice of venison.

In a hole, shaped like a mortar, cut in the trunk of a fallen tree, they pounded corn with a wooden pestle, and of the meal made cake. Alternately they danced and ate. Thus were the visitors from Texas entertained by the dusky sons and daughters of the Chicopees, and such is a description, as I saw it, of an Indian ball in the Pine Woods of Avoyelles.

In the autumn, I left the mills, and was employed at the opening. One day the mistress was urging Ford to procure a loom, in order that Sally might commence weaving cloth for the winter garments of the slaves. He could not imagine where one was to be found, when I suggested that the easiest way to get one would be to make it, informing him at the same time, that I was a sort of "Jack at all trades," and would attempt it, with his permission. It was granted very readily, and I was allowed to go to a neighboring planter's to inspect one before commencing the undertaking. At length it was finished and pronounced by Sally to be perfect. She could easily weave her task of fourteen yards, milk the cows, and have leisure time besides each day. It worked so well, I was continued in the employment of making looms, which were taken down to the plantation on the bayou.

At this time one John M. Tibeats, a carpenter, came to the opening to do some work on master's house. I was directed to quit the looms and assist him. For two weeks I was in his company, planing and matching boards for ceiling, a plastered room being a rare thing in the parish of Avoyelles.

John M. Tibeats was the opposite of Ford in all respects. He was a small, crabbed, quick–tempered, spiteful man. He had no fixed residence that I ever heard of, but passed from one plantation to another, wherever he could find employment. He was without standing in the community, not esteemed by white men, nor even respected by slaves. He was ignorant, withal, and of a revengeful disposition. He left the parish long before I did, and I know not whether he is at present alive or dead. Certain it is, it was a most unlucky day for me that brought us together. During my residence with Master Ford I had seen only the bright side of slavery. His was no heavy hand crushing us to the earth. He pointed upwards, and with benign and cheering words addressed us as his fellow–mortals, accountable, like himself, to the Maker of us all. I think of him with affection, and had my family been with me, could have borne his gentle servitude, without murmuring, all my days. But clouds were gathering in the horizon —forerunners of a pitiless storm that was soon to break over me. I was doomed to endure such bitter trials as the poor slave only knows, and to lead no more the comparatively happy life which I had led in the "Great Pine Woods."

CHAPTER 8. FORD'S EMBARRASSMENTS—THE SALE TO TIBEATS—THE CHATTEL MORTGAGE...

⊙ ⊙ ⊙

Ford's Embarrassments—The Sale To Tibeats—The Chattel Mortgage—Mistress Ford's Plantation On Bayou Boeuf—Description Of The Latter—Ford's Brother-In-Law, Peter Tanner—Meeting With Eliza—She Still Mourns For Her Children— Ford's Overseer Chapin—Tibeat's Abuse—The Keg Of Nails—The First Fight With Tibeats—His Discomfiture And Castigation—The Attempt To Hang Me—Chapin's Interference And Speech—Unhappy Reflections—Abrupt Departure Of Tibeats, Cook And Ramsay—Lawson And The Brown Mule—Message To The Pine Woods.

William Ford unfortunately became embarrassed in his pecuniary affairs. A heavy judgement was rendered against him in consequence of his having become security for his brother, Franklin Ford, residing on Red River, above Alexandria, and who had failed to meet his liabilities. He was also indebted to John M. Tibeats to a considerable amount in consideration of his services in building the mills on Indian Creek, and also a weaving–house corn–mill and other erections on the plantation at Bayou Boeuf, not yet completed. It was therefore necessary, in order to meet these demands, to dispose of eighteen slaves, myself among the number. Seventeen of them, including Sam and Harry, were purchased by Peter Compton, a planter also residing on Red River.

I was sold to Tibeats, in consequence, undoubtedly, of my slight skill as a carpenter. This was in the winter of 1842. The deed of myself from Freeman to Ford, as I ascertained from the public records in New- Orleans on my return, was dated June 23d, 1841. At the time of my sale to Tibeats, the price agreed to be given for me being more than the debt, Ford took a chattel mortgage of four hundred dollars. I am indebted for my life, as will hereafter be seen, to that mortgage.

I bade farewell to my good friends at the opening, and departed with my new master Tibeats. We went down to the plantation on Bayou Boeuf, distant twenty-seven miles from the Pine Woods, to complete the unfinished contract. Bayou Boeuf is a sluggish, winding stream—one of those stagnant bodies of water common in that region, setting back from Red River. It stretches from a point not far from Alexandra, in a south- easterly direction, and following its tortuous course, is more than fifty miles in length. Large cotton and sugar plantations line each shore, extending back to the borders of interminable swamps. It is alive with aligators, rendering it unsafe for swine, or unthinking slave children to stroll along its banks. Upon a bend in this bayou, a short distance from Cheneyville, was situated the plantation of Madam Ford—her brother, Peter Tanner, a great landholder, living on the opposite side.

On my arrival at Bayou Boeuf, I had the pleasure of meeting Eliza, whom I had not seen for several months. She had not pleased Mrs. Ford, being more occupied in brooding over her sorrows than in attending to her business, and had, in consequence, been sent down to work in the field on the plantation. She had grown feeble and emaciated, and was still mourning for her children. She asked me if I had forgotten them, and a great many times inquired if I still remembered how handsome little Emily was—how much Randall loved her—and wondered if they were living still, and where the darlings could then be. She had sunk beneath the weight of an excessive grief. Her drooping form and hollow cheeks too plainly indicated that she had well nigh reached the end of her weary road.

Ford's overseer on this plantation, and who had the exclusive charge of it, was a Mr. Chapin, a kindly-disposed man, and a native of Pennsylvania. In common with others, he held Tibeats in light estimation which fact, in connection with the four hundred dollar mortgage was fortunate for me.

I was now compelled to labor very hard. From earliest dawn until late at night, I was not allowed to be a moment idle. Notwithstanding which, Tibeats was never satisfied. He was continually cursing and complaining. He never spoke to me a kind word. I was his faithful slave, and earned him large wages every day, and yet I went to my cabin nightly, loaded with abuse and stinging epithets.

We had completed the corn mill, the kitchen, an so forth, and were at work upon the weaving house when I was guilty of an act, in that State punishable with death. It was my first fight with Tibeats. The weaving-house we were erecting stood in the orchard a few rods from the residence of Chapin, or the "great house," as it was called. One night, having worked until it was too dark to see, I was ordered by Tibeats to rise very early in the morning, procure a keg of nails from Chapin, and commence putting on the clapboards. I retired to the cabin extremely tired, and having cooked a supper of bacon and corn cake, and conversed a while with Eliza, who occupied the same cabin, as also did Lawson and his wife Mary, and a slave named Bristol, laid down upon the ground floor, little dreaming of the sufferings that awaited me on the morrow. Before daylight I was on the piazza of the "great house," awaiting the appearance of overseer Chapin. To have aroused him from his slumbers and stated my errand, would have been an unpardonable boldness. At length he came out. Taking off my hat, I informed him Master Tibeats had directed me to call upon him for a keg of nails. Going into the store- room, he rolled it out, at the same time saying, if Tibeats preferred a different size, he would endeavor to furnish them, but that I might use those until further directed. Then mounting his horse, which stood saddled and bridled at the door, he rode away into the field, whither the slaves had preceded him, while I took the keg on my shoulder, and proceeding to the weaving-house, broke in the head, and commenced nailing on the clapboards.

As the day began to open, Tibeats came out of the house to where I was, hard at work. He seemed to be that morning even more morose and disagreeable than usual. He was my master, entitled by law to my flesh and blood, and to exercise over me such tyrannical control as his mean nature prompted; but there was no law that could prevent my looking upon him with intense contempt. I despised both his disposition and his intellect. I had just come round to the keg for a further supply of nails, as he reached the weaving-house.

"I thought I told you to commence putting on weather-boards this morning," he remarked.

"Yes, master, and I am about it," I replied.

"Where?" he demanded.

"On the other side," was my answer.

He walked round to the other side, examined my work for a while, muttering to himself in a fault-finding tone.

"Didn't I tell you last night to get a keg of nails of Chapin?" he broke forth again.

"Yes, master, and so I did; and overseer said he would get another size for you, if you wanted them, when he came back from the field."

Tibeats walked to the keg, looked a moment at the contents, then kicked it violently. Coming towards me in a great passion, he exclaimed,

"G-d d—n you! I thought you knowed something."

I made answer, "I tried to do as you told me, master. I didn't mean anything wrong. Overseer said—" But he interrupted me with such a flood of curses that I was unable to finish the sentence. At length he ran towards the house, and going to the piazza, took down one of the overseer's whips.

The whip had a short wooden stock, braided over with leather, and was loaded at the butt. The lash was three feet long, or thereabouts, and made of raw-hide strands.

At first I was somewhat frightened, and my impulse was to run. There was no one about except Rachel, the cook, and Chapin's wife, and neither of them were to be seen. The rest were in the field. I knew he intended to whip me, and it was the first time any one had attempted it since my arrival at Avoyelles. I felt, moreover, that I had been faithful—that I was guilty of no wrong whatever, and deserved commendation rather than punishment. My fear changed to anger, and before he reached me I had made up my mind fully not to be whipped, let the result be life or death.

Winding the lash around his hand, and taking hold of the small end of the stock, he walked up to me, and with a malignant look, ordered me to strip.

"Master Tibeats, said I, looking him boldly in the face, "I will not." I was about to say something further in justification, but with concentrated vengeance, he sprang upon me, seizing me by the throat with one hand, raising the whip with the other, in the act of striking. Before the blow descended, however, I had caught him by the collar of the coat, and drawn him closely to me. Reaching down, I seized him by the ankle, and pushing him back with the other hand, he fell over on the ground. Putting one arm around his leg, and holding it to my breast, so that his head and shoulders only touched the ground, I placed my foot upon his neck. He was completely in my power. My blood was up. It seemed to course through my veins like fire. In the frenzy of my madness I snatched the whip from his hand. He struggled with all his power; swore that I should not live to see another day; and that he would tear out my heart. But his struggles and his threats were alike in vain. I cannot tell how many times I struck him. Blow after blow fell fast and heavy upon his wriggling form. At length he screamed—cried murder—and at last the blasphemous tyrant called on God for mercy. But he who had never shown mercy did not receive it. The stiff stock of the whip warped round his cringing body until my right arm ached.

Until this time I had been too busy to look about me. Desisting for a moment, I saw Mrs. Chapin looking from the window, and Rachel standing in the kitchen door. Their attitudes expressed the utmost excitement and alarm. His screams had been heard in the field. Chapin was coming as fast as he could ride. I struck him a blow or two more, then pushed him from me with such a well-directed kick that he went rolling over on the ground.

Rising to his feet, and brushing the dirt from his hair, he stood looking at me, pale with rage. We gazed at each other in silence. Not a word was uttered until Chapin galloped up to us.

"What is the matter?" he cried out.

"Master Tibeats wants to whip me for using the nails you gave me", I replied.

"What is the matter with the nails?" he inquired, turning to Tibeats.

Tibeats answered to the effect that they were too large, paying little heed, however, to Chapin's question, but still keeping his snakish eyes fastened maliciously on me.

"I am overseer here", Chapin began. "I told Platt to take them and use them, and if they were not of the proper size I would get others on returning from the field. It is not his fault. Besides, I shall furnish such nails as I please. I hope you will understand that, Mr. Tibeats."

Tibeats made no reply, but, grinding his teeth and shaking his fist, swore he would have satisfaction, and that it was not half over yet. Thereupon he walked away, followed by the overseer, and entered the house, the latter talking to him all the while in a suppressed tone, and with earnest gestures.

I remained where I was, doubting whether it was better to fly or abide the result, whatever it might be. Presently Tibeats came out of the house, and, saddling his horse, the only property he possessed besides myself, departed on the road to Chenyville.

When he was gone, Chapin came out, visibly excited, telling me not to stir, not to attempt to leave the plantation on any account whatever. He then went to the kitchen, and calling Rachel out, conversed with her some time. Coming back, he again charged me with great earnestness not to run, saying my master was a rascal; that he had left on no good errand, and that there might be trouble before night. But at all events, he insisted upon it, I must not stir.

As I stood there, feelings of unutterable agony overwhelmed me. I was conscious that I had subjected myself to unimaginable punishment. The reaction that followed my extreme ebullition of anger produced the most painful sensations of regret. An unfriended, helpless slave—what could I do, what could I say, to justify, in the remotest manner, the heinous act I had committed, of resenting a white man's contumely and abuse. I tried to pray—I tried to beseech my Heavenly Father to sustain me in my sore extremity, but emotion choked my utterance, and I could only bow my head upon my hands and weep. For at least an hour I remained in this situation, finding relief only in tears, when, looking up, I beheld Tibeats, accompanied by two horsemen, coming down the bayou. They rode into the yard, jumped from their horses, and approached me with large whips, one of them also carrying a coil of rope.

"Cross your hands", commanded Tibeats, with the addition of such a shuddering expression of blasphemy as is not decorous to repeat.

"You need not bind me, Master Tibeats, I am ready to go with you anywhere", said I.

One of his companions then stepped forward, swearing if I made the least resistance he would break my head—he would tear me limb from limb—he would cut my black throat—and giving wide scope to other similar expressions. Perceiving any importunity altogether vain, I crossed my hands, submitting humbly to whatever disposition they might please to make of me. Thereupon Tibeats tied my wrists, drawing the rope around them with his utmost strength. Then he bound my ankles in the same manner. In the meantime the other two had slipped a cord within my elbows, running it across my back, and tying it firmly. It was utterly impossible to move hand or foot. With a remaining piece of rope Tibeats made an awkward noose, and placed it about my neck.

"Now, then," inquired one of Tibeats' companions, "where shall we hang the nigger?"

One proposed such a limb, extending from the body of a peach tree, near the spot where we were standing. His comrade objected to it, alleging it would break, and proposed another. Finally they fixed upon the latter.

During this conversation, and all the time they were binding me, I uttered not a word. Overseer Chapin, during the progress of the scene, was walking hastily back and forth on the piazza. Rachel was crying by the kitchen door, and Mrs. Chapin was still looking from the window. Hope died within my heart. Surely my time had come. I should never behold the light of another day—never behold the faces of my children— the sweet anticipation I had cherished with such fondness. I should that hour struggle through the fearful agonies of death! None would mourn for me—none revenge me. Soon my form would be mouldering in that distant soil, or, perhaps, be cast to the slimy reptiles that filled the stagnant waters of the bayou! Tears flowed down my cheeks, but they only afforded a subject of insulting comment for my executioners.

At length, as they were dragging me towards the tree, Chapin, who had momentarily disappeared from the piazza, came out of the house and walked towards us. He had a pistol in each hand, and as near as I can now recall to mind, spoke in a firm, determined manner, as follows.

"Gentlemen, I have a few words to say. You had better listen to them. Whoever moves that slave another foot from where he stands is a dead man. In the first place, he does not deserve this treatment. It is a shame to murder him in this manner. I never knew a more faithful boy than Platt. You, Tibeats, are in the fault yourself. You are pretty much of a scoundrel, and I know it, and you richly deserve the flogging you have received. In the next place, I have been overseer on this plantation seven years, and, in the absence of William Ford, am master here. My duty is to protect his interests, and that duty I shall perform. You are not responsible–you are a worthless fellow. Ford holds a mortgage on Platt of four hundred dollars. If you hang him he loses his debt. Until that is canceled you have no right to take his life. You have no right to take it any way. There is a law for the slave as well as for the white man. You are no better than a murderer.

CHAPIN RESCUES SOLOMON FROM HANGING.

"As for you," addressing Cook and Ramsay, a couple of overseers from neighboring plantations, "as for you—begone! If you have any regard for your own safety, I say, begone."

Cook and Ramsay, without a further word, mounted their horses and rode away. Tibeats, in a few minutes, evidently in fear, and overawed by the decided tone of Chapin, sneaked off like a coward, as he was, and mounting his horse, followed his companions.

I remained standing where I was, still bound, with the rope around my neck. As soon as they were gone, Chapin called Rachel, ordering her to run to the field, and tell Lawson to hurry to the house without delay, and bring the brown mule with him, an animal much prized for its unusual fleetness. Presently the boy appeared.

"Lawson," said Chapin, "you must go to the Pine Woods. Tell your master Ford to come here at once —that he must not delay a single moment. Tell him they are trying to murder Platt. Now hurry, boy. Be at the Pine Woods by noon if you kill the mule."

Chapin stepped into the house and wrote a pass. When he returned, Lawson was at the door, mounted on his mule. Receiving the pass, he plied the whip right smartly to the beast, dashed out of the yard, and turning up the bayou on a hard gallop, in less time than it has taken me to describe the scene, was out of sight.

CHAPTER 9. THE HOT SUN—YET BOUND—THE CORDS SINK INTO MY FLESH...

⊙ ⊙ ⊙

The Hot Sun—Yet Bound—The Cords Sink Into My Flesh—Chapin's Uneasiness Speculation—Rachel, And Her Cup Of Water—Suffering Increases—The Happiness Of Slavery—Arrival Of Ford—He Cuts The Cords Which Bind Me, And Takes The Rope From My Neck—Misery—The Gathering Of The Slaves In Eliza's Cabin—Their Kindness—Rachel Repeats The Occurrences Of The Day—Lawson Entertains His Companions With An Account Of His Ride—Chapin's Apprehensions Of Tibeats— Hired To Peter Tanner—Peter Expounds The Scriptures—Description Of The Stocks.

As the sun approached the meridian that day it became insufferably warm. It's hot rays scorched the ground. The earth almost blistered the foot that stood upon it. I was without coat or hat, standing bareheaded, exposed to its burning blaze. Great drops of perspiration rolled down my face, drenching the scanty apparel wherewith I was clothed. Over the fence, a very little way off, the peach trees cast their cool, delicious shadows on the grass. I would gladly have given a long year of service to have been enabled to exchange the heated oven, as it were, wherein I stood, for a seat beneath their branches. But I was yet bound, the rope still dangling from my neck, and standing in the same tracks where Tibeats and his comrades left me. I could not move an inch, so firmly had I been bound. To have been enabled to lean against the weaving house would have been a luxury indeed. But it was far beyond my reach, though distant less than twenty feet. I wanted to lie down, but knew I could not rise again. The ground was so parched and boiling hot I was aware it would but add to the discomfort of my situation. If I could have only moved my position, however slightly, it would have been relief unspeakable. But the hot rays of a southern sun, beating all the long summer day on my bare head, produced not half the suffering I experienced from my aching limbs. My wrists and ankles, and the cords of my legs and arms began to swell, burying the rope that bound them into the swollen flesh.

All day Chapin walked back and forth upon the stoop, but not once approached me. He appeared to be in a state of great uneasiness, looking first towards me, and then up the road, as if expecting some arrival every moment. He did not go to the field, as was his custom. It was evident from his manner that he supposed Tibeats would return with more and better armed assistance, perhaps, to renew the quarrel, and it was equally evident he had prepared his mind to defend my life at whatever hazard. Why he did not relieve me—why he suffered me to remain in agony the whole weary day, I never knew. It was not for want of sympathy, I am certain. Perhaps he wished Ford to see the rope about my neck, and the brutal manner in which I had been bound; perhaps his interference with another's property in which he had no legal interest might have been a trespass, which would have subjected him to the penalty of the law. Why Tibeats was all day absent was another mystery I never could divine. He knew well enough that Chapin would not harm him unless he persisted in his design against me. Lawson told me afterwards, that, as he passed the plantation of John David Cheney, he saw the three, and that they turned and looked after him as he flew by. I think his supposition was, that Lawson had been sent out by Overseer Chapin to arouse the neighboring planters, and to call on them to come to his assistance. He, therefore, undoubtedly, acted on the principle, that "discretion is the better part of valor," and kept away.

But whatever motive may have governed the cowardly and malignant tyrant, it is of no importance. There I still stood in the noon–tide sun, groaning with pain. From long before daylight I had not eaten a morsel. I was growing faint from pain, and thirst, and hunger. Once only, in the very hottest portion of the day, Rachel, half fearful she was acting contrary to the overseer's wishes, ventured to me, and held a cup of water to my lips. The humble creature never knew, nor could she comprehend if she had heard them, the blessings I invoked upon her, for that balmy draught. She could only say, "Oh, Platt, how I do pity you," and then hastened back to her labors in the kitchen.

Never did the sun move so slowly through the heavens—never did it shower down such fervent and fiery rays, as it did that day. At least, so it appeared to me. What my meditations were—the innumerable thoughts that thronged through my distracted brain—I will not attempt to give expression to. Suffice it to say, during the whole long day I came not to the conclusion, even once, that the southern slave, fed, clothed, whipped and protected by his master, is happier than the free colored citizen of the North. To that conclusion I have never since arrived. There are many, however, even in the Northern States, benevolent and well-disposed men, who will pronounce my opinion erroneous, and gravely proceed to substantiate the assertion with an argument. Alas! they have never drank, as I have, from the bitter cup of slavery. Just at sunset my heart leaped with unbounded joy, as Ford came riding into the yard, his horse covered with foam. Chapin met him at the door, and after conversing a short time, he walked directly to me.

"Poor Platt, you are in a bad state," was the only expression that escaped his lips.

"Thank God!" said I, "thank God, Master Ford, that you have come at last."

Drawing a knife from his pocket, he indignantly cut the cord from my wrists, arms, and ankles, and slipped the noose from my neck. I attempted to walk, but staggered like a drunken man, and fell partially to the ground.

Ford returned immediately to the house, leaving me alone again. As he reached the piazza, Tibeats and his two friends rode up. A long dialogue followed. I could hear the sound of their voices, the mild tones of Ford mingling with the angry accents of Tibeats, but was unable to distinguish what was said. Finally the three departed again, apparently not well pleased.

I endeavored to raise the hammer, thinking to show Ford how willing I was to work, by proceeding with my labors on the weaving house, but it fell from my nerveless hand. At dark I crawled into the cabin, and laid down. I was in great misery—all sore and swollen—the slightest movement producing excruciating suffering. Soon the hands came in from the field. Rachel, when she went after Lawson, had told them what had happened. Eliza and Mary broiled me a piece of bacon, but my appetite was gone. Then they scorched some corn meal and made coffee. It was all that I could take. Eliza consoled me and was very kind. It was not long before the cabin was full of slaves. They gathered round me, asking many questions about the difficulty with Tibeats in the morning— and the particulars of all the occurrences of the day. Then Rachel came in, and in her simple language, repeated it over again—dwelling emphatically on the kick that sent Tibeats rolling over on the ground—whereupon there was a general titter throughout the crowd. Then she described how Chapin walked out with his pistols and rescued me, and how Master Ford cut the ropes with his knife, just as if he was mad.

By this time Lawson had returned. He had to regale them with an account of his trip to the Pine Woods—how the brown mule bore him faster than a "streak o' lightnin"—how he astonished everybody as he flew along—how Master Ford started right away—how he said Platt was a good nigger, and they shouldn't kill him, concluding with pretty strong intimations that there was not another human being in the wide world, who could have created such a universal sensation on the road, or performed such a marvelous John Gilpin feat, as he had done that day on the brown mule.

The kind creatures loaded me with the expression of their sympathy—saying Tibeats was a hard, cruel man, and hoping "Massa Ford" would get me back again. In this manner they passed the time, discussing, chatting, talking over end over again the exciting affair, until suddenly Chapin presented himself at the cabin door and called me.

"Platt," said he, "you will sleep on the floor in the great house to-night; bring your blanket with you."

I arose as quickly as I was able, took my blanket in my hand, and followed him. On the way he informed me that he should not wonder if Tibeats was back again before morning—that he intended to kill me—and that he did not mean he should do it without witnesses. Had he stabbed me to the heart in the presence of a hundred slaves, not one of them, by the laws of Louisiana, could have given evidence against him. I laid down on the floor in the "great house"—the first and the last time such a sumptuous resting place was granted me during my twelve years of bondage—and tried to sleep. Near midnight the dog began to bark. Chapin arose, looked from the window, but could discover nothing. At length the dog was quiet. As he returned to his room, he said,

"I believe, Platt, that scoundrel is skulking about the premises somewhere. If the dog barks again, and I am sleeping, wake me."

I promised to do so. After the lapse of an hour or more, the dog re-commenced his clamor, running towards the gate, then back again, all the while barking furiously.

Chapin was out of bed without waiting to be called. On this occasion, he stepped forth upon the piazza, and remained standing there a considerable length of time. Nothing, however, was to be seen, and the dog returned to his kennel. We were not disturbed again during the night. The excessive pain that I suffered, and the dread of some impending danger, prevented any rest whatever. Whether or not Tibeats did actually return to the plantation that night, seeking an opportunity to wreak his vengeance upon me, is a secret known only to himself, perhaps. I thought then, however, and have the strong impression still, that he was there. At all events, he had the disposition of an assassin— cowering before a brave man's words, but ready to strike his helpless or unsuspecting victim in the back, as I had reason afterwards to know.

At daylight in the morning, I arose, sore and weary, having rested little. Nevertheless, after partaking breakfast, which Mary and Eliza had prepared for me in the cabin, I proceeded to the weaving house and commenced the labors of another day. It was Chapin's practice, as it is the practice of overseers generally, immediately on arising, to bestride his horse, always saddled and bridled and ready for him— the particular business of some slave—and ride into the field. This morning, on the contrary, he came to the weaving house, asking if I had seen anything of Tibeats yet. Replying in the negative, he remarked there was something not right about the fellow— there was bad blood in him—that I must keep a sharp watch of him, or he would do me wrong some day when I least expected it.

While he was yet speaking, Tibeats rode in, hitched his horse, and entered the house. I had little fear of him while Ford and Chapin were at hand, but they could not be near me always.

Oh! how heavily the weight of slavery pressed upon me then. I must toil day after day, endure abuse and taunts and scoffs, sleep on the hard ground, live on the coarsest fare, and not only this, but live the slave of a blood-seeking wretch, of whom I must stand henceforth in continued fear and dread. Why had I not died in my young years—before God had given me children to love and live for? What unhappiness and suffering and sorrow it would have prevented. I sighed for liberty; but the bondman's chain was round me, and could not be shaken off. I could only gaze wistfully towards the North, and think of the thousands of miles that stretched between me and the soil of freedom, over which a *black* freeman may not pass.

Tibeats, in the course of half an hour, walked over to the weaving-house, looked at me sharply, then returned without saying anything. Most of the forenoon he sat on the piazza, reading a newspaper and conversing with Ford. After dinner, the latter left for the Pine Woods, and it was indeed with regret that I beheld him depart from the plantation.

Once more during the day Tibeats came to me, gave me some order, and returned.

During the week the weaving-house was completed —Tibeats in the meantime making no allusion whatever to the difficulty—when I was informed he had hired me to Peter Tanner, to work under another carpenter by the name of Myers. This announcement was received with gratification, as any place was desirable that would relieve me of his hateful presence.

Peter Tanner, as the reader has already been informed, lived on the opposite shore, and was the brother of Mistress Ford. He is one of the most extensive planters on Bayou Boeuf, and owns a large number of slaves.

Over I went to Tanner's, joyfully enough. He had heard of my late difficulties—in fact, I ascertained the flogging of Tibeats was soon blazoned far and wide. This affair, together with my rafting experiment, had rendered me somewhat notorious. More than once I heard it said that Platt Ford, now Platt Tibeats—a slave's name changes with his change of master—was "a devil of a nigger." But I was destined to make a still further noise, as will presently be seen, throughout the little world of Bayou Boeuf.

Peter Tanner endeavored to impress upon me the idea that he was quite severe, though I could perceive there was a vein of good humor in the old fellow, after all.

"You're the nigger," he said to me on my arrival —"You're the nigger that flogged your master, eh? You're the nigger that kicks, and holds carpenter Tibeats by the leg, and wallops him, are ye? I'd like to see you hold me by the leg—I should. You're a 'portant character—you're a great nigger—very remarkable nigger, ain't ye? I'd lash you—I'd take the tantrums out of ye. Jest take hold of my leg, if you please. None of your pranks here, my boy, remember *that*. Now go to work, you *kickin'* rascal," concluded Peter Tanner, unable to suppress a half-comical grin at his own wit and sarcasm.

After listening to this salutation, I was taken charge of by Myers and labored under his direction for a month, to his and my own satisfaction.

Like William Ford, his brother-in-law, Tanner was in the habit of reading the Bible to his slaves on the Sabbath, but in a somewhat different spirit. He was an impressive commentator on the New Testament. The first Sunday after my coming to the plantation, he called them together, and began to read the twelfth chapter of Luke. When he came to the 47th verse, he looked deliberately around him, and continued— "And that servant which knew his lord's will,"—here he paused, looking around more deliberately than before, and again proceeded—"which knew his lord's will, and prepared not himself"— here was another pause—"*prepared* not himself, neither did *according* to his will, shall be beaten with many stripes."

"D'ye hear that?" demanded Peter, emphatically. "*Stripes,*" he repeated, slowly and distinctly, taking off his spectacles, preparatory to making a few remarks.

"That nigger that don't take care—that don't obey his lord—that's his master—d'ye see?—that 'ere nigger shall be beaten with many stripes. Now, 'many' signifies a great many—forty, a hundred, a hundred and fifty lashes. That's Scripter!" and so Peter continued to elucidate the subject for a great length of time, much to the edification of his sable audience.

At the conclusion of the exercises, calling up three of his slaves, Warner, Will and Major or, he cried out to me—

"Here, Platt, you held Tibeats by the legs; now I'll see if you can hold these rascals in the same way, till I get back from meetin'."

Thereupon he ordered them to the stocks—a common thing on plantations in the Red River country. The stocks are formed of two planks, the lower one made fast at the ends to two short posts, driven firmly into the ground. At regular distances half circles are cut in the upper edge. The other plank is fastened to one of the posts by a hinge, so that it can be opened or shut down, in the same manner as the blade of a pocket-knife is shut or opened. In the lower edge of the upper plank corresponding half circles are also cut, so that when they close, a row of holes is formed large enough to admit a negro's leg above the ankle, but not large enough to enable him to draw out his foot. The other end of the upper plank, opposite the hinge, is fastened to its post by lock and key. The slave is made to sit upon the ground, when the uppermost prank is elevated, his legs, just above the ankles, placed in the sub-half circles, and shutting it down again, and locking it, he is held secure and fast. Very often the neck instead of the ankle is enclosed. In this manner they are held during the operation of whipping.

Warner, Will and Major, according to Tanner's account of them, were melon-stealing, Sabbath breaking niggers, and not approving of such wickedness, he felt it his duty to put them in the stocks.

Handing me the key, himself, Myers, Mistress Tanner and the children entered the carriage and drove away to church at Cheneyville. When they were gone, the boys begged me to let them out.

I felt sorry to see them sitting on the hot ground, and remembered my own sufferings in the sun. Upon their promise to return to the stocks at any moment they were required to do so, I consented to release them.

Grateful for the lenity shown them, and in order in some measure to repay it, they could do no less, of course, than pilot me to the melon- patch.

Shortly before Tanner's return, they were in the stocks again. Finally he drove up, and looking at the boys, said, with a chuckle,—

"Aha! ye havn't been strolling about much to-day, any way. I'*ll* teach you what's what. I'*ll* tire ye of eating water-melons on the Lord's day, ye Sabbath-breaking niggers."

Peter Tanner prided himself upon his strict religious observances he was a deacon in the church.

But I have now reached a point in the progress of my narrative, when it becomes necessary to turn away from these light descriptions, to the more grave and weighty matter of the second battle with Master Tibeats, and the flight through the great Pacoudrie Swamp.

⊙ ⊙ ⊙

CHAPTER 10. RETURN TO TIBEATS—IMPOSSIBILITY OF PLEASING HIM...

⊙ ⊙ ⊙

Return To Tibeats—Impossibility Of Pleasing Him—He Attacks Me With A Hatchet—The Struggle Over The Broad Axe—The Temptation To Murder Him— Escape Across The Plantation—Observations From The Fence—Tibeats Approaches, Followed By The Hounds-They Take My Track—Their Loud Yells—They Almost Overtake Me—I Reach The Water—The Pounds Confused—Moccasin Snake Alligators—Night In The "Great Pacoudrie Swamp"—The Sounds Of Life—North-West Course—Emerge Into The Pine Woods—The Slave And His Young Master— Arrival At Ford's—Food And Rest.

AT the end of a month, my services being no longer required at Tanner's I was sent over the bayou again to my master, whom I found engaged in building the cotton press. This was situated at some distance from the great house, in a rather retired place. I commenced working once more in company with Tibeats, being entirely alone with him most part of the time. I remembered the words of Chapin, his precautions, his advice to beware, lest in some unsuspecting moment he might injure me. They were always in my mind, so that I lived in a most uneasy state of apprehension and fear. One eye was on my work, the other on my master. I determined to give him no cause of offence, to work still more diligently, if possible, than I had done, to bear whatever abuse he might heap upon me, save bodily injury, humbly and patiently, hoping thereby to soften in some degree his manner towards me, until the blessed time might come when I should be delivered from his clutches.

The third morning after my return, Chapin left the plantation for Cheneyville, to be absent until night. Tibeats, on that morning, was attacked with one of those periodical fits of spleen and ill-humor to which he was frequently subject, rendering him still more disagreeable and venomous than usual.

It was about nine o'clock in the forenoon, when I was busily employed with the jack-plane on one of the sweeps. Tibeats was standing by the work-bench, fitting a handle into the chisel, with which he had been engaged previously in cutting the thread of the screw.

"You are not planing that down enough," said he.

"It is just even with the line," I replied.

"You're a d-d liar," he exclaimed passionately.

"Oh, well, master," I said, mildly, "I will plane it down more if you say so," at the same time proceeding to do as I supposed he desired. Before one shaving had been removed, however, he cried out, saying I had now planed it too deep—it was too small —I had spoiled the sweep entirely. Then followed curses and imprecations. I had endeavored to do exactly as he directed, but nothing would satisfy the unreasonable man. In silence and in dread I stood by the sweep, holding the jack-plane in my hand, not knowing what to do, and not daring to be idle. His anger grew more and more violent, until, finally, with an oath, such a bitter, frightful oath as only Tibeats could utter, he seized a hatchet from the work- bench and darted towards me, swearing he would cut my head open.

It was a moment of life or death. The sharp, bright blade of the hatchet glittered in the sun. In another instant it would be buried in my brain, and yet in that instant—so quick will a man's thoughts come to him in such a fearful strait—I reasoned with myself. If I stood still, my doom was certain; if I fled, ten chances to one the hatchet, flying from his hand with a too-deadly and unerring aim, would strike me in the back. There was but one course to take. Springing towards him with all my power, and meeting him full half-way, before he could bring down the blow, with one hand I caught his uplifted arm, with the other seized him by the throat. We stood looking each other in the eyes. In his I could see murder. I felt as if I had a serpent by the neck, watching the slightest relaxation of my gripe, to coil itself round my body, crushing and stinging it to death. I thought to scream aloud, trusting that some ear might catch the sound—but Chapin was away; the hands were in the field; there was no living soul in sight or hearing.

The good genius, which thus far through life has saved me from the hands of violence, at that moment suggested a lucky thought. With a vigorous and sudden kick, that brought him on one knee, with a groan, I released my hold upon his throat, snatched the hatchet, and cast it beyond reach.

Frantic with rage, maddened beyond control, he seized a white oak stick, five feet long, perhaps, and as large in circumference as his hand could grasp, which was lying on the ground. Again he rushed towards me, and again I met him, seized him about the waist, and being the stronger of the two, bore him to the earth. While in that position I obtained possession of the stick, and rising, cast it from me, also.

He likewise arose and ran for the broad-axe, on the work-bench. Fortunately, there was a heavy plank lying upon its broad blade, in such a manner that he could not extricate it, before I had sprung upon his back. Pressing him down closely and heavily on the plank, so that the axe was held more firmly to its place, I endeavored, but in vain, to break his grasp upon the handle. In that position we remained some minutes.

There have been hours in my unhappy life, many of them, when the contemplation of death as the end of earthly sorrow—of the grave as a resting place for the tired and worn out body—has been pleasant to dwell upon. But such contemplations vanish in the hour of peril. No man, in his full strength, can stand undismayed, in the presence of the "king of terrors." Life is dear to every living thing; the worm that crawls upon the ground will struggle for it. At that moment it was dear to me, enslaved and treated as I was.

Not able to unloose his hand, once more I seized him by the throat, and this time, with a vice-like gripe that soon relaxed his hold. He became pliant and unstrung. His face, that had been white with passion, was now black from suffocation. Those small serpent eyes that spat such venom, were now full of horror—two great white orbs starting from their sockets!

There was "a lurking devil" in my heart that prompted me to kill the human blood-hound on the spot—to retain the gripe on his accursed throat till the breath of life was gone! I dared not murder him, and I dared not let him live. If I killed him, my life must pay the forfeit—if he lived, my life only would satisfy his vengeance. A voice within whispered me to fly. To be a wanderer among the swamps, a fugitive and a vagabond on the face of the earth, was preferable to the life that I was leading.

My resolution was soon formed, and swinging him from the work-bench to the ground, I leaped a fence near by, and hurried across the plantation, passing the slaves at work in the cotton field. At the end of a quarter of a mile I reached the wood-pasture, and it was a short time indeed that I had been running it. Climbing on to a high fence, I could see the cotton press, the great house, and the space between. It was a conspicuous position, from whence the whole plantation was in view. I saw Tibeats cross the field towards the house, and enter it—then he came out, carrying his saddle, and presently mounted his horse and galloped away.

I was desolate, but thankful. Thankful that my life was spared,—desolate and discouraged with the prospect before me. What would become of me? Who would befriend me? Whither should I fly? Oh, God! Thou who gavest me life, and implanted in my bosom the love of life who filled it with emotions such as other men, thy creatures, have, do not forsake me. Have pity on the poor slave—let me not perish. If thou cost not protect me, I am lost—lost! Such supplications, silently and unuttered, ascended from my inmost heart to Heaven. But there was no answering voice—no sweet, low tone, coming down from on high, whispering to my soul, "It is

I, be not afraid." I was the forsaken of God, it seemed—the despised and hated of men!

In about three–fourths of an hour several of the slaves shouted and made signs for me to run. Presently, looking up the bayou, I saw Tibeats and two others on horse–back, coming at a fast gait, followed by a troop of dogs. There were as many as eight or ten. Distant as I was, I knew them. They belonged on the adjoining plantation. The dogs used on Bayou Boeuf for hunting slaves are a kind of blood–hound, but a far more savage breed than is found in the Northern States. They will attack a negro, at their master's bidding, and cling to him as the common bull- dog will cling to a four footed animal. Frequently their loud bay is heard in the swamps, and then there is speculation as to what point the runaway will be overhauled—the same as a New–York hunter stops to listen to the hounds coursing along the hillsides, and suggests to his companion that the fox will be taken at such a place. I never knew a slave escaping with his life from Bayou Bouef. One reason is, they are not allowed to learn the art of swimming, and are incapable of crossing the most inconsiderable stream. In their flight they can go in no direction but a little way without coming to a bayou, when the inevitable alternative is presented, of being drowned or overtaken by the dogs. In youth I had practiced in the clear streams that flow through my native district, until I had become an expert swimmer, and felt at home in the watery element.

I stood upon the fence until the dogs had reached the cotton press. In an instant more, their long, savage yells announced they were on my track. Leaping down from my position, I ran towards the swamp. Fear gave me strength, and I exerted it to the utmost. Every few moments I could hear the yelpings of the dogs. They were gaining upon me. Every howl was nearer and nearer. Each moment I expected they would spring upon my back—expected to feel their long teeth sinking into my flesh. There were so many of them, I knew they would tear me to pieces, that they would worry me, at once, to death. I gasped for breath—gasped forth a half–uttered, choking prayer to the Almighty to save me—to give me strength to reach some wide, deep bayou where I could throw them off the track, or sink into its waters. Presently I reached a thick palmetto bottom. As I fled through them they made a loud rustling noise, not loud enough, however, to drown the voices of the dogs.

Continuing my course due south, as nearly as I can judge, I came at length to water just over shoe. The hounds at that moment could not have been five rods behind me. I could hear them crashing and plunging through the palmettoes, their loud, eager yells making the whole swamp clamorous with the sound. Hope revived a little as I reached the water. If it were only deeper, they might loose the scent, and thus disconcerted, afford me the opportunity of evading them. Luckily, it grew deeper the farther I proceeded—now over my ankles—now half-way to my knees— now sinking a moment to my waist, and then emerging presently into more shallow places. The dogs had not gained upon me since I struck the water. Evidently they were confused. Now their savage intonations grew more and more distant, assuring me that I was leaving them. Finally I stopped to listen, but the long howl came booming on the air again, telling me I was not yet safe. From bog to bog, where I had stepped, they could still keep upon the track, though impeded by the water. At length, to my great joy, I came to a wide bayou, and plunging in, had soon stemmed its sluggish current to the other side. There, certainly, the dogs would be confounded —the current carrying down the stream all traces of that slight, mysterious scent, which enables the quick-smelling hound to follow in the track of the fugitive.

After crossing this bayou the water became so deep I could not run. I was now in what I afterwards learned was the "Great Pacoudrie Swamp." It was filled with immense trees—the sycamore, the gum, the cotton wood and cypress, and extends, I am informed, to the shore of the Calcasieu river. For thirty or forty miles it is without inhabitants, save wild beasts—the bear, the wild-cat, the tiger, and great slimy reptiles, that are crawling through it everywhere. Long before I reached the bayou, in fact, from the time I struck the water until I emerged from the swamp on my return, these reptiles surrounded me. I saw hundreds of moccasin snakes. Every log and bog—every trunk of a fallen tree, over which I was compelled to step or climb, was alive with them. They crawled away at my approach, but sometimes in my haste, I almost placed my hand or foot upon them. They are poisonous serpents—their bite more fatal than the rattlesnake's. Besides, I had lost one shoe, the sole having come entirely off, leaving the upper only dangling to my ankle.

I saw also many alligators, great and small, lying in the water, or on pieces of floodwood. The noise I made usually startled them, when they moved off and plunged into the deepest places. Sometimes, however, I would come directly upon a monster before observing it. In such cases, I would start back, run a short way round, and in that manner shun them. Straight forward, they will run a short distance rapidly, but do not possess the power of turning. In a crooked race, there is no difficulty in evading them.

About two o'clock in the afternoon, I heard the last of the hounds. Probably they did not cross the bayou. Wet and weary, but relieved from the sense of instant peril, I continued on, more cautious and afraid, however, of the snakes and alligators than I had been in the earlier portion of my flight. Now, before stepping into a muddy pool, I would strike the water with a stick. If the waters moved, I would go around it, if not, would venture through.

At length the sun went down, and gradually night's trailing mantle shrouded the great swamp in darkness. Still I staggered on, fearing every instant I should feel the dreadful sting of the moccasin, or be crushed within the jaws of some disturbed alligator. The dread of them now almost equaled the fear of the pursuing hounds. The moon arose after a time, its mild light creeping through the overspreading branches, loaded with long, pendent moss. I kept traveling forwards until after midnight, hoping all the while that I would soon emerge into some less desolate and dangerous region. But the water grew deeper and the walking more difficult than ever. I perceived it would be impossible to proceed much farther, and knew not, moreover, what hands I might fall into, should I succeed in reaching a human habitation. Not provided with a pass, any white man would be at liberty to arrest me, and place me in prison until such time as my master should "prove property, pay charges, and take me away." I was an estray, and if so unfortunate as to meet a law- abiding citizen of Louisiana, he would deem it his duty to his neighbor, perhaps, to put me forthwith in the pound. Really, it was difficult to determine which I had most reason to fear—dogs, alligators or men!

After midnight, however, I came to a halt. Imagination cannot picture the dreariness of the scene. The swamp was resonant with the quacking of innumerable ducks! Since the foundation of the earth, in all probability, a human footstep had never before so far penetrated the recesses of the swamp. It was not silent now—silent to a degree that rendered it oppressive,—as it was when the sun was shining in the heavens. My midnight intrusion had awakened the feathered tribes, which seemed to throng the morass in hundreds of thousands, and their garrulous throats poured forth such multitudinous sounds— there was such a fluttering of wings—such sullen plunges in the water all around me—that I was affrighted and appalled. All the fowls of the air, and all the creeping things of the earth appeared to have assembled together in that particular place, for the purpose of filling it with clamor and confusion. Not by human dwellings—not in crowded cities alone, are the sights and sounds of life. The wildest places of the earth are full of them. Even in the heart of that dismal swamp, God had provided a refuge and a dwelling place for millions of living things.

The moon had now risen above the trees, when I resolved upon a new project. Thus far I had endeavored to travel as nearly south as possible. Turning about I proceeded in a north-west direction, my object being to strike the Pine Woods in the vicinity of Master Ford's. Once within the shadow of his protection, I felt I would be comparatively safe.

My clothes were in tatters, my hands, face, and body covered with scratches, received from the sharp knots of fallen trees, and in climbing over piles of brush and floodwood. My bare foot was full of thorns. I was besmeared with muck and mud, and the green slime that had collected on the surface of the dead water, in which I had been immersed to the neck many times during the day and night. Hour after hour, and tiresome indeed had they become, I continued to plod along on my north-west course. The water began to grow less deep, and the ground more firm under my feet. At last I reached the Pacoudrie, the same wide bayou I had swam while "outward bound." I swam it again, and shortly after thought I heard a cock crow, but the sound was faint, and it might have been a mockery of the ear. The water receded from my advancing footsteps—now I had left the bogs behind me—now—now I was on dry land that gradually ascended to the plain, and I knew I was somewhere in the "Great Pine Woods."

Just at day-break I came to an opening—a sort of small plantation—but one I had never seen before. In the edge of the woods I came upon two men, a slave and his young master, engaged in catching wild hogs. The white man I knew would demand my pass, and not able to give him one, would take me into possession. I was too wearied to run again, and too desperate to be taken, and therefore adopted a ruse that proved entirely successful. Assuming a fierce expression, I walked directly towards him, looking him steadily in the face. As I approached, he moved backwards with an air of alarm. It was plain he was much affrighted—that he looked upon me as some infernal goblin, just arisen from the bowels of the swamp!

"Where does William Ford live?" I demanded, in no gentle tone.

"He lives seven miles from here," was the reply.

"Which is the way to his place?" I again demanded, trying to look more fiercely than ever.

"Do you see those pine trees yonder?" he asked, pointing to two, a mile distant, that rose far above their fellows, like a couple of tall sentinels, overlooking the broad expanse of forest.

"I see them," was the answer.

"At the feet of those pine trees," he continued, "runs the Texas road. Turn to the left, and it will lead you to William Ford's."

Without further parley, I hastened forward, happy as he was, no doubt, to place the widest possible distance between us. Striking the Texas road, I turned to the left hand, as directed, and soon passed a great fire, where a pile of logs were burning. I went to it, thinking I would dry my clothes; but the gray light of the morning was fast breaking away,—some passing white man might observe me; besides, the heat overpowered me with the desire of sleep; so, lingering no longer, I continued my travels, and finally, about eight o'clock, reached the house of Master Ford.

The slaves were all absent from the quarters, at their work. Stepping on to the piazza, I knocked at the door, which was soon opened by Mistress Ford. My appearance was so changed—I was in such a wobegone and forlorn condition, she did not know me. Inquiring if Master Ford was at home, that good man made his appearance, before the question could be answered. I told him of my flight, and all the particulars connected with it. He listened attentively, and when I had concluded, spoke to me kindly and sympathetically, and taking me to the kitchen, called John, and ordered him to prepare me food. I had; tasted nothing since daylight the previous morning.

When John had set the meal before me, the madam came out with a bowl of milk, and many little delicious dainties, such as rarely please the palate of a slave. I was hungry, and I was weary, but neither food nor rest afforded half the pleasure as did the blessed voices speaking kindness and consolation. It was the oil and the wine which the Good Samaritan in the "Great Pine Woods" was ready to pour into the wounded spirit of the slave, who came to him, stripped of his raiment and half-dead.

They left me in the cabin, that I might rest. Blessed be sleep! It visiteth all alike, descending as the dews of heaven on the bond and free. Soon it nestled to my bosom, driving away the troubles that oppressed it, and bearing me to that shadowy region, where I saw again the faces, and listened to the voices of my children, who, alas, for aught I knew in my waking hours, had fallen into the arms of that other sleep, from which they *never* would arouse.

⊙ ⊙ ⊙

CHAPTER 11. THE MISTRESS' GARDEN—THE CRIMSON AND GOLDEN FRUIT...

⊙ ⊙ ⊙

The Mistress' Garden—The Crimson And Golden Fruit—Orange And Pomegranate Trees—Return To Bayou Boeuf—Master Ford's Remarks On The Way—The Meeting With Tibeats—His Account Of The Chase—Ford Censure His Brutality—Arrival At The Plantation—Astonishment Of The Slaves On Seeing Me—The Anticipated Flogging—Kentucky John—Mr. Eldret, The Planter—Eldret's Sam—Trip To The "Big Cane Brake" The Tradition Of "Sutton's Field"—Forest Trees—Gnats And Mosqultos—The Arrival Of Black Women In The Big Cane—Lumber Women— Sudden Appearance Of Tibeats—His Provoking Treatment—Visit To Bayou Boeuf—The Slave Pass—Southern Hospitality—The Last Of Eliza—Sale To Edwin Epps.

AFTER a long sleep, sometime in the afternoon I awoke, refreshed, but very sore and stiff. Sally came in and talked with me, while John cooked me some dinner. Sally was in great trouble, as well as myself, one of her children being ill, and she feared it could not survive. Dinner over, after walking about the quarters for a while, visiting Sally's cabin and looking at the sick child, I strolled into the madam's garden. Though it was a season of the year when the voices of the birds are silent, and the trees are stripped of their summer glories in more frigid climes, yet the whole variety of roses were then blooming there, and the long, luxuriant vines creeping over the frames. The crimson and golden fruit hung half hidden amidst the younger and older blossoms of the peach, the orange, the plum, and the pomegranate; for, in that region of almost perpetual warmth, the leaves are falling and the buds bursting into bloom the whole year long.

I indulged the most grateful feelings towards Master and Mistress Ford, and wishing in some manner to repay their kindness, commenced trimming the vines, and afterwards weeding out the grass from among the orange and pomegranate trees. The latter grows eight or ten feet high, and its fruit, though larger, is similar in appearance to the jelly- flower. It has the luscious flavor of the strawberry. Oranges, peaches, plums, and most other fruits are indigenous to the rich, warm soil of Avoyelles; but the apple, the most common of them all in colder latitudes, is rarely to be seen.

Mistress Ford came out presently, saying it was praise-worthy in me, but I was not in a condition to labor, and might rest myself at the quarters until master should go down to Bayou Boeuf, which would not be that day, and it might not be the next. I said to her—to be sure, I felt bad, and was stiff, and that my foot pained me, the stubs and thorns having so torn it , but thought such exercise would not hurt me, and that it was a great pleasure to work for so good a mistress. Thereupon she returned to the great house, and for three days I was diligent in the garden, cleaning the walks, weeding the flower beds, and pulling up the rank grass beneath the jessamine vines, which the gentle and generous hand of my protectress had taught to clamber along the walls.

The fourth morning, having become recruited and refreshed, Master Ford ordered me to make ready to accompany him to the bayou. There was but one saddle horse at the opening, all the others with the mules having been sent down to the plantation. I said I could walk, and bidding Sally and John good-bye, left the opening, trotting along by the horse's side.

That little paradise in the Great Pine Woods was the oasis in the desert, towards which my heart turned lovingly, during many years of bondage. I went forth from it now with regret and sorrow, not so overwhelming, however, as if it had then been given me to know that I should never return to it again.

Master Ford urged me to take his place occasionally on the horse, to rest me; but I said no, I was not tired, and it was better for me to walk than him. He said many kind and cheering things to me on the way, riding slowly, in order that I might keep pace with him. The goodness of God was manifest, he declared, in my miraculous escape from the swamp. As Daniel came forth unharmed from the den of lions, and as Jonah had been preserved in the whale's belly, even so had I been delivered from evil by the Almighty. He interrogated me in regard to the various fears and emotions I had experienced during the day and night, and if I had felt, at any time, a desire to pray. I felt forsaken of the whole world, I answered him, and was praying mentally all the while. At such times, said he, the heart of man turns instinctively towards his Maker. In prosperity, and when there is nothing to injure or make him afraid, he remembers Him not, and is ready to defy Him; but place him in the midst of dangers, cut him off from human aid, let the grave open before him–then it is, in the time of his tribulation, that the scoffer and unbelieving man turns to God for help, feeling there is no other hope, or refuge, or safety, save in his protecting arm.

So did that benignant man speak to me of this life and of the life hereafter; of the goodness and power of God, and of the vanity of earthly things, as we journeyed along the solitary road towards Bayou Boeuf.

When within some five miles of the plantation, we discovered a horseman at a distance, galloping towards us. As he came near I saw that it was Tibeats! He looked at me a moment, but did not address me, and turning about, rode along side by side with Ford. I trotted silently at their horses' heels, listing to their conversation. Ford informed him of my arrival in the Pine Woods three days before, of the sad plight I was in, and of the difficulties and dangers I had encountered.

"Well," exclaimed Tibeats, omitting his usual oaths in the presence of

Ford, "I never saw such running before. I'll bet him against a hundred dollars, he'll beat any nigger in Louisiana. I offered John David Cheney twenty–five dollars to catch him, dead or alive, but he outran his dogs in a fair race. Them Cheney dogs ain't much, after all. Dunwoodie's hounds would have had him down before he touched the palmettoes. Somehow the dogs got off the track, and we had to give up the hunt. We rode the horses as far as we could, and then kept on foot till the water was three feet deep. The boys said he was drowned, sure. I allow I wanted a shot at him mightily. Ever since, I have been riding up and down the bayou, but had'nt much hope of catching him—thought he was dead, sartin. Oh, he's a cuss to run—that nigger is!"

In this way Tibeats ran on, describing his search in the swamp, the wonderful speed with which I had fled before the hounds, and when he had finished, Master Ford responded by saying, I had always been a willing and faithful boy with him; that he was sorry we had such trouble; that, according to Platt's story, he had been inhumanly treated, and that he, Tibeats, was himself in fault. Using hatchets and broad–axes upon slaves was shameful, and should not be allowed, he remarked. "This is no way of dealing with them, when first brought into the country. It will have a pernicious influence, and set them all running away. The swamps will be full of them. A little kindness would be far more effectual in restraining them, and rendering them obedient, than the use of such deadly weapons. Every planter on the bayou should frown upon such inhumanity. It is for the interest of all to do so. It is evident enough, Mr. Tibeats, that you and Platt cannot live together. You dislike him, and would not hesitate to kill him, and knowing it, he will run from you again through fear of his life. Now, Tibeats, you must sell him, or hire him out, at least. Unless you do so, I shall take measures to get him out of your possession."

In this spirit Ford addressed him the remainder of the distance. I opened not my mouth. On reaching the plantation they entered the great house, while I repaired to Eliza's cabin. The slaves were astonished to find me there, on returning from the field, supposing I was drowned. That night, again, they gathered about the cabin to listen to the story of my adventure. They took it for granted I would be whipped, and that it would be severe, the well-known penalty of running away being five hundred lashes.

"Poor fellow," said Eliza, taking me by the hand, "it would have been better for you if you had drowned. You have a cruel master, and he will kill you yet, I am afraid."

Lawson suggested that it might be, overseer Chapin would be appointed to inflict the punishment, in which case it would not be severe, whereupon Mary, Rachel, Bristol, and others hoped it would be Master Ford, and then it would be no whipping at all. They all pitied me and tried to console me, and were sad in view of the castigation that awaited me, except Kentucky John. There were no bounds to his laughter; he filled the cabin with cachinnations, holding his sides to prevent an explosion, and the cause of his noisy mirth was the idea of my outstripping the hounds. Somehow, he looked at the subject in a comical light. "I *know'd* dey would'nt cotch him, when he run cross de plantation. O, de lor', did'nt Platt pick his feet right up, tho', hey? When dem dogs got whar he was, he was'nt *dar*—haw, haw, haw! O, de lor' a' mity!"—and then Kentucky John relapsed into another of his boisterous fits.

Early the next morning, Tibeats left the plantation. In the course of the forenoon, while sauntering about the gin-house, a tall, good-looking man came to me, and inquired if I was Tibeats' boy, that youthful appellation being applied indiscriminately to slaves even though they may have passed the number of three score years and ten. I took off my hat, and answered that I was.

"How would you like to work for me?" he inquired.

"Oh, I would like to, very much," said I, inspired with a sudden hope of getting away from Tibeats.

"You worked under Myers at Peter Tanner's, didn't you?"

I replied I had, adding some complimentary remarks that Myers had made concerning me.

"Well, boy," said he, "I have hired you of your master to work for me in the "Big Cane Brake," thirty–eight miles from here, down on Red River."

This man was Mr. Eldret, who lived below Ford's, on the same side of the bayou. I accompanied him to his plantation, and in the morning started with his slave Sam, and a wagon–load of provisions, drawn by four mules, for the Big Cane, Eldret and Myers having preceded us on horseback. This Sam was a native of Charleston, where he had a mother, brother and sisters. He "allowed"—a common word among both black and white—that Tibeats was a mean man, and hoped, as I most earnestly did also, that his master would buy me.

We proceeded down the south shore of the bayou, crossing it at Carey's plantation; from thence to Huff Power, passing which, we came upon the Bayou Rouge road, which runs towards Red River. After passing through Bayou Rouge Swamp, and just at sunset, turning from the highway, we struck off into the "Big Cane Brake." We followed an unbeaten track, scarcely wide enough to admit the wagon The cane, such as are used for fishing–rods, were as thick as they could stand. A person could not be seen through them the distance of a rod. The paths of wild beasts run through them in various directions —the bear and the American tiger abounding in these brakes, and wherever there is a basin of stagnant water, it is full of alligators.

We kept on our lonely course through the "Big Cane" several miles, when we entered a clearing, known as "Sutton's Field." Many years before, a man by the name of Sutton had penetrated the wilderness of cane to this solitary place. Tradition has it that he fled thither, a fugitive, not from service, but from justice. Here he lived alone—recluse and hermit of the swamp—with his own hands planting the seed and gathering in the harvest. One day a band of Indians stole upon his solitude, and after a bloody battle, overpowered and massacred him. For miles the country round, in the slaves' quarters, and on the piazzas of "great houses," where white children listen to superstitious tales, the story goes, that that spot, in the heart of the "Big Cane," is a haunted place. For more than a quarter of a century, human voices had rarely, if ever, disturbed the silence of the clearing. Rank and noxious weeds had overspread the once cultivated field—serpents sunned themselves on the doorway of the crumbling cabin. It was indeed a dreary picture of desolation.

Passing "Sutton's Field," we followed a new-cut road two miles farther, which brought us to its termination. We had now reached the wild lands of Mr. Eldret, where he contemplated clearing up an extensive plantation. We went to work next morning with our cane-knives, and cleared a sufficient space to allow the erection of two cabins—one for Myers and Eldret, the other for Sam, myself, and the slaves that were to join us. We were now in the midst of trees of enormous growth, whose wide-spreading branches almost shut out the light of the sun, while the space between the trunks was an impervious mass of cane, with here and there an occasional palmetto.

The bay and the sycamore, the oak and the cypress, reach a growth unparalleled, in those fertile lowlands bordering the Red River. From every tree, moreover, hang long, large masses of moss, presenting to the eye unaccustomed to them, a striking and singular appearance. This moss, in large quantities, is sent north, and there used for manufacturing purposes.

We cut down oaks, split them into rails, and with these erected temporary cabins. We covered the roofs with the broad palmetto leaf, an excellent substitute for shingles, as long as they last.

The greatest annoyance I met with here were small flies, gnats and mosquitoes. They swarmed the air. They penetrated the porches of the ear, the nose, the eyes, the mouth. They sucked themselves beneath the skin. It was impossible to brush or beat them off. It seemed, indeed, as if they would devour us— carry us away piecemeal, in their small tormenting mouths.

A lonelier spot, or one more disagreeable, than the centre of the "Big Cane Brake," it would be difficult to conceive; yet to me it was a paradise, in comparison with any other place in the company of Master Tibeats. I labored hard, and oft–times was weary and fatigued, yet I could lie down at night in peace, and arise in the morning without fear.

In the course of a fortnight, four black girls came down from Eldret's plantation—Charlotte, Fanny, Cresia and Nelly. They were all large and stout. Axes were put into their hands, and they were sent out with Sam and myself to cut trees. They were excellent choppers, the largest oak or sycamore standing but a brief season before their heavy and well–directed blows. At piling logs, they were equal to any man. There are lumberwomen as well as lumbermen in the forests of the South. In fact, in the region of the Bayou Boeuf they perform their share of all the labor required on the plantation. They plough, drag, drive team, clear wild lands, work on the highway, and so forth. Some planters, owning large cotton and sugar plantations, have none other than the labor of slave women. Such an one is Jim Burns, who lives on the north shore of the bayou, opposite the plantation of John Fogaman.

On our arrival in the brake, Eldret promised me, if I worked well, I might go up to visit my friends at Ford's in four weeks. On Saturday night of the fifth week, I reminded him of his promise, when he told me I had done so well, that I might go. I had set my heart upon it, and Eldret's announcement thrilled me with pleasure. I was to return in time to commence the labors of the day on Tuesday morning.

While indulging the pleasant anticipation of so soon meeting my old friends again, suddenly the hateful form of Tibeats appeared among us. He inquired how Myers and Platt got along together, and was told, very well, and that Platt was going up to Ford's plantation in the morning on a visit.

"Poh, poh!" sneered Tibeats; "it isn't worth while —the nigger will get unsteady. He can't go."

But Eldret insisted I had worked faithfully—that he had given me his promise, and that, under the circumstances, I ought not to be disappointed. They then, it being about dark, entered one cabin and I the other. I could not give up the idea of going; it was a sore disappointment. Before morning I resolved, if Eldret made no objection, to leave at all hazards. At daylight I was at his door, with my blanket rolled up into a bundle, and hanging on a stick over my shoulder, waiting for a pass. Tibeats came out presently in one of his disagreeable moods, washed his face, and going to a stump near by, sat down upon it, apparently busily thinking with himself After standing there a long time, impelled by a sudden impulse of impatience, I started off.

"Are you going without a pass?" he cried out to me.

"Yes, master, I thought I would," I answered.

"How do you think you'll get there?" demanded he.

"Don't know," was all the reply I made him.

"You'd be taken and sent to jail, where you ought to be, before you got half-way there," he added, passing into the cabin as he said it. He came out soon with the pass in his hand, and calling me a "d–d nigger that deserved a hundred lashes," threw it on the ground. I picked it up, and hurried away right speedily.

A slave caught off his master's plantation without a pass, may be seized and whipped by any white man whom he meets. The one I now received was dated, and read as follows.

Platt has permission to go to Ford's plantation, on Bayou Boeuf, and return by Tuesday morning.

JOHN M. TIBEATS.

This is the usual form. On the way, a great many demanded it, read it, and passed on. Those having the air and appearance of gentlemen, whose dress indicated the possession of wealth, frequently took no notice of me whatever; but a shabby fellow, an unmistakable loafer, never failed to hail me, and to scrutinize and examine me in the most thorough manner. Catching runaways is sometimes a money-making business. If, after advertising, no owner appears, they may be sold to the highest bidder; and certain fees are allowed the finder for his services, at all events, even if reclaimed. "A mean white," therefore, —a name applied to the species loafer—considers it a god-send to meet an unknown negro without a pass.

There are no inns along the highways in that portion of the State where I sojourned. I was wholly destitute of money, neither did I carry any provisions, on my journey from the Big Cane to Bayou Boeuf; nevertheless, with his pass in his hand, a slave need never suffer from hunger or from thirst. It is only necessary to present it to the master or overseer of a plantation, and state his wants, when he will be sent round to the kitchen and provided with food or shelter, as the case may require. The traveler stops at any house and calls for a meal with as much freedom as if it was a public tavern. It is the general custom of the country. Whatever their faults may be, it is certain the inhabitants along Red River, and around the bayous in the interior of Louisiana are not wanting in hospitality.

I arrived at Ford's plantation towards the close of the afternoon, passing the evening in Eliza's cabin, with Lawson, Rachel, and others of my acquaintance. When we left Washington Eliza's form was round and plump. She stood erect, and in her silks and jewels, presented a picture of graceful strength and elegance. Now she was but a thin shadow of her former self. Her face had become ghastly haggard, and the once straight and active form was bowed down, as if bearing the weight of a hundred years. Crouching on her cabin floor, and clad in the coarse garments of a slave, old Elisha Berry would not have recognized the mother of his child. I never saw her afterwards. Having become useless in the cotton-field, she was bartered for a trifle, to some man residing in the vicinity of Peter Compton's. Grief had gnawed remorselessly at her heart, until her strength was gone; and for that, her last master, it is said, lashed and abused her most unmercifully. But he could not whip back the departed vigor of her youth, nor straighten up that bended body to its full height, such as it was when her children were around her, and the light of freedom was shining on her path.

I learned the particulars relative to her departure from this world, from some of Compton's slaves, who had come over Red River to the bayou, to assist young Madam Tanner during the "busy season." She became at length, they said, utterly helpless, for several weeks lying on the ground floor in a dilapidated cabin, dependent upon the mercy of her fellowthralls for an occasional drop of water, and a morsel of food. Her master did not "knock her on the head," as is sometimes done to put a suffering animal out of misery, but left her unprovided for, and unprotected, to linger through a life of pain and wretchedness to its natural close. When the hands returned from the field one night they found her dead! During the day, the Angel of the Lord, who moveth invisibly over all the earth, gathering in his harvest of departing souls, had silently entered the cabin of the dying woman, and taken her from thence. She was free at last!

Next day, rolling up my blanket, I started on my return to the Big Cane. After traveling five miles, at a place called Huff Power, the ever-present Tibeats met me in the road. He inquired why I was going back so soon, and when informed I was anxious to return by the time I was directed, he said I need go no farther than the next plantation, as he had that day sold me to Edwin Epps. We walked down into the yard, where we met the latter gentleman, who examined me, and asked me the usual questions propounded by purchasers. Having been duly delivered over, I was ordered to the quarters, and at the same time directed to make a hoe and axe handle for myself.

I was now no longer the property of Tibeats—his dog, his brute, dreading his wrath and cruelty day and night; and whoever or whatever my new master might prove to be, I could not, certainly, regret the change. So it was good news when the sale was announced, and with a sigh of relief I sat down for the first time in my new abode.

Tibeats soon after disappeared from that section of the country. Once afterwards, and only once, I caught a glimpse of him. It was many miles from Bayou Boeuf. He was seated in the doorway of a low groggery. I was passing, in a drove of slaves, through St. Mary's parish.

⊙ ⊙ ⊙

CHAPTER 12. PERSONAL APPEARANCE OF EPPS—EPPS, DRUNK AND SOBER...

⊙ ⊙ ⊙

Personal Appearance Of Epps—Epps, Drunk And Sober—A Glimpse Of His History—Cotton Growing—The Mode Of Ploughing And Preparing Ground—Of Planting—Of Hoeing, Of Picking, Of Treating Raw Hands—The Difference In Cotton Plckers—Patsey A Remarkable One—Tasked According To Ability—Beauty Of A Cotton Field—The Slave's Labors—Fear On Approaching The Ginhouse— Weighing—"Chores"—Cabin Life—The Corn Mill—The Uses Of The Gourd—Fear Of Oversleeping—Fear Continually—Mode Of Cultivating Corn—Sweet Potatoes— Fertility Of The Soil—Fattening Hogs—Preserving Bacon—Raising Cattle— Shooting-Matches—Garden Products—Flowers And Verdure.

EDWIN EPPS, of whom much will be said during the remainder of this history, is a large, portly, heavybodied man with light hair, high cheek bones, and a Roman nose of extraordinary dimensions. He has blue eyes, a fair complexion, and is, as I should say, full six feet high. He has the sharp, inquisitive expression of a jockey. His manners are repulsive and coarse, and his language gives speedy and unequivocal evidence that he has never enjoyed the advantages of an education. He has the faculty of saying most provoking things, in that respect even excelling old Peter Tanner. At the time I came into his possession, Edwin Epps was fond of the bottle, his "sprees" sometimes extending over the space of two whole weeks. Latterly, however, he had reformed his habits, and when I left him, was as strict a specimen of temperance as could be found on Bayou Boeuf When "in his Cups," Master Epps was a roystering, blustering, noisy fellow, whose chief delight was in dancing with his "niggers," or lashing them about the yard with his long whip, just for the pleasure of hearing them screech and scream, as the great welts were planted on their backs. When sober, he was silent, reserved and cunning, not beating us indiscriminately, as in his drunken moments, but sending the end of his rawhide to some tender spot of a lagging slave, with a sly dexterity peculiar to himself.

He had been a driver and overseer in his younger years, but at this time was in possession of a plantation on Bayou Huff Power, two and a half miles from Holmesville, eighteen from Marksville, and twelve from Cheneyville. It belonged to Joseph B. Roberts, his wife's uncle, and was leased by Epps. His principal business was raising cotton, and inasmuch as some may read this book who have never seen a cotton field, a description of the manner of its culture may not be out of place.

The ground is prepared by throwing up beds or ridges, with the plough—back–furrowing, it is called. Oxen and mules, the latter almost exclusively, are used in ploughing. The women as frequently as the men perform this labor, feeding, currying, and taking care of their teams, and in all respects doing the field and stable work, precisely as do the ploughboys of the North.

The beds, or ridges, are six feet wide, that is, from water furrow to water furrow. A plough drawn by one mule is then run along the top of the ridge or center of the bed, making the drill, into which a girl usually drops the seed, which she carries in a bag hung round her neck. Behind her comes a mule and harrow, covering up the seed, so that two mules three slaves, a plough and harrow, are employed in planting a row of cotton. This is done in the months of March and April. Corn is planted in February. When there are no cold rains, the cotton usually makes its appearance in a week. In the course of eight or ten days afterwards the first hoeing is commenced. This is performed in part, also, by the aid of the plough and mule. The plough passes as near as possible to the cotton on both sides, throwing the furrow from it. Slaves follow with their hoes, cutting up the grass and cotton, leaving hills two feet and a half apart. This is called scraping cotton. In two weeks more commences the second hoeing. This time the furrow is thrown towards the cotton. Only one stalk, the largest, is now left standing in each hill. In another fortnight it is hoed the third time, throwing the furrow towards the cotton in the same manner as before, and killing all the grass between the rows. About the first of July, when it is a foot high or thereabouts, it is hoed the fourth and last time. Now the whole space between the rows is ploughed, leaving a deep water furrow in the center. During all these hoeings the overseer or driver follows the slaves on horseback with a whip, such as has been described. The fastest hoer takes the lead row. He is usually about a rod in advance of his companions. If one of them passes him, he is whipped. If one falls behind or is a moment idle, he is whipped. In fact, the lash is flying from morning until night, the whole day long. The hoeing season thus continues from April until July, a field having no sooner been finished once, than it is commenced again.

In the latter part of August begins the cotton picking season. At this time each slave is presented with a sack. A strap is fastened to it, which goes over the neck, holding the mouth of the sack breast high, while the bottom reaches nearly to the ground. Each one is also presented with a large basket that will hold about two barrels. This is to put the cotton in when the sack is filled. The baskets are carried to the field and placed at the beginning of the rows.

When a new hand, one unaccustomed to the business, is sent for the first time into the field, he is whipped up smartly, and made for that day to pick as fast as he can possibly. At night it is weighed, so that his capability in cotton picking is known. He must bring in the same weight each night following. If it falls short, it is considered evidence that he has been laggard, and a greater or less number of lashes is the penalty.

An ordinary day's work is two hundred pounds. A slave who is accustomed to picking, is punished, if he or she brings in a less quantity than that. There is a great difference among them as regards this kind of labor. Some of them seem to have a natural knack, or quickness, which enables them to pick with great celerity, and with both hands, while others, with whatever practice or industry, are utterly unable to come up to the ordinary standard. Such hands are taken from the cotton field and employed in other business. Patsey, of whom I shall have more to say, was known as the most remarkable cotton picker on Bayou Boeuf. She picked with both hands and with such surprising rapidity, that five hundred pounds a day was not unusual for her.

Each one is tasked, therefore, according to his picking abilities, none, however, to come short of two hundred weight. I, being unskillful always in that business, would have satisfied my master by bringing in the latter quantity, while on the other hand, Patsey would surely have been beaten if she failed to produce twice as much.

The cotton grows from five to seven feet high, each stalk having a great many branches, shooting out in all directions, and lapping each other above the water furrow.

There are few sights more pleasant to the eye, than a wide cotton field when it is in the bloom. It presents an appearance of purity, like an immaculate expanse of light, new–fallen snow.

Sometimes the slave picks down one side of a row, and back upon the other, but more usually, there is one on either side, gathering all that has blossomed, leaving the unopened boils for a succeeding picking. When the sack is filled, it is emptied into the basket and trodden down. It is necessary to be extremely careful the first time going through the field, in order not to break the branches off the stalks. The cotton will not bloom upon a broken branch. Epps never failed to inflict the severest chastisement on the unlucky servant who, either carelessly or unavoidably, was guilty in the least degree in this respect.

The hands are required to be in the cotton field as soon as it is light in the morning, and, with the exception of ten or fifteen minutes, which is given them at noon to swallow their allowance of cold bacon, they are not permitted to be a moment idle until it is too dark to see, and when the moon is full, they often times labor till the middle of the night. They do not dare to stop even at dinner time, nor return to the quarters, however late it be, until the order to halt is given by the driver.

The day's work over in the field, the baskets are "toted," or in other words, carried to the gin-house, where the cotton is weighed. No matter how fatigued and weary he may be—no matter how much he longs for sleep and rest—a slave never approaches the gin-house with his basket of cotton but with fear. If it falls short in weight—if he has not performed the full task appointed him, he knows that he must suffer. And if he has exceeded it by ten or twenty pounds, in all probability his master will measure the next day's task accordingly. So, whether he has too little or too much, his approach to the gin-house is always with fear and trembling. Most frequently they have too little, and therefore it is they are not anxious to leave the field. After weighing, follow the whippings; and then the baskets are carried to the cotton house, and their contents stored away like hay, all hands being sent in to tramp it down. If the cotton is not dry, instead of taking it to the gin-house at once, it is laid upon platforms, two feet high, and some three times as wide, covered with boards or plank, with narrow walks running between them.

This done, the labor of the day is not yet ended, by any means. Each one must then attend to his respective chores. One feeds the mules, another the swine—another cuts the wood, and so forth; besides, the packing is all done by candle light. Finally, at a late hour, they reach the quarters, sleepy and overcome with the long day's toil. Then a fire must be kindled in the cabin, the corn ground in the small hand-mill, and supper, and dinner for the next day in the field, prepared. All that is allowed them is corn and bacon, which is given out at the corncrib and smoke-house every Sunday morning. Each one receives, as his weekly allowance, three and a half pounds of bacon, and corn enough to make a peck of meal.

That is all—no tea, coffee, sugar, and with the exception of a very scanty sprinkling now and then, no salt. I can say, from a ten years' residence with Master Epps, that no slave of his is ever likely to suffer from the gout, superinduced by excessive high living. Master Epps' hogs were fed on shelled corn—it was thrown out to his "niggers" in the ear. The former, he thought, would fatten faster by shelling, and soaking it in the water—the latter, perhaps, if treated in the same manner, might grow too fat to labor. Master Epps was a shrewd calculator, and knew how to manage his own animals, drunk or sober.

The corn mill stands in the yard beneath a shelter. It is like a common coffee mill, the hopper holding about six quarts. There was one privilege which Master Epps granted freely to every slave he had. They might grind their corn nightly, in such small quantities as their daily wants required, or they might grind the whole week's allowance at one time, on Sundays, just as they preferred. A very generous man was Master Epps!

I kept my corn in a small wooden box, the meal in a gourd; and, by the way, the gourd is one of the most convenient and necessary utensils on a plantation. Besides supplying the place of all kinds of crockery in a slave cabin, it is used for carrying water to the fields. Another, also, contains the dinner. It dispenses with the necessity of pails, dippers, basins, and such tin and wooden superfluities altogether.

When the corn is ground, and fire is made, the bacon is taken down from the nail on which it hangs a slice cut off and thrown upon the coals to broil. The majority of slaves have no knife, much less a fork. They cut their bacon with the axe at the woodpile. The corn meal is mixed with a little water, placed in the fire, and baked. When it is "done brown," the ashes are scraped off; and being placed upon a chip, which answers for a table, the tenant of the slave hut is ready to sit down upon the ground to supper. By this time it is usually midnight. The same fear of punishment with which they approach the gin-house, possesses them again on lying down to get a snatch of rest. It is the fear of oversleeping in the morning. Such an offence would certainly be attended with not less than twenty lashes.

With a prayer that he may be on his feet and wide awake at the first sound of the horn, he sinks to his slumbers nightly.

The softest couches in the world are not to be found in the log mansion of the slave. The one whereon I reclined year after year, was a plank twelve inches wide and ten feet long. My pillow was a stick of wood. The bedding was a coarse blanket, and not a rag or shred beside. Moss might be used, were it not that it directly breeds a swarm of fleas.

The cabin is constructed of logs, without floor or window. The latter is altogether unnecessary, the crevices between the logs admitting sufficient light. In stormy weather the rain drives through them, rendering it comfortless and extremely disagreeable. The rude door hangs on great wooden hinges. In one end is constructed an awkward fire–place.

An hour before day light the horn is blown. Then the slaves arouse, prepare their breakfast, fill a gourd with water, in another deposit their dinner of cold bacon and corn cake, and hurry to the field again. It is an offence invariably followed by a flogging, to be found at the quarters after daybreak. Then the fears and labors of another day begin; and until its close there is no such thing as rest. He fears he will be caught lagging through the day; he fears to approach the gin–house with his basket–load of cotton at night; he fears, when he lies down, that he will oversleep himself in the morning. Such is a true, faithful, unexaggerated picture and description of the slave's daily life, during the time of cotton– picking, on the shores of Bayou Boeuf.

In the month of January, generally, the fourth and last picking is completed. Then commences the harvesting, of corn. This is considered a secondary crop, and receives far less attention than the cotton. It is planted, as already mentioned, in February. Corn is grown in that region for the purpose of fattening hogs and feeding slaves; very little, if any, being sent to market. It is the white variety, the ear of great size, and the stalk growing to the height of eight, and often times ten feet. In August the leaves are stripped off, dried in the sun, bound in small bundles, and stored away as provender for the mules and oxen. After this the slaves go through the field, turning down the ear, for the purpose of keeping the rains from penetrating to the grain. It is left in this condition until after cotton-picking is over, whether earlier or later. Then the ears are separated from the stalks, and deposited in the corncrib with the husks on; otherwise, stripped of the husks, the weevil would destroy it. The stalks are left standing in the field.

The Carolina, or sweet potato, is also grown in that region to some extent. They are not fed, however, to hogs or cattle, and are considered but of small importance. They are preserved by placing them upon the surface of the ground, with a slight covering of earth or cornstalks. There is not a cellar on Bayou Boeuf. The ground is so low it would fill with water. Potatoes are worth from two to three "bits," or shillings a barrel; corn, except when there is an unusual scarcity, can be purchased at the same rate.

As soon as the cotton and corn crops are secured, the stalks are pulled up, thrown into piles and burned. The ploughs are started at the same time, throwing up the beds again, preparatory to another planting. The soil, in the parishes of Rapides and Avoyelles, and throughout the whole country, so far as my observation extended, is of exceeding richness and fertility. It is a kind of marl, of a brown or reddish color. It does not require those invigorating composts necessary to more barren lands, and on the same field the same crop is grown for many successive years.

Ploughing, planting, picking cotton, gathering the corn, and pulling and burning stalks, occupies the whole of the four seasons of the year. Drawing and cutting wood, pressing cotton, fattening and killing hog's, are but incidental labors.

In the month of September or October, the hogs are run out of the swamps by dogs, and confined in pens. On a cold morning, generally about New Year's day, they are slaughtered. Each carcass is cut into six parts, and piled one above the other in salt, upon large tables in the smoke-house.

In this condition it remains a fortnight, when it is hung up, and a fire built, and continued more than half the time during the remainder of the year. This thorough smoking is necessary to prevent the bacon from becoming infested with worms. In so warm a climate it is difficult to preserve it, and very many times myself and my companions have received our weekly allowance of three pounds and a half, when it was full of these disgusting vermin.

Although the swamps are overrun with cattle, they are never made the source of profit, to any considerable extent. The planter cuts his mark upon the ear, or brands his initials upon the side, and turns them into the swamps, to roam unrestricted within their almost limitless confines. They are the Spanish breed, small and spike–horned. I have known of droves being taken from Bayou Boeuf, but it is of very rare occurrence. The value of the best cows is about five dollars each. Two quarts at one milking, would be considered an unusual large quantity. They furnish little tallow, and that of a soft, inferior quality. Notwithstanding the great number of cows that throng the swamps, the planters are indebted to the North for their cheese and butter, which is purchased in the New–Orleans market. Salted beef is not an article of food either in the great house, or in the cabin.

Master Epps was accustomed to attend shooting matches for the purpose of obtaining what fresh beef he required. These sports occurred weekly at the neighboring village of Holmesville. Fat beeves are driven thither and shot at, a stipulated price being demanded for the privilege. The lucky marksman divides the flesh among his fellows, and in this manner the attending planters are supplied.

The great number of tame and untamed cattle which swarm the woods and swamps of Bayou Boeuf, most probably suggested that appellation to the French, inasmuch as the term, translated, signifies the creek or river of the wild ox.

Garden products, such as cabbages, turnips and the like, are cultivated for the use of the master and his family. They have greens and vegetables at all times and seasons of the year. "The grass withereth and the flower fadeth" before the desolating winds of autumn in the chill northern latitudes, but perpetual verdure overspreads the hot lowlands, and flowers bloom in the heart of winter, in the region of Bayou Boeuf.

There are no meadows appropriated to the cultivation of the grasses. The leaves of the corn supply a sufficiency of food for the laboring cattle, while the rest provide for themselves all the year in the evergrowing pasture.

There are many other peculiarities of climate, habit, custom, and of the manner of living and laboring at the South, but the foregoing, it is supposed, will give the reader an insight and general idea of life on a cotton plantation in Louisiana. The mode of cultivating cane, and the process of sugar manufacturing, will be mentioned in another place.

⊙ ⊙ ⊙

CHAPTER 13. THE CURIOUS AXE-HELVE— SYMPTOMS OF APPROACHING ILLNESS...

The Curious Axe-Helve—Symptoms Of Approaching Illness—Continue To Decline— The Whip Ineffectual—Confined To The Cabin—Visit By Dr. Wines—Art—Partial Recovery—Failure At Cotton Picking—What May Be Heard On Epps' Plantation— Lashes Graduated—Epps In A Whipping Mood—Epps In A Dancing Mood— Description Of The Dance—Loss Of Rest No Excuse—Epps' Characteristics—Jim Burns—Removal From Huff Power To Bayou Boeuf—Description Of Uncle Abram; Of Wiley; Of Aunt Phebe; Of Bob, Henry, And Edward; Of Petsey; With A Genealogical Account Of Each—Something Of Their Past History, And Peculiar Characteristics—Jealousy And Lust—Patsey, The Victim.

On my arrival at Master Epps', in obedience to his order, the first business upon which I entered was the making of an axe–halve. The handles in use there are simply a round, straight stick. I made a crooked one, shaped like those to which I had been accustomed at the North. When finished, and presented to Epps, he looked at it with astonishment, unable to determine exactly what it was. He had never before seen such a handle, and when I explained its conveniences, he was forcibly struck with the novelty of the idea. He kept it in the house a long time, and when his friends called, was wont to exhibit it as a curiosity.

It was now the season of hoeing. I was first sent into the corn–field, and afterwards set to scraping cotton. In this employment I remained until hoeing time was nearly passed, when I began to experience the symptoms of approaching illness. I was attacked with chills, which were succeeded by a burning fever. I became weak and emaciated, and frequently so dizzy that it caused me to reel and stagger like a drunken man. Nevertheless, I was compelled to keep up my row. When in health I found little difficulty in keeping pace with my fellow–laborers, but now it seemed to be an utter impossibility. Often I fell behind, when the driver's lash was sure to greet my back, infusing into my sick and drooping body a little temporary energy. I continued to decline until at length the whip became entirely ineffectual. The sharpest sting of the rawhide could not arouse me. Finally, in September, when the busy season of cotton picking was at hand, I was unable to leave my cabin. Up to this time I had received no medicine, nor any attention from my master or mistress. The old cook visited me occasionally, preparing me corn–coffee, and sometimes boiling a bit of bacon, when I had grown too feeble to accomplish it myself.

When it was said that I would die, Master Epps, unwilling to bear the loss, which the death of an animal worth a thousand dollars would bring upon him, concluded to incur the expense of sending to Holmesville for Dr. Wines. He announced to Epps that it was the effect of the climate, and there was a probability of his losing me. He directed me to eat no meat, and to partake of no more food than was absolutely necessary to sustain life. Several weeks elapsed, during which time, under the scanty diet to which I was subjected, I had partially recovered. One morning, long before I was in a proper condition to labor, Epps appeared at the cabin door, and, presenting me a sack, ordered me to the cotton field. At this time I had had no experience whatever in cotton picking. It was an awkward business indeed. While, others used both hands, snatching the cotton and depositing it in the mouth of the sack, with a precision and dexterity that was incomprehensible to me, I had to seize the boll with one hand, and deliberately draw out the white, gushing blossom with the other.

Depositing the cotton in the sack, moreover, was a difficulty that demanded the exercise of both hand and eyes. I was compelled to pick it from the ground where it would fall, nearly as often as from the stalk where it had grown. I made havoc also with the branches, loaded with the yet unbroken bolls, the long, cumbersome sack swinging from side to side in a manner not allowable in the cotton field. After a most laborious day I arrived at the gin-house with my load. When the scale determined its weight to be only ninety-five pounds, not half the quantity required of the poorest picker, Epps threatened the severest flogging, but in consideration of my being a "raw hand," concluded to pardon me on that occasion. The following day, and many days succeeding, I returned at night with no better success—I was evidently not designed for that kind of labor. I had not the gift—the dexterous fingers and quick motion of Patsey, who could fly along one side of a row of cotton, stripping it of its undefiled and fleecy whiteness miraculously fast. Practice and whipping were alike unavailing, and Epps, satisfied of it at last, swore I was a disgrace—that I was not fit to associate with a cotton-picking "nigger"— that I could not pick enough in a day to pay the trouble of weighing it, and that I should go into the cotton field no more. I was now employed in cutting and hauling wood, drawing cotton from the field to the gin- house, and performed whatever other service was required. Suffice to say, I was never permitted to be idle.

It was rarely that a day passed by without one or more whippings. This occurred at the time the cotton was weighed. The delinquent, whose weight had fallen short, was taken out, stripped, made to lie upon the ground, face downwards, when he received a punishment proportioned to his offence. It is the literal, unvarnished truth, that the crack of the lash, and the shrieking of the slaves, can be heard from dark till bed time, on Epps' plantation, any day almost during the entire period of the cotton-picking season.

The number of lashes is graduated according to the nature of the case. Twenty-five are deemed a mere brush, inflicted, for instance, when a dry leaf or piece of boll is found in the cotton, or when a branch is broken in the field; fifty is the ordinary penalty following all delinquencies of the next higher grade; one hundred is called severe; it is the punishment inflicted for the serious offence of standing idle in the field; from one hundred and fifty to two hundred is bestowed upon him who quarrels with his cabin-mates, and five hundred, well laid on, besides the mangling of the dogs, perhaps, is certain to consign the poor, unpitied runaway to weeks of pain and agony.

During the two years Epps remained on the plantation at Bayou Huff Power, he was in the habit, as often as once in a fortnight at least, of coming home intoxicated from Holmesville. The shooting-matches almost invariably concluded with a debauch. At such times he was boisterous and half-crazy. Often he would break the dishes, chairs, and whatever furniture he could lay his hands on. When satisfied with his amusement in the house, he would seize the whip and walk forth into the yard. Then it behooved the slaves to be watchful and exceeding wary. The first one who came within reach felt the smart of his lash. Sometimes for hours he would keep them running in all directions, dodging around the corners of the cabins. Occasionally he would come upon one unawares, and if he succeeded in inflicting a fair, round blow, it was a feat that much delighted him. The younger children, and the aged, who had become inactive, suffered then. In the midst of, the confusion he would slyly take his stand behind a cabin, waiting with raised whip, to dash it into the first black face that peeped cautiously around the corner.

At other times he would come home in a less brutal humor. Then there must be a merry-making. Then all must move to the measure of a tune. Then Master Epps must needs regale his melodious ears with the music of a fiddle. Then did he become buoyant, elastic, gaily "tripping the light fantastic toe" around the piazza and all thorough the house.

Tibeats, at the time of my sale, had informed him I could play on the violin. He had received his information from Ford. Through the importunities of Mistress Epps, her husband had been induced to purchase me one during a visit to New-Orleans. Frequently I was called into the house to play before the family, mistress being passionately fond of music.

All of us would be assembled in the large room of the great house, whenever Epps came home in one of his dancing moods. No matter how worn out and tired we were, there must be a general dance. When properly stationed on the floor, I would strike up a tune.

"Dance, you d–d niggers, dance," Epps would shout.

Then there must be no halting or delay, no slow or languid movements; all must be brisk, and lively, and alert. "Up and down, heel and toe, and away we go," was the order of the hour. Epps' portly form mingled with those of his dusky slaves, moving rapidly through all the mazes of the dance.

Usually his whip was in his hand, ready to fall about the ears of the presumptuous thrall, who dared to rest a moment, or even stop to catch his breath. When he was himself exhausted, there would be a brief cessation, but it would be very brief With a slash, and crack, and flourish of the whip, he would shout again, "Dance, niggers, dance," and away they would go once more, pell–mell, while I, spurred by an occasional sharp touch of the lash, sat in a corner, extracting from my violin a marvelous quick–stepping tune. The mistress often upbraided him, declaring she would return to her father's house at Cheneyville; nevertheless, there were times she could not restrain a burst of laughter, on witnessing his uproarious pranks. Frequently, we were thus detained until almost morning. Bent with excessive toil—actually suffering for a little refreshing rest, and feeling rather as if we could cast ourselves upon the earth and weep, many a night in the house of Edwin Epps have his unhappy slaves been made to dance and laugh.

Notwithstanding these deprivations in order to gratify the whim of an unreasonable master, we had to be in the field as soon as it was light, and during the day perform the ordinary and accustomed task. Such deprivations could not be urged at the scales in extenuation of any lack of weight, or in the cornfield for not hoeing with the usual rapidity. The whippings were just as severe as if we had gone forth in the morning, strengthened and invigorated by a night's repose. Indeed, after such frantic revels, he was always more sour and savage than before, punishing for slighter causes, and using the whip with increased and more vindictive energy.

Ten years I toiled for that man without reward. Ten years of my incessant labor has contributed to increase the bulk of his possessions. Ten years I was compelled to address him with down-cast eyes and uncovered head—in the attitude and language of a slave. I am indebted to him for nothing, save undeserved abuse and stripes.

Beyond the reach of his inhuman thong, and standing on the soil of the free State where I was born, thanks be to Heaven, I can raise my head once more among men. I can speak of the wrongs I have suffered, and of those who inflicted them, with upraised eyes. But I have no desire to speak of him or any other one otherwise than truthfully. Yet to speak truthfully of Edwin Epps would be to say—he is a man in whose heart the quality of kindness or of justice is not found. A rough, rude energy, united with an uncultivated mind and an avaricious spirit, are his prominent characteristics. He is known as a "nigger breaker," distinguished for his faculty of subduing the spirit of the slave, and priding himself upon his reputation in this respect, as a jockey boasts of his skill in managing a refractory horse. He looked upon a colored man, not as a human being, responsible to his Creator for the small talent entrusted to him, but as a "chattel personal," as mere live property, no better, except in value, than his mule or dog. When the evidence, clear and indisputable, was laid before him that I was a free man, and as much entitled to my liberty as he —when, on the day I left, he was informed that I had a wife and children, as dear to me as his own babes to him, he only raved and swore, denouncing the law that tore me from him, and declaring he would find out the man who had forwarded the letter that disclosed the place of my captivity, if there was any virtue or power in money, and would take his life. He thought of nothing but his loss, and cursed me for having been born free. He could have stood unmoved and seen the tongues of his poor slaves torn out by the roots—he could have seen them burned to ashes over a slow fire, or gnawed to death by dogs, if it only brought him profit. Such a hard, cruel, unjust man is Edwin Epps.

There was but one greater savage on Bayou Boeuf than he. Jim Burns' plantation was cultivated, as already mentioned, exclusively by women. That barbarian kept their backs so sore and raw, that they could not perform the customary labor demanded daily of the slave. He boasted of his cruelty, and through all the country round was accounted a more thorough-going, energetic man than even Epps. A brute himself, Jim Burns had not a particle of mercy for his subject brutes, and like a fool, whipped and scourged away the very strength upon which depended his amount of gain.

Epps remained on Huff Power two years, when, having accumulated a considerable sum of money, he expended it in the purchase of the plantation on the east bank of Bayou Boeuf, where he still continues to reside. He took possession of it in 1845, after the, holidays were passed. He carried thither with him nine slaves, all of whom, except myself, and Susan, who has since died, remain there yet. He made no addition to this force, and for eight years the following were my companions in his quarters, viz; Abram, Wiley, Phebe, Bob, Henry, Edward, and Patsey. All these, except Edward, born since, were purchased out of a drove by Epps during the time he was overseer for Archy B. Williams, whose plantation is situated on the shore of Red River, not far from Alexandria.

Abram was tall, standing a full head above any common man. He is sixty years of age, and was born in Tennessee. Twenty years ago, he was purchased by a trader, carried into South Carolina, and sold to James Buford, of Williamsburgh county, in that State. In his youth he was renowned for his great strength, but age and unremitting toil have somewhat shattered his powerful frame and enfeebled his mental faculties.

Wiley is forty-eight. He was born on the estate, of William Tassle, and for many years took charge of that gentleman's ferry over the Big Black River, in South Carolina.

Phebe was a slave of Buford, Tassle's neighbor, and having married Wiley, he bought the latter, at her instigation. Buford was a kind master, sheriff of the county, and in those days a man of wealth.

Bob and Henry are Phebe's children, by a former husband, their father having been abandoned to give place to Wiley. That seductive youth had insinuated himself into Phebe's affections, and therefore the faithless spouse had gently kicked her first husband out of her cabin door. Edward had been born to them on Bayou Huff Power.

Patsey is twenty–three—also from Buford's plantation. She is in no wise connected with the others, but glories in the fact that she is the offspring of a "Guinea nigger," brought over to Cuba in a slave ship, and in the course of trade transferred to Buford, who was her mother's owner.

This, as I learned from them, is a genealogical account of my master's shaves. For years they had been together. Often they recalled the memories of other days, and sighed to retrace their steps to the old home in Carolina. Troubles came upon their master Buford, which brought far greater troubles upon them. He became involved in debt, and unable to bear up against his failing fortunes, was compelled to sell these, and others of his slaves. In a chain gang they had been driven from beyond the Mississippi to the plantation of Archy B. Williams. Edwin Epps, who, for a long while had been his driver and overseer, was about establishing himself in business on his own account, at the time of their arrival, and accepted them in payment of his wages.

Old Abram was a kind–hearted being—a sort of patriarch among us, fond of entertaining his younger brethren with grave and serious discourse. He was deeply versed in such philosophy as is taught in the cabin of the slave; but the great absorbing hobby of Uncle Abram was General Jackson, whom his young master in Tennessee had followed to the wars. He loved to wander back, in imagination, to the place where he was born, and to recount the scenes of his youth during those stirring times when the nation was in arms. He had been athletic, and more keen and powerful than the generality of his race, but now his eye had become dim, and his natural force abated. Very often, indeed, while discussing the best method of baking the hoe–cake, or expatiating at large upon the glory of Jackson, he would forget where he left his hat, or his hoe, or his basket; and then would the old man be laughed at, if Epps was absent, and whipped if he was present. So was he perplexed continually, and sighed to think that he was growing aged and going to decay. Philosophy and Jackson and forgetfulness had played the mischief with him, and it was evident that all of them combined were fast bringing down the gray hairs of Uncle Abram to the grave.

Aunt Phebe had been an excellent field hand, but latterly was put into the kitchen, where she remained, except occasionally, in a time of uncommon hurry. She was a sly old creature, and when not in the presence of her mistress or her master, was garrulous in the extreme.

Wiley, on the contrary, was silent. He performed his task without murmur or complaint, seldom indulging in the luxury of speech, except to utter a wish that he was away from Epps, and back once more in South Carolina.

Bob and Henry had reached the ages of twenty and twenty–three, and were distinguished for nothing extraordinary or unusual, while Edward, a lad of thirteen, not yet able to maintain his row in the corn or the cotton field, was kept in the great house, to wait on the little Eppses.

Patsey was slim and straight. She stood erect as the human form is capable of standing. There was an air of loftiness in her movement, that neither labor, nor weariness, nor punishment could destroy. Truly, Patsey was a splendid animal, and were it not that bondage had enshrouded her intellect in utter and everlasting darkness, would have been chief among ten thousand of her people. She could leap the highest fences, and a fleet hound it was indeed, that could outstrip her in a race. No horse could fling her from his back. She was a skillful teamster. She turned as true a furrow as the best, and at splitting rails there were none who could excel her. When the order to halt was heard at night, she would have her mules at the crib, unharnessed, fed and curried before uncle Abram had found his hat. Not, however, for all or any of these, was she chiefly famous. Such lightning-like motion was in her fingers as no other fingers ever possessed, and therefore it was, that in cotton picking time, Patsey was queen of the field.

She had a genial and pleasant temper, and was faithful and obedient. Naturally, she was a joyous creature, a laughing , light-hearted girl, rejoicing in the mere sense of existence. Yet Patsey wept oftener, and suffered more, than any of her companions. She had been literally excoriated. Her back bore the scars of a thousand stripes; not because she was backward in her work, nor because she was of an unmindful and rebellious spirit, but because it had fallen to her lot to be the slave of a licentious master and a jealous mistress. She shrank before the lustful eye of the one, and was in danger even of her life at the hands of the other, and between the two, she was indeed accursed. In-the great house, for days together, there were high and angry words, poutings and estrangement, whereof she was the innocent cause. Nothing delighted the mistress so much as to see her suffer, and more than once, when Epps had refused to sell her, has she tempted me with bribes to put her secretly to death, and bury her body in some lonely place in the margin of the swamp. Gladly would Patsey have appeased this unforgiving spirit, if it had been in her power, but not like Joseph, dared she escape from Master Epps, leaving her garment in his hand. Patsey walked under a cloud. If she uttered a word in opposition to her master's will, the lash was resorted to at once, to bring her to subjection; if she was not watchful when about her cabin, or when walking in the yard, a billet of wood, or a broken bottle perhaps, hurled from her mistress' hand, would smite her unexpectedly in the face. The enslaved victim of lust and hate, Patsey had no comfort of her life.

These were my companions and fellow-slaves, with whom I was accustomed to be driven to the field, and with whom it has been my lot to dwell for ten years in the log cabins of Edwin Epps. They, if living, are yet toiling on the banks of Bayou Boeuf, never destined to breathe, as I now do, the blessed air of liberty, nor to shake off the heavy shackles that enthrall them, until they shall lie down forever in the dust.

⊙ ⊙ ⊙

CHAPTER 14. DESTRUCTION OF THE COTTON CROP IN 1845—DEMAND FOR LABORERS...

⊙ ⊙ ⊙

Destruction Of The Cotton Crop In 1845—Demand For Laborers In St. Mary's Parish—Sent Thither In A Drove—The Order Of The March—The Grand Coteau— Hired To Judge Turner On Bayou Salle—Appointed Driver In His Sugar House— Sunday Services Slave Furniture, How Obtained—The Party At Yarney's, In Centreville—Good Fortune—The Captain Of The Steamer—His Refusal To Secrete Me—Return To Bayou Boeuf—Sight Of Tibeats—Patsey's Sorrows—Tumult And Contention—Hunting The Coon And Opossum—The Cunning Of The Latter—The Lean Condition Of The Slave—Description Of The Fish Trap—The Murder Of The Man From Natchez—Epps Challenged By Marshall—The Influence Of Slavery—The Love Of Freedom.

THE first year of Epps' residence on the bayou, 1845, the caterpillars almost totally destroyed the cotton crop throughout that region. There was little to be done, so that the slaves were necessarily idle half the time. However, there came a rumor to Bayou Boeuf that wages were high, and laborers in great demand on the sugar plantations in St. Mary's parish. This parish is situated on the coast of the Gulf of Mexico, about one hundred and forty miles from Avoyelles. The Rio Teche, a considerable stream, flows through St. Mary's to the gulf.

It was determined by the planters, on the receipt of this intelligence, to make up a drove of slaves to be sent down to Tuckapaw in St. Mary's, for the purpose of hiring them out in the cane fields. Accordingly, in the month of September, there were one hundred and forty-seven collected at Holmesville, Abram, Bob and myself among the number. Of these about one-half were women. Epps, Alonson Pierce, Henry Toler, and Addison Roberts, were the white men, selected to accompany, and take charge of the drove. They had a two-horse carriage and two saddle horses for their use. A large wagon, drawn by four horses, and driven by John, a boy belonging to Mr. Roberts, carried the blankets and provisions.

About 2 o'clock in the afternoon, having been fed, preparations were made to depart. The duty assigned me was, to take charge of the blankets and provisions, and see that none were lost by the way. The carriage proceeded in advance, the wagon following; behind this the slaves were arranged, while the two horsemen brought up the rear, and in this order the procession moved out of Holmesville.

That night we reached a Mr. McCrow's plantation, a distance of ten or fifteen miles, when we were ordered to halt. Large fires were built, and each one spreading his blanket on the ground, laid down upon it. The white men lodged in the great house. An hour before day we were aroused by the drivers coming among us, cracking their whips and ordering us to arise. Then the blankets were rolled up, and being severally delivered to me and deposited in the wagon, the procession set forth again.

The following night it rained violently. We were all drenched, our clothes saturated with mud and water. Reaching an open shed, formerly a gin-house, we found beneath it such shelter as it afforded. There was not room for all of us to lay down. There we remained, huddled together, through the night, continuing our march, as usual, in the morning. During the journey we were fed twice a day, boiling our bacon and baking our corn-cake at the fires in the same manner as in our huts. We passed through Lafayetteville, Mountsville, New-Town, to Centreville, where Bob and Uncle Abram were hired. Our number decreased as we advanced—nearly every sugar plantation requiring the services of one or more.

On our route we passed the Grand Coteau or prairie, a vast space of level, monotonous country, without a tree, except an occasional one which had been transplanted near some dilapidated dwelling. It was once thickly populated, and under cultivation, but for some cause had been abandoned. The business of the scattered inhabitants that now dwell upon it is principally raising cattle. Immense herds were feeding upon it as we passed. In the centre of the Grand Coteau one feels as if he were on the ocean, out of sight of land. As far as the eye can see, in all directions, it is but a ruined and deserted waste.

I was hired to Judge Turner, a distinguished man and extensive planter, whose large estate is situated on Bayou Salle, within a few miles of the gulf. Bayou Salle is a small stream flowing into the bay of Atchafalaya. For some days I was employed at Turner's in repairing his sugar house, when a cane knife was put into my hand, and with thirty or forty others, I was sent into the field. I found no such difficulty in learning the art of cutting cane that I had in picking cotton. It came to me naturally and intuitively, and in a short time I was able to keep up with the fastest knife. Before the cutting was over, however, Judge Tanner transferred me from the field to the sugar house, to act there in the capacity of driver. From the time of the commencement of sugar making to the close, the grinding and boiling does not cease day or night. The whip was given me with directions to use it upon any one who was caught standing idle. If I failed to obey them to the letter, there was another one for my own back. In addition to this my duty was to call on and off the different gangs at the proper time. I had no regular periods of rest, and could never snatch but a few moments of sleep at a time.

It is the custom in Louisiana, as I presume it is in other slave States, to allow the slave to retain whatever compensation he may obtain for services performed on Sundays. In this way, only, are they able to provide themselves with any luxury or convenience whatever. When a slave, purchased, or kidnapped in the North, is transported to a cabin on Bayou Boeuf he is furnished with neither knife, nor fork, nor dish, nor kettle, nor any other thing in the shape of crockery, or furniture of any nature or description. He is furnished with a blanket before he reaches there, and wrapping that around him, he can either stand up, or lie down upon the ground, or on a board, if his master has no use for it. He is at liberty to find a gourd in which to keep his meal, or he can eat his corn from the cob, just as he pleases. To ask the master for a knife, or skillet, or any small convenience of the kind, would be answered with a kick, or laughed at as a joke. Whatever necessary article of this nature–is found in a cabin has been purchased with Sunday money. However injurious to the morals, it is certainly a blessing to the physical condition of the slave, to be permitted to break the Sabbath. Otherwise there would be no way to provide himself with any utensils, which seem to be indispensable to him who is compelled to be his own cook.

On cane plantations in sugar time, there is no distinction as to the days of the week. It is well understood that all hands must labor on the Sabbath, and it is equally well understood that those especially who are hired, as I was to Judge Turner, and others in succeeding years, shall receive remuneration for it. It is usual, also, in the most hurrying time of cotton–picking, to require the same extra service. From this source, slaves generally are afforded an opportunity of earning sufficient to purchase a knife, a kettle, tobacco and so forth. The females, discarding the latter luxury, are apt to expend their little revenue in the purchase of gaudy ribbons, wherewithal to deck their hair in the merry season of the holidays.

I remained in St. Mary's until the first of January, during which time my Sunday money amounted to ten dollars. I met with other good fortune, for which I was indebted to my violin, my constant companion, the source of profit, and soother of my sorrows during years of servitude. There was a grand party of whites assembled at Mr. Yarney's, in Centreville, a hamlet in the vicinity of Turner's plantation. I was employed to play for them, and so well pleased were the merry–makers with my performance, that a contribution was taken for my benefit, which amounted to seventeen dollars.

With this sum in possession, I was looked upon by my fellows as a millionaire. It afforded me great pleasure to look at it—to count it over and over again, day after day. Visions of cabin furniture, of water pails, of pocket knives, new shoes and coats and hats, floated through my fancy, and up through all rose the triumphant contemplation, that I was the wealthiest "nigger" on Bayou Boeuf.

Vessels run up the Rio Teche to Centreville. While there, I was bold enough one day to present myself before the captain of a steamer, and beg permission to hide myself among the freight. I was emboldened to risk the hazard of such a step, from overhearing a conversation, in the course of which I ascertained he was a native of tile North. I did not relate to him the particulars of my history, but only expressed an ardent desire to escape from slavery to a free State. He pitied me, but said it would be impossible to avoid the vigilant custom house officers in New- Orleans, and that detection would subject him to punishment, and his vessel to confiscation. My earnest entreaties evidently excited his sympathies, and doubtless he would have yielded to them, could he have done so with any kind of safety. I was compelled to smother the sudden flame that lighted up my bosom with sweet hopes of liberation, and turn my steps once more towards the increasing darkness of despair.

Immediately after this event the drove assembled at Centreville, and several of the owners having arrived and collected the monies due for our services we were driven back to Bayou Boeuf. It was on our return, while passing through a small village, that I caught sight of Tibeats, seated in the door of a dirty grocery, looking somewhat seedy and out of repair. Passion and poor whisky, I doubt not, have ere this laid him on the shelf.

During our absence, I learned from Aunt Phebe and Patsey, that the latter had been getting deeper and deeper into trouble. The poor girl was truly an object of pity. "Old Hogjaw," the name by which Epps was called, when the slaves were by themselves had beaten her more severely and frequently than ever. As surely as he came from Holmesville, elated with liquor—and it was often in those days—he would whip her, merely to gratify the mistress; would punish her to an extent almost beyond endurance, for an offence of which he himself was the sole and irresistible cause. In his sober moments he could not always be prevailed upon to indulge his wife's insatiable thirst for vengeance.

To be rid of Patsey—to place her beyond sight or reach, by sale, or death, or in any other manner, of late years, seemed to be the ruling thought and passion of my mistress. Patsey had been a favorite when a child, even in the great house. She had been petted and admired for her uncommon sprightliness and pleasant disposition. She had been fed many a time, so Uncle Abram said, even on biscuit and milk, when the madam, in her younger days, was wont to call her to the piazza, and fondle her as she would a playful kitten. But a sad change had come over the spirit of the woman. Now, only black and angry, fiends ministered in the temple of her heart, until she could look on Patsey but with concentrated venom.

Mistress Epps was not naturally such an evil woman, after all. She was possessed of the devil, jealousy, it is true, but aside from that, there was much in her character to admire. Her father, Mr. Roberts, resided in Cheneyville, an influential and honorable man, and as much respected throughout the parish as any other citizen. She had been well educated at some institution this side the Mississippi; was beautiful, accomplished, and usually good-humored. She was kind to all of us but Patsey—frequently, in the absence of her husband, sending out to us some little dainty from her own table. In other situations—in a different society from that which exists on the shores of Bayou Boeuf, she would have been pronounced an elegant and fascinating woman. An ill wind it was that blew her into the arms of Epps.

He respected and loved his wife as much as a coarse nature like his is capable of loving, but supreme selfishness always overmastered conjugal affection.

"He loved as well as baser natures can,

But a mean heart and soul were in that man."

He was ready to gratify any whim—to grant any request she made, provided it did not cost too much. Patsey was equal to any two of his slaves in the cotton field. He could not replace her with the same money she would bring. The idea of disposing of her, therefore, could not be entertained. The mistress did not regard her at all in that light. The pride of the haughty woman was aroused; the blood of the fiery southern boiled at the sight of Patsey, and nothing less than trampling out the life of the helpless bondwoman would satisfy her.

Sometimes the current of her wrath turned upon him whom she had just cause to hate. But the storm of angry words would pass over at length, and there would be a season of calm again. At such times Patsey trembled with fear, and cried as if her heart would break, for she knew from painful experience, that if mistress should work herself to the red- hot pitch of rage, Epps would quiet her at last with a promise that Patsey should be flogged a promise he was sure to keep. Thus did pride, and jealousy, and vengeance war with avarice and brute-passion in the mansion of my master, filling it with daily tumult and contention. Thus, upon the head of Patsey—the simpleminded slave, in whose heart God had implanted the seeds of virtue—the force of all these domestic tempests spent itself at last.

During the summer succeeding my return from St. Mary's parish, I conceived a plan of providing myself with food, which, though simple, succeeded beyond expectation. It has been followed by many others in my condition, up and down the bayou, and of such benefit has it become that I am almost persuaded to look upon myself as a benefactor. That summer the worms got into the bacon. Nothing but ravenous hunger could induce us to swallow it. The weekly allowance of meal scarcely sufficed to satisfy us. It was customary with us, as it is with all in that region, where the allowance is exhausted before Saturday night, or is in such a state as to render it nauseous and disgusting, to hunt in the swamps for coon and opossum. This, however, must be done at night, after the day's work is accomplished. There are planters whose slaves, for months at a time, have no other meat than such as is obtained in this manner. No objections are made to hunting, inasmuch as it dispenses with drafts upon the smoke-house, and because every marauding coon that is killed is so much saved from the standing corn. They are hunted with dogs and clubs, slaves not being allowed the use of fire-arms.

The flesh of the coon is palatable, but verily there is nothing in all butcherdom so delicious as a roasted 'possum. They are a round, rather long-bodied, little animal, of a whitish color, with nose like a pig, and caudal extremity like a rat. They burrow among the roots and in the hollows of the gum tree, and are clumsy and slow of motion. They are deceitful and cunning creatures. On receiving the slightest tap of a stick, they will roll over on the ground and feign death. If the hunter leaves him, in pursuit of another, without first taking particular pains to break his neck, the chances are, on his return, he is not to be found. The little animal has out witted the enemy —has "played 'possum"—and is off. But after a long and hard day's work, the weary slave feels little like going to the swamp for his supper, and half the time prefers throwing himself on the cabin floor without it. It is for the interest of the master that the servant should not suffer in health from starvation, and it is also for his interest that he should not become gross from over-feeding. In the estimation of the owner, a slave is the most serviceable when in rather a lean and lank condition, such a condition as the race-horse is in, when fitted for the course, and in that condition they are generally to be found on the sugar and cotton plantations along Red River.

My cabin was within a few rods of the bayou bank, and necessity being indeed the mother of invention, I resolved upon a mode of obtaining the requisite amount of food, without the trouble of resorting nightly to the woods. This was to construct a fish trap. Having, in my mind, conceived the manner in which it could be done, the next Sunday I set about putting it into practical execution. It may be impossible for me to convey to the reader a full and correct idea of its construction, but the following will serve as a general description.

A frame between two and three feet square is made, and of a greater or less height, according to the depth of water. Boards or slats are nailed on three sides of this frame, not so closely, however, as to prevent the water circulating freely through it. A door is fitted into the fourth side, in such manner that it will slide easily up and down in the grooves cut in the two posts. A movable bottom is then so fitted that it can be raised to the top of the frame without difficulty. In the centre of the movable bottom an auger hole is bored, and into this one end of a handle or round stick is fastened on the under side so loosely that it will turn. The handle ascends from the centre of the movable bottom to the top of the frame, or as much higher as is desirable. Up and down this handle, in a great many places, are gimlet holes, through which small sticks are inserted, extending to opposite sides of the frame. So many of these small sticks are running out from the handle in all directions, that a fish of any considerable dimensions cannot pass through without hitting one of them. The frame is then placed in the water and made stationary.

The trap is "set" by sliding or drawing up the door, and kept in that position by another stick, one end of which rests in a notch on the inner side, the other end in a notch made in the handle, running up from the centre of the movable bottom. The trap is baited by rolling a handful of wet meal and cotton together until it becomes hard, and depositing it in the back part of the frame. A fish swimming through the upraised door towards the bait, necessarily strikes one of the small sticks turning the handle, which displacing the stick supporting the door, the latter falls, securing the fish within the frame. Taking hold of the top of the handle, the movable bottom is then drawn up to the surface of the water, and the fish taken out. There may have been other such traps in use before mine was constructed, but if there were I had never happened to see one. Bayou Boeuf abounds in fish of large size and excellent quality and after this time

I w as very rarely in want of one for myself, or for my comrades. Thus a mine was opened—a new resource was developed, hitherto unthought of by the enslaved children of Africa, who toil and hunger along the shores of that sluggish, but prolific stream.

About the time of which I am now writing, an event occurred in our immediate neighborhood, which made a deep impression upon me, and which shows the state of society existing there, and the manner in which affronts are oftentimes avenged. Directly opposite our quarters, on the other side of the bayou, was situated the plantation of Mr. Marshall. He belonged to a family among the most wealthy and aristocratic in the country. A gentleman from the vicinity of Natchez had been negotiating with him for the purchase of the estate. One day a messenger came in great haste to our plantation, saying that a bloody and fearful battle was going on at Marshall's —that blood had been spilled—and unless the combatants were forthwith separated, the result would be disastrous.

On repairing to Marshall's house, a scene presented itself that beggars description. On the floor of one of the rooms lay the ghastly corpse of the man from Natchez, while Marshall, enraged and covered with wounds and blood, was stalking back and forth, "breathing out threatenings and slaughter." A difficulty had arisen in the course of their negotiation, high words ensued, when drawing their weapons, the deadly strife began that ended so unfortunately. Marshall was never placed in confinement. A sort of trial or investigation was had at Marksville, when he was acquitted, and returned to his plantation, rather more respected, as I thought, than ever, from the fact that the blood of a fellow being was on his soul.

Epps interested himself in his behalf, accompanying him to Marksville, and on all occasions loudly justifying him, but his services in this respect did not afterwards deter a kinsman of this same Marshall from seeking his life also. A brawl occurred between them over a gambling-table, which terminated in a deadly feud. Riding up on horseback in front of the house one day, armed with pistols and bowie knife, Marshall challenged him to come forth and make a final settlement of the quarrel, or he would brand him as a coward, and shoot him like a dog the first opportunity. Not through cowardice, nor from any conscientious scruples, in my opinion, but through the influence of his wife, he was restrained from accepting the challenge of his enemy. A reconciliation, however, was effected afterward, since which time they have been on terms of the closest intimacy.

Such occurrences, which would bring upon the parties concerned in them merited and condign punishment in the Northern States, are frequent on the bayou, and pass without notice, and almost without comment. Every man carries his bowie knife, and when two fall out, they set to work hacking and thrusting at each other, more like savages than civilized and enlightened beings.

The existence of Slavery in its most cruel form among them, has a tendency to brutalize the humane and finer feelings of their nature. Daily witnesses of human suffering—listening to the agonizing screeches of the slave—beholding him writhing beneath the merciless lash—bitten and torn by dogs—dying without attention, and buried without shroud or coffin—it cannot otherwise be expected, than that they should become brutified and reckless of human life. It is true there are many kind- hearted and good men in the parish of Avoyelles—such men as William Ford—who can look with pity upon the sufferings of a slave, just as there are, over all the world, sensitive and sympathetic spirits, who cannot look with indifference upon the sufferings of any creature which the Almighty has endowed with life. It is not the fault of the slaveholder that he is cruel, so much as it is the fault of the system under which he lives. He cannot withstand the influence of habit and associations that surround him. Taught from earliest childhood, by all that he sees and hears, that the rod is for the slave's back, he will not be apt to change his opinions in maturer years.

There may be humane masters, as there certainly are inhuman ones—there may be slaves well-clothed, well-fed, and happy, as there surely are those half-clad, half-starved and miserable; nevertheless, the institution that tolerates such wrong and inhumanity as I have witnessed, is a cruel, unjust, and barbarous one.

Men may write fictions portraying lowly life as it is, or as it is not—may expatiate with owlish gravity upon the bliss of ignorance—discourse flippantly from arm chairs of the pleasures of slave life; but let them toil with him in the field—sleep with him in the cabin—feed with him on husks; let them behold him scourged, hunted, trampled on, and they will come back with another story in their mouths. Let them know the *heart* of the poor slave—learn his secret thoughts—thoughts he dare not utter in the hearing of the white man; let them sit by him in the silent watches of the night—converse with him in trustful confidence, of "life, liberty, and the pursuit of happiness," and they will find that ninety-nine out of every hundred are intelligent enough to understand their situation, and to cherish in their bosoms the love of freedom, as passionately as themselves.

⊙ ⊙ ⊙

CHAPTER 15. LABORS ON SUGAR PLANTATIONS—THE MODE OF PLANTING...

⊙ ⊙ ⊙

Labors On Sugar Plantations—The Mode Of Planting Cane—Of Hoeing Cane—Cane Ricks—Cutting Cane—Description Of The Cane Knife Winrowing—Preparing For Succeeding Crops—Description Of Hawkins' Sugar Mill On Bayou Boeuf—The Christmas Holidays—The Carnival Season Of The Children Of Bondage—The Christmas Supper—Red, The Favorite Color—The Violin, And The Consolation It Afforded-The Christmas Dance—Lively, The Coquette—Sam Roberts, And His Rivals—Slave Songs—Southern Life As It Is—Three Days In The Year—The System Of Marriage—Uncle Abram's Contempt Of Matrimony.

IN consequence of my inability in cotton-picking, Epps was in the habit of hiring me out on sugar plantations during the season of cane-cutting and sugar-making. He received for my services a dollar a day, with the money supplying my place on his cotton plantation. Cutting cane was an employment that suited me, and for three successive years I held the lead row at Hawkins', leading a gang of from fifty to an hundred hands.

In a previous chapter the mode of cultivating cotton is described. This may be the proper place to speak of the manner of cultivating cane.

The ground is prepared in beds, the same as it is prepared for the reception of the cotton seed, except it is ploughed deeper. Drills are made in the same manner. Planting commences in January, and continues until

April. It is necessary to plant a sugar field only once in three years. Three crops are taken before the seed or plant is exhausted.

Three gangs are employed in the operation. One draws the cane from the rick, or stack, cutting the top and flags from the stalk, leaving only that part which is sound and healthy. Each joint of the cane has an eye, like the eye of a potato, which sends forth a sprout when buried in the soil. Another gang lays the cane in the drill, placing two stalks side by side in such manner that joints will occur once in four or six inches. The third gang follows with hoes, drawing earth upon the stalks, and covering them to the depth of three inches.

In four weeks, at the farthest, the sprouts appear above the ground, and from this time forward grow with great rapidity. A sugar field is hoed three times, the same as cotton, save that a greater quantity of earth is drawn to the roots. By the first of August hoeing is usually over. About the middle of September, whatever is required for seed is cut and tacked in ricks, as they are termed. In October it is ready for the mill or sugar-house, and then the general cutting begins. The blade of a cane-knife is fifteen inches long, three inches wide in the middle, and tapering towards the point and handle. The blade is thin, and in order to be at all serviceable must be kept very sharp. Every third hand takes the lead of two others, one of whom is on each side of him. The lead hand, in the first place, with a blow of his knife shears the flags from the stalk. He next cuts off the top down as far as it is green. He must be careful to sever all the green from the ripe part, inasmuch as the juice of the former sours the molasses, and renders it unsalable. Then he severs the stalk at the root, and lays it directly behind him. His right and left hand companions lay their stalks, when cut in the same manner, upon his. To every three hands there is a cart, which follows, and the stalks are thrown into it by the younger slaves, when it is drawn to the sugar- house and ground.

If the planter apprehends a frost, the cane is winrowed. Winrowing is the cutting the stalks at an early period and throwing them lengthwise in the water furrow in such a manner that the tops will cover the butts of the stalks. They will remain in this condition three weeks or a month without souring, and secure from frost. When the proper time arrives, they are taken up, trimmed and carted to the sugarhouse.

In the month of January the slaves enter the field again to prepare for another crop. The ground is now strewn with the tops, and flags cut from the past year's cane. On a dry day fire is set to this combustible refuse, which sweeps over the field, leaving it bare and clean, and ready for the hoes. The earth is loosened about the roots of the old stubble, and in process of time another crop springs up from the last year's seed. It is the same the year following; but the third year the seed has exhausted its strength, and the field must be ploughed and planted again. The second year the cane is sweeter and yields more than the first, and the third year more than the second.

During the three seasons I labored on Hawkins' plantation, I was employed a considerable portion of the time in the sugar–house. He is celebrated as the producer of the finest variety of white sugar. The following is a general description of his sugar–house and the process of manufacture.

The mill is an immense brick building, standing on the shore of the bayou. Running out from the building is an open shed, at least an hundred feet in length and forty or fifty feet in width. The boiler in which the steam is generated is situated outside the main building; the machinery and engine rest on a brick pier, fifteen feet above the floor, within the body of the building. The machinery turns two great iron rollers, between two and three feet in diameter and six or eight feet in length. They are elevated above the brick pier, and roll in towards each other. An endless carrier, made of chain and wood, like leather belts used in small mills, extends from the iron rollers out of the main building and through the entire length of the open shed. The carts in which the cane is brought from the field as fast as it is cut, are unloaded at the sides of the shed. All along the endless carrier are ranged slave children, whose business it is to place the cane upon it, when it is conveyed through the shed into the main building, where it falls between the rollers, is crushed, and drops upon another carrier that conveys it out of the main building in an opposite direction, depositing it in the top of a chimney upon a fire beneath, which consumes it. It is necessary to burn it in this manner, because otherwise it would soon fill the building, and more especially because it would soon sour and engender disease. The juice of the cane falls into a conductor underneath the iron rollers, and is carried into a reservoir. Pipes convey it from thence into five filterers, holding several hogsheads each. These filterers are filled with bone-black, a substance resembling pulverized charcoal. It is made of bones calcinated in close vessels, and is used for the purpose of decolorizing, by filtration, the cane juice before boiling. Through these five filterers it passes in succession, and then runs into a large reservoir underneath the ground floor, from whence it is carried up, by means of a steam pump, into a clarifier made of sheet iron, where it is heated by steam until it boils. From the first clarifier it is carried in pipes to a second and a third, and thence into close iron pans, through which tubes pass, filled with steam. While in a boiling state it flows through three pans in succession, and is then carried in other pipes down to the coolers on the ground floor. Coolers are wooden boxes with sieve bottoms made of the finest wire. As soon as the syrup passes into the coolers, and is met by the air, it grains, and the molasses at once escapes through the sieves into a cistern It is then white or loaf sugar of the finest kind—clear, clean, and as white as snow. When cool, it is taken out, packed in hogsheads, and is ready for market. The molasses is then carried from the cistern into the upper story again, and by another process converted into brown sugar.

There are larger mills, and those constructed differently from the one thus imperfectly described, but none, perhaps, more celebrated than this anywhere on Bayou Boeuf. Lambert, of New-Orleans, is a partner of Hawkins. He is a man of vast wealth, holding, as I have been told, an interest in over forty different sugar plantations in Louisiana.

The only respite from constant labor the slave has through the whole year, is during the Christmas holidays. Epps allowed us three—others allow four, five and six days, according to the measure of their generosity. It is the only time to which they look forward with any interest or pleasure. They are glad when night comes, not only because it brings them a few hours repose, but because it brings them one day nearer Christmas. It is hailed with equal delight by the old and the young; even Uncle Abram ceases to glorify Andrew Jackson, and Patsey forgets her many sorrows amid the general hilarity of the holidays. It —is the time of feasting, and frolicking, and fiddling—the carnival season with the children of bondage. They are the only days when they are allowed a little restricted liberty, and heartily indeed do they enjoy it.

It is the custom for one planter to give a "Christmas supper," inviting the shaves from neighboring plantations to join his own on the occasion; for instance, one year it is given by Epps, the next by Marshall, the next by Hawkins, and so on. Usually from three to five hundred are assembled, coming together on foot, in carts, on horseback, on mules, riding double and triple, sometimes a boy and girl, at others a girl and two boys, and at others again a boy, a girl and an old woman. Uncle Abram astride a mule, with Aunt Phebe and Patsey behind him, trotting towards a Christmas supper, would be no uncommon sight on Bayou Boeuf.

Then, too, "of all days i' the year," they array themselves in their best attire. The cotton coat has been washed clean, the stump of a tallow candle has been applied to the shoes, and if so fortunate as to possess a rimless or a crownless hat, it is placed jauntily on the head. They are welcomed with equal cordiality, however, if they come bare-headed and bare-footed to the feast. As a general thing, the women wear handkerchiefs tied about their heads, but if chance has thrown in their way a fiery red ribbon, or a cast-off bonnet of their mistress' grandmother, it is sure to be worn on such occasions. Red—the deep blood red—is decidedly the favorite color among the enslaved damsels of my acquaintance. If a red ribbon does not encircle the neck, you will be certain to find all the hair of their woolly heads tied up with red strings of one sort or another.

The table is spread in the open air, and loaded with varieties of meat and piles of vegetables. Bacon and corn meal at such times are dispensed with.

Sometimes the cooking is performed in the kitchen on the plantation, at others in the shade of wide branching trees. In the latter case, a ditch is dug in the ground, and wood laid in and burned until it is filled with glowing coals, over which chickens, ducks, turkeys, pigs, and not unfrequently the entire body of a wild ox, are roasted. They are furnished also with flour, of which biscuits are made, and often with peach and other preserves, with tarts, and every manner and description of pies, except the mince, that being an article of pastry as yet unknown among them. Only the slave who has lived all the years on his scanty allowance of meal and bacon, can appreciate such suppers. White people in great numbers assemble to witness the gastronomical enjoyments.

They seat themselves at the rustic table—the males on one side, the females on the other. The two between whom there may have been an exchange of tenderness, invariably manage to sit opposite; for the omnipresent Cupid disdains not to hurl his arrows into the simple hearts of slaves. Unalloyed and exulting happiness lights up the dark faces of them all. The ivory teeth, contrasting with their black complexions, exhibit two long, white streaks the whole extent of the table. All round the bountiful board a multitude of eyes roll in ecstacy. Giggling and laughter and the clattering of cutlery and crockery succeed. Cuffee's elbow hunches his neighbor's side, impelled by an involuntary impulse of delight; Nelly shakes her finger at Sambo and laughs, she knows not why, and so the fun and merriment flows on.

When the viands have disappeared, and the hungry maws of the children of toil are satisfied, then, next in the order of amusement, is the Christmas dance. My business on these gala days always was to play on the violin. The African race is a music-loving one, proverbially; and many there were among my fellow- bondsmen whose organs of tune were strikingly developed, and who could thumb the banjo with dexterity; but at the expense of appearing egotistical, I must nevertheless, declare, that I was considered the Ole Bull of Bayou Boeuf. My master often received letters, sometimes from a distance of ten miles, requesting him to send me to play at a ball or festival of the whites. He received his compensation, and usually I also returned with many picayunes jingling in my pockets—the extra contributions of those to whose delight I had administered. In this manner I became more acquainted than I otherwise would, up and down the bayou. The young men and maidens of Holmesville always knew there was to be a jollification somewhere, whenever Platt Epps was seen passing through the town with his fiddle in his hand. "Where are you going now, Platt?" and "What is coming off tonight, Platt?" would be interrogatories issuing from every door and window, and many a time when there was no special hurry, yielding to pressing importunities, Platt would draw his bow, and sitting astride his mule, perhaps, discourse musically to a crowd of delighted children, gathered around him in the street.

Alas! had it not been for my beloved violin, I scarcely can conceive how I could have endured the long years of bondage. It introduced me to great houses —relieved me of many days' labor in the field—supplied me with conveniences for my cabin—with pipes and tobacco, and extra pairs of shoes, and oftentimes led me away from the presence of a hard master, to witness scenes of jollity and mirth. It was my companion—the friend of my bosom triumphing loudly when I was joyful, and uttering its soft, melodious consolations when I was sad. Often, at midnight, when sleep had fled affrighted from the cabin, and my soul was disturbed and troubled with the contemplation of my fate, it would sing me a song of peace. On holy Sabbath days, when an hour or two of leisure was allowed, it would accompany me to some quiet place on the bayou bank, and, lifting up its voice, discourse kindly and pleasantly indeed. It heralded my name round the country—made me friends, who, otherwise would not have noticed me— gave me an honored seat at the yearly feasts, and secured the loudest and heartiest welcome of them all at the Christmas dance. The Christmas dance! Oh, ye pleasure-seeking sons and daughters of idleness, who move with measured step, listless and snail-like, through the slow-winding cotillon, if ye wish to look upon the celerity, if not the "poetry of motion"— upon genuine happiness, rampant and unrestrained— go down to Louisiana, and see the slaves dancing in the starlight of a Christmas night.

On that particular Christmas I have now in my mind, a description whereof will serve as a description of the day generally, Miss Lively and Mr. Sam, the first belonging to Stewart, the latter to Roberts, started the ball. It was well known that Sam cherished an ardent passion for Lively, as also did one of Marshall's and another of Carey's boys; for Lively was lively indeed, and a heart-breaking coquette withal. It was a victory for Sam Roberts, when, rising from the repast, she gave him her hand for the first "figure" in preference to either of his rivals. They were somewhat crest-fallen, and, shaking their heads angrily, rather intimated they would like to pitch into Mr. Sam and hurt him badly. But not an emotion of wrath ruffled the placid bosom of Samuel as his legs flew like drum-sticks down the outside and up the middle, by the side of his bewitching partner. The whole company cheered them vociferously, and, excited with the applause, they continued "tearing down" after all the others had become exhausted and halted a moment to recover breath. But Sam's superhuman exertions overcame him finally, leaving Lively alone, yet whirling like a top. Thereupon one of Sam's rivals, Pete Marshall, dashed in, and, with might and main, leaped and shuffled and threw himself into every conceivable shape, as if determined to show Miss Lively and all the world that Sam Roberts was of no account.

Pete's affection, however, was greater than his discretion. Such violent exercise took the breath out of him directly, and he dropped like an empty bag Then was the time for Harry Carey to try his hand; but Lively also soon out-winded him, amidst hurrahs and shouts, fully sustaining her well-earned reputation of being the "fastest gal" on the bayou.

One "set" off, another takes its place, he or she remaining longest on the floor receiving the most uproarious commendation, and so the dancing continues until broad daylight. It does not cease with the sound of the fiddle, but in that case they set up a music peculiar to themselves. This is called "patting," accompanied with one of those unmeaning songs, composed rather for its adaptation to a certain tune or measure, than for the purpose of expressing any distinct idea. The patting is performed by striking the hands on the knees, then striking the hands together, then striking the right shoulder with one hand, the left with the other—all the while keeping time with the feet, and singing, perhaps, this song;

"Harper's creek and roarin' ribber,

Thar, my dear, we'll live forebber;

Den we'll go to de Ingin nation,

All I walls in dis creation,

Is pretty little wife and big plantation.

Chorus. Up dat oak and down dat ribber,

Two overseers and one little nigger"

Or, if these words are not adapted to the tune called for, it may be that "Old Hog Eye" is—a rather solemn and startling specimen of versification, not, however, to be appreciated unless heard at the South. It runneth as follows;

"Who's been here since I've been gone?

Pretty little gal wid a josey on.

Hog Eye!

Old Hog Eye,

And Hosey too!

Never see de like since I was born,

Here come a little gal wid a josey on.

Hog Eye!

Old Hog Eye!

And Hosey too!"

Or, may be the following, perhaps, equally nonsensical, but full of melody, nevertheless, as it flows from the negro's mouth;

"Ebo Dick and Jurdan's Jo,

Them two niggers stole my yo'.

Chorus. Hop Jim along,

Walk Jim along,

Talk Jim along," etc.

Old black Dan, as black as tar,

He dam glad he was not dar.

Hop Jim along," etc.

During the remaining holidays succeeding Christmas, they are provided with passes, and permitted to go where they please within a limited distance, or they may remain and labor on the plantation, in which case they are paid for it. It is very rarely, however, that the latter alternative is accepted.

They may be seen at these times hurrying in all directions, as happy looking mortals as can be found on the face of the earth. They are different beings from what they are in the field; the temporary relaxation, the brief deliverance from fear, and from the lash, producing an entire metamorphosis in their appearance and demeanor. In visiting, riding, renewing old friendships, or, perchance, reviving some old attachment, or pursuing whatever pleasure may suggest itself; the time is occupied. Such is "southern life as it is" three days in the year, as I found it— the other three hundred and sixty-two being days of weariness, and fear, and suffering, and unremitting labor.

Marriage is frequently contracted during the holidays, if such an institution may be said to exist among them. The only ceremony required before entering into that "holy estate," is to obtain the consent of the respective owners. It is usually encouraged by the masters of female slaves. Either party can have as many husbands or wives as the owner will permit, and either is at liberty to discard the other at pleasure. The law in relation to divorce, or to bigamy, and so forth, is not applicable to property, of course. If the wife does not belong on the same plantation with the husband, the latter is permitted to visit her on Saturday nights, if the distance is not too far. Uncle Abram's wife lived seven miles from Epps', on Bayou Huff Power.

He had permission to visit her once a fortnight, but he was growing old, as has been said, and truth to say, had latterly well nigh forgotten her. Uncle Abram had no time to spare from his meditations on General Jackson—connubial dalliance being well enough for the young and thoughtless, but unbecoming a grave and solemn philosopher like himself.

⊙ ⊙ ⊙

CHAPTER 16. OVERSEERS—HOW THEY ARE ARMED AND ACCOMPANIED—THE HOMICIDE...

⊙ ⊙ ⊙

Overseers—How They Are Armed And Accompanied—The Homicide—His Execution At Marksville—Slave Drivers—Appointed Driver On Removing To Bayou Boeuff—Practice Makes Perfect—Epps's Attempt To Cut Platt's Throat—The Escape From Him—Protected By The Mistress—Forbids Reading And Writing—Obtain A Sheet Of Paper After Nine Years' Effort—The Letter—Armsby, The Mean White— Partially Confide In Him—His Treachery—Epps' Suspicions—How They Were Quieted—Burning The Letter—Armsby Leaves The Bayou—Disappointment And Despair.

WITH the exception of my trip to St. Mary's parish, and my absence during the cane-cutting seasons, I was constantly employed on the plantation of Master Epps. He was considered but a small planter, not having a sufficient number of hands to require the services of an overseer, acting in the latter capacity himself. Not able to increase his force, it was his custom to hire during the hurry of cotton-picking.

On larger estates, employing fifty or a hundred, or perhaps two hundred hands, an overseer is deemed indispensable. These gentlemen ride into the field on horseback, without an exception, to my knowledge, armed with pistols, bowie knife, whip, and accompanied by several dogs. They follow, equipped in this fashion, in rear of the slaves, keeping a sharp lookout upon them all. The requisite qualifications in an overseer are utter heartlessness, brutality and cruelty. It is his business to produce large crops, and if that is accomplished, no matter what amount of suffering it may have cost. The presence of the dogs are necessary to overhaul a fugitive who may take to his heels, as is sometimes the case, when faint or sick, he is unable to maintain his row, and unable, also, to endure the whip. The pistols are reserved for any dangerous emergency, there having been instances when such weapons were necessary. Goaded into uncontrollable madness, even the slave will sometimes turn upon his oppressor. The gallows were standing at Marksville last January, upon which one was executed a year ago for killing his overseer. It occurred not many miles from Epps' plantation on Red River. The slave was given his task at splitting rails. In the course of the day the overseer sent him on an errand, which occupied so much time that it was not possible for him to perform the task. The next day he was called to an account, but the loss of time occasioned by the errand was no excuse, and he was ordered to kneel and bare his back for the reception of the lash. They were in the woods alone—beyond the reach of sight or hearing. The boy submitted until maddened at such injustice, and insane with pain, he sprang to his feet, and seizing an axe, literally chopped the overseer in pieces. He made no attempt whatever at concealment, but hastening to his master, related the whole affair, and declared himself ready to expiate the wrong by the sacrifice of his life. He was led to the scaffold, and while the rope was around his neck, maintained an undismayed and fearless bearing, and with his last words justified the act.

Besides the overseer, there are drivers under him, the number being in proportion to the number of hands in the field. The drivers are black, who, in addition to the performance of their equal share of work, are compelled to do the whipping of their several gangs. Whips hang around their necks, and if they fail to use them thoroughly, are whipped themselves. They have a few privileges, however; for example, in cane- cutting the hands are not allowed to sit down long enough to eat their dinners. Carts filled with corn cake, cooked at the kitchen, are driven into the field at noon. The cake is distributed by the drivers, and must be eaten with the least possible delay.

When the slave ceases to perspire, as he often does when taxed beyond his strength, he falls to the ground and becomes entirely helpless. It is then the duty of the driver to drag him into the shade of the standing cotton or cane, or of a neighboring tree, where he dashes buckets of water upon him, and uses other means of bringing out perspiration again, when he is ordered to his place, and compelled to continue his labor.

At Huff Power, when I first came to Epps', Tom, one of Roberts' negroes, was driver. He was a burly fellow, and severe in the extreme. After Epps' removal to Bayou Boeuf, that distinguished honor was conferred upon myself. Up to the time of my departure I had to wear a whip about my neck in the field. If Epps was present, I dared not show any lenity, not having the Christian fortitude of a certain well–known Uncle Tom sufficiently to brave his wrath, by refusing to perform the office. In that way, only, I escaped the immediate martyrdom he suffered, and, withal, saved my companions much suffering, as it proved in the end. Epps, I soon found, whether actually in the field or not, had his eyes pretty generally upon us. From the piazza, from behind some adjacent tree, or other concealed point of observation, he was perpetually on the watch. If one of us had been backward or idle through the day, we were apt to be told all about it on returning to the quarters, and as it was a matter of principle with him to reprove every offence of that kind that came within his knowledge, the offender not only was certain of receiving a castigation for his tardiness, but I likewise was punished for permitting it.

If, on the other hand, he had seen me use the lash freely, the man was satisfied. "Practice makes perfect," truly; and during my eight years' experience as a driver, I learned to handle the whip with marvelous dexterity and precision, throwing the lash within a hair's breadth of the back, the ear, the nose, without, however, touching either of them. If Epps was observed at a distance, or we had reason to apprehend he was as sneaking somewhere in the vicinity, I would commence plying the lash vigorously, when, according to arrangement, they would squirm and screech as if in agony, although not one of them had in fact been even grazed. Patsey would take occasion, if he made his appearance presently, to mumble in his hearing some complaints that Platt was lashing them the whole time, and Uncle Abram, with an appearance of honesty peculiar to himself, would declare roundly I had just whipped them worse than General Jackson whipped the enemy at New-Orleans. If Epps was not drunk, and in one of his beastly humors, this was, in general, satisfactory. If he was, some one or more of us must suffer, as a matter of course. Sometimes his violence assumed a dangerous form, placing the lives of his human stock in jeopardy. On one occasion the drunken madman thought to amuse himself by cutting my throat.

He had been absent at Holmesville, in attendance at a shooting-match, and none of us were aware of his return. While hoeing by the side of Patsey, she exclaimed in a low voice, suddenly, "Platt, d'ye see old Hog-Jaw beckoning me to come to him?"

Glancing sideways, I discovered him in the edge of the field, motioning and grimacing, as was his habit when half-intoxicated. Aware of his lewd intentions, Patsey began to cry. I whispered her not to look up, and to continue at her work, as if she had not observed him. Suspecting the truth of the matter, however, he soon staggered up to me in a great rage.

"What did you say to Pats?" he demanded, with an oath. I made him some evasive answer, which only had the effect of increasing his violence.

"How long have you owned this plantation, say, you d—d nigger?" he inquired, with a malicious sneer, at the same time taking hold of my shirt collar with one hand, and thrusting the other into his pocket. "Now I'll cut your black throat; that's what I'll do," drawing his knife from his pocket as he said it. But with one hand he was unable to open it, until finally seizing the blade in his teeth, I saw he was about to succeed, and felt the necessity of escaping from him, for in his present reckless state, it was evident he was not joking, by any means. My shirt was open in front, and as I turned round quickly and sprang from him, while he still retained his gripe, it was stripped entirely from my back. There was no difficulty now in eluding him. He would chase me until out of breath, then stop until it was recovered, swear, and renew the chase again. Now he would command me to come to him, now endeavor to coax me, but I was careful to keep at a respectful distance. In this manner we made the circuit of the field several times, he making desperate plunges, and I always dodging them, more amused than frightened, well knowing that when his sober senses returned, he would laugh at his own drunken folly. At length I observed the mistress standing by the yard fence, watching our half–serious, half–comical manoeuvres. Shooting past him, I ran directly to her. Epps, on discovering her, did not follow. He remained about the field an hour or more, during which time I stood by the mistress, having related the particulars of what had taken place. Now, *she* was aroused again, denouncing her husband and Patsey about equally. Finally, Epps came towards the house, by this time nearly sober, walking demurely, with his hands behind his back, and attempting to look as innocent as a child.

As he approached, nevertheless, Mistress Epps began to berate him roundly, heaping upon him many rather disrespectful epithets, and demanding for what reason he had attempted to cut my throat. Epps made wondrous strange of it all, and to my surprise, swore by all the saints in the calendar he had not spoken to me that day.

"Platt, you lying nigger, *have I*?" was his brazen appeal to me.

It is not safe to contradict a master, even by the assertion of a truth. So I was silent, and when he entered the house I returned to the field, and the affair was never after alluded to.

Shortly after this time a circumstance occurred that came nigh divulging the secret of my real name and history, which I had so long and carefully concealed, and upon which I was convinced depended my final escape. Soon after he purchased me, Epps asked me if I could write and read, and on being informed that I had received some instruction in those branches of education, he assured me, with emphasis, if he ever caught me with a book, or with pen and ink, he would give me a hundred lashes. He said he wanted me to understand that he bought "niggers" to work and not to educate. He never inquired a word of my past life, or from whence I came. The mistress, however, cross-examined me frequently about Washington, which she supposed was my native city, and more than once remarked that I did not talk nor act like the other "niggers," and she was sure I had seen more of the world than I admitted.

My great object always was to invent means of getting a letter secretly into the post-office, directed to some of my friends or family at the North. The difficulty of such an achievement cannot be comprehended by one unacquainted with the severe restrictions imposed upon me. In the first place, I was deprived of pen, ink, and paper. In the second place, a slave cannot leave his plantation without a pass, nor will a post-master mail a letter for one without written instructions from his owner. I was in slavery nine years, and always watchful and on the alert, before I met with the good fortune of obtaining a sheet of paper. While Epps was in New-Orleans, one winter, disposing of his cotton, the mistress sent me to Holmesville, with an order for several articles, and among the rest a quantity of foolscap. I appropriated a sheet, concealing it in the cabin, under the board on which I slept.

After various experiments I succeeded in making ink, by boiling white maple bark, and with a feather plucked from the wing of a duck, manufactured a pen. When all were asleep in the cabin, by the light of the coals, lying upon my plank couch, I managed to complete a somewhat lengthy epistle. It was directed to an old acquaintance at Sandy Hill, stating my condition, and urging him to take measures to restore me to liberty. This letter I kept a long time, contriving measures by which it could be safely deposited in the post-office. At length, a low fellow, by the name of Armsby, hitherto a stranger, came into the neighborhood, seeking a situation as overseer. He applied to Epps, and was about the plantation for several days. He next went over to Shaw's, near by, and remained with him several weeks. Shaw was generally surrounded by such worthless characters, being himself noted as a gambler and unprincipled man. He had made a wife of his slave Charlotte, and a brood of young mulattoes were growing up in his house. Armsby became so much reduced at last, that he was compelled to labor with the slaves. A white man working in the field is a rare and unusual spectacle on Bayou Boeuf. I improved every opportunity of cultivating his acquaintance privately, desiring to obtain his confidence so far as to be willing to intrust the letter to his keeping. He visited Marksville repeatedly, he informed me, a town some twenty miles distant, and there, I proposed to myself, the letter should be mailed.

Carefully deliberating on the most proper manner of approaching him on the subject, I concluded finally to ask him simply if he would deposit a letter for me in the Marksville post-office the next time he visited that place, without disclosing to him that the letter was written, or any of the particulars it contained; for I had fears that he might betray me, and knew that some inducement must be held out to him of a pecuniary nature, before it would be safe to confide in him. As late as one o'clock one night I stole noiselessly from my cabin, and, crossing the field to Shaw's, found him sleeping on the piazza. I had but a few picayunes—the proceeds of my fiddling performances, but all I had in the world I promised him if he would do me the favor required. I begged him not to expose me if he could not grant the request. He assured me, upon his honor, he would deposit it in the Marksville post-office, and that he would keep it an inviolable secret forever. Though the letter was in my pocket at the time, I dared not then deliver it to him, but stating I would have it written in a day or two, bade him good night, and returned to my cabin. It was impossible for me to expel the suspicions I entertained, and all night I lay awake, revolving in my mind the safest course to pursue. I was willing to risk a great deal to accomplish my purpose, but should the letter by any means fall into the hands of Epps, it would be a death-blow to my aspirations. I was "perplexed in the extreme."

My suspicions were well-founded, as the sequel demonstrated. The next day but one, while scraping cotton in the field, Epps seated himself on the line fence between Shaw's plantation and his own, in such a position as to overlook the scene of our labors. Presently Armsby made his appearance, and, mounting the fence, took a seat beside him. They remained two or three hours, all of which time I was in an agony of apprehension.

That night, while broiling my bacon, Epps entered the cabin with his rawhide in his hand.

"Well, boy," said he, "I understand I've got a larned nigger, that writes letters, and tries to get white fellows to mail 'em. Wonder if you know who he is?"

My worst fears were realized, and although it may not be considered entirely creditable, even under the circumstances, yet a resort to duplicity and downright falsehood was the only refuge that presented itself.

"Don't know nothing about it, Master Epps," I answered him, assuming an air of ignorance and surprise; "Don't know nothing at all about it, sir."

"Wan't you over to Shaw's night before last?" he inquired.

"No, master," was the reply.

"Hav'nt you asked that fellow, Armsby, to mail a letter for you at Marksville?"

"Why, Lord, master, I never spoke three words to him in all my life. I don't know what you mean."

"Well," he continued, "Armsby told me to-day the devil was among my niggers; that I had one that needed close watching or he would run away; and when I axed him why, he said you come over to Shaw's, and waked him up in the night, and wanted him to carry a letter to Marksville. What have you got to say to that, ha?"

"All I've got to say, master," I replied, "is, there is no truth in it. How could I write a letter without any ink or paper? There is nobody I want to write to, 'cause I haint got no friends living as I know of. That Armsby is a lying, drunken fellow, they say, and nobody believes him anyway. You know I always tell the truth, and that I never go off the plantation without a pass. Now, master, I can see what that Armsby is after, plain enough. Did'nt he want you to hire him for an overseer?"

"Yes, he wanted me to hire him," answered Epps.

"That's it," said I, "he wants to make you believe we're all going to run away, and then he thinks you'll hire an overseer to watch us. He just made that story out of whole cloth, 'cause he wants to get a situation. It's all a lie, master, you may depend on't."

Epps mused awhile, evidently impressed with the plausibility of my theory, and exclaimed,

"I'm d—d, Platt, if I don't believe you tell the truth. He must take me for a soft, to think he can come it over me with them kind of yarns, musn't he? Maybe he thinks he can fool me; maybe he thinks I don't know nothing—can't take care of my own niggers, eh! Soft soap old Epps, eh! Ha, ha, ha! D—n Armsby! Set the dogs on him, Platt," and with many other comments descriptive of Armsby's general character, and his capability of taking care of his own business, and attending to his own "niggers," Master Epps left the cabin. As soon as he was gone I threw the letter in the fire, and, with a desponding and despairing heart, beheld the epistle which had cost me so much anxiety and thought, and which I fondly hoped would have been my forerunner to the land of freedom, writhe and shrivel on its bed of coals, and dissolve into smoke and ashes. Armsby, the treacherous wretch, was driven from Shaw's plantation not long subsequently, much to my relief, for I feared he might renew his conversation, and perhaps induce Epps to credit him.

I knew not now whither to look for deliverance. Hopes sprang up in my heart only to be crushed and blighted. The summer of my life was passing away; I felt I was growing prematurely old; that a few years more, and toil, and grief, and the poisonous miasma of the swamps would accomplish their work on me—would consign me to the grave's embrace, to moulder and be forgotten. Repelled, betrayed, cut off, from the hope of succor, I could only prostrate myself upon the earth and groan in unutterable anguish. The hope of rescue was the only light that cast a ray of comfort on my heart. That was now flickering, faint and low; another breath of disappointment would extinguish it altogether, leaving me to grope in midnight darkness to the end of life.

⊙ ⊙ ⊙

CHAPTER 17. WILEY DISREGARDS THE COUNSELS OF AUNT PHEBE AND UNCLE...

⊙ ⊙ ⊙

Wiley Disregards The Counsels Of Aunt Phebe And Uncle Abram, And Is Caught By The Patrollers—The Organization And Duties Of The Latter—Wiley Runs Away— Speculations In Regard To Him—His Unexpected Return—His Capture On The Red River, And Confinement In Alexandria Jail—Discovered By Joseph B. Roberts Subduing Dogs In Anticipation Of Escape—The Fugitives In The Great Pine Woods—Captured By Adam Taydem And The Indians—Augustus Killed By Dogs— Nelly, Eldret's Slave Woman—The Story Of Celeste—The Concerted Movement— Lew Cheney, The Traitor—The Idea Of Insurrection.

THE year 1850, down to which time I have now arrived, omitting many occurrences uninteresting to the reader, was an unlucky year for my companion Wiley, the husband of Phebe, whose taciturn and retiring nature has thus far kept him in the background. Notwithstanding Wiley seldom opened his mouth, and revolved in his obscure and unpretending orbit without a grumble, nevertheless the warm elements of sociality were strong in the bosom of that silent "nigger" In the exuberance of his self-reliance, disregarding the philosophy of Uncle Abram, and setting the counsels of Aunt Phebe utterly at naught, he had the fool-hardiness to essay a nocturnal visit to a neighboring cabin without a pass.

So attractive was the society in which he found himself, that Wiley took little note of the passing hours, and the light began to break in the east before he was aware. Speeding homeward as fast as he could run, he hoped to reach the quarters before the horn would sound; but, unhappily, he was spied on the way by a company of patrollers.

How it is in other dark places of slavery, I do not know, but on Bayou Boeuf there is an organization of patrollers, as they are styled, whose business it is to seize and whip any slave they may find wandering from the plantation. They ride on horseback, headed by a captain, armed, and accompanied by dogs. They have the right, either by law, or by general consent, to inflict discretionary chastisement upon a black man caught beyond the boundaries of his master's estate without a pass, and even to shoot him, if he attempts to escape. Each company has a certain distance to ride up and down the bayou. They are compensated by the planters, who contribute in proportion to the number of slaves they own. The clatter of their horses' hoofs dashing by can be heard at all hours of the light, and frequently they may be seen driving a slave before them, or leading him by a rope fastened around his neck, to his owner's plantation.

Wiley fled before one of these companies, thinking he could reach his cabin before they could overtake him; but one of their dogs, a great ravenous hound, griped him by the leg, and held him fast. The patrollers whipped him severely, and brought him, a prisoner, to Epps. From him he received another flagellation still more severe, so that the cuts of the lash and the bites of the dog rendered him sore, stiff, and miserable, insomuch he was scarcely able to move It was impossible in such a state to keep up his row, and consequently there was not an hour in the day but Wiley felt the sting of his master's rawhide on his raw and bleeding back. His sufferings became intolerable, and finally he resolved to run away. Without disclosing his intentions to run away even to his wife Phebe, he proceeded to make arrangements for carrying his plan into execution. Having cooked his whole week's allowance, he cautiously left the cabin on a Sunday night, after the inmates of the quarters were asleep. When the horn sounded in the morning, Wiley did not make his appearance. Search was made for him in the cabins, in the corn-crib, in the cotton-house, and in every nook and corner of the premises. Each of us was examined, touching any knowledge we might have that could throw light upon his sudden disappearance or present whereabouts. Epps raved and stormed, and mounting his horse, galloped to neighboring plantations, making in inquiries in all directions. The search was fruitless. Nothing whatever was elicited, going to show what had become of the missing man. The dogs were led to the swamp, but were unable to strike his trail. They would circle away through the forest, their noses to the ground, but invariably returned in a short time to the spot from whence they started.

Wiley had escaped, and so secretly and cautiously as to elude and baffle all pursuit. Days and even weeks passed away, and nothing could be heard of him. Epps did nothing but curse and swear. It was the only topic of conversation among us when alone. We indulged in a great deal of speculation in regard to him, one suggesting he might have been drowned in some bayou, inasmuch as he was a poor swimmer; another, that perhaps he might have been devoured by alligators, or stung by the venomous moccasin, whose bite is certain and sudden death. The warm and hearty sympathies of us all, however, were with poor Wiley, wherever he might be. Many an earnest prayer ascended from the lips of Uncle Abram, beseeching safety for the wanderer.

In about three weeks, when all hope of ever seeing him again was dismissed, to our surprise, he one day appeared among us. On leaving the plantation, he informed us, it was his intention to make his way back to South Carolina—to the old quarters of Master Buford. During the day he remained secreted, sometimes in the branches of a tree, and at night pressed forward through the swamps. Finally, one morning, just at dawn, he reached the shore of Red River. While standing on the bank, considering how he could cross it, a white man accosted him, and demanded a pass. Without one, and evidently a runaway, he was taken to Alexandria, the shire town of the parish of Rapides, and confined in prison. It happened several days after that Joseph B. Roberts, uncle of Mistress Epps, was in Alexandria, and going into the jail, recognized him. Wiley had worked on his plantation, when Epps resided at Huff Power. Paying the jail fee, and writing him a pass, underneath which was a note to Epps, requesting him not to whip him on his return, Wiley was sent back to Bayou Boeuf. It was the hope that hung upon this request, and which Roberts assured him would be respected by his master, that sustained him as he approached the house. The request, however, as may be readily supposed, was entirely disregarded. After being kept in suspense three days, Wiley was stripped, and compelled to endure one of those inhuman floggings to which the poor slave is so often subjected. It was the first and last attempt of Wiley to run away. The long scars upon his back, which he will carry with him to the grave, perpetually remind him of the dangers of such a step.

There was not a day throughout the ten years I belonged to Epps that I did not consult with myself upon the prospect of escape. I laid many plans, which at the time I considered excellent ones, but one after the other they were all abandoned. No man who has never been placed in such a situation, can comprehend the thousand obstacles thrown in the way of the flying slave. Every white man's hand is raised against him — the patrollers are watching for him—the hounds are ready to follow on his track, and the nature of the country is such as renders it impossible to pass through it with any safety. I thought, however, that the time might come, perhaps, when I should be running through the swamps again. I concluded, in that chase, to be prepared for Epps' dogs, should they pursue me. He possessed several, one of which was a notorious slave-hunter, and the most fierce and savage of his breed. While out hunting the coon or the opossum, I never allowed an opportunity to escape, when alone, of whipping them severely. In this manner I succeeded at length in subduing them completely. They feared me, obeying my voice at once when others had no control over them whatever. Had they followed and overtaken me, I doubt not they would have shrank from attacking me.

Notwithstanding the certainty of being captured, the woods and swamps are, nevertheless, continually filled with runaways. Many of them, when sick, or so worn out as to be unable to perform their tasks, escape into the swamps, willing to suffer the punishment inflicted for such offences, in order to obtain a day or two of rest.

While I belonged to Ford, I was unwittingly the means of disclosing the hiding-place of six or eight, who had taken up their residence in the "Great Pine Woods." Adam Taydem frequently sent me from the mills over to the opening after provisions. The whole distance was then a thick pine forest. About ten o'clock of a beautiful moonlight night, while walking along the Texas road, returning to the mills, carrying a dressed pig in a bag swung over my shoulder, I heard footsteps behind me, and turning round, beheld two black men in the dress of slaves approaching at a rapid pace. When within a short distance, one of them raised a club, as if intending to strike me; the other snatched at the bag. I managed to dodge them both, and seizing a pine knot, hurled it with such force against the head of one of them that he was prostrated apparently senseless to the ground. Just then two more made their appearance from one side of the road. Before they could grapple me, however, I succeeded in passing them and taking to my heels, fled, much affrighted, towards the mills. When Adam was informed of the adventure, he hastened straightway to the Indian village, and arousing Cascalla and several of his tribe, started in pursuit of the highwaymen. I accompanied them to the scene of attack, when we discovered a puddle of blood in the road, where the man whom I had smitten with the pine knot had fallen. After searching carefully through the woods a long time, one of Cascalla's men discovered a smoke curling up through the branches of several prostrate pines, whose tops had fallen together. The rendezvous was cautiously surrounded, and all of them taken prisoners. They had escaped from a plantation in the vicinity of Lamourie, and had been secreted there three weeks They had no evil design upon me, except to frighten me out of my pig. Having observed me passing towards Ford's just at night-fall, and suspecting the nature of my errand, they had followed me, seen me butcher and dress the porker, and start on my return. They had been pinched for food, and were driven to this extremity by necessity. Adam conveyed them to the parish jail, and was liberally rewarded.

Not unfrequently the runaway loses his life in the attempt to escape. Epps' premises were bounded on one side by Carey's, a very extensive sugar plantation. He cultivates annually at least fifteen hundred acres of cane, manufacturing twenty-two or twenty-three hundred hogsheads of sugar; an hogshead and a half being the usual yield of an acre. Besides this he also cultivates five or six hundred acres of corn and cotton. He owned last year one hundred and fifty three field hands, besides nearly as many children, and yearly hires a drove during the busy season from this side the Mississippi.

One of his negro drivers, a pleasant, intelligent boy, was named Augustus. During the holidays, and occasionally while at work in adjoining fields, I had an opportunity of making his acquaintance, which eventually ripened into a warm and mutual attachment. Summer before last he was so unfortunate as to incur the displeasure of the overseer, a coarse, heartless brute, who whipped him most cruelly. Augustus ran away. Reaching a cane rick on Hawkins' plantation, he secreted himself in the top of it. All Carey's dogs were put upon his track—some fifteen of them—and soon scented his footsteps to the hiding place. They surrounded the rick, baying and scratching, but could not reach him. Presently, guided by the clamor of the hounds, the pursuers rode up, when the overseer, mounting on to the rick, drew him forth. As he rolled down to the ground the whole pack plunged upon him, and before they could be beaten off, had gnawed and mutilated his body in the most shocking manner, their teeth having penetrated to the bone in an hundred places. He was taken up, tied upon a mule, and carried home. But this was Augustus' last trouble. He lingered until the next day, when death sought the unhappy boy, and kindly relieved him from his agony.

It was not unusual for slave women as well as slave men to endeavor to escape. Nelly, Eldret's girl, with whom I lumbered for a time in the "Big Cane Brake," lay concealed in Epps' corn crib three days. At night, when his family were asleep, she would steal into the quarters for food, and return to the crib again. We concluded it would no longer be safe for us to allow her to remain, and accordingly she retraced her steps to her own cabin.

But the most remarkable instance of a successful evasion of dogs and hunters was the following.

Among Carey's girls was one by the name of Celeste. She was nineteen or twenty, and far whiter than her owner, or any of his offspring. It required a close inspection to distinguish in her features the slightest trace of African blood. A stranger would never have dreamed that she was the descendant of slaves. I was sitting in my cabin late at night, playing a low air on my violin, when the door opened carefully, and Celeste stood before me. She was pale and haggard. Had an apparition arisen from the earth, I could not have been more startled.

"Who are you?" I demanded, after gazing at her a moment.

"I'm hungry; give me some bacon," was her reply.

My first impression was that she was some deranged young mistress, who, escaping from home, was wandering, she knew not whither, and had been attracted to my cabin by the sound of the violin. The coarse cotton slave dress she wore, however, soon dispelled such a supposition.

"What is your name?" I again interrogated.

"My name is Celeste," she answered. "I belong to Carey, and have been two days among the palmettoes. I am sick and can't work, and would rather die in the swamp than be whipped to death by the overseer. Carey's dogs won't follow me. They have tried to set them on. There's a secret between them and Celeste, and they won't mind the devilish orders of the overseer. Give me some meat—I'm starving."

I divided my scanty allowance with her, and while partaking of it, she related how she had managed to escape and described the place of her concealment. In the edge of the swamp, not half a mile from Epps' house, was as a large space, thousands of acres in extent, thickly covered with palmetto. Tall trees, whose long arms interlocked each other, formed a canopy above them, so dense as to exclude the beams of the sun. It was like twilight always, even in the middle of the brightest day. In the centre of this great space, which nothing but serpents very often explore—a sombre and solitary spot—Celeste had erected a rude hut of dead branches that had fallen to the ground, and covered it with the leaves of the palmetto. This was the abode she had selected. She had no fear of Carey's dogs, any more than I had of Epps'. It is a fact, which I have never been able to explain, that there are those whose tracks the hounds will absolutely refuse to follow. Celeste was one of them.

For several nights she came to my cabin for food. On one occasion our dogs barked as she approached, which aroused Epps, and induced him to reconnoitre the premises. He did not discover her, but after that it was not deemed prudent for her to come to the yard. When all was silent I carried provisions to a certain spot agreed upon, where she would find them.

In this manner Celeste passed the greater part of the summer. She regained her health, and became strong and hearty. At all seasons of the year the howlings of wild animals can be heard at night along the borders of the swamps. Several times they had made her a midnight call, awakening her from slumbers with a growl. Terrified by such unpleasant salutations, she finally concluded to abandon her lonely dwelling; and, accordingly, returning to her master, was scourged, her neck meanwhile being fastened in the stocks, and sent into the field again.

The year before my arrival in the country there was a concerted movement among a number of slaves. on Bayou Boeuf, that terminated tragically indeed. It was, I presume, a matter of newspaper notoriety at the time, but all the knowledge I have of it, has been derived from the relation of those living at that period in the immediate vicinity of the excitement. It has become a subject of general and unfailing interest in every slave-hut on the bayou, and will doubtless go down to succeeding generations as their chief tradition. Lew Cheney, with whom I became acquainted

—a shrewd, cunning negro, more intelligent than the generality of his race, but unscrupulous and full of treachery—conceived the project of organizing a company sufficiently strong to fight their way against all opposition, to the neighboring territory of Mexico.

A remote spot, far within the depths of the swamp, back of Hawkins' plantation, was selected as the rallying point. Lew flitted from one plantation to another in the dead of night, preaching a crusade to Mexico, and, like Peter the Hermit, creating a furor of excitement wherever he appeared. At length a large number of runaways were assembled; stolen mules, and corn gathered from the fields, and bacon escaped from smoke-houses, had been conveyed into the woods. The expedition was about ready to proceed when their hiding place was discovered. Lew Cheney, becoming convinced of the ultimate failure of his project, in order to curry favor with his master, and avoid the consequences which he foresaw would follow, deliberately determined to sacrifice all his companions. Departing secretly from the encampment, he proclaimed among the planters the number collected in the swamp, and, instead of stating truly the object they had in view, asserted their intention was to emerge from their seclusion the first favorable opportunity, and murder every white person along the bayou.

Such an announcement, exaggerated as it passed from mouth to mouth, filled the whole country with terror. The fugitives were surrounded and taken prisoners, carried in chains to Alexandria, and hung by the populace. Not only those, but many who were suspected, though entirely innocent, were taken from the field and from the cabin, and without the shadow of process or form of trial, hurried to the scaffold. The planters on Bayou Boeuf finally rebelled against such reckless destruction of property, but it was not until a regiment of soldiers had arrived from some fort on the Texan frontier, demolished the gallows, and opened the doors of the Alexandria prison, that the indiscriminate slaughter was stayed. Lew Cheney escaped, and was even rewarded for his treachery. He is still living, but his name is despised and execrated by all his race throughout the parishes of Rapides and Avoyelles.

Such an idea as insurrection, however, is not new among the enslaved population of Bayou Boeuf. More than once I have joined in serious consultation, when the subject has been discussed, and there have been times when a word from me would have placed hundreds of my fellow-bondsmen in an attitude of defiance Without arms or ammunition, or even with them, I saw such a step would result in certain defeat, disaster and death, and always raised my voice against it.

During the Mexican war I well remember the extravagant hopes that were excited. The news of victory filled the great house with rejoicing, but produced only sorrow and disappointment in the cabin. In my opinion—and I have had opportunity to know something of the feeling of which I speak—there are not fifty slaves on the shores of Bayou Boeuf, but would hail with unmeasured delight the approach of an invading army.

They are deceived who flatter themselves that the ignorant and debased slave has no conception of the magnitude of his wrongs. They are deceived who imagine that he arises from his knees, with back lacerated and bleeding, cherishing only a spirit of meekness and forgiveness. A day may come—it will come, if his prayer is heard—a terrible day of vengeance when the master in his turn will cry in vain for mercy.

CHAPTER 18. O'NEIL, THE TANNER—ONVERSATION WITH AUNT PHEBE...

⊙ ⊙ ⊙

O'Neil, The Tanner—Conversation With Aunt Phebe Overheard—Epps In The Tanning Business—Stabbing Of Uncle Abram—The Ugly Wound-Epps Is Jealous— Patsey Is Missing—Her Return From Shaw's—Harriet, Shaw's Black Wife—Epps Enraged—Patsey Denies His Charges—She Is Tied Down Naked To Four Stakes— The Inhuman Flogging—Flaying Of Patsey—The Beauty Of The Day—The Bucket Of Salt Water—The Dress Stiff With Blood—Patsey Grows Melancholy—Her Idea Of God And Eternity—Of Heaven And Freedom—The Effect Of Slave-Whipping—Epps' Oldest Son—"The Child Is Father To The Man."

WILEY suffered severely at the hands of Master Epps, as has been related in the preceding chapter, but in this respect he fared no worse than his unfortunate companions. "Spare the rod," was an idea scouted by our master. He was constitutionally subject to periods of ill-humor, and at such times, however little provocation there might be, a certain amount of punishment was inflicted. The circumstances attending the last flogging but one that I received, will show how trivial a cause was sufficient with him for resorting to the whip.

A Mr. O'Neil, residing in the vicinity of the Big Pine Woods, called upon Epps for the purpose of purchasing me. He was a tanner and currier by occupation, transacting an extensive business, and intended to place me at service in some department of his establishment, provided he bought me. Aunt Phebe, while preparing the dinner-table in the great house, overheard their conversation. On returning to the yard at night, the old woman ran to meet me, designing, of course, to overwhelm me with the news. She entered into a minute repetition of all she had heard, and Aunt Phebe was one whose ears never failed to drink in every word of conversation uttered in her hearing. She enlarged upon the fact that "Massa Epps was g'wine to sell me to a tanner ober in de Pine Woods," so long and loudly as to attract the attention of the mistress, who, standing unobserved on the piazza at the time, was listening to our conversation.

"Well, Aunt Phebe," said I, "I'm glad of it. I'm tired of scraping cotton, and would rather be a tanner. I hope he'll buy me."

O'Neil did not effect a purchase, however, the parties differing as to price, and the morning following his arrival, departed homewards. He had been gone but a short time me, when Epps made his appearance in the field. Now nothing will more violently enrage a master, especially Epps, than the intimation of one of his servants that he would like to leave him. Mistress Epps had repeated to him my expressions to Aunt Phebe the evening previous, as I learned from the latter afterwards, the mistress having mentioned to her that she had overheard us. On entering the field, Epps walked directly to me.

"So, Platt, you're tired of scraping cotton, are you? You would like to change your master, eh? You're fond of moving round—traveler—ain't ye? Ah, yes—like to travel for your health, may be? Feel above cotton-scraping, I 'spose. So you're going into the tanning business? Good business—devilish fine business. Enterprising nigger! B'lieve I'll go into that business myself. Down on your knees, and strip that rag off your back! I'll try my hand at tanning."

I begged earnestly, and endeavored to soften him with excuses, but in vain. There was no other alternative; so kneeling down, I presented my bare back for the application of the lash.

"How do you like *tanning*?" he exclaimed, as the rawhide descended upon my flesh. "How do you like *tanning*?" he repeated at every blow. In this manner he gave me twenty or thirty lashes, incessantly giving utterance to the word "*tanning*," in one form of expression or another. When sufficiently "tanned," he allowed me to arise, and with a half- malicious laugh assured me, if I still fancied the business, he would give me further instruction in it whenever I desired. This time, he remarked, he had only given me a short lesson in "tanning "—the next time he would "curry me down."

Uncle Abram, also, was frequently treated with great brutality, although he was one of the kindest and most faithful creatures in the world. He was my cabin-mate for years. There was a benevolent expression in the old man's face, pleasant to behold. He regarded us with a kind of parental feeling, always counseling us with remarkable gravity and deliberation.

Returning from Marshall's plantation one afternoon, whither I had been sent on some errand of the mistress, I found him lying on the cabin floor, his clothes saturated with blood. He informed me that he had been stabbed! While spreading cotton on the scaffold, Epps came home intoxicated from Holmesville. He found fault with every thing, giving many orders so directly contrary that it was impossible to execute any of them. Uncle Abram, whose faculties were growing dull, became confused, and committed some blunder of no particular consequence. Epps was so enraged thereat, that, with drunken recklessness, he flew upon the old man, and stabbed him in the back. It was a long, ugly wound, but did not happen to penetrate far enough to result fatally. It was sewed up by the mistress, who censured her husband with extreme severity, not only denouncing his inhumanity, but declaring that she expected nothing else than that he would bring the family to poverty— that he would kill all the slaves on the plantation in some of his drunken fits.

It was no uncommon thing with him to prostrate Aunt Phebe with a chair or stick of wood; but the most cruel whipping that ever I was doomed to witness —one I can never recall with any other emotion than that of horror—was inflicted on the unfortunate Patsey.

It has been seen that the jealousy and hatred of Mistress Epps made the daily life of her young and agile slave completely miserable. I am happy in the belief that on numerous occasions I was the means of averting punishment from the inoffensive girl. In Epps' absence the mistress often ordered me to whip her without the remotest provocation. I would refuse, saying that I feared my master's displeasure, and several times ventured to remonstrate with her against the treatment Patsey received. I endeavored to impress her with the truth that the latter was not responsible for the acts of which she complained, but that she being a slave, and subject entirely to her master's will, he alone was answerable.

At length "the green–eyed monster" crept into the soul of Epps also, and then it was that he joined with his wrathful wife in an infernal jubilee over the girl's miseries.

On a Sabbath day in hoeing time, not long ago, we were on the bayou bank, washing our clothes, as was our usual custom. Presently Patsey was missing. Epps called aloud, but there was no answer. No one had observed her leaving the yard, and it was a wonder with us whither she had gone. In the course of a couple of hours she was seen approaching from the direction of Shaw's. This man, as has been intimated, was a notorious profligate, and withal not on the most friendly terms with Epps. Harriet, his, wife, knowing Patsey's troubles, was kind to her, in consequence of which the latter was in the habit of going over to see her every opportunity. Her visits were prompted by friendship merely, but the suspicion gradually entered the brain of Epps, that another and a baser passion led her thither—that it was not Harriet she desired to meet, but rather the unblushing libertine, his neighbor. Patsey found her master in a fearful rage on her return. His violence so alarmed her that at first she attempted to evade direct answers to hi his questions, which only served to increase his suspicions. She finally, however, drew herself up proudly, and in a spirit of indignation boldly denied his charges.

"Missus don't give me soap to wash with, as she does the rest," said Patsey, "and you know why. I went over to Harriet's to get a piece," and saying this, she drew it forth from a pocket in her dress and exhibited it to him. "That's what I went to Shaw's for, Massa Epps," continued she; "the Lord knows that was all."

"You lie, you black wench!" shouted Epps.

"I don't lie, massa. If you kill me, I'll stick to that."

"Oh! I'll fetch you down. I'll learn you to go to Shaw's. I'll take the starch out of ye," he muttered fiercely through his shut teeth.

Then turning to me, he ordered four stakes to be driven into the ground, pointing with the toe of his boot to the places where he wanted them. When the stakes were driven down, he ordered her to be stripped of every article of dress. Ropes were then brought, and the naked girl was laid upon her face, her wrists and feet each tied firmly to a stake. Stepping to the piazza, he took down a heavy whip, and placing it in my hands, commanded me to lash her. Unpleasant as it was, I was compelled to obey him. Nowhere that day, on the face of the whole earth, I venture to say, was there such a demoniac exhibition witnessed as then ensued.

Mistress Epps stood on the piazza among her children, gazing on the scene with an air of heartless satisfaction. The slaves were huddled together at a little distance, their countenances indicating the sorrow of their hearts. Poor Patsey prayed piteously for mercy, but her prayers were vain. Epps ground his teeth, and stamped upon the ground, screaming at me, like a mad fiend, to strike harder.

"Strike harder, or your turn will come next, you scoundrel," he yelled.

"Oh, mercy, massa!—oh! have mercy, do. Oh, God! pity me," Patsey exclaimed continually, struggling fruitlessly, and the flesh quivering at every stroke.

THE STAKING OUT AND FLOGGING OF THE GIRL PATSEY.

When I had struck her as many as thirty times, I stopped, and turned round toward Epps, hoping he was satisfied; but with bitter oaths and threats, he ordered me to continue. I inflicted ten or fifteen blows more. By this time her back was covered with long welts, intersecting each other like net work. Epps was yet furious and savage as ever, demanding if she would like to go to Shaw's again, and swearing he would flog her until she wished she was in h—l. Throwing down the whip, I declared I could punish her no more. He ordered me to go on, threatening me with a severer flogging than she had received, in case of refusal. My heart revolted at the inhuman scene, and risking the consequences, I absolutely refused to raise the whip. He then seized it himself, and applied it with ten-fold greater force than I had. The painful cries and shrieks of the tortured Patsey, mingling with the loud and angry curses of Epps, loaded the air. She was terribly lacerated—I may say, without exaggeration, literally flayed. The lash was wet with blood, which flowed down her sides and dropped upon the ground. At length she ceased struggling. Her head sank listlessly on the ground. Her screams and supplications gradually decreased and died away into a low moan. She no longer writhed and shrank beneath the lash when it bit out small pieces of her flesh. I thought that she was dying!

It was the Sabbath of the Lord. The fields smiled in the warm sunlight—the birds chirped merrily amidst the foliage of the trees—peace and happiness seemed to reign everywhere, save in the bosoms of Epps and his panting victim and the silent witnesses around him. The tempestuous emotions that were raging there were little in harmony with the calm and quiet beauty of the day. I could look on Epps only with unutterable loathing and abhorrence, and thought within myself—"Thou devil, sooner or later, somewhere in the course of eternal justice, thou shalt answer for this sin!"

Finally, he ceased whipping from mere exhaustion, and ordered Phebe to bring a bucket of salt and water. After washing her thoroughly with this, I was told to take her to her cabin. Untying the ropes, I raised her in my arms. She was unable to stand, and as her head rested on my shoulder, she repeated many times, in a faint voice scarcely perceptible, "Oh, Platt—oh, Platt!" but nothing further. Her dress was replaced, but it clung to her back, and was soon stiff with blood. We laid her on some boards in the hut, where she remained a long time, with eyes closed and groaning in agony. At night Phebe applied melted tallow to her wounds, and so far as we were able, all endeavored to assist and console her. Day after day she lay in her cabin upon her face, the sores preventing her resting in any other position.

A blessed thing it would have been for her—days and weeks and months of misery it would have saved her—had she never lifted up her head in life again. Indeed, from that time forward she was not what she had been. The burden of a deep melancholy weighed heavily on her spirits. She no longer moved with that buoyant and elastic step—there was not that mirthful sparkle in her eyes that formerly distinguished her. The bounding vigor—the sprightly, laughter-loving spirit of her youth, were gone. She fell into a mournful and desponding mood, and often times would start up in her sleep, and with raised hands, plead for mercy. She became more silent than she was, toiling all day in our midst, not uttering a word. A care-worn, pitiful expression settled on her face, and it was her humor now to weep, rather than rejoice. If ever there was a broken heart— one crushed and blighted by the rude grasp of suffering misfortune—it was Patsey's.

She had been reared no better than her master's beast—looked upon merely as a valuable and handsome animal—and consequently possessed but a limited amount of knowledge. And yet a faint light cast its rays over her intellect, so that it was not wholly dark. She had a dim perception of God and of eternity, and a still more dim perception of a Saviour who had died even for such as her. She entertained but confused notions of a future life—not comprehending the distinction between the corporeal and spiritual existence. Happiness, in her mind, was exemption from stripes—from labor—from the cruelty of masters and overseers. Her idea of the joy of heaven was simply rest, and is fully expressed in these of a melancholy bard;

"I ask no paradise on high,

With cares on earth oppressed,

The only heaven for which I sigh,

Is rest, eternal rest."

It is a mistaken opinion that prevails in some quarters that the slave does not understand the term— does not comprehend the idea of freedom. Even on Bayou Boeuf, where I conceive slavery exists in its most abject and cruel form—where it exhibits features altogether unknown in more northern States— the most ignorant of them generally know full well its meaning. They understand the privileges and exemptions that belong to it—that it would bestow upon them the fruits of their own labors, and that it would secure to them the enjoyment of domestic happiness. They do not fail to observe the difference between their own condition and the meanest white man's, and to realize the injustice of the laws which place it in his power not only to appropriate the profits of their industry, but to subject them to unmerited and unprovoked punishment, without remedy, or the right to resist or to remonstrate.

Patsey's life, especially after her whipping, was one long dream of liberty. Far away, to her fancy an immeasurable distance, she knew there was a land of freedom. A thousand times she had. heard that somewhere in the distant North there were no slaves—no masters. In her imagination it was an enchanted region, the Paradise of the earth. To dwell where the black man may work for himself—live in his own cabin—till his own soil, was a blissful dream of Patsey's—a dream, alas! the fulfillment of which she can never realize.

The effect of these exhibitions of brutality on the household of the slave-holder, is apparent. Epps' oldest son is an intelligent lad of ten or twelve years of age. It is pitiable, sometimes, to see him chastising, for instance, the venerable Uncle Abram. He will call the old man to account, and if in his childish judgement it is necessary, sentence him to a certain number of lashes, which he proceeds to inflict with much gravity and deliberation. Mounted on his pony, he often rides into the field with his whip, playing the overseer, greatly to his father's delight. Without discrimination, at such times, he applies the rawhide, urging the slaves forward with shouts, and occasional expressions of profanity, while the old man laughs, and commends him as a thorough-going boy.

"The child is father to the man," and with such training, whatever may be his natural disposition, it cannot well be otherwise than that, on arriving at maturity, the sufferings and miseries of the slave will be looked upon with entire indifference. The influence of the iniquitous system necessarily fosters an unfeeling and cruel spirit, even in the bosoms of those who, among, their equals, are regarded as humane and generous.

Young Master Epps possessed some noble qualities, yet no process of reasoning could lead him to comprehend, that in the eye of the Almighty there is no distinction of color. He looked upon the black man simply as an animal, differing in no respect from any other animal, save in the gift of speech and the possession of somewhat higher instincts, and, therefore, the more valuable. To work like his father's mules— to be whipped and kicked and scourged through life— to address the white man with hat in hand, and eyes bent servilely on the earth, in his mind, was the natural and proper destiny of the slave. Brought up with such ideas—in the notion that we stand without the pale of humanity—no wonder the oppressors of my people are a pitiless and unrelenting race.

⊙ ⊙ ⊙

CHAPTER 19. AVERY, ON BAYOU ROUGE— PECULIARITY OF DWELLINGS...

⊙ ⊙ ⊙

Avery, On Bayou Rouge—Peculiarity Of Dwellings—Epps Builds A New House— Bass, The Carpenter—His Noble Qualities—His Personal Appearance And Eccentricities—Bass And Epps Discuss The Question Of Slavery—Epps' Opinion Of Bass—I Make Myself Known To Him—Our Conversation—His Surprise—The Midnight Meeting On The Bayou Bank—Bass' Assurances—Declares War Against-Slavery—Why I Did Not Disclose My History—Bass Writes Letters—Copy Of His Letter To Messrs. Parker And Perry—The Fever Of Suspense—Disappointments— Bass Endeavors To Cheer Me—My Faith In Him.

IN the month of June, 1852, in pursuance of a previous contract, Mr. Avery, a carpenter of Bayou Rouge, commenced the erection of a house for Master Epps. It has previously been stated that there are no cellars on Bayou Boeuf; on the other hand, such is the low and swampy nature of the ground, the great houses are usually built upon spiles. Another peculiarity is, the rooms are not plastered, but the ceiling and sides are covered with matched cypress boards, painted such color as most pleases the owner's taste. Generally the plank and boards are sawed by slaves with whip-saws, there being no waterpower upon which mills might be built within many miles. When the planter erects for himself a dwelling, therefore, there is plenty of extra work for his slaves. Having had some experience under Tibeats as a carpenter, I was taken from the field altogether, on the arrival of Avery and his hands.

Among them was one to whom I owe an immeasurable debt of gratitude. Only for him, in all probability I should have ended my days in slavery. He was my deliverer a man whose true heart overflowed with noble and generous emotions. To the last moment of my existence I shall remember him with feelings of thankfulness. His name was Bass, and at that time he resided in Marksville. It will be difficult to convey a correct impression of his appearance or character. He was a large man, between forty and fifty years old, of light complexion and light hair. He was very cool and self-possessed, fond of argument, but always speaking with extreme deliberation. He was that kind of person whose peculiarity of manner was such that nothing he uttered ever gave offence. What would be intolerable, coming from the lips of another, could be said by him with impunity. There was not a man on Red River, perhaps, that agreed with him on the subject of politics or religion, and not a man, I venture to say, who discussed either of those subjects half as much. It seemed to be taken for granted that he would espouse the unpopular side of every local question, and it always created amusement rather than displeasure among his auditors, to listen to the ingenious and original manner in which he maintained the controversy. He was a bachelor—an "old bachelor," according to the true acceptation of the term—having no kindred living, as he knew of, in the world. Neither had he any permanent abiding place—wandering from one State to another, as his fancy dictated. He had lived in Marksville three or four years, and in the prosecution of his business as a carpenter; and in consequence, likewise, of his peculiarities, was quite extensively known throughout the parish of Avoyelles. He was liberal to a fault; and his many acts of kindness and transparent goodness of heart rendered him popular in the community, the sentiment of which he unceasingly combated.

He was a native of Canada, from whence he had wandered in early life, and after visiting all the principal localities in the northern and western States, in the course of his peregrinations, arrived in the unhealthy region of the Red River. His last removal was from Illinois. Whither he has now gone, I regret to be obliged to say, is unknown to me. He gathered up his effects and departed quietly from Marksville the day before I did, the suspicions of his instrumentality in procuring my liberation rendering such a step necessary. For the commission of a just and righteous act he would undoubtedly have suffered death, had he remained within reach of the slavewhipping tribe on Bayou Boeuf.

One day, while working on the new house, Bass and Epps became engaged in a controversy, to which, as will be readily supposed, I listened with absorbing interest. They were discussing the subject of Slavery.

"I tell you what it is Epps," said Bass, "it's all wrong—all wrong, sir—there's no justice nor righteousness in it. I wouldn't own a slave if I was rich as Croesus, which I am not, as is perfectly well understood, more particularly among my creditors. There's another humbug—the credit system—humbug, sir; no credit—no debt. Credit leads a man into temptation. Cash down is the only thing that will deliver him from evil.

But this question of Slavery; what right have you to your niggers when you come down to the point?"

"What right!" said Epps, laughing; "why, I bought 'em, and paid for 'em."

Of *course* you did; the law says you have the right to hold a nigger, but begging the law's pardon, it lies. Yes, Epps, when the law says that it's a liar, and the truth is not in it. Is every thing right because the law allows it? Suppose they'd pass a law taking away your liberty and making you a slave?"

"Oh, that ain't a supposable case," said Epps, still laughing; "hope you don't compare me to a nigger, Bass."

"Well," Bass answered gravely, "no, not exactly. But I have seen niggers before now as good as I am, and I have no acquaintance with any white man in these parts that I consider a whit better than myself. Now, in the sight of God, what is the difference, Epps, between a white man and a black one?"

"All the difference in the world," replied Epps. "You might as well ask what the difference is between a white man and a baboon. Now, I've seen one of them critters in Orleans that knowed just as much as any nigger I've got. You'd call them feller citizens, I s'pose?"—and Epps indulged in a loud laugh at his own wit.

"Look here, Epps," continued his companion; "you can't laugh me down in that way. Some men are witty, and some ain't so witty as they think they are. Now let me ask you a question. Are all men created free and equal as the Declaration of Independence holds they are?"

"Yes," responded Epps, "but all men, niggers, and monkeys ain't;" and hereupon he broke forth into a more boisterous laugh than before.

"There are monkeys among white people as well as black, when you come to that," coolly remarked Bass. "I know some white men that use arguments no sensible monkey would. But let that pass. These niggers are human beings. If they don't know as much as their masters, whose fault is it? They are not allowed to know anything. You have books and papers, and can go where you please, and gather intelligence in a thousand ways. But your slaves have no privileges. You'd whip one of them if caught reading a book. They are held in bondage, generation after generation, deprived of mental improvement, and who can expect them to possess much knowledge? If they are not brought down to a level with the brute creation, you slaveholders will never be blamed for it. If they are baboons, or stand no higher in the scale of intelligence than such animals, you and men like you will have to answer for it. There's a sin, a fearful sin, resting on this nation, that will not go unpunished forever. There will be a reckoning yet—yes, Epps, there's a day coming that will burn as an oven. It may be sooner or it may be later, but it's a coming as sure as the Lord is just."

"If you lived up among the Yankees in New-England," said Epps, "I expect you'd be one of them cursed fanatics that know more than the constitution, and go about peddling clocks and coaxing niggers to run away."

"If I was in New–England," returned Bass, "I would be just what I am here. I would say that Slavery was an iniquity, and ought to be abolished. I would say there was no reason nor justice in the law, or the constitution that allows one man to hold another man in bondage. It would be hard for you to lose your property, to be sure, but it wouldn't be half as hard as it would be to lose your liberty. You have no more right to your freedom, in exact justice, than Uncle Abram yonder. Talk about black skin, and black blood; why, how many slaves are there on this bayou as white as either of us? And what difference is there in the color of the soul? Pshaw! the whole system is as absurd as it is cruel. You may own niggers and be hanged, but I wouldn't own one for the best plantation in Louisiana."

"You like to hear yourself talk, Bass, better than any man I know of. You would argue that black was white, or white black, if any body would contradict you. Nothing suits you in this world, and I don't believe you will be satisfied with the next, if you should have your choice in them."

Conversations substantially like the foregoing were not unusual between the two after this; Epps drawing him out more for the purpose of creating a laugh at his expense, than with a view of fairly discussing the merits of the question. He looked upon Bass, as a man ready to say anything merely for the pleasure of hearing his own voice; as somewhat self–conceited, perhaps, contending against his faith and judgment, in order, simply, to exhibit his dexterity in argumentation.

He remained at Epps, through the summer, visiting Marksville generally once a fortnight. The more I saw of him, the more I became convinced he was a man in whom I could confide. Nevertheless, my previous ill– fortune had taught me to be extremely cautious. It was not my place to speak to a white man except when spoken to, but I omitted no opportunity of throwing myself in his way, and endeavored constantly in every possible manner to attract his attention. In the early part of August he and myself were at work alone in the house, the other carpenters having left, and Epps being absent in the field. Now was the time, if ever, to broach the subject and I resolved to do it, and submit to whatever consequences might ensue. We were busily at work in the afternoon, when I stopped suddenly and said—

"Master Bass, I want to ask you what part of the country you came from?"

"Why, Platt, what put that into your head?" he answered. "You wouldn't know if I should tell you." After a moment or two he added—"I was born in Canada; now guess where that is."

"Oh, I know where Canada is," said I, "I have been there myself."

"Yes, I expect you are well acquainted all through that country", he remarked, laughing incredulously.

"As sure as I live, Master Bass," I replied, "I have been there. I have been in Montreal and Kingston, and Queenston, and a great many places in Canada, and I have been in York State, too—in Buffalo, and Rochester, and Albany, and can tell you the names of the villages on the Erie canal and the Champlain canal."

Bass turned round and gazed at me a long time without uttering a syllable.

"How came you here?" he inquired, at length,

"Master Bass," I answered, "if justice had been done, I never would have been here."

"Well, how's this?" said he. "Who are you? You have been in Canada sure enough; I know all the places you mention. How did you happen to get here? Come, tell me all about it."

"I have no friends here," was my reply, "that I can put confidence in. I am afraid to tell you, though I don't believe you would tell Master Epps if I should."

He assured me earnestly he would keep every word I might speak to him a profound secret, and his curiosity was evidently strongly excited. It was a long story, I informed him, and would take some time to relate it. Master Epps would be back soon, but if he would see me that night after all were asleep, I would repeat it to him. He consented readily to the arrangement, and directed me to come into the building where we were then at work, and I would find him there. About midnight, when all was still and quiet, I crept cautiously from my cabin, and silently entering the unfinished building, found him awaiting me.

After further assurances on his part that I should not be betrayed, I began a relation of the history of my life and misfortunes. He was deeply interested asking numerous questions in reference to localities and events. Having ended my story I besought him to write to some of my friends at the North, acquainting them with my situation, and begging them to forward free papers, or take such steps as they might consider proper to secure my release. He promised to do so, but dwelt upon the danger of such an act in case of detection, and now impressed upon me the great necessity of strict silence and secrecy. Before we parted our plan of operation was arranged.

We agreed to meet the next night at a specified place among the high weeds on the bank of the bayou, some distance from master's dwelling. There he was write down on paper the names and address of several persons, old friends in the North, to whom he would direct letters during his next visit to Marksville. It was not deemed prudent to meet in the new house, inasmuch as the light it would be necessary to use might possibly be discovered. In the course of the day I managed to obtain a few matches and a piece of candle, unperceived, from the kitchen, during a temporary absence of Aunt Phebe. Bass had pencil and paper in his tool chest.

At the appointed hour we met on the bayou bank, and creeping among the high weeds, I lighted the candle, while he drew forth pencil and paper and prepared for business. I gave him the names of William Perry, Cephas Parker and Judge Marvin, all of Saratoga Springs, Saratoga county, New-York. I had been employed by the latter in the United States Hotel, and had transacted business with the former to a considerable extent, and trusted that at least one of them would be still living at that place. He carefully wrote the names, and then remarked, thoughtfully—

"It is so many years since you left Saratoga, all these men may be dead, or may have removed. You say you obtained papers at the custom house in New-York. Probably there is a record of them there, and I think it would be well to write and ascertain."

I agreed with him, and again repeated the circumstances related heretofore, connected with my visit to the custom house with Brown and Hamilton. We lingered on the bank of the bayou an hour or more, conversing upon the subject which now engrossed our. thoughts. I could no longer doubt his fidelity, and freely spoke to him of the many sorrows I had borne in silence, and so long. I spoke of my wife and children, mentioning their names and ages, and dwelling upon the unspeakable happiness it would be to clasp them to my heart once more before I died. I caught him by the hand, and with tears and passionate entreaties implored him to befriend me—to restore me to my kindred and to liberty—promising I would weary Heaven the remainder of my life with prayers that it would bless and prosper him. In the enjoyment of freedom—surrounded by the associations of youth, and restored to the bosom of my family—that promise is not yet forgotten, nor shall it ever be so long as I have strength to raise my imploring eyes on high.

"Oh, blessings on his kindly voice and on his silver hair, And blessings on his whole life long, until he meet me there."

He overwhelmed me with assurances of friendship and faithfulness, saying he had never before taken so deep an interest in the fate of any one. He spoke of himself in a somewhat mournful tone, as a lonely man, a wanderer about the world—that he was growing old, and must soon reach the end of his earthly journey, and lie down to his final rest without kith or kin to mourn for him, or to remember him—that his life was of little value to himself, and henceforth should be devoted to the accomplishment of my liberty, and to an unceasing warfare against the accursed shame of Slavery.

After this time we seldom spoke to, or recognized each other. He was, moreover, less free in his conversation with Epps on the subject of Slavery. The remotest suspicion that there was any unusual intimacy — any secret understanding between us—never once entered the mind of Epps, or any other person, white or black, on the plantation.

I am often asked, with an air of incredulity, how I succeeded so many years in keeping from my daily and constant companions the knowledge of my true name and history. The terrible lesson Burch taught me, impressed indelibly upon my mind the danger and uselessness of asserting I was a freeman. There, was no possibility of any slave being able to assist me, while, on the other hand, there was a possibility of his exposing me. When it is recollected the whole current of my thoughts, for twelve years, turned to the contemplation of escape, it will not be wondered at, that I was always cautious and on my guard. It would have been an act of folly to have proclaimed my right to freedom; it would only have subjected me to severer scrutiny—probably have consigned me to some more distant and inaccessible region than even Bayou Boeuf. Edwin Epps was a person utterly regardless of a black man's rights or wrongs—utterly destitute of any natural sense of justice, as I well knew. It was important, therefore, not only as, regarded my hope of deliverance, but also as regarded the few personal priviliges I was as permitted to enjoy, to keep from him the history of my life.

The Saturday night subsequent to our interview at the water's edge, Bass went home to Marksville. The next day, being Sunday, he employed himself in his own room writing letters. One he directed to the Collector of Customs at New–York, another to Judge Marvin, and another to Messrs. Parker and Perry jointly. The latter was the one which led to my recovery. He subscribed my true name, but in the postscript intimated I was not the writer. The letter itself shows that he considered himself engaged in a dangerous undertaking—no less than running "the risk of his life, if detected." I did not see the letter before it was mailed, but have since obtained a copy, which is here inserted;

"Bayou Boeuf, August 15, 1852.

"Mr. WILLIAM PERRY or Mr. CEPHAS PARKER.

"Gentlemen—It having been a long time since I have seen or heard from you, and not knowing that you are living, it is with uncertainty that I write to you, but the necessity of the case must be my excuse.

"Having been born free, just across the river from you, I am certain you must know me, and I am here now a slave. I wish you to obtain free papers for me, and forward them to me at Marksville, Louisiana, Parish of Avoyelles, and oblige

"Yours, SOLOMON NORTHUP.

"The way I came to be a slave, I was taken sick in Washington City, and was insensible for some time. When I recovered my reason, I was robbed of my free–papers, and in irons on my way to this State, and have never been able to get any one to write for me until now; and he that is writing for me runs the risk of his life if detected."

The allusion to myself in the work recently issued, entitled "A Key to Uncle Tom's Cabin," contains the first part of this letter, omitting the postscript. Neither are the full names of the gentlemen to whom it is directed correctly stated, there being a slight discrepancy, probably a typographical error. To the postscript more than to the body of the communication am I indebted for my liberation, as will presently be seen.

When Bass returned from Marksville he informed me of what he had done. We continued our midnight consultations, never speaking to each other through the day, excepting as it was necessary about the work. As nearly as he was able to ascertain, it would require two weeks for the letter to reach Saratoga in due course of mail, and the same length of time for an answer to return. Within six weeks, at the farthest, we concluded, an answer would arrive, if it arrived at all. A great many suggestions were now made, and a great deal of conversation took place between us, as to the most safe and proper course to pursue on receipt of the free papers. They would stand between him and harm, in case we were overtaken and arrested leaving the country altogether. It would be no infringement of law, however much it might provoke individual hostility, to assist a freeman to regain his freedom.

At the end of four weeks he was again at Marksville, but no answer had arrived. I was sorely disappointed, but still reconciled myself with the reflection that sufficient length of time had not yet elapsed— that there might have been delays—and that I could not reasonably expect one so soon. Six, seven, eight, and ten weeks passed by, however, and nothing came. I was in a fever of suspense whenever Bass visited Marksville, and could scarcely close my eyes until his return. Finally my master's house was finished, and the time came when Bass must leave me. The night before his departure I was wholly given up to despair. I had clung to him as a drowning man clings to the floating spar, knowing if it ships from his grasp he must forever sink beneath the waves. The all–glorious hope, upon which I had laid such eager hold, was crumbling to ashes in my hands. I felt as if sinking down, down, amidst the bitter waters of Slavery, from the unfathomable depths of which I should never rise again.

The generous heart of my friend and benefactor was touched with pity at the sight of my distress. He endeavored to cheer me up, promising to return the day before Christmas, and if no intelligence was received in the meantime, some further step would be undertaken to effect our design. He exhorted me to keep up my spirits—to rely upon his continued efforts in my behalf, assuring me, in most earnest and impressive language, that my liberation should, from thenceforth, be the chief object of his thoughts.

In his absence the time passed slowly indeed. I looked forward to Christmas with intense anxiety and impatience. I had about given up the expectation of receiving any answer to the letters. They might have miscarried, or might have been misdirected.

Perhaps those at Saratoga, to whom they had been addressed, were all dead; perhaps, engaged in their pursuits they did not consider the fate of an obscure, unhappy black man of sufficient importance to be noticed. My whole reliance was in Bass. The faith I had in him was continually re–assuring me, and enabled me to stand up against the tide of disappointment that had overwhelmed me.

So wholly was I absorbed in reflecting upon my situation and prospects, that the hands with whom I labored in the field often observed it. Patsey would ask me if I was sick, and Uncle Abram, and Bob, and Wiley frequently expressed a curiosity to know what I could be thinking about so steadily. But I evaded their inquiries with some light remark, and kept my thoughts locked closely in my breast.

⊙ ⊙ ⊙

CHAPTER 20. BASS FAITHFUL TO HIS WORD— HIS ARRIVAL ON CHRISTMAS EVE...

⊙ ⊙ ⊙

Bass Faithful To His Word—His Arrival On Christmas Eve—The Difficulty Of Obtaining An Interview—The Meeting In The Cabin—Non-Arrival Of The Letter— Bass Announces His Intention To Proceed North—Christmas—Conversation Between Epps And Bass—Young Mistress M'coy, The Beauty Of Bayou Boeuf—The "Ne Plus Ultra" Of Dinners—Music And Dancing—Presence Of The Mistress—Her Exceeding Beauty—The Last Slave Dance—William Pierce—Oversleep Myself—The Last Whipping—Despondency—The Cold Morning—Epps' Threats—The Passing Carriage—Strangers Approaching Through The Cotton-Field—Last Hour On Bayou Boeuf.

FAITHFUL to his word, the day before Christmas, just at night-fall, Bass came riding into the yard.

"How are you," said Epps, shaking him by the hand, "glad to see you." He would not have been very glad had he known the object of his errand.

"Quite well, quite well," answered Bass. "Had some business out on the bayou, and concluded to call and see you, and stay over night."

Epps ordered one of the slaves to take charge of his horse, and with much talk and laughter they passed into the house together; not, however, until Bass had looked at me significantly, as much as to say, "Keep dark, we understand each other." It was ten o'clock at night before the labors of the day were performed, when I entered the cabin. At that time Uncle Abram and Bob occupied it with me. I laid down upon my board and feigned I was asleep. When my companions had fallen into a profound slumber, I moved stealthily out of the door, and watched, and listened attentively for some sign or sound from Bass. There I stood until long after midnight, but nothing could be seen or heard. As I suspected, he dared not leave the house, through fear of exciting the suspicion of some of the family. I judged, correctly, he would rise earlier than was his custom, and take the opportunity of seeing me before Epps was up. Accordingly I aroused Uncle Abram an hour sooner than usual, and sent him into the house to build a fire, which, at that season of the year, is a part of Uncle Abram's duties.

I also gave Bob a violent shake, and asked him if he intended to sleep till noon, saying master would be up before the mules were fed. He knew right well the consequence that would follow such an event, and, jumping to his feet, was at the horse–pasture in a twinkling.

Presently, when both were gone, Bass slipped into the cabin.

"No letter yet, Platt," said he. The announcement fell upon my heart like lead.

"Oh, do write again, Master Bass," I cried; "I will give you the names of a great many I know. Surely they are not all dead. Surely some one will pity me."

"No use," Bass replied, "no use. I have made up my mind to that. I fear the Marksville post–master will mistrust something, I have inquired so often at his office. Too uncertain—too dangerous."

"Then it is all over," I exclaimed. "Oh, my God, how can I end my days here!"

"You're not going to end them here," he said, "unless you die very soon. I've thought this matter all have come to a determination. There are more ways than one to manage this business, and a better and surer way than writing letters. I have a job or two on hand which can be completed by March or April. By that time I shall have a considerable sum of money, and then, Platt, I am going to Saratoga myself."

I could scarcely credit my own senses as the words fell from his lips. But he assured me, in a manner that left no doubt of the sincerity of his intention, that if his life was spared until spring, he should certainly undertake the journey.

"I have lived in this region long enough," he considered; "I may as well be in one place as another. For a long time I have been thinking of going back more to the place where I was born. I'm tired of Slavery as well as you. If I can succeed in getting you away from here, it will be a good act that I shall like to think of all my life. And I shall succeed, Platt;

I'm bound to do it. Now let me tell you what I want. Epps will be up soon, and it won't do to be caught here. Think of a great many men at Saratoga and Sandy Hill, and in that neighborhood, who once knew you.

I shall make excuse to come here again in the course of the winter, when I will write down their names. I will then know who to call on when I go north. Think of all you can. Cheer up! Don't be discouraged. I'm with you, life or death. Good-bye. God bless you," and saying this he left the cabin quickly, and entered the great house.

It was Christmas morning—the happiest day in the whole year for the slave. That morning he need not hurry to the field, with his gourd and cotton-bag. Happiness sparkled in the eyes and overspread the countenances of all. The time of feasting and dancing had come. The cane and cotton fields were deserted. That day the clean dress was to. be donned—the red ribbon displayed; there were to be re-unions, and joy and laughter, and hurrying to and fro. It was to be a day of liberty among the children of Slavery. Wherefore they were happy, and rejoiced.

After breakfast Epps and Bass sauntered about the yard, conversing upon the price of cotton, and various other topics.

"Where do your niggers hold Christmas?" Bass inquired.

"Platt is going to Tanners to-day. His fiddle is in great demand. They want him at Marshall's Monday, and Miss Mary McCoy, on the old Norwood plantation, writes me a note that she wants him to play for her niggers Tuesday."

"He is rather a smart boy, ain't he?" said Bass. "Come here, Platt," he added, looking at me as I walked up to them, as if he had never thought before to take any special notice of me.

"Yes," replied Epps, taking hold of my arm and feeling it, "there isn't a bad joint in him. There ain't a boy on the bayou worth more than he is—perfectly sound, and no bad tricks. D—n him, he isn't like other niggers; doesn't look like 'em—don't act like 'em. I was offered seventeen hundred dollars for him last week."

"And didn't take it?" Bass inquired, with an air of surprise.

"Take it—no; devilish clear of it. Why, he's a reg'lar genius; can make a plough beam, wagon tongue—anything, as well as you can. Marshall wanted to put up one of his niggers agin him and raffle for them, but I told him I would see the devil have him first."

"I don't see anything remarkable about him," Bass observed.

"Why, just feel of him, no," Epps rejoined. "You don't see a boy very often put together any closer than he is. He's a thin-skin'd cuss, and won't bear as much whipping as some; but he's got the muscle in him, and no mistake.

Bass felt of me, turned me round, and made a thorough examination, Epps all the while dwelling on my good points. But his visitor seemed to take but little interest finally in the subject, and consequently it was dropped. Bass soon departed, giving me another sly look of recognition and significance, as he trotted out of the yard.

When he was gone I obtained a pass, and started for Tanner's—not Peter Tanner's, of whom mention has previously been made, but a relative of his. I played during the day and most of the night, spending the next day, Sunday, in my cabin. Monday I crossed the bayou to Douglas Marshall's, all Epps' slaves accompanying me, and on Tuesday went to the old Norwood place, which is the third plantation above Marshall's, on the same side of the water.

This estate is now owned by Miss Mary McCoy, a lovely girl, some twenty years of age. She is the beauty and the glory of Bayou Bouef. She owns about a hundred working hands, besides a great many house servants, yard boys, and young children. Her brother–in–law, who resides on the adjoining estate, is her general agent. She is beloved by all her slaves, and good reason indeed have they to be thankful that they have fallen into such gentle hands. Nowhere on the bayou are there such feasts, such merrymaking, as at young Madam McCoy's. Thither, more than to any other place, do the old and the young for miles around love to repair in the time of the Christmas holiday; for nowhere else can they find such delicious repasts; nowhere else can they hear a voice speaking to them so pleasantly. No one is so well beloved—no one fills so large a space in the hearts of a thousand slaves, as young Madam McCoy, the orphan mistress of the old Norwood estate.

On my arrival at her place, I found two or three hundred had assembled. The table was prepared in a long building, which she had erected expressly for her slaves to dance in. It was covered with every variety of food the country afforded, and was pronounced by general acclamation to be the rarest of dinners. Roast turkey, pig, chicken, duck, and all kinds of meat, baked, boiled, and broiled, formed a line the whole length of the extended table, while the vacant spaces were filled with tarts, jellies, and frosted cake, and pastry of many kinds. The young mistress walked around the table, smiling and saying a kind word to each one, and seemed to enjoy the scene exceedingly.

When the dinner was over the tables were removed to make room for the dancers. I tuned my violin and struck up a lively air; while some joined in a nimble reel, others patted and sang their simple but melodious songs, filling the great room with music mingled with the sound of human voices and the clatter of many feet.

In the evening the mistress returned, and stood in the door a long time, looking at us. She was magnificently arrayed. Her dark hair and eyes contrasted strongly with her clear and delicate complexion. Her form was slender but commanding, and her movement was a combination of unaffected dignity and grace. As she stood there, clad in her rich apparel, her face animated with pleasure, I thought I had never looked upon a human being half so beautiful. I dwell with delight upon the description of this fair and gentle lady, not only because she inspired me with emotions of gratitude and admiration, but because I would have the reader understand that all slave-owners on Bayou Boeuf are not like Epps, or Tibeats, or Jim Burns. Occasionally can be found, rarely it may be, indeed, a good man like William Ford, or an angel of kindness like young Mistress McCoy.

Tuesday concluded the three holidays Epps yearly allowed us. On my way home, Wednesday morning, while passing the plantation of William Pierce, that gentleman hailed me, saying he had received a line from Epps, brought down by William Varnell, permitting him to detain me for the purpose of playing for his slaves that night. It was the last time I was destined to witness a slave dance on the shores of Bayou Boeuf. The party at Pierce's continued their jollification until broad daylight, when I returned to my master's house, somewhat wearied with the loss of rest, but rejoicing in the possession of numerous bits and picayunes, which the whites, who were pleased with my musical performances, had contributed.

On Saturday morning, for the first time in years, I overslept myself. I was frightened on coming out of the cabin to find the slaves were already in the field. They had preceded me some fifteen minutes. Leaving my dinner and water-gourd, I hurried after them as fast as I could move. It was not yet sunrise, but Epps was on the piazza as I left the hut, and cried out to me that it was a pretty time of day to be getting up. By extra exertion my row was up when he came out after breakfast. This, however, was no excuse for the offence of oversleeping. Bidding me strip and lie down, he gave me ten or fifteen lashes, at the conclusion of which he inquired if I thought, after that, I could get up sometime in the morning. I expressed myself quite positively that I could, and, with back stinging with pain, went about my work.

The following day, Sunday, my thoughts were upon Bass, and the probabilities and hopes which hung upon his action and determination. I considered the uncertainty of life; that if it should be the will of God that he should die, my prospect of deliverance, and all expectation of happiness in this world, would be wholly ended and destroyed. My sore back, perhaps, did not have a tendency to render me unusually cheerful. I felt down–hearted and unhappy all day long, and when I laid down upon the hard board at night, my heart was oppressed with such a load of grief; it seemed that it must break.

Monday morning, the third of January, 1853, we were in the field betimes. It was a raw, cold morning, such as is unusual in that region. I was in advance, Uncle Abram next to me, behind him Bob, Patsey and Wiley, with our cotton–bags about our necks. Epps happened (a rare thing, indeed,) to come out that morning without his whip. He swore, in a manner that would shame a pirate, that we were doing nothing. Bob ventured to say that his fingers were so numb with cold he couldn't pick fast. Epps cursed himself for not having brought his rawhide, and declared that when he came out again he would warm us well; yes, he would make us all hotter than that fiery realm in which I am sometimes compelled to believe he will himself eventually reside.

With these fervent expressions, he left us. When out of hearing, we commenced talking to each other, saying how hard it was to be compelled to keep up our tasks with numb fingers; how unreasonable master was, and speaking of him generally in no flattering terms. Our conversation was interrupted by a carriage passing rapidly towards the house. Looking up, we saw two men approaching us through the cotton– field.

Having now brought down this narrative to the last hour I was to spend on Bayou Boeuf—having gotten through my last cotton picking, and about to bid Master Epps farewell—I must beg the reader to go back with me to the month of August; to follow Bass' letter on its long journey to Saratoga; to learn the effect it produced—and that, while I was repining and despairing in the slave hut of Edwin Epps, through the friendship of Bass and the goodness of Providence, all things were working together for my deliverance.

⊙ ⊙ ⊙

CHAPTER 21. THE LETTER REACHES SARATOGA—IS FORWARDED TO ANNE...

⊙ ⊙ ⊙

The Letter Reaches Saratoga—Is Forwarded To Anne—Is Laid Before Henry B. Northup—The Statute Of May 14, 1840—Its Provisions—Anne's Memorial To The Governor—The Affidavits Accompanying It—Senator Soule's Letter—Departure Of The Agent Appointed By The Governor—Arrival At Marksville—The Hon. John P. Waddill—The Conversation On New-York Politics—It Suggests A Fortunate Idea— The Meeting With Bass—The Secret Out—Legal Proceedings Instituted—Departure Of Northup And The Sheriff From Marksville For Bayou Boeuf—Arrangements On The Way—Reach Epps' Plantation—Discover His Slaves In The Cotton-Field—The Meeting—The Farewell.

I AM indebted to Mr. Henry B. Northup and others for many of the particulars contained in this chapter.

The letter written–by Bass, directed to Parker and Perry, and which was deposited in the post–office in Marksville on the 15th day of August, 1852, arrived at Saratoga in the early part of September. Some time previous to this, Anne had removed to Glens Falls, Warren county, where she had charge of the kitchen in Carpenter's Hotel. She kept house, however, lodging with our children, and was only absent from them during such time as the discharge of her duties in the hotel required.

Messrs. Parker and Perry, on receipt of the letter, forwarded it immediately to Anne. On reading it the children were all excitement, and without delay hastened to the neighboring village of Sandy Hill, to consult Henry B. Northup, and obtain his advice and assistance in the matter.

Upon examination, that gentleman found among the statutes of the State an act providing for the recovery of free citizens from slavery. It was passed May 14, 1840, and is entitled "An act more effectually to protect the free citizens of this State from being kidnapped or reduced to slavery." It provides that it shall be the duty of the Governor, upon the receipt of satisfactory information that any free citizen or inhabitant of this State, is wrongfully held in another State or Territory of the United States, upon the allegation or pretence that such person is a slave, or by color of any usage or rule of law is deemed or taken to be a slave, to take such measures to procure the restoration of such person to liberty, as he shall deem necessary. And to that end, he is authorized to appoint and employ an agent, and directed to furnish him with such credentials and instructions as will be likely to accomplish the object of his appointment. It requires the agent so appointed to proceed to collect the proper proof to establish the right of such person to his freedom; to perform such journeys, take such measures, institute such legal proceedings, etc., as may be necessary to return such person to this State, and charges all expenses incurred in carrying the act into effect, upon moneys not otherwise appropriated in the treasury.[1]

It was necessary to establish two facts to the satisfaction of the Governor: First, that I was a free citizen of New-York; and secondly, that I was wrongfully held in bondage. As to the first point, there was no difficulty, all the older inhabitants in the vicinity being ready to testify to it. The second point rested entirely upon the letter to Parker and Perry, written in an unknown hand, and upon the letter penned on board the brig Orleans, which, unfortunately, had been mislaid or lost.

A memorial was prepared, directed to his excellency, Governor Hunt,

1 See Appendix A

setting forth her marriage, my departure to Washington city; the receipt of the letters; that I was a free citizen, and such other facts as were deemed important, and was signed and verified by Anne. Accompanying this memorial were several affidavits of prominent citizens of Sandy Hill and Fort Edward, corroborating fully the statements it contained, and also a request of several well known gentlemen to the Governor, that Henry B. Northup be appointed agent under the legislative act.

On reading the memorial and affidavits, his excellency took a lively interest in the matter, and on the 23d day of November, 1852, under the seal of the State, "constituted, appointed and employed Henry B. Northup, Esq., an agent, with full power to effect" my restoration, and to take such measures as would be most likely to accomplish it, and instructing him to proceed to Louisiana with all convenient dispatch.[2]

The pressing nature of Mr. Northup's professional and political engagements delayed his departure until December. On the fourteenth day of that month he left Sandy Hill, and proceeded to Washington. The Hon. Pierre Soule, Senator in Congress from Louisiana, Hon. Mr. Conrad, Secretary of War, and Judge Nelson, of the Supreme Court of the United States, upon hearing a statement of the facts, and examining his commission, and certified copies of the memorial and affidavits, furnished him with open letters to gentlemen in Louisiana, strongly urging their assistance in accomplishing the object of his appointment.

Senator Soule especially interested himself in the matter, insisting, in forcible language, that it was the duty and interest of every planter in his State to aid in restoring me to freedom, and trusted the sentiments of honor and justice in the bosom of every citizen of the commonwealth would enlist him at once in my behalf. Having obtained these valuable letters, Mr. Northup returned to Baltimore, and proceeded from thence to Pittsburgh. It was his original intention, under advice of friends at Washington, to go directly to New Orleans, and consult the authorities of

2 See Appendix B

that city. Providentially, however, on arriving at the mouth of Red River, he changed his mind. Had he continued on, he would not have met with Bass, in which case the search for me would probably have been fruitless.

Taking passage on the first steamer that arrived, he pursued his journey up Red River, a sluggish, winding stream, flowing through a vast region of primitive forests and impenetrable swamps, almost wholly destitute of inhabitants. About nine o'clock in the forenoon, January 1st, 1853, he left the steamboat at Marksville, and proceeded directly to Marksville Court House, a small village four miles in the interior.

From the fact that the letter to Messrs. Parker and Perry was post-marked at Marksville, it was supposed by him that I was in that place or its immediate vicinity. On reaching this town, he at once laid his business before the Hon. John P. Waddill, a legal gentleman of distinction, and a man of fine genius and most noble impulses. After reading the letters and documents presented him, and listening to a representation of the circumstances under which I had been carried away into captivity, Mr. Waddill at once proffered his services, and entered into the affair with great zeal and earnestness. He, in common with others of like elevated character, looked upon the kidnapped with abhorrence. The title of his fellow parishioners and clients to the property which constituted the larger proportion of their wealth, not only depended upon the good faith in which slave sales were transacted, but he was a man in whose honorable heart emotions of indignation were aroused by such an instance of injustice.

Marksville, although occupying a prominent position, and standing out in impressive italics on the map of Louisiana, is, in fact, but a small and insignificant hamlet. Aside from the tavern, kept by a jolly and generous boniface, the court house, inhabited by lawless cows and swine in the seasons of vacation, and a high gallows, with its dissevered rope dangling in the air, there is little to attract the attention of the stranger.

Solomon Northup was a name Mr. Waddill had never heard, but he was confident that if there was a slave bearing that appellation in Marksville or vicinity, his black boy Tom would know him. Tom was accordingly called, but in all his extensive circle of acquaintances there was no such personage.

The letter to Parker and Perry was dated at Bayou Boeuf. At this place, therefore, the conclusion was, I must be sought. But here a difficulty suggested itself, of a very grave character indeed. Bayou Boeuf, at its nearest point, was twenty–three miles distant, and was the name applied to the section of country extending between fifty and a hundred miles, on both sides of that stream. Thousands and thousands of slaves resided upon its shores, the remarkable richness and fertility of the soil having attracted thither a great number of planters. The information in the letter was so vague and indefinite as to render it difficult to conclude upon any specific course of proceeding. It was finally determined, however, as the only plan that presented any prospect of success, that Northup and the brother of Waddill, a student in the office of the latter, should repair to the Bayou, and traveling up one side and down the other its whole length, inquire at each plantation for me. Mr. Waddill tendered the use of his carriage, and it was definitely arranged that they should start upon the excursion early Monday morning.

It will be seen at once that this course, in all probability, would have resulted unsuccessfully. It would have been impossible for them to have gone into the fields and examine all the gangs at work. They were not aware that I was known only as Platt; and had they inquired of Epps himself, he would have stated truly that he knew nothing of Solomon Northup.

The arrangement being adopted however , there was nothing further to be done until Sunday had elapsed. The conversation between Messrs. Northup and Waddill, in the course of the afternoon, turned upon New–York politics.

"I can scarcely comprehend the nice distinctions and shades of political parties in your State," observed Mr. Waddill. "I read of soft–shells and hard–shells, hunkers and barnburners, woolly–heads and silver–grays, and am unable to understand the precise difference between them. Pray, what is it?"

Mr. Northup, re–filling his pipe, entered into quite an elaborate narrative of the origin of the various reactions of parties, and concluded by saying there was another party in New–York, known as free–soilers or abolitionists. "You have seen none of those in this part of the country, I presume?" Mr. Northup remarked.

"Never, but one," answered Waddill, laughingly. "We have one here in Marksville, an eccentric creature, who preaches abolitionism as vehemently as any fanatic at the North. He is a generous, inoffensive man, but always maintaining the wrong side of an argument. It affords us a deal of amusement. He is an excellent mechanic, and almost indispensable in this community. He is a carpenter. His name is Bass."

Some further good–natured conversation was had at the expense of Bass' peculiarities, when Waddill all at once fell into a reflective mood, and asked for the mysterious letter again.

"Let me see—l–e–t m–e s–e–e!" he repeated, thoughtfully to himself, running his eyes over the letter once more. "'Bayou Boeuf, August 15.' August 15—post–marked here. 'He that is writing for me—' Where did Bass work last summer?" he inquired, turning suddenly to his brother.

His brother was unable to inform him, but rising, left the office, and soon returned with the intelligence that "Bass worked last summer somewhere on Bayou Boeuf."

"He is the man," 'bringing down his hand emphatically on the table,' "who can tell us all about Solomon Northup," exclaimed Waddill.

Bass was immediately searched for, but could not be found. After some inquiry, it was ascertained he was at the landing on Red River. Procuring a conveyance, young Waddill and Northup were not long in traversing the few miles to the latter place. On their arrival, Bass was found, just on the point of leaving, to be absent a fortnight or more. After an introduction, Northup begged the privilege of speaking to him privately a moment. They walked together towards the river, when the following conversation ensued.

"Mr. Bass," said Northup, "allow me to ask you if you were on Bayou Boeuf last August?"

"Yes, sir, I was there in August," was the reply.

"Did you write a letter for a colored man as that place to some gentleman in Saratoga Springs?"

"Excuse me, sir, if I say that is none of your business," answered Bass, stopping and looking his interrogator searchingly in the face.

"Perhaps I am rather hasty, Mr. Bass; I beg your pardon; but I have come from the State of New-York to accomplish the purpose the writer of a letter dated the 15th of August, post-marked at Marksville, had in view. Circumstances have led me to think that you are perhaps the man who wrote it. I am in search of Solomon Northup. If you know him, I beg you to inform me frankly where he is, and I assure you the source of any information you may give me shall not be divulged, if you desire it not to be."

A long time Bass looked his new acquaintance steadily in the eyes, without opening his lips. He seemed to be doubting in his own mind if there was not an attempt to practice some deception upon him. Finally he said, deliberately—

"I have done nothing to be ashamed of I am the man who wrote the letter. If you have come to rescue Solomon Northup, I am glad to see you."

"When did you last see him, and where is he?" Northup inquired.

"I last saw him Christmas, a week ago to-day. He is the slave of Edwin Epps, a planter on Bayou Boeuf, near Holmesville. He is not known as

Solomon Northup; he is called Platt."

The secret was out—the mystery was unraveled. Through the thick, black cloud, amid whose dark and dismal shadows I had walked twelve years, broke the star that was to light me back to liberty. All mistrust and hesitation were soon thrown aside, and the two men conversed long and freely upon the subject uppermost in their thoughts. Bass expressed the interest he had taken in my behalf—his intention of going north in the Spring, and declaring that he had resolved to accomplish my emancipation, if it were in his power. He described the commencement and progress of his acquaintance with me, and listened with eager curiosity to the account given him of my family, and the history of my early life. Before separating, he drew a map of the bayou on a strip of paper with a piece of red chalk, showing the locality of Epps' plantation, and the road leading most directly to it.

Northup and his young companion returned to Marksville, where it was determined to commence legal proceedings to test the question of my right to freedom. I was made plaintiff, Mr. Northup acting as my guardian, and Edwin Epps defendant. The process to be issued was in the nature of replevin, directed to the sheriff of the parish, commanding him to take me into custody, and detain me until the decision of the court. By the time the papers were duly drawn up, it was twelve o'clock at night—too late to obtain the necessary signature of the Judge, who resided some distance out of town. Further business was therefore suspended until Monday morning.

Everything, apparently, was moving along swimmingly, until Sunday afternoon, when Waddill called at Northup's room to express his apprehension of difficulties they had not expected to encounter. Bass had become alarmed, and had placed his affairs in the hands of a person at the landing, communicating to him his intention of leaving the State. This person had betrayed the confidence reposed in him to a certain extent, and a rumor began to float about the town, that the stranger at the hotel, who had been observed in the company of lawyer Waddill, was after one of old

Epps, slaves, over on the bayou. Epps was known at Marksville, having frequent occasion to visit that place during the session of the courts, and the fear entertained by Mr. Northup's adviser was, that intelligence would be conveyed to him in the night, giving him an opportunity of secreting me before the arrival of the sheriff.

This apprehension had the effect of expediting matters considerably. The sheriff, who lived in one direction from the village, was requested to hold himself in readiness immediately after midnight, while the Judge was informed he would be called upon at the same time. It is but justice to say, that the authorities at Marksville cheerfully rendered all the assistance in their power.

As soon after midnight as bail could be perfected, and the Judge's signature obtained, a carriage, containing Mr. Northup and the sheriff, driven by the landlord's son, rolled rapidly out of the village of Marksville, on the road towards Bayou Boeuf.

It was supposed that Epps would contest the issue involving my right to liberty, and it therefore suggested itself to Mr. Northup, that the testimony of the sheriff, describing my first meeting with the former, might perhaps become material on the trial. It was accordingly arranged during the ride, that, before I had an opportunity of speaking to Mr. Northup, the sheriff should propound to me certain questions agreed upon, such as the number and names of my children, the name of my wife before marriage, of places I knew at the North, and so forth. If my answers corresponded with the statements given him, the evidence must necessarily be considered conclusive.

At length, shortly after Epps had left the field, with the consoling assurance that he would soon return and *warm* us, as was stated in the conclusion of the preceding chapter, they came in sight of the plantation, and discovered us at work. Alighting from the carriage, and directing the driver to proceed to the great house, with instructions not to mention to any one the object of their errand until they met again, Northup and the sheriff turned from the highway, and came towards us across the cotton field. We observed them, on looking up at the carriage—one several rods in advance of the other. It was a singular and unusual thing to see white men approaching us in that manner, and especially at that early hour in the morning, and Uncle Abram and Patsey made some remarks, expressive of their astonishment. Walking up to Bob, the sheriff inquired.

"Where's the boy they call Platt?"

"Thar he is, massa," answered Bob, pointing to me, and twitching off his hat.

I wondered to myself what business he could possibly have with me, and turning round, gazed at him until he had approached within a step. During my long residence on the bayou, I had become familiar with the face of every planter within many miles; but this man was an utter stranger—certainly I had never seen him before.

"Your name is Platt, is it?" he asked.

"Yes, master," I responded.

Pointing towards Northup, standing a few rods distant, he demanded—"Do you know that man?"

I looked in the direction indicated, and as my eyes rested on his countenance, a world of images thronged my brain; a multitude of well-known faces—Anne's, and the dear children's, and my old dead father's; all the scenes and associations of childhood and youth; all the friends of other and happier days, appeared and disappeared, flitting and floating like dissolving shadows before the vision of my imagination, until at last the perfect memory of the man recurred to me, and throwing up my hands towards Heaven, I exclaimed, in a voice louder than I could utter in a less exciting moment—

"Henry B. Northup! Thank God—thank God!"

In an instant I comprehended the nature of his business, and felt that the hour of my deliverance was at hand. I started towards him, but the sheriff stepped before me.

"Stop a moment," said he; "have you any other name than Platt?"

"Solomon Northup is my name, master," I replied.

"Have you a family?" he inquired.

"I had a wife and three children."

"What were your children's names?"

"Elizabeth, Margaret and Alonzo."

"And your wife's name before her marriage?"

"Anne Hampton."

"Who married you?"

"Timothy Eddy, of Fort Edward."

"Where does that gentleman live?" again pointing to Northup, who remained standing in the same place where I had first recognized him.

"He lives in Sandy Hill, Washington county, New York," was the reply.

He was proceeding to ask further questions, but I pushed past him, unable longer to restrain myself. I seized my old acquaintance by both hands. I could not speak. I could not refrain from tears.

"Sol," he said at length, "I'm glad to see you."

I essayed to make some answer, but emotion choked all utterance, and I was silent. The slaves, utterly confounded, stood gazing upon the scene, their open mouths and rolling eyes indicating the utmost wonder and astonishment. For ten years I had dwelt among them, in the field and in the cabin, borne the same hardships, partaken the same fare, mingled my griefs with theirs, participated in the same scanty joys; nevertheless, not until this hour, the last I was to remain among them, had the remotest suspicion of my true name, or the slightest knowledge of my real history been entertained by any one of them.

Not a word was spoken for several minutes, during which time I clung fast to Northup, looking up into his face, fearful I should awake and find it all a dream.

"Throw down that sack," Northup added, finally; "your cotton-picking days are over. Come with us to the man you live with."

I obeyed him, and walking between him and the sheriff, we moved towards the great house. It was not until we had proceeded some distance that I had recovered my voice sufficiently to ask if my family were all living. He informed me he had seen Anne, Margaret and Elizabeth but a short time previously; that Alonzo was also living, and all were well. My mother, however, I could never see again. As I began to recover in some measure from the sudden and great excitement which so overwhelmed me, I grew faint and weak, insomuch it was with difficulty I could walk. The sheriff took hold of my arm and assisted me, or I think I should have fallen. As we entered the yard, Epps stood by the gate, conversing with the driver. That young man, faithful to his instructions, was entirely unable to give him the least information in answer to his repeated inquiries of what was going on. By the time we reached him he was almost as much amazed and puzzled as Bob or Uncle Abram.

Shaking hands with the sheriff, and receiving an introduction to Mr. Northup, he invited them into house, ordering me, at the same time, to bring in some wood. It was some time before I succeeded in cutting an armful, having, somehow, unaccountably lost the power of wielding the axe with any manner of precision. When I entered with it at last, the table was strewn with papers, from one of which Northup was reading. I was probably longer than necessity required, in placing the sticks upon the fire, being particular as to the exact position of each individual one of them. I heard the words, "the said Solomon Northup," and "the deponent further says," and "free citizen of New-York," repeated frequently, and from these expressions understood that the secret I had so long retained from Master and Mistress Epps, was finally developing. I lingered as long as prudence permitted, and was about leaving the room, when Epps inquired,

"Platt, do you know this gentleman?"

"Yes, master," I replied, "I have known him as long as I can remember."

"Where does he live?"

"He lives in New-York."

"Did you ever live there?"

"Yes, master—born and bred there."

"You was free, then. Now you d—d nigger," he exclaimed, "why did you not tell me that when I bought you?"

"Master Epps," I answered, in a somewhat different tone than the one in which I had been accustomed to address him "Master Epps, you did not

take the trouble to ask me; besides, I told one of my owners— the man that kidnapped me—that I was free, and was whipped almost to death for it."

SCENE IN THE COTTON FIELD, SOLOMON DELIVERED UP

"It seems there has been a letter written for you by somebody. Now, who is it?" he demanded, authoritatively. I made no reply.

"I say, who wrote that letter?" he demanded again.

"Perhaps I wrote it myself", I said.

"You haven't been to Marksville post–office and back before light, I know."

He insisted upon my informing him, and I insisted I would not. He made many vehement threats against the man, whoever he might be, and intimated the bloody and savage vengeance he would wreak upon him, when he found him out. his whole manner and language exhibited a feeling of anger towards the unknown person who had written for me, and of fretfulness at the idea of losing so much property. Addressing Mr. Northup he swore if he had only had an hour's notice of his coming, he would have saved him the trouble of taking me back to New–York; that he would have run me into the swamp, or some other place out of the way, where all the sheriffs on earth couldn't have found me.

I walked out into the yard, and was entering the kitchen door, when something struck me in the back. Aunt Phebe, emerging from the back door of the great house with a pan of potatoes, had thrown one of them with unnecessary violence, thereby giving me to understand that she wished to speak to me a moment confidentially. Running up to me, she whispered in my ear with great earnestness,

"Lor a' mity, Platt! what d'ye think? Dem two men come after ye. Heard 'em tell masse you free— got wife and tree children back thar whar you come from. Goin' wid 'em? Fool if ye don't—wish I could go," and Aunt Phebe ran on in this manner at a rapid rate.

Presently Mistress Epps made her appearance in the kitchen. She said many things to me, and wondered why I had not told her who I was. She expressed her regret, complimenting me by saying she had rather lose any other servant on the plantation. Had Patsey that day stood in my place, the measure of my mistress' joy would have overflowed. Now there was no one left who could mend a chair or a piece of furniture—no one who was of any use about the house—no one who could play for her on the violin —and Mistress Epps was actually affected to tears.

Epps had called to Bob to bring up his saddle horse. The other slaves, also, overcoming their fear of the penalty, had left their work and come to the yard. They were standing behind the cabins, out of sight of Epps. They beckoned me to come to them, and with all the eagerness of curiosity, excited to the highest pitch, conversed with and questioned me. If I could repeat the exact words they uttered, with the same emphasis—if I could paint their several attitudes, and the expression of their countenances—it would be indeed an interesting picture. In their estimation, I had suddenly arisen to an immeasurable height—had become a being of immense importance.

The legal papers having been served, and arrangements made with Epps to meet them the next day at Marksville, Northup and the sheriff entered the carriage to return to the latter place. As I was about mounting to the driver's seat, the sheriff said I ought to bid Mr. and Mrs. Epps good bye. I ran back to the piazza where they were standing, and taking off my hat, said,

"Good–bye, missis."

"Good–bye, Platt," said Mrs. Epps, kindly.

"Good–bye, master."

"Ah! you d—d nigger," muttered Epps, in a surly, malicious tone of voice, "you needn't feel so cussed tickled—you ain't gone yet—I'll see about this business at Marksville to–morrow."

I was only a "*nigger*" and knew my place, but felt as strongly as if I had been a white man, that it would have been an inward comfort, had I dared to have given him a parting kick. On my way back toward the carriage, Patsey ran from behind a cabin and threw her arms about my neck.

"Oh! Platt," she cried, tears streaming down her face, "you're goin' to be free—you're goin' way off yonder where we'll neber see ye any more. You've saved me a good many whipping, Platt; I'm glad you're goin' to be free—but oh! de Lord, de Lord! what'll become of me?"

I disengaged myself from her, and entered the carriage. The driver cracked his whip and away we rolled. I looked back and saw Patsey, with drooping head, half reclining on the ground; Mrs. Epps was on the piazza; Uncle Abram, and Bob, and Wiley, and Aunt Phebe stood by the gate, gazing after me. I waved my hand, but the carriage turned a bend of the bayou, hiding them from my eyes forever.

We stopped a moment at Carey's sugar house, where a great number of slaves were at work, such an establishment being a curiosity to a Northern man. Epps dashed by us on horseback at full speed—on the way, as we learned next day, to the "Pine Woods," to see William Ford, who had brought me into the country.

Tuesday, the fourth of January, Epps and his counsel, the Hon. E. Taylor,

Northup, Waddill, the Judge and sheriff of Avoyelles, and myself, met in a room in the village of Marksville. Mr. Northup stated the facts in regard to me, and presented his commission, and the affidavits accompanying it. The sheriff described the scene in the cotton field. I was also interrogated at great length. Finally, Mr. Taylor assured his client that he was satisfied, and that litigation would not only be expensive, but utterly useless. In accordance with his advice, a paper was drawn up and signed by the proper parties, wherein Epps acknowledged he was satisfied of my right to freedom, and formally surrendered me to the authorities of New–York. It was also stipulated that it be entered of record in the recorder's office of Avoyelles.[3]

Mr. Northup and myself immediately hastened to the landing, and taking passage on the first steamer that arrived, were soon floating down Red River, up which, with such desponding thoughts, I had been borne twelve years before.

3 See Appendix C

CHAPTER 22. ARRIVAL IN NEW-ORLEANS— GLIMPSE OF FREEMAN...

⊙ ⊙ ⊙

Arrival In New-Orleans—Glimpse Of Freeman—Genois, The Recorder—His Description Of Solomon—Reach Charleston—Interrupted By Custom House Officers—Pass Through Richmond—Arrival In Washington—Burch Arrested— Shekels And Thorn—Their Testimony—Burch Acquitted—Arrest Of Solomon—Burch Withdraws The Complaint—The Higher Tribunal—Departure From Washington— Arrival At Sandy Hill—Old Friends And Familiar Scenes—Proceed To Glens Falls— Meeting With Anne, Margaret, And Elizabeth—Solomon Northup Staunton— Incidents—Conclusion.

As the steamer glided on its way towards New-Orleans, perhaps I was not happy—perhaps there was no difficulty in restraining myself from dancing round the deck—perhaps I did not feel grateful to the man who had come so many hundred miles for me—perhaps I did not light his pipe, and wait and watch his word, and run at his slightest bidding. If I didn't—well, no matter.

We tarried at New-Orleans two days. During that time I pointed out the locality of Freeman's slave pen, and the room in which Ford purchased me. We happened to meet Theophilus in the street, but I did not think it worth while to renew acquaintance with him. From respectable citizens we ascertained he had become a low, miserable rowdy—a broken-down, disreputable man.

We also visited the recorder, Mr. Genois, to whom Senator Soule's letter was directed, and found him a man well deserving the wide and honorable reputation that he bears. He very generously furnished us with a sort of legal pass, over his signature and seal of office, and as it contains the recorder's description of my personal appearance, it may not be amiss to insert it here. The following is a copy;

"State of Louisiana—City of New-Orleans

Recorder's Office, Second District.

"To all to whom these presents shall come:-

"This is to certify that Henry B. Northup, Esquire, of the county of Washington, New-York, has produced before me due evidence of the freedom of Solomon, a mulatto man, aged about forty-two years, five feet, seven inches and six lines, woolly hair, and chestnut eyes, who is a native born of the State of New-York. That the said Northup, being about bringing the said Solomon to his native place, through the southern routes, the civil authorities are requested to let the aforesaid colored man Solomon pass unmolested, he demeaning well and properly.

"Given under my hand and the seal of the city of New-Orleans this 7th January, 1853.

[L. S.] "TH. GENOIS, Recorder."

On the 8th we came to Lake Pontchartrain, by railroad, and, in due time, following the usual route, reached Charleston. After going on board the steamboat, and paying our passage at this city, Mr. Northup was called upon by a custom-house officer to explain why he had not registered his servant. He replied that he had no servant—that, as the agent of New-York, he was accompanying a free citizen of that State from slavery to freedom, and did not desire nor intend to make any registry whatever. I conceived from his conversation and manner, though I may perhaps be entirely mistaken, that no great pains would be taken to avoid whatever difficulty the Charleston officials. might deem proper to create. At length, however, we were permitted to proceed, and, passing through Richmond, where I caught a glimpse of Goodin's pen, arrived in Washington January

17th, 1853.

We ascertained that both Burch and Radburn were still residing in that city. Immediately a complaint was entered with a police magistrate of Washington, against James H. Burch, for kidnapping and selling me into slavery. He was arrested upon a warrant issued by Justice Goddard, and returned before Justice Mansel, and held to bail in the sum of three thousand dollars. When first arrested, Burch was much excited, exhibiting the utmost fear and alarm, and before reaching the justice's office on Louisiana Avenue, and before knowing the precise nature of the complaint, begged the police to permit him to consult Benjamin O. Shekels, a slave trader of seventeen years, standing, and his former partner. The latter became his bail.

At ten o'clock, the 18th of January, both parties appeared before the magistrate. Senator Chase, of Ohio, Hon. Orville Clark, of Sandy Hill, and Mr. Northup acted as counsel for the prosecution, and Joseph H. Bradley for the defence.

Gen. Orville Clark was called and sworn as a witness, and testified that he had known me from childhood, and that I was a free man, as was my father before me. Mr. Northup then testified to the same, and proved the facts connected with his mission to Avoyelles.

Ebenezer Radburn was then sworn for the prosecution, and testified he was forty–eight years old; that he was a resident of Washington, and had known Burch fourteen years; that in 1841 he was keeper of Williams' slave pen; that he remembered the fact of my confinement in the pen that year. At this point it was admitted by the defendant's counsel, that I had been placed in the pen by Burch in the spring of 1841, and hereupon the prosecution rested.

Benjamin O. Shekels was then offered as a witness by the prisoner. Benjamin is a large, coarse–featured man, and the reader may perhaps get a somewhat correct conception of him by reading the exact language he used in answer to the first question of defendant's lawyer. He was asked the place of his nativity, and his reply, uttered in a sort of rowdyish way, was in these very words—

"I was born in Ontario county, New–York, and *weighed fourteen pounds!"*

Benjamin was a prodigious baby! He further testified that he kept the Steamboat Hotel in Washington in 1841, and saw me there in the spring of that year. He was proceeding to state what he had heard two men say, when Senator Chase raised a legal objection, to wit, that the sayings of third persons, being hearsay, was improper evidence. The objection was overruled by the Justice, and Shekels continued, stating that two men came to his hotel and represented they had a colored man for sale; that they had an interview with Burch; that they stated they came from Georgia, but he did not remember the county; that they gave a full history of the boy, saying he was a bricklayer, and played on the violin; that Burch remarked he would purchase if they could agree; that they went out and brought the boy in, and that I was the same person. He further testified, with as much unconcern as if it was the truth, that I represented I was born and bred in Georgia; that one of the young men with me was my master; that I exhibited a great deal of regret at parting with him, and he believed "got into tears!"—nevertheless, that I insisted my master had a right to sell me; that he ought to sell me; and the remarkable reason I gave was, according to Shekels, because he, my master, "had been gambling and on a spree!"

He continued, in these words, copied from the minutes taken on the examination; "Burch interrogated the boy in the usual manner, told him if he purchased him he should send him south. The boy said he had no objection, that in fact he would like to go south. Burch paid $650 for him, to my knowledge. I don't know what name was given him, but think it was not Solomon. Did not know the name of either of the two men. They were in my tavern two or three hours, during which time the boy played on the violin. The bill of sale was signed in my bar–room. It was a printed blank, filled up by Burch. Before 1838 Burch was my partner. Our business was buying and selling slaves. After that time he was a partner of Theophilus

Freeman, of New-Orleans. Burch bought here— Freeman sold there!"

Shekels, before testifying, had heard my relation of the circumstances connected with the visit to Washington with Brown and Hamilton, and therefore, it was, undoubtedly, he spoke of "two men," and of my playing on the violin. Such was his fabrication, utterly untrue, and yet there was found in Washington a man who endeavored to corroborate him.

Benjamin A. Thorn testified he was at Shekels' in 1841, and saw a colored boy playing on a fiddle. "Shekels said he was for sale. Heard his master tell him he should sell him. The boy acknowledged to me he was a slave. I was not present when the money was paid. Will not swear positively this is the boy. The master *came near shedding tears; I think the boy did!* I have been engaged in the business of taking slaves south, off and on, for twenty years. When I can't do that I do something else."

I was then offered as a witness, but, objection being made, the court decided my evidence inadmissible. It was rejected solely on the ground that I was a colored man—the fact of my being a free citizen of New- York not being disputed.

Shekels having testified there was a bill of sale executed, Burch was called upon by the prosecution to produce it, inasmuch as such a paper would corroborate the testimony of Thorn and Shekels. The prisoner's counsel saw the necessity of exhibiting it, or giving some reasonable explanation for its non-production. To effect the latter, Burch himself was offer- as a witness in his own behalf It was contended by counsel for the people, that such testimony should not be allowed—that it was in contravention of every rule of evidence, and if permitted would defeat the ends of justice. His testimony, however, was received by the court! He made oath that such a bill of sale had been drawn up and signed, *but he had lost it, and did not know what had become of it!* Thereupon the magistrate was requested to dispatch a police officer to Burch's residence, with directions to bring his books, containing his bills of sales for the year 1841. The request was granted, and before any measure could be taken to prevent it, the officer had obtained possession of the books, and brought them into court. The sales for the year 1841 were found, and carefully examined, but no sale of myself, by any name, was discovered!

Upon this testimony the court held the fact to be established, that Burch came innocently and honestly by me, and accordingly he was discharged.

An attempt was then made by Burch and his satellites, to fasten upon me the charge that I had conspired with the two white men to defraud him—with what success, appears in an extract taken from an article in the New-York Times, published a day or two subsequent to the trial; "The counsel for the defendant had drawn up, before the defendant was discharged; an affidavit, signed by Burch, and had a warrant out against the colored man for a conspiracy with the two white men before referred to, to defraud Burch out of six hundred and twenty-five dollars. The warrant was served, and the colored man arrested and brought before officer Goddard. Burch and his witnesses appeared in court, and H. B. Northup appeared as counsel for the colored man, stating he was ready to proceed as counsel on the part of the defendant, and asking no delay whatever. Burch, after consulting privately a short time with Shekels, stated to the magistrate that he wished him to dismiss the complaint, as he would not proceed farther with it. Defendant's counsel stated to the magistrate that if the complaint was withdrawn, it must be without the request or consent of the defendant. Burch then asked the magistrate to let him have the complaint and the warrant, and he took them. The counsel for the defendant objected to his receiving them, and insisted they should remain as part of the records of the court, and that the court should endorse the proceedings which had been had under the process. Burch delivered them up, and the court rendered a judgement. of discontinuance by the request of the prosecutor, and filed it in his office."

There may be those who will affect to believe the statement of the slave-trader—those, in whose minds his allegations will weigh heavier than mine. I am a poor colored man—one of a down-trodden and degraded race, whose humble voice may not be heeded by the oppressor—but knowing the truth, and with a full sense of my accountability, I do solemnly declare before men, and before God, that any charge or assertion, that I conspired directly or indirectly with any person or persons to sell myself; that any other account of my visit to Washington, my capture and imprisonment in Williams, slave pen, shall is contained in these pages, is utterly and absolutely false. I never played on the violin in Washington. I never was in the Steamboat Hotel, and never saw Thorn or Shekels, to my knowledge, in my life, until last January. The story of the trio of slave-traders is a fabrication as absurd as it is base and unfounded. Were it true, I should not have turned aside on my way back to liberty for the purpose of prosecuting Burch. I should have *avoided* rather than sought him. I should have known that such a step would have resulted in rendering me infamous. Under the circumstances —longing as I did to behold my family, and elated with the prospect of returning home—it is an outrage upon probability to suppose I would have run the hazard, not only of exposure, but of a criminal prosecution and conviction, by voluntarily placing myself in the position I did, if the statements of Burch and his confederates contain a particle of truth. I took pains to seek him out, to confront him in a court of law, charging him with the crime of kidnapping; and the only motive that impelled me to this step, was a burning sense of the wrong he had inflicted upon me, and a desire to bring him to justice. He was acquitted, in the manner, and by such means as have been described. A human tribunal has permitted him to escape; but there is another and a higher tribunal, where false testimony will not prevail, and where I am willing, so far at least as these statements are concerned, to be judged at last.

We left Washington on the 20th of January, and proceeding by the way of Philadelphia, New-York, and Albany, reached Sandy Hill in the night of the 21st. My heart overflowed with happiness as I looked around upon old familiar scenes, and found myself in the midst of friends of other days. The following morning I started, in company with several acquaintances, for Glens Falls, the residence of Anne and our children.

As I entered their comfortable cottage, Margaret was the first that met me. She did not recognize me. When I left her, she was but seven years old, a little prattling girl, playing with her toys. Now she was grown to womanhood—was married, with a bright-eyed boy standing by her side. Not forgetful of his enslaved, unfortunate grand-father, she had named the child Solomon Northup Staunton. When told who I was, she was overcome with emotion, and unable to speak. Presently Elizabeth entered the room, and Anne came running from the hotel, having been informed of my arrival. They embraced me, and with tears flowing down their cheeks, hung upon my neck. But I draw a veil over a scene which can better be imagined than described.

When the violence of our emotions had subsided to a sacred joy—when the household gathered round the fire, that sent out its warm and crackling comfort through the room, we conversed of the thousand events that had occurred—the hopes and fears, the joys and sorrows, the trials and troubles we had each experienced during the long separation. Alonzo was absent in the western part of the State. The boy had written to his mother a short time previous, of the prospect of his obtaining sufficient money to purchase my freedom. From his earliest years, that had been the chief object of his thoughts and his ambition. They knew I was in bondage. The letter written on board the brig, and Clem Ray himself , had given them that information. But where I was, until the arrival of Bass' letter, was a matter of conjecture. Elizabeth and Margaret once returned from school— so Anne informed me—weeping bitterly. On inquiring the cause of the children's sorrow, it was found that, while studying geography, their attention had been attracted to the picture of slaves working in the cotton-field, and an overseer following them with his whip. It reminded them of the sufferings father might be, and, as it happened, actually was, enduring in the South. Numerous incidents, such as these, were related—incidents showing they still held me in constant remembrance, but not, perhaps, of sufficient interest to the reader, to be recounted.

RIVAL HOME, AND FIRST MEETING WITH HIS WIFE AND CHILDREN

My narrative is at an end. I have no comments to make upon the subject of Slavery. Those who read this book may form their own opinions of the "peculiar institution." What it may be in other States, I do not profess to know; what it is in the region of Red River, is truly and faithfully delineated in these pages. This is no fiction, no exaggeration. If I have failed in anything, it has been in presenting to the reader too prominently the bright side of the picture. I doubt not hundreds have been as unfortunate as myself; that hundreds of free citizens have been kidnapped and sold into slavery, and are at this moment wearing out their lives on plantations in Texas and Louisiana. But I forbear. Chastened and subdued in spirit by the sufferings I have borne, and thankful to that good Being through whose mercy I have been restored to happiness and liberty, I hope henceforward to lead an upright though lowly life, and rest at last in the church yard where my father sleeps.

ROARING RIVER.

A REFRAIN OF THE RED RIVER PLANTATION.

ROARING RIVER.

A Refrain Of The Red River Plantation

"Harper's creek and roarin' ribber,

Thar, my dear, we'll live forebber;

Den we'll go to de Ingin nation,

All I want in dis creation,

Is pretty little wife and big plantation.

CHORUS.

Up dat oak and down dat ribber,

Two overseers and one little nigger."

⊙ ⊙ ⊙

APPENDIX A

An act more effectually to protect the free citizens of this State from being kidnapped, or reduced to Slavery.

[Passed May 14, 1840]

The People of the State of New–York, represented in Senate and Assembly, do enact as follows;

Whenever the Governor of this State shall receive information satisfactory to him that any free citizen or any inhabitant of this State has been kidnapped or transported away out of this State, into any other State or Territory of the United States, for the purpose of being there held in slavery; or that such free citizen or inhabitant is wrongfully seized, imprisoned or held in slavery in any of the States or Territories of the United States, on the allegation or pretence that such a person is a slave, or by color of any usage or rule of law prevailing in such State or Territory, is deemed or taken to be a slave, or not entitled of right to the personal liberty belonging to a citizen; it shall be the duty of the said Governor to take such measures as he shall deem necessary to procure such person to be restored to his liberty and returned to this State. The Governor is hereby authorized to appoint and employ such agent or agents as he shall deem necessary to effect the restoration and return of such person; and shall furnish the said agent with such credentials and instructions as will be likely to accomplish the object of his appointment. The Governor may determine the compensation to be allowed to such agent for his services besides his necessary expenses.

Such agent shall proceed to collect the proper proof to establish the right of such person to his freedom, and shall perform such journeys, take such measures, institute and procure to be prosecuted such legal proceedings, under the direction of the Governor, as shall be necessary to procure such person to be restored to his liberty and returned to this State.

The accounts for all services and expenses incurred in carrying this act into effect shall be audited by the Comptroller, and paid by the Treasurer on his warrant, out of any moneys in the treasury of this State not otherwise appropriated. The Treasurer may advance, on the warrant of the Comptroller, to such agent, such sum or sums as the Governor shall certify to be reasonable advances to enable him to accomplish the purposes of his appointment, for which advance such agent shall account, on the final audit of his warrant.

This act shall take effect immediately.

APPENDIX B

Memorial of Anne.

To His Excellency, the Governor of the State of New-York,

The memorial of Anne Northup, of the village of Glens Falls, in the county of Warren, State aforesaid, respectfully sets forth—

That your memorialist, whose maiden name was Anne Hampton, was forty-four years old on the 14th day of March last, and was married to Solomon Northup, then of Fort Edward, in the county of Washington and State aforesaid, on the 25th day of December, A. D. 1828, by Timothy Eddy, then a Justice of the Peace. That the said Solomon, after such marriage, lived and kept house with your memorialist in said town until 1830, when he removed with his said family to the town of Kingsbury in said county, and remained there about three years, and then removed to Saratoga Springs in the State aforesaid, and continued to reside in said Saratoga Springs and the adjoining town until about the year 1841, as near as the time can be recollected, when the said Solomon started to go to the city of Washington, in the District of Columbia, since which time your memorialist has never seen her said husband.

And your memorialist further states, that in the year 1841 she received information by a letter directed to Henry B. Northup, Esq., of Sandy Hill, Washington county, New-York, and post-marked at New-Orleans, that said Solomon had been kidnapped in Washington, put on board of a vessel, and was then in such vessel in New-Orleans, but could not tell how he came in that situation, nor what his destination was.

That your memorialist ever since the last mentioned period has been wholly unable to obtain any information of where the said Solomon was, until the month of September last, when another letter was received from the said Solomon, post-marked at Marksville, in the parish of Avoyelles, in the State of Louisiana, stating that he was held there as a slave, which statement your memorialist believes to be true.

That the said Solomon is about forty-five years of age, and never resided out of the State of New-York, in which State he was born, until the time he went to Washington city, as before stated. That the said Solomon Northup is a free citizen of the State of New-York, and is now wrongfully held in slavery, in or near Marksville, in the parish of Avoyelles, in the State of Louisiana, one of the United States of America, on the allegation or pretence that the said Solomon is a slave.

And your memorialist further states that Mintus Northup was the reputed father of said Solomon, and was a negro, and died at Fort Edward, on the 22d day of November, 1829; that the mother of said Solomon was a mulatto, or three quarters white, and died in the county of Oswego, New-York, some five or six years ago, as your memorialist was informed and believes, and never was a slave.

That your memorialist and her family are poor and wholly unable to pay or sustain any portion of the expenses of restoring the said Solomon to his freedom.

Your excellency is entreated to employ such agent or agents as shall be deemed necessary to effect the restoration and return of said Solomon Northup, in pursuance of an act of the Legislature of the State of New-York, passed May 14th, 1840, entitled "An act more effectually to protect the free citizens of this State from being kidnapped or reduced to slavery." And your memorialist will ever pray.

(Signed,) ANNE NORTHUP.

Dated November 19,1852.

STATE OF NEW–YORK.

Washington county, ss.

Anne Northup, of the village of Glens Falls, in the county of Warren, in said State, being duly sworn, doth depose and say that she signed the above memorial, and that the statements therein contained are true.

(Signed,) ANNE NORTHUP.

Subscribed and sworn before me this 19th November, 1852.

CHARLES HUGHES, Justice Peace.

We recommend that the Governor appoint Henry B. Northup, of the village of Sandy Hill, Washington county, New–York, as one of the agents to procure the restoration and return of Solomon Northup, named in the foregoing memorial of Anne Northup.

Dated at Sandy Hill, Washington Co., N. Y.,

November 20, 1852. (Signed,)

PETER HOLBROOK, DANIEL SWEET,

B. F. HOAG, ALMON CLARK,

CHARLES HUGHES, BENJAMIN FERRIS,

E. D. BAKER, JOSIAH H. BROWN

ORVILLE CLARK.

STATE OF NEW–YORK.

Washington County, ss.

Josiah Hand, of the village of Sandy Hill, in said county, being duly sworn, says, he is fifty–seven years old, and was born in said village, and has always resided there; that he has known Mintus Northup and his son Solomon, named ; in the annexed memorial of Anne Northup, since previous to the year 1816; that Mintus Northup then, and until the time of his death, cultivated a farm in the towns of Kingsbury and Fort Edward, from the time deponent first knew him until he died; that said Mintus and his wife, the mother of said Solomon Northup, were reported to be free citizens of New-York, and deponent believes they were so free; that said Solomon Northup was born in said county of Washington, as deponent believes, and was married Dec. 25th, 1828, in Fort Edward aforesaid, and his said wife and three children—two daughters and one son— are now living in Glens Falls, Warren county, New-York, and that the said Solomon Northup always resided in said county of Washington, and its immediate vicinity, until about 1841, since which time deponent has not seen him, but deponent has been credibly informed, and as he verily believes truly, the said Solomon is now wrongfully held as a slave in the State of Louisiana. And deponent further says that Anne Northup, named in the said memorial, is entitled to credit, and deponent believes the statements contained in her said memorial are true.

(Signed,) JOSIAH HAND.

Subscribed and sworn before me this 19th day of November, 1852, CHARLES HUGHES, Justice Peace.

STATE OF NEW-YORK.

Washington county, ss.

Timothy Eddy, of Fort Edward, in said county, being duly sworn, says he is now over—years old, and has been a resident of said town more than— years last past, and that he was well acquainted with Solomon Northup, named in the annexed memorial of Anne Northup, and with his father, Mintus Northup, who was a negro,—the wife of said Mintus was a mulatto woman; that said Mintus Northup and his said wife and family, two sons, Joseph and Solomon, resided in said town of Fort Edward for several years before the year 1828, and said Mintus died in said town A. D. 1829, as deponent believes. And deponent further says that he was a Justice of the Peace in said town in the year 1828, and as such Justice of the Peace, he, on the 25th day of Dec'r, 1828, joined the said Solomon Northup in marriage with Anne Hampton, who is the same person who has subscribed the annexed memorial. And deponent expressly says, that said Solomon was a free citizen of the State of New–York, and always lived in said State, until about the year A. D. 1840, since which time deponent has not seen him, but has recently been informed, and as deponent believes truly, that said Solomon Northup is wrongfully held in slavery in or near Marksville, in the parish of Avoyelles, in the State of Louisiana. And deponent further says, that said Mintus Northup was nearly sixty years old at the time of his death, and was, for more than thirty years next prior to his death, a free citizen of the State of New– York.

And this deponent further says, that Anne Northup, the wife of said Solomon Northup, is of good character and reputation, and her statements, as contained in the memorial hereto annexed, are entitled to full credit.

(Signed,) TIMOTHY EDDY.

Subscribed and sworn before me this 19th day of November, 1852, TIM'Y STOUGHTON, Justice.

STATE OF New–York.

Washington County, ss.

Henry B. Northup, of the village of Sandy Hill, in said county, being duly sworn, says, that he is forty–seven years old, and has always lived in said county; that he knew Mintus Northup, named in the annexed memorial, from deponent's earliest recollection until the time of his death, which occurred at Fort Edward, in said county, in 1829; that deponent knew the children of said Mintus, viz, Solomon and Joseph; that they were both born in the county of Washington aforesaid, as deponent believes; that deponent was well acquainted with said Solomon, who is the same person named in the annexed memorial of Anne Northup, from his childhood; and that said Solomon always resided in said county of Washington and the adjoining counties until about the year 1841; that said Solomon could read and write; that said Solomon and his mother and father were free citizens of the State of New-York; that sometime about the year 1841 this deponent received a letter from said Solomon, post-marked New-Orleans, stating that while on business at Washington city, he had been kidnapped, and his free papers taken from him, and he was then on board a vessel, in irons, and was claimed as a slave, and that he did not know his destination, which the deponent believes to be true, and he urged this deponent to assist in procuring his restoration to freedom; that deponent has lost or mislaid said letter, and cannot find it; that deponent has since endeavored to find where said Solomon was, but could get no farther trace of him until Sept. last, when this deponent ascertained by a letter purporting to have been written by the direction of said Solomon, that said Solomon was held and claimed as a slave in or near Marksville, in the parish of Avoyelles, Louisiana, and that this deponent verily believes that such information is true, and that said Solomon is now wrongfully held in slavery at Marksville aforesaid.

(Signed,) HENRY B. NORTHUP.

Subscribed and sworn to before me this 20th day of November, 1852,

CHARLES HUGHES, J.P.

STATE OF NEW-YORK.

Washington County, ss

Nicholas C. Northup, of the visage of Sandy Hill, in said county, being duly sworn, cloth depose and say, that he is now fifty-eight years of age, and has known Solomon Northup, mentioned in the annexed memorial of Ann Northup, ever since he was born. And this deponent saith that said Solomon is now about forty-five years old, and was born in the county of Washington aforesaid, or in the county of Essex, in said State, and always resided in the State of New-York until about the year 1841, since which time deponent has not seen him or known where he was, until a few weeks since, deponent was informed, and believes truly, that said Solomon was held in slavery in the State of Louisiana. Deponent further says, that said Solomon was married in the town of Fort Edward, in said county, about twenty-four years ago, and that his wife and two daughters and one son now reside in the village of Glens Falls, county of Warren, in said State of New-York. And this deponent swears positively that said Solomon N Northup is a citizen of said State of New-York, and was born free, and from his earliest infancy lived and resided in the counties of Washington, Essex, Warren and Saratoga, in the State of New-York, and that his said wife and children have never resided out of said counties since the time said Solomon was married; that deponent knew the father of said Solomon Northup; that said father was a negro named Mintus Northup, and died in the town of Fort Edward, in the county of Washington, State of New-York, on the 22d day of November, A. D. 1829, and was buried in the grave-yard in Sandy Hill aforesaid; that for more than thirty years before his death he lived in the counties of Essex, Washington and Rensselaer and State of New-York, and left a wife, and two sons, Joseph and the said Solomon, him surviving; that the mother of said Solomon was a mulatto woman, and is now dead, and died, as deponent believes, in Oswego county, New-York, within five or six years past. And this deponent further states, that the mother of the said Solomon Northup was not a slave at the time of the birth of said Solomon Northup, and has not been a slave at any time within the last fifty years.

(Signed,) N. C. NORTHUP.

Subscribed and sworn before me this 19th day of November, 1852, CHARLES HUGHES, Justice Peace.

STATE OF NEW-YORK.

Washington County, ss.

Orville Clark, of the village of Sandy Hill, in the. county of Washington, State of New-York, being duly sworn, doth depose and say—that he, this deponent, is over fifty years of age; that in the years 1810 and 1811, or most of the time of those years, this deponent resided at Sandy Hill, aforesaid, and at Glens Falls; that this deponent then know Mintus Northup, a black or colored man; he was then a free man, as this deponent believes and always understood; that the wife of said Mintus Northup, and mother of Solomon, was a free woman; that from the year 1818 until the time of the death of said Mintus Northup, about the year 1829, this deponent was very well acquainted with the said Mintus Northup; that he was a respectable man in the community in which he resided, and was a free man, so taken and esteemed by all his acquaintances; that this deponent has also been and was acquainted with his son Solomon Northup, from the said year 1818 until he left this part of the country, about the year 1840 or 1841; that he married Anne Hampton, daughter of William Hampton, a near neighbor of this deponent; that the said Anne, wife of said Solomon, is now living and resides in this vicinity; that the said Mintus Northup and William Hampton were both reputed and esteemed in this community as respectable men. And this deponent saith that the said Mintus Northup and his family, and the said William Hampton and his family, from the earliest recollection and acquaintance of this deponent with him (as far back as 1810,) were always reputed, esteemed, and taken to be, and this deponent believes, truly so, free citizens of the State of New-York. This deponent knows the said William Hampton, under the laws of this State, was entitled to vote at our elections, and he believes the said Mintus Northup also was entitled as a free citizen with the property qualification. And this deponent further saith, that the said Solomon Northup, son of said Mintus, and husband of said Anne Hampton when he left this State, was at the time thereof a free citizen of the State of New-York. And this deponent further saith, that said Anne Hampton, wife of Solomon Northup, is a respectable woman, of good character, and I would believe her statements, and do believe the facts set forth in her memorial to his excellency, the Governor, in relation to her said husband, are true.

(Signed,) ORVILLE CLARK.

Sworn before me, November 19th, 1852.

U. G. PARIS, Justice of the Peace.

STATE OF NEW–YORK.

Washington County, ss.

Benjamin Ferris, of the village of Sandy Hill, in said county, being duly sworn, doth depose and say—that he is now fifty–seven years old, and has resided in said village forty–five years; that he was as well acquainted with Mintus Northup, named in the annexed memorial of Anne Northup, from the year 1816 to the time of his death, which occurred at Fort Edward, in the fall of 1829; that he knew the children of the said Mintus, namely, Joseph Northup and Solomon Northup, and that the said Solomon is the same person named in said memorial; that said Mintus resided in the said county of Washington to the time of his death, and was, during all that time, a free citizen of the said State of New–York, as deponent verify believes; that said memorialist, Anne Northup, is a woman of good character, and the statement contained in her memorial is entitled to credit.

(Signed) BENJAMIN FERRIS.

Sworn before me, November 19th, 1852.

U. G. PARIS, Justice of the Peace.

STATE OF NEW–YORK.

Executive Chamber, Albany, Nov. 30, 1852.

I hereby certify that the foregoing is a correct copy of certain proofs filed in the Executive Department, upon which I have appointed Henry B. Northup an Agent of this State, to take proper proceedings in behalf of Solomon Northup there in mentioned.

(Signed,) WASHINGTON HUNT.

By the Governor.

J. F. R., Private Secretary.

STATE OF NEW–YORK.

Executive Department.

WASHINGTON HUNT, Governor of the State of New–York, to whom it may concern, greeting,

Whereas, I have received information on oath, which is satisfactory to me, that Solomon Northup, who is a free citizen of this State, is wrongfully held in slavery, in the State of Louisiana.

And whereas, it is made my duty, by the laws of this State, to take such measures as I shall deem necessary to procure any citizen so wrongfully held in slavery, to be restored to his liberty and returned to this State.

Be it known, that in pursuance of chapter 375 of the laws of this State, passed in 1840, I have constituted, appointed and employed Henry B. Northup, Esquire, of the county of Washington, in this State, an Agent, with full power to effect the restoration of said Solomon Northup, and the said Agent is hereby authorized and empowered to institute such proper and legal proceedings, to procure such evidence, retain such counsel, and finally to take such measures as will be most likely to accomplish the object of his said appointment.

He is also instructed to proceed to the State of Louisiana with all convenient dispatch, to execute the agency hereby created.

In witness whereof, I have hereunto subscribed my name, [L.S.] and affixed the privy seal of the State, at Albany, this 23d day of November, in the year of our Lord 1852.

(Signed,) WASHINGTON HUNT.

JAMES E. RUGGLES, Private Secretary.

⊙ ⊙ ⊙

APPENDIX C

⊙ ⊙ ⊙

State of Louisiana.

Parish of Avoyelles.

Before me, Aristide Barbin, Recorder of the parish of Avoyelles, personally came and appeared Henry B. Northup, of the county of Washington, State of New-York, who hath declared that by virtue of a commission to him as agent of the State of New-York, given and granted by his excellency, Washington Hunt, Governor of the said State of New- York, bearing date the 23d day of November, 1852, authorizing and empowering him, the said Northup, to pursue and recover from slavery a free man of color, called Solomon Northup, who is a free citizen of the State of New-York, and who was kidnapped and sold into slavery, in the State of Louisiana, and now in the possession of Edwin Epps, of the State of Louisiana, of the Parish of Avoyelles; he, the said agent, hereto signing, acknowledges that the said Edwin has this day given and surrendered to him as such agent, the said Solomon Northup, free man of color, as aforesaid, in order that he be restored to his freedom, and carried back to the said State of New-York, pursuant to said commission, the said Edwin Epps being satisfied from the proofs produced by said agent, that the said Solomon Northup is entitled to his freedom. The parties consenting that a certified copy of said power of attorney be annexed to this act.

Done and signed at Marksville, parish of Avoyelles, this fourth day of January, one thousand eight hundred and fifty-three, in the presence of the undersigned, legal and competent witnesses, who have also hereto signed.

(Signed,)

HENRY B. NORTHUP.

EDWIN EPPS.

ADE. BARBIN, Recorder.

Witnesses:

H. TAYLOR,

JOHN P. WADDILL.

STATE OF LOUISIANA.

Parish of Avoyelles.

I do hereby certify the foregoing to be a true and correct copy of the original on file and of record in my office.

Given under my hand and seal of office as Recorder [L. S.] in and for the parish of Avoyelles, this 4th day of January, A. D. 1853.

(Signed,) ADE. BARBIN, Recorder.

THE END

www.ingramcontent.com/pod-product-compliance
Lightning Source LLC
LaVergne TN
LVHW041736060526
838201LV00046B/824
* 9 7 8 9 3 9 0 8 9 6 6 0 8 *